Environmental Management

Ajith Sankar R.N.
Organic Farmer
and
Founder–Ekatwa

OXFORD
UNIVERSITY PRESS

OXFORD
UNIVERSITY PRESS

Oxford University Press is a department of the University of Oxford.
It furthers the University's objective of excellence in research, scholarship,
and education by publishing worldwide. Oxford is a registered trade mark of
Oxford University Press in the UK and in certain other countries.

Published in India by
Oxford University Press
YMCA Library Building, 1 Jai Singh Road, New Delhi 110001, India

ISBN-13: 978-0-19-945891-2
ISBN-10: 0-19-945891-X

Typeset in Baskerville
by ADoT Publishing Services, Chennai
Printed in India by Magic International, Greater Noida

Preface

Thank you for reading this textbook.

Every generation believes that it is living in unique times. We too, are no different, and we have reasons to support our belief. No other generation in the history of mankind had access to the kind of physical comforts that we enjoy now. The accessibility to various lifestyle choices is so mind-boggling that we remain unfulfilled even after spending a full day in a shopping mall looking for clothes to wear for a special occasion. However, this obsession for physical comfort and gratifying the cravings of the mind also causes suffering, not just to oneself, but to all. As the acquisitive drive is on an increase, it impacts the balance of the universe. The growing human population and its demands on the planet, tend to exacerbate this imbalance.

We are witnessing an increasing prevalence of extreme weather conditions to such an extent that we have become numb to those affected by these disasters. We are going through an extinction wave where the loss of species is thousand times the normal rate, and where forest area equivalent to that of a football field is being destroyed every second! The planet is witnessing the existence of conditions vastly different from those observed in the last 6,50,000 years. Industries ranging from insurance to winter tourism are being negatively affected by this imbalance. In this context, shouldn't 'Environmental Management' be a discipline that takes centre stage, especially in institutions that groom people on management and leadership? This is happening gradually, though many a times, not out of a conscious and mindful choice, but because of a forced compulsion. I have stoically acknowledged the shift in global warming discussions—from attempts to mitigate global warming to that of adaptation measures—a shift that is also partially driven by the melancholic acceptance and certainty by the global community, that we have irresponsibly created certain planetary phenomena that are now irreversible.

What is unique about climatic and environmental effects is that they are not constrained by national and geographic boundaries, but affect both at the macro and micro levels. While the drying up of rivers in the rice bowl district of Palakkad in Kerala can be considered a regional issue, this is also partially caused by the same phenomenon that melts the Arctic ice. Melting of Himalayan glaciers not just affects Indians, but directly affects citizens of other countries, and also has the potential to indirectly affect global commodity prices. Ill health resulting from the usage of the endosulfan pesticide may be projected as regional, but it will affect all the regions to where the crops subjected to this pesticide are exported. Plastic disposal is an issue for most local bodies of governance, but soon these disposed plastics reach oceans, form garbage patches, affect aquatic life forms, and re-enter the food chain, thereby affecting humans again. This textbook delves into such environmental issues that affect us all.

Clearly, the situation is grave. However, human beings have the inherent capability to be optimistic even in the gravest of the situations. Viktor Frankl should be nodding; and I have evidence(s) to support this. *Ecosia.org*, a less than ten member start-up that runs a search engine donates almost 50% of its advertisement revenue to green projects, and has contributed more than 15 crores of rupees in the initial five years of its existence. Shubendu Sharma has been creating urban forests through his venture *Afforestt*, and Veni Madhvi has been nurturing sacred groves through *Vedic Vanas*. We see the increasing popularity of organic products, the emergence of eco-labels that support socially responsible and environment-friendly business practices, and governments choosing to promote mass rapid transportation systems. More than 50 lakh people from around the world have supported a Greenpeace online campaign to create a global sanctuary in the Arctic region. Countries such as Ecuador and Bolivia have given legal rights to nature itself. United Nations and civil society groups have been facilitating dialogues and discussion resulting in global treaties that promote sustainable development. In addition to introducing the reader to similar developments that give hope and reasons to cheer, the textbook also explores the connection between business and sustainability practices, including the oft-repeated 'business case'.

The textbook team has endeavoured to make this work beneficial for many in the following ways:

- Attempt was made to make the textbook as comprehensive as possible, while acknowledging that a boundary needs to be drawn for any topic, including *Environmental Management*. Thus, a reader would discover that, along with the existence of the conventional topics such as bio-diversity, waste management, renewable energy, polluter pays principle, energy efficiency, disaster management, negative externalities, and many more, the textbook also delves into emerging and specialized areas, ideas, and topics, such as 5Rs, genuine progress indicator, spirituality and ecology, reading a sustainability report, etc.
- The content of the textbook is supported by research, and significant efforts have gone into developing research-based content.
- A number of examples indicating the practice of environmental management have been provided. These examples, both Indian and global, are worthy of emulation. Some of these examples, which have been provided in boxed contents, are spread across various chapters, and need not have direct connection to that specific chapter, though they do have connection with the overall theme of the textbook.
- In addition to these examples, the textbook also has an exclusive section that offers detailed case studies and shorter caselets and the online resources centre has an Instructor's manual and PowerPoint presentations. This will aid the faculty members to facilitate discussions amongst the students.
- The language used is simple, so that even a high-school student will be able to understand the ideas presented. Even the style used in footnotes is to communicate utility and ease of use, and not a blind adherence to any particular referencing style, except in those cases where the copyright holders asked the referencing to be done in a specific way.
- Attempts were made to make the textbook content presentable and welcoming. A number of visual images and photographs have been used so that the reader is able to receive the message effectively and with emotional connect. We have gone

also attempting to keep the cost of the textbook affordable, so that a large number of students and readers can access the book.

We have aimed to create a textbook that is world class. This book has happened because of the efforts and sacrifice of innumerable beings—those who offered food to the author thereby sustaining his body, those who provided the content and knowledge resources free of cost, those who were displaced from their lands due to the construction of power projects that generated electricity to power the laptop and internet that supported this textbook-writing effort, those who offered the possibility of creating this textbook, those who willed that this textbook be published, those who contributed to the improvisation and publication of this textbook, those who dedicated their life for noble causes that are being chronicled in the textbook, those who provided the supportive infrastructure, and more.

I've observed that, for some of the most inspiring creations that have happened in India, it has been difficult to find the name of the creator/inventor/discoverer associated with that work. While their works benefitted the world, the creators chose to remain anonymous. With the passage of time, their names dissolved into the Universe. Due to my admiration to that practice and respect for such individuals, I pondered over the possibility of following their footsteps, on whether an author's name really needs to be included. The answer was Yes—that I need to attribute an author's name—primarily due to the concern and consideration for easing the rigours of daily existence for many. However, the dilemma on whether my decision is ideal continues.

This work is a *yagna* or a sacrifice (sacrifice, from its Latin roots, means, to make a process holy or sacred). The author will not be taking any royalty from the sales of the textbook. The author's royalty is being channelized towards subsidizing the cost of the textbook.

Punya (merits) accrued in a sacrifice is to be shared for the common good and well-being of all species. This is done through extending an invite to all to participate in this sacrifice, and by creating opportunities for all to contribute to the fulfilment of its objectives. I've given my efforts to this *yagna* and continue to do so. If you are convinced that this work is worthy of respect, I invite you to join in this endeavour. You can share this book with your friends and well-wishers, gift copies of this book to many, write reviews about this book, promote this book among your circles, make postings about this book in social media and 'like' it, recommend this book to students, faculty members, and academic institutions, and most importantly, incorporate learnings from this book in your own life, on a daily basis (Do not miss the section on Reflective Questions, Recommended Books, and Recommended Documentaries/Movies at the end of various chapters).

This textbook is dedicated to *The Universal Feminine*.

Thank you.

Ajith

Features of the Book

Dedicated chapters to important concepts

Contains important chapters that lay emphasis on companies/industries finding solutions to various environmental issues

5   BUSINESS AND SUSTAINABILITY

6   PROCESSES, TOOLS, AND STANDARDS FOR ENVIRONMENTAL MANAGEMENT

In 2014, Tata Global Beverages Limited (formerly Tata Tea Limited), joined the Tea 2030 partnership. The partnership will focus on (a) sustainable production that benefits the communities and the natural environment where tea is cultivated, (b) engaging consume so that they demand more sustainable tea, and (c) providin values to all players in the supply chain. Other members of this alliance include Unilever, Rainfor Alliance, Fairtrade International, Yorkshire Tea, Finlays, the Ethical Tea Partnership, and IDH Sustainable Trade Initiative.

On 23 September 2013, Indian Institution of Corporate Affairs (IICA) and Bombay Stock Exchange (BSE) Ltd. entered into an arrangement to develop a Corporate Social Responsibility (CSR) index for Indian companies listed in BSE.

Side bars

Contains numerous side bars throughout the book with interesting/informative facts to build the students' interest in the subject

Images

Contains numerous vivid images that attempt to give a broader perspective to the concepts discussed

FIG. 1.1[7]   Male, the capital of the Maldives

TABLE 3.3[58] Average noise levels (in decibels) at different places of Delhi

Location	2012		2013	
	Average day	Deepavali day	Average day	Deepavali day
Lajpat Nagar	58			
East Arjun Nagar	57			
Mayur Vihar Phase – II	48			
Pitam Pura	56			
Kamla Nagar	61			
Dilshad Garden	58			
Ansari Nagar	58			
Connaught Place	64			

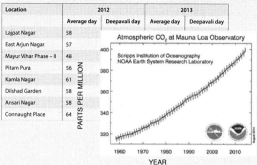

FIG. 3.10[97] CO_2 concentrations measured at the Mauna Loa observatory, Hawaii

Figures and Tables

Every chapter contains several figures and tables to support the concepts discussed

Chapter-end exercises

Provides exhaustive chapter-end exercises such as multiple-choice questions, short answer, long answer, and reflective type questions, as well as take-home activities for students to test their understanding

CHAPTER SUMMARY

- Pollution refers to the contamination in a natural substance that interferes with the health of any living organism or cause harmful environmental
- Marine Pollution occurs due to the introduction of unnatural materials like pesticides, industrial and agricultural waste, and chemicals that are

KEYWORDS

- Pollution
- Air pollution

Multiple-choice Questions

1. _____ is harmful for plant and animal 1 peeling of paint, affect soil chemistry.
   (a) Acid rain
   (b) Soil pollution
   (c) Water pollution
   (d) Degradation

Short Answer Questions

1. Define pollution and its types.

Long Answer Questions

1. What is meant by ecological footprint? its significance? How is it different from footprint?

Reflective Question

You would have noticed that the societal trend

Take-home Activity

Select any natural ecosystem near your educational

Recommended Book

1. Pathak, Bindheshwar, *The Road to Freedom: A Sociological Study on the Abolition of Scavenging in India*, Motilal Banarsidass, 2000.

Recommended Documentaries/Movies

1. Minus One Project of Samsung Printers, 2012 (This short clipping is available for water/ and https://www.youtube.com/ watch?v=Se12y9hSOM0), Duration: 8 minutes

Additional resources

Each chapter provides a selection of recommended books, videos, and documentary films for interested readers to learn more about the subject

Case Studies and Caselets

An exclusive section that details environmental management techniques and sustainable practices adopted by various organizations is included

CASE STUDY 1

THE STORY OF ETHICUS—INDIA'S FIRST ETHICAL FASHION BRAND[1]

"We have got this big problem with our lifestyle, which is not eco-friendly. Ethicus is not just about the fabric, it is not just about organic cotton, it is about a new kind of lifestyle. The very process is organic. In my tenure, I've been focusing on socially and environmentally responsible designs. Ethicus was very much related to this ideology, they are socially and environment responsible, and it an ideal company that ways I visited their entire set up and it was very encouraging

Rahul Mishra, Fashion Designer, explaining his association with Ethicus

CASELET 1

AAROGYAPACHA AND JEEVANI

In December 1987, a group of researchers, led by Dr P Pushpangadan from The Tropical Botanical Gardens Research Institute (TBGRI), traveled to the forests of Western Ghat section in southern Kerala as part of All India Coordinated Research Project on Ethnobiology (AICRPE). Kani tribe, a tribe indigenous to the region, was a nomadic community of approximately 16,000 people. 'We went there to survey the Kani tribal settlements, but we got exhausted after a long walk. When they saw us tired, some of the Kani tribesmen, who were our guides, offered us fruits of a plant. We ate them and

Brief Contents

Preface   *iii*
Features of the Book   *vi*
Detailed Contents   *ix*

 1. Realm of Ecology and Ecosystems   1
 2. Spiritual Perspectives on Environment   38
 3. Environmental Issues   107
 4. Natural Resources Management   155
 5. Business and Sustainablity   200
 6. Processes, Tools, and Standards for Enviromental Management   255
 7. Waste Management Systems and Practices   303
 8. Biodivesity   329
 9. Environmental Ethics   369
10. Environmental Laws, Policies, and Treaties   411
11. Environmental Economics and Green Economy   433
12. Realm of Ecology and Ecosystems   467

Index   *585*

Detailed Contents

Preface   iii
Features of the Book   vi
Brief Contents   viii

1. Realm of Ecology and Ecosystems   1
Definition and Etymology   1
Scope and Importance   2
Evolution of Sustainable Development   7
 Sustainable Development Timeline   7
 Evolution of Green Movement in India   18
 Principal Objectives of National Environment Policy
  2006   21
 National Action Plan on Climate Change   22
 National Water Policy (2012)   23
Concept of Ecosystem   25
 Structure and Function   25
 Energy Flow   26
 Food Chain, Food Web and Producers, Consumers,
  and Decomposers   27
 Ecological Succession   29
 Limiting Factors, Law of Minimum, and Law of
  Tolerance   30
 Carrying Capacity   30
 Various Ecosystems and Their Features   31

2. Spiritual Perspectives on Environment   38
India's Heritage in Environment   38
 Nakshatra and Trees Associated with Them   47
 Sacred Forests/Sacred Groves of India   49
 Benefits of Sacred Groves   52
Indian Culture and Worship of Nature   55
Deep Ecology and Reverential Ecology   58
Gaia Hypothesis   63
Farming in Harmony with Nature   65
 Introduction to Sustainable Farming   65
 Differences Between Organic and Conventional Farming   68
 Natural Farming   71
 Permaculture   73
The Role of Vegetarianism   74

 Ways to Save the Planet through Your Plate   80
Religious Perspectives on Earth and Nature   82
 Buddhist Declaration on Climatic Change   83
 Hindu Declaration on Climate Change   86
 Jain Declaration on Nature   87
 Jain Teachings   88
 Jain Code of Conducts   92
 Muslim Declaration on Nature   93
 The St Francis Pledge   96
 Church of South India Statement   97
 Jewish Declaration on Nature   100

3. Environmental Issues   107
Background: Definition of Pollution,
  Environment, and Pollutants   107
Types of Pollution: Causes and Effects   108
 Air Pollution   108
 Ozone Imbalance and Ozone Depletion   109
 Acid Rain   111
 Water Pollution   112
 Use and Over-utilization of Surface and Ground
  Water Resource   113
 Floods and Drought   114
 Conflicts Over Water   115
 Dams: Benefits and Problems   118
 Resettlement and Rehabilitation of People: Its Problems
  and Concerns   118
 Successful Models of Water Resource Management   119
 Soil Pollution   120
 Marine Pollution, Algal Bloom, and Ocean
  Acidification   120
 Noise Pollution   124
 Thermal Pollution   125
 Light Pollution   126
Nuclear Hazards and Accidents   127

Human Interference with the Natural Environment
and its Impact   129
Implications of Human Population Growth   129
Animal and Human Conflict   131
Impact of Technology on Environment   133
*Bioaccumulation, Bioconcentration, and
Biomagnification   134*
Greenhouse Effect, Global Warming, and
Anthropogenic Climate Change   136
Positive Feedback in Climatology   141
Melting of Polar Ice: The Arctic and the Antarctic   141
Impact of Climate Change on India   145
Disaster Management   146
Floods   147
Earthquakes   148
Cyclones   148
Landslides   148
Common Relief Materials Required After
Natural Disasters   150

4. Natural Resources Management   155
Energy Resources and Growing Energy Needs   155
Demand and Supply of Fossil Fuels   156
*Problems Related to Demand and Supply of Fossil
Fuel-based Energy   157*
Renewable and Non-renewable Energy Sources   158
Market and Usage of Alternate Energy Sources   158
Energy Intensity, Carbon Intensity, and Energy
Efficiency   166
Food Resources and World Food Problems   169
*Changes Caused by Modern Agriculture and its Effects—
Water Logging and Salinity   172*
*Problems Related to Extensive Usage of Fertilizers
and Pesticides   173*
Mineral Resources   174
Use and Exploitation of Mineral Resources   174
*Environmental Effects of Extracting and Using Mineral
Resources   175*
Forest Resources   176
Use and Exploitation of Forest Resources   176
Deforestation   179
Water Resources   181
Water Footprint   181

*Water Conservation, Rain Water Harvesting, and
Watershed Management   185*
Indigenous Water Conservation Systems in India   186
Water Harvesting Techniques   191
Land Management   193
Land Degradation, Desertification, and Soil Erosion   194

5. Business and Sustainability   200
Economy—'A Wholly Owned Subsidiary of the
Natural Environment'   202
Sustainable Development and its Background—
Brundtland Commission and Rio Summit   201
The Business Case for Sustainability   203
Strategies for Sustainable Development   205
*Integrating Environmental Sustainability into Core Business
Practices   206*
Extended Producer Responsibility   207
Poverty Alleviation and Bottom of Pyramid Models   209
Cleaner Production   209
*Cradle to Cradle Design and Sustainable Products
and Services   210*
Bio-mimicry   211
Green Vehicles and Electric Mobility   213
Green Buildings and Natural Buildings   214
Natural Buildings—Tools and Techniques   218
Green Investing/Socially Responsible Investing   221
Carbon Offsetting and Carbon Neutrality   223
Climate Registry   224
Green Businesses and their Growth   225
Brand Strategy and Sustainability   227
Why Green Marketing?   229
Green Rankings   232
Eco-labels and Environmentally Preferred
Purchasing   233
Sustainability/Environmental Reporting
Standards and Certifications   239
Triple Bottom Line Reporting   239
Sustainability Reporting Initiatives   241

**6. Processes, Tools, and Standards for
Environmental Management   255**
Introduction   255
Environmental Management System   255

Environmental Risk Management   257
Environmental Design Management   258
Industrial Ecology and Tools for Measuring
    Environmental Impacts   259
Ecological Footprint   261
Carbon Footprint and Carbon Dioxide Equivalent   263
Life Cycle Analysis   264
Ecosystem Services and Valuation   267
Benefit-cost Analysis or Cost-benefit Analysis   276
Stakeholder Analysis   278
Total Value Chain Analysis   278
EROEI—Energy Returned on Energy Invested   279
Carbon Rating   279
Environmental Impact Assessment and Auditing   279
Checklists for Applying Environmental Clearance   280
General Checklist   280
*Checklist of Environmental Impacts (Only for Construction
    Projects)   286*
Structure of EIA Document   291
Environmental Auditing   292
Environmental Decision Making   293
Sustainability Reporting Best Practice Questions   293
How to Read a Sustainability Report   295

7. Waste Management Systems and Practices   303
Introduction   303
Consumerism and Waste Products   304
Generation and Characteristics of Waste   304
Types of Waste   306
Solid Waste   306
Industrial Waste   306
Construction and Demolition Waste   306
Special Wastes   307
Hazardous Waste: Management and Treatment   307
Waste Management—Collection, Storage,
    Transport, and Disposal   308
Waste Disposal Practices   309
Urban Waste Management   314
Integrated Waste Management   317
Policies on Waste Management   319

8. Biodiversity   329
Introduction   329

Genetic, Species, and Ecosystem Diversity   331
*Value of Biodiversity: Consumptive Use, Productive Use,
    Social, Ethical, Aesthetic, and Option Values   331*
Biodiversity at Global, National, and Local Levels   334
Bio-geographical Classification of India   334
India as a Mega-diversity Nation   334
Hotspots of Biodiversity   337
Threats to Biodiversity   337
Habitat Loss and Destruction   338
Poaching of Wildlife and Human–Wildlife Conflicts   340
Exploitation of Natural Resources   341
Invasive Species   343
Climate Change, Pollution, and Contamination   343
Conservation of Biodiversity   344
*Conservation Status of a Species and the IUCN
    Red List   344*
Aichi Biodiversity Targets   345
Endangered and Endemic Species of India   348
Ecosystem Management   348
Forests and Woodlands   350
Forest Management and Wildlife Management   351
Rainforests, Deforestation, and Afforestation   353
Wetlands and Mangroves   354
Wildlife and its Protection   356
Wildlife Conservation in India   359
Wasteland Reclamation   362
People's Biodiversity Register   362

9. Environmental Ethics   369
Anthropocentrism and Ecocentrism   369
Earth Charter   370
Preamble   371
Principles   372
The Way Forward   377
Role of Consumers and Investors in Making
    Businesses Sustainable   377
Shareholder Resolutions   380
Equitable use of Resources for
    Sustainable Lifestyles   387
*Role of an Individual in the Conservation of Natural
    Resources and in Preventing Pollution   388*
Locavorism   394
Unsustainable Dietary Habits   395

Food Miles and Slow Food Movement   398
Role of NGOs   400
Green Governance   401
Convention of Biological Diversity   402
Akwé: Kon Guidelines   402
Tkarihwaié:ri Code Of Ethical Conduct   403

10. Environmental Laws, Policies, and Treaties   411
Introduction   411
Chronology of Environmental Laws in India   413
General   413
Forests and Wildlife   414
Water   415
Air   415
Domestic Laws   416
Environmental Protection Act   416
Air (Prevention and Control of Pollution) Act   416
Water (Prevention and Control of Pollution) Act   416
Wild Life Protection Act   417
Forest Conservation Act   417
Clearance/Permissions for Establishing Industry   418
Issues Involved in Enforcement of Environmental
    Legislation   418
Public Interest Litigations   420
International Agreements, Laws, and Treaties   420
International Agreements and Laws   421
Global Developments   426

11. Environmental Economics and Green Economy   433
Environmental Economics   433
Sustainability and Enhanceability   434
Ecological Economics and Green Economy   435
Externalization   436
Examples of Negative Spatial Externalization   437
Cost of Pollution   439
True Cost Economics   440
Responses to Market Failures   441
Common Types of Market Failures in the Context

of Sustainability   441
Responses to Market Failures   442
Club of Rome and Limits to Growth   448
Development Indices and Alternative
    Growth Indicators   449
Genuine Progress Indicator   451
Gross National Happiness   452
Natural Capital   455
Role of Incentives in Enforcing
    Environmental Quality   457
*Reducing Emissions from Deforestation and
    Degradation   457*
Payments for Ecosystem Services (PES)   458
*How Payment for Ecosystem Services Can Benefit
    Poor   461*
Need for Regulatory and Operational Changes in
    Financial Markets and Economy   461

12. Case Studies and Caselets   467
Case Study 1 – The Story of Ethicus—India's First
    Ethical Fashion Brand   468
Case Study 2 – Walmart's Environmental Strategy 487
Case Study 3 – Making Sustainability a Strategy: The
    Case of Interface   500
Case Study 4 – Compensation for Watershed Services
    at Los Negros, Bolivia   510
Case Study 5 – Radiant Clothing: Communicating the
    Value of an Environment-based Strategy   518
Case Study 6 – Project Greenhands   530
Caselet 1 – Aarogyapacha and Jeevani   557
Caselet 2 – East Kolkata Wetlands   559
Caselet 3 – Narmada Bachao Andolan and the Sardar
    Sarovar Dam Project   563
Caselet 4 – Example of Sustainable Transportation:
    Green Tomato Cars, Nextbike, TransMilenio, Delhi
    Metro Rail, and Nature Air   569
Caselet 5 – The Natural Step   578
Caselet 6 – Siachen Peace Park   582

Index   585

1

REALM OF ECOLOGY AND ECOSYSTEMS

Samudra Vasane Devi
Parvatha Sthana Mandale
Vishnu Patnee Namasthubhyam
Paada Sparsam Kshamaswa me

After reading this chapter, the reader will be able to understand the following:
- Definition, concepts, scope, and importance of ecology and ecosystems
- What the various ecosystems are
- Evolution of concepts and practices related to sustainable development at a national and international level
- National Environmental Policy, National Action Plan on Climate Change, and National Water Policy

Oh Mother Earth! O Great Goddess shining in the apparel of the ocean and conveying maternal love through the beautiful hills which are your limbs! I bow unto Thee, the beloved consort of Lord Vishnu, who sustains the whole creation! Mother, forgive me, as I touch you with my feet!

This prayer, *Bhumi Vandanam* (Salutation to Mother Earth), is chanted by many *Bharatheeyas* (Indians) as they wake up from their sleep and before they place their feet on the ground. It is a paradox that a culture rooted in such lofty thoughts is now in a situation where even holy rivers such as the Ganga and the Yamuna have high levels of pollution.

DEFINITION AND ETYMOLOGY

The word 'ecology' has its origins in the Greek and German languages. The word 'Oecology' evolved from the German word 'Okologie', a term coined by Ernst Haeckel, a German biologist and philosopher. 'Oikos', in Greek, means house or household. In ancient Greece, the family unit was large and 'oikos' referred to the house, the extended family, farmland, etc. Thus, ecology could refer to writings, discourses, collections, science, or the study of the household. Ecology is the study of the interlinkages between living organisms along with their physical, chemical, and biological environment.

Though ecology and environment are used synonymously, there is a difference in their meaning. Ecology, as a sub-discipline of biology, is related with the study of life. Ecology, therefore,

is closely related to evolutionary biology, physiology, and genetics. The study of ecology explores the movement of energy and materials through living communities, the distribution of organisms and bio-diversity, and the life process and adaptations of organisms. An ecosystem is a biological community along with its physical environment. Living and non-living entities are connected through nutrient cycles and energy flows. Environment refers to the aggregation of surroundings, conditions, and influences in relation to a considered entity. The National Environment Policy (NEP), 2006, refers to 'Environment' as that which 'comprises all entities, natural or manmade, external to oneself, and their interrelationships, which provide value, now or perhaps in the future, to humankind'. The policy document also states that 'Environmental concerns relate to their degradation through actions of humans'. Environmental management is a branch of study that deals with managing the resources of the planet in a way that benefits the well-being of all species, and sustains resources for use by future generations.

SCOPE AND IMPORTANCE

Since the industrial revolution, nations have taken the path of growing their economies without any regard for the environment. This was particularly so for nations in Europe, the Americas, and other rich countries. An example of this negligence is indicated by the incident of a river catching fire—the highly polluted Cuyahoga River, Ohio, USA—as recently as in 1969. The TIME magazine reported, 'No Visible Life. Some river! Chocolate-brown, oily, bubbling with subsurface gases, it oozes rather than flows. "Anyone who falls into the Cuyahoga does not drown", Cleveland's citizens joke grimly. "He decays."'[1] This was true for all nations. Such negligence and exploitation has resulted in species becoming extinct.

Human intervention has resulted in a massive decline of bio-diversity due to habitat destruction, the release of toxins, the usage and release of harmful chemicals, over-harvesting, and more. The extinction of species is a natural phenomenon and massive bio-diversity losses have occurred five times in the past 540 million years. However, the current ongoing massive decline, referred to as the 'sixth extinction wave'[2], is the first wave to occur during the existence of human beings and has been induced by their behaviour. This extinction wave is the greatest since the dinosaurs disappeared 65 million years ago.[3] It is now estimated that species are becoming extinct at 1000 times the natural rate.[4] Biologists have mentioned that if this continues unabated, it could

---

1 http://www.time.com/time/magazine/article/0,9171,901182,00.html, last accessed on 24 June 2012.

2 Gerardo Ceballos, Andrés García, Paul R. Ehrlich, 'The Sixth Extinction Crisis: Loss of Animal Populations and Species', *Journal of Cosmology*, Vol 8, 2010, pp. 1821–1831.

3 *Millennium Ecosystem Assessment: A Toolkit for Understanding and Action*, Island Press, March 2007, http://islandpress.org/assets/library/27_matoolkit.pdf, last accessed on 8 August 2011.

4 http://news.bbc.co.uk/2/hi/science/nature/8449506.stm, last accessed on 27 September 2012.

5 Gerardo Ceballos, Andrés García, Paul R. Ehrlich, 'The Sixth Extinction Crisis: Loss of Animal Populations and Species', *Journal of Cosmology*, Vol 8, 2010, pp. 1821–1831.

be a harbinger of the downfall of the human civilization and the premature demise of billions of people.[5] The Fifth Assessment Report of the Intergovernmental Panel on Climate Change (IPCC) states that 'The atmospheric concentrations of carbon dioxide (CO2), methane, and nitrous oxide have increased to levels unprecedented in at least the last 800,000 years. CO2 concentrations have increased by 40 per cent since pre-industrial times, primarily due to fossil fuel emissions and secondarily due to net land use change emissions. The ocean has absorbed about 30 per cent of the emitted anthropogenic carbon dioxide, causing ocean acidification.'[6] The report also predicts the continuing warming of the global ocean. Global warming will also result in ice melting at an abnormal rate (Refer Fig. 1.1.). As heat from the surface of the ocean penetrates into the deep ocean, ocean currents and circulation will get affected.

FIG. 1.1[7] Male, the capital of the Maldives

Due to climate change and the expected rise of water levels, Maldives, an island inhabited by more than 300,000 people, is expected to be submerged within a century.

In 2005, more than a thousand of the world's leading biological scientists released *The Millennium Ecosystem Assessment*. They analysed the state of the planet's ecosystem and provided guidelines for decision-makers. *The Millennium Ecosystem Assessment* states, 'In the last half-century, people have made unprecedented changes to the planet's ecosystems — largely to meet rising demands for food, fresh water, fibre, and energy' and adds that almost 60 per cent of the ecosystem services examined as part of the *Millennium Ecosystem*

---

6 http://www.ipcc.ch/news_and_events/docs/ar5/ar5_wg1_headlines.pdf, last accessed on 6 October 2013.

7 Photo by Shahee Illyas, used with permission. Image source: http://commons.wikimedia.org/wiki/File:Male-total. jpg#mediaviewer/File:Male-total.jpg, last accessed on 14 July 2014.

Assessment were degraded or were used in unsustainable ways.[8] The assessment found that of the 24 ecosystem services measured, only four showed an improvement during the previous 50 years and 15 ecosystem services were in serious decline. A key finding of the report is that 'Pressures on ecosystems will grow significantly worse during the first half of this century, unless human attitudes and actions change'.[9]

As per the United Nations Environment Programme Finance Initiative, 2010, human activity in 2008 amounted to $6.6 trillion in global environmental damage, 33 per cent of which was caused by 3,000 of the world's largest publicly traded organizations. The *Living Planet Report 2010*, released by the World Wide Fund for Nature, the Global Footprint Network, and the Zoological Society of London, indicated that the ecological footprint exceeded the earth's bio-capacity by 50 per cent (refer Fig. 1.2). This meant that it takes 1.5 years for the Earth to produce the resources that humanity currently consumes in one year. The report goes on to state that we would be requiring one more planet by 2030, if we continued our lifestyle of 'business as usual'. 'If everyone in the world lived like an average resident of the United States or the United Arab Emirates, then a bio-capacity equivalent to more than 4.5 Earths would be required to keep up with humanity's consumption and CO2 emissions,' says the *Living Planet Report*.[10]

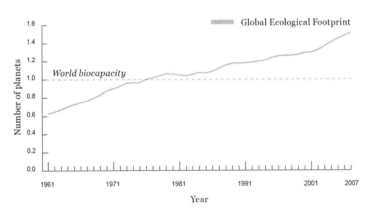

Global Ecological Footprint

Human demand on the biosphere more than doubled between 1961 and 2007 (Global Footprint Network, 2010)

FIG. 1.2 Global ecological footprint

Source: WWF 2012. Living Planet Report 2010. WWF International, Gland, Switzerland[11]

---

8 *Millennium Ecosystem Assessment: A Toolkit for Understanding and Action*, Island Press, March 2007, http://islandpress.org/assets/library/27_matoolkit.pdf, last accessed on 8 August 2011.

9 *Millennium Ecosystem Assessment: A Toolkit for Understanding and Action*, Island Press, March 2007, http://islandpress.org/assets/library/27_matoolkit.pdf, last accessed on 8 August 2011.

10 http://wwf.panda.org/about_our_earth/all_publications/living_planet_report/2010_lpr/lpr_2010_media_center/, last accessed on 27 May 2011.

11 *Living Planet Report 2010*, http://awsassets.panda.org/downloads/wwf_lpr2010_lr_en.pdf, last accessed on 8 October 2013. Used with permission.

Two decades ago, the month of February in Mumbai was known for the blooming of coral trees (*Erythrina indica*) and for rosy pastors (*Pastor roseus*), and the birds that inhabit these trees. However, it has now been noted that these trees now bloom less frequently and the number of these birds in the ecosystem has decreased. As human beings exploit one ecosystem service, it invariably results in the destruction of another ecosystem service. For example, mining done to extract metals has resulted in soil erosion, a loss of biodiversity, and the contamination of soil, groundwater, and surface water by chemicals from mining processes. Exploiting the ecosystem today may result in improving material well-being and removing poverty, but such exploitation cannot continue for long. One cannot continue to extract precious metals from a single ore for a long time. To solve some of today's problems, we are depleting the ecological resources of tomorrow. An example could be the increasing prevalence of the number of deep bore wells or drilled wells in India. Bore wells and drilled wells access water that has accumulated below impermeable rocks over thousands of years. This has resulted in a steep drop in the water table[12,13,14,15] and reports indicate a significant drying up of India's water table.[16] A study conducted by the Uttar Pradesh state groundwater department states that groundwater availability (up to a depth of 5 metres), declined 21.65–59.85% during the pre-monsoon period from 1984 to 2006. The decline was 52.2–91.5% during the post-monsoon period.[17] Such a depletion of ecological resources will have serious repercussions for future generations and their well-being.

Many a time, the negative impact of ecosystem and climate change is felt by people living away from those enjoying the benefits of natural services. When we speed comfortably in our cars fuelled by petroleum products, the environmental price is paid by those in nations such as Sudan, Ecuador, or Nigeria[18]. There have been instances where rivers get polluted due to oil extraction which has affected the health of those who are dependent on the river water. It may not seem like too much of a waste to keep the lights switched on while leaving a room. However, a look behind the scene will lead us to discover that a significant portion of India's electricity is powered by coal-based power plants, a major source of carbon emissions. While we enjoy the comfort of electricity, the health of the people living near the power plant is affected by the emissions from the power plants. 'The world's poor, especially subsistence farmers and pastoralists are the first to

12 http://articles.timesofindia.indiatimes.com/2009-06-27/allahabad/28169537_1_tubewells-water-table-water-level, last accessed on 4 October 2011.

13 http://articles.timesofindia.indiatimes.com/2011-04-07/ranchi/29392204_1_water-harvesting-rain-water-water-table, accessed on 4 October 2011.

14 http://articles.timesofindia.indiatimes.com/2010-02-02/delhi/28125128_1_water-table-water-supply-mgd,   last accessed on 4 October 2011.

15 http://www.hindu.com/2009/07/19/stories/2009071957040400.htm, last accessed on 4 October 2011.

16 http://www.deccanherald.com/content/56673/indias-ground-water-table-dry.html, last accessed on 5 October 2011.

17 http://articles.timesofindia.indiatimes.com/2011-06-11/lucknow/29646511_1_ground-water-water-table-canal-water, last accessed on 4 October 2011.

18 http://www.unep.org/newscentre/default.aspx?DocumentID=2649&ArticleID=8827,last accessed on 17 August 2011.

If everyone in the world lived like an average resident of the United States or the United Arab Emirates, a bio-capacity equivalent to more than 4.5 Earths would be required to keep up with humanity's consumption and CO_2 emissions.

suffer from the loss of services provided by ecosystems and biodiversity—in other words, the free benefits of nature. These include food and fuel-wood from forests, the flow of water and nutrients from forest to field, flood control, drought control, and soil retention provided by forests, fish from the ocean, and so on,' says Pavan Sukhdev, Founder-CEO of GIST Advisory, an environmental consulting firm, and former Managing Director–Global Markets Division, Deutsche Bank.[19] Kabir Sanjay Bavikatte, Legal Advisor–National Biodiversity Authority, India and Lawyer–Natural Justice, says 'For many communities, the ecosystem is the greatest and the most reliable service provider, providing goods and services in ways that governments cannot. A loss of biodiversity means that those who are reliant on natural ecosystems for their livelihoods will have no alternative but to either relocate to cities or rely on a country's social welfare resources to survive.'[20]

As per a report by 'The Economics of Ecosystems and Bio-diversity' (TEEB)[21], 47 per cent of the gross domestic product (GDP) of the poor in India comes from ecosystem services. The NEP 2006 acknowledges environmental degradation as a major causal factor in enhancing and perpetuating poverty, particularly among the rural poor, when such degradation impacts soil fertility, the quantity and quality of water, air quality, forests, wildlife, and fisheries. A number of environment-health factors are closely linked with dimensions of poverty (e.g., malnutrition or the lack of access to clean energy and water). Environmental factors are estimated to be responsible for nearly 20 per cent of the burden of disease in India. 'For millions of the world's poorest people, healthy ecosystems are a matter of survival; starvation looms when a fishery fails; cholera spreads when waste-filtering wetlands are lost. Even in wealthier industrialized countries, degraded ecosystems take a devastating toll on human health. Air and water pollution are linked to an explosion of asthma and other respiratory problems, and an increased risk of cancer and heart disease. Epidemics rage when natural systems are disrupted. For example, the emergence of Lyme disease in the US has been linked to a loss of habitat and a diminished diversity of species,' reports a publication of the Millennium Ecosystem Assessment.[22] The dominant theme of the NEP 2006 is that while the conservation of environmental resources is necessary to secure livelihoods and the well-being of all,

19 http://pavansukhdev.com/2011/04/05/%E2%80%9Cto-make-poverty-history-make-nature-the-future%E2%80%9D/, last accessed on 25 May 2011.

20 Kabir Sanjay Bavikatte, *Green Governance Foundations for a Green Economy*, The Hindu Survey of the Environment 2012.

21 TEEB (2010) *The Economics of Ecosystems and Biodiversity: Mainstreaming the Economics of Nature: A Synthesis of the Approach, Conclusions and Recommendations of TEEB*, Available at http://www.teebweb.org/wp-content/uploads/Study%20 and%20Reports/Reports/Synthesis%20report/TEEB%20Synthesis%20Report%202010.pdf, last accessed on 14 July 2014.

22 *Millennium Ecosystem Assessment: A Toolkit for Understanding and Action*, Island Press, March 2007, http://www.unpei.org/ sites/default/files/PDF/ecosystems-economicanalysis/MEA-A-Toolkit.pdf, last accessed on 14 July 2014.

the most secure basis for conservation is to ensure that people dependent on particular resources obtain better livelihoods through conservation itself, than by degrading resources. For the economically poor of the world, many environmental problems are problems of poverty. Unsafe drinking water and inadequate sewage facilities could be considered as grave environmental health threats facing them. Figure 1.3 shows an image of an oil spill in Nigeria.

FIG. 1.3[23] Oil spill in Ogoniland, Nigeria

EVOLUTION OF SUSTAINABLE DEVELOPMENT

Words such as 'sustainable development', 'organic farming', etc., have gained increasing popularity. However, a deeper exploration would reveal that farming, prior to the arrival of industrialization and applications of synthetic chemicals and pesticides, was always organic. Development was meant to be fruitful, to benefit all members of the community, including all the species. The advent of industrial revolution changed many of these ideas. The following time-line focuses on developments after the emergence of industrial development.

Sustainable Development Timeline[24]

1862

Josh Ruskin's book, *Unto This Last*, spoke about the destructive effects of unrestricted industrialism on human beings and the natural world. This essay influenced personalities like Mahatma Gandhi, who suggested a lifestyle in harmony with the environment.

---

23 Image source: http://www.unep.org/newscentre/default.aspx?DocumentID=2649&ArticleID=8827, last accessed on 17 August 2011. Used with permission.

24 Adapted from http://www.iisd.org/pdf/2009/sd_timeline_2009.pdf, last accessed on 24 April 2012. Used with permission.

1948

The International Union for Conservation of Nature and Natural Resources (IUCN), an international organization dedicated for the conservation of the integrity and diversity of nature was founded.

1962

Silent Spring, by Rachel Carson, brought together research on toxicology, ecology, and epidemiology to suggest that agricultural pesticides were building to catastrophic levels, and were linked to the damage to animal species and human health. The book specifically documented the effects of pesticide abuse on birds. It also influenced the decision to ban the usage of dichlorodiphenyltrichloroethane (DDT) in USA in 1972.

1967

The Environmental Defense Fund (EDF) was formed in the USA to pursue legal solutions to environmental damage. The EDF went to court to stop the Suffolk County Mosquito Control Commission from spraying DDT on Long Island's marshes. (www.environmentaldefense.org)

1968

- The Intergovernmental Conference for Rational Use and Conservation of the Biosphere was organized by UNESCO. Early discussions were held on the concept of ecologically sustainable development. (www.unesco.org)
- Paul Ehrlich published *The Population Bomb*, on the connection among human population, resource exploitation, and the environment.
- The Apollo lunar mission by NASA sent the first 'Earthrise' picture (Refer Fig. 1.4), which was considered to be one of the most influential environmental photographs. It was said that this picture influenced the start of the 'Earth Day' event in 1970, now celebrated across countries on April 22.

1969

- Friends of the Earth was formed as an advocacy organization dedicated to the prevention of environmental degradation, the preservation of diversity, and the role of citizens in decision-making. (www.foe.org)
- The National Environmental Policy Act was passed in the United States, making it one of the first countries to establish a national legislative framework to protect the environment. The law set the basis for environmental impact assessment (EIA) in the world.
- The pollution of the river Rhine in Europe, due to the usage of the pesticide Endosulfan, resulted in the death of more than 20 million fish and the contamination of the river.

1970

- The First Earth Day was held as a national teach-in on the environment. An estimated 20 million people participated in peaceful demonstrations across the United States. (www.earthday.net)

FIG. 1.4[25] First 'earthrise' picture sent by the Apollo Lunar mission

- The Natural Resources Defense Council was formed with a staff of lawyers and scientists to push for comprehensive U.S. environmental policy. (www.nrdc.org)

1971

- Greenpeace was started in Canada and launched an aggressive agenda to stop environmental damage through civil protests and non-violent interference. (www.greenpeace.org)
- The Organization for Economic Co-operation and Development (OECD) Council advocated the polluter pays principle—those causing pollution should pay the resulting costs.

1972

- The UN Conference on the Human Environment and United Nations Environment Programme (UNEP) held in Stockholm was rooted in the pollution and acid rain problems of northern Europe. This conference resulted in the establishment of many national environmental protection agencies and the UNEP(www.unep.org).

---

25 http://www.hq.nasa.gov/office/pao/History/alsj/a410/AS8-14-2383HR.jpg, last accessed on 6 August 2014. Copyright free image from NASA.

Infosys Technologies Ltd, plans to go carbon-neutral by 2018. As part of this goal, the company is in the process of sourcing 100% of its electricity requirements from renewable resources. Infosys, from 2007-08 to 2011-12, reduced its per capita, per month electricity consumption by 32.67%, GHG emissions by 25.67%, and water consumption by 22.87%.

- Club of Rome published the controversial *Limits to Growth* report, which predicted dire consequences if growth did not slow down. Northern countries criticized the report for not including technological solutions; southern countries were incensed because it advocated the abandonment of economic development. (www.clubofrome.org)

1973

- The United States enacted the Endangered Species Act and became one of the first countries to implement legal protection for its heritage of fish, wildlife, and plants.
- The *Chipko* movement was born in India in response to deforestation and environmental degradation. These women's actions influenced both forestry and women's participation in environmental issues. (www.rightlivelihood.org/recip/chipko.htm)
- The Organization of the Petroleum Exporting Countries (OPEC) oil crisis fuelled the limits-to-growth debate.

1974

- Rowland and Molina released work on chlorofluorocarbons (CFCs) in the scientific journal *Nature*, calculating that continued use of CFCs at current rates would critically deplete the ozone layer.
- The Latin American World Model was developed by the Fundación Bariloche. It is the South's response to *Limits to Growth* and calls for growth and equity for the Third World (www.fundacionbariloche.org.ar/LP-mod-latinoam.htm).

1975

- The Convention on International Trade in Endangered Species of Flora and Fauna (CITES) came into force. (www.cites.org)
- The Worldwatch Institute was established in the United States to raise public awareness of global environmental threats and to catalyse effective policy responses; it began publishing its annual report *The State of the World* in 1984. (www.worldwatch.org)

1976

Habitat, the UN Conference on Human Settlements, was the first global meeting to link the environment with human settlement.

1977

- The Green Belt Movement was started in Kenya, using community tree planting to prevent desertification. (www.greenbeltmovement.org)
- The UN Conference on Desertification was held.

1978

The OECD Directorate of the Environment re-launched research on environmental and economic linkages. (www.oecd.org)

1979

- *Banking on the Biosphere*, the IIED report on practices of nine multilateral development agencies including the World Bank, set the stage for reforms that are still under way.
- The Three Mile Island nuclear accident occurred in Pennsylvania, United States.

1980

- The International Union for the Conservation of Nature (IUCN) released the *World Conservation Strategy* report. The section 'Towards Sustainable Development' identified the main agents of habitat destruction as poverty, population pressure, social inequity, and trading regimes. The report called for a new international development strategy to redress inequities. (www.iucn.org)
- The Independent Commission on International Development Issues published *North-South: A Programme for Survival* (Brandt Report), calling for a new economic relationship between North and South.
- The Center for Science and Environment (CSE), one of the leading public interest research and advocacy organizations in India started functioning.

1981

The World Health Assembly unanimously adopted the Global Strategy for Health for All by the Year 2000, which affirmed that the major social goal of governments should be for all people to attain a level of health that would permit them to lead socially and economically productive lives. (www.who.org)

1982

- The World Resources Institute was established in the United States. It began publishing biennial assessments of world resources in 1986. (www.wri.org)
- The UN Convention on the Law of the Sea (UNCLOS) was signed[26]. It established material rules concerning environmental standards and enforcement provisions dealing with marine pollution. (www.un.org/depts/los)
- The international debt crisis erupted and threatened the world's financial system. It turned the 1980s into a lost decade for Latin America and other developing regions.
- The UN World Charter for Nature (WCN)[27] adopted the principle that every form of life is unique and should be respected regardless of its value to humankind.

---

26 http://www.un.org/Depts/los/convention_agreements/texts/unclos/closindx.htm, last accessed on 18 September 2014.

27 http://www.un.org/documents/ga/res/37/a37r007.htm, last accessed on 18 September 2014.

It called for an understanding of our dependence on natural resources and the need to control our exploitation of them. (www.un.org/documents/ga/res/37/a37r007.htm) India has ratified UNCLOS and voted for WCN.

1983

- Development Alternatives was established in India. It fostered a new relationship among people, technology, and the environment in the South. (www.devalt.org)
- The Grameen Bank was established to provide credit to the poorest of the poor in Bangladesh, launching a new understanding of the role of microcredit in development. (www.grameen-info.org)

1984

- A toxic chemical leak left 10,000 dead and 300,000 injured in Bhopal, India. (www.bhopal.net)
- A drought in Ethiopia resulted in between 250,000 and 1 million people dying of starvation.
- The International Conference on Environment and Economics held by the OECD concluded that the environment and economics should be mutually reinforcing.

1985

- Responsible Care, an initiative of the Canadian Chemical Producers, provided a code of conduct for chemical producers and has now been adopted in many countries. (www.ccpa.ca)
- A meeting in Austria of the World Meteorological Society, the UNEP, and the International Council of Scientific Unions reported on the build-up of carbon dioxide and other greenhouse gases in the atmosphere. These gases predict global warming.
- The Antarctic ozone hole was discovered by British and American scientists.

1986

The Chernobyl nuclear station accident generated a massive toxic radioactive explosion.

1987

- Our Common Future (Brundtland Report), a report of the World Commission on Environment and Development weaved together social, economic, cultural, and environmental issues and global solutions. It popularized the term 'sustainable development'.
- The OECD Development Advisory Committee created guidelines for environment and development in bilateral aid policies. (www.oecd.org/dac)
- The Montreal Protocol on Substances that Deplete the Ozone Layer was adopted. (http://ozone.unep.org)

1988

- Chico Mendes, a Brazilian rubber tapper fighting the destruction of the Amazon rainforest, was assassinated. Scientists used satellite photos to document what the Amazon fires were doing to the rainforest. (www.chicomendes.com)
- The Intergovernmental Panel on Climate Change (IPCC) was established to assess the most up-to-date scientific, technical, and socioeconomic research in the field. (www.ipcc.ch)

1989

- The Exxon Valdez tanker ran aground, dumping 11 million gallons of oil into Alaska's Prince William Sound. (www.evostc.state.ak.us)
- The Stockholm Environmental Institute was established as an independent institute for carrying out global and regional environmental research. (www.sei.se)

1990

The UN Summit for Children was held, an important recognition of the impact of the environment on future generations. (www.unicef.org/wsc)

1991

- The Canadian East coast cod fishery collapsed when only 2,700 tonnes of spawning biomass were left after a harvest of 190,000 tonnes.
- Hundreds of oil fires burnt in Kuwait for months following the Persian Gulf War.
- The Protocol on Environmental Protection to the Antarctic Treaty[28] was signed in 1991. India has ratified the treaty.

1992

- The Business Council for Sustainable Development published *Changing Course*, and established business interests in promoting sustainable development practices. (www.wbcsd.ch)
- The Earth Summit held in Rio de Janeiro, had 172 governments participating of which 108 countries sent their heads of government. Formally known as the UN Conference on Environment and Development (UNCED), agreements were reached on the action plan Agenda 21 and on the Convention on Biological Diversity, the Framework Convention on Climate Change, and the non-binding Forest Principles.

1993

The first meeting of the UN Commission on Sustainable Development was established as a follow-up to UNCED, to enhance international cooperation, and to rationalize intergovernmental decision-making capacity. (www.un.org/esa/sustdev)

---

28 http://www.antarctica.ac.uk/about_antarctica/geopolitical/treaty/update_1991.php, last accessed on 18 September 2014.

In 2010, Washington DC imposed a 5-cent fee for every disposable plastic bag given to customers. Proceeds from this fine were channelized into cleaning up the Anacostia River that flows through Washington DC. Following the imposition of the fee, consumer bag usage came down from 22.5 million per month to 3 million.

1994

- The Global Environment Facility was established, restructuring billions of dollars in aid to give more decision-making powers to developing countries. (www.gefweb.org)
- China's Agenda 21, a white paper on the population, environment, and development of the People's Republic of China, was published. China set an international example for national strategies for sustainable development.

1995

- The execution of Ken Saro-Wiwa in Nigeria brought international attention to the link between human rights, environmental justice, security, and economic growth.
- The World Trade Organization (WTO) was established, and formally recognized the link between trade, environment, and development. (www.wto.org)

1995

The World Summit for Social Development was held in Copenhagen. It was the first time that the international community expressed a clear commitment in eradicating poverty absolutely. (www.un.org/esa/socdev/wssd/index.html)

1996

ISO 14001 was formally adopted as a voluntary international standard for corporate environmental management systems. (www.iso.org)

1997

Asia experienced ecological and financial chaos. Land clearing fires intensified by El Niño-induced drought resulted in a haze blanketing the region and cost US$3 billion in health costs and fire-related damage. Concurrently, the market crashed, raising questions about currency speculation and the need for government economic reforms.

1998

- Controversies arose over genetically modified (GM) organisms. Global environmental and food security concerns were raised, and the European Union blocked imports of GM crops from North America. Farmers in developing countries rebelled against 'terminator technology', a technology where seeds will not germinate.
- Due to unusually severe weather conditions, China experienced the worst floods in decades, two-thirds of Bangladesh was underwater for several months from monsoons, hurricane Mitch destroyed parts of Central America, 54 countries

Pancha Bhuta Suprabhatam
(Greetings to the Five Elements
of the Universe)

Prithvi saGandha
SarasasthatAapaha

Sparsascha Vayur Jwalitham cha
Tejah

Nabhah sa Sabdam Mahataa sa
Daiva

Kurvantu sarve Mama
Suprabhaatam

Earth, with its quality of smell;
Water, with its quality of taste; Air,
with its quality of touch; Fire, with
its quality of brilliance; and Space,
with its quality of sound. May all
these elements along with the
Cosmic Mind, make my morning
auspicious.

were hit by floods and 45 by drought, and the global temperature reached the highest ever recorded. (http://lwf.ncdc.noaa.gov/oa/climate/research/1998/ann/extremes98.html)

1999

- The Dow Jones Sustainability Index was launched. The first of its kind, the tool provided guidance to investors looking for profitable companies following sustainable development principles. (www.sustainability-index.com)
- The third WTO Ministerial Conference was held in Seattle. Thousands of demonstrators protested the negative effects of globalization and the growth of global corporations. Along with deep conflicts among WTO delegates, they scuttled the negotiations. The first of many anti-globalization protests, the demonstrations signalled a new era of confrontation between disaffected stakeholders and those in power. (www.iisd.org/trade/wto/seattleandsd.htm)

2000

- The UN Millennium Development Goals were defined. The largest-ever gathering of world leaders agreed to a set of time-bound and measurable goals for combating poverty, hunger, disease, illiteracy, environmental degradation, and discrimination against women, to be achieved by 2015. (www.un.org/millenniumgoals)
- Miss Waldron's red colobus monkey was declared extinct, the first extinction in several centuries of a member of the primate order, to which humans belong. According to the IUCN Red List, 11,046 species are now threatened with extinction.
- The Bharat Stage Emission Standards were introduced

2001

- 9/11, the attack on the World Trade Center and the Pentagon led to stock markets and economies stumbling.
- The Fourth Ministerial Conference of the WTO was held in Doha, Qatar, and recognized environmental and developmental concerns in its final declaration.

2002

- The World Summit on Sustainable Development was held in Johannesburg, marking 10 years since the UNCED. In a climate of frustration at the lack of

Wipro Limited was ranked the leading global company in the 'Greenpeace Guide to Greener Electronics', which was released in November 2012. HP and Nokia were ranked second and third in the rankings.

government progress, the summit promoted 'partnerships' as a non-negotiated approach to sustainability. (www.worldsummit2002.org)

- The Global Reporting Initiative released guidelines for reporting on the economic, environmental, and social dimensions of business activities. (www.globalreporting.org)

2003

India started the National Bio-diversity Authority, located in Chennai.

2004

- Wangari Muta Maathai was awarded the Nobel Peace Prize. The founder of the Green Belt Movement in Kenya, she was the first environmentalist to be awarded a Nobel Prize. (http://nobelprize.org/peace/laureates/2004)
- There was a HIV/AIDS pandemic in sub-Saharan Africa. In 2004 alone, 2.5 million people in the region died of AIDS, and over three million became newly infected. With only 10 per cent of the world's population, the region was home to more than 60 per cent of all people living with HIV. (www.unaids.org)

2005

- The Kyoto Protocol entered into force. It legally bound developed countries to the goal of reducing greenhouse gas emissions, and established the Clean Development Mechanism for developing countries.
- The Millennium Ecosystem Assessment was released. 1,300 experts from 95 countries provided scientific information concerning the consequences of ecosystem change for human well-being.

2006

- The Stern report made the convincing economic case that the costs of inaction on climate change would be up to 20 times greater than the measures required to address the issue today (www.sternreview.org.uk).
- NASA reported that the ozone layer was recovering, due in part to the reduced concentrations of CFCs, phased out under the Montreal Protocol. (http://science.nasa.gov/headlines/y2006/26may_ozone.htm)
- Project Greenhands, an environmental initiative of the Isha Foundation, created a Guinness World Record in planting tree saplings. Members of the foundation planted more than 8.56 lakh saplings on a single day. By March 2015, Project Greenhands had organized the planting of more than two crore saplings.
- The Mahatma Gandhi National Rural Employment Guarantee Act was launched.

2007

- Public attention to climate change increased. Former U.S. Vice President Al Gore's documentary, *An Inconvenient Truth*, won an Academy Award, and the IPCC's alarming forecasts about the planet's health made headlines. The IPCC and Gore shared the Nobel Peace Prize. (www.ipcc.ch)
- More signs of ecosystem stress emerged. In addition to an earlier prediction that fish stocks could disappear in 50 years, scientists said sharks and bee colonies were also at risk.

2008

- World food, fuel, and financial crises converged. Global food prices increased 43 per cent in one year; the growing energy demand in China, India, and elsewhere sent energy prices soaring; financial institutions faltered over the collapse of mortgage lending in the United States, and markets tumbled, sending the world into recession.
- Green economy ideas entered the mainstream. National governments invested a portion of their economic stimulus in environmental actions and a low-carbon economy and green growth became new objectives for the future economy. (www.oecd.org/dataoecd/58/34/44077822.pdf)
- Urbanization increased. For the first time in history, more than 50 per cent of the world's population lived in towns and cities. (www.unfpa.org/pds/urbanization. htm)

2009

- The Australian drought that commenced in 2003 led to the worst wildfires in history.
- The G20 promised to phase out fossil fuel subsidies. Experts estimated that annual subsidies could amount to $500 billion, equal to 1 per cent of world GDP.[29] As per the International Energy Agency (IEA), $409 bn was spent in 2010 to subsidize fossil fuels. This was an increase from $300 bn in 2009. The IEA also estimated that this global subsidy could increase to $600 bn in 2012.[30]
- Connectivity throughout the world exceeded predictions. About 60 per cent of world's people had mobile phones, and 25 per cent were on the Internet. Social networking was directly influencing citizen engagement, from the Obama presidential campaign to the contested Iranian election.
- At the Copenhagen climate negotiations, the domestic targets and actions of large emitters such as the United States and China took centre stage, but the international process continued to be seen as critical in measuring whether

---

29 www.globalsubsidies.org/files/assets/I_policy_brief_on_G-20_Announcement_Oct_09-1.pdf, last accessed on August 22, 2012.
30 http://www.bnef.com/PressReleases/view/224, last accessed on August 22, 2012.

those actions were meeting the global reductions that science demanded. The outcomes of the Copenhagen negotiations were unclear—the process may have been in trouble but the Copenhagen Accord itself may have been a breakthrough in terms of engaging developing countries. (www.iisd.ca/climate/cop15/)

- The website GoodGuide.com was launched. It enabled consumers to receive information on the health, environmental, and social impact of products that a consumer intended to buy. The company also launched mobile applications whereby this information could be collected by scanning the barcode of the consumer product.

2010
- India launched the National Green Tribunal.
- India set up an expert group to provide a roadmap for a Green National Accounting (GNA) system.

2013
- India banned animal testing in the manufacture of cosmetics including lipsticks, eye make-up, and toothpaste.
- India passed the Right to Fair Compensation and Transparency in Land Acquisition, Rehabilitation and Resettlement Act with provisions for fairer compensation, and increased transparency during land acquisition during the setting up of industries. This act replaced the Land Acquisition Act of 1894.

Evolution of Green Movement in India

The environmental movement in India recorded a major event in 1730. Abhay Singh, Maharajah of Jodhpur required timber for burning lime for the construction of his new palace. His soldiers reached Khejarli, a village in the district of Jodhpur. This region was inhabited by Bishnois, a Hindu sect that does not allow the killing of wildlife and the cutting of trees. The Bishnois are guided by the 29 (Bish–twenty, noi – nine) principles given by Guru Jambheshwar, and these principles centre mainly on living a life respecting nature. The name of the village Khejarli was derived from the Khejri tree that grows in abundance in the village. As the soldiers started the process of felling the trees, Amrita Devi, a mother of three, protested, against the tree felling. It is said that she preferred to give up her life rather than seeing the trees chopped. Amrita Devi was beheaded and the tree felling continued. Her daughters soon joined in and met with the same end. The news spread, and soon, more Bishnois, 363 in all, became martyrs. The tree felling party went back to Jodhpur and told the Maharajah about the incident. Maharaja Abhay Singh, apologized and issued a decree that prohibited the cutting of green trees and the hunting of animals in the Bishnoi villages. This event has been considered to be the inspiration for the Chipko (hug) movement that started in the Garhwal Himalayas of Uttarakhand in the early 1970s.

Chipko Movement

The Chipko movement was a socio-ecological movement driven by the awareness against tree felling carried out by the government contractors in the region. The decreasing forest cover resulted in soil erosion and water shortages, which resulted in the farmers giving up their traditional livelihood practices such as raising livestock and collecting firewood and fodder. The destruction of the green cover also resulted in landslides and floods. This led the natives to organize themselves in protest. The initial protests started in 1971. Members of the Dasholi Gram Swarajya Sangh (DGSS) hugged trees (*chipko*) as a non-violent protest action, to force contractors to retreat. Such protests spread across the region. The protest that started at the town Chamoli Gopeshwar soon spread to other regions. In 1974, loggers arrived to start cutting trees as a part of logging operations in Reni village. DGSS workers and the men of Reni village were duped by the contractors into going to another region for a fictitious compensation payment. The women of the village refused to fell the trees and instead, started hugging them to stop the trees from being felled. They kept an all-night vigil. When the men returned and the message spread nearby regions, more people joined the protest. After four days, the contractors and loggers had to leave. This incident led the Chief Minister of the state (Hemwati Nandan Bahuguna) to set up a committee, which after studying the issue, ruled in favour of the villagers. Within a decade, similar protests took place across the Uttarakhand Himalayas. In 1977, in one such protest, women started tying *Rakhis* to the trees that were meant to be cut. The Chipko movement soon encompassed activities that included protesting against limestone mining, energy conservation, water management, and afforestation. Some of the heroes of this struggle included Gaura Devi, Sudesha Devi, Bachni Devi, Chandi Prasad Bhatt, Sundarlal Bahuguna, Govind Singh Rawat, Dhoom Singh Negi, Shamsher Singh Bisht, and Ghanasyam Raturi.

Save Silent Valley

It was during the same period that a similar movement was taking place in the southern part of India, in the Nilgiris. In 1973, the Kerala State Electricity Board (KSEB) decided to construct a dam across the *Kunthipuzha* (translated from Malayalam, it means River Kunthi), one of the major rivers originating at Silent Valley, located in the Niligiri Hills region of Palakkad district, Kerala. The region consisted of *shola* forests and was known locally as *Sairandhrivanam*, named after Sairandhri (also known as Draupadi), the wife of the *Pandavas*. Legend has it that as part of their 13-year travels, the *Pandavas* travelled south and reached this region. This region is a treasure house of fauna and flora, including medicinal plants. *Hydnocarpus*, an evergreen forest tree whose seeds provide the oil that can be used to treat leprosy, and *Rauvolfia serpentina*, a shrub used for treating high blood

In May 2013, the gram panchayat of Gerethang village in western Sikkim, India, passed a resolution to not use any paper or styrofoam plates, mugs, plastic spoons, etc., at social gatherings. The resolution also included the decision not to sell such materials in any shops. Instead, of such materials, a self-help group will produce and supply leaf-based products.

pressure are a few examples. Varieties of wild pepper, cardamom, black gram, rice, and bean have been found in this region. This region was also inhabited by the lion-tailed macaque (Fig. 1.5), the great Indian hornbill, and the Nilgiri *Tahr*. The dam was expected to have a height of 130 metres, and would have resulted in 8.3 km² of virgin rainforest getting destroyed. A paucity of funds resulted in delays in construction and the KSEB decided to resume construction in 1976. During this period, tree felling was being carried on in the valley. A call for the conservation of this forest came from poets, academicians, and conservationists. It was during this period that the Indira Gandhi intervened. She, as the Prime Minister, had formed the National Committee for Environmental Planning and Co-ordination, which was looking for places in the Western Ghats suitable for conservation. The search led to Silent Valley as an ideal place for conservation. In 1977, the Kerala Forest Research Institute (KFRI) compiled the initial assessment report, which mentioned that the region had the 'largest chunk of continuous evergreen forest without any human interference in the country'.[31] In 1978, the Government of India gave its

FIG. 1.5[32] Lion-tailed macaque, found in Silent Valley, is among the rarest and most threatened of primates

31 http://www.indianexpress.com/news/a-silent-revolution/541546/2, last accessed on 30 May 2011.
32 Photo by Aaron Logan. Used with permission. Image source: 'Lightmatter lion-tailed macaque'. Licensed under Creative Commons Attribution 2.0 via Wikimedia Commons - http://commons.wikimedia.org/wiki/File:Lightmatter_lion-tailed_macaque.jpg#mediaviewer/File:Lightmatter_lion-tailed_macaque.jpg, last accessed on 14 July 2014.

sanction to the Silent Valley National Park Project, with the condition that the state government enact legislation to protect the ecosystem. In the same year, the International Union for Conservation of Nature and Natural Resources (IUCN) passed a resolution that supported the conservation of the region. In 1979, the government of Kerala passed legislation protecting Silent Valley, however excluding the electric project area from the protected area. Although the cutting of forests continued in the excluded area, the High Court of Kerala passed an order against this, following the filing of a petition of writ. The High Court soon lifted the ban, but Indira Gandhi, the Prime Minister, requested the state government to stop further action in the valley, until a comprehensive study was done. Soon a multi-disciplinary committee, chaired by Dr MGK Menon, was created and submitted a report. Following the study of the report, the dam project was abandoned. On November 15, 1984 the Silent Valley forests were declared a National Park and on September 1, 1986 the National Park was also designated the core area of the Nilgiri Biosphere Reserve. In 2007, a 147.22 km² buffer zone was approved by the Kerala Cabinet.

Principal Objectives of National Environment Policy 2006[33]

- Conservation of critical environmental resources—To protect and conserve critical ecological systems and resources, and invaluable natural and man-made heritage, that is essential for life support, livelihoods, economic growth, and a broad conception of human well-being.
- Intra-generational equity: Livelihood Security for the Poor—To ensure equitable access to environmental resources, and quality for all sections of society, and in particular, to ensure that poor communities, which are most dependent on environmental resources for their livelihoods, are assured secure access to these resources.
- Inter-generational equity—To ensure judicious use of environmental resources to meet the needs and aspirations of present and future generations.
- Integration of environmental concerns in economic and social development—To integrate environmental concerns into policies, plans, programs, and projects for economic and social development.
- Efficiency in environmental resource use—To ensure efficient use of environmental resources in the sense of reduction in their use per unit of economic output, to minimize adverse environmental impacts.
- Environmental governance—To apply the principles of good governance (transparency, rationality, accountability, reduction in time and costs, participation, and regulatory independence) to the management and regulation of use of environmental resources.

---

33 http://www.moef.nic.in/downloads/about-the-ministry/introduction-nep2006e.pdf, last accessed on 17 July 2014.

- Enhancement of resources for environmental conservation—To ensure higher resource flows, comprising finance, technology, management skills, traditional knowledge, and social capital, for environmental conservation through mutually beneficial multi-stakeholder partnerships between local communities, public agencies, the academic and research community, investors, and multilateral and bilateral development partners.

National Action Plan on Climate Change

The National Action Plan on Climate Change (NAPCC) outlines the strategies, policies and programs adopted by India to address climate mitigation and adaptation. Released in 2008, NAPCC is guided by the following principles:[34]

- Protecting the poor and vulnerable sections of society through an inclusive and sustainable development strategy, sensitive to climate change.
- Achieving national growth objectives through a qualitative change in direction that enhances ecological sustainability, leading to further mitigation of greenhouse gas emissions.
- Devising efficient and cost-effective strategies for end user Demand Side Management.
- Deploying appropriate technologies for both adaptation and mitigation of greenhouse gases emissions extensively as well as at an accelerated pace.
- Engineering new and innovative forms of market, regulatory, and voluntary mechanisms to promote sustainable development.
- Effecting implementation of programs through unique linkages, including civil society and local government institutions, and through public private partnership.
- Welcoming international cooperation for research, development, sharing, and transfer of technologies enabled by additional funding and a global IPR regime that facilitates technology transfer to developing countries under the UNFCCC.

As part of NAPCC, eight national missions are designed and these national missions form the core of the action plan. These missions[35], their objectives and the organizations responsible for its implementation are indicated in Table 1.1.

TABLE 1.1 National missions, objectives, and responsible organizations

S. no.	Mission	Objective	Responsible entity
1	National Solar Mission	20,000 MW of solar power by 2020	Ministry of New and Renewable Energy
2	National Mission for Enhanced Energy Efficiency	10,000 MW of EE savings by 2020	Ministry of Power

(Contd)

34 http://pmindia.nic.in/Pg01-52.pdf, last accessed on 26 September 2012.
35 http://www.moef.nic.in/sites/default/files/presnt_CC.pdf, last accessed on 19 July 2013.

3	National Mission on Sustainable Habitat	EE in residential and commercial buildings, public transport, Solid waste management	Ministry of Urban Development
4	National Water Mission	Water conservation, river basin management	Ministry of Water Resources
5	National Mission for Sustaining the Himalayan Ecosystem	Conservation and adaptation practices, glacial monitoring	Ministry of Science and Technology
6	National Mission for a Green India	6 million hectares of afforestation over degraded forest lands by the end of the 12th Plan	Ministry of Environment and Forests
7	National Mission for Sustainable Agriculture	Drought proofing, risk management, agricultural research	Ministry of Agriculture
8	National Mission on Strategic Knowledge for Climate Change	Vulnerability assessment, research and observation, data management	Ministry of Science and Technology

Missions 1, 2, and 3 are focused on mitigation while Missions 3, 4, 5, 6, and 7 are focused on adaptation strategies.

National Water Policy (2012)

The salient features[36] of the National Water Policy, released in 2012, by the Ministry of Water Resources, Government of India, are as follows:

- To ensure that the Centre, the states, and various governance institutions provide access to a minimum quantity of potable water for essential health and hygiene to all its citizens, available within easy reach of the household.
- To evolve a National Framework Law.
- To recognize water as a sustainer of life and ecology.
- To manage water as a community resource, held by the state, under public trust doctrine to achieve food security, livelihood, and equitable and sustainable development for all.
- To keep a portion of river flows aside to meet ecological needs ensuring that the low and high flow releases are proportional to the natural flow regime, including base flow contribution in the low flow season through regulated ground water use.
- To develop water footprints and water footprints to be included in the project appraisal and environment impact assessment (EIA) for water uses, particularly for industrial projects.

36 Adapted from the policy document available at http://wrmin.nic.in/writereaddata/NationalWaterPolicy/NWP2012Eng6495132651.pdf, last accessed on 16 July 2014.

- To assess and review the availability of water resources and their use by various sectors at periodic intervals.
- To revive traditional water harvesting structures and water bodies.
- To sensitize and encourage the community to adapt first to the utilization of water as per local availability, before water is provided through long distance transfer.
- To price water in a way that ensures efficient usage of water and also conservation of water.
- To arrive at a fair pricing for water for drinking, sanitation, agricultural, and industrial purposes and to arrive at this pricing through an independent statutory Water Regulatory Authority, set up by each State, after wide ranging consultation with all stakeholders.
- To determine water charges on a volumetric basis.
- To incentivize the recycle and reuse of water.
- To regulate the usage of electricity to minimize the overdrawing of groundwater.
- To give statutory powers to Water Users Associations (WUAs) to collect and retain a portion of water charges, manage the volumetric quantum of water allotted to them, and maintain the distribution system in their jurisdiction. WUAs should be given the freedom to fix rates subject to floor rates determined by Water Regulatory Authorities.
- To establish a National Water Informatics Center to collect and maintain hydrologic data from the country.
- To release all hydrological data in the public domain.
- To manage water resources projects and services with community participation.
- To establish a Water Disputes Tribunal at the centre.
- To explore the possibilities of involving the private sector in water resources projects and services, with accountability to democratically elected local bodies.
- To provide improved water supply in rural areas with proper sewerage facilities.
- To incentivize sewerage systems with decentralized sewage treatment plants and least water intensive sanitation.
- To focus on collecting surface water for urban and rural water supply.
- To promote the reuse of urban water effluents from kitchens and bathrooms, after treatment.
- To use urban domestic water systems to collect and publish water accounts and water audit reports.
- To promote rainwater harvesting and desalinization in urban and industrial areas.
- To integrate urban water supply and sewage treatment schemes and to include sewerage charges in water supply bills.
- To prevent the industries from using more water within the plant, to avoid treatment, or to pollute groundwater.

- To allow industries in water-scarce regions to withdraw only make-up water and to ensure that industries have the obligation to return only effluents treated to a specified standard back into the hydrologic system.
- To plan water resources projects considering the social and environmental aspects in addition to techno-economic considerations in consultation with project-affected and beneficiary families.
- To not allow encroachments, and diversion of water bodies (such as rivers, lakes, tanks, ponds, etc.,) and drainage channels (irrigated areas as well as urban area drainage).
- To strictly regulate urban settlements, encroachments, and any developmental activities in the protected upstream areas of reservoirs or water bodies, and key aquifer recharge areas.
- To ensure that various planning processes take into consideration the environmental needs of Himalayan regions, aquatic ecosystems, wet lands, and embanked flood plains.
- To prevent the pollution of water sources and water bodies. To evolve a periodic system of inspection by third parties and to take stringent punitive action against the persons responsible for pollution.
- To ensure that industrial effluents, local cesspools, and chemical and fertilizer residues do not reach the ground water.
- To promote training and academic courses in water management.
- To start applied research in water management.
- To start a national campaign for water literacy.
- To establish an autonomous center for research in water policy.
- To conduct quality improvement programs for water planners and managers.
- To provide grants to states to update infrastructure and management practices, to prepare annual water balances and accounts for the site and basin, to prepare hydrologic balances for water systems, etc.

CONCEPT OF ECOSYSTEM

An ecosystem refers to the biological environment of an area that consists of living organisms, and its interaction with non-living physical components such as air, soil, sunlight, and water. Examples of ecosystems include agro-ecosystem, aquatic ecosystem, chaparral, coral reefs, desert, freshwater ecosystem, human ecosystem, littoral zone, marine ecosystem, pond ecosystem, prairie, rainforest, riparian zone, savanna, steppe, taiga, tundra, and urban ecosystem.

Structure and Function

The structure of an ecosystem is influenced by the systematic physical organization of the biotic (related to living organisms) and abiotic (related to non-living—physical and chemical factors) components of that ecosystem. The flow of nutrients between biotic and abiotic components is referred to as the biogeochemical cycle. Some of the major biogeochemical cycles include the carbon cycle, nitrogen cycle, phosphorus cycle, sulphur cycle, oxygen cycle, and water cycle.

Two processes happen simultaneously in an ecosystem—the biogeochemical cycle and the energy flow that happens amongst the autotrophs, heterotrophs, and decomposers (Refer to the section Food Chain, Food Web and Producers, Consumers, and Decomposers for details on autotrophs, heterotrophs, and decomposers). These two processes constitute the functions of an ecosystem.

An ecosystem can be represented in a trophic structure that depicts the relationship between producers and consumers. The trophic structure and function of an ecosystem is graphically represented as an ecological pyramid (Fig. 1.6) also referred to as a trophic pyramid/energy pyramid/Eltonian pyramid (named after Dr Charles Elton, the British ecologist who devised the pyramid). Each trophic level has a certain mass of nutrients (such as carbon, nitrogen, calcium, phosphorous, etc.,), which are referred to as 'standing state' and a certain mass of living material, which is referred to as 'standing crop' (biomass). The pyramids of number, biomass, and productivity represent the population number, the amount of biomass and the amount of productivity, respectively. Biomass pyramids indicate the amount of biomass at each trophic level, while productivity pyramids show the production of biomass or its turnover.

Energy Flow

The sun plays the prime role in any discussion related to the energy flow in the ecosystem. No wonder that ancient cultures and their people paid obeisance to the sun. Light from the sun provides energy for green plants to engage in photosynthesis, which results in the production of glucose that is stored as starch. In the presence of sunlight and a pigment called chlorophyll, plants convert water and carbon dioxide to form glucose and oxygen. This can be expressed as follows:

$$6CO_2 + 6H_2O + \text{sunlight} + \text{chlorophyll} \rightarrow C_6H_{12}O_6 + 6O_2$$

The energy stored in plants, which are consumed by animals and human beings, breaks down the glucose through the process of respiration and releases the energy needed for the plants' sustenance. This can be expressed as follows:

$$C_6H_{12}O_6 + 6O_2 \rightarrow 6CO_2 + 6H_2O + \text{energy}$$

The accumulation of energy in plants will be in the form of starch, and the transfer of this accumulated energy from plants, which are the primary producers, to other life forms is referred to as an energy flow. The flow of energy through a food chain is referred to as an energy flow. Ecologists also refer to energy flow as calorific flow.

Energy is transferred from one trophic level to another trophic level. It is estimated that 90 per cent of the energy is lost at each level in the form of heat or incompletely digested food. Thus, in a food chain that involves the primary producer, the primary consumer, the secondary consumer, and the tertiary consumer, the primary consumer receives only 10 per cent of the energy produced by the primary producer. The secondary consumer and the tertiary consumer receive only 1 per cent and 0.1 per cent of the energy produced by the primary producer.

Food Chain, Food Web and Producers, Consumers, and Decomposers

The base of the pyramid is often formed by primary producer organisms such as green plants. The first level is referred to as the first trophic level. Following the primary producers are the primary consumers (herbivores), secondary consumers, and tertiary consumers, who will occupy the top of the pyramid. Autotrophs like plants are considered to be primary producers and occupy the first level as they obtain energy directly from an energy source like sunlight. Autotrophs such as plants or algae are the producers in a food chain. They are capable of producing their own food and in order to produce it, do not rely on organic compounds or carbon sources as an energy source. Autotrophs are organisms that produce complex organic compounds such as carbohydrates, fats, and proteins from simple inorganic molecules using energy from light (by photosynthesis) or inorganic chemical reactions (chemosynthesis).

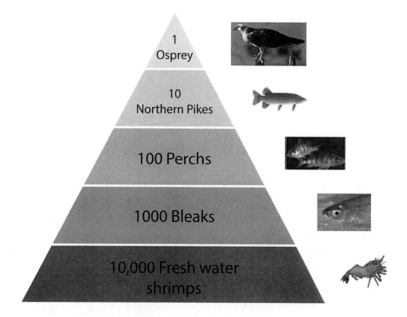

FIG. 1.6[37] Trophic pyramid

_____

37 Sources of various public domain photos used in the image: http://en.wikipedia.org/wiki/File:
Alburnus.jpg, http://en.wikipedia.org/wiki/File:Heterocarpus_ensifer.jpg, http://en.wikipedia.org/wiki/
File:YellowPerch.jpg, http://en.wikipedia.org/wiki/File:Esox_lucius1.jpg, http://commons.wikimedia.org/
wiki/File:Pandion_haliaetus_NBII.jpg, http://commons.wikimedia.org/wiki/File:KopAlver.jpg, last accessed
on 7 August 2014.

The food linkage between various trophic levels is referred to as the food chain and the network connecting various food chains is referred to as the food web. Links are trophic interactions directed from prey to predator. A chain is a sequence of links that starts at a basal species and ends with a consumer species. Food chains are directional paths of trophic energy, or equivalently, sequences of links that start with basal species, such as producers or fine organic matter, and end with consumer organisms.[38] A food chain is a linear sequence that starts from a species that eats no other species (like plants) and ends with a species that is eaten by no other species in the web. Species like plants are referred to as producers as they utilize solar energy to produce food and are not dependent on other organisms. Food chains typically start with a producer. In a food chain, all organisms other than the organisms at the first level are referred to as consumers as they consume some other organism. Chain length is measured by the number of links in the sequence from producers or fine organic matter to consumers. A web's average chain length is the average number of links in every chain connecting all consumers to basal species.[39] Raymond Lindeman, in his now famous research paper 'The Tropic-Dynamic Aspect of Ecology'[40] spoke about the energy flow in ecosystems and gave the 10 per cent law suggesting that only 10 per cent of energy is transferred to the next trophic level. Therefore, plants can store only 10 per cent of the energy from the sun. Herbivores or primary consumers have access only to this 10 per cent of this energy while the remaining 90 per cent is dissipated as heat. There is further energy loss of 90 per cent as one move from the level of a primary consumer to that of a secondary consumer (Fig. 1.6).

The health of the organism at the top of the food chain is indicative of the health of the entire ecosystem. For example, the tiger is considered to be an apex predator. It is also referred to as a top predator or a top-level predator or an alpha predator. A tiger can exist only if there is a healthy availability of other species in the ecosystem, and thus the existence of the tiger is an indicator of the health of the ecosystem, and the conservation of the tiger results in the conservation of species across all trophic levels. Due to this reason, Project Tiger, a project launched by the Government of India in 1973 aiming at the conservation of tigers, also aims at maintaining the natural habitat of tigers and rectifying the damage done to the habitat. In the formative years of this project, there were nine tiger reserves, which have increased to 46 in 2014[41].

---

38 Neo D. Martines, 'Artifacts or Attributes? Effects of Resolution on the Little Rock Lake Food Web', *Ecological Monographs*, 61(4), 1991.

39 Neo D. Martines, 'Artifacts or Attributes? Effects of Resolution on the Little Rock Lake Food Web', *Ecological Monographs*, 61(4), 1991.

40 Lindeman, Raymond L., 'The Trophic-Dynamic Aspect of Ecology', *Ecology*, 23(4), 1942, pp. 399–417.

41 http://projecttiger.nic.in/content/107_1_Background.aspx, last accessed on 14 July 2014.

In 2012, LG Electronics USA launched consumer goods (an OLED TV, LCD Computer Monitor, a refrigerator, a washing machine, and a smartphone) that carry the CarbonFree logo, a certification from CarbonFund.org foundation that certifies a product to be carbon neutral, a feat achieved by the company offsetting or reducing emissions associated with the product. Life Cycle Analysis (LCAs) of the products, from extraction of raw materials to product disposal, will be carried out to determine the emissions caused by these products. LG is working with E-Stewards Initiative to engage in e-waste recycling.

Ecological Succession

Ecological succession refers to the process of change undergone by a biotic community during a period of time. Usually such changes are orderly and predictable. For example, a deciduous forest community could be destroyed by a wildfire. Though the trees and plants are destroyed, the soil is very much alive, now with added nutrients derived from the fallen trees. Soon, grasses and bushes start growing, followed by fast-growing trees. Under the fast-growing trees grow the slow-growing shade tolerant trees. As days go by, the fast-growing trees are dwarfed by deciduous trees. This results in the death of the fast-growing shade intolerant trees. Now, the situation is conducive for another wild-fire, resulting in the repetition of the entire cycle.

Periodic fires in forest ecosystems help to maintain the habitat. Such naturally occurring fires promote diversity of the forest ecosystem. Examples of how a forest fire helps to maintain the habitat and ecological succession are as follows:

- Natural fires near the Great Lakes[42] ecosystem in USA usually occur every 125-180 years. The seed of the jack pine, which is found in this region, is aided by fire. The seeds are found inside the cones in the tree and these cones remain closed for many years. The heat from the fire opens the cones and releases the seeds onto the ground. The seeds of the jack pine can withstand significantly high heat exposure. Along with the burning of the mature tree, the fire also burns the existing vegetation and litter on the ground. This way, the seeds are provided with soil that is high in minerals.
- In regions like Alaska, the decay of vegetation is slow because of the cold conditions. Thus the availability of nutrients for life is also slow. A natural fire results in the release of a significant amount of nutrients, resulting in a fresh growth of plants, which results in food for animal life.

While natural fires result in ecological succession, a human induced fire causes harm. In USA, almost 80,000 wildfires are recorded each year and burn more than 6.5 million acres of forests and grasslands annually.[43] It has been estimated that nine out of ten wildfires in USA are caused by humans.[44]

---

42 Located in the US–Canada border, these five lakes consists of Lake Superior, Lake Michigan, Lake Huron, Lake Erie, and Lake Ontario. They form the largest group of freshwater lakes on the planet.
43 http://www.smokeybear.com/resources/Smokey%20TG%20BW.pdf, last accessed on 4 July 2012.
44 http://www.smokeybear.com/resources/Smokey%20TG%20BW.pdf, last accessed on 4 July 2012.

Ecological succession can be of three types – primary, secondary, and cyclic. Primary succession occurs in an environment where conditions suitable for biotic growth are created anew. An example could be an area where there has been a flow of lava to a region where soil did not exist, or an area from where a glacier has retreated. Following the cooling of lava, pioneer organisms like lichen and fungus may start growing. In due course of time, these pioneer organisms are replaced by grass and other pioneer plants, which will soon be replaced by other plants and animals. In secondary succession, there is an interruption to an already established ecosystem, for example, a forest fire burning away the existing biotic connections and paving the way for new ones. Primary succession usually takes a longer period of time as compared to secondary succession. Cyclic succession is the gradual, organic change in vegetation and species that occurs in an area when there is little disturbance to the ecosystem.

Limiting Factors, Law of Minimum, and Law of Tolerance

The Law of Tolerance, as proposed by V.E. Shelford states that the abundance in the population of an organism depends on the extent to which a complex of conditions is satisfied. Each organism has ranges of tolerance, which are the upper and lower limits of a range of environmental factors such as light, temperature, availability of water, and food, that contribute to the existence of the organism. Organisms with a wide range of tolerance will increase in their population while those organisms that have a narrow range of tolerance will have a restricted population. Limiting factors are those factors that regulate the population of an organism when they occur in excess or are insufficient. The Law of the Minimum, as proposed by Justus von Liebig states that growth in the population of an organism is limited by the factor that is the most deficient (at a minimum) in the environment that sustains the organism. The law of the minimum was originally meant only for the plant kingdom. Shelford expanded the Law of the Minimum to include the animal kingdom.

In 2013, the Government of India banned the establishment of dolphinariums for commercial entertainment, private or public exhibition, and for interaction purposes. The ban is applicable not just to dolphins, but all marine mammals. In its statement, the Government of India said that it is morally unacceptable to keep dolphins captive for entertainment purposes. India is one of four countries in the world (the others being Costa Rica, Hungary, and Chile) to ban such shows.

Carrying Capacity

Carrying capacity refers to the maximum population density of a given species that a given environment can support. It is also referred to as the maximal load in an environment. The carrying capacity for each species in a habitat is different because of the difference in the requirements for food, shelter, and social requirements. Technology and behavioural intervention has played an important role in impacting the carrying capacity of the world. The use of fertilizers, composting, greenhouses, land reclamation, etc., has increased the carrying capacity of the world. However, many of these interventions have resulted in negatively impacting the life of other living organisms and in the degradation of the planet. For example, while the increased use of fertilizers has resulted in increased food production, it has also resulted in an enormous usage of water and fossil fuels, from which fertilizers are made. Similarly, land reclamation has resulted in the destruction of wetlands, which have provided ecosystem services such as flood control, groundwater replenishment, and water purification.

Various Ecosystems and Their Features

Forest Ecosystem

A forest is an area with a high density of trees (for more details, including the definition and classification of forests, refer to the chapter on bio-diversity). Forests cover 30 per cent of the total land area and 9.4 per cent of the planet's surface. They cover 90 per cent of the world's terrestrial biodiversity. A forest consists of the upper tree layer, also referred to as the canopy or overstory, and the lower tree layer or the understory. The understory consists of the following: (a) shrub layer, (b) herb layer, and (c) the moss layer with soil microbes. Human induced factors that affect forests include deforestation through logging and forest fires, the introduction of foreign tree species, and environmental fallouts like acid rain. However, at least some of these negative interventions can be offset by allowing for the regrowth of the forest. Forests that have regrown after major human induced or natural disturbances are referred to as secondary forests. The forests that have not undergone such disturbances are referred to as primary forests or old growth forests.

Grassland Ecosystem

Geographical regions dominated by grasses are referred to as grasslands. The height of the vegetation in this land can vary. Grasslands support diverse wildlife and can be classified as follows: (a) tropical and subtropical grasslands, (b) temperate grasslands, (c) flooded grasslands, (d) montane grasslands, (e) Tundra grasslands, and (f) desert and xeric grasslands. Some of the mammals found in grasslands include wildebeest (gnu), American bison, giant anteater, and Dzungarian horse. Grasslands could occur as a result of animal movement and behaviour. For example, the bush elephants of Africa are known to eat the saplings of acacia plants preventing them from maturing into trees. These elephants are also known for ripping plants and pulling down trees. The ecosystem in grasslands is also influenced by human intervention including farming and making provision for the grazing of domesticated animals.

The world's tallest grasslands are the Terai-Duar grasslands located at the base of the Himalayas. These grasslands stretch through Bhutan, Nepal, and India. Grasses in this grassland include *baruwa* and *kans* grass. The region is also known for the one-horned rhinoceros, Bengal tigers, Indian leopards, and Asian elephants. Some of the other species of wildlife found in the grasslands of India include the Indian bison, Indian water buffalo, nilgai, Bengal florican, lesser florican, pygmy hog, hispid hare, hog deer, and swamp deer (*barasingha*).[45]

---

45 http://www.planningcommission.nic.in/aboutus/committee/wrkgrp11/tf11_grass.pdf, last accessed on 17 July 2014.

Desert Ecosystem

A desert is a geographical region that receives extremely low precipitation. Regions with precipitation less than 250 millimetres (10 inches), are considered to be true deserts, while those regions that receive precipitation between 250 millimetres and 500 millimetres are considered to be semi-deserts or steppes. These regions lose more moisture than they receive. Deserts occupy one-third of the total land area of the planet. Only 20 per cent of the earth's deserts are covered by sand. Deserts can be classified as hot and cold deserts. Hot deserts are found in the tropical region. The Saharan desert, Arabian desert, and Thar desert in India, are examples. Cold deserts are typically located at higher altitudes than hot deserts. They may also be part of the rain-shadow region of high mountains. For example, Ladakh is a high-altitude cold desert located in the northern part of India with Himalayan ranges creating a rain-shadow region in Ladakh (refer to Fig. 1.7 for another example of a locale with a rain-shadow region on one side and perennial rivers on the windward side). While deserts have relatively thin flora cover, they are diverse. Desert animals in hot deserts usually remain hidden during daylight hours because of the heat conditions prevailing in the desert and the need of water. Two of the largest deserts of the world are cold deserts–the Antarctic and the Arctic. The largest hot desert is the Saharan Desert.

In the Thar desert region of India, 23 species of lizard and 25 species of snakes have been found[46]. Mammalian varieties found in this region consist of 41 species[47] and include the blackbuck, Indian gazelle, and the Indian wild ass. The lack of water in this region ensured that the conversion of grassland to cropland was slow, thereby resulting in the survival of these animals. 141 species[48] of migratory and resident birds, including species of eagles, falcons, harriers, and vultures, have been recorded in the Thar desert. Despite the extreme climate, the Thar desert region is also one of the most densely populated regions of the world, with a human population of 84–90 per sq. km. as compared to 3–6 per sq. km. in other deserts.

Aquatic Ecosystem

An ecosystem associated with a body of water is referred to as an aquatic ecosystem (refer to Fig. 1.8 for an aquatic ecosystem). Two of the major aquatic ecosystems are marine ecosystems and freshwater ecosystems. While marine ecosystems cover approximately 71 per cent of the earth's surface and contain 97 per cent of the planet's water, freshwater

---

46 http://edugreen.teri.res.in/explore/life/thar.htm, last accessed on 17 July 2014.
47 http://www.undp.org/content/dam/undp/documents/projects/IND/00057823_Project%20Document%20-%20 71579.pdf, last accessed on 17 July 2014.
48 http://www.undp.org/content/dam/undp/documents/projects/IND/00057823_Project%20Document%20-%20 71579.pdf, last accessed on 17 July 2014.

FIG. 1.7[49] An image from Tirunelveli district in Tamilnadu, India, depicting the Agasthyamalai hills. While the Agasthyamalai hills create a rain-shadow for the Tirunelveli region, the hills are also the source for rivers (Thamirabarani, Karamana, and Neyyar) and medicinal plants on the windward side of the hills.

ecosystems cover 0.8 per cent of the planet's surface and contain 0.009 per cent of the planet's water. Marine ecosystems include oceans, estuaries, lagoons, mangroves, the deep sea, the sea floor, coral reefs, and more.

---

49 Photo by Arun Ganesh, used with permission. Image source: 'Agasthyamalai range and Tirunelveli rainshadow' by w:user:PlaneMad - Photo by w:user:PlaneMad. Licensed under Creative Commons Attribution-Share Alike 3.0 via Wikimedia Commons - http://commons.wikimedia.org/wiki/File:Agasthyamalai_range_and_Tirunelveli_rainshadow.jpg#mediaviewer/File:Agasthyamalai_range_and_Tirunelveli_rainshadow.jpg, last accessed on 26 September 2012.

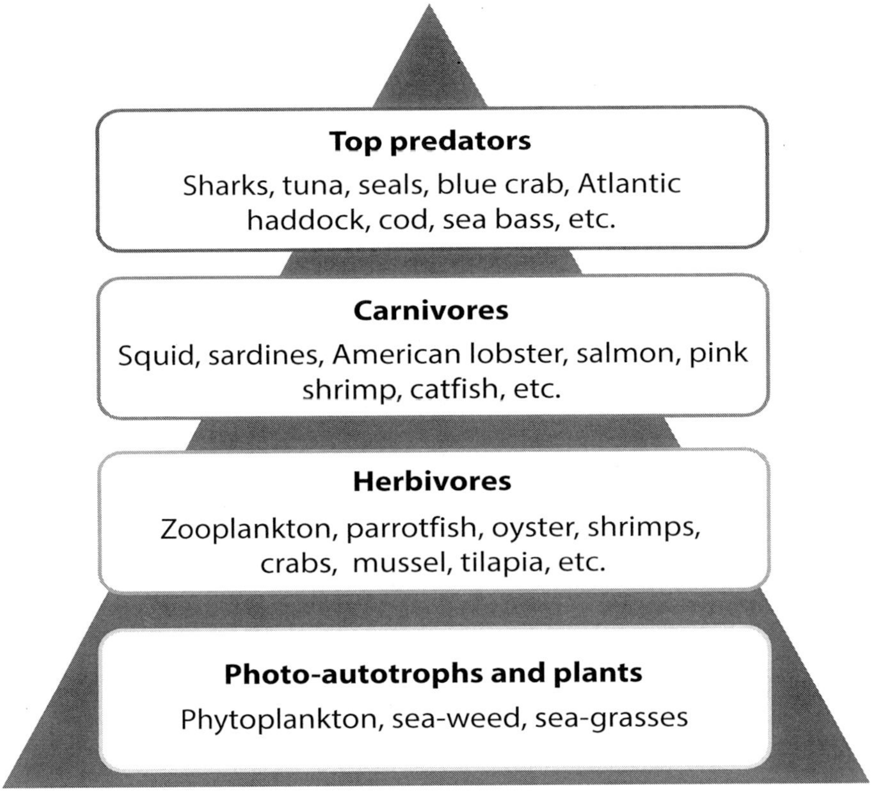

Top predators
Sharks, tuna, seals, blue crab, Atlantic haddock, cod, sea bass, etc.

Carnivores
Squid, sardines, American lobster, salmon, pink shrimp, catfish, etc.

Herbivores
Zooplankton, parrotfish, oyster, shrimps, crabs, mussel, tilapia, etc.

Photo-autotrophs and plants
Phytoplankton, sea-weed, sea-grasses

FIG. 1.8 Aquatic ecosystems

Though freshwater ecosystems cover only a miniscule part of the earth's surface, they contain 41 per cent of the world's known fish species. Fresh water ecosystems can be classified into the lentic ecosystem, lotic ecosystem, and wetland ecosystem. The lentic ecosystem consists of water bodies with slow moving water. This includes ponds, pools, and lakes. The backwaters and lagoons of Kerala fall into this category. The lotic ecosystem refers to water bodies with rapidly moving water, such as streams and rivers. Wetlands are areas where water and soil are in close proximity. Types of wetland include swamps, marshes, fens, and bogs. Wetlands are considered to be the top productive natural ecosystems. In addition to providing a number of ecosystem services, they also support a large number of animal and plant species. The *Sundarbans* in Bengal are known for their wetlands with mangrove forests. Freshwater ecosystems perform important ecosystem services including recycling nutrients, purifying water, recharging of ground water, controlling floods, and providing a habitat for a variety of wildlife.

CHAPTER SUMMARY

- Ecology, from the context of its root words, refers to writings/discourses/collections/science/study of the household. Ecology is the study of the interlinkages between living organisms along with their physical, chemical, and biological environment.
- Environment management is a branch of study that deals with managing the resources of the planet in a way that benefits the well-being of all species; and sustains resources for use by future generations.
- Human intervention has resulted in a massive decline of biodiversity due to habitat destruction, release of toxins, the usage and release of harmful chemicals, over-harvesting, and more.
- As per a report from 'The Economics of Ecosystems and Biodiversity' (TEEB), 47 per cent of the GDP of the poor in India comes from ecosystem services.
- The *Chipko* movement was a socio-ecological movement driven by awareness against tree-felling carried out by government contractors in the region.
- An ecosystem refers to the biological environment of an area that consists of living organisms, and its interaction with the non-living physical components such as air, soil, sunlight, and water.
- The energy stored in the plants that are consumed by animals and human beings, breaks down glucose through the process of respiration and releases the energy needed for their sustenance. This can be expressed as follows:

$C_6H_{12}O_6 + 6O_2 \rightarrow 6CO_2 + 6H_2O + energy$

- The base of the pyramid is often formed by the primary producers, primary consumers, secondary consumers, and tertiary consumers.

- Ecological succession refers to the process of change undergone by a biotic community in a period of time.
- The Law of Tolerance, as proposed by V. E. Shelford states that the abundance in the population of an organism depends on the extent to which a complex of conditions is satisfied.
- The Law of the Minimum, as proposed by Justus von Liebig states that the growth in the population of an organism is limited by the factor that is the most deficient (at a minimum) in the environment that sustains the organism.
- Carrying capacity refers to the maximum population density of a given species that a given environment can support. It is also referred to as the maximal load in an environment.
- A forest is an area with a high density of trees. Forests cover 30 per cent of total land area and 9.4 per cent of the planet's surface.
- Geographical regions dominated by grasses are referred to as grasslands. The height of the vegetation in this land can vary. Grasslands support diverse wildlife and can be classified as follows: (a) tropical and subtropical grasslands, (b) temperate grasslands, (c) flooded grasslands, (d) montane grasslands, (e) Tundra grasslands, and (f) desert and xeric grasslands.
- A desert is a geographical region that receives extremely low precipitation.
- An ecosystem associated with a body of water is referred to as an aquatic ecosystem. Two of the major aquatic ecosystems are marine ecosystems and freshwater ecosystems.

KEYWORDS

Ecology	Food web
Ecological succession	Law of Minimum
Ecosystem	Law of Tolerance
Environment management	Sustainable development
Food chain	

EXERCISES

Multiple-choice Questions

1. 'Oikos', in Greek means
   (a) house or household   (c) freedom
   (b) creation   (d) environment
2. The *Chipko* movement was a socio-ecological
   movement driven by
   (a) awareness against tree-felling
   (b) planting green trees
   (c) voicing for human rights
   (d) saving animals
3. The objective of the National Environment
   Policy 2006 was
   (a) conservation of critical environmental
       resources
   (b) integration of environmental concerns in
       economic and social development
   (c) efficiency in environmental resource use
   (d) enhancement of resources for
       environmental conservation
   (e) all of these
4. The National Action Plan on Climate Change
   (NAPCC) is guided by the following principle:
   (a) Protecting the poor and vulnerable sections
       through an inclusive and sustainable
       development strategy, sensitive to climate
       change
   (b) Inter-generational equity
   (c) Intra-generational equity
   (d) Forming multilateral and bilateral
       development partners
5. _____ refers to a biological environment of
   an area that consists of living organisms and its
   interaction with non-living physical components.
   (a) Ecosystem   (c) Food web
   (b) Food chain   (d) Bioaccumulation

6. Energy stored in plants, breaks down glucose
   through the process of respiration and releases
   the energy needed for their sustenance and can
   be expressed as
   (a) $C_6H_{12}O_6 + 6O_2 \rightarrow 6CO_2 + 6H_2O + energy$
   (b) $C_6H_{12}O_6 + 6O_2 \rightarrow 6CO_2 + 6H_2O + glucose$
   (c) $C_6H_{12}O_5 + 6O_2 \rightarrow 5CO_2 + 6H_2O + energy$
   (d) $C_6H_{12}O_6 + 6O_2 \rightarrow 6CO_2 + 5H_2O +$
       carbohydrates
7. The base of the pyramid is often formed by the
   (a) primary producers, primary consumers,
       secondary consumers, and tertiary
       consumers
   (b) primary consumers, the primary producers,
       secondary consumers, and tertiary consumers
   (c) primary producers, primary consumers,
       tertiary consumers, and secondary consumers
   (d) tertiary consumers, primary producers,
       primary consumers, and secondary
       consumers
8. _____ refers to the process of change
   undergone by a biotic community in a period of
   time.
   (a) Ecological succession   (c) Ecology
   (b) Environment succession   (d) Food web
9. The maximum population density of a given
   species that a given environment can support is
   referred to as
   (a) carrying capacity   (c) bio-diversity
   (b) withholding capacity   (d) ecosystem
10. _____ ecosystem includes oceans,
    estuaries, lagoons, mangroves, deep sea, sea
    floor, coral reefs, and more.
    (a) Marine   (c) Grassland
    (b) Forest   (d) Deep

Short Answer Questions

1. Define etymology, ecology, and environmental
   management.
2. Describe the evolution of green movement in
   India.
3. What do you mean by food chain and food
   web?
4. Define the Law of Minimum and the Law of
   Tolerance.

Long Answer Questions

1. Explain the evolution of sustainable development.
2. Explain the National Environmental Policy (NEP) 2006 and the National Action Plan on Climate Change (NAPCC).
3. Explain the concept of ecosystem, its structure, functions, and various types of ecosystem.
4. Explain ecological succession.
5. Explain the energy flow in the ecosystem.

Reflective Question

1. The Living Planet Report states that 'If everyone in the world lived like an average resident of the United States or the United Arab Emirates, then a bio-capacity equivalent to more than 4.5 Earths would be required to keep up with humanity's consumption and CO_2 emissions'. How can we, as humanity, and you, as a citizen, make a transition to a sustainable way of being and living?

Take-home Activity

1. Make a food chain for each of the following. You should use examples local to your region:
   (a) Desert food chain
   (b) Aquatic food chain

Web Reading

1. Silent Valley: 25 years of an ecological triumph http://www.livemint.com/Home-Page/ZTKhUS56VU5MODk8aYxb2J/Silent-Valley-25-years-of-an-ecological-triumph.html, last accessed on 18 September 2014.
2. World Business Council for Sustainable Development (WBCSD) Case Studies on bio-diversity and eco-system services, stakeholder consultation and ecosystem accounting http://www.wbcsd.org/Pages/EDocument/EDocumentDetails.aspx?ID=14923, last accessed on 18 September 2014.

Recommended Books

1. Jared Diamond, *Collapse: How Societies Choose to Fail or Survive*, Penguin Books, 2005.
2. John Robbins, *The Food Revolution*, Magna Publisher, 2001.
3. David Suzuki and Amanda McConnell, *The Sacred Balance*, Greystone Books, 2007.
4. Henry David Thoreau, *Walden; or, Life in the Woods*, GBD Publications, 2010.

Recommended Documentary/ Movie:

1. *An Inconvenient Truth*. Dir. Davis Guggenheim. Paramount Classics, 2006.

Answers to Mutiple-choice Questions:
   1(a)   2(a)   3(e)   4(a)   5(a)   6(a)   7(a)   8(a)   9(a)   10(a)

SPIRITUAL PERSPECTIVES ON ENVIRONMENT

After reading the chapter, the reader will be able to understand the following:

- How the ethos and culture of India respect every being of this planet, living, and non-living
- Introduction to sustainable farming methods such as natural farming and organic farming
- How a plant-based diet is friendlier to the planet
- Declaration given by various religions on nature and climate change

The word 'Hindu' entered the English language in the seventeenth century. It came from the Persians, whose Muslim descendants ruled India for close to a thousand years. They derived it from the river Indus, which flows through the north-western plains of the subcontinent and gave its name to the land and its people. How apt that in naming the religion of India, we should call it after its bioregion. Hindus, with their reverence for sacred rivers, mountains, forests, and animals, have always been close to nature.... If Hinduism can be given a legitimate name, it is 'Sanatan Dharma', which is used by many Hindus today. Roughly translated, this means 'the eternal essence of life'. The essence is not limited only to humans. It is the essential quality that unites all beings—human, animal, or plant—with the universe that surrounds them and ultimately with the original source of their existence, the Godhead. This perception of underlying unity is what causes Hindus to steadfastly refuse to separate their religion from their daily life, or to separate their own faith from the other great traditions of the world. To them all religions are a part of the process of discovering the unity of God, humanity, and nature.[1]

INDIA'S HERITAGE IN ENVIRONMENT

In the speech delivered at the 2009 World Parliament of Religions, Swami Sandeepananda Giri, Founder, School of Bhagavad Gita, said, 'All the Indian scriptures took birth in the forests and among nature, in the presence of plants, animals, and all the forces of nature'.[2] Prof G.D. Sharma says, 'The first thing to observe is that the fountainhead of our culture is not in the city but in the *Aranyaka*. In the forests, there was a lot of open space. The trees and plants, rivers and lakes, had

---

1 Ranchor Prime, Vedic Ecology: Practical Wisdom for Surviving the 21st Century, Mandala Publishing, 2002.
2 http://www.schoolofbhagavadgita.org/pdf/Speech-parliament-of-world-religion.pdf, last accessed on 28 April 2010.

Most Indian epics, Puranas (mythologies) and scriptures begin with an appeal for the divine incarnation to heal and save the Earth. The five elements even assumed God like forms and were given names. Why! Even names like *Vishwamitra*, which means friend of the universe, are proof that the ancient wise sages and men respected, worshipped, and loved nature.

abundant scope for man to coexist with them'.[3] 'Protection of Nature is our culture. Only India has such a culture. If there is a word like '*Aranyaka*' in any of the old literatures, it is only in India', says poet Sugathakumari.[4] All the four Vedas—Rig, Sama, Yajur, and Atharva—have a number of hymns dedicated to the natural deities. Indra, considered as the deity associated with rains, has the largest number of hymns attached to him.[5] Rigveda mentions flora species such as lotus, bamboo, various types of grasses, ashvatta, and fauna such as peacocks, swans, water buffaloes, bulls, lions, boars, camels, and elephants. Atharvaveda mentions a range of flora and fauna. Swami Sandeepananda Giri adds, 'Most Indian epics, Puranas (mythologies), and scriptures begin with an appeal for the divine incarnation to heal and save the Earth. The five elements even assumed God-like forms and were given names. Why! Even names like *Vishwamitra*, which means friend of the universe, are proof that the ancient wise sages and men respected, worshipped and loved nature'.[6] The Earth is considered as the Mother of all mothers — *Bhu Mata* or *Prithvi Ma*. Even now, whenever a new building or house is constructed, *Bhoomi Puja* is performed.

Thiruvalluvar's *Kural* (also referred to as *Thirukural*) mentions that the existence of sparkling water, open space (arable lands), hills, and forests constitute a fort (Verse 742).[7] The culture of India associated rivers to the quality of creation and sustenance of life. A motherly nature has been ascribed to the rivers. Thus, most of the major rivers of India have been given a feminine name.[8] Releasing waste to the rivers was considered a sin. While taking bath in the house, one is suggested to cultivate the feeling that the water poured on the body has the presence of the holy rivers such as Ganga, Yamuna, Godavari, Saraswathi, Narmada, Sindhu, and Kaveri. This is done through invoking *Nadee Vandanam* or 'Remembrance of Rivers', which is as follows:

> *Gangecha Yamune Devi*
> *Godaavari Saraswathi*
> *Narmade Sindhu Kaaveri*
> *Thirthesmin Sannidhim Kuru*

3 G D Sharma, Management and the Indian Ethos, Rupa and Co., 2004
4 The Prayer of India, *Piravi*, October 2009.
5 http://www.cbseacademic.in/web_material/Circulars/2012/68_KTPI/Module_5.pdf, last accessed on 22 November 2012.
6 http://www.schoolofbhagavadgita.org/pdf/Speech-parliament-of-world-religion.pdf, last accessed on 28 April 2010.
7 Manineerum Mannum Malaiyum Aninizhar, Kaatum Utaiya Tharan
8 Lalitha Vaidyanathan, Environmentalism in Hinduism, Paper presented at the workshop of EARTHWARE on 'Traditional belief and Religious Approaches to Environmental Preservation', organized by UNESCO and ANTARA at Trawas, East Jawa, Indonesia, April 11–15, 1994.

(I invoke, in this water, the holy presence of Goddess Ganga, Yamuna, Godavari, Saraswathi, Narmada, Sindhu, and Kaveri.)

The worship and veneration of trees is a custom found in many cultures of the world (Fig. 2.1). It is done as a respect for the life-giving quality of the tree and the fertility of the earth. Scriptures speak about celestial trees that connect beings of all kinds. The tree marks a sacred centre. The whole of Auroville is centred on a Banyan tree. Lord Shiva as Dakshinamurthy is depicted as sitting in silence under *Ashwath Vriksha* (a name for Pipal/Bodhi tree/*Ficus religiosa*). Worship of Pipal trees was a ritual, and *Brahma Purana* referred to Pipal as the king of trees. We can find that many villages also have Banyan trees as their centre. A Banyan tree at Kurukshetra is also said to have witnessed the *Gitopadesa*.[9] The Banyan tree is found in the imagery of Kabbalah, the mystical aspect of Judaism.[10] One tradition of Buddhist thought believes that it was the Bodhi Tree, a Banyan tree of the species of Sacred Fig (under which Gautama, The Buddha experienced enlightenment), which inspired Gautama, The Buddha, to spread the message of Dharma (*Dhamma*) to all, rather than remaining in meditative absorption (*Pratyeka Buddha*). In the account given by Ashvaghosha about the events in the life of Gautama, The Buddha, he speaks about a female deity in the woods who supported Siddhartha's (former name of Gautama, The Buddha) determination in his quest for awakening.

FIG. 2.1[11] The entrance of Anjumoorthy Temple, Palakkad, Kerala. Note the two Banyan trees flanking the entrance of the temple.

---

9 http://www.freewebs.com/balakrishnanmuniapan/Kurukshetra%20-%20The%20Land%20of%20Gita.pdf, last accessed on 28 April 2010.
10 http://www.khandro.net/nature_trees.htm, last accessed on 28 April 2010.
11 Photo by Ajith Sankar R N

Swami Chinmayananda says,[12]

'It is the tradition of Hindu thought from the early days of the Vedas to consider the entire universe in the form of a tree. Not only in the Vedas, we find the same tradition of referring to this universal symbol, both in its erect and inverted position, in Buddhist, Gnostic, Hermitic, Christian, and Islamic religious books also.

The Maitreyopanishad speaks of one Asvattha tree identified with Om. The Rig Veda asks: 'What is that tree out of which heaven and earth are fashioned?' In Mundakopanishad, again, there is the picture of the tree referred to. In the Mahabharata, in its Asvatthama-parva, we find a full description of the Brahma-vrksa. In Vishnu Sahasranama, Tree is counted as one of the names of the Supreme Lord. In the later literature, the conception changed, and we find the same tree standing inverted, representing the entire finite world of plurality. The Kathopanishad conceives it, and the Svetasvatara Upanishad refers to it, and in the Gita, we find an exhaustive description of it.

The finite world of plurality is conceived of as an Asvattha tree because a Banyan tree can be considered relatively immortal due to its long days of existence. Again, there is no single tree which can be otherwise quoted which has such a large number of branches and leaves which are ever in a state of agitation, with so many adventitious roots flowing out of its branches to embrace the Mother Earth and make its shady grounds a thousand-pillared hall of noisy confusions! The very name of the tree, Asvattha, also has, in the construction of its nomenclature, a meaning well-suited for the purpose: Sva means 'tomorrow', ttha means 'existence'. 'Svattha' means, therefore, 'that which exists tomorrow also;' when the negative sense 'A' is prefixed it becomes 'Asvattha, meaning, 'that which will not exist tomorrow' - that which is finite.

This Tree of Universe, representing in itself the entire world of objects, is vitalised by the eternal, all-pervading consciousness which is the goal of Rsi-s struggling on the path of self-realisation.

Every Hindu is supposed to have the sacred plant 'tulsi' in their house. In the morning, salutation is given to the *tulsi* as a symbol of respect to the entire plant kingdom and the plant aspect of nature. A lamp is also lighted near the tulsi plant symbolising that the light of life is being continuously supported by the plant kingdom. The *Tulsi Stotram* (Hymn to Tulsi) is as below:

NamasTulasi Kalyaani
Namo Vishnu Priye Subhe
Namo Moksha Prade Devi
Nama: Sampath Pradaayini

The hymn could be translated as:

Salutations to the Tulsi, the auspicious one,
Salutations to the one, who is the beloved of Vishnu,
Salutations to the Goddess, who offers liberation,
Salutations to the one, who bestows wealth.

---

12 Swami Chinmayananda, Discourses on Taittiriya Upanishad, Central Chinmaya Mission Trust, Mumbai, 2008. Used with permission.

Offering of food is made to the trees, which has been associated with wisdom and immortality. People believe that trees are the abode of deities. In India, *Yaksha* or *Yakshasi* (fairy or spirit beings) are said to occupy trees. Deep Narayan Pandey, in his paper *Sacred Water and Sanctified Vegetation: Tanks and Trees in India* states that 'Sacred trees symbolize specific arrays of human conditions, possibilities, and anticipation'. Married women, as part of their *vrata* (fasting) honouring Savithri who brought back the life of her husband from Yama, offer their prayers to the Banyan tree (It was under the Banyan tree that Satyavan, Savithri's husband, regained life).

In Tamilnadu, there are famous temples associated with veneration of trees. The *Ekambareswarar* temple located at Kanchipuram has a 3500–year-old mango tree. The main deity of Thiruvanaikaval located at Tiruchirapalli is *Jambukeswara*, representing the element water. This deity is depicted sitting under a *jambu* (black plum) tree, which grows over a small stream that engulfs the deity during the rainy season. The Chidambaram temple is associated with the legend of Lord Shiva entering the mangrove forest. Pichavaram, located near Chidambaram, is the second largest mangrove forest in the world. The temples of Chidambaram, Kalahasti Nathar, Thiruvannamalai Arunachaleswara, Thiruvanaikaval Jambukeswara, and Kanchi Ekambareswara represent the five elements of space/ether, wind/air, fire, water, and earth.

Lord Vishnu is associated with the Bargad, Gular, and Pipal, Lord Shiva with Bel, Maulashri, Rudraksha, and Lord Dattatreya with Gular. Trees in Tamilnadu are also associated with local deities, in addition to Gods who are widely revered. *Arkamma* is the Goddess associated with the *erukku* plant, while *Panaiveriyamman* is a Goddess associated with the Palmyra palm (*panai*). *Puliyidaivalaiyamman* is the Goddess associated with tamarind tree (*Pula*) while Goddess *Kadambariyamman* is associated with the *Kadamba* tree. Sal, deodar, rudraksha, bel, ashok, kadam, and pipal are considered sacred at different parts of India. Plants are also offered protection during certain vulnerable stages of their life. The Kols of Vindhya Hills do not eat the unripe fruits of wood apple and Indian gooseberry before the Dussehra festival (October). Such an action ensured that viable seeds are produced from the fruits. If consumed otherwise, seed cannot be produced, and the species will become extinct. Indian Fig (*Vad/Vat*), Pipal, Gular (*dumber*), and Indian frankincense (*Salai*) are given protection in the Aravallis and is considered sacred in other parts of India too. The scriptures say that one tree is equal to ten sons. *Arthashastra* prescribes fines for those who destroy trees, groves, and forests (Table 2.1).

In Vedic literature (8000–1000 BC), especially in Atharvaveda (1000 BC), plants are considered as deities. There are *Suktas* to *vanaspatis*[13] like Ashvatta (III 6) and others and qualities of living beings are attributed to them. These deities are invoked to cure

---

13 Vanaspati, in Sanskrit, refers to large trees.

TABLE 2.1[14] Fines for destroying trees in *Arthashastra*

Protection of plants		
	Nature of offence	**Punishment prescribed**
1	Felling a living tree for (a) establishing mine, factory or constructing big bridge/dam etc. (b) firewood	(a) Offender should be condemned as a degraded person (XI. 64). (b) Offender should be condemned as a degraded person (XI. 65)
2	Cutting down fruit-laden tree or shrub or twine or climber or flowering herb	Offender should recite certain *Rks* for hundred times (XI. 143)
3	Destroying plants—cultivated or monocarpous or wild	To atone for the sin, the offender has to attend on a cow throughout a whole day, and undergo penance by subsisting only on milk (XI. 145)
Protection of animals		
	Nature of offence	**Punishment prescribed**
1	Teasing the animals	Punishment should be commensurate with the gravity of the offence (VIII. 286)
2	Wounding, injuring leading to blood-shed, etc.	Cost of the treatment should be borne by the offender (VIII. 287)
3	If other animals are harmed because of untrained driver of a vehicle	Owner of the vehicle is to pay a fine of two hundred *panas* (VIII 293)
4	Causing harm to animals like cow, elephant, camel, horse, etc.	Owner is to pay a fine of five hundred *panas* (VIII 296)
5	(a) Causing violence to small animals (b) Harming ass, goat, cattle	Offender has to pay a fine of: (a) 50 *panas* (VIII. 297) (b) Five *masas* of silver (c) One *masa* (VIII. 298)
6	Knowingly killing *marjara* (cat), *nakula* (mongoose), *manduka* (toad), *svaan* (dog), *godha* (iguana), *uluka* (owl), *kaka* (crow)	Offender should perform *caandraavana vrata*

diseases. Ancient India had a discipline of study related to plants known as *Vrikshayurveda*, the science of plant life. 'Ayur'means 'Life', and it is fair to conclude that Indian tradition was aware that plants had life.

14 Priyadarsan Sensarma , 'Conservation of Biodiversity in Manu-Samhita', *Indian Journal of History and Science*, Vol. 33(4), 1998, pp. 270–271. http://www.new1.dli.ernet.in/data1/upload/insa/INSA_2/20005a60_267.pdf, last accessed on 22 November 2012. Used with permission.

However, it was only a century ago, it was proven through the means of observational and measured science. In 1900, at the International Congress of Physics, Paris, France, Jagadish Chandra Bose presented the research paper 'On the similarity of effect of electric stimulus on inorganic and living substances'. J C Bose compared the response of metals, plants, and animals to electrical, chemical, and mechanical stimuli and documented them in his book 'Response in the Living and Non-Living'. He found that plants respond to stimuli as if they have nervous systems like animals and proved that plants can 'feel pain and understand affection and other feelings'. He also proved that plants had finer senses like responding to melodious music and harsh noise. In the former case, the plants grew faster while in the latter case, the growth of the plants was stunted. Bose also proved that even the non-living matters such as metals and stones also respond to stimuli (though very inertly) in a way similar to the muscular responses of the living.

In Yaska's[15] Nirukta (a treatise on etymology and semantics of Vedic words), 'being' or life is said to have six modifications (*shad bhaavavikaarah*) of jayate, asti, viparinamite, vardhate, apakshiyate, and mriyate (birth, existence, change/evolution/transformation, growth, decay, and death). Since plants are born, they exist, change, grow, decay, and die, they are considered as 'beings'. The ancient texts also classify living beings as *Sthavara* (static) and *Jangama* (moving). Trees belong to the first category. In Mahabharatha (Shanti Parva, Chapter 184), Sage Bharadwaja asks Sage Bhrigu on 'whether or not trees have life?' and the sage responds saying that trees do have life[16] and considering them lifeless is only ignorance (*jivam pashyaami vrikshaanaam achaitanyam na vidyate*). Ayurveda and Smritis of Manu describe four categories of living beings—*jarayuja, andaja, swedaja,* and *udbhijja*—those born from womb, egg, sweat, and the ground. Plants have been considered to be part of the fourth category.

In September 2012, Stellar Energy, a USA-based large-scale solar energy integrator, announced the installation of 3692 solar modules on the rooftop of MBS Media, the production studio of James Cameron, who is directing the movies Avatar 2 and Avatar 3, as part of the Avatar trilogy. The solar modules are capable of generating 960 kW of solar power.

In Ayurveda, Charaka defines 'living organism' as one that has body, sense organs, mind, and soul (*sharirendriyasattvatmasamyogadhari jivitam*). The idea that plants have body is self-evident, and that they have sense organs, too, is explained with reasons in Mahabharata (Shanti parva) passage:

- *Creeper entwines her coil round the tree 'finding' its path all over. The blind cannot find their path. Therefore, plants can see.*
- *After a harsh sound of stormy wind, fire, or thunder, the flowers and leaves of trees fall off apparently out of scare. Obviously they can hear and react to sound.*
- *Trees react to good and bad smell and through fumigation by various materials can be cured of their diseases. Hence, they can smell.*

---

15 A grammarian from India. He preceded Panini, another famous grammarian. Yaska is thought to have lived around 6th-7th century BC.
16 http://www.sacred-texts.com/hin/m12/m12b011.htm, last accessed on 4 November 2012. Contents available in this website are in the public domain, unless otherwise stated.

- *Leaves, flowers, fruits, and bark of trees dry up and fall down with heat. It is the sense of 'touch' that reacts to heat and cold. So trees can feel touch.*
- *Trees 'drink' water with their roots ('padapa', a tree, is so called because it consumes its nourishment with 'feet'—padaih pibati). They are subject to diseases and can be treated by mixing remedial materials in the water that they consume. Responding to such treatment is a proof of their having the sense of taste.*
- *Trees can feel happiness and sorrow, which is a function of mind. Therefore, they have mind.*
- *The above mentioned sense organs and mind cannot function without a sentient substratum. Hence trees must have a soul, too.*

Brhatsamhita of Varahamihira, who lived in the sixth century, contains a chapter titled *Vrikshayurveda*. In the opening verse Varahamihira states, 'After studying various sastras of the ancient sages and after being convinced about their authenticity, I propose to explain the same in a clear manner in this composition which is neither too brief nor too exhaustive (Chapter 1, verse 2). While this communicates that the science of *Vrikshayurveda* could have been well developed even before the sixth century, we do not have many texts related to that antiquity preserved. *Vrikshayurveda* of Surapala is an ancient Sanskrit text that deals with the science of plant life. The manuscript of the text was found at the Bodleian Library, Oxford, UK. In 1996, Asian Agri-History Foundation (AAHF) published an English translation of Vrikshayurveda of Surapala.

The below excerpt is a translated version of Verses 9-23 from Surapala's Vrikshayurveda, translated by Nalini Sadhale,[17] former Professor and Head, Department of Sanskrit, Osmania University, Hyderabad.

A person is honored in *Vaikuntha* for as many thousand years as the days he resides in a house where tulsi is grown.

And if one properly grows *bilva*, which pleases Lord Siva, in his family, the goddess of riches resides permanently passes on to the sons and grandsons.

He who plants even a single *asvattha*, wherever it may be, as per the prescribed mode, goes to the abode of Hari.

He who has planted *dhatri* has performed several sacrifices. He has donated the earth. He would be considered a celibate forever.

He who plants a couple of banyan trees as per the prescribed mode would go to the abode of Siva and many heavenly nymphs will attend upon him.

After planting neem trees, a person well-versed in dharma attains the abode of Sun. Indeed! He resides there for a long period.

By planting four *plaksa* trees, a person doubtlessly obtains the fruits of Rajasuya sacrifice.

He who plants five or six mango trees attains the abode of Garuda and lives happily forever like gods.

---

17 Sadhale, Nalini (Tr.), 1996, Surapala's Vrikshayurveda (The Science of Plant Life by Surapala), Agri-History Bulletin No.1, Asian Agri-History Foundation, Secunderabad, 500009, India. Used with permission.

Plastic bag trivia

Two million plastic bags are in use each minute and one trillion plastic bags are used worldwide.

It has been found that every square mile of the ocean contains 46,000 pieces of floating plastic.

Almost 100,000 sea turtles die every year due to strangulation by plastic bags.

Source: http://www.learnstuff.com/ suffocating-the-world/

One should plant seven *palasa* trees or even one. One attains the abode of Brahma and enjoys the company of gods by doing so.

He who himself plants eight *udumbara* trees or even prompts someone to plant them, rejoices in the lunar world.

He who has planted *madhuka* has propitiated Parvati, has become free from diseases, and has worshipped all deities.

If one plants *ksirini*, *dadimi*, *rambha*, *priyala*, and *panasa*, one experiences no affliction for seven births.

He who has knowingly or unknowingly planted *ambu* is respected as a recluse even while staying in the house.

By planting all kinds of other trees, useful for fruits and flowers, a person gets a reward of thousand cows adorned with jewels.

By planting one *asvattha*, one *picumanda*, one *nyagrodha*, ten tamarind trees, the group of three, viz., *kapittha*, bilva, and *amalaka*, and five mango trees, one never visits hell.

In the same book, in a commentary given by Sri K L Mehra titled 'Biodiversity Perspective', it is mentioned that Vrikshayurveda 'mainly deals with various species of trees and their healthy growth and productivity. The text mentions about 170 species of plants, including herbs, shrubs, and trees. There are 325 systematically arranged verses, beginning with a salutation to Lord Ganesha, followed by glorification of trees, and composition on tree planting and production. Various chapters deal with the raising of orchards, agri-horticulture, and tree planting near houses. Special references are made to procuring, preserving, and treatment of seeds and planting materials, preparation of pits for planting; selection of land (soil); methods of irrigation and ways to locate groundwater; nourishment and fertilizers; diseases of plants and plant protection; laying out of gardens and orchards; creation of agricultural/horticultural wonders; use of plant species as indicators of crop and animal production; and description of sacred plants'.[18]

The translators of Surapala's Vrikshayurveda states that they are not aware of any other attempt in the world by which plant disorders were classified into two groups; i.e., internal and external, before the time of Surapala. It is also significant that physiology of trees was considered similar to those of humans. The *tridhatu* theory of Ayurveda was applied to plants—the internal disorders of trees were attributed to *vata*, *kapha*, and *pitta* kinds as had been done in case of humans. A balance of *vata*, *kapha*, and *pitta* indicates health, and a vitiation of any one or more of them indicates disease.

---

18 Sadhale, Nalini (Tr.) (1996), 'Surapala's Vrikshayurveda (The Science of Plant Life by Surapala)', *Agri-History Bulletin No.1*, Asian Agri-History Foundation, Secunderabad, 500009, India. Used with permission.

Planting a tree is described as a happy and solemn occasion to be celebrated after ascertaining an auspicious day and time. The suggestion here is that plants are like members of the family and deserve similar attention.

Nakshatra and Trees Associated With Them

While planting and nurturing any tree is encouraged, individuals are especially urged to plant trees related to their *Nakshatra*. This process helps in accruing merit in this life and after life. Certain trees are associated with each of the 27 Nakshatra, referred in Jyothisha, the astrological system prevalent in India (Table 2.2).

TABLE 2.2 Trees associated with Nakshatra referred in Jyothisha, the astrological system prevalent in India

Star	Name of the tree in various Indian languages	English name	Botanical name
Ashvini/Aswathy/ Ashwini	Kanjiram/Yetti/Etti/ Kuchala	Strychnine	*Strychnos Nux-vomica*
Bharani	Nelli/Perunelli/Aavali/ Amla/Amalaki	Indian Gooseberry/ Amla	*Phyllanthus emblica/ Emblica officinalis*
Karthika/Krittika	Athi/Ambar/Udumbara/ Gular	Cluster Fig/Country Fig/Fig	*Ficus glomerata/Ficus racemosa*
Rohini	Njaval/Jambhali/ Perunjaval	Jamun/Black Plum	*Eugenia Jaambolana/ Syzygium cuminii*
Makayiram/ Mrigashirsha	Karingali /Karungali/ Kher	Cutch Tree/ Milmesha/Ebony	*Acacia catechu/ Diospyros ebunum*
Thiruvathira/ Aardra	Kari /Kumbil/ Karai/Thippilli/ Agar/Krushnagus/ Agalichandanum/Akil/ Sen Santhanam/Aguru/	Cashmere Tree/ Long Pepper/ Red Sandal	*Diospyros melanoxylon/ Ptero carpus santalinus/ Aquillaria agallocha*
Punartham/ Punarpusam/ Punarvasu	Mula/Moongil/Velu	Bamboo	*Bambusa vulgais/ Bamboosa arundinorea*
Pooyam/ Pusam/ Pushya	Arayal/Arasamaram/ Pimpal/Pipal/Aal	Sacred Fig/ Peepal/ Ficus	*Ficus religiosa*

(Contd)

TABLE 2.2 *(Contd)*

Star	Name of the tree in various Indian languages	English name	Botanical name
Aayilyam/ Aashlesha	Punna /Punnai/ Nagapoo/Naagchafa/ Nagkeshar/Nahar	Messua Tree/ Alexandrian Laurel/ Beauty Leaf Poon	*Calophyllum indophyllum/ Mesua ferrea*
Makam/ Magha/ Magam	Peral/Alamaram/Vatt/ Bargad	Banyan Tree/ Indian Fig	*Ficus benghalensis*
Pooram/ Purva Phalguni/ Poorva	Plasu/Chamata/Palas/ Khakda/Modugu/ Murikku/Parasu/ Polash/Desuka Jhad/ Dhak/Chalcha	Flame of the Forest/ Parrot Tree	*Butea monosperma*
Uthram/ Uttara/ Phalguni/ Uthiram	Ithi/Itti/Arali/Payari	Indian Laurel/ Rose Laurel/ Indian Cleaner	*Ficus tinctoria/ Nerium indicum/ Ficus arnattiana*
Atham/ Astham/ Hasta	Ambazham/Marima/ Nalini/Kaatuma/Velam/ Chameli/Mulla/Mullai	Hog Plum, Neem/ Royal Jasmine	*Spondias pinnata / Azadirachta indica/ Jasminum grandiflorum*
Chithira/ Chitra/ Chithirai	Koovalam /Vilvam/Bel/ Bilvam/Bilwa/	Beal Tree/Bengal Quince/Stone Apple/ Wood Apple	*Aegle marmelos*
Chothy/ Swathi/ Suvathi	Maruthu/ Neermaruthu/ Marutham/ Jarul/Arjun	Arjuna Tree / Queen's Flower	*Terminalia Arjuna/ Lagerstroemia speciosa*
Visakham/ Vishaka	Dadhipala/ Vayamkatha/ Vilamaram/Kaith/ Naagkeshar/Nahar	Governor's Plum/ Wood Apple/ Ceylon Ironwood/ Indian rose chestnut	*Feronia elephantum/ Feronia limonia/ Mesua ferrea/ Limonia acidissima*
Anizham/ Anusham/ Anuradha	Elanji/Magizh/ Magizham/Maulshree/ Naagkeshar	Bullet Wood Tree	*Mimusops elengi/ Mesua ferrea*
Thrikketta/ Kettai/ Jyeshta/ Ketta	Vetti/Pachotti/ Kuttipala/Prayan/ Sambar	Bodh Tree/ Stunted Jack	*Aporusa lindleyana/ Calammus rotang/ Connatus wightii*

(Contd)

Moolam/ Mula	Kunthirikkam / Veluthakunthirikom/ Acha/Anjan/ Mamaram/Raal/Sal/ Shala/Ashvakarna/	White Dammar/ Hardwickia/ Mango Tree/ Sal Tree	*Boswellia serrata/ Mangiferus indicus/ Shorea robusta/ Hardwickia binate*
Pooradam/ Purva Ashada	Aattupala/Aatrupalai/ Samudrakai/ Vanchikodi/Vet	Fish Poison Tree/ Tinospora	*Salix tetraspeama/Tinos pora cardifodia/Calamus pseudo-tenuis*
Uthradam/Uttar Ashada	Plavu /Pila/Pala/Sakkai Pala/Phanas	Jack Fruit Tree/ Bread Fruit	*Artocarpus heterophyllus/ Autocarpus cummunis*
Thiruvonam/ Sravana	Erukku/Vellerukku/Rui	Gigantic Swallow/ Swallow Wort	*Calotropis procera/ Calotropis gigantea*
Avittam/ Dhanishta/ Shravishtha	Muringa/Paarampu/ Muringai/Vanni/Vilayti kikar/Shashi	Indian Gum Tree/ Indian Mesquit/ Kejari	*Moringa oleifera/Prosopis cinenaria/Prosepsis speciosa/Prosopis juliflora*
Chathayam/ Sathayam/ Satabisha/ Shatataraka	Kadambu/Kadambam/ Katampu/Valanch	Kadam Tree/ Indian Oak	*Anthocephalus cadambu/Mitragyna parviflora/Neolamarckia cadamba*
Pooruruttathi/ Purva Badrapada	Mavu/Maamaram/ Maruthu/Aamra	Mango Tree/ Arjun Tree	*Magnifera Indica/ Terminalia arjuna*
Uthruttathi/ Uttra Badrapada	Aryaveppu/Veppu/ Vembu/Kadu nimbi	Margosa Tree/ Neem	*Azadiracta indica/ Agadirachta indica*
Revathi	Eluppa/Iluppai/Moha	Indian Butter Tree/ Maduca	*Madhuca longifolia/ Maduca indica*

Note: For a few *Nakshatra*, the trees recommended may vary depending on traditions/regions. The above table is only indicative, and the author, after referring multiple sources, has made an attempt to include all the trees recommended for a *Nakshatra*.

Sacred Forests/Sacred Groves of India

One of the traditional conservation practices among indigenous communities in certain parts of the world that contributed to the conservation and protection of biodiversity was the preservation of small forest patches by dedicating them to the local deities. Such forest patches are called 'sacred groves'. Sacred groves used to be spaces for contemplation and meditation. Sacred groves consisted of a few trees to lush forests spanning several acres that are usually dedicated to local folk deities (Ayyanar, Amman, or *Vanadevatas*).

FIG. 2.2 [20] *'The Sacred Hindoo Grove near Chandod on the Banks of the Nerbudda',*
drawn in 1782 by James Forbes, a British artist and writer.

Groves can also exist around temples and near the burial or cremation grounds (Fig. 2.2). 'This preservation of the entire vegetation in association with a deity is quite a distinct phenomenon from the preservation of isolated specimens of sacred tree species like peepal *Ficus religiosa* or umber *Ficus glomerata* which are often preserved and worshipped even without any association with a deity', says Madhav Gadgil and VD Vartak, in their article 'The Sacred Groves of Western Ghats in India'.[19]

Sacred groves existed in a variety of forms and places—the scrub forest in Rajasthan to the rainforests in Kerala (Table 2.3). The reported number of sacred groves in India comes to approximately 14,000. More than 1000 deities have been associated with sacred groves that exist in Kerala and Karnataka. Evolution of culture has been influenced by these sacred groves—*Theyyam* from Kerala and *Nagmandalam* from Karnataka. Folk dances and rituals form an important aspect of the culture influenced by sacred groves. References to sacred groves were made in Kalidasa's *Vikramurvashiiya.*

---

19 Madhav Gadgil and VD Vartak, 'The Sacred Groves of Western Ghats in India', Economic Botany, Vol 30(2), April-June 1976, pp. 152–60.
20 'ChandodSacredGrove' by James Forbes - Drawn by James Forbes, Bombay 1782. Oriental Memoirs, Vol. III, 1813. Licensed under Public domain via Wikimedia Commons - http://commons.wikimedia.org/wiki/File:ChandodSacredGrove.jpg#mediaviewer/File:ChandodSacredGrove.jpg, last accessed on 14 July 2014.

TABLE 2.3 Regions where concentration of sacred groves are high and
the local names for sacred forests

Region/State	Local names of sacred groves/sacred forests
Andhra Pradesh	Pavithravana
Arunachal Pradesh	Gumpa forests (attached to Buddhist monasteries)
Assam	Than, Madaico
Chhattisgarh	Sarna, Devlas, Mandar, Budhadev
Goa	Deorai, Pann
Gujarat	–
Haryana	–
Himachal Pradesh	Deo Bhumi
Jharkhand	Sarna
Karnataka	Devara Kadu, Devkad
Kerala	Kavu, Sarppakkavu
Madhya Pradesh	Devkot, Matikot, Devsthali, Budhadev
Maharashtra	Deorai, Devrai, Devgudi
Manipur	Gamkhap, Mauhak (sacred bamboo reserves)
Meghalaya	Law Lyngdhoh, Law Kyntang, Law Niam
Orissa	Jahera, Thakuramma
Puducherry	Kovil Kadu
Rajasthan	Oran, Kenkri, Jogmaya, Vani, Devbani, Shamlat deh
Sikkim	Gumpa forests (attached to Buddhist monasteries)
Tamilnadu	Swami shola, Kovilkadu
Uttarakhand	Deo Bhumi, Bugyal (sacred alpine meadows)
West Bengal	Garamthan, Harithan, Jahera, Sabitrithan, Santalburithan

Initiatives are happening to bring reusability in the usage and distribution of purified drinking water. In January 2015, the Government of Bihar banned the usage of plastic water bottles during meetings organized by government departments. Usage of steel tumblers and flasks were recommended, in lieu of plastic bottles.

Sanctity associated with the sacred groves differed—in some of the groves, people were not allowed even to take dry foliage and fallen fruits. The people who lived near those groves believed that disturbances in the grove will offend the local deity, and that would cause calamities, diseases, and failure of crops. An example for practice of such non-interference is the Garo and the Khasi tribes of north-eastern India. Unlike them, the Gonds of central India prohibited the cutting of a tree or its branches, yet allowed the usage of fallen parts from the tree.

Benefits of Sacred Groves

• These groves played the repository for Ayurvedic medicines, fruits, honey, etc.

• The sacred groves maintained floral and faunal diversity and were the refuge of endemic species of the region.

• Water bodies such as ponds, streams, or springs were associated with sacred groves. These helped to meet the water requirements of the people living nearby. The green cover of the region helped in recharging these water bodies and also in increasing the water table.

• The vegetative cover reduced the soil erosion, improved the soil stability of the region, and controlled desertification of the region.

Sacred forests exist in other parts of the world too. Researchers have found that 'Sacred forests are keystone structures for forest bird conservation in south-west China's Himalayan Mountains'[21] In a drought year, increased number of birds were using these forest patches, suggesting the possibility that birds may be using these sacred forests as refuges during times of extreme weather. The sacred forests also had higher variety of bird species as compared to other areas. Speaking at the Parliament of World Religions, held between December 3–9, 2009, Swami Sandeepananda Giri, Founder, School of Bhagavad Gita, says,[22]

> Today's world is full of talk, talk, talk. Back home in India, I saw a big advertisement of a telecom company that says, 'Talk more!' As it is we talk too much, and because we are always talking, we never listen; What saddens me is that because we never listen, we miss out a lot of things in our lives especially what Nature is saying to us. This is another sad consequence of our modern lifestyle. In ancient times the sages were fine-tuned to Nature—they heard and listened. Their deep and quiet wisdom was a result of hearing and listening,

---

21 http://www.sciencedirect.com/science/article/pii/S0006320713001961, last accessed on 18 July 2013.
22 http://www.schoolofbhagavadgita.org/pdf/Speech-parliament-of-world-religion.pdf, last accessed on 2 May 2014.

To the Hindu sage, 'hearing each other' means not just humans hearing humans. It signifies hearing the whole universe with utmost reverence, attention and concentration.

and this was reflected in their hymns and worship. They heard, they listened, and they sang in glory:

Om bhadram karnebhih shrunuyaama devaah
Bhadram pashyemaakshabhiryajatraah
Sthirairangaistushtuvaamsastanoobhih
Vyashema devahitam yadaayuh
Swasti na indro vridhashravaah
Swasti nah pooshaa vishwavedaah
Swasti nastaarkshyo arishtanemih
Swasti no brihaspatir dadhaatu.
Om shantih, shantih, shantih!

This shloka was recited by our rishis to nature through which they appealed, 'May our ears rejoice from hearing your voices'. 'May we see what is auspicious'.

To the Hindu sage 'hearing each other' means not just humans hearing humans. It signifies hearing the whole universe with utmost reverence, attention, and concentration. When in meditation, one can hear and see even the quiet blooming of a flower. Every bit of Nature would have much to tell us—the seas, rivers, plants, and animals—even the tiny ant. And they would especially tell us how much they suffer today, and how this suffering would spell disaster for the whole of mankind and the universe.

Warren Buffet, the acclaimed investor, as part of his India visit, during March 2011, planted a tree sapling at Bangalore, and mentioned, '... Somebody planted a tree for me long ago in the form of an educational institution, and I sat under that tree, metaphorically. The same happened in one area after another in my life'.[23] Sri Sathya Sai Baba says that Nature is the best example of selfless service. The work ethos of India is built on the adage of *Paropakaaraartham Idam Shareeram* (This body is meant for the service of others). The *Rishis* say that there are four Mothers, in addition to the Mother who has given birth to the body. They are Mother Cow, Mother Earth, Motherland, and Mother Veda (Sacred Scriptures). In the *Anusasana Parva* of Mahabharata, Section LXXVI, it is said that 'The cow is my mother. The bull is my sire'. Lord Krishna is also known as Govinda—protector of the cows. Shiva is said to ride on Nandi. In ancient rural India, every household had a few cows that provided a constant supply of milk and a few bulls that helped as draft animals. It is a habit in rural households to feed cows with leftover food items. Cows also consume food items like grass, a seemingly trivial object. Cows transform them to products that are healthy and wholesome for human beings and other beings. Cow dung is often used as manure and has insect repellent properties. It is

---

23 Asha Rai & Vinay Kamat, Life's about planting trees for others: Warren Buffett, Times of India, Coimbatore, last accessed on 24 March 2011. http://timesofindia.indiatimes.com/business/india-business/Lifes-about-planting-trees-for-others-Warren-Buffett/articleshow/7776690.cms, last accessed on 25 March 2011.

also an important component in low input agricultural practices and organic farming. Organic farmers like Subhash Palekar, Shanta Ramaswamy, and P. Gomathinayagam vouch for the use of cow dung and cow urine in the role of sustainable farm practices. Subhash Palekar opined that the dung generated by one cow is enough to manure 30 acres of land.[24, 25, 26, 27] By converting that which is *Nikrushta* to that which is *Utkrishta*, the cow can be considered as a symbolism of transforming the *Nikrushta* aspect of a human personality (baser instincts/inferior aspects of one's personality) to that of an *Utkrishta* (the finer/subtler) aspect of human personality. Cows are a symbolic emblem of selfless duty (*Paropakaaraartham Idam Shareeram*). There is a saying that people learn by observing. The presence of cows in households made people appreciate the nuances of selfless service.

Other animals were also given prominence in the social structure of India, and this has got reflected in epics and *Puranas*. Ranchor Prime, author of the book Vedic Ecology,[28] mentions, 'Animals played an important part in Rama's adventures. Hanuman the monkey was his dearest servant and best devotee. Rama's army was made up of monkeys. A vulture named Jatayu gave his life to try and save Sita from being kidnapped. Jambavan the bear helped in the battle on Lanka. The role of these animals in helping Rama has given special status to all their kind, especially to monkeys'.

Associating animals and birds as *Vahanas* of Gods and Goddesses and the resulting feeling of sacredness ensured the conservation of these animals and birds (Table 2.4). In a module, 'Indian Traditional Knowledge on Environmental Conservation',[29] published by Central Board of Secondary Education (CBSE), it is stated '…snake's association with god Siva and snake (or Naga) worship was a conscious effort by our saints to preserve the animal, who otherwise incites fear and persecution because of its perceived venomous nature. In fact, snakes are an important link in the food cycle and play a significant role in maintaining the ecological balance'. The Aachaaraanga Sutra, a Jain text, states that 'a wise man should not act sinfully towards plants, nor cause others to act so, nor allow others to act so'.[30] 'While Jainism preaches complete non-violence, Buddhism follows the middle path and states that killing of animals or felling of trees should not be done until absolutely necessary', states CBSE in their module, 'Indian Traditional Knowledge on Environmental Conservation'.[31]

24 The Hindu, http://www.hinduonnet.com/2006/03/16/stories/2006031616430300.htm, last accessed on 27 April 2010.

25 The Hindu, http://www.thehindu.com/thehindu/mp/2009/07/18/stories/2009071851650600.htm, last accessed on 27 April 2010.

26 The Hindu, http://www.hinduonnet.com/seta/2004/03/11/stories/2004031101521400.htm, last accessed on 27 April 2010.

27 The Hindu, http://www.hinduonnet.com/2008/03/22/stories/2008032250220200.htm, last accessed on27 April 2010.

28 Ranchor Prime, Vedic Ecology: Practical Wisdom for Surviving the 21st Century, Mandala Publishing, 2002

29 http://www.cbseacademic.in/web_material/Circulars/2012/68_KTPI/Module_5.pdf, last accessed on 22 November 2012.

30 http://www.sacred-texts.com/jai/sbe22/sbe2207.htm, last accessed on 23 November 2012.

31 http://www.cbseacademic.in/web_material/Circulars/2012/68_KTPI/Module_5.pdf, last accessed on 22 November 2012.

TABLE 2.4 Some of the deities and *Vahanas* associated with them

Name of the deity	Name of the Vahana	Species
Ganesha	Mushika/Ulaka	Mouse/rat
Vishnu, Krishna, Vaishnavi	Garuda	Eagle
Shiva	Nandi	Bull
Karthik (Karthikeya/Karthik/Murugan/Skanda)	Parvani	Peacock
Brahma	Kalahamsa	Swan
Durga	Manasthala	Lion
Indra	Airavat	Elephant
Kama	Suka	Parrot
Lakshmi	Uluka	Owl
Rati		Pigeon
Kubera		Man
Agni		Ram (Male Sheep)
Saraswati	Hansa	Swan

INDIAN CULTURE AND WORSHIP OF NATURE

The culture of India assigns life to even the seemingly inanimate objects. Hence, life is associated not just with animals or plants, but also with rivers, mountains, stones, etc. In the villages of India, it is a commonplace to see worship of stones anointed with oil, as an offering to the spirit within the stone. A tree could be adopted as a son through a ritual known as *taruputravidhi*. *Upanayana* (initiation) was conducted for trees like pipal, and marriage was performed between Banyan tree and neem tree. Thus, rituals usually associated with humans were extended to include the plant kingdom too. It should not come as a surprise that the existence of life on plants was explained in modern scientific parlance by Jagadish Chandra Bose.

Mata Amritanandamayi says, 'The relationship between man and Nature is like the relationship between Pindanda, the microcosm and Brahmanda, the macrocosm. Our ancestors understood this and so they included nature worship in religious practices. The idea behind all religious practices was to closely associate human beings with

Speaking about the habit inculcated in him by his elders, Swami Swaroopananda, Acharya, Chinmaya Mission, says,

When we were growing up, our grandmother told us everyday to put water on at least one tree. It was in the name of worship. 'Go, go, there is the peepal tree.' Now we realize that peepal tree is the maximum oxygen giver, right? In India, we are not blind worshippers. You nourish the tree, and the tree nourishes you.

nature. By establishing a loving relationship between man and nature, they ensured both the balance of nature and the progress of the human race. Ancients loved and worshipped trees and plants such as the Banyan tree, Bilwa, and tulsi, not because the trees bore fruit and helped them to make a profit, but because ancients knew that they were connected. Indic scriptures suggest that a householder should perform the pancha yajnas or five daily sacrifices.... Bhuta yajna is the last sacrifice; it is to serve all living beings as embodiments of the Universal Being. This is done through the feeding of and caring for animals and plants. Earlier, family members never ate before feeding domestic birds and animals. They would also water their plants and trees before eating. In those days, worshipping nature and natural phenomenon were part and parcel of human life. People were always eager to please Nature in gratitude for her kind gifts. Bhuta yajna brings about the consciousness of the unity of all life'.[32]

Frank Dixon, Former Director–Research, Innovest Venture Partners (the largest sustainability research firm in the world) has this to say about India, 'India has many strengths that make it one of the greatest countries in the world. I believe India's greatest strength is the Indian people, in particular their spiritual devotion and purity. Many Indians see beyond illusion and understand the deeper meaning is best displayed by the custom of bowing of life. Perhaps this to the God within when greeting another person. Many Western people visit India to find spiritual inspiration, clarity, and renewal. This focus on the deeper reality of humanity's oneness with nature and each other is needed to address growing environmental and social problems around the world. The Indian people model the peace, wisdom, love, and respect needed to achieve the beautiful, prosperous, and sustainable world that all humanity seeks'.[33]

As everything in nature is reverberating with life, respect for creation becomes a natural byproduct. Ayurveda states that 'even when one takes any leaf or any part of a plant one must mentally pray and ask for pardon for breaking the leaf for medicinal purposes, so that the plants are not shocked'. This interconnectedness among humans and plants could have revealed to the ancestors, the medicinal virtues associated with many plants. 'From a seemingly simple curry leaf regularly used for good seasoning to carefully selected leafy shoots of 'agase' for preparing a special curry on the day of Ekadashi, from a glass of refreshing lime juice for indigestion to steaming hot coriander 'kashayam' for fever, from freshly prepared bolus of 'nelanelli' chutney for liver infection to the triphala linctus at bedtime to overcome constipation, from sandalwood paste for skin care to bhringamalaka taila for hair care, from the fresh twigs of

Earlier, family members never ate before feeding domestic birds and animals. They would also water their plants and trees before eating. In those days, worshipping Nature and natural phenomenon were part and parcel of human life.

---

32 Mata Amritanandamayi, How We Relate to Life, The Speaking Tree, Times of India, 16 March 2011. Used with permission.

33 As communicated to the author.

The following is a quote from Calvin, in the comic strip *Calvin and Hobbes* (written and illustrated by Bill Watterson).

I was reading about how countless species are being pushed towards extinction by man's destruction of forests. Sometimes I think the surest sign that intelligent life exists elsewhere in the universe is that none of it has tried to contact us.

neem hung across the main doorway on the traditional new year day, to the shoot tips of banni tree exchanged with friends on the day of dusserah, be it a familiar household formulation, or a prescribed drug, or a traditional cosmetic, or a special culinary preparation, or a customary observance rooted in our traditions, medicinal plants have come a long way to have found very significant position in our lifestyles'.

One of the personalities in Indian epics, who is yet to be discovered in the context of leading a life in reverence to Mother Nature is Balaram, elder brother of Lord Krishna. While Krishna fought a war against the tyranny of kings like Kansa and Jarasandha, Balaram's war was against the tyranny of materialism on the planet.[34] While the Kurukshetra war was going on, Balaram leaves on a pilgrimage performing *Yagnas* and *Daanam* (acts of charity). While the war creates all kinds of disturbances, *Yagnas* creates positive energy. Thus, Balaram is performing an endeavour of *Pratikraman* in response to *Atikraman*.[35] Popular stories indicate the contempt Balaram had towards the limiting short-sighted lifestyles of Yadavas. It is said that Balaram and his wife Revati stayed out of Dwaraka and engaged themselves in sustainable farming practices ('organic farming').

Rituals of Indian tradition indicate the necessity to purify both the outer environment and the inner environment. Pollution of space was not just about the external space, it was also about the inner space, by acting on thoughts that may cause harm. Purification of the inner environment was done by tapping and nurturing noble thoughts and care for all, and being in stillness. The culture has suggested that a sincere spiritual aspirant is bound to benefit from a Sattwik, plant-based diet. It is also suggested that one can develop pure thoughts by having pure food. The life of the plants itself provides food for thought on how a human being can lead his/her life. Thus, spirituality and care for nature were not distinct aspects, and were interconnected.

Yagnas (Yagnam/Homam) were conducted to purify the atmosphere. As a part of the process, dried leaves of herbs were burned along with ghee. These yagnas had other benefits too. William Miller, a consultant on values-centred innovation,[36] had this to say about *Athi Rudra Maha Yagna* that was held at Prasanthi Nilayam,[37] 'I realized that this grand, self-purifying event incorporates two metaphors that prepared me for how

34 Mala Kapadia, Mahabharata to Copenhagen: The Untold Story of Balaram, Conference Paper presented at the International Conference on 'Indian Management for Global Effectiveness: Insights from the Mahabharata' held at Indian Business Academy, Bangalore on February 19 and 20, 2010

35 Mala Kapadia, Mahabharata to Copenhagen: The Untold Story of Balaram, Conference Paper presented at the International Conference on 'Indian Management for Global Effectiveness: Insights from the Mahabharata' held at Indian Business Academy, Bangalore on February 19 and 20, 2010

36 www.VCIhome.com

37 The ashram of Sri Sathya Sai Baba. Prasanthi Nilayam means 'Abode of Peace'.

to participate: that I could use the sacrificial ceremonies to 'wash myself clean of my errors in life' and to 'offer into God's 'refining fire'... Also, I kept in mind the Sanskrit verse we chant every day—'Loka Samastha, Sukhino Bhavantu'—'May all beings in all the worlds be happy'. Since that is the purpose of this Yagna, I felt attuned to whatever has been happening, even without mentally understanding everything... It will remain an ongoing process in my heart. I will simply continue to focus on asking God to make me pure so I can be an instrument of peace'.[38]

While such vedic practices exhort an individual to develop one's capability to discriminate between that which is ephemeral and that which is eternal, the modern day individual is bombarded with one message—of conspicuous consumption. Kalle Lasn, founder of Adbusters magazine, says 'Advertisements are the most prevalent and toxic of the mental pollutants. From the moment your alarm sounds in the morning to the wee hours of late night TV, commercial pollution floods your brain at the rate of about three thousand marketing messages per day. Every day an estimated 12 billion display ads, 3 million radio commercials, and more than 200,000 TV commercials are dumped into North America's collective unconscious'.[39] Advertising message is so prevalent and spread across that we have not understood the impact that advertising is having on our decisions. An average American, by the time he reaches college, would have spent three to four hours a week watching TV ads, about 100,000 of them,[40] and during the course of his life, watches three years of advertising on television.[41] These advertisements all preach a variation of the same underlying social message: satisfaction through purchase. Such a constant propaganda barrage may well induce us to consume more than we otherwise would.[42]

DEEP ECOLOGY AND REVERENTIAL ECOLOGY

The term 'Deep Ecology' was coined by the Norwegian philosopher Arne Næss in 1973. Arne Næss contrasted deep ecology with shallow environmentalism/conventional environmentalism/anthropocentric environmentalism. The term 'Anthropocentric' referred to a situation where everything was looked from the perspective of the human species. Anthropocentric environmentalism was concerned with the conservation of the environment only from a materialist and consumer-oriented outlook. An example of such environmentalism could be the obsession to plant decorative trees that do not grow high, and do not shed too many leaves. 'The fact that these trees are avoided by all natural forms of life since they are alien species is possibly seen as a boon by car owners who are known to complain about bird droppings', says Lyla Bavadam, Deputy Editor, *Frontline*.[43] Deep ecology had a more holistic view of the world and had the understanding that the separate parts of the ecosystem which also included

---

38 http://media.radiosai.org/journals/Vol_04/01SEP06/CoverStory_Army.htm, last accessed on 1 November 2012.
39 Kalle Lasn, Culture Jam: The Uncooling of America, William Morrow & Company, November 1999.
40 Eban S Goodstein, Economics and the Environment, Wiley, 2011.
41 Jean Kilbourne, Can't Buy My Love: How Advertising Changes the Way We Think and Feel, Touchstone, 2000.
42 Eban S Goodstein, Economics and the Environment, Wiley, 2011.

the humans, functioned as a whole. Deep Ecology could thus be defined as, an ecological philosophy that recognizes that all life has a right to exist, no species is more important or less important than another, and the instrumental utility provided by a species to human needs is irrelevant when recognizing the inherent worth of all living beings. Deep Ecology respects the interdependence of organisms.

Deep ecologists state that humans have no right to reduce the richness and diversity of life forms of nature, other than to satisfy *vital* human needs. Unfortunately, human interference in non-human world is excessive and it is worsening. Deep ecologists desire for policy changes that appreciate an ideological shift that appreciates quality of life rather than standard of living. 'We think that all our natural world, all our forests and rivers, all our earth and animals, are for us... they are ours, and we can use them for our benefit. Even the environmentalists, use a very rational, scientific,and human-centred approach—that we have to preserve the earth and its environment, we have to take care of the forests, rivers, and animals. But the reason we have to conserve them, preserve them, and take care of them is because we can use them for human benefit. So forests are a medicine chest for humans and so on... That is shallow ecology. Deep ecology goes a bit further and says Earth is not here just for us. There are 8.4 million species on this Earth, and they have as much intrinsic value and right to be and live, undisturbed, unpolluted, uncontaminated, as human beings have a right to live. So giving nature its rightful place and giving nature its intrinsic value is the main idea of Deep Ecology', says Satish Kumar, Editor-in-Chief, *Resurgence Magazine*, a magazine considered as the artistic and spiritual voice of the green movement in United Kingdom.[44]

The authors presume that Indian spiritual philosophy and practice have elevated ecological considerations to a higher dimension. It is interesting to hear what Deepak Chopra has to say about 'environment'. In an interview to Big Picture TV, he says,

In September 2013, HP set specific greenhouse gas emissions reduction goals for its suppliers and business partners. The goal is a 20% reduction in emissions by 2020, with 2010 as the base year. HP has more than 1,000 production suppliers and thousands of non-production suppliers.

'Both the biological organism and what we call 'environment' are differentiated patterns of behaviour of a single reality, whether you call that reality Gaia, whether you call that Planet Earth or you call that the Sentient Universe, we are all differentiated patterns of a single Consciousness. So, you don't look at that tree and say, 'Oh, that's the environment'. That tree is your lungs. If it didn't breathe, you wouldn't breathe. And if you didn't breathe, it wouldn't breathe. It is inseparable. The earth is your body. The rivers and waters of our planet are your circulation. Pollute them, you'll pollute your circulation. The air is your breath. The energies of the universe are your emotions. The information states of the universe are your thoughts. There is no difference between an electromagnetic synaptic

43 Lyla Bavadam, The changing urban landscape, The Hindu Survey of the Environment 2012, 2012.
44 http://www.bigpicture.tv/?id=3117, last accessed on 24 March 2012.

FIG. 2.3[46] An Asian Palmyra palm tree

storm in your brain and an electromagnetic synaptic storm in the sky. There is no inside, there is no outside. There is a single reality that is differentiating into the observer and the observed, the perceiver and the perceived, the subjective reality and the objective reality'.[45]

Quoting a Bhagavad Gita verse (3:10), Swami Chinmayananda says, 'Even when the Creator, the Total-mind, puts up the show of the Universe of the Five Elements and brings forth the living organisms along with man, on this stage of life to work, to strive, and to achieve, he creates also Yajna, "the spirit of self-dedicated activities". The Yajna-spirit is seen everywhere: the Sun shines, the Moon appears, the Sea throbs, the Earth bears—all in a spirit of sacrifice and self-dedicated motherly love with never even a trace of attachment of any kind of self-arrogating motive. The whole world of cosmic powers, and nature's phenomena function instinctively in the service of all. Even before life could appear on the face of the earth, the elemental forces had prepared in the sacred spirit-of-dedication. Even when life developed and multiplied, at all levels, we can easily recognize different degrees of Yajna-activities, which keep up the harmonious growth of existence... The Creator created the world along with the "spirit-of-service" and the "capacity-for-sacrifice"... The Law of Seva is faithfully followed by every sentient and insentient member of the cosmos instinctively. Man alone is given the freedom to act as he likes and to the extent he disobeys this Universal Law-of-Sacrifice, Yajna, to that extent he comes to suffer, because he, with his arrogant and egoistic actions, brings discord in the harmony of the existence around him'.[47]

---

45 http://www.bigpicture.tv/?id=3214, last accessed on 26 June 2010.
46 Photo: Ajith Sankar R N
47 Swami Chinmayanada, The Holy Geeta, Central Chinmaya Mission Trust, 2006

An interview with Satish Kumar, Editor-in-Chief, *Resurgence Magazine*.

Be Eco-centric, Not Ego-centric

The 'Earth Pilgrim' Satish Kumar was ordained as a Jain monk at nine, but at 18, was inspired by Mahatma Gandhi to re-enter worldly life and work in Vinoba Bhave's land reform movement. In 1962, he walked from India to the US and presented 'peace tea' to leaders of nuclear armed nations. In 1973, renowned economist EF Schumacher persuaded Satish Kumar to live in England arguing, 'there are many Gandhians in India, we need one in England'. Satish took over as editor of *Resurgence* magazine, started by Schumacher to promote his alternative vision of economics enshrined in 'Small is Beautiful'. Over the years, Kumar has inspired the international green movement towards a spiritual orientation, termed as deep or reverential ecology. In 1991, he founded an international centre for learning—Schumacher College in Devon. His books include *You are Therefore I am*, *The Buddha*, *The Terrorist*, and most recently, *Earth Pilgrim*, also a BBC film on his life watched by over 3.6 million viewers.

You are working on an ecological interpretation of the Bhagavad Gita...

The Bhagavad Gita has many dimensions of personal development and liberation, and of how we relate to the world. For example, it says people depend on food, food depends on rain, and rain depends on people following the law of the universe, which is the wheel of time. The wheel means that nature moves in a cyclical, not linear, manner. In a cyclical system everything returns, renews, and nourishes itself. You plant a seed and it becomes a plant, then a tree, which produces a flower which becomes a seed again. At the moment, the world is following a linear pattern, not the Gita's law of nature. We take from nature; use, and throw away. This is why there is global warming and climate change.

What does it mean—to be an 'earth pilgrim'?

For the pilgrim, the destination, the result, is not so important. This is also mentioned in the Bhagavad Gita. The fruit of your action is inconsequential; the spirit with which you do something is important. When your consciousness is a pilgrim's consciousness, your whole life becomes a pilgrimage. A touristic mind is ego-centric, whereas a pilgrim's mind is eco-centric. Ego is about 'me', separate from you. 'Eco' is relational—it comes from' the Greek term oikos—'home'. Home is a place of relationship. We are all related. My footprint on the earth is light because I see the earth as sacred. The pilgrim does not harm, or minimizes the harm and has a light footprint, whereas the tourist is not interested in not harming. If we live on the earth as pilgrims, then we do not harm, and we will not be harmed.

How can we awaken ourselves to the ecological implications of the way we live and consume?

The pilgrim's approach is one of restraint and knowing the abundant gifts of nature. Nature is generous, intelligent, and conscious. As the Upanishads say the whole universe is divine. Our share in nature's abundance is only to meet our vital needs, so that there is enough for everybody. Nature is resilient because it depends on what is available, on the resources of the place. If we humans live by the sun, rain, air, wind, and soil which are around us, we too, will be resilient, sustainable, and spiritual. If we consume in that spirit—buy what is made locally, through the energy of rain, wind, and sun—then life can sustain. If we don't live on what the universe provides us on our doorstep, for instance sunshine, and go deep underground for oil, we are not in harmony with natural order.

You bring together soil and soul, whereas spirituality is usually focused on self-realization and not on realizing our inter-connectedness with everything else...

Reality is both inner and outer. Soul is the inner quality and soil is the outer quality. Conventional spirituality has become limited to the soul and to personal salvation. Spirituality has become the idea of the inner without the outer. Inner and outer being two sides of the same coin, our personal happiness is not separate from the well-being of the earth. Soil represents outer reality. If we take care of the soil or environment our soul will also be strong and nourished. A new spirituality is needed—eco-spirituality, where 'eco' denotes relationship with the outer world without which our inner world will be poor.

Ecology also needs to become spiritually sensitive...

We see the natural world only as a source of our consumerist way of life and want to protect it for selfish reasons. From a spiritual approach, nature has rights just as human beings have rights. Belief in the intrinsic sacredness of the earth is spiritual ecology. It is fine to go to temples or do yoga, but then, do you pollute the environment? This split between inner and outer is what I'm trying to heal.

There has been a twin movement in your life—the broad-basing of spirituality and the deepening of ecology...

Yes. My monastic order was oriented towards personal salvation. The world is bondage; keep your back towards it and your face towards moksha. That way, spirituality becomes world-denying. My focus has been on living lightly; and spiritually. If you do everything with a spiritual consciousness, you transform ordinary activity into spiritual practice. This in turn transforms your inner world, where doing no harm on the outside becomes a way of being liberated from fear, anxiety, and ego. A journey like this is cyclical—it is not outer or inner, but a cycle of outer-inner, outer-inner. That is the wheel of dharma.

Could there be a uniquely Indian response to the economic crisis?

An important figure in Indian spirituality is the dancing Shiva. Instead of growth we should have a 'dancing economy'. In growth economy you have to keep growing linearly because if you stop, there is a recession and unemployment. In a finite world, you cannot grow infinitely. We can change this with the metaphor of the dancing Shiva, and create a dancing economy. Dance is joyful and cyclical. You can have activities—arts, crafts, making things, farming—but in a dancing, cyclical way. A dancing economy is a spiritual economy while a growth economy is a materialistic economy.

(This interview, done by Swati Chopra, was first published in 'The Speaking Tree' (a *Times of India* publication) dated 4 July 2010.)[48]

GAIA HYPOTHESIS

The air is his breath, the trees are the hairs of his body,
The oceans his waist, the hills and mountains are his bones.
The rivers are the veins of the Cosmic person,
His movements are the passing of ages.
Srimad Bhagavatam, 2.1.32-33

In 1970s, James Lovelock came out with Gaia Hypotheses where he proposed that Earth was a complete system and everything in the ecosphere was interdependent and equally necessary for maintaining life on Earth. As the hypothesis has since been supported by a number of experiments and provided predictions, it has been referred to as Gaia Theory.

Some of the highlights of the hypothesis are as follows:

- Earth is a living system!!!
- The system seeks an environment optimal for contemporary life.
- This living system has automatically controlled global temperature, atmospheric content, ocean salinity, and other factors that maintain its own habitability.
- The theory argues that organic and inorganic components of Earth evolved together as a single, living, and self-regulating system.

James Lovelock says, 'The Gaia hypothesis suppose(s) that the atmosphere, the oceans, the climate, and the crust of the Earth are regulated at a state comfortable for life because of the behaviour of living organisms. Specifically, the Gaia hypothesis said that the temperature, oxidation state, acidity, and certain aspects of the rocks and waters are at any time kept constant, and that this homeostasis is maintained by active feedback processes operated automatically and unconsciously the biota. Solar energy sustains comfortable conditions for life. The conditions are only constant in the short term and evolve in synchrony with the changing needs of the biota as it evolves. Life and its environment are so closely coupled that evolution concerns Gala, not the organisms or the environment taken separately'.[49]

---

48 Used with permission
49 James Lovelock, The Ages of Gaia: A Biography of Our Living Earth, Bantam Books, 1 March 1990

In western thought, this hypothesis was a radical move from earlier ideas, which considered every entity to be independent of the other and focused on satisfying its own needs, independent of the needs of others. Gaia hypothesis resulted in recognition of the effect that one's action have on the other. This idea necessitated a rethink on the tenets of individual and organizational behaviour.

The name 'Gaia' was derived from the primordial Earth Goddess of ancient Greek religion. As per Greek mythology, this goddess drew the living world forth from Chaos, the formless or void state that preceded the creation of the universe. The prefix 'Ge' in Geology and Geography is taken from the root word in Greek for Earth.

Examples of Gaian processes can include the following:

1. Oxygen Balance—Dr James Lovelock suggested that Gaia is at work to keep the oxygen content of the atmosphere high and within the range that all oxygen-breathing animals require. Lovelock states that the stability of earth's atmosphere is not due to chemical equilibrium as it happens in planets without life. After Fluorine, Oxygen is the most reactive element, and thus there is a high possibility of oxygen combining with gases and minerals of Earth's atmosphere and crust. Still, in Earth, oxygen constitutes 20.95%. In contrast, the atmospheres of Venus and Mars contain zero per cent of free oxygen.

2. Temperature Balance—Gaia theory visualizes the system regulating the surface temperature of Earth within a narrow range, between 10°C and 20°C, for a period of over three billion years. Since the beginning of life on earth, the solar luminosity has increased by 25%.[50] Gaia theory argues that even if one ignores the long-term increasing trend of sun's luminosity, the temperature of this planet would vary far more, as it happens on the surface of a planet like Mars, where in the summers and in the equator, the temperature may vary between 20°C in day to −90°C in the night. The balance and stability of Earth's temperature are maintained by varying the amount of CO_2 in the atmosphere. The drop in the atmosphere's ability to absorb/retain the increased solar radiation is due to a global decline in CO_2 levels over that time. The excess carbon in the atmosphere was locked in various parts of Earth and only the carbon required to manage plant life was retained in the atmosphere. The biosphere would have attempted to fix CO_2 in the form of the calcium carbonate of marine shells, chalk, limestone, oil, coal, and organic material dispersed in rock matter. It is also propounded that phytoplankton, the microscopic organisms that can be found in the uppermost sunlit layer of water bodies, release dimethyl sulphide (DMS) into air which gets converted to sulphuric acid which becomes the nuclei for

In July 2012, Alameda County, a county in the state of California, USA, passed a new policy asking pharmaceutical companies to pay for the collection and disposal of the unused/expired medicines manufactured by them. This policy was based on the idea of extended producer responsibility. Alameda county has been facing issues related to illicit usage of these medicines. Water bodies and landfills got poisoned as residues from these medicines reached them.

---

50 http://www.nature.com/nature/journal/v277/n5698/abs/277640a0.html, last accessed on 23 October 2014

cloud condensation. This nuclei help in producing thicker clouds, blocks the rays from the sun, and cools the ocean. The CLAW hypothesis stated that there is a feedback loop operating between ocean ecosystems and the climate of the earth; this stabilized the temperature of the earth. As per the CLAW hypothesis, an increase in the available energy from sun results in an increase in the growth rate of phytoplankton or increased enhanced photosynthesis. This contributes to the increased presence of DMS which in turns contributes to an increase in a cloud reflecting more solar radiation. In the same manner, a decrease in the sun's energy results in decreased reflection of solar radiation.

3. Salinity in oceans has been constant at about 3.4% for a very long time.[51] As most cells do not generally tolerate values above 5%, this stability in oceanic environments is important. However, it has been a mystery on how this stability in oceanic salinity has been maintained despite possibilities of increased oceanic salinity due to the flow of river salts to the ocean. Natural geological weathering and geographical phenomenon like lava releases salts into the water bodies that carry these salts to the oceans. A theory has been propounded that salt flats that are hosts to dense patches of bacteria, may be absorbing the salts in the water bodies by trapping salts and other minerals to form a sheath within which the bacterial colonies live.

As our consumption increases and the global energy demand increases, we are opening up areas where nature stored carbon. This results in the accelerated burning of CO_2 which makes the earlier roles played by nature difficult. In 2006, James Lovelock also proposed the anti-CLAW hypothesis. If global warming increases, it leads to water stratification, a situation that retards water mixing and nutrient mixing between various layers of water bodies, including oceans. This would lead to a reduction in the supply of nutrients from the deeper layer of oceans resulting in the reduction of phytoplankton activity, thereby a fall in the production of DMS, a fall in cloud condensation nuclei, decrease in the reflection of radiation. Thus, the acceptance of radiation increases, and the planet warms further contributing to further water stratification and accelerated collapse.

FARMING IN HARMONY WITH NATURE

Introduction to Sustainable Farming

> *... species are not in competition with each other to survive. Species are in a continuous dance of mutuality, reciprocity, and connectivity. There is an old Indian, Hindu idea - of Dance of Shiva. If you go to Indian temples, you will see statues of Dancing Shiva. Dancing Shiva is the nature of the universe. Everything is dancing with each other. The species connect with each other. So this eternal dance is going on - of connectivity, of inter-dependence, of mutuality, of reciprocity.*[52]
> Satish Kumar, Editor-in-Chief, *Resurgence Magazine*

---

51 Tyler Volk, Toward a Future for Gaia Theory, Climatic Change, Volume 52, Issue 4, pp 423-430, 1 March 2002.
52 http://www.bigpicture.tv/?id=3117, last accessed on 24 March 2012.

Siachen Glacier is the highest battle-ground on earth. Soldiers suffer more from inhospitable weather conditions as compared to attack from enemy. Both India and Pakistan spend enormous amounts of money to maintain military presence in the region. This military presence is contributing to the waste dumping and destruction of the pristinity and purity of the region. There have been proposals towards the creation of trans-boundary peace park in the Siachen Glacier region.

The Millennium Ecosystem Assessment states that between 1950 and 1980, more land was converted to cropland than in the eighteenth and the first half of the nineteenth centuries combined and nearly one-fourth of the land on the surface of earth is now cultivated. 'As the use of synthetic fertilizers has grown, humans have doubled the amount of nitrogen in the environment. Nitrogen in our air and water cause asthma and respiratory disease, blue-baby syndrome, cancer, and other chronic diseases', states the assessment.[53] A study, published in 2004, which compared U.S. Department of Agriculture data on vegetable nutrients between 1950 and 1999, indicated that there has been a decline of nutrient values in foods (protein, calcium, phosphorus, iron, riboflavin, and ascorbic acid). The researchers believed that the reason for such a decrease could be selective breeding, as growers and researchers focus on producing crops that yield more fruit, a process that resulted in growers not focusing on nutrient content.[54]

Organic farming incorporates farming that works in harmony with nature—both living and non-living. Such a practice involves farming techniques that do not harm nature or exploitation. Historically, farming was done organically. The technological advances made during World War II led to changes in farming practices. Ammonium nitrite used as an oxidizing agent in explosives was later made to be used as nitrogen-based fertilizer. Organophosphates, used in nerve gases, soon became the basis of many insecticides and herbicides. Organic farming aims to take a break from the usage of such chemicals and fertilizers. The organic farming practice also includes good animal husbandry. In India, cow dung is the major manure used in organic farming. Some inputs given by farmers in organic farming utilize only natural materials. This includes indigenous microorganism (IMO), which is collected from nearby fields or forests using a wooden lunch box with steamed rice. Other inputs include fermented plant juice (FPJ), oriental herbal nutrient (OHN), etc.

Some of the advantages of organic farming are as follows:

1. Improved soil fertility and bio-diversity

Organic farming is done taking into consideration the local climate factors such as rainfall, temperature, and soil type. Taking into consideration these factors, the decision is made on which crop to be cultivated. All the crops

53 Millennium Ecosystem Assessment: A Toolkit for Understanding and Action, Island Press, March 2007, http://islandpress.org/assets/library/27_matoolkit.pdf, last accessed on 8 August 2011.

54 Davis D, Changes in USDA Food Composition Data for 43 Garden Crops, 1950 to 1999, Journal of the American College of Nutrition, 2004, Web Article can be accessed at http://www.jacn.org/content/23/6/669.full

don't suit all the places. In organic farming, the crop most suitable to local climatic conditions are cultivated. Methods to improve its effectiveness are adopted by the farmers. Crop rotation and multiple cropping are done in organic farming.

The exclusive usage of organic manure nourishes the soil leading to the well-being of natural habitat in the area. It has been suggested that organic farming increased the on-farm biodiversity by almost 30%.[55] Remnants of vegetables, fruits, and other organic waste are converted to compost which is used as manure. In organic farming, crop nutrition is done by planting sub plants in between the main crops. This results in nitrogen fixation. Crop rotation is also done to avoid planting the same crops every year as cultivation of the same crop reduces soil fertility. The nutrition requirement for every crop is different, and thus, crop rotation enhances soil fertility. In the case of vegetables, crops rotation is done in 3–4 years.

Mulching, the process of putting a protective cover over the soil (mimicking the leaf cover found on the forest floors), is done, and this process results in reduced evaporation and watering needs. This also reduces the growth of weeds and stops sudden changes in soil temperatures. Mulching can also be done by recycling grass clippings. Grass clippings have 75–85% moisture content which returns to the soil as they decompose. Also, as they decompose these grass clippings release nutrients such as nitrogen, potassium, and phosphorous.

2. Avoidance of chemical pesticides and fertilizers

Instead of using chemical pesticides, which have been proven to be harmful for human beings and other living beings, natural pesticides may be used in organic farming to control diseases and weeds. Some plants have enzymes that have insecticidal properties. These enzymes are extracted and used as natural pesticides. In-organic farm, natural predators like rodents are allowed to grow in the farm and these rodents kill the so-called pests. Chemical fertilizers adversely affect the nutrient content of the soil. The micro-organisms in the soil are killed and the rejuvenation process of the nutrient quality of the soil is reduced. Usage of fertilizers and pesticides pollutes the soil and during rainfall, the water soon washes away these chemicals to nearby water bodies such as a pond, well or a river. The air in the region also gets affected. All these affect the health of many living beings, including humans. In organic farming, the ecological balance of the region is maintained. Organic farming, thus does not affect the food cycle. Fertilizers are made from fossil fuels, a reduction in the consumption of fertilizers also results in the reduced use for fossil fuels and the reduction in its usage can move up to 50%.[56]

---

55 http://www.worldwatch.org/certified-organic-farmland-still-lagging-worldwide, last accessed on 28 January 2013.
56 http://www.worldwatch.org/certified-organic-farmland-still-lagging-worldwide, last accessed on 28 January 2013.

3. Improved health

In a study, made by School of Agriculture, Food and Rural Development, Newcastle University, and published in April 2011, it was indicated that organic food could increase the life expectancy by 17 days for women and 25 days for men. The study also suggested that using organic food may result in increased availability of vitamin C and other key nutrients in the food.[57] Usage of organic food also provides protection from toxic or chemical residues that may accumulate in the body.

A study done, in 1998, by Iowa State University at the Neely-Kinyon Memorial Research and Demonstration Farm, indicated that the profit per acre, generated in organic farming is higher as compared to conventional farming.[58] A 30 year side-by-side research between conventional and organic farming, done by Rodale Institute, a Kutztown, US-based organization engaged in organic research, resulted in the below conclusions:[59]

- Yield from organic farming match yields from conventional farming
- Organic farming outperforms conventional farming, during years of drought
- Organic farming systems build rather than deplete soil organic matter
- Organic farming is considered more efficient as it uses 45% less energy
- Greenhouse gas emissions in conventional farming systems were 40% higher
- Organic farming systems are more profitable

Nutritive cycle theory—Nutritive cycle theory acknowledges the need to provide different type of nutrients at different life stages of a plant. Based on the growth stage of the plant, the quantity and type of nutrients varies. Crops tend to require nitrogen during its earlier stages of growth, when the plant is building its body. Phosphoric compounds are required in adult stage, and this is the stage when the plant is preparing for reproduction. Calcium and potassium are required during maturity. Knowing this, the farmers adopt a practice where the appropriate input is provided at the appropriate stage.

Differences Between Organic and Conventional Farming

The differences between organic and conventional farming are listed in Table 2.5.

In response to a question posed in the Lok Sabha, Government of India mentioned that 'the area under organic cultivation including fruits and vegetables has been increasing in the country over the years. It stood at 10.86 lakh hectares as on 31.03.2010. Exports of organic agricultural produce are also increasing year to year'.[60] In 2004-05, the area under organic cultivation was 42,000 hectares. This is an approx 2400% increase in a period of 6 years.

57 http://www.tandfonline.com/doi/abs/10.1080/07352689.2011.554417, last accessed on 1 September 2011.

58 http://www.leopold.iastate.edu/sites/default/files/pubs-and-papers/2003-03-fundamentals-organic-agriculture.pdf, last accessed on 15 April 2013.

59 http://66.147.244.123/~rodalein/wp-content/uploads/2012/12/FSTbookletFINAL.pdf, last accessed on 28 January 2013.

60 http://pib.nic.in/newsite/erelease.aspx?relid=73642, last accessed on 23 April 2012.

TABLE 2.5 Differences between organic and conventional farming

	Organic farming	Conventional farming
Objective	Organic farming is about feeding the soil.	Conventional farming is about feeding the plants
Practices	Use of organic inputs, minimum external inputs, and crop rotation. The compost/organic manure are generated from the waste from our daily life (banana peel, fruits, and vegetable skins, etc.)	Heavy usage of synthetic chemicals and pesticides
Market	Niche market	High volume production
Products	Good in taste, flavour, and nutrition	Contain toxic residues
Technology	Less mechanization	Mechanized production
Size	Primarily owned by small and marginal farmers	Large-scale farms (especially in western countries), tied to major food corporations
Impact on the environment	Farming in harmony with the ecosystem, not against it. Could even enhance the ecosystem balance.	Damages the ecosystem
Cost of farming	Low, as there is very less usage of external inputs	High, as there is high usage of external inputs
Sustainability	No/very less usage of external inputs. Hence, sustainable.	Highly energy intensive. Driven by fertilisers made from petroleum products. Not sustainable.

As per the FiBL-IFOAM survey, the following are some statistics (Table 2.6)[61] related to organic cultivation at various geographic locations.

A report by Organic World highlights that certified organic land makes only 0.9% of global agricultural land.[62] 37 million hectares of land in the world has been organically farmed. This is a three-fold increase in the area under organic cultivation, starting 1999. As per the report, India (400,551 farmers), Uganda (188,625), and Mexico

---

61 Used with permission. FiBL and IFOAM (2012): Dynamic data table with key data from the FiBL-IFOAM survey. Published at the Organic World website, maintained by the Research Institute of Organic Agriculture FiBL, Frick, Switzerland. Available at http://www.organic-world.net/statistics-data-tables-dynamic.html, last accessed on 23 April 2012.

62 http://www.organic-world.net/fileadmin/documents/yearbook/2012/fibl-ifoam-2012-summary.pdf, last accessed on 28 January 2012.

TABLE 2.6 Organic cultivation statistics at various geographic locations

Region		Area (hectare)	% Organic	Producers
Africa				
	2005	489,949.00	0.1	132,409
	2010	1,075,830.00	0.12	539,402
Asia				
	2005	2,678,700.00	0.25	173,332
	2010	2,778,290.00	0.2	460,762
Europe				
	2005	6,762,680.00	1.37	187,820
	2010	10,002,100.00	2.1	277,362
Latin America				
	2005	5,056,160.00	0.83	185,909
	2010	8,389,460.00	1.36	272,232
Northern America				
	2005	2,219,640.00	0.57	12,111
	2010	2,652,620.00	0.68	16,870
Oceania				
	2005	11,762,700.00	2.57	2689
	2010	12,145,000.00	2.87	8483

(128,826) had the highest number of certified organic producers. Laura Reynolds, a staff researcher with Worldwatch Institute's Food and Agriculture Program says, 'Although organic agriculture often produces lower yields on land that has recently been farmed conventionally, it can outperform conventional practices—especially in times of drought—when the land has been farmed organically for a longer time'. She adds, 'Conventional agricultural practices often degrade the environment over both the long and short term through soil erosion, excessive water extraction, and biodiversity loss'.[63]

Natural Farming

Natural farming is an ecological farming propounded by a Japanese farmer and philosopher, Masanobu Fukuoka (1913–2008) (Fig. 2.4). Natural farming has also been referred to as 'Do nothing farming', 'Fukuoka method', etc. Natural farming has significant amount of similarities with organic farming. One can even state that natural farming is an advanced step of organic farming. A number of practices followed in organic farming are followed in natural farming also. 'It is better to maintain soil productivity by adopting organic farming for at least three years before switching over to natural farming',[64] explains Kailash Murthy, a bank employee who found his interest in natural farming. Fukuoka had mentioned that natural farming is not really a do-nothing technique. '(natural farming) actually involves a process of bringing your mind as closely in line as possible with the natural functioning of the environment... The real path to natural farming requires that a person know what unadulterated nature is, so that he or she can instinctively understand what needs to be done—and what must not be done—to work in harmony with its processes'.[65]

Some of the attributes of natural farming are as follows:

1. Natural farming is done with the belief that respecting the nature of life is the effective way to achieve optimum quality and yield. Natural farming opposes human exploitation of life.

2. No usage of synthetic chemicals and pesticides. In natural farming, weeds and rodents are used to maintain ecological balance. In farms that practices natural farming, we can find grass growing between the fruit trees. These grasses results in increased percolation of rainwater to the ground, holds moisture, prevents erosion, propagates the growth of microorganisms, and finally, produces organic fertilizers.

   In addition, light, aroma, and poisonous plants may be used to manage pests. Due to the same, the fruits may have some natural stripes, spots or insect bites. This is an indication for the zero usage of chemicals.

3. No input or very minimum inputs. Any minimum input is provided from natural materials. Unlike organic farming, in natural farming, not even organic manure or organic pesticides are used.

4. In natural farming, no tillage is done. Tillage may degrade the physical characteristics of the soil and the flow of nutrients. It can also result in a change

63 http://www.worldwatch.org/achieving-sustainable-food-system-organic-farming, last accessed on 3 February 2013.
64 http://www.hindu.com/seta/2009/06/11/stories/2009061150191600.htm, last accessed on 25 April 2012.
65 http://fukuokafarmingol.info/faplow.html, last accessed on 14 July 2014.

FIG. 2.4. Masanobu Fukuoka, at Bija Vidyapeeth,
Dehradun, India, in 2002[66]

in the social chemistry. Tilling also uproots all plants in the area, thereby turning these roots as food for bacteria and fungi. This damages the ability of these plants to aerate the soil. Living roots drill millions of tiny holes in the soil and provide oxygen.

5. In natural farming, farmers make what they need. All/most of the materials/ inputs given to the farm are made from materials available in the farm.

Kailash Murthy has been practising natural farming at his farm located in Doddinduvadi village, Kollegal taluk, Chamarajanagar district, Karnataka. He has found that yield from his farm are higher than farms in his neighbourhood areas that are cultivated conventionally. In his farm, Kailash Murthy has grown 33 quintals of paddy in an acre while his neighbours grow 18 quintals using synthetic chemical fertilizers.[67] This is opposite to the common perception that organic farms and natural farms yield lesser. The author of this textbook has observed that, in some farms, there

---

66 Photo by Vasanth. Used with permission. Image Source: http://naturalfarming.org/node/9. Used with permission. last accessed on 14 July 2014.

67 http://www.hindu.com/2009/01/19/stories/2009011952860300.htm, last accessed on 25 April 2012.

'Suppose if we destroy the weeds and organic matter from the soil, the animals and insects depending on that organic matter as their food, will attack our crop. They need food. They will change their food habits. Then we are going to face a lot of problem. So, in my farm I am providing also for animals and insects. I am maintaining one crop for me. Among the millions in diversity, we are one. So, am maintaining one crop for me, and leaving the rest for others'.

has been a drop in the yield after converting to organic or natural farming. However, the input costs in these farms have also gone down significantly. Thus, the farmers were able to experience more than offset the drop in revenues due to lesser yield, and they had a higher net income while practising organic/natural farming as compared to conventional farming. Kailash Murthy says, 'Suppose if we destroy the weeds and organic matter from the soil, the animals and insects depending on that organic matter as their food, will attack our crop. They need food. They will change their food habits. Then we are going to face a lot of problems. So, in my farm I am providing also for animals and insects. I am maintaining one crop for me. Among the millions in diversity, we are one among them. So, am maintaining one crop for me, and leaving the rest for others'.[68]

In Fukuoka's writings about natural farming, readers can find a connection between farming and a sense of sacredness. The following two quotations from *The One-Straw Revolution* exemplify this:

1. Speaking biologically, fruit in a slightly shrivelled state is holding its respiration and energy consumption down to the lowest possible level. It is like a person in meditation: his metabolism, respiration, and calorie consumption reach an extremely low level. Even if he fasts, the energy within the body will be conserved. In the same way, when mandarin oranges grow wrinkled, when fruit shrivels, when vegetables wilt, they are in the state that will preserve their food value for the longest possible time.

2. The ultimate goal of farming is not the growing of crops, but the cultivation and perfection of human beings.

Permaculture

Permaculture is to create an agricultural practice modelled from natural ecosystems. Permaculture is a combination of two words—*Perma*nent Agri*culture*. Bill Mollison, who coined the word (along with David Holmgren), says, 'Permaculture is a philosophy of working with, rather than against nature; of protracted and thoughtful observation rather than protracted and thoughtless labour; and of looking at plants and animals in all their functions, rather than treating any area as a single project system'.[69] The three broad maxims that guide Permaculture are:

---

68 http://www.youtube.com/watch?v=FcxxVjQTO8Q, last accessed on 13 September 2013.
69 http://www.shirleymaclaine.com/articles/environment/article-292, last accessed on 15 April 2013.

- Care for the earth
- Care for the people
- Fair share (setting limits to consumption and reproduction, and to redistribute surplus)

The 12 design principles[70] of Permaculture are:

- Observe and interact
- Catch and store energy
- Obtain a yield
- Apply self-regulation and accept feedback
- Use and value renewable resources & services
- Produce no waste
- Design from patterns to details
- Integrate rather than segregate
- Use small and slow solutions
- Use and value diversity
- Use edges and value the marginal
- Creatively use and respond to change

> The ultimate goal of farming is not the growing of crops, but the cultivation and perfection of human beings.

Some of the common practices involved in permaculture are agro-forestry, Hügelkultur,[71] natural building, rainwater harvesting, sheet mulching, managed intensive rotational grazing, and keyline design.

THE ROLE OF VEGETARIANISM

One should treat animals such as deer, camels, asses, monkeys, mice, snakes, birds, and flies exactly like one's own children. How little difference there actually is between children and these innocent animals.
Srimad Bhagavatam, 7.14-9

Environmental Working Group (EWG), a Washington-based not-for-profit organization, in partnership with CleanMetrics, an environmental analysis and consulting firm did a lifecycle assessment study among 20 types of food sources that provides proteins. The study, which was done in the USA, found that lamb, beef, cheese, pork, and farmed salmon generated the highest greenhouse gases (Fig. 2.5). Lamb, beef, cheese, and pork also had the worst environmental impacts. While the global population has almost doubled in the last four decades, production of meat has tripled during this period.[72] This jump in production has serious negative impact on the environment. Production of meat protein required 6–20 times as much fossil

---

70 For more details about each of these design principles, one may refer to http://holmgren.com.au/wp-content/uploads/2013/02/Essence_of_Pc_EN.pdf, last accessed on 15 April 2013.

71 To increase water retention in the soil, wood is buried underground. As the wood decompose, its porous structure acts as a sponge.

72 http://www.worldwatch.org/global-meat-production-and-consumption-continue-rise-1, last accessed on 30 April 2012.

fuel in comparison with the production of soy protein, on a per kg basis.[73] In 2008, meat production contributed 15–24% of the greenhouse gas emissions.[74] In 2005, the Food and Agriculture Organization of the United Nations mentioned that 'Expanding livestock production is one of the main drivers of the destruction of tropical rain forests in Latin America, which is causing serious environmental degradation in the region'.[75] This livestock production was mainly meant for human consumption.[76] It has also been estimated that livestock contribute, directly and indirectly, to about 9% of total anthropogenic CO_2 emissions, 37% of methane emissions, and 65% of nitrous oxide emissions.[77]

As part of the natural process, animals existed in harmony with the natural environment. When the animal population increased, there was an increase in the

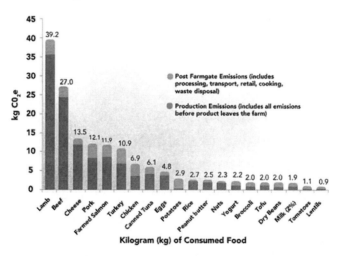

CO_2 **(Equivalent) emissions for various foods.**

FIG. 2.5 [78] CO_2 (equivalent) emissions for various foods

73 Nathan Fiala, 'Meeting the Demand: An Estimation of Potential Future Greenhouse Gas Emissions from Meat Production', *Ecological Economics*, Vol. 67(3), 2008.

74 Nathan Fiala, 'Meeting the Demand: An Estimation of Potential Future Greenhouse Gas Emissions from Meat Production', *Ecological Economics* Vol. 67(3), 2008.

75 http://www.fao.org/newsroom/en/news/2005/102924/, last accessed on 31 March 2012.

76 http://www.fao.org/newsroom/en/news/2005/102924/, last accessed on 31 March 2012.

77 H Steinfeld *et al.*, Livestock's Long Shadow: Environmental Issues and Options. Livestock, Environment and Development, FAO, 2006.

78 Source: From the report 'Meat Eater's Guide to Climate Change + Health', Available at http://breakingnews.ewg.org/meateatersguide/a-meat-eaters-guide-to-climate-change-health-what-you-eat-matters/climate-and-environmental-impacts/, last accessed on 2 Accessed on October 2, 2013. Copyright © Environmental Working Group, www.ewg.org. Used with permission.

consumption of plants in the natural environment. This increased consumption resulted in decreased availability of plant-based food. As the availability of food came down, the animal population decreased. Thus, the balance was maintained. However, human intervention, driven by increased demand for animal flesh due to appetite driven by taste sensations, resulted in factory farming.

In factory farming, animals are grown in an artificial environment where the animals have to be provided with food. For this provision, grains and grasses were grown in a large scale. Forest lands were thus diverted to farm lands for grains and grasses. Unique plant species that played significant roles in balancing the ecosystem were thus lost. Further, artificial stimulants were fed or injected to these factory-farmed animals, including livestock. The dung produced by these animals is not suitable for sustaining life in the local ecosystem. In the USA, in 2011, antibiotics sold towards meat and poultry production (29.9 million pounds) is four times the amount of antibiotics sold to treat sick people (7.7 million pounds).[79] As per the research done by World Watch Institute, 'Seventy-five per cent of the antibiotics used on livestock are not absorbed by the animals and are excreted in waste, posing a serious risk to public health'.[80] Misuse of antibiotics amongst livestock animals will result in the development of antibiotic-resistant infections in people.[81]

It has also been found that producing nutrients in plant form requires less water than producing it in animal form (Table 2.7). Also, raising animals for food requires more land than growing crops. It has also been noted that plant-based foods emit less of CO_2 as compared to animal products. John Robbins and Dean Ornish, in their book, *Food Revolution*,[82] states that it takes 16 pounds of grain to make one pound of beef, and livestock eat 70% of all the grains produced in the world. They also state that more chickens are killed in US every year than the entire human population of the world.

Satish Kumar, a Jain monk who also edits the *Resurgence* magazine[83] comments, 'The Isa Upanishad tells us that everything, from a blade of grass to the whole cosmos, is the home of God. God lives in every corner of existence. Therefore, the whole creation is sacred. The Ganges is the symbol of that Holy Spirit which permeates through every river and Holy Mountain. Kailash is the holy mountain, but all mountains are holy because God lives there. The cow is holy because ultimately all the animal kingdom is holy. This sense of the sacred in the whole creation is fundamental to our relationship with nature. Western civilization considers human life to be sacred, but Hindus have gone much further and said that not only human life but all life is sacred. Therefore

---

79 http://www.pewhealth.org/reports-analysis/issue-briefs/antibiotics-and-industrial-farming-101-85899466272, last accessed on 28 December 2013.

80 http://www.worldwatch.org/global-meat-production-and-consumption-continue-rise-1, last accessed on 30 April 2012.

81 http://www.pewhealth.org/reports-analysis/issue-briefs/antibiotics-and-industrial-farming-101-85899466272, last accessed on 28 December 2013.

82 Conari Press, September 2010

83 A UK based bi-monthly magazine that is often described as the artistic and spiritual voice of the green movement.

all life forms, not just human beings, must be revered and respected. This is the reason for being vegetarian, which is ecological in the deepest sense. Animal life should not be taken for our own purposes, nor should it be artificially created, as it is in the West where millions of cattle, pigs, and chicken are reared for slaughter in factory farms. There should be a natural pattern of birth and death in the forest, on the land, in the air, and sea. Rearing animals for our own use is not natural'.[84]

As per Ayurveda, *Agni* (Root of the English word 'ignite') or 'digestive fire' is responsible for absorbing the nutrients and essential elements required by the body, and also for burning the waste. Ayurveda states that strong Agni leads to well-being while a weak Agni leads to *ama* or toxic residue in our cells. *Ojas* is the subtle substance extracted from digested food. *Ojas* brings clarity to mind, sustains the physical body and balances the emotions. In order to promote the creation and flow of *Ojas* through the body, Ayurveda recommends a diet focused on Sattwik foods. The body can easily digest Sattwik food. This diet will include organic milk, rice, fruits, sesame, almonds etc. It is difficult and sometimes impossible to create *Ojas* from items like processed food (canned,

TABLE 2.7 [85] Water requirements for the production of various items eaten by humans (cubic metre of water per tonne of production)

	Hoekstra & Hung (2003)	Chapagain & Hoekstra (2003)	Zimmer & Renault (2003)	Oki et al. (2003)	Average
Beef		15,977	13,500	20,700	16,726
Pork		5906	4600	5900	5469
Cheese		5288			5288
Poultry		2828	4100	4500	3809
Eggs		4657	2700	3200	3519
Rice	2656		1400	3600	2552
Soybeans	2300		2750	2500	2517
Wheat	1150		1160	2000	1437
Maize	450		710	1900	1020
Milk		865	790	560	738
Potatoes	160		105		133

84 Ranchor Prime, Vedic Ecology: Practical Wisdom for Surviving the 21st Century, Mandala Publishing, 2002
85 Author adaptation from Virtual Water Trade: Proceedings of the International Expert Meeting on Virtual Water Trade, February 2003, Available at www.waterfootprint.org/Reports/Report12.pdf, last accessed on 31 March 2012.

frozen, and reheated), leftovers (old/stale food), meat, poultry, fish, fried, oily, cheese, and items with an excess of sour or salty tastes. Also, consuming alcohol and smoking cigarettes destroys *Ojas*. Hence, maintaining a diet that produce maximum *Ojas* will help in creating an evolved body and mind. Actions disrupting the digestive fire will include eating too fast, overeating, lack of attention to food while eating (such as having food and watching TV, chit-chatting while eating etc.), immoral emotions and actions, eating when upset, etc.

The Bhagavad Gita suggests that one should evolve to those foods, which are wholesome and pleasing to the heart. The Gita also says that foods that are too bitter, too sour, salty, hot, pungent, dry, and burning cause distress, misery, and disease. The Gita goes on to state that food prepared more than 3 hours before being eaten, food that is decomposed and putrid is dear to those in the mode of darkness.

We will listen to what Ricardo Levy, Acting CEO, Catalytica Energy Systems Inc., Mountain View, CA, Unites States would like to share with us:

'I think that longing and belonging are two of the most important concepts. Our longings are windows into our spirituality. In a sense they are interlinked with two aspects of belonging: love and compassion. It's all a marvelous intertwining circle. One of my favourite quotes from Abraham Yoshua Heschel is: Needs are spiritual opportunities. I find this so true, just as longings are also opportunities for us to learn about our spirituality'.

'Another quote that is a bit longer also expresses this same concept about needs. It comes from the Hindu book Will I be the Hero of My Own Life?*:*

> *We are such creatures of wants that even simple things like being hungry set up an intense inner vibration from which our mechanism speaks. Generally speaking we then just want to respond to that vibration to feed the system. Rarely do we take the time to observe the nature of the vibration itself. We do not use the hunger as an opportunity to understand our own essence and the dynamics at work in us. We don't let the vibration intensify and change to reveal its subtler component. Were we to do so, we would begin to recognise the nature of wanting itself, independent of its particular form'.*[86]

Holy books like Bible promote a sentient diet. A vegetarian diet is in alignment with the central biblical principle of stewardship. In *Are we good stewards of God's creation?*[87] It is stated, 'In Eden, all creatures lived peacefully, and God told both humans and animals to consume only plant foods (Genesis 1:29–31). Several prophecies, like Isaiah 11:6–9, foresee a return to this vegetarian world, where the wolf, lamb, lion, cow, bear, snake, and little child all coexist peacefully'. A number of Christians believe that one should strive towards the harmonious world Isaiah envisioned, to try to live in accordance with the prayer that Jesus

86 Quotations extracted from the public knowledge base of the 'Spiritual Based Leadership Research Programme' are © 2006 by the Global Dharma Center (GDC). GDC retains the copyright to all excerpts from this knowledge base.

87 http://www.all-creatures.org/cva/AWGSGC-Mar07.pdf, last accessed on 28 April 2010.

taught, 'Thy kingdom come, Thy will be done, On earth as it is in heaven' (Matt. 6:10).

In the Bible, there is a mention of an incident that happened after the resurrection of Jesus Christ. The below is the quotation from the Amplified Bible:

> *'And behold, that very day two of [the disciples] were going to a village called Emmaus, [which is] about seven miles from Jerusalem.*
>
> *And they were talking with each other about all these things that had occurred.*
>
> *And while they were conversing and discussing together, Jesus Himself caught up with them and was already accompanying them.*
>
> *But their eyes were held, so that they did not recognize Him....*
>
> *....Then they drew near the village to which they were going, and He acted as if He would go further.*
>
> *But they urged and insisted, saying to Him, Remain with us, for it is toward evening, and the day is now far spent. So He went in to stay with them.*
>
> *And it occurred that as He reclined at table with them, He took [a loaf of] bread and praised [God] and gave thanks and asked a blessing, and then broke it and was giving it to them.*
>
> *When their eyes were [instantly] opened and they [clearly] recognized Him, and He vanished ([i]departed invisibly)'.*

Luke 24: 13-16, 28-31

The following is an excerpt (permitted to reprint) from 'Are we good stewards of God's creation?' published by the Christian Vegetarian Association (http://www.all-creatures.org/cva/honoring.htm, Accessed on April 28, 2010)

Adam's 'dominion' over animals (Gen.1:26, 28), we believe, conveys sacred stewardship, since God immediately afterward prescribed a vegetarian diet (1:29-30) in a world God found 'very good' (1:31). Created in God's image of love (1 John 4:4), we are called to be caretakers of God's Creation, not tyrants over God's creatures.

Genesis 1:21-22 relates that, before God created humanity, God regarded the animals 'good' and blessed them. Further evidence that we should consider animals as inherently valuable comes from Genesis 2:18-19, which indicates that God made animals as Adam's helpers and companions: 'Then the Lord God said,' It is not good that man should be alone; I will make him a helper fit for him'. So out of the ground the Lord God formed every beast of the field and every bird of the air, and brought them to the man to see what he would call them...' (RSV). Adam named the animals, which we believe shows concern and friendship. We don't name the animals we eat.

God endowed pigs, cattle, sheep, and all farmed animals with their own desires and needs, which is apparent when these animals are given an opportunity to enjoy life. For example, pigs are as curious, social, and intelligent as cats or dogs. Pigs can even play some video games better than monkeys. Similarly, chickens enjoy one another's company and like to play, dust bathe, and forage for food. Jesus compared his love for us to a hen's love for her chicks (Luke 13:34).

The Bible do not mention on what caused his disciples to recognize him. Could it be the unique way in which Jesus broke the bread, a way that nobody else can imitate? An embodiment of Divine sees Divinity in everything. The way Jesus broke the bread could be incomparable. He would have broken the bread with utmost respect, reverence, and prayerfulness, as if the bread was His father Himself.

Research studies suggest that vegetarianism plays a vital role in facilitating spiritually, ecologically sustainable behaviour (Narayanan Y, Marinova D, 2006).[88] Dr R K Pachauri, Chairman, Intergovernmental Panel on Climate Change (IPCC) and Director General of TERI, states, 'In my view an important component of lifestyle changes relates to changes in diet, which in fact may bring about an improvement in human health. In the case of meat consumption, there are benefits not only to the individual who reduces consumption of meat, but clear advantages in terms of reducing greenhouse gas (GHG) emissions'.[89] In his blog 'Lifestyle Changes for A Healthy Planet', Pachauri explains how a vegetarian diet helps the planet.[90]

Ways to Save the Planet through Your Plate

Eat More Pulses

Eat protein sources from lower down the food chain, such as pulses and nuts. Su Taylor, Spokesperson, Vegetarian Society of United Kingdom, explains: 'Grains, pulses, and nuts have a much smaller carbon footprint than meat products by about a factor of three and are ideal as foods for human consumption'.[91]

Choose Seasonal and Local; If possible, Buy Organic

If you have visited a modern supermarket, you would have noticed fruits of all varieties and sizes, from all parts of the world. Have you thought where these foods came from and how much distance they would have travelled? By eating seasonal produces, and especially that which is grown locally, you'll not only be supporting local economy and providing for local employment, you will also be reducing the carbon footprint and reducing the food miles. Visit a farmers market or a weekly market to source local produces. Organic food products should actually cost lesser, as the input cost is less in organic farming. In many retail stores, the organic food products are sold with a price that is almost par with non-organic products. However, in some retail outlets, it is priced significantly higher (niche marketing?). If you can afford to go organic, buy organic, and buy organic products that are produced as close to the point of purchase as possible.

88 Wooltorton, S. and Marinova, D. (Eds), *Sharing wisdom for our future. Environmental education in action: Proceedings of the 2006 Conference of the Australian Association of Environmental Education.*

89 http://blog.rkpachauri.org/blog/4/Lifestyle-Changes-for-A-Healthy-Planet.htm

90 The blog mentions, 'An interesting comparison between a vegetarian meal and a beef steak, for instance, was provided by The New York Times in its issue of 27 January 2008 which is revealing. A meal consisting of 1 cup of broccoli, 1 cup of eggplant, 4 ounces cauliflower and 8 ounces of rice results in 0.4 pounds of emissions of CO_2 equivalent. On the other hand a 6 ounce beef steak results in 10 pounds of CO_2 equivalent emissions, which amount to 25 times that of the vegetarian meal with which the comparison was made'.

91 http://blogs.worldwatch.org/nourishingtheplanet/wp-content/uploads/2012/01/Can-becoming-a-vegetarian-help-save-the-planet-The-Ecologist-meat-vso.pdf, last accessed on 30 April 2012.

Be Bold, Go Vegetarian; If Not, Increase the Number of Meat-free Days in Your Life
Paul McCartney, the musician of the Beatles fame, has been campaigning for 'Meat Free
Mondays'. The McCartney family says, 'In 2009, we launched the Meat Free Monday
campaign as a simple and straightforward idea to show everyone the value of eating
less meat—and to make it easier for us all to do so'.[92] India has produced towering
personalities, and also popular personalities, who've been vegetarians (Table 2.8).

An issue paper released by Natural Resources Defense Council (NRDC), related to
food wastage in the USA, states, 'Much of the needed food production can be traced
back to increased meat consumption, either the meat itself or the crops required
to feed livestock. Animal products require 4–40 times the calories to produce than
they provide in nutrition when eaten, mainly due to the crops they consume. If all
of the crop production currently allocated to animal feed were directly consumed by
humans, global food production would increase by some two billion tons and food
calories would increase by 49%. This becomes more important when considering
the projections that, barring any shift in diets, worldwide meat consumption could
increase 40% by 2050 (from a 2000 baseline). Although not the focus of this paper,
an important step in ensuring food security will be to move diets away from animal
products, thus increasing the efficiency of our food system in terms of calories
delivered'.[93]

TABLE 2.8 Few of the famous personalities who practised a vegetarian diet

Albert Einstein	Amala Akkineni	Amitabh Bachchan	Anil Kumble
Annie Besant	APJ Abdul Kalam	Asoka, the Great	Bill Clinton
Brad Pitt	Bryan Adams	Carl Lewis	Confucius
Deepak Chopra	Franz Kafka	Gautama, The Buddha	Gautam Adani
George Bernard Shaw	George Harrison	Greg Chappell	Harsha Bhogle
Jane Godall	Julia 'Butterfly' Hill	Jiddu Krishnamurti	John the Baptist
Kabir	Kumaramangalam Birla	Lakshmi Mittal	Leonardo Da Vinci
Leo Tolstoy	Lord Swaraj Paul	Mahatma Gandhi	Mahavira
Martina Navratilova	Mata Amritanandamayi	Michael Bolton	Mike Tyson
Nikola Tesla	Paramahansa Yogananda	Paul McCartney	Plutarch
Pythagoras	Rabindranath Tagore	Ramana Maharshi	Romain Rolland

(Contd)

92　http://www.meatfreemondays.com/index.cfm, last accessed on 30 April 2012.
93　http://www.nrdc.org/food/files/wasted-food-IP.pdf, last accessed on 18 January 2013.

Sachin Tendulkar	Sadhguru Jaggi Vasudev	Saint Angela de Merici	Saint Catherine of Siena
Saint Francis of Paola	Saint John de Brito	Saint Mathew	Saint Richard of Chichester
Sant Kirpal Singhji	Scott Adams	Shania Twain	Shashi Tharoor
SP Balasubramanyam	Srinivasa Ramanujan	Sri Sathya Sai Baba	Sri Sri Ravishankar
Swami Prabhupada	Swami Chinmayananda	Swami Dayananda Saraswathi	Swami Sivananda
Thich Nhat Hanh	Tulsi Tanti	Venkatesh Prasad	Venugopal Dhoot
Viswanathan Anand	Virender Sehwag	Yehudi Menuhin	William Blake

RELIGIOUS PERSPECTIVES ON EARTH AND NATURE

Religion is one of the oldest organizations in the recorded history, and continues to be a great influencer for the majority of the human population. People also put their

FIG. 2.6 [94] Buddhist teachers and monks in Bangkok, Thailand, come together as part of a merit-making ceremony to honour the souls of poached African elephants. As per World Wide Fund for Nature (WWF), Thailand is the world's largest unregulated ivory market and also a major destination for ivory poached from Africa.

94 Image Courtesy: WWF Thailand. Used with permission. Source: http://worldwildlife.org/stories/buddhist-teachers-deliver-powerful-message-against-illegal-ivory-trade, last accessed on 6 May 2013. For more details, https://www.facebook.com/wwfthailand

trust and faith on religious teaching and its leaders than other structures or groups. More importantly, the essence of most religions, if put into practice, will pave the way for a sustainable future. Some most inspiring thoughts about sustainability are found in the scriptures of the world and are told and preached by the mystics of various spiritual organizations and religious traditions. Religions thus have a leading role to play in re-connecting human beings to the ecosystems on whom the human beings depend upon. Taken together, various religious institutions would also be one of the largest stockholders of the world, and would be having significant amount of assets. By connecting with nature, religions have an opportunity to discover deeper meanings of their own traditions. Organizations like 'The Alliance of Religions and Conservation' works to build alliances between faith communities and conservation groups.

Buddhist Declaration on Climatic Change[95]

The Declaration that follows, The Time to Act is Now, is a pan-Buddhist statement by Zen teacher Dr David Tetsuun Loy and senior Theravadin teacher Ven. Bhikkhu Bodhi, with scientific inputs from Dr John Stanley. The Dalai Lama blessed the Declaration by signing it.

Today, we live in a time of great crisis, confronted by the gravest challenge that humanity has ever faced: the ecological consequences of our own collective karma. The scientific consensus is overwhelming: human activity is triggering environmental breakdown on a planetary scale. Global warming, in particular, is happening much faster than previously predicted, most obviously at the North Pole. For hundreds of thousands of years, the Arctic Ocean has been covered by an area of sea-ice as large as Australia—but now this is melting rapidly. In 2007, the Intergovernmental Panel on Climate Change (IPCC) forecast that the Arctic might be free of summer sea ice by 2100. It is now apparent that this could occur within a decade or two. Greenland's vast ice-sheet is also melting more quickly than expected. The rise in sea-level this century will be at least one metre—enough to flood many coastal cities and vital rice-growing areas like the Mekong Delta in Vietnam.

Glaciers all over the world are receding quickly. If current economic policies continue, the glaciers of the Tibetan Plateau, source of the great rivers that provide water for billions of people in Asia, are likely to disappear by mid-century. Severe drought and crop failures are already affecting Australia and Northern China. Major reports—from the IPCC, United Nations, European Union, and International Union for Conservation of Nature—agree that, without a collective change of direction, dwindling supplies of water, food, and other resources could create famine conditions, resource battles, and mass migration by mid-century—perhaps by 2030, according to the UK's chief scientific advisor.

---

95 Used with permission. The declaration can be accessed at http://www.ecobuddhism.org/bcp/all_content/buddhist_declaration/

In December 2011, Kohls, a US-based retail chain, announced that its customers will be able to recharge their electric vehicles (EV) for free at 33 Kohls stores as part of the company's pilot program to introduce EV chargers in its outlets. Other US-based retailing companies that introduced EV chargers include IKEA, Lowe's and Walgreens. Walgreens plans to install charging stations at 800 stores.

Global warming plays a major role in other ecological crises, including the loss of many plant and animal species that share this Earth with us. Oceanographers report that half the carbon released by burning fossil fuels has been absorbed by the oceans, increasing their acidity by about 30%. Acidification is disrupting calcification of shells and coral reefs, as well as threatening plankton growth, the source of the food chain for most life in the sea.

Eminent biologists and U.N. reports concur that 'business-as-usual' will drive half of all species on Earth to extinction within this century. Collectively, we are violating the first precept—'do not harm living beings'—on the largest possible scale. And we cannot foresee the biological consequences for human life when so many species that invisibly contribute to our own well-being vanish from the planet.

Many scientists have concluded that the survival of human civilization is at stake. We have reached a critical juncture in our biological and social evolution. There has never been a more important time in history to bring the resources of Buddhism to bear on behalf of all living beings. The four noble truths provide a framework for diagnosing our current situation and formulating appropriate guidelines—because the threats and disasters we face ultimately stem from the human mind, and therefore require profound changes within our minds. If personal suffering stems from craving and ignorance—from the three poisons of greed, ill will, and delusion—the same applies to the suffering that afflicts us on a collective scale. Our ecological emergency is a larger version of the perennial human predicament. Both as individuals and as a species, we suffer from a sense of self that feels disconnected not only from other people but from the Earth itself. As Thich Nhat Hanh has said, 'We are here to awaken from the illusion of our separateness'. We need to wake up and realize that the Earth is our mother as well as our home—and in this case the umbilical cord binding us to her cannot be severed. When the Earth becomes sick, we become sick, because we are part of her.

Our present economic and technological relationships with the rest of the biosphere are unsustainable. To survive the rough transitions ahead, our lifestyles and expectations must change. This involves new habits as well as new values. The Buddhist teaching that the overall health of the individual and society depends upon inner well-being, and not merely upon economic indicators, helps us determine the personal and social changes we must make.

Individually, we must adopt behaviours that increase everyday ecological awareness and reduce our 'carbon footprint'. Those of us in the advanced economies need to retrofit and insulate our homes and workplaces for energy efficiency; lower thermostats in winter and raise them in summer; use high efficiency light bulbs and appliances; turn off unused electrical appliances; drive the most fuel-efficient cars possible, and reduce meat consumption in favor of a healthy, environmentally-friendly plant-based diet.

These personal activities will not by themselves be sufficient to avert future calamity. We must also make institutional changes, both technological and economic. We must 'de-carbonize' our energy systems as quickly as feasible by replacing fossil fuels with renewable energy sources that are limitless, benign, and harmonious with nature. We especially need to halt the construction of new coal plants, since coal is by far the most polluting and most dangerous source of atmospheric carbon. Wisely utilized, wind power, solar power, tidal power, and geothermal power can provide all the electricity that we require without damaging the biosphere. Since up to a quarter of world carbon emissions result from deforestation, we must reverse the destruction of forests, especially the vital rainforest belt where most species of plants and animals live.

It has recently become quite obvious that significant changes are also needed in the way our economic system is structured. Global warming is intimately related to the gargantuan quantities of energy that our industries devour to provide the levels of consumption that many of us have learned to expect. From a Buddhist perspective, a sane and sustainable economy would be governed by the principle of sufficiency: the key to happiness is contentment rather than an ever-increasing abundance of goods. The compulsion to consume more and more is an expression of craving, the very thing the Buddha pinpointed as the root cause of suffering.

Instead of an economy that emphasizes profit and requires perpetual growth to avoid collapse, we need to move together towards an economy that provides a satisfactory standard of living for everyone while allowing us to develop our full (including spiritual) potential in harmony with the biosphere that sustains and nurtures all beings, including future generations. If the political leaders are unable to recognize the urgency of our global crisis, or unwilling to put the long-term good of humankind above the short-term benefit of fossil-fuel corporations, we may need to challenge them with sustained campaigns of citizen action.

Dr James Hansen of NASA and other climatologists have recently defined the precise targets needed to prevent global warming from reaching catastrophic 'tipping points'. For human civilization to be sustainable, the safe level of CO_2 in the atmosphere is no more than 350 parts per million (ppm). This target has been endorsed by the Dalai Lama, along with other Nobel laureates and distinguished scientists. Our current situation is particularly worrisome in that the present level is already 387 ppm, and has been rising at 2 ppm per year. We are challenged not only to reduce carbon emissions, but also to remove large quantities of carbon gas already present in the atmosphere.

As signatories to this statement of Buddhist principles, we acknowledge the urgent challenge of climate change. We join with the Dalai Lama in endorsing the 350 ppm target. In accordance with Buddhist teachings, we accept our individual and collective responsibility to do whatever we can to meet this target, including (but not limited to) the personal and social responses outlined above.

We have a brief window of opportunity to take action, to preserve humanity from imminent disaster and to assist the survival of the many diverse and beautiful forms of life on Earth. Future generations, and the other species that share the biosphere with us, have no voice to ask for our compassion, wisdom, and leadership. We must listen to their silence. We must be their voice, too, and act on their behalf.

Hindu Declaration on Climate Change[96]

(Convocation of Hindu Spiritual Leaders, Parliament of the World's Religions, Melbourne, Australia, 8 December 2009)

Earth, in which the seas, the rivers, and many waters lie, from which arise foods and fields of grain, abode to all that breathes and moves, may She confer on us Her finest yield.
Bhumi Suktam, Atharva Veda xii.1.3

The Hindu tradition understands that a man is not separate from nature, that we are linked by spiritual, psychological, and physical bonds with the elements around us. Knowing that the Divine is present everywhere and in all things, Hindus strive to do no harm. We hold a deep reverence for life and an awareness that the great forces of nature—the earth, the water, the fire, the air, and space—as well as all the various orders of life, including plants and trees, forests, and animals, are bound to each other within life's cosmic web.

Our beloved Earth, so touchingly looked upon as the Universal Mother, has nurtured the mankind through millions of years of growth and evolution. Now centuries of rapacious exploitation of the planet have caught up with us, and a radical change in our relationship with nature is no longer an option. It is a matter of survival. We cannot continue to destroy nature without also destroying ourselves. The dire problems besetting our world—war, disease, poverty, and hunger—will all be magnified many fold by the predicted impacts of climate change.

The nations of the world have yet to agree upon a plan to ameliorate man's contribution to this complex change. This is largely due to powerful forces in some nations which oppose any such attempt, challenging the very concept that unnatural climate change is occurring. Hindus everywhere should work towards an international consensus. Humanity's very survival depends upon our capacity to make a major transition of consciousness, equal in significance to earlier transitions from nomadic to agricultural, agricultural to industrial, and industrial to technological. We must transit to complementarity in place of competition, convergence in place of conflict, holism in place of hedonism, and optimization

---

96 Used with permission from Parliament of World Religions (www.parliamentofreligions.org); Also available at http://www.hinduismtoday.com/pdf_downloads/hindu-climate-change-declaration.pdf, last accessed on 5 October 2011.

Below is a reader's comment to a news article indicating that the ski industry in USA has suffered $1 billion loss and dropped 27,000 jobs, over the last decade, due to diminished snowfall patterns.

All of the species on this Earth, save one, live with about the same energy footprint as when they first appeared. My belief is that this is the energy footprint that was designed to be sustainable. We, humankind, have increased this initial energy footprint by orders of magnitude...

in place of maximization. We must, in short, move rapidly towards a global consciousness that replaces the present fractured and fragmented consciousness of the human race.

Mahatma Gandhi urged, 'You must be the change you wish to see in the world'. If alive today, he would call upon Hindus to set the example, to change our lifestyle, to simplify our needs and restrain our desires. As one-sixth of the human family, Hindus can have a tremendous impact. We can and should take the lead in Earth-friendly living, personal frugality, lower power consumption, alternative energy, sustainable food production, and vegetarianism, as well as in evolving technologies that positively address our shared plight. Hindus recognize that it may be too late to avert drastic climate change. Thus, in the spirit of vasudhaiva kutumbakam, 'the whole world is one family', Hindus encourage the world to be prepared to respond with compassion to such calamitous challenges such as population displacement, food and water shortage, catastrophic weather, and rampant disease.

Sanatana Dharma envisions the vastness of God's manifestation and the immense cycles of time in which it is perfectly created, preserved, and destroyed, again and again, every dissolution being the preamble to the next creative impulse. Notwithstanding this spiritual reassurance, Hindus still know we must do all that is humanly possible to protect the Earth and her resources for the present as well as future generations.

Jain Declaration on Nature[97]

(In 1990, Institute of Jainology, in consultation with many Jain communities, initiated the preparation of Jain Declaration on Nature, which defines the essential Jain values, the concepts of nature, ecology, and the environment. The process involved the participation of some 30 Jain scholars with final editing by Dr L M Singhvi. This document was presented to HRH Prince Philip, the President of the World Wide Fund for Nature (WWF), on 23 October 1990 at Buckingham Palace in the presence of 21 leaders representing Jain communities across the world.)

The Jain tradition which enthroned the philosophy of ecological harmony and non-violence as its lodestar flourished for centuries side-by-side with other schools of thoughts in ancient India. It formed a vital part of the mainstream of ancient

---

97 Source: Originally published by Institute of Jainology Ltd, Unit 18, Silicon Business Centre, 28 Wadsworth Road, Perivale, Greenford, Middlesex UB6 7JZ, Also available at http://www.jainology.org/publications/jain-delaration-on-nature/, last accessed on 26 May 2011, Used with permission.

Indian life, contributing greatly to its philosophical, artistic, and political heritage. During certain periods of Indian history, many ruling elites as well as large sections of the population were Jains, followers of the Jinas (Spiritual Victors).

The ecological philosophy of Jainism which flows from its spiritual quest has always been central to its ethics, aesthetics, art, literature, economics, and politics. It is represented in all its glory by the 24 Jinas or Tirthankaras (Path-finders) of this era whose example and teachings have been its living legacy through the millennia.

Although the ten million Jains estimated to live in modern India constitute a tiny fraction of its population, the message and motifs of the Jain perspective, its reverence for life in all forms, its commitment to the progress of human civilization, and to the preservation of the natural environment continues to have a profound and pervasive influence on Indian life and outlook.

In the twentieth century, the most vibrant and illustrious example of Jain influence was that of Mahatma Gandhi, acclaimed as the Father of the Nation. Gandhi's friend, Srimad Rajchandra, was a Jain. The two great men corresponded, until Rajchandra's death, on issues of faith and ethics. The central Jain teaching of ahimsa (non-violence) was the guiding principle of Gandhi's civil disobedience in the cause of freedom and social equality. His ecological philosophy found apt expression in his observation that the greatest work of humanity could not match the smallest wonder of nature.

Jain Teachings

1. Ahimsa (non-violence)

The Jain ecological philosophy is virtually synonymous with the principle of ahimsa (non-violence) which runs through the Jain tradition like a golden thread.

'Ahimsa parmo dharmah' (Non-violence is the supreme religion).

Mahavira, the 24th and last Tirthankara (Path-finder) of this era, who lived 2500 years ago in north India, consolidated the basic Jain teachings of peace, harmony, and renunciation, taught two centuries earlier by the Tirthankara Parshva, and for thousands of years previously by the 22 other Tirthankaras of this era, beginning with Adinatha Rishabha. Mahavira threw new light on the perennial quest of the soul with the truth and discipline of ahimsa. He said:

'There is nothing so small and subtle as the atom or any element as vast as space. Similarly, there is no quality of soul more subtle than non-violence and no virtue of spirit greater than reverence for life'.

Ahimsa is a principle that Jains teach and practice not only towards human beings but towards all nature. It is an unequivocal teaching that is at once ancient and contemporary.

The scriptures tell us:

'All the Arhats (Venerable Ones) of the past, present, and future discourse, counsel, proclaim, propound and prescribe thus in unison:

Do not injure, abuse, oppress, enslave, insult, torment, torture or kill any creature or living being'.

In this strife torn world of hatred and hostilities, aggression and aggrandizement, and of unscrupulous and unbridled exploitation and consumerism, the Jain perspective finds the evil of violence writ large.

The teaching of ahimsa refers not only to wars and visible physical acts of violence but to violence in the hearts and minds of human beings, their lack of concern and compassion for their fellow humans and for the natural world. Ancient Jain texts explain that violence (Ahimsa) is not defined by actual harm, for this may be unintentional. It is the intention to harm, the absence of compassion, which makes action violent. Without violent thought there could be no violent actions. When violence enters our thoughts, we remember Tirthankara Mahavira's words:

'You are that which you intend to hit, injure, insult, torment, persecute, torture, enslave or kill'.

2. Parasparopagraho jivanam (interdependence)

Mahavira proclaimed a profound truth for all times to come when he said:

'One who neglects or disregards the existence of earth, air, fire, water, and vegetation disregards his own existence which is entwined with them'.

Jain cosmology recognizes the fundamental natural phenomenon of symbiosis or mutual dependence, which forms the basis of the modern day science of ecology. It is relevant to recall that the term 'ecology' was coined in the latter half of the nineteenth century from the Greek word oikos, meaning `home', a place to which one returns. Ecology is the branch of biology which deals with the relations of organisms to their surroundings and to other organisms.

The ancient Jain scriptural aphorism *Parasparopagraho jivanan* (All life is bound together by mutual support and interdependence) is refreshingly contemporary in its premise and perspective. It defines the scope of modern ecology while extending it further to a more spacious 'home'. It means that all aspects of nature belong together and are bound in a physical as well as a metaphysical relationship. Life is viewed as a gift of togetherness, accommodation, and assistance in a universe teeming with interdependent constituents.

3. Anekantavada (the doctrine of manifold aspects)

The concept of universal interdependence underpins the Jain theory of knowledge, known as *anekantavada* or the doctrine of manifold aspects. *Anekantavada* describes the world as a multifaceted, ever-changing reality with infinity of viewpoints depending on the time, place, nature, and state of the one who is the viewer and that which is viewed.

This leads to the doctrine of *syadvada* or relativity, which states that truth, is relative to different viewpoints (*nayas*). What is true from one point of view is open to question from another. Absolute truth cannot be grasped from any particular viewpoint alone because absolute truth is the sum total of all the different viewpoints that make up the universe.

Because it is rooted in the doctrines of *anekantavada* and *syadvada*, Jainism does not look upon the universe from an anthropocentric, ethnocentric, or egocentric viewpoint. It takes into account the viewpoints of other species, other communities and nations, and other human beings.

4. Samyaktva (equanimity)

The discipline of non-violence, the recognition of universal interdependence, and the logic of the doctrine of manifold aspects, lead inexorably to the avoidance of dogmatic, intolerant, inflexible, aggressive, harmful, and unilateral attitudes towards the world around. It inspires the personal quest of every Jain for samyaktva (equanimity) towards both jiva (animate beings) and ajiva (inanimate substances and objects). It encourages an attitude of give and take and of live and let live. It offers a pragmatic peace plan based, not on the domination of nature, nations or other people, but on equanimity of mind devoted to the preservation of the balance of the universe.

5.Jiva-daya (compassion, empathy, and charity)

Although the term 'ahimsa' is stated in the negative (a=non, himsa=violence), it is rooted in a host of positive aims and actions which have great relevance to contemporary environmental concerns.

Ahimsa is an aspect of daya (compassion, empathy, and charity), described by a great Jain teacher as 'the beneficent mother of all beings' and 'the elixir for those who wander in suffering through the ocean of successive rebirths'.

Jiva-daya means caring for and sharing with all living beings, tending, protecting, and serving them. It entails universal friendliness (maitri), universal forgiveness (kshama), and universal fearlessness (abhaya).

Jains, whether monks, nuns or householders, therefore, affirm prayerfully and sincerely, that their heart is filled with forgiveness for all living beings, and that they have sought and received the forgiveness of all beings, that they crave the friendship of all beings, that all beings give them their friendship and that there is not the slightest feeling of alienation or enmity in their heart for anyone or anything. They also pray that forgiveness and friendliness may reign throughout the world and that all living beings may cherish each other.

Jain Cosmology

Jains do not acknowledge an intelligent first cause as the creator of the universe. The Jain theory is that the universe has no beginning or end. It is traced to jiva and ajiva, the two everlasting, uncreated, independent, and coexisting categories. Consciousness is jiva. That which has no consciousness is ajiva.

There are five substances of ajiva:

Dharma—the medium of motion

Adharma—the medium of rest

Akasha—space

Pudgala—matter

Kala—time

Pudgala (matter) has form and consists of individual atoms (paramanu) and conglomerates of atoms (skandha) which can be seen, heard, smelt, tasted, and/or touched. According to Jains, energy, or the phenomena of sound, darkness, shade, heat, light, and the like, is produced by conglomerates of atoms.

The jiva (soul) has no form but, during its worldly career, it is vested with a body and becomes subject to an inflow of karmic 'dust' (asravas). These are the subtle material particles that are drawn to a soul because of its worldly activities. The asrawas bind the soul to the physical world until they have brought about the karmic result when they fall away 'like ripe fruit' by which time other actions have drawn more asravas to the soul.

With the exception of the Arihantas (the Ever Perfect) and the Siddhas (the Liberated), who have dispelled the passions which provide the 'glue' for the asravas, all souls are in karmic bondage to the universe. They go through a continuous cycle of death and rebirth in a personal evolution that can lead at last to moksha (eternal release). In this cycle there are countless souls at different stages of their personal evolution; earth-bodies, water-bodies, fire-bodies, air-bodies, vegetable-bodies, and mobile bodies ranging from bacteria, insects, worms, birds, and larger animals to human beings, infernal beings, and celestial beings.

The Jain evolutionary theory is based on a grading of the physical bodies containing souls according to the degree of sensory perception. All souls are equal but are bound by varying amounts of asravas (karmic particles) which is reflected in the type of body they inhabit. The lowest form of physical body has only the sense of touch. Trees and vegetation have the sense of touch and are therefore able to experience pleasure and pain, and have souls. Mahavira taught that only the one who understood the grave demerit and detriment caused by destruction of plants and trees understood the meaning and merit of reverence for nature. Even metals and stones might have life in them and should not be dealt with recklessly.

Above the single-sense jivas are micro-organisms and small animals with two, three or four senses. Higher in the order are the jivas with five senses. The highest grade of animals and human beings also possess rationality and intuition (manas). As a highly evolved form of life, human beings have a great moral responsibility in their mutual dealings and in their relationship with the rest of the universe.

In December 2011, Chilean government launched a campaign, 'In summer, no ties' asking Chilean men to take off their ties during the summer season. The campaign mentioned that removing ties will result in reduced usage of air conditioning and cooling. According to the Chilean Ministry, estimated savings could touch 10 million dollars in a 3-month period. This campaign has followed similar campaigns in countries like Japan and Spain.

It is this conception of life and its eternal coherence, in which human beings have an inescapable ethical responsibility, which made the Jain tradition a cradle for the creed of environmental protection and harmony.

Jain Code of Conducts

1. The five vrata (vows)

The five vratas (vows) in the Jain code of conduct are:

Non-violence in thought, word and deed

To seek and speak the truth

To behave honestly and never to take anything by force or theft

To practice restraint and chastity in thought, word, and deed

To practice non-acquisitiveness

The vow of ahimsa is the first and pivotal vow. The other vows may be viewed as aspects of ahimsa which together form an integrated code of conduct in the individual's quest for equanimity and the three jewels (ratna-traya) of right faith, right knowledge, and right conduct.

The vows are undertaken at an austere and exacting level by the monks and nuns and are then called maha-vratas (great vows). They are undertaken at a more moderate and flexible level by householders and called the anu-vratas ('atomic' or basic vows).

Underlying the Jain code of conduct is the emphatic assertion of individual responsibility towards one and all. Indeed, the entire universe is the forum of one's own conscience. The code is profoundly ecological in its secular thrust and its practical consequences.

2. Kindness to animals

The transgressions against the vow of non-violence include all forms of cruelty to animals and human beings. Many centuries ago, Jains condemned as evil the common practice of animal sacrifice to the gods. It is generally forbidden to keep animals in captivity, to whip, mutilate or overload them or to deprive them of adequate food and drink. The injunction is modified in respect of domestic animals to the extent that they may be roped or even whipped occasionally but always mercifully with due consideration and without anger.

3. Vegetarianism

Except for allowing themselves a judicious use of one-sensed life in the form of vegetables, Jains would not consciously take any life for food or sport. As a community they are strict vegetarians, consuming neither meat, fish nor eggs. They confine themselves to vegetable and milk products.

4. Self-restraint and avoidance of waste

By taking the basic vows, the Jain laity endeavors to live a life of moderation and restraint and to practice a measure of abstinence and austerity. They must not procreate indiscriminately lest they overburden the universe and its resources. Regular periods of fasting for self-purification are encouraged.

In their use of the earth's resources Jains take their cue from 'the bee [that] sucks honey in the blossoms of a tree without hurting the blossom and strengthens itself'. Wants should be reduced, desires curbed, and consumption levels kept within reasonable limits. Using any resource beyond one's needs and misuse of any part of nature is considered a form of theft. Indeed, the Jain faith goes one radical step further and declares unequivocally that waste and creating pollution are acts of violence.

5. Charity

Accumulation of possessions and enjoyment for personal ends should be minimized. Giving charitable donations and one's time for community projects generously is a part of a Jain householder's obligations. That explains why the Jain temples and pilgrimage centers are well endowed and well managed. It is this sense of social obligation born out of religious teachings that has led the Jains to found and maintain innumerable schools, colleges, hospitals, clinics, lodging houses, hostels, orphanages, relief and rehabilitation camps for the handicapped, old, sick, and disadvantaged as well as hospitals for ailing birds and animals. Wealthy individuals are advised to recognize that beyond a certain point their wealth is superfluous to their needs and that they should manage the surplus as trustees for social benefit.

The five fundamental teachings of Jainism and the five-fold Jain code of conduct outlined in this Declaration are deeply rooted in its living ethos in unbroken continuity across the centuries. They offer the world today a time-tested anchor of moral imperatives and a viable route plan for humanity's common pilgrimage for holistic environmental protection, peace, and harmony in the universe.

Muslim Declaration on Nature[98]

(Authored by His Excellency Dr. Abdullah Omar Naseef, Secretary General, Muslim World League, 1986.)

The essence of Islamic teaching is that the entire universe is Allah's creation. Allah makes the waters flows upon the earth, upholds the heavens, makes the rain fall and keeps the boundaries between day and night. The whole of the rich and wonderful universe belongs to Allah, its Maker. It is Allah who created the plants and the animals in their pairs and gave them the means to multiply. Then Allah created mankind—a very special creation because mankind alone was created with reason and the power to think and even the means to turn against his Creator.

---

98 Used with permission. Credits: The Alliance of Religions and Conservation (ARC). Content sourced from http://www.arcworld.org/faiths.asp?pageID=132, last accessed on 26 May 2011.

Mankind has the potential to acquire a status higher than that of the angels or sink lower than the lowest of the beasts.

The word 'Islam' has the dual meaning of submission and peace. Mankind is special, a very particular creation of Allah. But still we are Allah's creation and we can only properly understand ourselves when we recognize that our proper condition is one of submission to Allah who made us.

And only when we submit to the Will of Allah can we find peace: peace within us as individuals, peace between man and man, and peace between man and nature. When we submit to the Will of Allah, we become aware of the sublime fact that all our powers, potentials, skills, and knowledge are granted to us by Allah. We are His servants and when we are conscious of that, when we realize that all our achievements derive from the Mercy of Allah, and when we return proper thanks and respect and worship to Allah for our nature and creation, then we become free. Our freedom is that of being sensible, aware, and responsible trustees of Allah's gifts and bounty.

For the Muslim, mankind's role on earth is that of a Khalifah - vicegerent or trustee of Allah. We are Allah's stewards and agents on Earth. We are not masters of this Earth; it does not belong to us to do what we wish. It belongs to Allah and He has entrusted us with its safekeeping. Our function as vicegerents, Khalifahs of Allah, is only to oversee the trust. The khalifah is answerable for his/her actions, for the way in which he/she uses or abuses the trust of Allah.

Islam teaches us that we have been created by Allah, that we will return to Allah for Judgement, and that we are accountable for our deeds as well as our omissions. The khalifah will have to render an account of how he treated the trust of Allah on the Day of Reckoning. The notion that describes the accountability of the khalifah is akhirah (the Hereafter). Islam is the guidance of how to live today so that we can face the akhirah: it is the Message which informs us of what will be involved in that reckoning.

The central concept of Islam is Tawhid - the Unity of Allah. Allah is Unity and His Unity is also reflected in the unity of mankind, and the unity of man and nature. His trustees are responsible for maintaining the unity of His creation, the integrity of the Earth, its flora and fauna, its wildlife and natural environment. Unity cannot be had by discord, by setting one need against another; it is maintained by balance and harmony. Therefore, Muslims say that Islam is the middle path, and we will be answerable for how we have walked this path and how we have maintained balance and harmony in the whole of creation around us.

So unity, trusteeship, and accountability, that are tawhid, khalifah, and akhirah, the three central concepts of Islam, are also the pillars of the environmental ethics of Islam. They constitute the basic values taught by the Qur'an. It is these values which led Muhammad, (peace be upon him), the Prophet of Islam, to say:

'Whosoever plants a tree and diligently looks after it until it matures and bears fruit is rewarded', and 'If a Muslim plants a tree or sows a field and men and beasts and birds eat from it, all of it is a charity on his part', and again, 'The world is green and beautiful, and Allah has appointed you as His stewards over it'. Environmental consciousness is born when such values are adopted and become an intrinsic part of our mental and physical make-up.

And these are not remote, other-worldly notions; they concern us here and now. If you were to ask me what the notion of the Hereafter has to do with here and now, my answer might surprise you. I would say nuclear power and biotechnology. Both of these are very present here-and-now issues. Both have benefits and costs. Both have implications for the health and well being of mankind and nature. If I sincerely intend to be Allah's khalifa, His steward on Earth, then I must have an opinion about them and prepare myself to make choices about them, because I will be accountable for what mankind has wrought with these devices in the Hereafter.

Islam is a very practical world view. It seeks, in all its principles and injunctions, to give pragmatic shapes to its concepts and values. Indeed, the notions of tawhid and khalifah have been translated into practical injunctions in the Shari'ah (Islamic Law). Surah Shari'ah institutions as haram zones, inviolate areas within which development is prohibited to protect natural resources, and hima, reserves established solely for the conservation of wildlife and forests, form the core of the environmental legislation of Islam.

The classical Muslim jurist, Izzad-Din Ibn Abdas-Salam, used these aspects of the Shari'ah when he formulated the bill of legal rights of animals in the thirteenth century. Similarly, numerous other jurists and scholars developed legislations to safeguard water resources, prevent over-grazing, conserve forests, limit the growth of cities, protect cultural property, and so on. Islam's environmental ethics then are not limited to metaphysical notions; they provide a practical guide as well.

Muslims need to turn to this nexus of values, this way of understanding themselves and their environment. The notions of unity, trusteeship, and accountability should not be reduced to matters of personal piety; they must guide all aspects of their life and work. Shari'ah should not be relegated just to issues of crime and punishment; it must also become the vanguard for environmental legislation.

We often say that Islam is a complete way of life, by which it is meant that our ethical system provides the bearings for all our actions. Yet our actions often undermine the very values we cherish. Often while working as scientists or technologists, economists or politicians, we act contrary to the environmental dictates of Islam. We must imbibe these values into our very being. We must judge our actions by them. They furnish us with a world-view which enables us to ask environmentally appropriate questions, to draw up the right balance sheet of possibilities, and to properly weigh the environmental costs and benefits of what we want, what we can do within the ethical boundaries established by Allah, without violating the rights of His other creations.

If we use the same values, the same understanding in our work as scientist or technologist, economist or politician, as we do to know ourselves as Muslims—those who submit themselves to the Will of Allah—then, I believe, we will create a caring and practical way of being, doing and knowing; a true Islamic alternative to the environmentally destructive thought and actions which dominates the world today.

The St Francis Pledge

The St Francis[99] Pledge is created by the Catholic Coalition on Climate Change, an organization that includes a number of Catholic organizations based in USA. This organization launched the Catholic Climate Covenant that 'seeks to show respect for God's creation by focusing on the link between creation and poverty embodied in the life and ministry of St. Francis and the words of the Psalmist 'The earth is the Lord's and all it holds' (Psalm 24:1). The St. Francis Pledge is a part of this covenant. One can join the Catholic Climate Covenant by taking the St. Francis Pledge. Those who would like to join the Covenant will be asked to fulfill all five elements of the Pledge, which is as follows:

Starting 11 December 2011, 'The National', an English language newspaper from UAE and owned by Abu Dhabi media, started printing on 100% recycled paper.

I/We Pledge to:

PRAY and reflect on the duty to care for God's Creation and protect the poor and vulnerable.

LEARN about and educate others on the causes and moral dimensions of climate change.

ASSESS how we —as individuals and in our families, parishes, and other affiliations – contribute to climate change by our own energy use, consumption, waste, etc.

ACT to change our choices and behaviors to reduce the ways we contribute to climate change.

ADVOCATE for Catholic principles and priorities in climate change discussions and decisions, especially as they impact those who are poor and vulnerable.

---

99 In the book 'What did Jesus mean by that?! Exploring the universal truth of Jesus' teachings', Debra and William Miller states 'St. Francis of Assisi (1181-1226 CE) was a Christian Saint and mystic. He was a great charismatic and Christ-like figure of utter humility and simplicity that created a new spiritual consciousness in the Christian West. He is known for his sense of God's all-pervading presence and his freshness of vision and intense love for all of God's creatures.'

Church of South India Statement[100][101]

By Bishop Thomas Samuel
   Madhya Kerala Diocese, April 2008
   (This is an adaptation of the concluding address of Bishop Thomas Samuel at the end of the Seven Day International Ecological Conferences organized by CSI Madhya Kerala Diocese in February 2008.)

The Background

One of the reasons for the present ecological crisis is greed. It is greed that causes people to exploit resources. It is greed that means there is not enough. And the over-exploitation of resources is causing imbalances in nature. As Mahatma Gandhi said: 'The earth provides enough to satisfy everyone's need, but not everyone's greed'.

We believe that environmental problems are more spiritual than technological. And we believe that God calls us now to confess and repent of attitudes which devalue creation. Forgetting that 'the earth is the Lord's', we have often simply used creation, while forgetting our responsibility to care for it.

The Aim

Our aim is to keep this beautiful world beautiful, and not to turn it into a wasteland.

Our Covenants

In the Bible, there are covenants and laws and statutes to be observed if the earth and its inhabitants are to experience oneness and harmony. And the most important covenant is between God and humanity. We are God's gardeners, and when we forget this, not only does the earth suffer, but all creation suffers, because all things are connected.

The Bible says the Earth is the Lord's and that God is the owner of this universe.

We believe that God loves creation and wants its life to flourish. No creature is different in God's sight. Every creature has its own dignity and its own rights, because all are included in God's covenant.

So it is said in the story of Noah: 'Behold', says God, 'I establish my covenant with you and your descendants after you, and every living creature' (Gen 9: 9-10).

The fundamental human rights come from this covenant 'with us'. The rights of future generations come from the covenant 'with us and our descendants'. The rights of nature come from the covenant 'with us and our descendants and with every living

---

100 The Church of South India is the result of the union of churches of varying traditions: Anglican, Methodist, Congregational, Presbyterian, and Reformed.

101 Used with permission. Credits: The Alliance of Religions and Conservation (ARC). Content sourced from http://www.arcworld.org/faiths.asp?pageID=133, last accessed on 6 November 2012.

creature'. Before God, the creator, we and our descendants and every living creature are equal partners of God's covenant. Nature is not our property.

Instead, all living beings must be respected by humanity as God's partners in the covenant. Whoever destroys nature destroys himself/herself. Whoever injures the dignity of the animals injures God.

The Role of Faith

Our actions and attitudes toward the Earth need to proceed from the centre of our faith, and be rooted in the fullness of God's revelation in Christ and the Scriptures. We seek carefully to learn all that the Bible tells us about the Creator, creation, and the human task. In our life and words we declare that full good news for all creation is still waiting 'with eager longing for the revealing of the children of God', (Rom.8:19).

In Hinduism there is no separation between the Divine and nature. Both are the same aspects of the same reality. Like the ocean, Brahma the Creator is the unmanifest depths of the sea. Everything is Brahman, or as it is said; 'Sarvam Khalvidam Brahma'.

Everything is the very aspect of the same reality, and everything is sacred. Christians too can share in this Vedic vision of unity which is the basis for an ecological approach, in which human beings can honour the entire universe. There are many sacred places to Hindus. Christians too sing of the beauty of the earth but seem to have no difficulty in polluting that which is holy. We should not ignore our high calling. All things are connected.

The Importance of Hope

We refuse to succumb to despair: remember Abraham who hoped against hope. There is hope for the future. If we can live out this vision in our daily lives and can communicate it to others in word and action then we can play a powerful role in creating an attitude of reverence for the earth. Attitude is very important in ecology: it affects everything, including, perhaps most importantly in this debate and issue, how we see things in this world. John 3:16 is probably the best known verse in the New Testament: 'God so loved the World that he gave his only begotten son that whoever believes in him may not perish but have eternal life'.

Have you noticed that the verse does not say: 'God so loved humans ...', but 'God so loved the world'... the whole cosmos? John proclaims that God's love is not restricted to the human race; it extends to all aspects of life. And this verse may be seen to contain considerable implications for our attitudes to the environment.

We need to recognize that what we do with God's creation around us will have a tremendous effect, for good or ill, on the lives of our grandchildren and on the generations of their children and grandchildren. By our attitude to God's creation now, we determine the nature of the society that will be inherited later this century by the children of our children.

Will it be a society that has to contend with—to be content with—pollution of the air, the earth, the rivers and the seas? Or will it be a society which retains the fullness with which God has endowed it and to which the psalmist refers when he proclaims: 'The earth and its fullness are the Lord's'?

How We Can Help

Here are some of the ways in which we in the Church of South India can help.

- We can learn to eat lower on the food chain: reducing the animal products in our diet is perhaps the single most-effective step we can make
- We can practice energy conservation: let us use less heat, less light, and less air-conditioning.
- We can plant trees.
- We can change our driving habits.
- We can influence the government.
- We can develop our thoughts on eco-spirituality.
- We can participate in recycling.
- We can volunteer in local cleanup programmes.
- We can join environmental groups.
- As church leaders and church members we can take a leadership role in persuading others to do the same.
- And perhaps most important of all, we can evaluate our own life styles, our desires, our aims, and our relationships with creation. We can help lead others to think about what is most important in their own lives: what do they really value?

A Parable for the Environment

There was a wise man, a hermit in the Himalayas, and people used to go to him to find answers. One day a little boy thought of an idea for tricking the hermit. 'I'm going to get a small bird and hold it in my hand', he told his friends in the village. 'And I will say: is it dead or is it alive? And if he says it is dead then I will release it, and if he says it is alive then I will crush it'. So the boy went to see the wise man, and he did what he had boasted. But the hermit looked into his eyes and could see what he was planning.

'It will be', said the wise man, 'what you want it to be'.

And this story illustrates what we can do about the environment. It will be what we want it to be. If we can have a vision and communicate it to others, then we will have a powerful role in transmitting a sense of reverence for this world.

Jewish Declaration on Nature[102]

(By Rabbi Arthur Hertzberg, Vice-President, World Jewish Congress)

'Whoever is merciful to all creatures is a descendant of our ancestor Abraham' (Bezoh 32b).

In the sacred writings of Judaism, Jews are described over and over again as 'merciful people, the children of merciful people'. (Yebamot 79a, Shabbat 133b). The Talmud even tells us (Shabbat 151b) that heaven rewards the person who has concern and compassion for the rest of creation, but this assurance of reward is not the major moral thrust of Jewish teaching. Our tradition emphasizes that Jews are commanded to do what is moral, 'not for the sake of receiving a reward' (Abot 1:3). The good is necessary even when it does not redound to our immediate, personal benefit.

When God created the world, so the Bible tells us, He made order out of the primal chaos. The sun, the moon, and the stars, plants, animals, and ultimately man, were each created with a rightful and necessary place in the universe. They were not to encroach on each other, 'Even the divine teaching, the Torah, which was revealed from on high, was given in a set measure' (Vayikra Rabbah 15:2) and even these holy words may not extend beyond their assigned limit. 'And the Lord took man and put him in the Garden of Eden, to tend it and guard it' (Genesis 2:15).

Soon Adam, man, the one creature who is most godlike, gave names to all of creation, as God looked on and approved'. And the name that Adam gave to each living being has remained its name' (Genesis 2:19) forever. In the Kabbalistic teaching, as Adam named all of God's creatures, he helped define their essence. Adam swore to live in harmony with those whom he had named. Thus, at the very beginning of time, man accepted responsibility before God for all of creation.

Judaism, of course, knows the doctrine of the world beyond death, but its central concern is with life in this world. The tzaddik, the righteous Jew, is not a pillar saint who has withdrawn from the world. He is someone whose conduct in the very midst of life helps to establish that which seems impossible—one can live in this world of righteousness without encroaching on the rights of other people, or of any of God's creatures.

The festivals of the Jewish religion do call upon us to stand before God, in the awe at His majesty, trembling before His judgements, but that is not the dominant mood of the Jewish faith. The festivals celebrate, in joy, the cycle of the seasons of nature. The rabbis even insisted that: 'He who has denied himself any one of the rightful joys in this world is a sinner' (Baba Kama 91b). The highest form of obedience to God's commandments is to do them not in mere acceptance but in the nature of union with

102 Credits: The Alliance of Religions and Conservation (ARC), Used with permission. Content sourced from http://www.arcworld.org/faiths.asp?pageID=159, last accessed on 6 November 2012.

Him. In such a joyous encounter between man and God, the very rightness of the world is affirmed.

The encounter of God and man in nature is thus conceived in Judaism as a seamless web with man as the leader and custodian of the natural world. Even in the many centuries when Jews were most involved in their immediate dangers and destiny, this universalist concern has never withered. In this century, Jews have experienced the greatest tragedy of their history when one third of their people were murdered by unnatural men and, therefore, we are today particularly sensitive to the need for a world in which each of God's creations in what He intended it to be. Now, when the whole world is in peril, when the environment is in danger of being poisoned and various species, both plant and animal, are becoming extinct, it is our Jewish responsibility to put the defence of the whole of nature at the very centre of our concern.

And yet it must be said, in all truth, that this question of man's responsibility to the rest of creation cannot be defined by simply expressing our respect for all of nature. There is a tension at the centre of the Biblical tradition, embedded in the very story of creation itself, over the question of power and stewardship. The world was created because God willed it, but why did He will it? Judaism has maintained, in all its versions, that this world is the arena that God created for man, half beast and half angel, to prove that he could behave as a moral being. The Bible did not fail to demand even of God Himself that He be bound, as much as man, by the law of morality. Thus, Abraham stood before God, after He announced that He was about to destroy the wicked city of Sodom, and Abraham demanded of God Himself that He produce moral justification for this act: 'Shall not judge of all the earth do justice?' (Genesis 18:25). Comparably, man was given dominion over nature, but he was commanded to behave towards the rest of creation with justice and compassion. Man lives, always, in tension between his power and the limits set by conscience.

Man's carnivorous nature is not taken for granted, or praised, in the fundamental teachings of Judaism. The rabbis of the Talmud told that men were vegetarians in earliest times, between creation and the generation of Noah. In the twelfth century Maimonides, the greatest of all rabbinic scholars, explained that animal sacrifices had been instituted in ancient Judaism as a concession to the prevalent ancient practice of making such offerings to the pagan gods (Mareh Nebuhim 111:32). The implication is clear, that Judaism was engaged in weaning men from such practices.

Judaism as a religion offers the option of eating animal flesh, and most Jews do, but in our own century there has been a movement towards vegetarianism among very pious Jews. A whole galaxy of central rabbinic and spiritual teachers, including several past and present Chief Rabbis of the Holy Land, have been affirming vegetarianism as the ultimate mean of the Jewish moral teaching. They have been proclaiming the autonomy of all living creatures as the value which our religious tradition must now teach to all of its believers. Let this affirmation resound this day and in the days to come. Let it be heard by all our brethren, wherever they may be, as the commandment which we must strive to realize. This cannot be achieved in one generation, and it will not happen through pressure from within or without. Jews will move increasingly to vegetarianism out of their deepening knowledge of what their tradition commands, as they understand it in this age.

Our ancestor Abraham inherited his passion for nature from Adam. The later rabbis never forgot it. Some twenty centuries ago they told the story of two men who were out on the water in a rowboat. Suddenly, one of them started to see under his feet. He maintained that it was his right to do whatever he wished with the place which belonged to him. The other answered him that they were in the rowboat together; the hole that he was making would sink both of them. (Vayikra Rabbah 4:6).

We have a responsibility to life, to defend it everywhere, not only against our own sins but also against those of others. We are all passengers together in this same fragile and glorious world. Let us safeguard our rowboat and let us row together.

CHAPTER SUMMARY

- All the four Vedas—Rig, Sama, Yajur, and Atharva—have a number of hymns dedicated to the natural deities.
- Worship of pipal trees was a ritual, and Brahma Purana referred to pipal as the king of trees.
- In India, Yaksha or Yakshasi (fairy or spirit beings) are said to occupy trees.
- The scriptures say that one tree is equal to 10 sons. While planting and nurturing any tree is encouraged, individuals are especially urged to plant trees related to their Nakshatra. This process helps in accruing merit in this life and after life.
- Sacred groves consisted of a few trees to lush forests spanning several acres that are usually dedicated to local folk deities (Ayyanar, Amman, or Vanadevatas). Groves can also exist around temples and near the burial or cremation grounds.
- A tree could be adopted as a son through a ritual known as taruputravidhi. Upanayana (initiation) was conducted for trees like pipal, and marriage was performed between Banyan tree and neem tree.
- Ayurveda states that 'even when one takes any leaf or any part of a plant one must mentally pray and ask for pardon for breaking the leaf for medicinal purposes, so that the plants are not shocked'.
- Yagnas (Yagnam/Homam) were conducted to purify the atmosphere. As a part of the process, dried leaves of herbs were burned along with ghee.
- Deep ecology is a contemporary ecological philosophy that recognizes an inherent worth of all living beings, regardless of their instrumental utility to human needs. The philosophy emphasizes the interdependence of organisms within ecosystems and that of ecosystems with each other within the biosphere.
- The term 'Anthropocentric' referred to a situation where everything was looked from the perspective of the human species.
- James Lovelock came out with Gaia Hypotheses where he proposed that Earth was a complete system and everything in the ecosphere was interdependent and equally necessary for maintaining life on Earth.
- Ancient India had a discipline of study related to plants known as Vrikshayurveda, the science of plant life. 'Ayur' means 'Life' and it is fair to conclude that Indian tradition was aware that plants had life.

- Organic farming incorporates farming that works in harmony with nature—both living and non-living. Such a practice involves farming techniques that do not harm nature or exploitation.
- Natural farming is an ecological farming propounded by a Japanese farmer and philosopher, Masanobu Fukuoka (1913–2008). Natural farming has also been referred to as 'Do Nothing Farming', and 'Fukuoka Method'.
- As per Ayurveda, Agni (Root of the English word 'ignite') or 'digestive fire' is responsible for absorbing the nutrients and essential elements required by the body, and also for burning the waste.
- Bhagavad Gita suggests that one should evolve to those foods which are wholesome and pleasing to the heart. The Gita also says that foods that are too bitter, too sour, salty, hot, pungent, dry, and burning cause distress, misery, and disease.
- Hinduism advocates that Earth, in which the seas, the rivers, and many waters lie, from which arise foods and fields of grain, abode to all that breathes and moves, may She confer on us Her finest yield.
- The Jain tradition which enthroned the philosophy of ecological harmony and non-violence as its lodestar flourished for centuries side by side with other schools of thought in ancient India. The ecological philosophy of Jainism which flows from its spiritual quest has always been central to its ethics, aesthetics, art, literature, economics, and politics. It is represented in all its glory by the 24 Jinas or Tirthankaras (Path finders) of this era whose example and teachings have been its living legacy through the millennia.
- The essence of Islamic teaching is that the entire universe is Allah's creation. Allah makes the waters flows upon the earth, upholds the heavens, makes the rain fall, and keeps the boundaries between day and night. The whole of the rich and wonderful universe belongs to Allah, its Maker.
- The St. Francis Pledge is created by the Catholic Coalition on Climate Change, an organization that includes a number of Catholic organizations based in USA. This organization launched the Catholic Climate Covenant that 'seeks to show respect for God's creation by focusing on the link between creation and poverty embodied in the life and ministry of St. Francis and the words of the Psalmist 'The earth is the Lord's and all it holds' (Psalm 24:1).
- 'Whoever is merciful to all creatures is a descendant of our ancestor Abraham'. (Bezoh 32b). In the sacred writings of Judaism, Jews are described over and over again as 'merciful people, the children of merciful people' (Yebamot 79a, Shabbat 133b). Judaism as a religion offers the option of eating animal flesh, and most Jews do, but in our own century there has been a movement towards vegetarianism among very pious Jews.

KEYWORDS

- Conventional farming
- Deep ecology
- Gaia hypothesis
- Natural farming
- Organic farming
- Reverential ecology
- Sacred forest
- Sacred grove
- Sustainable farming
- Vegetarianism
- Vrikshayurveda

EXERCISES

Multiple-choice Questions

1. _____ consisted of a few trees to lush forests spanning several acres that are usually dedicated to local folk deities.
   (a) Sacred groves
   (b) Grassland ecosystem
   (c) Forest ecosystem
   (d) Deep ecology

2. *Paropakaaraartham Idam Shareeram* means
   (a) God is everywhere.
   (b) This body is meant for the service of others.
   (c) Do not harm animals.
   (d) One can do anything to attain one's needs.

3. _____, which is to serve all living beings as embodiments of the Universal Being, brings about the consciousness of the unity of all life.
   (a) Bhuta yajna
   (b) Upanishads
   (c) Ayurveda
   (d) Service to nature

4. Gaia hypothesis states that
   (a) Earth is a living system.
   (b) The system seeks an environment optimal for contemporary life.
   (c) This living system has automatically controlled global temperature, atmospheric content, ocean salinity, and other factors, that maintain its own habitability.
   (d) The theory argues that organic and inorganic components of Earth evolved together as a single, living, self-regulating system.
   (e) All of these

5. Ancient India had a discipline of study related to plants known as
   (a) Vrikshayurveda
   (b) Nirukta
   (c) Jangama
   (d) Charaka

6. Use of organic inputs, minimum external inputs, crop rotation is done in
   (a) Conventional farming
   (b) Organic farming
   (c) Bio-concentration
   (d) None of these

7. 'Earth, in which the seas, the rivers, and many waters lie, from which arise foods and fields of grain, abode to all that breathes and moves, may She confer on us Her finest yield' is followed in
   (a) Hinduism   (c) Buddhism
   (b) Jainism   (d) Christianity

8. The ecological philosophy of this religion is represented in all its glory by the 24 Jinas or *Tirthankaras* and promotes ecological harmony and non-violence.
   (a) Hinduism   (c) Buddhism
   (b) Jainism   (d) Christianity

9. Unity, trusteeship, and accountability (tawhid, khalifah, and akhirah) are the pillars of the environmental ethics of this religion.
   (a) Hinduism
   (b) Jainism
   (c) Islam
   (d) Christianity

10. 'The earth is the Lord's and all it holds' (Psalm 24:1) is followed in
    (a) Hinduism   (c) Islam
    (b) Jainism   (d) Christianity

11. 'Whoever is merciful to all creatures is a descendant of our ancestor Abraham' (Bezoh 32b) is followed in
    (a) Hinduism
    (b) Jainism
    (c) Islam
    (d) Judaism

Short Answer Questions

1. Enlist few nakshatras and trees associated with them.
2. Describe the punishment prescribed in Manusmriti for offense towards plants, and animals.
3. Explain the differences between organic and conventional farming.
4. Name some of the deities and Vahanas associated with them.
5. Explain the teachings in Maitreyopanishad, Mundakopanishad, Kathopanishad, and Svetasvatara Upanishad towards nature.

Long Answer Questions

1. Detail about the sacred forests/sacred groves of India.
2. Explain on how our Indian culture gives emphasis towards worshipping nature.
3. Explain deep ecology and reverential ecology.
4. What do you mean by Gaia hypothesis. State with examples.
5. Give examples from Vedic literature, on how human beings can live in harmony with the nature?
6. Compare and contrast organic, natural, and conventional farming.
7. Describe the role of vegetarianism and its advantages, and impact in the society and individual.
8. Explain in detail the perspectives of various religions on earth and nature.

Reflective Question

1. Do you agree with the Gaia hypothesis that Earth is a living system or that earth is alive? Why or why not? If the earth has a life/soul, how would that change the way you relate to the world? How would your perspectives about lifestyle or consumption change if you experience that earth is also alive?

Take-home Activities

1. Compare and contrast the attitude that religions from India had towards nature with those of Native Americans and Australian aborigines.
2. Create an organic vegetable garden at your home/campus/roof-top/terrace/other places. Document the various activities that you have done—Soil preparation, collection of organic seeds, indigenous pest control methods without the usage of pesticides, harvesting, and more.
3. Make a team of three or four students. Visit:
   (a) Two agricultural fields of organic/ natural farmers or
   (b) Two organic retail outlets or
   (c) One organic/natural farmer and an organic retail outlet (the retail outlet should not be owned by the farmer you are visiting).

Do a SWOT analysis. Give your perspectives, opinions, conclusions—based on your visit and the primary data that you have collected during that visit. Make a 30 min presentation in the class. These retail outlets/agricultural fields can be located anywhere in the world. All the team members should visit both the locations— no sub-allocation of work. Outlets/fields that are visited by one group of students should not be repeated by another student group.

Web Reading

1. On Vegetarianism - http://michaelbluejay.com/veg/

Recommended Books

1. Nanditha Krishna, *Sacred Animals of India*, Penguin Books India, New Delhi, 2010.
2. Masanobu Fukuoka, *The One Straw Revolution*, Other India Press, 1992.
3. Ranchor Prime, *Vedic Ecology: Practical Wisdom for Surviving the 21ˢᵗ century*, Mandala Publishing, 2002.

Recommended Documentaries/Movies/Short Films

1. *Home*. Dir. Yann Arthus-Bertrand. Europa Corp., 2006. (This documentary is available for free viewing in YouTube).
2. *Earthlings*. Dir. Shaun Monson. Nation Earth, 2005. (This documentary is available for free viewing in YouTube). Duration: 95 minutes.
3. *Kailash Murthy and Natural Farming*, Available in YouTube at https://www.youtube.com/watch?v=Uop6tpKhbPo, Duration: 14 minutes
4. *Using Mulch in your Vegetable Garden*, Available in YouTube at https://www.youtube.com/watch?v=g88mnfse2QY, Duration: 4 minutes
5. *Sathish Kumar speaking about Deep Ecology*, Available in YouTube at https://www.youtube.com/watch?v=MlmTLvHMg-g, Duration: 8 minutes
6. *Do Trees Communicate*, Available in YouTube at https://www.youtube.com/watch?v=-8SORM4dYG8, Duration: 5 minutes
7. *James Lovelock explains Gaia Hypothesis in a conversation with David Suzuki*, Available in YouTube at https://www.youtube.com/watch?v=44yiTg7cOVI, Duration: 4 minutes

Answers to Mutiple-choice Questions:

1(a)   2(b)   3(a)   4(e)   5(a)   6(b)   7(a)   8(b)   9(c)   10(d)   11(d)

3

ENVIRONMENTAL ISSUES

'Such a wonderful tree, Mom!' shouted Arya when he looked up at the huge banyan tree in the garden.
'Yes such huge branches and such beautiful leaves,' added Lila.
'And such a huge trunk mom, it's so wonderful!' Arya said while hugging the tree trunk fondly.
'But my son, do you see what supports all this?' Lila asked Arya and then pointed to some of the roots of the tree that had sprung above the ground. Arya looked at them curiously.[1]

After reading the chapter, the reader will be able to understand the following:
- Causes and aspects of pollution
- Environmental issues like ozone depletion, global warming and its impacts, acid rain, ocean acidification, algal bloom, ground water depletion, bio-accumulation, and more
- Successful practices in water management
- Management of disasters

BACKGROUND: DEFINITION OF POLLUTION, ENVIRONMENT, AND POLLUTANTS

Pollution refers to the contamination in a natural substance that interferes with the health of any living organism or cause harmful environmental effects. India's Environmental Protection Act (1986) refers to 'Environment' as that which includes water, air and land and the inter-relationship, which exists among and between water, air and land, and human beings, other living creatures, plants, microorganism and property. 'Environmental Pollutant' is defined as any solid, liquid or gaseous substance present in such concentration as may be, tend to be, injurious to the environment. The same act refers to 'Environmental Pollution' as the presence in the environment of any environmental pollutant.

In 1971, Paul R Ehrlich and John P Holdren[2] suggested how environmental impact is influenced by the growing population of human beings, affluence, and technology. This was used as:

$$I = P \times A \times T$$

1 Jeetendra Jain, *Joy24x7*, Jaico Publishing House, 2008. Used with permission.
2 Paul R. Ehrlich, John P. Holdren, Impact of population growth, Science, 1971.

where I is Human Impact, P is Population, A is Affluence, and T is the (resource intensity in the usage of) Technology.

Human population is on an exponential increase and average consumption of each person on the increase, thereby resulting in a strong negative impact on the planet. An increase in the technology efficiency can reduce the environmental impact. With 'P' and 'A' on a strong upward trend, 'T' has to fall significantly, just to ensure that 'I' is maintained at the same levels. However, that has not been the case and all the variables have been on an increase.

TYPES OF POLLUTION: CAUSES AND EFFECTS

Air Pollution

Air pollution refers to the contamination in air that interferes with the health of living organisms like human beings. Air pollution can be due to the release of various forms of gases, soot, various particulate matter, etc. Air pollution affects all forms of living beings and their interdependent relationships. It has been noted that air pollution, in the form of diesel exhausts, reduce the ability of honeybees to recognize the floral odours.[3] Such a change could impact the capability of honeybees to engage in pollination, an important ecosystem service, which, as per the estimates given by the researchers, is valued at €153 billion a year, and almost 70% of the world's principal food crops and 35% of the global food production relying upon pollination. The steep increase in the number of vehicles is causing harm to many species. As per the Motor Vehicle Department of Kerala, the number of vehicles in Kerala in 2000–01 was 20,97,863 while in 2013–14, it went up to 87,51,895, which is almost a four-fold increase (317%).[4] An increase in the usage of automobiles has been recorded across the country. As per Society of Indian Automobile Manufacturers (SIAM), the vehicle sales trend went up by 85% to 17,815,618 in 2012–13 from 9,654,435 in 2007–08.[5]

Between 2001 and 2011, the total number of registered vehicles in India went up from 5,49,91,000 to 14,18,66,000, which is a 158% increase. It has been found that more than 95% of vehicles registered in India are private vehicles.[6]

Air pollution is also caused by industries, especially those related to oil and gas and fertilisers. Coal-fired power plants are another source of air pollution. A Greenpeace report released in 2013 stated, 'In 2011–12, particulate emissions from coal-fired

---

3 Robbie D. Girling, Inka Lusebrink, Emily Farthing, Tracey A. Newman, Guy M. Poppy, Diesel exhaust rapidly degrades floral odours used by honeybees, Scientific Reports 3, Ocotber 2013, doi:10.1038/srep02779, Also available at http://www.nature.com/srep/2013/131003/srep02779/full/srep02779.html, last accessed on 10 October 2013.

4 CM Jino, Vahanaperuppam Nalirattiyaladhikam, Mathrubhumi, 29 April 2014.

5 http://www.siamindia.com/scripts/domestic-sales-trend.aspx,n last accessed on 18 August 2014.

6 http://articles.economictimes.indiatimes.com/2012-01-04/news/30588978_1_private-vehicles-public-transport-licences, last accessed on 18 August 2014.

power plants, resulted in an estimated 80,000–115,000 premature deaths and more than 20 million asthma cases, which cost the public and the government an estimated ₹16,000–23,000 crores. The largest impact of these emissions is felt over the states of Delhi, Haryana, Maharashtra, Madhya Pradesh, Chhattisgarh, Indo-Gangetic plain, and most of central-east India.[7] Air pollution could also be caused by local events like the celebration of festivals. Table 3.1 indicates the increase in the level of pollutants in Delhi, during the Deepavali day, as measured by the Central Pollution Control Board (CPCB). Significant amount of pollution could also be caused by exceptional events like wars (Fig. 3.1).

TABLE 3.1[8]   Level of pollutants during exceptional events

Sulphur dioxide (SO$_2$)				
(Units in microgram per cubic metre)	2012		2013	
	Normal day	Deepavali day	Normal day	Deepavali day
Concentration range for various locations in Delhi	4–24	13–63	4–5	5–56
Particulate matter (PM10)				
(Units in microgram per cubic metre)	2012		2013	
	Normal day	Deepavali day	Normal day	Deepavali day
Concentration range for various locations in Delhi	452–648	748–951	163–441	796–1,138

Ozone Imbalance and Ozone Depletion

Ozone layer, which occurs 15 miles above sea level, acts as a protective layer for earth by acting as a shield against the excessive ultra-violet radiation entering into the planet from the outer space. Ozone layer is found as part of the stratosphere. There has been a decline in the total volume of ozone at the rate of about 4% per decade since the late 1970s. It has also been found that there has been a reduction in ozone over earth's Polar Regions. This phenomenon is referred to as the ozone hole. The ozone thinning

---

7 http://www.greenpeace.org//india/en/publications/Coal-Kills/, last accessed on 18 August 2014.
8 http://www.cpcb.nic.in/upload/Latest/Latest_82_DeepawaliPressRelease2013.pdf, last accessed on 6 November 2013.

or destruction is caused by halogens from man-made halocarbons like CFCs, freons, and halons. Depletion of ozone will result in the planet and its organisms getting exposed to increased ultra-violet (UV-B) radiation, which may cause skin cancer, cataracts, damages to plant kingdom, and reduction in plankton population.

There is also ground level ozone, which is created due to the reactions between oxides of nitrogen (NOx) and volatile organic compounds (VOC). Automobile emissions are major sources of both NOx and VOC. Ground level ozone can cause respiratory troubles, chest pain, coughing, irritation in throat, and can affect the functioning of the lungs. In addition to affecting human beings, ground level ozone can also affect vegetation. As per US EPA, it leads to 'reduced agricultural crop and commercial forest yields, reduced growth and survivability of tree seedlings, and increased susceptibility to diseases, pests, and other stresses such as harsh weather. In the US alone, ground-level ozone is responsible for an estimated US$500 million in reduced crop production each year. Ground-level ozone also damages the foliage of

FIG. 3.1[9] Fires from Kuwaiti oil wells, created by the retreating Iraqi defence forces, during the Gulf War 1990–91, resulted in increasing the pollution levels.

9 'BrennendeOelquellenKuwait1991' by United States ArmyOriginal uploader was St.Krekeler at de.wikipedia - Originally from de.wikipedia; description page is/was here.(Original text : US Army, Tech. SGT Perry Heimer). Licensed under Public domain via Wikimedia Commons - http://commons.wikimedia.org/wiki/File:BrennendeOelquellen Kuwait1991.jpg#mediaviewer/File:BrennendeOelquellenKuwait1991.jpg, last accessed on 8 August 8, 2014.

trees and other plants, affecting the landscape of cities, national parks and forests, and recreation areas.'[10]

Usage of paints that are low in VOC, reducing automobile pollution through walking, using of public transportation, and bicycling are some of the ways through which one can help in reducing the harmful effects of ozone imbalance.

Acid Rain

Emissions of CO_2, sulphur dioxide, and nitrogen oxide react with water in atmosphere to produce acids that drop down during rain, snowfall, fog, dew, etc. Acid rain is harmful for plant and animal life and also for infrastructure—it can corrode steel structures, erode statues, and peeling of paint (Fig. 3.2). Acid rain can also affect the soil chemistry. While acid rain does not directly impact the human health, the particulate matter responsible for acid rain can cause heart and lung problems. The main cause of acid rain is human induced, through the release of nitrogen and sulphur compounds from vehicles, factories, and power plants. Natural phenomena that contribute to acid rain includes volcanic emission.

FIG. 3.2[11] Effects of acid rain, on the forests of Jizera Mountains, Czech Republic

---

10 http://www.epa.gov/oar/oaqps/gooduphigh/bad.html, last accessed on 19 August 2014.
11 'Acid rain woods1' by Nipik 22:01, 10 July 2006 (UTC) - Own work. Licensed under Public domain via Wikimedia Commons - http://commons.wikimedia.org/wiki/File:Acid_rain_woods1.JPG#mediaviewer/File:Acid_rain_woods1.JPG, Accessed on May 14, 2012.

Water Pollution

Due to the high population and the resulting release of high levels of untreated sewage, most of the rivers in India are polluted (Fig. 3.3). Flooding also moves garbage from the land to the water bodies like rivers, ponds, and lakes. A Central Pollution Control Board (CPCB) report, Status of Water Quality in India – 2011,[12] states that the organic pollution is the predominant pollution of aquatic resources. Suneel Pandey, Fellow, Centre for Environmental Studies, The Energy and Resources Institute (TERI) says, 'Out of total riverine length of approximately 45,000 km in our country, 14% of riverine length is severely polluted (BOD[13] more than 6 mg/l), and 19% is moderately polluted (BOD 3–6 mg/l).'[14] Pristine rivers will have a BOD value that is below 1 mg/L. In 2009, CPCB estimated that the sewage generation from Class-I cities and Class-II towns[15] together is 38,255 MLD (million litres per day), while only 11,788 MLD is being treated for pollution—approximately one-third is treated for pollution while the other two-third is not.[16,17] For domestic waste water treatment, setting up of decentralized treatment systems for clusters of approximately 100–200 households is considered an optimum solution.

While organic pollution could be a predominant contributor to water pollution, industrial effluents can also pollute water bodies. In a toxicological study conducted by Salim Ali Centre for Ornithology and Natural History (SACON)[18], in mid-2000s, it was found that 1,700 fishes belonging to 66 species collected from 170 wetlands from 14 states of India had both pesticides and heavy metal content, and consumption of these fish on a regular basis would lead to health problems.[19, 20, 21]

While the annual per capita availability of renewable freshwater in India was 6,042 cubic metres in 1947, it has fallen to 1,845 cubic metres in 2007. By 2025, the total water demand of the country will be 1,050 bcm (billion cubic metres) while the total utilizable water resources will be 1,122 bcm. With an increase in population, the demand will move beyond what is available, and thus the country will have to face an acute water crisis. As per CPCB, water requirement in India, in 2050, will be 1,450 cubic km/yr, while the estimated utilizable water resource potential through conventional

12 http://www.cpcb.nic.in/upload/NewItems/NewItem_198_Status_of_WQ_in_India_2011.pdf, last accessed on 19 August 2014.
13 BOD refers to Biochemical Oxygen Demand and is the amount of dissolved oxygen in water.
14 Suneel Pandey, Saving good water, The Hindu Survey of the Environment 2012, 2012.
15 Reference based on the 2001 census that refers to 498 class-I cities and 410 class-II towns.
16 http://www.cpcb.nic.in/upload/NewItems/NewItem_153_Foreword.pdf, last accessed on 30 September 2012.
17 http://pib.nic.in/newsite/PrintRelease.aspx?relid=77736, last accessed 30 September 2012.
18 A center for research in ornithology and natural history, located at Anaikatty, Coimbatore, India.
19 http://envfor.nic.in/report/0203/chap-08.htm, last accessed on 28 September 2012.
20 http://www.hindu.com/2005/02/16/stories/2005021605811200.htm, last accessed on 28 September 2012.
21 V S Vijayan, Turning wetlands into badlands, The Hindu Survey of the Environment 2012, 2012.

development strategies is only 1,122 cubic km/yr.[22] All these indicate the importance of water harvesting, conservation of water resources, treatment of waste water, and importance of not releasing waste into water bodies.

Use and Over-utilization of Surface and Ground Water Resource

Surface water is the water available in rivers, lakes, and wetlands. Surface water is replenished through precipitation (rain and snow) and lost through evaporation, seepage, and discharge to larger water bodies. Fresh water located below the surface is ground water. It is also called as sub-surface water. Seepage from surface water leads to the formation of ground water. Ground water can have seepage to the oceans or it can also form springs. Of the total global water availability, only 2.5% belongs to the category of fresh water, while the rest belongs to oceans and other saline water. Out of this 2.5%, glaciers and ice caps constitute 68.7%. Ground water constitutes 30.1%, and surface/other water constitutes 1.2%.

FIG. 3.3[23] Pollution in Oshiwara River, Mumbai

---

22 http://www.cpcb.nic.in/upload/NewItems/NewItem_198_Status_of_WQ_in_India_2011.pdf, last accessed on 19 August 2014.

23 "Oshiwara river" by User;Jan jrg - Own work. Licensed under Public domain via Wikimedia Commons - http://commons.wikimedia.org/wiki/File:Oshiwara_river.JPG#mediaviewer/File:Oshiwara_river.JPG

Fresh water is used for agricultural, industrial, household, and recreational purposes. Usage of water has been growing at a rate that is more than double the rate of population increase in the last century.[24] As per the Food and Agricultural Organization of the United Nations (FAO), 71% of water that is withdrawn from the planet goes towards agricultural purpose, while 20% goes towards an industrial purpose, and 9% for domestic purposes.[25] In the Indian subcontinent, the contribution to agriculture, industry, and domestic demands contributes to 92%, 3%, and 5% of the total withdrawn water.[26] While industries are improving their water efficiency, the overall consumption of water is going up. The global population is on an increase with population predicted to touch approximately 9 billion by 2050.[27] To feed this population, increased amount of food production would be required; a need that will also require increased water resources. It has been noted that the usage of groundwater has exceeded the replenishment and recharge levels in many cities and regions.[28] Over-use of ground water, also referred to as over-drafting, result in the lowering of water tables, beyond the reach of existing wells. As the water table goes down, one may receive water that has increasing presence of elements such as arsenic and fluoride, which are more prevalent at deeper levels. As water table goes down, rivers dry up. Water normally percolates to streams and rivers and augments the water flow in the river. However, as water table goes down, the process reverses and water from rivers seeps down to regions nearby, resulting in the drying up of the river. As the river dries up, the shrubs, the trees, and the water-dependent species also disappear. Over-utilization of water can result in the following:

- Fall in water table.
- Intrusion of salt water into the ground water—with ground water on a reduction, there is the intrusion of salt water from the sea. This is especially found in the coastal regions.
- Drying up of bore wells.
- Pollution of water—as the ground water gets dried up, the water with fertiliser content seeps through the ground and pollutes the ground water.

Floods and Drought

As per the European Union Floods Directive,[29] flood means 'the temporary covering by water of land not normally covered by water.' Floods can be caused by heavy rainfall, which could be exacerbated by the release of water from dams, melting of snow, and extreme weather events such as a tsunami or a cyclone. While the flood directive acknowledges that floods are natural phenomena that are difficult to prevent, activities such as the expansion

---

24 http://www.unwater.org/statistics_use.html, last accessed on 13 November 2012.

25 http://www.fao.org/nr/water/aquastat/countries_regions/asia/index4.stm, last accessed on 13 November 2012.

26 http://www.fao.org/nr/water/aquastat/countries_regions/asia/index4.stm, last accessed on 13 November 2012.

27 http://www.un.org/apps/news/story.asp?NewsID=13451&Cr=population&Cr1, last accessed on November 13, 2012.

28 http://www.unwater.org/statistics_use.html, last accessed on 13 November 2012.

29 http://eur-lex.europa.eu/LexUriServ/LexUriServ.do?uri=OJ:L:2007:288:0027:0034:EN:PDF, last accessed on 13 November 2012.

of human settlements, growth of economic assets in the floodplains, and changes of land use resulting in the reduction of the natural water retention contribute to an increase in the likelihood and adverse impacts of flood events. The directive further states that it can cause fatalities, displacement of people, damage to the environment, and compromise economic development. The directive has also defined *flood risk* as the combination of the probability of a flood event and of the potential adverse consequences for human health, the environment, cultural heritage, and economic activity associated with a flood event. Approaches to reduce the occurrence of floods can be through afforestation and creation of water management channels.

Drought is a situation that occurs when a region faces a deficiency in water supply, primarily due to lesser than average precipitation. Droughts could extend over years and can cause mass migrations and humanitarian problems. The effects of drought can increase due to water intensive cropping patterns and over-exploitation of water resources. Droughts can result in the following:

- Reduced food production and yield
- Damage to terrestrial and aquatic ecosystems
- Dust storms, erosions, and increased possibility of wildfires
- Famine, malnutrition, dehydration, and other diseases
- Social unrests and wars as people start engaging in conflicts over limited resources that satisfies basic needs

Mitigation of drought effects can be done through rainwater harvesting, construction of water storage structures, afforestation, and sustainable irrigation practices like drip irrigation.

Conflicts Over Water

With freshwater resources being limited, unevenly distributed, yet important, there is increasing pressure on having access to this limited supply. The conflicts could occur between countries or within the countries. Agreements could be reached between the entities to avert such conflicts. The Indus Waters Treaty is an example of such an agreement reached between India and Pakistan in 1960. This treaty was facilitated by the World Bank. Conflicts could also occur within a country, as occurred in the case of Karnataka and Tamilnadu over the sharing of the water of River Kaveri. Pacific Institute,[30] an Oakland, California-based research organization, states that water conflicts could be due to (a) the need for control of water resources, its supply and access, (b) military reasons, where water is used as a weapon during military action, (c) political tool to achieve political gains, (d) terrorist activities, where water resources, its supply, and infrastructure are used as targets and tools to create disruption, and (e) development disputes where water resources and systems are sources of disputes in the context of societal development. Table 3.2 lists out some of the water related conflict details, related to India as maintained by the Pacific Institute.

---

30 http://pacinst.org/

TABLE 3.2[31] Conflicts related to water in India

1947 onwards	Partition divides the Ganges River between Bangladesh and India; construction of the Farakka barrage by India, beginning in 1962, increases tension; short-term agreements settle dispute in 1977–82, 1982–84, and 1985–88, and 30-year treaty is signed in 1996.
1947–1960s	Partition leaves Indus basin divided between India and Pakistan; disputes over irrigation water ensue, during which India stems flow of water into irrigation canals in Pakistan. Indus Waters Agreement reached in 1960 after 12 years of World Bank-led negotiations.
1991–2007	Violence erupts when Karnataka rejects an interim order handed down by the Cauvery Waters Tribunal, set up by the Indian Supreme Court. The Tribunal was established in 1990 to settle two decades of dispute between Karnataka and Tamil Nadu over irrigation rights to the Cauvery river.
1999–1999	Three people died and 20 were injured in December 1999 in Falla, Gujarat when the police open fired on 300 people protesting against the state government's decision to reserve water from the nearby Kankavati Dam for Jamnagar—a neighbouring town. The dam had become the only source of water for about 60 villages near Falla, and shortages and overdraft of groundwater contributed to a water crisis.
2002	Two people were killed and 25 others injured in Kashmir when police fired at a group of villagers clashing over water sharing. The incident took place in a Garend village in a dispute over sharing water from an irrigation stream.
2002	Continuing violence over the allocation of the Cauvery (Kaveri) River between Karnataka and Tamil Nadu. Riots, property destruction, more than 30 injuries, arrests through September and October.
2002	A camp of the Assam Rifles of the Indian military at Yairipok in Thoubal district with a mission to protect a water reservoir is attacked by suspected terrorists who fired grenades and other explosives on 27th January. Later, a spokesman for the United National Liberation Front (UNLF) claimed that the attack was carried out by its armed wing, the Manipur People's Army, which has been fighting for what it called an 'Independent Manipur.'
2004	Twelve Indian security forces were killed by an IED planted in an underground water pipe during 'counter-insurgency operation in Khanabal area in Anantnag district.'
2004	Four people were killed in October and more than 30 injured in November in ongoing protests by farmers over allocations of water from the Indira Ghandi Irrigation Canal in Sriganganagar district, which borders Pakistan. Authorities imposed curfews on the towns of Gharsana, Raola, and Anoopgarh.
2007	Thousands of farmers breached security and stormed the area of Hirakud dam to protest allocation of water to industry. Minor injuries were reported during the conflict between the farmers and police.
2009	A family in Madhya Pradesh state in India is killed by a small mob for illegally drawing water from a municipal pipe. Others ran to collect water for themselves before the pipe ran out. Drought and inequality in water distribution led to increasing conflict in the region. Indian media report more than 50 violent clashes in the state capital, Bhopal during May alone. Since January, 12 people have been killed and even more injured.

(Contd)

31 Adaptation from http://www2.worldwater.org/conflict/list/, last accessed on 20 August 2014. Used with permission.

2009	Police clash with hundreds of Mumbai residents protesting water cuts. One man is killed and a dozen others injured. Mumbai authorities are forced to ration supplies after the worst monsoon season in decades.
2010	A protest about water shortages in the National Capital Territory of Delhi in India led to violence. Erratic water supply and cutoffs in the Kondli area of Mayur Vihar in East Delhi causes a violent protest and several injuries.
2010	At least three deaths and dozens of injuries are reported during protests over land and water given away for a power plant in Sompeta in Srikakulam district in Andhra Pradesh, India.
2012	Thousands of farmers in Karnataka try to prevent the release of water from two dams (Krishna Raja Sagar, and Kabini) on the Cauvery river. Injuries to protestors and police were reported. The water releases were ordered by the Indian Supreme Court, which required Karnataka to deliver water downstream state of Tamil Nadu despite severe drought. The dispute continues later in the year when Karnataka again halts releases.
2012	Scuffles and protests break out around New Delhi during the summer of 2012 as residents surround water delivery trucks and fight over water. The summer was the hottest in 33 years, leading to extensive energy and water shortages.
2012	Violence erupts in the latest event in the dispute between Pakistan and India over the waters of the Indus Basin. Pakistani militants attack and sabotage water systems, flood protection works, and dams in the Wullar Lake region of northern Kashmir. They attack engineers and workers and detonate explosives at the unfinished Tulbul Navigation Lock/Wullar Dam. Pakistan claims the new dam violates the Indus Water Treaty by cutting flows to Pakistan.
2012	Militants block work at the Wullar Conservation Project (Wullar Dam) construction site in the Baramulla District of India—a project opposed by Pakistan. Officials suggest that these militants may have been sent by Pakistan because of their concerns that the project is in violation of Pakistani interests under the Indus Water Treaty of 1960. Sources said that eight of the 16 militants who stopped work of the Project were Pakistani nationals. India says the dam is not in violation of the Treaty and would, if completed, be used only for transportation purposes. Pakistan believes the Indian control over Jehulm waters has the potential to disrupt the Pakistan-Upper Jhelum Canal, Upper Chenab Canal, and the Lower Bari Doab Canal.
2012	Women from the village of Rasooh are reportedly assaulted for attempting to take water from a village well. The tensions over water are related to long-standing tensions between caste groups but have been worsened by drought and water shortage.
2013	An acute water shortage in Ahmednagar district, Maharashtra, India leads to fights among locals and one death. The government expresses concern about large-scale public unrest due to a severe drought and major water shortages.
2013	Tensions continue between India and Pakistan over access and control of the Siachen Glacier in Kashmir, with a demand by Pakistan that India withdraw troops stationed there.
2014	Tensions revived in the area of Jammu and Kashmir in early 2014 when upper caste women reportedly restrict access to higher quality water sources.

Dams: Benefits and Problems

Dams have been built across the world due to the following benefits:

- Power Generation—Dams provide an opportunity to generate hydroelectric power.
- Drinking water supply
- Irrigation—Dams control the flow of water and stores it. This stored water is used for irrigation and agricultural purposes.
- Flood control
- Recreation and tourism—Although dams are not built for promoting tourism, dams do attract people for aesthetic pleasures.

However, dams have also been known for creating a number of problems:

- Loss of archaeological and cultural sites and specimens underwater
- Loss of habitat for many species that may be endangered
- Changes in the topography of rivers downstream and changes in their water flow
- Displacement of people—It is estimated 40–80 million people have been physically displaced from their homes as part of dam construction.[32]
- Possibilities of dam failure

Resettlement and Rehabilitation of People: Its Problems and Concerns

Individuals and communities are forced out of their homeland in the name of economic development. This is being done mainly due to the following reasons:

- Construction of dams, hydro-projects, and irrigation projects
- Land acquisition for industrial development, including creation of Special Economic Zones (SEZs), technology parks and more
- Development of transportation infrastructure including roadways, railways, and canals.
- Extraction, transportation, and management of energy and minerals. This includes mining and maintenance of power plants.
- Creation of military installations and testing grounds for military related activities.

In rare occasions, displacement of people also happens due to forestry and conservation-related projects. For example, forest dwellers may be induced to move out of a forest region if that region is made into a protected area. It has been estimated[33, 34, 35] that 15 million people every year are affected by 'Development- Induced Displacement.'

---

32 http://www.internationalrivers.org/resources/the-world-commission-on-dams-framework-a-brief-introduction-2654, last accessed on 13 November 2012.

33 B. Terminski, Environmentally-Induced Displacement. Theoretical Frameworks and Current Challenges, Liege, 2012.

34 M.M. Cernea, Development-induced and conflict-induced IDPs: bridging the research divide, Forced Migration Review, Special Issue, December 25-27, 2006.

35 A. Oliver-Smith (ed.), Development & Dispossession: The Crisis of Forced Displacement and Resettlement (School for Advanced Research Advanced Seminar), 2009.

It is said that almost 50 million Indians have been displaced from their native regions due to big projects[36] and almost 1–2 million people were displaced for the Sardar Sarovar Dam project.

Successful Models of Water Resource Management[37]

- Pani Panchayats, is a water resource management model in Maharashtra and was started by a social worker, Vilasrao Salunkhe and his wife Kalpanatai Salunkhe. This endeavour started in 1973 (after the 1972 drought), and motivated villagers to pool their efforts to harness their meagre water resources for common good. This community-based water council endeavour is now taken forward by Gram Gaurav Pratisthan, Pune. As part of the Pani Panchayat model, co-operatives based on the concept of managing water resources at the community level on the principle of equal sharing and distribution are formed. For more details about the principles that guide the functioning of Pani Panchayat, refer http://www.panipanchayat.org/principle.html
- Rajiv Gandhi Watershed Management Mission programme launched in 1994 by the Madhya Pradesh government aimed at a bottom-up approach. The program aimed for labour intensive land and water management. As part of the mission, committee of people were elected on a watershed basis. The mission supported them with financial and technical support. Activities of this mission were executed through the creation of the watershed communities, which consisted of user groups, self-help groups and credit groups. This committee organized community meetings, planning, execution of watershed plans, the distribution of funds to community groups, maintenance of records, and implementation of the project. For more details, refer http://www.watermissionmp.org
- In addition to being a political activist, Anna Hazare is also known for his work associated with the development of Ralegan Siddhi, a village in Maharashtra. The community watershed development programmes undertaken in this village has been one of the earliest reported successful interventions in India. The watershed development programme has facilitated the overall development of the village. For more details, refer http://www.annahazare.org/ralegan-siddhi.html

There has been attempts to project bottled water as a panacea for the water-related issues that people are facing today. A document[38] related to 'The Bellagio Conversations' states, 'water that has been packaged in a modern container, shipped, and heavily marketed is perceived as superior, safer, more convenient, and ready for

---

36 http://www.planningcommission.nic.in/reports/articles/ncsxna/art_dam.pdf, last accessed on 22 November 2012.

37 This section is an improvement of an excerpt from the "Water Resources" section of the State of the Environment Report released by the Karnataka Government. This report is available at http://parisara.kar.nic.in/PDF/waterresources.pdf

38 http://www.cifor.org/pes/publications/pdf_files/Bellagio%20Conversations%20PWS%202008.pdf, last accessed on 22 November 2012.

consumption. Users have no problem paying high prices for bottled water, and are often unaware that watershed restoration could secure similar water quality, at a fraction of the price.' The document also notes that making natural watersheds more effective has the capability to significantly meet human needs at a cost lower than the technology intensive conventional alternatives. A case in example is what happened in New York. By investing US$1 billion towards the watershed protection and restoration in the Catskill Mountains, a region near New York that also has a forest preserve, the New York City Department for Environment Protection (NYC DEP) was able to save the city US$6–$10 billion that would have gone to build a water filtration plant that would have also cost US$300–$500 million to operate on an annual basis.[39,40,41]

Soil Pollution

Soil pollution is caused due to the usage of human-made chemicals that are not natural to the soil. Soil contamination can alter the soil chemistry, resulting in the change of metabolism of microorganisms and anthropods. This will thus affect organisms in the next level of the food chain. It has been found that the concentration of the chemicals becomes higher as one moves to higher levels of the food web. The concentration of DDT has resulted in the weakening of eggshells leading to increased rates of mortality for the chicks.

Some of the causes for soil pollution are as follows:

Usage of pesticides and fertilisers	Dumping of waste and effluents, including industrial and e-waste	Dumping of oil and fuel-related material
Seepage of contaminated surface water to subsurface strata	Acid rain	Genetically modified plants and produces
Release from industrial accidents	Nuclear waste	Altering the nature of soil due to mining practices

Marine Pollution, Algal Bloom, and Ocean Acidification

The value provided by oceans in terms of goods and services itself amount to US$3 trillion annually,[42] in addition to services that can never be accounted for. However, the intervention of humans are affecting the oceans. Marine pollution occurs due to the

39 http://aswm.org/wordpress/the-compleat-wetlander-where-have-all-the-wetlands-gone-why-does-it-matter/, last accessed on 22 November 2012.
40 http://suprememastertv.com/bbs/board.php?bo_table=pe&wr_id=131&goto_url=, last accessed on 22 November 2012.
41 http://www.theriverstrust.org/seminars/archive/water/WRT_WATER_PES_Guide_27-06-12_A3.pdf, last accessed on 22 November 2012.
42 Governing the high seas: In deep water, The Economist, Feb 22nd 2014; Also available at http://www.economist.com/news/international/21596990-humans-are-damaging-high-seas-now-oceans-are-doing-harm-back-deep-water, last accessed on 11 May 2014.

introduction of unnatural materials like pesticides, industrial, agricultural waste, and chemicals that are introduced into the oceans. Pollution can come from land-based sources like sewerage and industrial waste discharges, or it could also be caused by wind-blown debris. Many of the toxins are consumed by planktons and other small organisms in the ocean. The Monterey Bay Aquarium Research Institute (MBARI) has recorded evidence of man-made debris and trash up to 13,000 feet below sea level and 300 miles offshore from waters off of central and southern California, the Pacific Northwest, Hawaii, and the Gulf of California.[43] Waste in the sea can also be carried by waves and finally deposited in the seashore (Fig. 3.4), and these wastes can be harmful to sea-based beings (Fig. 3.5).

FIG. 3.4[45] Waste on the Hawaaiin coastline

FIG. 3.5[46] Remnants of a Laysan Albatross (found in the North Pacific) chick, which was accidentally fed with plastic by its parents resulting in death

43 http://www.mbari.org/news/news_releases/2013/deep-debris/deep-debris-release.html, last accessed on 4 July 2013.

Surface runoff of water, if it is from farming sources, carries nutrients with it. As the nutrient-rich water enters the ocean, algae and phytoplankton rapidly increase its population resulting in algal bloom. Some of these algal blooms may be harmful as they affect other organisms due to the release of natural toxins, oxygen depletion, and affecting the physiological structure of other organisms. Consumption of the available oxygen in the sea by the algae results in the area becoming a dead zone for other forms of marine life. An example of such a dead zone is near the Gulf of Mexico, located near Cuba and the USA. The dead zone, which now covers 6,700 square miles, is caused by the nitrates and phosphorous flowing to the Gulf of Mexico, primarily for the state of Illinois, Iowa, and Indiana. *The Economist* magazine writes, 'Invasive species of many kinds are moved around the world by human activity–and do an estimated US$100 billion of damage to oceans each year. Farmers dump excess fertilizer into rivers, which finds its way to the sea; there cyanobacteria (blue-green algae) feed on the nutrients, proliferate madly and reduce oxygen levels, asphyxiating all sea creatures. In 2008, there were over 400 'dead zones' in the oceans. Polluters pumped out CO_2, which dissolves in seawater, producing carbonic acid. That in turn has increased ocean acidity by over a quarter since the start of the industrial revolution. In 2012, scientists found pteropods (a kind of sea snail) in the Southern Ocean with partially dissolved shells.'[44]

Shipping also creates an environmental impact on the water bodies. Ships normally take ballast water from the coastal water of one region/country and releases in another port. This water can include invasive and non-native species that cause economic and ecological damage to aquatic ecosystems of other countries/regions. Collusions between ships and aquatic animals have resulted in serious harm and death to these animals. It has been estimated that shipping contributes 18-30% of the pollution caused by nitrogen oxide (NOX) emissions and contributed 9% of the pollution caused by sulphur oxide emissions.[47] It also contributes to 3.5–4% of all climate change emissions.[48] A study done by the Earth Systems Research

44 Governing the high seas: In deep water, The Economist, Feb 22nd 2014; Also available at http://www.economist.com/news/international/21596990-humans-are-damaging-high-seas-now-oceans-are-doing-harm-back-deep-water, last accessed on 11 May 2014.

45 Image Source: "Marine debris on Hawaiian coast" by NOAA - http://marinedebris.noaa.gov/marinedebris101/photos_ecosys.html. Licensed under Public domain via Wikimedia Commons - http://commons.wikimedia.org/wiki/File:Marine_debris_on_Hawaiian_coast.jpg#mediaviewer/File:Marine_debris_on_Hawaiian_coast.jpg, last accessed Accessed on 10 February 10, 2010.

46 Image Source: "Albatross chick plastic" by Duncan Wright - USFWS. Licensed under Public domain via Wikimedia Commons - http://commons.wikimedia.org/wiki/File:Albatross_chick_plastic.jpg#mediaviewer/File:Albatross_chick_plastic.jpg , last accessed Accessed on 10 February 10, 2010.

47 http://www.guardian.co.uk/environment/2009/apr/09/shipping-pollution, last accessed on 17 November 2012.

48 http://www.guardian.co.uk/environment/2009/apr/09/shipping-pollution, last accessed on 17 November 2012.

Laboratory[49] concluded that the commercial shipping liners of the world created as much pollution as half the total number of automobiles of this world.[50] There are also instances where oil tankers create oil spills, which have disastrous consequences (Fig. 3.6). Ships also dump black water (waste water from toilets and medical uses) and grey water (waste water from cleaning activities, and showers) to the water bodies. The ships may also release bilge water (the mixture of water and oil, which emerges from leaks from machinery, engines, and maintenance activities) to the sea.[51]

FIG. 3.6[52] Birds killed as a result of the Exxon–Valdez oil spill

49 http://www.esrl.noaa.gov/
50 http://www.guardian.co.uk/environment/2009/mar/31/noaa-pollution-florida-freighters-tankers-cruise-ships, last accessed on 17 November 2012.
51 http://usatoday30.usatoday.com/travel/news/2002/2002-11-08-cruises-1acover.htm, last accessed on 17 November 2012.
52 Image Source: http://en.wikipedia.org/wiki/File:EVOSWEB_013_oiled_bird3.jpg, last accessed Accessed on 17 November 17, 2012.

Ocean acidification increases as the presence of atmospheric CO_2 is on a rise, resulting in the absorption of this CO_2 to the ocean's surface. As pH levels of seawater decreases, the water is more acidic. Ocean acidification has a number of impacts on marine population. Some of them are as follows:

- Disrupts the olfactory ability (pertaining to the sensual capability of smell) of fishes to detect predators.[53,54]
- Affects the shells of the marine organisms. A research study indicated that the shells of many of the marine organizations got weakened (including those of corals, clams, oysters, scallops, and urchins), while some of the marine organism built heavier shells (lobsters and crabs).[55]
- It was also found that ocean acidification increases the anxiety level of the fishes.[56]

Noise Pollution

Noise pollution is the displeasing sounds that can cause harm or affect the balance of human beings and other life forms. Noise pollution can affect the cardio-vascular systems of human beings, contribute to arterial diseases, and cause noise-induced hearing loss. It can also cause annoyance and aggression, hypertension, sleep disturbances, and high-stress levels. Among animals and birds, it can lead to permanent hearing loss, interference with their navigating capabilities, and predator or prey detection capabilities. Most of the noise pollution is machine created. Researchers from Universities of Exeter and Bristol have found that marine noise pollution, also caused by ships, are causing a reduction in the survival possibilities of marine creatures like eels. When exposed to noise, eels were caught more than twice as quickly by the predators[57]. Sometimes, the traffic noise overwhelms the mating calls of the birds and could affect bird populations. Noise also makes animals and birds to communicate louder as otherwise their voice will be masked by human induced noises. When one species starts speaking loudly, it will mask the voice of other species, which will be forced to communicate louder. All in all, the whole ecosystem starts speaking louder.

Many festivals and celebrations contribute to noise pollution, due the usage of crackers. Bursting of crackers is gradually becoming a norm for many festivals and fairs, irrespective of religions. Hindu monks like Swami Bhoomananda Theertha from

53 Danielle L. Dixson, Philip L. Munday, Geoffrey P. Jones, Ocean acidification disrupts the innate ability of fish to detect predator olfactory cues, Ecology Letters, Volume 13, Issue 1, January 2010, pages 68-75. Also available at http://onlinelibrary.wiley.com/doi/10.1111/j.1461-0248.2009.01400.x/abstract, last accessed on 06 December 2013.

54 Philip L. Mundaya, Danielle L. Dixsona, Jennifer M. Donelsona, Geoffrey P. Jonesa, Morgan S. Pratchetta, Galina V. Devitsinac, Kjell B. Døvingd, Ocean acidification impairs olfactory discrimination and homing ability of a marine fish, PNAS, Vol. 106, No. 6, February 10, 2009. Also available at http://www.pnas.org/content/106/6/1848.abstract, last accessed on 6 December 2013.

55 http://conservationmagazine.org/2010/01/shell-game/, last accessed on 6 December 2013.

56 http://conservationmagazine.org/2013/11/ocean-acidification-makes-fish-anxious/, last accessed on 6 December 2013.

57 http://www.bris.ac.uk/news/2014/august/eels-and-noise.html, last accessed on 8 August 2014.

TABLE 3.3[58]   Average noise levels (in decibels) at different places of Delhi

Location	2012		2013	
	Average day	Deepavali day	Average day	Deepavali day
Lajpat Nagar	58	81	56	79
East Arjun Nagar	57	74	59	72
Mayur Vihar Phase – II	48	73	60	83
Pitam Pura	56	75	61	73
Kamla Nagar	61	80	63	81
Dilshad Garden	58	78	59	80
Ansari Nagar	58	76	56	81
Connaught Place	64	69	69	74
I T O	70	71	67	69

Monitoring time: 18:00 hours to 24:00 hours

Narayanashrama Tapovanam[59] has questioned the necessity to spend (and waste) huge amount of money on crackers. While monitoring the noise levels in Delhi, on normal days and on Deepavali days, Central Pollution Control Board has found an increase in the noise levels on Deepavali days (Table 3.3). Bursting of crackers affect the peaceful living of birds and many animal species. As bursting of crackers extends through the evening, it affects the restfulness and sleep of birds. As dogs are sensitive to sound, they run haywire affected by the bursting sound. An important ritual for every Hindu is to engage in *Bhoota Pooja*—the worship of every element of this Universe, including beings of all species. Hindus also worship animals and birds as *Vahanas* of Gods and Goddesses. It is no wonder that many sincere Hindus tend to avoid participating in such and similar practices that cause harm to all species.

Thermal Pollution

Thermal pollution refers to the deterioration of water quality due to changes in the water temperature that is primarily human induced. Sources of thermal pollution caused by warm water will include:
- Release of water used as a coolant in power plants and industrial plants such as petroleum refineries, chemical plants, steel mills, and paper mills. Thermal plume from coal-fired power plants also contribute to increase in water temperature.
- Rainwater run-off from urban areas

---

58 http://www.cpcb.nic.in/upload/Latest/Latest_82_DeepawaliPressRelease2013.pdf, last accessed on 6 November 2013.
59 http://narayanashramatapovanam.org/

In both the cases, especially the first one, water now has a higher temperature. When it is released into the natural water environment, it will affect the existence of oxygen in the water by decreasing the level of dissolved oxygen in water. Many aquatic organisms fail to reproduce at higher temperatures. Changes in the species composition of coral reefs and coral bleaching are also observed. Coral bleaching refers to the coral reefs getting a lighter or white appearance. The corals have a relationship with unicellular organisms known as zooxanthellae, which gives corals its varied colours. When the conditions necessary to sustain zooxanthellae are not maintained, bleaching of the corals occurs.

Similar to warm water pollution, release of unnatural cold water can also affect the life. Release of cold water from reservoirs to rivers and streams that have warmer water; have resulted in the reduction/elimination of fish species of the region.

Light Pollution

Alteration of natural light levels due to the intervention of human beings through the projection of artificial lights is known as light pollution. It is caused due to ineffective designs in lighting systems that project excessive and misdirected light, especially upward into the sky, where such a light is not required. Such obtrusive lights change the light levels and affects living patterns followed by many life forms during its migration, reproduction, and feeding practices. Light pollution is also known as photo-pollution or luminous pollution. There are organizations like the 'International Dark-Sky Association' that works to preserve and protect the natural dark environments available in the night (Fig. 3.7). Such initiatives have resulted in increasing the visibility of stars during the night, the reduction in the usage of energy, and a reduction in the effects of unnatural lighting. Earth Hour, an initiative by World Wide Fund for Nature (WWF), is an event that has helped in promoting these objectives. Those who enjoy watching the stars and the sky in the night, and to learn from those views, finds artificial lighting to be obtrusive.[60, 61, 62]

While usage of artificial lighting systems has its advantages, it is life threatening for certain species. Two examples are that of turtles and salmons. Leatherback turtles are the deepest diving among all air-breathing animals and are also the most migratory among all turtles. Mother turtles lay eggs on the beaches. After hatching, the baby turtles emerge from the nest at the nighttime, as temperature tends to be cooler. These baby turtles use moonlight and the reflection of the moon on the water to find their way to the sea. Researchers[63] have observed that artificial lighting in the beaches results in these baby turtles getting misdirected to land, thereby becoming a prey to predators or dying of dehydration. It has also been found that the migratory timing and behaviour of young

60 http://stargazing.co.nz/our-sky/, last accessed on 20 August 2014.
61 http://www.ehow.com/list_5969818_benefits-star-gazing.html, last accessed on 20 August 2014.
62 http://chellean.wordpress.com/2011/09/15/star-gazing-in-a-world-of-light-pollution/, last accessed on 20 August 2014.
63 Marina Zheleva, The dark side of light. Light pollution kills leatherback turtle hatchlings, Biodiscovery 2012; 3: 4. Also available at http://www.biodiscoveryjournal.co.uk/Article/The-dark-side-of-light, last accessed on 26 August 2013.

(wild Atlantic) salmons could be influenced by street lighting and such changes may impact the fitness of these young salmons.[64]

NUCLEAR HAZARDS AND ACCIDENTS

Sustained nuclear fission is used to generate electricity through the production of heat. Usage of nuclear energy has been a consistent source of debate. While organizations like International Atomic Energy Agency (IAEA) and World Nuclear Association (a group of

FIG. 3.7[65]   A campaign poster by Need-Less (http://www.need-less.org.uk)

---

64 Riley W.D., Bendall B., Ives M.J., Edmonds N.J., Maxwell D.L., ' Street Lighting Disrupts the Diel Migratory Pattern of Wild Atlantic Salmon, *Salmo salar* L., Smolts Leaving Their Natal Strem', *Aquaculture*, Vols 330-333, 2012, pp. 74-81. Abstract available at http://www.sciencedirect.com/science/article/pii/S0044848611009690, last accessed on 23 August 2013.

65 http://www.need-less.org.uk/posters%20page.html, last accessed on 23 August 2013. Used with permission.

companies associated with nuclear power production) communicate that nuclear energy is an energy source that does not produce carbon emissions, there are organizations like Greenpeace and Nuclear Information and Resource Service (NIRS) who are concerned with the security and safety related to power plants. Nuclear power accidents include the Three Mile Island accident in the US (1979), Chernobyl disaster in Ukraine (part of former USSR, 1986), and the Fukushima Daiichi Nuclear disaster in Japan (2011) (Fig. 3.8). Following a nuclear blast caused by the explosion of a nuclear weapon or due to a nuclear reaction that occurs in an unsafe environment, the radioactive residual material reaches the atmosphere creates radioactive contamination in soil and aquifers, and these will remain affected for years to come. Severe radiation can also cause mutation among humans and animals resulting in physiological deformities. It has been found that, in the first four years following the Chernobyl disaster in Ukraine, nearly 350 animals born in the Narodychi region of Ukraine had gross deformities such as missing or extra limbs, missing eyes, heads or ribs, or deformed skulls. This was in contrast to the region registering only three abnormal births in the five years prior to the disaster. Even after more than 25 years of the Chernobyl accident, birds living near the affected area are affected by cataract, an ailment related to the eye. It was found that the incidence of cataracts among 1100 free-living birds increased with the level of background radiation.[66] More than 35% of these 1100 birds were affected by cataract.[67]

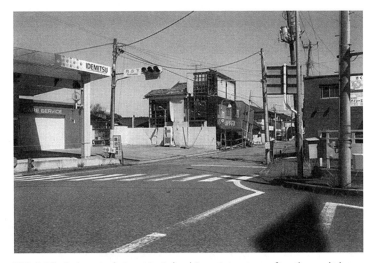

FIG. 3.8[68] A deserted street in Fukushima, two years after the meltdown of the Fukushima nuclear power plant

66 Mousseau TA, Moller AP, Elevated Frequency of Cataracts in Birds from Chernobyl. PLoS ONE 8(7), 2013. Also available at http://www.plosone.org/article/info%3Adoi%2F10.1371%2Fjournal.pone.0066939, last accessed on 16 August 2013.
67 Mousseau TA, Moller AP, Elevated Frequency of Cataracts in Birds from Chernobyl. PLoS ONE 8(7), 2013. Also available at http://www.plosone.org/article/info%3Adoi%2F10.1371%2Fjournal.pone.0066939, last accessed on 16 August 2013.
68 Photo by Guldo Van Nispen, Used with permission, Available at https://www.flickr.com/photos/vannispen/ 8648177528, last accessed Accessed on 02 August 2, 2014.

During November 2013, the Australian state of Tasmania announced that it will aim for 100% renewable energy by 2020. Tasmania has already achieved emission reductions of about 34% against the 1990 baseline.

Nuclear power generation, as well as research-related endeavours, usually creates radio-active wastes as by-products. More than 95% of the total radioactivity produced during nuclear power generation is related to 'high-level' waste,[69] a term that refers to the highly radioactive fission products and trans-uranic elements generated in the reactor core of nuclear reactors. To produce 1000 MW(e) of electricity from a nuclear power station, approximately 30 tonnes of high-level solid-packed waste and 300 cubic metres of low and intermediate level waste is generated per year. Globally, nuclear power plants produce approximately 10,000 m^3 of high-level waste on an annual basis. While ascertaining the feasibility of creating a nuclear waste repository in Yucca mountain located in southern Nevada, Environmental Protection Authority (EPA) of the USA, was ascertaining the radiation emission for a period of 10,000 years to 10,00,000 years.[70] Such long-term impacts and concerns about nuclear accidents[71] have created unpopularity about nuclear power in the minds of people.

HUMAN INTERFERENCE WITH THE NATURAL ENVIRONMENT AND ITS IMPACT

The absence of a spiritual relationship to the land renders the land without a soul, with something that can be commodified, can be abused, can be destroyed because it has no relationship to humans.[72]

Chris Peters, Pohlik-lah/Karuk leader and director of the non-profit Seventh Generation Fund for Indian Development

Implications of Human Population Growth

Human population, which crossed seven billion in 2011,[73] is expected to reach approximately nine billion by 2050.[74] Increasing population will put stress on the availability of drinking water, sanitation networks, and will result in migration to cities and urbanization. While we are aware of the major changes that may occur as part of the increasing human population, there are a number of implications that goes unnoticed. Through a survey in the Mediterranean coast of the Iberian Peninsula, it was found that the availability of sea-shells in the coastline was three times more abundant three decades ago. This fall is primarily driven by the seemingly innocent activity of tourists picking up few seashells from the seashore, as a souvenir. However, as the number of visitors to the beaches across the world

69 http://www.world-nuclear.org/info/inf04.html, last accessed on 25 December 2012.

70 http://nepis.epa.gov/Exe/ZyPDF.cgi/9101MCB9.PDF?Dockey=9101MCB9.PDF, last accessed 10 May 2014.

71 http://en.wikipedia.org/wiki/Nuclear_and_radiation_accidents, last accessed on 25 December 2012.

72 http://www.globalonenessproject.org/sites/default/files/education/resources/livingonenessstudyguide.pdf, last accessed on 28 May 2013. Used with permission.

73 http://www.worldometers.info/world-population/, last accessed on 11 December 2012.

74 http://www.worldometers.info/world-population/, last accessed on 11 December 2012.

reaches millions, the collection in the number of seashells jumps significantly. Seashells play a variety of roles, such as algae use them as a shelter, birds use them to build nests, and hermit crabs carry them as armour. The data also indicated that an increase in the number of tourists resulted in a decrease in the number of seashells available on the shore.[75]

India already is facing the troubles associated with the depletion of groundwater supplies. Though India has only 2.4% of the planet's total land area, its current population size of 1.2 billion constitutes almost 17% of the global population. Increased population will also result in demand for more technological gadgets and lifestyle-related comforts, all contributing to increased wastage and emissions. With increasing population, the demand on the resources of the planet will also increase. *National Geographic Magazine*, in a report that speaks about the prevalent seafood crisis, states, 'Too many hooks in the water. That's the problem with today's fisheries. Working from small pole-and-line boats to giant industrial trawlers, fishermen remove more than 170 billion pounds of wildlife a year from the seas.'[76]

Sadhguru Jaggi Vasudev, Founder, Isha Foundation, says, 'The tree population should increase, human population has to come down. We have bred irresponsibly. In the last 100 years, i.e., in the beginning of the century, we were just 1.5 billion. Today we are 7 billion plus. United Nations is making predictions that by 2050 we will be 9.6 billion people. 9.6 billion people means we will have to live with 40% less resource than what we are enjoying now. When I say resource, I am not talking about oil or gold or something. I am talking about food that you eat, water that you drink, and the air that you breathe. This is going to be a serious problem. So 9.6 billion people in another 40 years, not even 40, in 36 years, is a dangerous bomb sitting in front of us. Either we curtail this consciously or Nature is going to do it to us in a very cruel manner. If we do it consciously, we can call ourselves human beings. If Nature does it for us, we are just creatures on this planet.'[77]

Interestingly, Tenzin Gyatso, the 14th Dalai Lama, popularly referred to as Dalai Lama, has mentioned, '*The best way to birth control is that there are more monks!*'[78]

Tenzin Gyatso, the 14th Dalai Lama ("Dalai Lama"), has mentioned, *"The best way to birth control is that there are more monks!"*

Tenzin Gyatso, the 14th Dalai Lama, popularly referred to as Dalai Lama, says,'...As I mentioned earlier, family planning should be encouraged. From a Buddhist perspective, it is quite simple. Each human life is very precious. From this perspective, it is better to avoid or control birth, but today there are 1.5 billion[79] precious lives—too many precious lives! As a result it is not only one or two precious human

---

75 Michal Kowalewski, Rosa Domnech, Jordi Martinell, "Vanishing Clams on an Iberian Beach: Local Consequences and Global Implications of Accelerating Loss of Shells to Tourism", PLoS ONE 9(1), 2014. Also available at http://www.plosone.org/article/info%3Adoi%2F10.1371%2Fjournal.pone.0083615.

76 http://ngm.nationalgeographic.com/2010/10/seafood-crisis/greenberg-text/1, last accessed on 3 February 2013.

77 http://www.ecowalkthetalk.com/blog/2012/09/01/sadhguru-jaggi-vasudev-project-green-hands-and-tree-planting-in-tamil-nadu/, last accessed on 1 October 2012.

78 The Dalai Lama said he was "optimistic" about the evolution of mankind, http://www.wreporter.com/world/the-dalai-lama-said-he-was-optimistic-about-the-evolution-of-mankind/, last accessed on 1 October 2012.

79 This speech was given on September 28, 1996, as part of the "Endangered Tibet" Conference in Snlnn, Australia.

lives that are at stake, but the question is of the survival of humanity at large. So therefore the conclusion we arrive at is that we must take family planning very seriously, if we are to save the prosperity of the entire humanity, preferably through non-violent means, not through abortion or killing, but by some other means. I often half-jokingly say... more monks and nuns. That is the most non-violent arid effective method. So if you can't become a monk or a nun, then practice other non-violent methods of birth control.'[80]

Animal and Human Conflict

With an increase in the human population, human habitat also expands. As this expansion intrudes into the wildlife territory (Fig. 3.9), there is an increased interaction between humans and animals that can result in a negative impact on wildlife or humans. A factsheet from the WWF states, 'From tigers killing cattle in Malaysia and elephants trampling fields in Kenya to sun bears destroying corn crops in Colombia and wolves attacking sheep in Italy …it happens around the world, affects rich and poor, and is bad news for all concerned.'[81] Some of the negative impacts of such an interaction are:

FIG. 3.9[82] Forest destruction for slash-and-burn agriculture, a technique that involves destruction of forests/trees to create agricultural land

---

80 http://www.dalailama.com/messages/environment/tibets-environment, last accessed on 1 October 2012.

81 http://awsassets.panda.org/downloads/human_animal_conflict_factsheet2006.pdf

82 Photo by Matt Zimmerman, Used with permission, Image Source: https://www.flickr.com/photos/16725630@ N00/1524189000, last accessed Accessed on 2 August 2, 2014.

- Loss of life or injury for human beings, wild animals, and domesticated animals
- Damage to agricultural produces and crops
- Damage to habitats
- Damage to human property

Primarily there are three ways through which the human–animal conflicts are reduced—(a) give priority to human beings to the detriment of animals and its ecosystems, (b) give priority to animals and its ecosystems, with human beings being asked to relocate, and (c) trying to promote peaceful co-existence amongst humans, animals, and their ecosystems. In many cases, the focus will be on promoting peaceful co-existence.

Some of the practices adopted to reduce human–animal conflicts include:

- Promoting livelihoods that do not result in a conflict between animals and wildlife. An example could be an eco-tourism project where the native tribal population operates a wildlife safari on top of the elephants. Eco-friendly development of villages around protected areas to elicit co-operation of local community in the management of the protected areas.
- Creating a network of protected areas and wildlife corridors. Rejuvenating the travel paths used by wildanimals for their seasonal movement. This would reduce the need for the wildanimals to seek travel paths through human habitats.
- Improving the availability of natural food and water to reduce the movement of animals from the forests to the human habitations. Afforestation and planting endeavours of native trees could be done to provide increased food sources and living spaces for wildanimals.
- Creating buffer zones between human settlements/agricultural regions and protected regions/forests.
- Farmers are encouraged to grow crops that are not liked by wildanimals.
- Farms are designed in a way that will result in the early detection of the arrival of wildlife. Warning systems like manned watchtowers and observers are kept. Firecrackers, electrical fences, solar fences, and boundary walls are used to reduce human–animal conflict. In many countries of African continent, chilli and tobacco-based deterrents are kept to keep elephants out of fields.
- Educating people about the need to conserve wildlife and forests. Educating people, staff from the forest department, and police about the measures that could be taken to reduce conflict with wild animals.
- Relocating animals to other parks and sanctuaries if they have reached a maximum number.
- Research on the food habits of the animal predators.
- Developing facilities to immobilize problematic animals through tranquilization, relocating them to rescue centres, and releasing them to their natural habitats.
- Involving voluntary organizations and research/academic institutions in the management of protected areas.
- Provision for insurance schemes and financial aid through compensations.

> To butcher an innocent animal in front of the all-merciful God or Goddess, and style it as devotion, hoodwinking the gullible minds, and terrorizing those who resist or dissuade the move is too derogatory.
> *Swami Bhoomananda Theertha, Narayanashrama Tapovanam.*

- Many animals, especially those in the wild are killed due to superstitious beliefs. Thus, it is necessary to create opportunities where people can tune to the deeper essence of religions. Condemning animal sacrifices in Hindu temples, a press statement was released by Hindu Navotthana Pratishthan. Swami Bhoomananda Theertha from Narayanasharama Tapovanam, said, 'To butcher an innocent animal in front of the all-merciful God or Goddess and style it as devotion, hoodwinking the gullible minds, and terrorising those who resist or dissuade the move is too derogatory.'[83]

Impact of Technology on Environment

Positive Impacts

- Technology has been of help in improving the impact assessment of any 'developmental' project on environment.
- Technology has helped to increase the efficiency of various machines. This includes an efficiency increase in the combustion engine, resulting in a reduction in emissions from the engine. The fuel efficiency of passenger cars, on average, has increased from 15 mpg in 1970 to 24 mpg currently, which is a performance improvement of almost 60%. (It would be interesting to note that during this period the number of car registrations happening per year went up from 1,23,479 in 1970 to 6,81,154, in 2009, which is an increase of 452%.[84] This huge increase in the usage of cars has negated all efficiency gains made).
- Technology has resulted in new tools such as sensors, e-market places, etc. that has contributed to more efficient operations.

Negative Impacts

- Increased use of technology has resulted in more widespread logging.
- Increased energy consumption, increased familiarity and usage of electronic gadgets, motor vehicles, and household appliances like air-conditioners, etc. has resulted in increased release of greenhouse gas emissions resulting in the depletion of the stratospheric ozone layer and increased global warming.
- Technology has aided increased exploitative extraction of mineral wealth from the planet. Areas that were pristine and inaccessible, for example, the Arctic region, is now prone to mining and energy exploration due to latest technologies.
- Chemical contamination of the natural environment—Many of the metals found in gadgets poison water and land. Drinking water (groundwater and

---

83 http://narayanashramatapovanam.org/institution/nt-activities/socio-cultural-activities/139-outlawed-animal-slaughter-in-hindu-temples-.html, last accessed on 20 August 2014.
84 http://info.ornl.gov/sites/publications/files/Pub31202.pdf, last accessed on 29 April 2013.

surface water) are contaminated due to increased mining as advancements in mining technologies helps the miners to expand their areas of operations. Toxic waste is released to the natural environment through the usage of pesticides.

- With increasing demand for raw materials and the availability of technology to develop resource bases that will provide those raw materials, loss of habitat or alteration in habitat has become the norm. Construction of extractive infrastructure and infrastructure that supports them (pipelines) have caused physical disruption of wildlife habitats and this affects the migratory movement of animals and birds.

- Technologically driven industrial units may not align with a region's historical, visual and aesthetic sense.

- Technology-driven operations can result in over-extraction of natural resources (over-fishing), loss of livelihoods, and relocation of people.

- Risks in human health and safety due to exposure to hazardous chemicals.

Bioaccumulation, Bioconcentration, and Biomagnification

Absorption of a toxic substance in an organism, at a rate higher than the rate at which this toxic substance is lost from the body of the organism is referred to as *bioaccumulation*. As per the US Geological Survey, bioaccumulation refers to the 'biological sequestering of a substance at a higher concentration than that at which it occurs in the surrounding environment or medium. Also, the process whereby a substance enters organisms through the gills, epithelial tissues, dietary, or other sources.'[85] The Environmental Protection Agency (EPA) of USA defines Bioaccumulation as a 'general term describing a process by which chemicals are taken up by an organism either directly from exposure to a contaminated medium or by consumption of food containing the chemical.'[86]

Bioconcentration, though similar to bioaccumulation, is specifically related to the accumulation of the substance from water. In bioaccumulation, the substance can be taken from all sources, both dietary and non-dietary—air, food, water etc. EPA defines bioconcentration as 'a process by which there is a net accumulation of a chemical directly from an exposure medium into an organism.' It is also defined as the process of accumulation of water-borne chemicals by fish and other aquatic animals through non-dietary routes.[87]

Maersk Line, the largest container shipping company in the world by revenue, announced in 2013, that it achieved its 2020 target of reducing carbon emissions by 25% from 2007 levels, eight years ahead of schedule.

Biomagnification refers to the occurrence of higher concentration of a particular chemical substance in the higher levels of a food chain. Biomagnification is also

---

85 http://water.usgs.gov/nawqa/glos.html, last accessed on 4 December 2012.

86 http://www.epa.gov/oswer/riskassessment/glossary.htm#b, last accessed Accessed on 04 December 4, 2012.

87 Barron, M.G. 'Bioconcentration–Will Water-borne Organic Chemicals Accumulate in Aquatic Animals?' *Environmental Science & Technology*, Vol. 24(11) 1990, pp. 1612-1618.

referred to as bioamplification or biological magnification. The following are some of the definitions of biomagnification:

- The sequence of processes in an ecosystem by which higher concentrations of a particular chemical, like the pesticide DDT, are reached in organisms higher up the food chain, generally through a series of prey-predator relationships.
- Result of the process of bioaccumulation and biotransfer by which tissue concentrations of chemicals in organisms at one trophic level exceed tissue concentrations in organisms at the next lower trophic level in a food chain.[88]
- Biomagnification is the process whereby the tissue concentrations of a contaminant increase as it passes up the food chain through two or more trophic levels.[89]

Biomagnification can occur due to the low probability/impossibility of the accumulated chemical to be broken down or degrade during the process. Bioconcentration and bio-accumulation occur within an organization, while biomagnification occurs across various levels in the food chain. It has been noted that increased usage of DDT has resulted in decreased population of some of the carnivorous birds (bald eagles, peregrine falcons), while their population recovered following a ban on the usage DDT in agriculture, in America.[90] DDT has a half-life of 15 years, and Table 3.4 indicates the residue that remains through the years, during the process of using 100 kg of DDT.[91] The table indicates that, of the 100 kg of DDT used, almost 1 kg continues to be remain unbroken as residue, even after 100 years

TABLE 3.4 Residue remains during the process of 100 kg of DDT

Year	Amount remaining (kg)
0	100
15	50
30	25
45	12.5
60	6.25
75	3.13
90	1.56
105	0.78
120	0.39

---

88 http://www.epa.gov/oswer/riskassessment/glossary.htm, last accessed on 3 December 2012.

89 Nowell L.H., Capel P.D., Dileanis P.D., Pesticides in Stream Sediment and Aquatic Biota--Distribution, Trends, and Governing Factors: Boca Raton, Fla., CRC Press, *Pesticides in the Hydrologic System Series,* Vol. 4, p. 1040.

90 http://users.rcn.com/jkimball.ma.ultranet/BiologyPages/D/DDTandTrophicLevels.html, last accessed on 04 December 2012.

91 http://www.marietta.edu/~biol/102/2bioma95.html, last accessed on 04 December 2012.

GREENHOUSE EFFECT, GLOBAL WARMING, AND ANTHROPOGENIC CLIMATE CHANGE

Climate change refers to significant changes in measure related to climate. This could be changes in temperature, precipitation such as rainfall and snow, and changes in wind patterns. Earth's systems are always undergoing change and these changes could extend from decades to centuries (like ice ages). Such changes are usually gradual and are caused by natural factors like changes in sun's intensity. However, since the beginning of the industrial revolution, human beings have been repeatedly intervening in the rhythms of the nature through deforestation, burning of fossil fuels, reckless extraction of natural resources, and finally waste disposal. One such human-induced change ('anthropogenic') in climate is global warming.

Global warming is the increase in the temperature near the surface of the planet and atmosphere due to increased greenhouse gas emissions. Greenhouse gases such as CO_2, water vapour, methane, and nitrous oxide raise the temperature in lower atmosphere by trapping the heat. Citing an IPCC report, *The Telegraph* reported, 'The UN Intergovernmental Panel on Climate Change (IPCC) also said there was 95% likelihood that global warming is caused by human activities. That was the highest assessment so far from the IPCC, which put the figure at 90% in a previous report in 2007, 66% in 2001, and just over 50% in 1995.'[92] Considering that IPCC reports involves consultation and reviewing by a large number of scientists, IPCC estimations are conservative,[93] and there has been criticisms that these reports do not take into consideration the worst case scenarios.[94]

Increased emission of CO_2 is considered one of the main reasons for global warming. In 2010, the annual growth rate of atmospheric CO_2 was 2.36±0.09 parts per million, resulting in the atmospheric CO_2 concentration moving up to 389.6 ppm, 39% above the concentration that was prevalent during the beginning of the industrial revolution—about 278 ppm in 1750. In the first half of 2012, CO_2 concentration in Alaska touched 400 ppm and also in regions such as Greenland, Norway, Iceland, and Mongolia.[95] The present concentration is also the highest during at least the previous 800,000 years. The growth rate in carbondioxide was also the largest growth rate in the past decade. Global Carbon Project, an international collaboration of scientists tracking the carbon numbers, released this data. They mentioned, 'The average for the decade 2000–2009 was 1.9±0.1 ppm per year, 1.5±0.1 ppm for the decade 1990–1999, and 1.6±0.1 for the decade 1980–1989.'[96] Fig. 3.10 indicates the CO_2 concentrations measured at the Mauna Loa observatory, Hawaii.

---

92 http://www.telegraph.co.uk/earth/environment/climatechange/10248747/Climate-change-forecast-for-2100-is-floods-and-heat-...-and-its-mans-fault.html, last accessed on 01 September 2013.

93 http://e360.yale.edu/content/feature.msp?id=2698, last accessed on 06 October 2013.

94 http://e360.yale.edu/feature/has_the_un_climate_panel_now_outlived_its_usefulness/2696/, last accessed on 06 October 2013.

95 http://www.csmonitor.com/Science/2012/0531/Climate-change-Arctic-passes-400-parts-per-million-milestone, last accessed on 24 June 2012.

96 http://www.globalcarbonproject.org/carbonbudget/10/hl-full.htm#AtmosphericEmissions, last accessed on 07 December 2011.

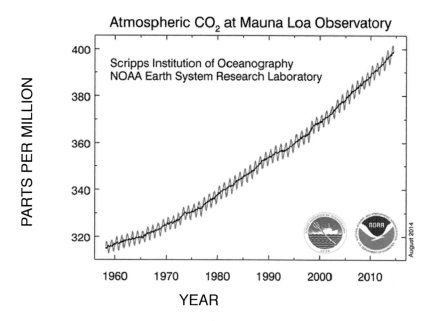

FIG. 3.10[97] CO_2 concentrations measured at the Mauna Loa observatory, Hawaii

An increased presence of atmospheric CO_2 caused due to human activity results in a change in temperature and weather patterns. Increased CO_2 emissions are driven by increasing burning of fossil fuels to supply power or to run automobiles. The biggest global contributors to CO_2 from burning fossil fuels were China (27%), United States (14%), European Union (10%), and India (6%). However, per capita emissions in India were extremely low as compared to China, the USA or many European countries (Table 3.5). Between 2012 and 2013, fossil fuel-based carbon emissions in China and India increased by 5.9% and 7.7%, respectively, while there was a decrease in fossil fuel-based carbon emissions in the USA and Europe, with a decrease of 3.7% and 1.8%.[98] Being one of the top three emitters of the world (Table 3.6), yet with one of lowest emissions per person, India has a significant role in leading the world in global negotiations related to climate and environment.

'Warming of the climate system is unequivocal, and since the 1950s, many of the observed changes are unprecedented over decades to millennia. The atmosphere and ocean have warmed, the amounts of snow and ice have diminished, sea level has risen, and the concentrations of greenhouse gases have increased,' states the IPCC

---

97 www.esrl.noaa.gov/gmd/webdata/ccgg/trends/co2_data_mlo.png, Image available in the public domain, last accessed on 2 August 2014.
98 http://www.globalcarbonproject.org/carbonbudget/13/files/UEA_CarbonBudget2013_UK.pdf, last accessed on 21 August 2014.

TABLE 3.5[99] Territorial Emissions per capita for some of the countries

Country	tCO$_2$/person	Country	tCO$_2$/person	Country	tCO$_2$/person	Country	tCO$_2$/person
Qatar	40	Poland	8.3	Mauritius	3.3	Zimbabwe	0.7
Kuwait	30	Iran	7.8	Jordan	3.1	Bhutan	0.7
Brunei	24	Malaysia	7.4	Syria	2.9	Sri Lanka	0.6
UAE	19	Denmark	7.4	Singapore	2.7	Bangladesh	0.4
Oman	19	Seychelles	7.3	Botswana	2.6	Cameroon	0.3
Bahrain	18	China	6.6	Egypt	2.6	Cambodia	0.3
Saudi Arabia	17	Spain	6.0	Peru	2.1	Afghanistan	0.3
USA	17	Hong Kong	5.5	Uruguay	2.0	Sudan	0.3
Australia	17	France	5.3	Macao	2.0	Kenya	0.3
Canada	15	Sweden	5.2	Indonesia	1.9	Myanmar	0.2
Russia	13	Portugal	5.0	Vietnam	1.8	Zambia	0.2
Norway	12	Switzerland	4.7	India	1.7	Nepal	0.1
Taiwan	11	Thailand	4.7	Costa Rica	1.7	Tanzania	0.1
Netherlands	10	Mongolia	4.3	Bolivia	1.6	Uganda	0.1
Israel	9.6	Turkey	4.3	Yemen	1.0	Burkna Faso	0.1
Japan	9.2	Maldives	3.5	Pakistan	0.9	Malawi	0.1
Germany	8.7	Cuba	3.5	Philippines	0.9	Somalia	0.1

TABLE 3.6[100] Countries leading in CO$_2$ emissions (kt)

Country	Kt	Country	Kt	Country	Kt
China	82,86,892	Germany	7,45,384	Saudi Arabia	4,64,481
USA	54,33,057	Iran	5,71,612	South Africa	4,60,124
India	20,08,823	South Korea	5,67,567	Mexico	4,43,674
Russia	17,40,776	Canada	4,99,137	Indonesia	4,33,989
Japan	11,70,715	UK	4,93,505	Brazil	4,19,754

Fifth Assessment Report.[101] National Climate Assessment and Development Advisory Committee (NCADAC), established under the US Department of Commerce supported through the National Oceanic and Atmospheric Administration (NOAA) states, 'U.S. average temperature has increased by about 1.5°F since 1895; more than 80% of this increase has occurred since 1980. The most recent decade was the nation's hottest on

---

99 Data Source: http://www.globalcarbonatlas.org/?q=emissions, last accessed on 21 August 2014.
100 http://data.worldbank.org/indicator/EN.ATM.CO2E.KT/countries, last accessed on 21 August 2014.
101 http://www.ipcc.ch/news_and_events/docs/ar5/ar5_wg1_headlines.pdf, last accessed on 06 October 2013.

record.'[102] It also states, 'Global climate is changing, and this is apparent across the US in a wide range of observations. The climate change of the past 50 years is primarily due to human activities, predominantly the burning of fossil fuels.'

Increases of temperature by every degree will be having serious repercussions on the planet (Fig. 3.11). Jeremy Rifkin, Economist, Founder and President of the Foundation on Economic Trends says, 'It (climate change) is impacting agriculture dramatically. This is the most dangerous period in human history. If we go up 3°C in a century, it takes us back 3 million years. The big deal here is the water cycle. Everything survives by the way this is conditioned. For every 1°C rise in temperature, the atmosphere absorbs 7% more precipitation from the ground and the water cycle gets unstable. The ecosystem can't catch up to this. Scientists at the UN say, we are in the early stages of the sixth extinction of life in 450 million years. That is unbelievable.'[103] The NCADAC report states that extreme weather and climate events have increased in recent decades, and there is evidence that many of these increases are related to human activities.[104] 'The climate negotiators heading to Copenhagen in December must accept the fact that the world's carbon emissions must eventually stop—and stop completely. There is no sustainable per capita carbon emission level because it is the total amount of carbon emitted that counts,' says Myles Allen, Climate Dynamics group—Department of Atmospheric, Oceanic, and Planetary Physics Department, University of Oxford.[105]

A study,[106] published in the journal '*Proceedings of the National Academy of Sciences of the United States of America*' (PNAS), found that a one degree Celsius rise in global temperature could result in a two to seven-fold increase in the frequency of storms of the magnitude of Hurricane Katrina, which caused a damage of US$81 billion and death of 1,833 people, in 2005. Quantifying future flood losses (due to climate change, growing population, etc.) in 136 largest coastal cities of the world, a research paper published in *Nature Climate Change* indicates that it would increase to US$52 billion per year by 2050, from the current levels of approximately US$6 billion per year.[107] With the number of storms on the increase, it has been found that 'Climate change that increases the frequency and intensity of storms results in more reproductive failure of Magellanic penguins, a

Mr Veerappa Moily, when he was the Petroleum Minister, Govt of India, announced every Wednesday of the week as 'Bus Day', where the ministry officials and public sector enterprises under the Petroleum Ministry, were suggested to use public transportation (such as bus or train), bicycles or car pools. This was done to promote fuel conservation.

102 http://ncadac.globalchange.gov/download/NCAJan11-2013-publicreviewdraft-chap1-execsum.pdf, last accessed on 17 January 2013.

103 Yashodhara Dasgupta, Suneera Tandon, India can lead this new revolution, BusinessWorld, 20 February 2012.

104 http://ncadac.globalchange.gov/download/NCAJan11-2013-publicreviewdraft-chap1-execsum.pdf, last accessed on 17 January 2013.

105 http://www.ipsnews.net/2009/10/climate-change-four-degrees-of-devastation/, last accessed on 1 March 2013.

106 http://www.pnas.org/content/early/2013/03/14/1209980110, last accessed on 30 March 2013.

107 Stephane Hallegatte, Colin Green, Robert J. Nicholls, Jan Corfee-Morlot, Future flood losses in major coastal cities, Nature Climate Change, 3, 2013, 802-806, Also available at http://www.nature.com/nclimate/journal/v3/n9/full/nclimate1979.html, last accessed on 1 September 2013.

pattern likely to apply to many species breeding in the region. Climate variability has already lowered reproductive success of Magellanic penguins and is likely undermining the resilience of many other species.'[108]

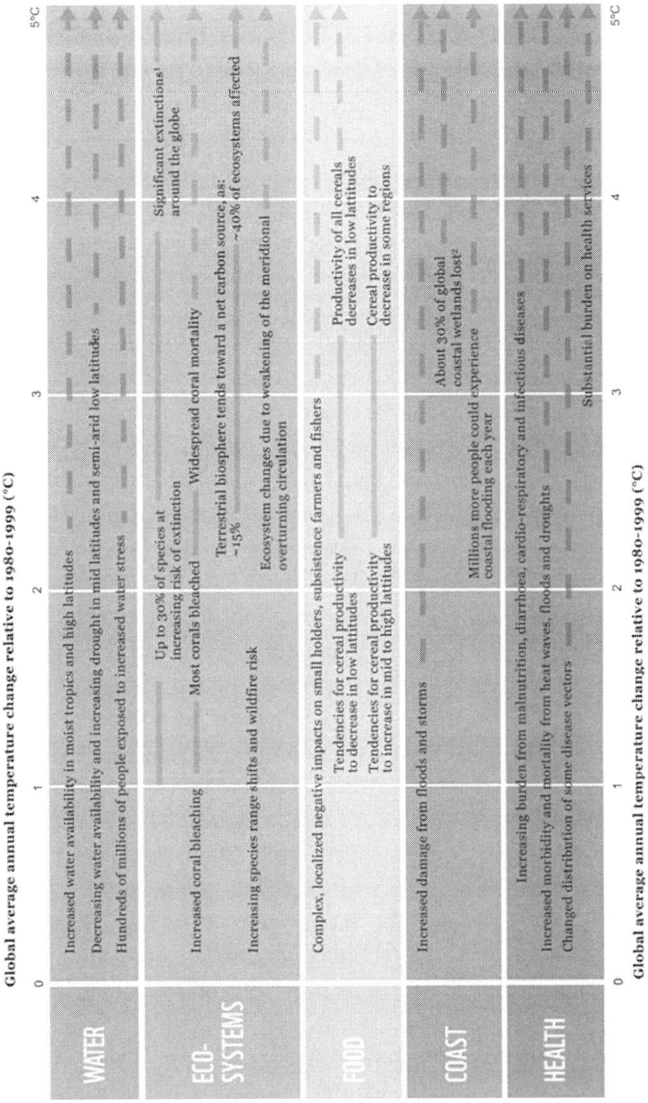

FIG. 3.11[109] Impact of temperature changes

108 P. Dee Boersma, Ginger A. Rebstock, Climate Change Increases Reproductive Failure in Magellanic Penguins, PLoS ONE 9(1), 2014, Also available at http://www.plosone.org/article/info%3Adoi%2F10.1371%2Fjournal.pone.0085602, last accessed on 19 February 2014.

109 WWF. 2012. *Living Planet Report 2012*. WWF International, Gland, Switzerland. Used with permission. Available at http://wwf.panda.org/about_our_earth/all_publications/living_planet_report/

Positive Feedback in Climatology

The mechanisms in a system, including that of climate, that amplify or diminish the effects of change are referred to as feedbacks. If the feedback amplifies the earlier process, it is referred to as a positive feedback while diminishing the earlier process is referred to as a negative feedback. As per Intergovernmental Panel on Climate Change (IPCC), 'An interaction mechanism between processes in the climate system is called a climate feedback, when the result of an initial process triggers changes in a second process that in turn influences the initial one. A positive feedback intensifies the original process, and a negative feedback reduces it.'[110]

Some of the examples of positive feedbacks could be as follows:

- A warmer atmosphere will result in increased melting of ice. As ice melts, darker surfaces (in comparison to ice) such as land and water start appearing. Darker surfaces have less reflective capability of sunlight as compared to ice. Due to the lowered reflective capability, sunlight gets retained near the surface of the planet. This contributes to a further increase in the atmospheric temperature, which contributes to a further increase in the melting of the ice, which contributes to an increase in warming, and the cycle continues.
- As atmospheric temperature increases, increased evaporation occurs. This results in increased greenhouse effect, leading to more warming. Increased warming contributes to an increase in the atmospheric temperature. The cycle continues.

Melting of Polar Ice: The Arctic and the Antarctic

The result of global warming has been clearly visible in the Polar Regions of the world. The Arctic region is warming up almost twice as the rest of the planet. It has been noted that while the temperature in the lower atmosphere has increased by 0.7°C, on a global average, since the 1950s, the temperature in Greenland has increased by 1.5°C. A 2°C increase in global temperature would result in the Arctic warming by 3–6°C. This is because the global climate system shifts heat from the much hotter equator to the colder polar region. The polar regions of Antarctica and Arctic region have been known for their massive ice shelves. This rising temperature has resulted in the loss of sea ice and melting of the ice sheets. 'Over the last two decades, the Greenland and Antarctic ice sheets have been losing mass, glaciers have continued to shrink almost worldwide, and Arctic sea ice and Northern Hemisphere spring snow cover have continued to decrease in extent,' says the IPCC Fifth Assessment Report.[111]

Wipro with second rank, Tata Consultancy Services with 11th rank, and Infosys with 19th rank were among the top 20 in the Newsweek's Green Rankings of Global Companies for 2012.

Snow and ice reflect more solar heat as compared to land or water. When snow and ice melts, it is replaced by water or land, that is darker as compared to snow and ice, and this

---

110 http://www.ipcc.ch/ipccreports/tar/wg1/518.htm, last accessed on 8 November 2012.
111 http://www.ipcc.ch/news_and_events/docs/ar5/ar5_wg1_headlines.pdf, last accessed on 6 October 2013.

dark surface absorbs more heat that causes further warming in the microclimate and thus more melting of snow and ice which results in more warming. This becomes a cyclical loop. Permafrost, which is the earth material at or below 0°C for two or more consecutive years, will start thawing due to an increase in temperature resulting in the release of methane (Methane traps heat 25 times in comparison to CO_2) and carbondioxide held within the permafrost. The increased release contributes to the warming. The ground ice in the permafrost will also melt. The last time Arctic permafrost thawed (55 million years ago), it contributed to a global temperature increase of 5°C. Inter-governmental Panel on Climate Change (IPCC) indicates that when the Polar Regions were significantly warmer as compared to what it is today, and this was 125,000 years ago, increased inflow of water resulted in the sea levels going up by 4–6 metres. Such an increase can result in inundation of megacities such as New York, London, Shanghai, Florida, Dubai, and Mumbai resulting in the displacement of millions of people. Brian Fagan, Author and Emeritus Professor of Anthropology at the University of California, Santa Barbara says, 'An estimated 17–40 million people in Bangladesh will be affected if current projections of the effects of sea level rise become reality. As the land is gradually lost to rising salinity and the ocean, with no prospect of recovery, there remains but one option for many Bangladeshis—to move away completely. The effects are somewhat akin to those experienced by small, low-lying islands like the Maldives or Tuvalu in the Central Pacific.'[112] The Fifth Assessment Report of IPCC states that 'the rate of sea level rise since the mid-19th century has been larger than the mean rate during the previous two millennia.'[113]

The satellite data from National Snow and Ice Data Centre of USA shows that ice in the Arctic has shrunk below the long-term average. The area covered by snow in the month of June is approximately one-fifth less than the area covered by snow in the 1960s. Since the satellite monitoring of sea ice started in 1979, it has been found that the sea ice has shrunk by 12% a decade. The summer sea ice is at its lowest levels for at least 2000 years. A melting Arctic may disrupt the mixing of the Oceanic currents—the mixing of the cold polar water with the warm water from the tropical region. *The Economist* magazine reported, 'Melting sea ice will not affect global sea levels, because floating ice displaces its own mass in seawater. But melting glaciers will.'[114] This will have a debilitating effect on the Arctic habitats.

Erik Conway Historian from NASA's Jet Propulsion Laboratory reports, 'Gravity data collected from space using NASA's Grace satellite show that Antarctica has been losing more than a hundred cubic kilometres (24 cubic miles) of ice each year since 2002.'[115] It has also been noted the ice loss in Antarctica is not a linear trend—a similar loss every year. Instead, the ice loss is increasing with time (Fig. 3.12). The warming of the Antarctic

112 http://e360.yale.edu/feature/as_extreme_weather_increases_bangladesh_braces_for_the_worst/2659/, last accessed on 11 June 2013.

113 http://www.ipcc.ch/news_and_events/docs/ar5/ar5_wg1_headlines.pdf, last accessed on 6 October 2013.

114 The Melting North, *The Economist*, Vol 403, Number 8789, June 16, 2012.

115 http://climate.nasa.gov/news/242, last accessed on 25 December 2012.

peninsula, 'among the highest seen anywhere on Earth in recent times' will result in the 'loss of a unique landscape and biota'[116]

It has been found that three penguin species – Adélie, Chinstrap, and Gentoo – that share the Western Antarctic Peninsula for breeding grounds have been affected due to the changes in the temperatures. Ecology, the journal of 'Ecological Society of America' states, 'Results from integrated analyses confirm that Pygoscelis adeliae (Adélie Penguins) are decreasing at almost all locations on the Antarctic Peninsula. Results also resolve previously contradictory studies and unambiguously establish that P. antarctica (Chinstrap Penguins), thought to benefit from decreasing sea ice, are instead declining regionally. In contrast, another open-water species, P. papua (Gentoo Penguin), is increasing in abundance and expanding southward.'[118] This is because the resident Gentoo population is able to adapt to the local conditions. They prefer areas with less sea ice, while the other two species require more sea ice for their life cycle.[119]

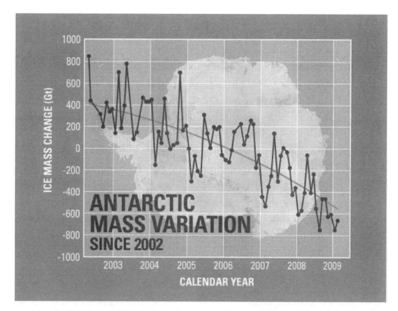

FIG. 3.12[117] Ice loss in Antarctica is increasing with time

116 http://www.antarctica.ac.uk//bas_research/science/climate/antarctic_peninsula.php, last accessed on 25 December 2012.

117 http://climate.nasa.gov/news/242, last accessed on 10 May 2014. Used with permission.

118 Heather J. Lynch, Ron Naveen, Philip N. Trathan, and William F. Fagan, "Spatially Integrated Assessment Reveals Widespread Changes in Penguin Populations on the Antarctic Peninsula", *Ecology*, Vol 93(6), 2012, pp. 1367-1377.

119 http://commcgi.cc.stonybrook.edu/am2/publish/General_University_News_2/Stony_Brook_University_Professor_Tracks_Antarctic_Penguin_Breeding_Cycles.shtml, last accessed on 19 January 2013.

In addition to Penguins, there are other species who are also affected by changes in polar ice. A study[120] has found that the rate of ice cover has a strong influence on harp seal stranding rates on the east coast of the USA from 1991 to 2010. The researchers state that 'Yearling seals are particularly vulnerable to decreases in ice cover, which could largely explain the observed increases in seal strandings during light ice years. Decreased ice cover and early thawing will force pups into the water earlier, potentially before they are able to fully fend for themselves.'[121]

Melting of Arctic sea ice makes life difficult for a number of other species including animals like Caribou. Researchers have suggested that 'sea ice decline has the potential to influence ecological dynamics in terrestrial Arctic systems'.[122] They have noted the possibility that the loss of Arctic ice leads to temperature increase in inlands resulting in the early emergence of plants that Caribou calves used to feed on. Though the plants were emerging earlier, the birth period for Caribou calves remained as usual, resulting in these calves missing on food. It has been noted that the date of emergence of these plants were advancing (becoming early) every year. As the gap between the birth of the Caribou calves and the plant species widens, it becomes increasingly difficult for the calves to find food, resulting in their death.

The cost of melting Arctic will be stratospheric. It has been calculated that the release of methane, occurring due to the thawing of permafrost beneath the East Siberian Sea/ East Siberian Arctic Shelf (northern Russia), will cost the world almost $60 trillion (Note: to be understood in the context that the size of the world economy in 2012 was about $70 trillion). This cost has been estimated based on the effect of greenhouse gas emissions on health, crops, the occurrence of extreme weather, and other climate risks and its impacts on infrastructure. Researchers suggest that 'the economic consequence will be distributed around the globe,' with almost 80% of them occurring 'in the poorer economies of Africa, Asia, and South America.'[123] The costs related to physical changes for the entire Arctic region would be significantly higher. Being aware of the importance of protecting the Arctic region, there has been a call from the global community to declare the Arctic as a global sanctuary. 'Save the Arctic' (http://www.savethearctic.org/), a campaign by Greenpeace International, an environmental not-for-profit organization, has received online support from more than 65 lakh citizens from around the world (Fig. 3.13).

120 Brianne K. Soulen, Kristina Cammen, Thomas F. Schultz, David W. Johnston, Factors Affecting Harp Seal (Pagophilus groenlandicus) Strandings in the Northwest Atlantic, PLoS ONE 8(7), 2013. Also available at http://www.plosone.org/article/info%3Adoi%2F10.1371%2Fjournal.pone.0068779, last accessed on 26 July 2013.

121 Brianne K. Soulen, Kristina Cammen, Thomas F. Schultz, David W. Johnston, Factors Affecting Harp Seal (Pagophilus groenlandicus) Strandings in the Northwest Atlantic, PLoS ONE 8(7), 2013. Also available at http://www.plosone.org/article/info%3Adoi%2F10.1371%2Fjournal.pone.0068779, last accessed on 26 July 2013.

122 Jeffrey T. Kerby, Eric Post, Advancing plant phenology and reduced herbivore production in a terrestrial system associated with sea ice decline, Nature Communications 4, October 2013, Also available at http://www.nature.com/ncomms/2013/131001/ncomms3514/full/ncomms3514.html, last accessed on 10 October 2013, doi: 10.1038/ncomms3514.

123 Gail Whiteman, Chris Hope, Peter Wadhams, Climate science: Vast costs of Arctic change, Nature, 499, July 2013, 401-403. Also available at http://www.nature.com/nature/journal/v499/n7459/full/499401a.html, last accessed on 16 August 2013.

FIG. 3.13[124] Greenpeace Poster about the 'Save the Arctic' campaign

Impact of Climate Change on India

As per a 2011 report[125] released by the Met Office Hadley Centre, UK, India may face a number of negative impacts due to human-induced climate change. It has been suggested that, by the end of the 21st century, India would witness increased frequency in extreme (and currently rare) floods. A general increase in mean and extreme precipitation is also expected. Climate change could also result in increased water stress and climate change could also worsen food security of the nation. It has been noted that, for the period 1970–2009, an increase in the number of hot days and a decrease in the number of cool days have been observed in India. There was also a decrease in the frequency of cool nights. There was also a decrease in the number of cool days. The World Bank has suggested that India could be facing extreme heat, changing rainfall patterns, increased draught conditions, falling water tables, glacier melt in the Himalayan region and its impact on various rivers, increased spread of diseases, malnutrition, and difficulties in areas related to Agriculture and Food Security, Energy Security, and Water Security.[126]

---

124 Used with permission from Greenpeace.
125 www.metoffice.gov.uk/media/pdf/7/i/India.pdf, last accessed on 5 May 2013.
126 http://www.worldbank.org/en/news/feature/2013/06/19/india-climate-change-impacts, last accessed on 21 August 2014.

DISASTER MANAGEMENT

Disaster management can involve the phases of (a) Mitigation, (b) Preparedness, (c) Response, and (d) Recovery. Mitigation involves risk identification and assessment practices. It involves knowing about the potential risks involved. Preparedness is about planning for the response actions when disaster occurs. This can also include getting the equipments ready and the practices to be followed during a disaster. Rehearsal and evacuation plans, maintenance of emergency communication and power systems, and installation of advanced warning systems are part of the preparedness phase. Following the disaster, the primary focus of the response phase would be on meeting the basic needs of the affected population. The phase will include search and rescue (SAR) practices to help people who are in distress, distribution of relief, creation of disaster impact reports, disposal of dead bodies and animal carcasses, restoration of transportation facilities and critical infrastructure (like water supply, power, telephone services), and arrangements for sanitation and hygiene. Recovery phase will include post-disaster assessment and assistance to the affected people. Reconstruction processes during this phase can be done by taking into consideration the local needs and usage of materials that are indigenous.

Disaster management strategies can include the following:

- Assessment of Risk—Ascertaining information related to the occurrence of disasters in a particular area in its historical past, collecting information about the geographical nature and the ecosystem of the region, information about the spread of the population in the area, and collecting information about potential hazards in the region could contribute to the assessment of risk
- Usage of appropriate technology for weather forecasting, disaster prediction and warning, and dissemination of information
- Awareness training to the general public and to the officials
- Institutional mechanisms to promote and support inter-department coordination among the governmental departments
- Usage of resources in the context of risk assessment
- Designing and construction of disaster-resistant buildings, and structural improvement of old buildings

There are certain measures that an individual can take for any disaster. This includes:

- Stocking one's home with emergency supplies—clean water that will meet the requirement for 3 days, non-perishable food for 3 days, first-aid kid, battery-operated radio, etc.
- Keeping the tanks of your vehicle filled so that the vehicle is ready during an emergency
- Monitoring weather updates through television or radio
- Turning off cooking gas, electricity, and water. Disconnecting electric appliances

Internet Joke

Somewhere in the universe, two planets met at a dinner table. The first planet asked: 'How are you?'

'Not so well', replied the second planet, 'as I've got the Homo Sapiens.'

- Post-disaster, drink only boiled or purified water.
- Do not intrude or interfere with damaged power-lines
- Ascertain whether the locality/home is in a disaster-prone area
- Create an emergency rescue plans, routes of evacuation, and know the route to rescue shelters
- If asked to evacuate by the authorities, take only the essential items

Through the Disaster Management Act, 2005, Government of India created a National Disaster Management Authority (NDMA), which is headed by the Prime Minister. The Act also entails the creation of State Disaster Management Authorities (SDMAs) that will be headed by the Chief Ministers and District Disaster Management Authorities (DDMAs) that will be headed by the district collectors. NDMA has been assigned the responsibility of devising the policies, plans, and guidelines for disaster management and the implementation of effective response during disasters. Data could be collected from land-based, sea-based, and space-based observational systems. This could include data from meteorological satellites, weather stations, rain gauges, wind profilers, radars located in ships and in the coasts, ocean data buoys, and reports from World Meteorological Organization and Indian Meteorological Department can aid in predictions.

Gruesome, narrow, and selfish as it may sound, researchers[127] have found that there is an increased possibility that people may migrate towards environment friendly attitudes when they are personally affected by a climatic event. Following the devastation caused by Hurricane Sandy in the East Coast region of the USA, the residents of New Jersey developed preference towards the politician who has environment-friendly views and perspectives. The researchers suggested that their study 'results suggest that direct experience with extreme weather can increase pro-environmentalism.' So, does that mean that we should desire for disasters to happen?

Floods

Methods of flood control include dams, self-closing flood barrier, river defence (bunds, and weirs), and coastal defence (beach nourishment, barrier islands, and sea walls). Dams that are constructed with the sole intention of flood control are referred to as dry dams. Dry dams allow the water to flow freely during normal conditions, and during flood conditions, hold back excess water, and release it in a controlled manner. During a flood situation, individuals are advised to stay away from floodwaters. As part of the flood response preparation, the authorities should locate high-rise places and communicate the existence of these locations to the citizens.

---

127 Laurie A. Rudman, Meghan C. McLean, Martin Bunzl, When Truth Is Personally Inconvenient, Attitudes Change: The Impact of Extreme Weather on Implicit Support for Green Politicians and Explicit Climate-Change Beliefs, Psychological Science, September 20, 2013, doi: 10.1177/0956797613492775; Abstract available at http://pss. sagepub.com/content/early/2013/09/19/0956797613492775.abstract, last accessed on 4 October 2013.

Earthquakes

The measures that should be undertaken to mitigate the impacts of an earthquake are as follows:

Prior to an earthquake

- Train the people on how to respond during an earthquake through conducting earthquake drills.
- Earthquake proof your building:
    - During earthquakes, more harm is caused by the movement of household items or man-made structures rather than the movement of earth. Hence, it is advisable to remove, move, fix, screw or latch items that are likely to break or cause injury should they fall on living beings.
    - Heavy objects could be moved to lower levels.
    - Objects should not stuff the exits and pathways.
- Always keep a first-aid kit and an emergency supply of food and water.

During an earthquake

- If you are inside a building, drop to the ground and take cover by getting under a sturdy table/desk/bench. Stay under cover till the shaking stops.
- If you are outside a building, move into the open, away from equipments, electricity wires, streetlights, trees, fences, and objects placed at a height. Stay in the open till the shaking stops.

Cyclones

Cyclones are known by various names—hurricane, tropical cyclone, typhoon, storm, or tropical depression, depending on the location of its occurrence and its strength. Cyclones are associated with thunders, strong winds and, heavy rains. These storm systems have a low pressure centre, referred to as an 'eye.' As with other natural phenomenon, the destructive effects of cyclones can be mitigated by forewarning systems that will help people to move away from the expected impact area (Fig. 3.14).

It is important to make the necessary arrangements for proper transportation through removing the obstructions and debris in the roads—fallen electric poles, trees, etc. Appropriate coordination between governmental machinery and non-governmental organizations should happen to ensure efficient distribution of government aid and aid from the public. Intra-governmental co-ordination among the police, irrigation, roads, agriculture, civil supplies, and medical departments should happen.

Landslides

Landslides are caused due to the change in the stability of a slope and this could be due to a number of factors, including groundwater pressure, loss of vegetation, and weakening of the toe of the slope. Landslides could also occur due to over-exploitation of groundwater, improper mining, construction of dams, and tunnelling. Human interventions aggravate the possibilities of a landslide occurring. This could include

FIG. 3.14[128] Traffic jam, caused due to the evacuation of citizens following a hurricane forewarning

interventions aggravate the possibilities of a landslide occurring. This could include agricultural and construction activities. Some of the regions of north-eastern part of India that has been termed as 'very high hazard zones' by the Geological Survey of India (GSI) have been denuded of protective vegetal cover, which has been reduced to less than 30 per cent, which is less than half of what would be considered desirable. This region was earlier known for its lush vegetation due to high rainfall. Landslide reduction and mitigation practices can include the following:

- Preparation of landslide hazard maps for hilly regions where human inhabitation is prevalent
- Preparation of landslide hazard maps of all river basins located in hilly regions
- Preventing settlements and infrastructure development in vulnerable areas
- Remediation practices includes:
  - Correction of slope geometry
  - Providing protection to the toe of the slope
  - Management of surface and sub-surface water
  - Reinforcing techniques such as nailing, bolting, anchoring, micro-piling, application of geo-grids
  - Afforestation

128 "Residents evacuating ahead of hurricane bret" by Dave Gatley - This image is from the FEMA Photo Library.. Licensed under Public domain via Wikimedia Commons - http://commons.wikimedia.org/wiki/File:Residents_evacuating_ahead_of_hurricane_bret.jpg#mediaviewer/File:Residents_evacuating_ahead_of_hurricane_bret.jpg, last accessed Accessed on 7 August 2014.

Figures 3.15 and 3.16[129] show details of loss events in 1980–2013

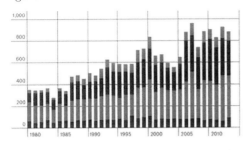

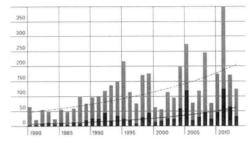

 Geophysical events: Earthquake, tsunami, volcanic eruption

 Meteorological events: Tropical storm, extratropical storm, convective storm, local storm

 Hydrological events: Flooding, mass movement

 Climatological events: Extreme temperatures, drought, wildfire

 Overall losses (2013 values)*

 Of which insured losses (2013 values)*

-- Trend: Overall losses

– Trend: Insured losses

* Values adjusted for inflation using the Consumer Price Index (CPI) of each country.

FIG. 3.15 Number of loss events 1980–2013

FIG. 3.16 Overall losses and unsured losses1980–2013 (in US$ bn)

COMMON RELIEF MATERIALS REQUIRED AFTER NATURAL DISASTERS

Table 3.7 lists some of the common relief materials required in the aftermath of weather phenomena that affect human populations.

Importantly, there should be enthusiastic professionals and volunteers to aid the affected people and also to take preventive steps to stop the spread of epidemics. Arrangements should be made to bury the dead bodies, lest it cause the spread of diseases.

TABLE 3.7 Common relief materials required in the aftermath of weather phenomena affect humans

Blankets and woolens	Bedspread and towels	Umbrellas and raincoats	Tarpaulins	Buckets and Mugs
Transportation vehicles	Soap, toothpaste	Mats	Footwear	Dress materials
Food grade non-toxic water bottles	Biscuits, noodles, corn flakes, baby food, powdered milk	Torchlight, batteries, lanterns	Candles, matchbox	Dry ration (rice, pulses, cooking oil)

(Contd)

129 Source: Munic Re

Mosquito repellents and mosquito nets	Cooking and eating Utensils - pans (*Tawa*), pressure cookers, wok (*Kadhai*), cooking pots, spoons, knife, plates, glass	Disinfectants, anti-septic creams, adhesive bandages, water purifier tablets, glucose, first-aid kits	Tent Materials	Drinking water facilities
Gunny bags	Cooking fuel	Communication equipment like mobile phones	Solar operated equipments	Alternate power sources like generators

CHAPTER SUMMARY

- Pollution refers to the contamination in a natural substance that interferes with the health of any living organism or cause harmful environmental effects.
- Air pollution refers to the contamination in air that interferes with the health of living organisms like human beings.
- Ozone layer, which occurs 15 miles above sea level, acts as a protective layer for earth by acting as a shield against the excessive ultra-violet radiation entering into the planet from outer space. Ozone layer is found as part of the stratosphere.
- Emissions of CO_2, sulphur dioxide, and nitrogen oxide react with water in atmosphere to produce acids that drop down during rain, snowfall, fog, dew, etc. Acid rain is harmful for plant and animal life and for infrastructure—it can corrode steel structures, erode statues, and peeling of paint.
- Drought is a situation that occurs when a region faces a deficiency in water supply, primarily due to lesser than average precipitation.
- Soil pollution is caused due to the usage of human made chemicals that are not natural to the soil.

- Marine pollution occurs due to the introduction of unnatural materials like pesticides, industrial and agricultural waste, and chemicals that are introduced to the oceans.
- Noise pollution is the displeasing sounds that can cause harm or affect the balance of human beings and other life forms. Most of the noise pollution is machine created.
- Thermal pollution refers to the deterioration of water quality due to changes in the water temperature that is primarily human induced.
- Similar to warm water pollution, release of unnatural cold water can also affect life. Release of cold water from reservoirs to rivers and streams that have warmer water; have resulted in the reduction/elimination of fish species of the region.
- Sustained nuclear fission is used to generate electricity through the production of heat. Usage of nuclear energy has been a consistent source of debate.
- Nuclear power generation, as well as research related endeavours, usually creates radioactive wastes as by-products. More than 95% of the total radioactivity produced during nuclear power generation is related to 'high-level' waste.

- Human population, which crossed seven billion in 2011, is expected to reach 9.2 billion by 2050. Increasing population will put stress on availability of drinking water, sanitation networks and will result in migration to cities and urbanisation.
- Absorption of a toxic substance in an organism, at a rate higher than the rate at which this toxic substance is lost from the body of the organism is referred to as bioaccumulation.
- Bioconcentration, though similar to bioaccumulation, is specifically related to the accumulation of the substance from water. In bioaccumulation, the substance can be taken from all sources, both dietary and non-dietary—air, food, water, etc.
- Biomagnification refers to the occurrence of higher concentration of a particular chemical substance in

the higher levels of a food chain. Biomagnification is also referred to as bioamplification or biological magnification.
- Disaster Management can involve the phases of (a) Mitigation, (b) Preparedness, (c) Response, and (d) Recovery.
- Methods of flood control include dams, self-closing flood barrier, river defence (bunds and weirs) and coastal defence (beach nourishment, barrier islands, and sea walls).
- Landslides are caused due the change in the stability of a slope and this could be due to a number of factors including groundwater pressure, loss of vegetation and weakening of the toe of the slope. Human interventions aggravate the possibilities of a landslide occurring.

KEYWORDS

- Acid rain
- Air pollution
- Anthropogenic climate change
- Bioaccumulation
- Bioconcentration
- Biomagnification
- Global warming

- Marine pollution
- Noise pollution
- Ozone depletion
- Soil pollution
- Thermal pollution
- Water pollution

EXERCISES

Multiple-choice Questions

1. _____ is harmful for plant and animal life and can corrode steel structures, erode statues and peeling of paint, affect soil chemistry.
   - (a) Acid rain
   - (b) Soil pollution
   - (c) Water pollution
   - (d) Degradation
2. _____ is a situation that occurs when a region faces a deficiency in water supply,

   primarily due to lesser than average precipitation.
   - (a) Drought
   - (b) Flood
   - (c) Erosion
   - (d) Social unrest
3. Dams are used for
   - (a) Power generation
   - (b) Drinking water supply

(c) Irrigation

(d) All of these

4. _____ occurs due to the introduction of unnatural materials like pesticides, industrial, and agricultural waste, and chemicals that are introduced to the oceans.

(a) Air pollution

(b) Noise pollution

(c) Soil pollution

(d) Marine pollution

5. _____ refers to the deterioration of water quality due to changes in the water temperature that is primarily human induced.

(a) Air pollution

(b) Noise pollution

(c) Thermal pollution

(d) Marine pollution

6. Absorption of a toxic substance in an organism, at a rate higher than the rate at which this toxic substance is lost from the body of the organism is referred to as

(a) Bioaccumulation

(b) Biodegradation

(c) Bioconcentration

(d) Biomagnification

7. _____ though similar to bioaccumulation, is specifically related to the accumulation of the substance from water

(a) Bioaccumulation

(b) Biodegradation

(c) Bioconcentration

(d) Biomagnification

8. _____ refers to the occurrence of higher concentration of a particular chemical substance in the higher levels of a food chain.

(a) Bioaccumulation

(b) Biodegradation

(c) Bioconcentration

(d) Biomagnification

9. _____ can involve the phases of (a) Mitigation, (b) Preparedness, (c) Response, and (d) Recovery

(a) Disaster management

(b) Biodegradation

(c) Bioconcentration

(d) Air pollution

10. _____ are caused due the change in the stability of a slope and this could be due to a number of factors including groundwater pressure, loss of vegetation and weakening of the toe of the slope.

(a) Landslides

(b) Flood

(c) Drought

(d) Famine

Short Answer Questions

1. Define pollution and its types.
2. Mention any three nuclear power accidents.
3. Describe one of the successful models in water resource management.
4. Describe marine pollution and algal bloom.
5. List any common ten relief materials required immediately after natural disasters.

Long Answer Questions

1 Write an essay about the impacts of the anthropogenic climate change.
2. What are the practices adopted to reduce human-animal conflict?
3. Differentiate bioaccumulation, bio-concentration, and biomagnification.

Reflective Question

1. The following is an excerpt from 'Living Oneness: Restoring Wholeness in a Fragmented World', a study guide released by 'A Global Oneness Project'.

> The death toll of the December 2004 tsunami caused by the Indian Ocean earthquake with an epicenter off the coast of Sumatra, Indonesia was near 230,000. But the Moken people, the 2,000–3,000 indigenous sea gypsies who reside where the tsunami was most destructive, survived with only the death of one boy. These ancient people know the sea, and spend seven or eight months a year living on their boats - which

> they identify as extensions of their own human bodies. It was their intimate relationship with the sea and its life that alerted them to the coming tsunami and inspired a retreat to higher ground or out beyond the waves that saved their population.

The story of the Moken captivated the imagination of many. How did they know the tsunami was coming? What wisdom do they draw upon that alerted them? What sense perceptions were at work?[130]

Recommended Books

1. Jean Giono, *The Man Who Planted Trees*, Shambhala, 1953.
2. Ramachandra Guha, *How Much Should a Person Consume?: Environmentalism in India and the United States*, University of California Press, 2006.
3. Peter M. Senge, Bryan Smith, Sara Schley, Joe Laur, Nina Kruschwitz, *The Necessary Revolution: How Individuals And Organizations Are Working Together to Create a Sustainable World*, Crown Business, 2008.
4. Colin Beavan, *No Impact Man*, Farrar, Straus and Giroux, 2009.

Videos on Worldwide Web

1. *Why the Oceans Matter?* Available at http://www.youtube.com/watch?v=ycHt8De_S1w (Duration: 3 minutes).
2. 3D volumetric representation of CO_2 emissions emitted by New York City. Available at http://www.youtube.com/watch?v=DtqSIplGXOA (Duration: 3 minutes).
3. *Trash in the deep sea: Bringing a hidden problem to light.* Available at http://www.youtube.com/watch?v=mOZngsJU2k0 (Duration: 4 minutes).
4. *A Song of our Warming Planet.* Available at http://www.youtube.com/watch?v=5t08CLczdK4 (Duration: 4 minutes).
5. *The Power of Water - Ed Begley, Jr. in conversation with Sadhguru Jaggi Vasudev.* Available at http://www.youtube.com/watch?v=sbUtgWPBGjY (Duration: 9 minutes).
6. *Losing the Dark*, Available at http://www.youtube.com/watch?v=dd82jaztFIo (Duration: 6 minutes).

Answers to Mutiple-choice Questions:

1(a)   2(a)   3(d)   4(d)   5(c)   6(a)   7(c)   8(d)   9(a)   10(a)

---

130 http://www.globalonenessproject.org/sites/default/files/education/resources/livingonenessstudyguide.pdf, last accessed on 28 May 2013. Used with permission.

4 NATURAL RESOURCES MANAGEMENT

Our ancestors viewed the earth as rich and bountiful, which it is. Many people in the past also saw nature as inexhaustibly sustainable, which we now know is the case only if we care for it. It is not difficult to forgive destruction in the past, which resulted from ignorance. Today, however, we have access to more information, and it is essential that we re-examine ethically what we have inherited, what we are responsible for, and what we will pass on to coming generations. "[1]

Tenzin Gyatso
His Holiness, the 14th Dalai Lama

After reading the chapter, the reader will be able to understand the following:
- Importance of renewable energy in meeting the growing energy needs of the world
- Various types of renewable energy markets
- Concept of water footprint
- Importance of indigenous water harvesting systems

ENERGY RESOURCES AND GROWING ENERGY NEEDS

On the last Saturday of every March, World Wide Fund for Nature (WWF) organizes Earth Hour, a lights-off event that encourages people and organizations to switch off their non-essential lights for one hour, and to adopt longer-lasting sustainable changes. Many have criticized the necessity of such events in a country like India where many cities have daily power shortages that last for many hours and many villages that are yet to see electrification. However, energy demand and production in India has been on an increase, driven by an energy-driven lifestyle, increased number of villages being connected to the electricity grid, and demand from the industrial sector. A similar surge in energy demand and consumption is witnessed across the globe, as people of developing countries are adopting an increasingly energy-driven lifestyle. The energy production and consumption between years 1990 and 2010 along with the projections for 2015 and 2020 are shown in Table 4.1, as per the BP 'Statistical Review of the World Energy 2012'.

---

1 http://www.dalailama.com/messages/environment/an-ethical-approach, last accessed on 28 March 2013.

TABLE 4.1 Energy production and consumption between 1990 and 2020

Units in million tonnes oil equivalent/year	1990	1995	2000	2005	2010	2015*	2020*
Total renewables production in the world	28.1	36.1	51.2	83.1	158.6	264.1	432.7
Total energy production in the world	**8206.5**	**8592.7**	**9387.0**	**10867.2**	**12145.6**	**13565.8**	**14685.1**
Percentage of renewables, as part of total energy production	0.3	0.4	0.5	0.8	1.3	1.9	2.9
Percentage increase in energy production, every five years		4.7	9.2	15.8	11.8	11.7	8.3
Percentage increase in renewables production, every five years		28.5	41.8	62.3	90.9	66.5	63.8

Note: Part of the data used in the aforementioned table has been sourced from *BP Statistical Review of World Energy 2012.*[2]

*Data used for years 2015 and 2020 are projections.

Demand and Supply of Fossil Fuels

The production and consumption of fossil-based fuels is shown in the following table (Table 4.2).

TABLE 4.2 Fossil-based fuel's consumption and production

Million tonnes oil equivalent/year	1990	1995	2000	2005	2010	2015 *	2020 *
Total oil consumption	3141.5	3262.8	3562.4	3888.5	3968.8	4076.6	4261.8
Total natural gas consumption	1769.5	1927	2176.2	2511.2	2858.1	3331.6	3684.7
Total coal consumption	2220.3	2256.2	2399.7	3012.9	3555.8	4053.3	4396.7

(Contd)

2 http://www.indiaenvironmentportal.org.in/files/file/statistical_review_of_world_energy_full_report_2012.pdf, last accessed on 30 August 2014. Used with permission.

Total oil production	3171.8	3284.4	3611.8	3906.6	3913.7	4089.4	4262.8
Total natural gas production	1790.2	1910.6	2178.7	2507.8	2880.9	3325.5	3712.5
Total coal production	2267.1	2266	2352.5	3064.4	3731.4	4252	4426

Note: Data used in the aforementioned table has been sourced from *BP Statistical Review of World Energy 2012*.[3]

*Data used for years 2015 and 2020 are projections.

Problems Related to Demand and Supply of Fossil Fuel-based Energy

As per the estimates made by International Energy Agency (IEA) in mid-2011, energy related carbon dioxide emissions in 2010 were the highest in history.[4] Of the estimated CO_2 emissions, 44 per cent came from coal, 36 per cent was contributed by oil, and 20 per cent from natural gas. On a per capita basis, OECD countries collectively emitted 10 tonnes annually, while China and India emitted 5.8 tonnes and 1.5 tonnes respectively. While 40 per cent of total emissions came from OECD countries, they accounted only for 25 per cent growth emissions as compared to 2009. Non-OECD countries such as China and India saw stronger increases in emissions as their economic growth accelerated. As per the IEA's *World Energy Outlook 2011*, global energy demand is bound to increase one-third between 2010 and 2035. Of this, 50 per cent will be powered by China and India.

Over the past decade, from 2000–2010, coal accounted for nearly half of the increase in global energy use (see Fig. 4.1).

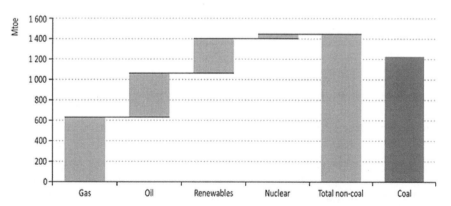

FIG. 4.1[5] Incremental world primary energy demand of fuel in 2000–2010

3 http://www.indiaenvironmentportal.org.in/files/file/statistical_review_of_world_energy_full_report_2012.pdf, last accessed on 30 August 2014. Used with permission.

4 http://www.iea.org/newsroomandevents/news/2011/may/name,19839,en.html, last accessed on 30 August 2014. Used with permission.

5 http://www.worldenergyoutlook.org/media/weowebsite/2011/key_graphs.pdf, last accessed on 4 May 2014. Used with permission.

India has a unique situation when it comes to energy management. Despite almost 40 crore people in India living without access to electricity, electricity shortage in the country is estimated at 2535 GW.[6] In the next decade, the electricity requirement in India is expected to more than double. Significant amount of electricity is produced from fossil-based fuel sources like petroleum products. Through imports, they achieve 80 per cent of their oil needs, which is a strategic risk. However, using fossil-based fuel sources for energy needs also has high ecological risks, including contributing to climate change.

Renewable and Non-renewable Energy Sources

Renewable energy sources refers to those energy sources that last for a relatively longer period of time, like thousands of years, unlike non-renewable energy sources that deplete over centuries or sometimes even decades. Examples of renewable energy sources include wind power, solar energy, tidal waves, etc. These sources rely on naturally existing energy flows and their usage is non-depleting or they get replaced at a rate faster than their usage. Non-renewable energy sources are primarily petroleum reserves or coal reserves, and extraction of these sources results in a permanent reduction in their availability. Renewable energy sources are also referred to as alternative energy and their capture and creation are usually more environment-friendly than the non-renewable energy sources.

Market and Usage of Alternate Energy Sources

Alternate energy sources like solar, wind, tidal, and biomass do not produce emissions like fossil fuel industries and they are natural sources for generation. European Union has set a target of '20-20-20', which indicates that its objective is to reduce carbon dioxide emissions by 20 per cent and generate 20 per cent of its energy needs from renewable energy by 2020, with the current renewable energy generation being just seven per cent. Countries like US, China, and India are also implementing plans that focus on increased power generation from renewable energy. *The Economist* says, 'Private insurers say that last year (2012) was the second-most-expensive in American history for disasters related to climate change, costing them $139 billion. But private insurance paid only a quarter of these costs, leaving taxpayers to cover the rest. By comparison, funding renewable energy properly seems rather cheap.'[7] With organizations improving on their sustainability related practices, one can find many companies sourcing only electricity made from renewable sources (see Table 4.3).

6 http://mnre.gov.in/file-manager/UserFiles/presentations-pwc-workshop-06092012/MNRE.pdf, last accessed on 24 December 2012.

7 http://www.economist.com/news/united-states/21579046-wind-power-doing-well-it-still-relies-irregular-and-short-term-subsidies-blown, last accessed on 12 June 2013.

TABLE 4.3[8]   Top 25 organizations in USA that use only green power

Name of the organization	Annual power usage (kWh)	Power providers	Green power resources
Intel Corporation	3,102,050,000	Sterling Planet, PNM, and On-site Generation	Biogas, biomass, small-hydro, solar, and wind
Kohl's Department Stores	1,536,529,000	Nexant, Sterling Planet, Renewable Choice Energy, 3Degrees, and On-site Generation	Solar
Staples	635,951,792	Renewable Choice Energy, 3Degrees, Sterling Planet, Avista Utilities, Pacific Power, Tennessee Valley Authority, Portland General Electric, On-site Generation, and Florida Power and Light	Biogas, solar, and wind
Unilever	514,825,000	Renewable Choice Energy, and 3Degrees	Biomass and wind
District of Columbia	459,000,000	Washington Gas Energy Services	Wind
TD Bank, NA	270,866,241	Renewable Choice Energy and On-site Generation	Solar and wind
U.S. Environmental Protection Agency	247,496,852	Sterling Planet, Pacific Power, 3Degrees, On-site Generation, and Minnesota Power	Biogas, Biomass, Solar, and Wind
DHL	209,871,000	JustGreen	Wind
State Street Corporation	205,000,000	Element Markets	Wind
Pearson	175,000,000	3Degrees	Geothermal, small-hydro, solar, and wind
Metropolitan Pier and Exposition Authority	160,874,258	Sterling Planet	Wind
Georgetown University	152,370,500	Hess Energy Marketing	Various
Deutsche Bank	150,000,000	3Degrees	Wind
NYSE Euronext	126,169,000	Green Mountain Energy	Wind
Steelcase Inc.	121,067,000	Renewable Choice Energy	Wind

(Contd)

8 http://www.epa.gov/greenpower/toplists/partner100.htm, last accessed on 12 April 2014, inputs from EPA are made available in the public domain.

TABLE 4.2 *(Contd)*

Name of the organization	Annual power usage (kWh)	Power providers	Green power resources
The World Bank Group	118,881,000	Nexant	Wind
Washington Real Estate Investment Trust	116,970,368	Renewable Choice Energy	Wind
Drexel University	96,678,000	Community Energy	Solar and wind
Herman Miller Inc.	86,500,000	Element Markets, Native Energy, and Wolverine Power Marketing Cooperative	Biomass and wind
SAP America	86,000,000	Renewable Choice Energy	Wind
Powdr	80000000	Renewable Choice Energy	Wind
Keurig Green Mountain, Inc.	78,819,183	Native Energy and On-site Generation	Solar and wind
Mohawk Fine Papers Inc.	78,000,000	Nexant, Renewable Choice Energy, Carbon Solutions Group, and Greenlight Energy	Wind
Datapipe, Inc.	75,189,998	Noble Americas Energy Solutions	Various
Port of Portland	75,070,343	NextEra Energy Resources and On-site Generation	Solar and wind

As per the Ministry of New and Renewable Energy, Government of India, India's total installed capacity of power generation, by the end of October 2012, was 2,10,544 MW. Of this, the contribution of renewable energy was about 12.5 per cent (26,267 MW). In the past one decade, there has been a growth of more than 666 per cent in the renewable energy capacity of India, from 3.9 GW in 2002–03 to 29.9 GW in January 2013.[9,10] The government has made a target of generating 30,000 MW of renewable energy as part of the 12th five year plan period. As per Bloomberg New Energy Finance, clean energy investment in India outpaced the rest of the world, primarily driven by the increased cost-competitiveness in wind and solar projects.[11] In 2011, clean energy investments in India reached $10.3 billion, a 52 per cent increase from the previous year. The most efficiently operated renewable energy projects in India produce power at a cost that varies from ₹2.70 to ₹4.00 per kilowatt-hour (kWh), compared to coal energy that cost ₹1.90 to ₹4.80 kWh.[12]

Solar   Solar energy is considered to be an abundant form of energy. The global energy demand in 2020 is expected to be 20 TW, which is only 0.02 per cent of the

---

9 http://www.rtcc.org/2013/10/28/indias-solar-capacity-passes-2gw-milestone/, last accessed on 7 February 2014.

10 http://mnre.gov.in/mission-and-vision-2/achievements/, last accessed on 7 February 2014.

11 http://www.bnef.com/PressReleases/view/186, last accessed on 22 August 2012.

12 Narasimhan, T E 2012, Affordable wind energy not just hot air, The Economic Times, Chennai, 20 August 2012.

annual irradiation of sunlight to earth's surface, at 120,000 TW. This is also equivalent to the energy produced by approximately 120 million coal power plants. It is thus noted that one hour of solar irradiation on this planet is enough to power humanity's energy needs for 2020. It has also been assessed that this 20 TW can be produced in a plot of 830 square kilometre with 1600 hours of solar exposure, with a conservative 15 per cent efficiency.[13] Electricity is produced from solar energy through photo-voltaic cells or through solar-thermal techniques, which uses heaters and turbines. In addition to producing electricity, solar energy is also used for a number of other activities including heating, cooking, etc. (See Fig. 4.2).

A press release by the Solar Energy Industries Association mentions that solar energy installations in USA soared by 109 per cent in 2011 to 1855 megawatts. US Solar Market Insight forecast 2012 as a strong year with installations reaching more than 2800 megawatts. Beyond 2012, the report forecasts installations to continue their ascendancy at a compound annual growth rate of 30 per cent through 2016.

One of the national missions under India's National Action Plan on climate change is Jawaharlal Nehru National Solar Mission (JNNSM). JNNSM aims to deploy 22,000 MW of solar power by 2022 (see Table 4.4).

FIG. 4.2 [14] The solar bowl used in the solar kitchen at Auroville, India. It concentrates sunlight on a movable receiver and produces steam that is used for cooking

13 Roland Berger Strategy Consultants, *Green Growth, Green Profit*, First Edition, Palgrave Macmillan, Basingstoke, 2011.
14 Photo by John Harper, Image Source: http://en.wikipedia.org/wiki/File:Auroville_Solar_Bowl.JPG, Accessed on August 2, 2014.

TABLE 4.4 Targets of JNNSM

	Target for phase I (2010-13)	Target for phase II (2013-17)	Target for phase III (2017-22)
Solar collectors	7 million sq. metre	15 million sq. metre	20 million sq. metre
Off-grid solar application	200 MW	1000 MW	2000 MW
Grid solar power (large plants, rooftop and distribution grid plants)	1100 MW	4000–10,000 MW	20,000 MW
Solar lighting system	5 million	10 million	20 million

Source: Ministry of New and Renewable Energy, Government of India.[15]

There has been a significant growth in solar power installations in India. Cumulatively, it has been 3 MW, 11 MW, 36 MW, and 930 MW in years 2008–09, 2009–10, 2010–11, and 2011–12 respectively.[16] It has been noted that feed-in-tariffs, in 2011, for large-scale solar power plants (5 MW and above) has reduced to an average of ₹8.77 per kWh from ₹18.00 per kWh in 2009. With the prices dropping by half, this is among the lowest tariffs anywhere in the world, primarily contributed by competitive bidding and a sharp fall in the process of solar PV globally. KPMG estimates that *grid parity* (the price at which the cost of power sourced from a renewable energy source is less than or equal to the price of purchasing power from the electricity grid) for utility scale solar power in India could happen by 2017[17] (see Table 4.5). This estimation is based on an expected annual increase of 4-5.5% on the cost of conventional electricity and a 5–7% annual decline in solar power prices driven by increasing economies of scale in manufacturing and R&D driven technology advancements leading to improved conversion efficiency. Grid parity for retail level projects is expected to happen earlier, depending on the tariffs charged for various consumer categories. KPMG also estimates that the total solar market potential in India will be approximately 12,500 MW by 2016–17. In September 2012, a company won a 25 MW solar project in the state of Odisha, India, by quoting a tariff of ₹7.00 a unit, the lowest in the Indian solar power industry.[18] Deutsche Bank states that 'grid parity has been reached in India despite the high cost of capital of 10–12%'.[19] Cost of solar power, in the global markets, including that of USA (see Table 4.6) is also expected to reduce.

---

15 http://mnre.gov.in/file-manager/UserFiles/presentations-pwc-workshop-06092012/MNRE.pdf, last accessed on 23 December 2012.

16 http://mnre.gov.in/file-manager/UserFiles/presentations-pwc-workshop-06092012/MNRE.pdf, last accessed on 24 December 2012.

17 http://www.kpmg.com/IN/en/IssuesAndInsights/ArticlesPublications/Documents/Rising-sun-2-full.pdf, last accessed on 5 May 2014.

18 http://www.thehindubusinessline.com/industry-and-economy/article3954786.ece, last accessed on 2 October 2012.

19 http://www.pv-magazine.com/news/details/beitrag/deutsche-bank--sustainable-solar-market-expected-in-2014_100010338, last accessed on 6 March 2013.

TABLE 4.5[20] Solar PV tariff's in India

Solar PV Tariff's (in ₹)	Round-I (Dec-2010)	Round-II (Dec-2011)
Highest tariff	12.75	9.44
Lowest tariff	10.95	7.49
Median tariff	12.12	8.91
Marginal retail power tariff	5.50–7.50	

TABLE 4.6[21] Total installed PV system prices and costs of electricity (global average)

Year	System price ($/W)	LCOE range (cents/kWh)
2007	$7.20	24–42
2008	$7.00	23–41
2009	$5.12	17–31
2010	$4.55	15–28
2011	$3.47	12–23
2012	$2.58	9–18
2013*	$2.33	8–17
2014*	$2.10	7–15
2015*	$1.89	6–14
2016*	$1.75	6–14
2017*	$1.61	6–13
2018*	$1.49	5–12
2019*	$1.38	5–12
2020*	$1.27	4–11
2021*	$1.17	4–11
2022*	$1.07	4–10

*Data used for the years are an estimation. Discount rate is assumed at 4 per cent, capacity factor at 16–26 per cent, and O&M cost at $6–60/kW.

Wind In Denmark, 28 per cent of the country's electricity supply is met by wind power. As per the statistics of World Wind Energy Association[22], a non-profit association representing the wind power sector, the worldwide wind capacity surpassed 318 gigawatt (318,530 megawatt) by the end of 2013. About 72 per cent of the total

20 http://www.kpmg.com/IN/en/IssuesAndInsights/ArticlesPublications/Documents/Rising-sun-2-full.pdf, last accessed on 5 May 2014. Used with permission.
21 Source: Clean Energy Trends 2013, http://www.cleanedge.com/sites/default/files/CETrends2013_Final_Web.pdf, last accessed on 2 October 2013. Used with permission.
22 http://www.wwindea.org

global wind capacity was represented by the five top wind markets—China, USA, Germany, Spain, and India. 34% of the energy produced by Denmark comes from wind power.[23]

In countries like India, a situation has already reached where the cost of wind power is now at par with the price of coal-fired energy. On average, the generation cost for wind energy would be ₹3.5–3.6 per kWh while for coal it should be ₹4 per kWh. Almost 30 per cent of electricity demand of Tamilnadu is met by wind energy.[24] While the Centre for Wind Energy Technology (CWET), Chennai, has calculated India's wind energy potential between 49,000 MW (49 GW) and 102,000 MW (102 GW),[25] other experts have postulated the potential between 2000–3000 GW.[26] Roland Berger Strategy Consultants[27] estimates that India's wind power capacity could reach 40 GW by 2022. India, with its vast 7000 mile long coastline also has significant off-shore wind power potential.

There have been significant improvements in wind energy technology. 'Today's turbines have, on average, a technical capacity eight times larger than they had in 1990, and generate 17 times more power,' says an article in *The Economist*.[28]

Other renewable energy sources like tidel and bio-mass   It has been estimated that India has a potential of generating about 8000 MW tidal energy. Approximately 7000 MW of this potential exists in the Gulf of Khambhat, Gujarat, 1200 MW in the Gulf of Kutch, Gujarat, and approximately 100 MW in the Gangetic delta in the Sunderbans region of West Bengal. Worldwatch Institute has reported that 836 million people in India rely on traditional biomass for energy needs.[29] Ministry of New and Renewable Energy (MNRE) of Government of India has estimated that 32 per cent of the total primary energy needs are from biomass while 70 per cent of the country's population depends on biomass for their energy needs.[30] Biomass refers to organic materials that could be used for generating energy through their usage as fuel. It could also refer to biodegradable wastes. Some of the biogas materials include bagasse, coffee and tea waste, coconut shells, cotton stalk, de-oiled cakes, groundnut shells, hay/straw, jute wastes, husk of rice and soya, paper mill waste, saw dust, wild bushes, etc. The availability of biomass in the country is about 500 million metric tonnes on an annual basis. Surplus biomass availability is 120–150 million metric tonnes annually and this could offer a power generation potential of 18,000 MW. It has also been estimated

23 http://www.wwindea.org/webimages/WWEA_WorldWindReportKeyFigures_2013.pdf, last accesssed on 1 September 2014.

24 Narasimhan, T E 2012, Affordable wind energy not just hot air, *The Economic Times*, Chennai, 20 August 2012.

25 http://www.cwet.tn.nic.in/html/departments_ewpp.html, last accessed on 22 December 2012.

26 http://wwindea.org/home/index.php?option=com_content&task=view&id=352&Itemid=40, last accessed on 22 December 2012.

27 Roland Berger Strategy Consultants, *Green Growth, Green Profit*, First Edition, Palgrave Macmillan, Basingstoke, 2011.

28 http://www.economist.com/news/united-states/21579046-wind-power-doing-well-it-still-relies-irregular-and-short-term-subsidies-blown, last accessed on 12 June 2013.

29 http://www.worldwatch.org/energy-poverty-remains-global-challenge-future, last accessed on 22 January 2013.

30 http://www.mnre.gov.in/schemes/grid-connected/biomass-powercogen/, last accessed on 22 January 2013.

In 2013, France decided to turn off lights of all non-residential buildings an hour after the last worker leaves. Exterior and shop window lighting has to be turned off by 1.00 am. Shop window lighting can be switched on only from 7.00 am or an hour before opening time. French government hopes that this would help in reducing the negative impact artificial lights have on ecosystems and wildlife, and sleep patterns of human beings.

that an additional 5000 MW could be generated through bagasse-based cogeneration in the sugar mills of the country.[31] MNRE mentions that 130 biomass power projects with a potential of 999 MW and 158 bagasse cogeneration projects in sugar mills with a potential of 1666.0 MW have been installed in India and feeds power to the grid.[32]

Compressed natural gas (CNG) Though CNG is fossil-fuel based, it is considered a cleaner fuel as it emits lesser amount of pollutants like carbon dioxide, carbon monoxide, sulphur oxides, nitrogen oxides, and particulate matter, in comparison with other fuels like petrol. It is made by compressing natural gas to less than 1 per cent of its volume at standard atmospheric pressure.

Waste-to-energy It is estimated that 69 million (690 lakh) tonnes of solid waste is generated annually from urban India. This is approximately 0.5 kilogram of municipal solid waste (MSW) per person per day.[33] A report by Global Initiative for Restructuring Environment and Management (GIREM), an industry body states that an Indian, on an average, is generating about 500 gm of waste every day, while urban India is generating 703 lakh tonnes of solid waste annually.[34] According to Energy Alternatives India, a Chennai based consulting firm, urban India generates 55 million (550 lakh) tonnes of municipal solid waste and 38 billion litre of sewage on an annual basis.[35] One of the ways through which an attempt is made to dispose waste is by burning them. This is known as incineration and involves the combustion of organic substances that are part of the waste materials. During the process of Waste-to-Energy (WE), electric energy or heat energy is created from incineration. This energy recovery process is also known as Energy from Waste (EW). Though incineration can be one of the options to manage waste, it is not considered by many to be an effective waste management process.[36] What is recommended is the prevention and minimization of waste, reuse, and recycling. A reader commented to an article on the possible impact that waste-to-energy power plants in Delhi may have on the rag-pickers, '…allow the trash to be picked up and sorted by the rag pickers and then use the worthless remainder to fuel the plant.'[37]

---

31 http://www.mnre.gov.in/schemes/grid-connected/biomass-powercogen/, last accessed on 22 January 2013.

32 http://www.mnre.gov.in/schemes/grid-connected/biomass-powercogen/, last accessed on 22 January 2013.

33 http://articles.timesofindia.indiatimes.com/2012-09-01/mumbai/33534839_1_solid-waste-incinerators-recyclers, last accessed on 21 January 2012.

34 http://www.thehindu.com/sci-tech/energy-and-environment/article3896812.ece, last accessed on 21 January 2013.

35 http://www.renewableenergyworld.com/rea/news/article/2013/01/india-waste-manager-seeks-200-million-ipo-to-finance-waste-to-energy-plant, last accessed on 21 January 2013.

36 http://en.wikipedia.org/wiki/Waste-to-energy_plant#Arguments_against_incineration, last accessed on 21 January 2013.

37 http://www.huffingtonpost.com/2012/09/21/india-garbage-energy-plan_n_1902433.html, last accessed on 21 January 2013.

ENERGY INTENSITY, CARBON INTENSITY, AND ENERGY EFFICIENCY

As per the office of Energy Efficiency and Renewable Energy (EERE), US Department of Energy, energy intensity refers to 'The amount of energy used in producing a given level of output or activity. It is measured by the quantity of energy required to perform a particular activity (service), expressed as energy per unit of output or activity measure of service,'[38] whereas energy efficiency can be defined for a component or service as 'the amount of energy required in the production of that component or service; for example, the amount of steel that can be produced with one billion Btu of energy. Energy efficiency is improved when a given level of service is provided with reduced amounts of energy inputs, or services, or products are increased for a given amount of energy input.'[39] Energy intensity is usually used as a macro-economic parameter, to measure the energy efficiency of a nation's economy. Carbon intensity refers to the amount of carbon emissions released per unit of GDP or per unit of energy consumed for an activity.

Difference between Energy Efficiency and Energy Intensity[40]

The following are the differences between energy efficiency and energy intensity as stated by the office of EERE, US Department of Energy.

Efficiency improvements in processes and equipment and other explanatory factors can contribute to observed changes in energy intensity. Within the category 'other explanatory factors' we can identify two separate effects: structural changes and behavioural factors (discussed further in point 2).

1. Declines in energy intensity are a proxy for efficiency improvements, provided (a) energy intensity is represented at an appropriate level of disaggregation to provide meaningful interpretation and (b) other explanatory and behavioural factors are isolated and accounted for.

    Energy efficiency refers to the activity or product that can be produced with a given amount of energy; for example, the number of tons of steel that can be melted with a megawatt hour of electricity. At the level of a specific technology, the difference between efficiency and energy intensity is insignificant—one is simply the inverse of the other. In this example, energy intensity is the number of megawatt hours used to melt one ton of steel.

    At the level of the aggregate economy (or even at the level of an end-use sector) energy efficiency is not a meaningful concept because of the heterogeneous nature of the output. The production of a huge number of

---

38 http://www1.eere.energy.gov/analysis/eii_trend_definitions.html, last accessed on 20 October 2013. Content available in the public domain.

39 http://www1.eere.energy.gov/analysis/eii_trend_definitions.html, last accessed on 20 October 2013. Content available in the public domain.

40 http://www1.eere.energy.gov/analysis/eii_trend_definitions.html, last accessed on 20 October 2013. Content available in the public domain.

goods, the mixing of the transport of freight and people, and the variety of housing and climates makes an aggregate energy intensity number based on gross domestic product (GDP), a number that disguises rather than illuminates. A simple intensity measure can be calculated (as energy/GDP), but this number has little information content without the underlying sector detail.

The distinction between energy intensity and energy efficiency is important when multiple technologies or multiple products underline what is being compared. While it would not be sensible to compare the energy efficiency of steel production with the energy efficiency of ethanol production, it is possible to examine the energy intensity of all manufacturing.

2. Other explanatory factors cause changes in the energy use that have no bearing on the efficiency with which energy is used. These changes may be structural, behavioural, or due to factors like the weather, over which we have no control. These are sometimes collectively referred to as structural elements and they give rise to a change in energy use per unit measure of output, but do not reflect improvements in the underlying efficiency of energy use. A few examples of these are as follows:

(a) Structural changes in the economy are major movements in the composition of the economy and in any of the end-use sectors that can affect energy intensity but are not related to energy efficiency improvements. In the industrial sector, a shift in manufacturing emphasis from the energy intensive industries—primary metal, chemicals, and forest products—to less energy-intensive industries such as transportation equipment or food would cause a decline in the index of energy intensity that does not necessarily reflect an increase in energy efficiency. By the same token, if the population shifts to warmer climates, both commercial and residential heating intensity in the winter will decline, but air conditioning intensity in the summer will likely increase. Similarly, if the number of people in a household changes, overall energy use is also likely to change. We think of changes in the industry structure, shifts in regional population, and changes in household size as the structural components of 'other explanatory factors' changes.

(b) Changes in energy use per unit measure of output that are a result of behavioural factors also may not reflect improvements in the underlying efficiency of energy use. For example, it is well known that as people age, they will use more electricity or fuel to warm their home during the winter. While the efficiency of heating equipment in the building has not changed, the energy intensity of the house has increased to maintain a suitable living environment (conditioned space). It is sometimes difficult to separate people's behaviour from structural change such as demographic changes, like the aging of the population, may be contributing factors to the behavioural changes.

(c) There are also changes over which we have little or no control. Weather is the classic example. Yet changes in weather can have a profound effect on the amount of energy used, especially for space conditioning of homes and businesses. It is for these reasons that the national system of energy intensity indicators presented on this website has attempted to build up the aggregate numbers from the sector details. By building up from the details and incorporating changes in other explanatory factors (to the extent these factors can be identified from the available data), the measures of intensity more closely approximate changes in the underlying efficiency of energy use.

The following data (see Table 4.7), available at India's Ministry of Environment and Forests[41] website, indicates that the energy intensity and carbon intensity of the country is poised to reduce in the years ahead while the aggregate GHG emissions and per capita GHG emissions are bound to increase.

TABLE 4.7 Intensity and aggregate emissions for India, projected

	NCAER CGE model	TERI MoEF model	IRADe AA model	TERI Poznan model	McKinsey India model
GHG emissions in 2030–31 (CO_2 or CO_2e) (billion tons)	4.00 billion tons of CO_2e	4.9 billion tons (in 2031–32)	4.23 billion tons	7.3 billion tons in 2031–32	5.7 billion tons
Per capita GHG emissions in 2030–31 (CO_2 or CO_2e)	2.77 tons CO_2e per capita	3.4 tons CO_2e per capita (in 2031–32)	2.9 tons CO_2e per capita	5.0 tons CO_2e per capita (in 2031-32)	3.9 tons CO_2e per capita (2030), all GHGs
CAGR of GDP till 2030–31, %	8.84%	8.84%	7.66%	8.2%	7.51%
Fall in energy intensity	3.85% per annum (compounded annual decline rate)	From 0.11 in 2001–02 to 0.06 in 2031–32 kgoe per $ GDP at PPP	From 0.1 to 0.04 kgoe per $ GDP at PPP	From 0.11 in 2001-02 to 0.08 in 2031–32 kgoe per $ GDP at PPP	Approximately 2.3% per annum between 2005 and 2030
Fall in CO_2 (or CO_2e) intensity	From 0.37 kg CO_2e to 0.15 kg CO_2e per $ GDP at PPP from 2003–04 to 2030–31.	From 0.37 to 0.18 kg CO_2 per $ GDP at PPP from 2001–02 to 2031–32	From 0.37 to 0.18 Kg CO_2 per $ GDP at PPP from 2003–04 to 2030–31	From 0.37 to 0.28 kg CO_2 per $ GDP at PPP from 2001–02 to 2031–32	Approximately 2% per annum between 2005 and 2030 (at PPP GDP, constant USD 2005 prices)

---

41 http://www.moef.nic.in/sites/default/files/GHG_presentation.pdf, last accessed on 19 July 2013.

Bureau of Energy Efficiency (BEE), through the National Productivity Council (NPC), has conducted a study that estimated the electricity saving potential in key sectors. The study identified a saving potential of 75.4 billion kWh through the implementation of energy efficiency measures in these sectors. These savings should be understood in the context of national electricity deficit being 73.1 billion kWh, reported during 2007-08.[42]

The National Mission for Enhanced Energy Efficiency (NMEEE) plans to encourage the market for energy efficiency measures, which is estimated to be around ₹74,000 crores.[43] Through this mission, by 2015, 23 million tons of oil-equivalent to fuel savings (coal, gas, and petroleum products) is expected to be achieved every year and an avoided capacity addition of over 19,000 MW. Through this process, the government estimates an annual carbon dioxide emission of 98.55 million tons.[44] Through this mission, the government has launched the Perform Achieve and Trade (PAT) initiative, which has set targets for mandatory energy savings, for a number of companies from eight sectors—thermal power plants, iron and steel, aluminium, cement, chlor-alkali, pulp and paper, textile, and fertilizer sectors. The scheme also plans for tradable energy savings certificates. Units that achieve savings more than the target can trade the savings certificates with units that underperformed. The mission has also developed two fiscal instruments—Partial Risk Guarantee Fund (PRGF) and Venture Capital Fund for Energy Efficiency (VCFEE).

There has been criticism about using carbon intensity and energy intensity as indicators that mark progress in mitigating the negative effects of anthropogenic climate change and global warming. While countries have been able to reduce their carbon intensity and energy intensity, the aggregate emissions continue to rise, resulting in increased release of greenhouse gases into the atmosphere.

FOOD RESOURCES AND WORLD FOOD PROBLEMS

An issue paper released by Natural Resources Defense Council (NRDC) states, 'Getting food from the farm to our fork eats up 10 per cent of the total US energy budget, uses 50 per cent of US land, and swallows 80 per cent of all freshwater consumed in the US. Yet, 40 per cent of food in the US today goes uneaten. This not only means that Americans are throwing out the equivalent of US$165 billion each year, but also that the uneaten food ends up rotting in landfills as the single largest component of US municipal solid waste where it accounts for almost 25 per cent of US methane emissions. Reducing food losses by just 15 per cent would be enough food to feed more than 25 million Americans every year at a time when one in six Americans lack a secure supply of food to their tables.' The report also adds that, 'the average American consumer wastes 10 times as much food as someone in Southeast Asia, up 50 per cent from Americans in the

---

42 http://pib.nic.in/newsite/erelease.aspx?relid=55875, last accessed on 11 February 2013.
43 http://pib.nic.in/newsite/erelease.aspx?relid=55875, last accessed on 11 February 2013.
44 http://pib.nic.in/newsite/erelease.aspx?relid=55875, last accessed on 11 February 2013.

1970s.'[45]. It was stated in the report *Global Food; Waste Not, Want Not*, published by UK's Institution of Mechanical Engineers, that, 'We produce about four billion metric tonnes of food per annum. Yet due to poor practices in harvesting, storage, and transportation, as well as market and consumer wastage, it is estimated that 30-50 per cent (or 1.2–2 billion tonnes) of all food produced never reaches a human stomach. Furthermore, this figure does not reflect the fact that large amounts of land, energy, fertilizers, and water have also been lost in the production of foodstuffs which simply end up as waste.'[46]

The following table (see Table 4.8) shows some statistics compiled by United Nations' World Food Programme (WFP).[47]

TABLE 4.8 Statistics on world hunger

1.	Some 805 million people in the world do not have enough food to lead a healthy active life. That's about one in nine people on earth.
2.	The vast majority of the world's hungry people live in developing countries, where 13.5 percent of the population is undernourished.
3.	Poor nutrition causes nearly half (45%) of the deaths in children under five—3.1 million children each year.
4.	One out of six children—roughly 100 million—in developing countries is underweight.
5.	One in four of the world's children is stunted. In developing countries the proportion can rise to one in three.
6.	66 million primary school-age children attend classes hungry across the developing world, with 23 million in Africa alone.

It has been estimated that food wasted in the US itself amounts to US$165 billion annually.[48] Some of the policy level initiatives suggested to reduce the wastage of food include:

- Conducting a study of food losses through the system, from production to post-consumption.
- Establishing food waste reduction goals at the national and local levels, and implementing food waste prevention programmes.
- Enabling recovery and distribution of food.
- Improving public awareness about the wastage of food and how reducing food wastage can have a positive impact on alleviating hunger, benefitting the environment, and reducing costs.

Specific steps that could be undertaken to reduce the wastage of food include:

- Revising aesthetic standards—Food retailers with multiple number of retailing outlets demand food products that are similar in size and shape and are

---

45 http://www.nrdc.org/food/files/wasted-food-IP.pdf, last accessed on 17 January 2013.
46 http://www.imeche.org/knowledge/themes/environment/global-food, last accessed on 18 January 2013.
47 http://www.wfp.org/hunger/stats, Used with permission, last accessed on 18 January 2013.
48 http://www.nrdc.org/food/files/wasted-food-IP.pdf, last accessed on 17 January 2013.

aesthetically appealing. This puts pressure on the farmers to harvest only homogenous looking food products, and many a times the rest of the food products go waste. Such concerns are more prevalent in US and European markets where farmers may choose not to harvest crops that are off-grade. The report *Global Food; Waste Not, Want Not*, published by UK's Institution of Mechanical Engineers, adds, 'Major supermarkets, in meeting consumer expectations, will often reject entire crops of perfectly edible fruit and vegetables at the farm because they do not meet exacting marketing standards for their physical characteristics, such as size and appearance. For example, up to 30 per cent of the UK's vegetable crop is never harvested as a result of such practices. Globally, retailers generate 1.6 million tonnes of food waste annually in this way.'[49] Consumers can also start exercising their discriminatory capability to purchase food that are healthy, even if the food products does not look visually attractive.

- Applying discrimination while shopping, cooking, and eating—Avoiding impulse buys and falling a prey to marketing tricks. Planning prior hand for what to shop by using shopping lists and planning for meals would result in conscious purchasing rather than impulse buying. '...commonly used sales promotions frequently encourage customers to purchase excessive quantities which, in the case of perishable foodstuffs, inevitably generate wastage in the home. Overall between 30 per cent and 50 per cent of what has been bought in developed countries is thrown away by the purchaser.'[50] Also, while cooking, one can make optimum usage of trimmings and peelings, as they contain significant amount of nutrition. There are restaurants that encourage guests to take the leftover food home rather than wasting it. Each of us can promote the practice of taking the left over food to our home rather than wasting it in the restaurants and eateries.

- Encouraging regional or local food distribution—Promotion of food markets locally and regionally would result in alleviation of losses associated with fresh food products that have lower shelf-life.

- Menu Planning—Restaurants can use 'specials' to make effective use of food inventory that may soon go waste. They can also plan for repurposing food, half-order options, reducing the size of the food portions while allowing the customers to go for optional refills. Organizations that are engaged in food production and can influence them (restaurants, culinary institutes, and trade associations), can impart training on menu planning and inventory planning that will result in a reduction of food wastage.

Reduction in food wastage will also result in more efficient and effective usage of land, water, and energy. This is important in the context of the perspective that extreme

---

49 http://www.imeche.org/knowledge/themes/environment/global-food, last accessed on 18 January 2013.

50 http://www.imeche.org/knowledge/themes/environment/global-food, last accessed on 18 January 2013.

temperature patterns (that have become increasingly prevalent) have negatively affected food production in some countries. Extreme temperatures have affected maize production in France.[51] Currently, the food production system of the world is utilizing almost 4.9 Gha of the 10 Gha usable land surface available. It would be extremely difficult to increase the farming area any further, without affecting the other ecosystems. Increased prevalence of animal-based diet, and thus the increasing meat production, will demand more water and energy—for example, production of beef entails 50 times the usage of water in comparison with that of vegetables.[52] Estimates indicate that approximately 7–10 calories of input are required to produce one calorie of food, with the highest energy required for production of meat like beef (35 calories) while plant crop requires much lesser (three calories). Increasing consumption of animal-based diet would also demand extensive land use as livestock farming demands increased land use. 'One hectare of land can, for example, produce rice or potatoes for 19-22 people per annum. The same area will produce enough lamb or beef for only one or two people. Considerable tensions are likely to emerge, as the need for food competes with demands for ecosystem preservation and biomass production as a renewable energy source,' states UK's Institution of Mechanical Engineers.[53] About 70 per cent of the 3.8 trillion m^3 of water used by humans per annum is consumed by the global agricultural sector.[54]

Changes Caused by Modern Agriculture and its Effects—Water Logging and Salinity

Some of the practices associated with modern agriculture have contributed to the increase in the quantity of food production and this has gone to feed increasing human population. However, this has happened at a huge cost to the environment. This increase in food production has happened with the extensive usage of fertilizers and pesticides. Application of fertilizers has contributed to an increase in the production of food. However, experiences of various farmers indicates that the continuous usage of fertilizers, through many years, will result in food production reaching a plateau, and the land erodes its natural fertility.[55, 56, 57] Usage of fertilizers also entails the need for high water usage. Modern agriculture practices persuaded the construction of big dams. Construction of big dams and the resulting flood irrigation gave an option for food producers to shift to crops that require high usage of water content. Such irrigation also resulted in water logging, a state where soil is saturated with water, thus retarding the growth of plants. Water logging also contributed to increased salinity, as

51 http://www.met.reading.ac.uk/~ed/home/hawkins_etal_2012_GCB.pdf, last accessed on 24 January 2013.

52 http://www.imeche.org/knowledge/themes/environment/global-food, last accessed on 18 January 2013.

53 http://www.imeche.org/knowledge/themes/environment/global-food, last accessed on 18 January 2013.

54 http://www.imeche.org/knowledge/themes/environment/global-food, last accessed on 18 January 2013.

55 http://www.youtube.com/watch?v=Uop6tpKhbPo, last accessed on 14 February 2013.

56 http://www.youtube.com/watch?v=FcxxVjQTO8Q, last accessed on 14 February 14 2013.

57 http://www.youtube.com/watch?v=Yg3-7DcCkPE, last accessed on 14 February 2013.

During the Apple Inc.'s annual general meeting for 2014, Tim Cook, CEO, mentioned to the investors, 'If you're in Apple for only a week or two months, I would encourage you not to invest in Apple.' He said, 'We are here for the long term.' This came in the context of an investor group asking Tim to engage only in those activities that were profitable for the company and questioning Cook's stance that the company's sustainability programs and goals (like sourcing of 100 per cent of its power from green sources) were good for the company's bottom-line. Tim Cook also added, 'If you want me to do things only for ROI (Return on Investment) reasons, you should get out of this stock.'

the dissolved salts in the irrigated water remains in the soil after the water has been evaporated.

Problems Related to Extensive Usage of Fertilizers and Pesticides

Fertilizers can be organic or inorganic in nature. However, the usage of synthetic fertilizers has become increasingly prevalent and one associates fertilizers to synthetic fertilizers. The following are the causes of usage of synthetic fertilizers:

- Oxygen depletion in oceans, resulting in reduction of oceanic flora and fauna—oceanic dead zones
- Leaching of fertilizer into groundwater
- Fertilizer dependency
- Soil acidification and nutrient imbalance
- Contribution to greenhouse gases
- Pesticides have been known for causing harm to the environment and human health. Based on the extent of their usage, pesticides can affect the nervous system, cause irritation to skin and eyes, can be carcinogenic in nature, and can also affect

the hormonal or endocrinal system.[58] One of the studies synthesized, 'Strong evidence of association with pesticide exposure was found for all neurologic outcomes, genotoxicity, and 4 of 6 reproductive effects: birth defects, fetal death, altered growth, and other outcomes. Exposure to pesticides generally doubled the level of genetic damage as measured by chromosome aberrations in lymphocytes... rates of dermatitis were higher among those who had had high exposure to pesticides on the job.'[59] The following are the causes of usage of pesticides.

- Blue baby syndrome—Newborn babies with heart defects
- Accumulation of heavy metals and radio-active elements in various life forms
- Increased pest fitness—Pests that survive pesticide spray give birth to 'superpests', the pests that are highly resistant to the existing pesticides.
- Extinction of 'non-target' organisms—Many pesticides kill not only the organisms that cause harm to the crops, but also a broad range of organisms, which are useful to the sustenance of the eco-system.

58 http://www.epa.gov/pesticides/health/human.htm, last accessed on 12 February 2013.

59 http://www.ncbi.nlm.nih.gov/pmc/articles/PMC2231436/, last accessed on 14 February 2013.

60 http://www.nytimes.com/2013/03/29/science/earth/soaring-bee-deaths-in-2012-sound-alarm-on-malady.html?pagewanted=all, last accessed on 16 July 2013.

61 http://www.nytimes.com/2012/03/30/science/neocotinoid-pesticides-play-a-role-in-bees-decline-2-studies-find.html, last accessed on 16 July 2013.

The harmful effects of Endosulfan usage in the district of Kasargod, Kerala, have been well documented. Decrease in bee population, reported from many parts of the world, has been linked to the usage of pesticides.[60,61] Agricultural Research Service, the research division of the United States Department of Agriculture states, 'Bee pollination is responsible for more than US$15 billion in increased crop value each year. About one mouthful in three in our diet directly or indirectly benefits from honeybee pollination. Commercial production of many specialty crops like almonds and other tree nuts, berries, fruits, and vegetables are dependent on pollination by honeybees. These are the foods that give our diet diversity, flavour, and nutrition.'[62]

MINERAL RESOURCES

Mineral resources are the abiotic natural resources that exist in the world. Metals such as gold, copper, tin, etc., are derived from these mineral resources. Mining and oil and gas drilling are part of the extractive industries. While usage of these mineral resources has made our life comfortable, but the exploitation and extraction of these resources are causing concern on whether it would be possible for the planet to sustain future generations.[63] An increase in gadget-driven lifestyle results in the usage and thus mining of rare earth elements, which are not easy to source. Thus, in addition to the increasing demand for minerals, increasing mining is also driven by our lifestyle.

Use and Exploitation of Mineral Resources

The intimate connection between human beings and nature is ingrained in many of us, at an intuitive level. During his high school days, the author of this textbook saw the usage 'exploiting natural resources' in his geography textbook. The author started thinking about why a violent and degrading word such as 'exploit' was being used. The same thought was shared by a batch-mate of the author's. Well, having been young with receptive and impressionable minds, they were yet to be introduced to the worldly way of looking at nature—as a commodity to be exploited. Al Gore, former US Vice President who won the Nobel Peace Prize in 2007 (and known for creating awareness about global warming through his role in the Oscar award winning documentary *An Inconvenient Truth*) states in his book *Earth in Balance: Ecology and the Human Spirit*, 'The more deeply I search for

Bee pollination is responsible for more than US$15 billion in increased crop value each year. About one mouthful in three in our diet directly or indirectly benefits from honeybee pollination. Commercial production of many specialty crops like almonds and other tree nuts, berries, fruits, and vegetables are dependent on pollination by honeybees.

---

62 http://www.ars.usda.gov/News/docs.htm?docid=15572, last accessed on 16 July 2013.
63 http://www.unece.org/oes/nutshell/2004-2005/focus_sustainable_development.html, last accessed on 16 February 2013.

the roots of the global environmental crisis, the more I am convinced that it is an outer manifestation of an inner crisis, that is, for lack of a better word, spiritual.'

Environmental Effects of Extracting and Using Mineral Resources

The New Delhi based Centre for Science and Environment (CSE) conducted an analysis of the environment and forest clearances granted by the Indian government during the 11th five-year plan—between 2007 and 2011. Studying the sectors related to thermal power, hydropower, cement, iron and steel, and mining, CSE states that the scale of clearances has been unprecedented.[64] Forest clearance was granted to 8284 projects during this period and 203,576 hectare (ha) of forest land was diverted (see Table 4.9). For easier comparison, this land area is equivalent to almost 290,000 football fields. As *The Hindu Survey of the Environment 2012* laments, 'As you drive through the hills of Meghalaya, almost imperceptibly you accumulate on yourself a layer of black. Symbolic of the death of the forests that covered these hills—the fine black dust shroud of hills once green; coal dust. The Jaintia and Khasi hills of Meghalaya have been stripped bare of their once luxuriant forest cover, perfectly denuded to get to the deposits of coals that lie beneath. Over the years, mountain after mountain has been hacked, until nothing but the black remains. The story is much the same in other parts of India. Shades differ, red replaces black when mining for iron. Then there are colours of hematite, bauxite, manganese, and limestone. The list goes on.'[65] Some of the environmental effects of extraction and usage of mineral resources include:

- Large scale deforestation
- Defacement of the landscape—With the removal of the top-soil, to facilitate mining of the area, the landscape gets badly affected.
- Pollution of water bodies—Drainage from mines affects the water bodies that are located nearby.
- Air pollution—During the process of extraction and usage, particulate matter and harmful pollutants are released into the air.

TABLE 4.9 Diversion of Forestlands in the past two decades

Period/Year	Forestland diverted (in hectares)
1981–1992	198,421.19
8th Five Year Plan (1992–1997)	84,587.07
9th Five Year Plan (1997–2002)	147,397.57
10th Five Year Plan (2002–2007)	196,262.32
11th Five Year Plan (2007–2012)	204,425.06

Source: Centre for Science and Environment, New Delhi[66]

---

64 http://www.cseindia.org/userfiles/EIA_forest_clearances.pdf, last accessed on 20 September 2012.
65 Krishnadas, Meghna, and Nisarg Prakash 2012, Mining your business, *The Hindu Survey of the Environment 2012*.
66 http://www.cseindia.org/userfiles/EIA_forest_clearances.pdf, last accessed on 20 September 2012. Used with permission.

Diversion of Forest Land to Mining

When mineral resources are extracted, the top soil is affected. It takes centuries to form a fertile top soil. Mining results in removal of forest cover through cutting trees that took ages to grow. As nutrients get removed from the eco system, nature cycles get affected. Lack of trees and other flora result in run-off of rainwater and soil erosion. As the percolation of water reduces, there is a reduction in water table, thereby affecting water bodies and river systems. Soil erosion results in increased deposit of sediments in streams and water bodies, thereby choking aquatic beings living in these water bodies. Many birds and animals lose their habitats as trees are brought down. It has been noted that access roads and constructions near the forest area that has been allocated to mining results in a sudden increase in human activities like settlements, collection of forest produces, dumping of wastage near the region, increased irresponsible tourism, etc.

FOREST RESOURCES

Forests have been considered as treasure houses throughout the world so much so that mythical stories from various cultural traditions had characters that protect the forests from exploitation. Details related to the importance of forests have been provided throughout this textbook.

Use and Exploitation of Forest Resources

It is estimated that the livelihood of almost 1.6 billion people depends on the forests.[67] Up to 80 per cent of the population in developing countries depends on non-timber forest products for economic subsistence and for nutrition.[68] Food and Agricultural Organisation of the United Nations (FAO) has listed out the names of trees that are used in agro-forestry systems, firewood, food production, for non-wood forest products, fodder, poles, shade and shelter, timber, medicinal purposes, amenities and aesthetic purposes, and for conservation and environmental protection.[69]

Access to natural environment also provides health benefits for people. Researchers have found an increase in human mortality related to cardiovascular and lower-respiratory-tract illness in regions infested with the emerald ash borer, an invasive insect, which has killed 100 million ash trees since it got accidently introduced to the US states of Illinois, Indiana, Michigan, and Ohio. It was also found that the magnitude of this effect was greater as infestation progressed and in regions with above-average median household income. 'Across the 15 states in the study area, the borer was associated with an additional 6,113 deaths related to illness of the lower respiratory system, and 15,080

67 http://wwf.panda.org/about_our_earth/about_forests/importance/economicforest/, last accessed on 16 February 2013.

68 http://wwf.panda.org/about_our_earth/about_forests/importance/economicforest/, last accessed on 16 February 2013.

69 http://www.fao.org/docrep/005/AC850E/ac850e09.htm, last accessed on 16 February 2013.

cardiovascular-related deaths,' states the researcher.[70] It was concluded that 'the loss of trees to the emerald ash borer increased mortality related to cardiovascular and lower-respiratory-tract illness. This finding adds to the growing evidence that the natural environment provides major public health benefits.'[71]

In a study done by USDA Forest Service and Davey Institute, the researchers found that trees, annually removed 4.7–64.5 tonnes of particles, which were not bigger than 2.5 microns.[72] The researchers estimated this service to be worth US$1.1 million to US$60.1 million. Green spaces have also been able to contribute to improving the well-being of people. Research evidence exists, which indicates that 'individuals have both lower mental distress and higher well-being when living in urban areas with more green space.'[73] Evidence also exists to indicate that 'the mental health benefits of green space are not only immediate, but sustainable over long periods of time.'[74]

Among the many services that the forests provide, some include:

- Preservation and regeneration of nutrients in soil
- Climatic control
- Storage of genes
- Provision of clean air and water
- Reduction of soil erosion
- Preventing floods by reducing the surface run-off of water
- Reduction in the creation of drought
- Preserving nutrients in soil
- Maintenance of soil structure
- Providing food, fuel-wood, timber, fodder, dyes, tannins, fibre, gums, resins, medicinal plants, fruits, raw materials for a number of industries, and other goods and services for people and livestock.
- Habitat for millions of wild animals and plants
- Acting as wind-breaks

It is this recognition of the importance of forests that prompted Ecosia.org, a search engine, to donate 80 per cent of its advertisement revenue for its first five years of existence, to programmes that support afforestation and tree planting (see Fig. 4.3).

70 Donovan, Geoffrey H, David T Butry, Yvonne L Michael, Jeffrey P Prestemon, Andrew M. Liebhold, Demetrios Gatziolis, and Megan Y. Mao, The Relationship Between Trees and Human Health: Evidence from the Spread of the Emerald Ash Borer, *American Journal of Preventive Medicine*, Vol. 44, Issue 2, pp. 139-145, February 2013.

71 Donovan, Geoffrey H, David T Butry, Yvonne L Michael, Jeffrey P Prestemon, Andrew M. Liebhold, Demetrios Gatziolis, and Megan Y. Mao, The Relationship Between Trees and Human Health: Evidence from the Spread of the Emerald Ash Borer, *American Journal of Preventive Medicine*, Vol. 44, Issue 2, pp. 139-145, February 2013.

72 Nowaka, David J, Satoshi Hirabayashib, Allison Bodineb, and Robert Hoehna 2013, *Environmental Pollution*, Vol. 178, July 2013, pp. 395-402.

73 White,Mathew P, Ian Alcock, Benedict W Wheeler, Michael H Depledge 2013, Would You Be Happier Living in a Greener Urban Area? A Fixed-Effects Analysis of Panel Data, *Psychological Science*, 23 April 2013. Also available at http://pss.sagepub.com/content/early/2013/04/23/0956797612464659.abstract

74 http://www.eurekalert.org/pub_releases/2014-01/uoe-gsd010314.php, last accessed on 29 January 2014.

Ecosia, in five years, has donated more than ₹15 crores to such programs, thereby being an inspiration for a number of business organizations and individuals. Ecosia currently contributes more than 50% of its revenues and more than 80% of its surplus income to green causes.[75]

FIG. 4.3[76]   A poster released by Ecosia.org communicating the uniqueness of their company

---

75 http://www.treehugger.com/clean-technology/green-search-engine-ecosia-donates-over-160000-by-1st-birthday. html, last accessed on 1 September 2014.

76 Used with permission.

Deforestation

Deforestation is the removal of a forest or trees from a piece of land, which is converted to non-forest uses that may include farms, ranches, and urban use (see Fig. 4.4). World Wide Fund for Nature (WWF) states that 13 million hectares of forests are converted or lost each year.[77] Deforestation could be done for the following reasons:

- To be used as firewood
- To be used as timber
- To clear land for usage as
    - human settlements
    - grazing field for animals
    - mining, quarrying, irrigation, and industrial projects
    - agricultural land

FIG. 4.4[78] Deforestation

---

77 http://wwf.panda.org/about_our_earth/about_forests/importance/forestspeople/, last accessed on 16 February 2013.

78 Photo by Victor David Helzberg, used with permission. Image source: https://www.flickr.com/photos/crustmania/233523196/, last accessed on 2 August 2014.

Effects of Deforestation, Timber Extraction, Mining, and Dams on Forest and Tribal People

- There is an increase in soil erosion, intensification of floods, and possible desertification—The presence of trees and the fallen leaves reduce the surface run-off of water. As the trees are felled, the soil gets washed away more easily.
- There is a fall in the ground water levels and destruction of perennial rivers—The presence of flora and the fallen leaves acts as a natural barrier to the surface run-off of water. As more water penetrates through the soil, underground water storage increases. This also creates perennial rivers. With deforestation, seepage of water reduces, and recharging of underground reservoirs also stops.
- There is migration of tribal population—With sources of food and livelihood resources dwindling, there will be migration of tribal population.
- There is a decrease in rainfall—Extensive presence of flora in forests contributes to high level of transpiration. With the felling of forests, there is a reduction in rainfall.
- There is extinction of species and loss of biodiversity.
- Climatic change accelerates.
- There are long-term economic losses.
- Mining could result in extensive deforestation and degradation of land.
- Mining also results in the release of pollutants.
- Mining and related activities release greenhouse and other toxic gases like the emission of methane during coal mining.
- Creation of dams results in the submergence of large tracts of areas contributing to deforestation and loss of biodiversity.

It has been found that secondary forests (the land where there is the growth of the second generation of forests, after the initial deforestation of tropical forests) have less capability to hold carbon (carbon sequestration). It was found that the total carbon content in a secondary forest is only around 80 per cent of that of the primary forest, even after about 80 years. Secondary forests only had one-fourth of the amount of species that were present in the primary forests. Researchers speculate that it may take more than 150 years for secondary forests to have a bio-diversity level that is comparable to that of the secondary forest, and they also add that it may well be impossible for a secondary forest to replenish all the biodiversity that existed in the primary forests, as many species may not have the possibility to return to the area where the primary forests existed.[79]

---

79 http://phys.org/news/2013-11-rainforest-carbon-recovers-faster-biodiversity.html, last accessed on 21 November 2013.

WATER RESOURCES

Increasing population and increasing consumption has led to a dwindling of water resources. Water bodies almost in all parts of the world have been meeting with destruction. For example, the volume and the surface area of Lake Akeshir, in Turkey, have gradually decreased over the last three decades, and the lake finally dried up in 2008.[80] Lake Chad, which covered about 9700 square miles (25,000 sq. km) in 1963, has shrunk to one-twentieth of its size now. This decline has contributed to failures in agriculture, death of livestock, and fisheries.[81] Researchers who have studied the 241 lakes, near the Asian Gobi Desert region of China, have found that '121 of the 241 lakes became fully desiccated at the end of the 2000s. Our results confirmed the prevalence of drought-induced lake shrinkage and desiccation at a regional scale, which has been sustained since the year 2000, and highlighted an accelerated shrinkage of individual lakes by human water use in the agriculture-dominated regions.'[82]

Water Footprint

Water footprint is the volume of water used for a product/service that is consumed. This is measured in water volume consumed (evaporated) and/or polluted. While calculating a water footprint, three components are taken into consideration—blue water footprint, green water footprint, and grey water footprint.

- Blue water footprint is the volume of freshwater that evaporated from surface water and ground water.
- Green water footprint is the volume of water evaporated from rainwater stored in the soil as soil moisture.
- Grey water footprint is the volume of polluted water associated with the production. It is estimated as the volume of water required to dilute pollutants to maintainthe water quality at or above the agreed water quality standards.

The 2012 Living Planet Report states that of the total global water footprint, 92 per cent is caused due to agricultural production.[83] Table 4.10 shows the water footprint of some of the crops, crop products, and animal products.

---

80 Sener, Erhan, Aysen Davraz, and Sehnaz Sener 2010, Investigation of Aksehir and Eber Lakes (SW Turkey) Coastline Change with Multitemporal Satellite Images, *Water Resources Management*, March 2010, Vol. 24, Issue 4, pp. 727-745.

81 http://news.nationalgeographic.com/news/2001/04/0426_lakechadshrinks.html, last accessed on 24 October 2013.

82 Liu, Hongyan, Yi Yin, Shilong Piao, Fengjun Zhao, Mike Engels, and Philippe Ciais 2013, Disappearing Lakes in Semiarid Northern China: Drivers and Environmental Impact, *Environmental Science & Technology*, 1 October 2013. Also available at http://pubs.acs.org/doi/abs/10.1021/es305298q, last accessed on 24 October 2013.

83 http://awsassets.panda.org/downloads/1_lpr_2012_online_full_size_single_pages_final_120516.pdf, last accessed on 18 February 2013.

TABLE 4.10[84] Average water footprint of some crops, derived crop products, and animal products (m³/ton) in India during 1996–2005

Crop product	Average water footprint (m³/ton)	Water footprint component	Average water footprint (m³/ton)	Animal product
Wheat	643	Green	3206	Swine, pure, for breeding
	1162	Blue	688	
	294	Grey	328	
Rice in the husk, paddy	1394	Green	3647	Sheep, live
	452	Blue	262	
	224	Grey	154	
Barley	1247	Green	2668	Goats, live
	780	Blue	238	
	96	Grey	8	
Maize	2225	Green	5246	Poultry, live
	103	Blue	671	
	195	Grey	599	
Millet	3719	Green	885	Milk, fat cont.1% or less
	76	Blue	130	
	233	Grey	63	
Sorghum	5694	Green	4377	Cheese
	98	Blue	657	
	233	Grey	310	
Potatoes	221	Green	4888	Birds' eggs, in shell
	36	Blue	635	
	34	Grey	542	
Sweet potatoes	587	Green	6644	Bovine animals
	12	Blue	299	
	67	Grey	123	
Sugar cane	122	Green	2028	Cherries
	141	Blue	660	
	17	Grey	177	

(Contd)

84 Sources: (1) Mekonnen, MM, and AY Hoekstra 2010, The green, blue and grey water footprint of crops and derived crop products, *Value of Water Research Report Series No. 47*, UNESCO-IHE, Delft, the Netherlands. (2) Mekonnen, MM and AY Hoekstra 2010, The green, blue and grey water footprint of farm animals and animal products, *Value of Water Research Report Series No. 48*, UNESCO-IHE, Delft, the Netherlands. (3) A detailed report can be downloaded from http://www.waterfootprint.org/Reports/Report47-WaterFootprintCrops-Vol1.pdf, last accessed on 4 February 2013. Used with permission.

Refined sugar	1034	Green	289	Pineapples
	1197	Blue	31	
	143	Grey	48	
Soybeans	4242	Green	293	Papayas
	23	Blue	45	
	145	Grey	25	
Groundnuts in shell	2871	Green	1440	Ginger
	340	Blue	61	
	210	Grey	175	
Castor oil seed	7624	Green	1440	Turmeric
	1422	Blue	61	
	203	Grey	175	
Cotton, not carded or combed	14680	Green	305	Bananas, including plantains
	4222	Blue	170	
	2183	Grey	26	
Cabbages	70	Green	802	Oranges
	50	Blue	3	
	33	Grey	76	
Lettuce	518	Green	1381	Apples
	19	Blue	421	
	108	Grey	123	
Tomatoes	126	Green	2127	Apricots
	58	Blue	615	
	43	Grey	184	
Cauliflowers and broccoli	223	Green	95	Celery
	6	Blue	50	
	39	Grey	53	
Cucumbers and gherkins	246	Green	95	Carrots and turnips
	81	Blue	50	
	112	Grey	53	
Garlic	368	Green	440	Peas
	370	Blue	13	
	165	Grey	84	
Beans	998	Green		
	26	Blue		
	262	Grey		

Eight Mighty Rivers that Ran Dry Due to Overuse

Rivers across the world are drying up due to human interventions, including groundwater extraction, re-routing of rivers, construction of structures on the river, and destruction of greenery in the nearby regions. The following rivers ran dry due to such activities by humans.

1. Colorado River (Fig. 4.5)
2. Indus
3. Amu Darya

FIG. 4.5[85] River Colorado

---

85 Photo by Jason Hollinger, used with permission. *Source*: https://www.flickr.com/photos/7147684@N03/910681223/, last accessed on 5 August 2014.

4. Syr Darya
5. Rio Grande
6. Yellow
7. Teesta
8. Murray

Water Conservation, Rain Water Harvesting, and Watershed Management

'Peninsular rivers like Krishna, Godavari, and Cauvery no longer touch the seas. Outfalls of Krishna have reached near zero in summer. In the fertile Godavari delta, coastal erosion is eating into the land due to the absence of sufficient sediments and flows from upstream. Most of the endemic fish species are dwindling due to the numerous obstacles to their migration route and lack of water,' says Latha Anantha, Director of River Research Centre and Parineeta Dandekar, Member of River Research Centre.[86] Water conservation encompasses the policies, strategies, and activities to manage fresh water as a sustainable resource to protect the water environment and to meet the current and future human demands. Of the total water available in the planet, only 2.5 per cent is freshwater. However, only 1 per cent of the total freshwater is accessible for human usage. It has been noted that while the world population has doubled in the last 40 years, the usage of water has quadrupled. As the population increases by another one billion by 2025, it will require an additional 1 trillion cubic metres of water for agricultural usage.[87] There is a need to increase the efficiency while using water. Irrigation techniques like flood irrigation uses a lot of water as compared to spray irrigation and drip irrigation. It is important that we move to efficient usage of water resources like drip irrigation.

Rainwater harvesting includes the techniques and processes of accumulating and storing rainwater for future use. Rainwater harvesting is a cost-effective way of raising the water table. The harvested water can be used for both domestic and irrigation related activities. Rainwater harvesting provides water that do not contain (or almost negligible traces of) dissolved minerals/salts/heavy metals. Rainwater harvesting structures usually have three components—(a) the area used for rainwater collection, also referred to as catchment area, (b) the rainwater collection device (such as tanks and pits), and (c) the conveyance system that is used to transport the water collected from the catchment area to the collection device. The following are some of the ways in which rainwater harvesting could be done.

- Growing flora—trees, shrubs, etc.
- Roofwater collection
- Bunding and terracing
- Farming

---

86 Anantha, Latha, and Parineeta Dandekar 2012, The Science and Politics of River Flows, The Hindu Survey of the Environment 2012, .

87 http://livinggreenmag.com/2012/10/26/energy-ecology/the-global-water-crisis-infographic/, last accessed on 20 February 2013.

- Contour trenching
- Contour farming
- Ponds and tanks
- Diversion bunds
- Check dams/sub-surface dams/diaphragm dams

While all of the aforementioned methods would be of help in rainwater harvesting, one of the most effective methods for large-scale rainwater harvesting is the conservation of forests. For example, Shola forests are known for acting like sponge—they absorb and retain water during rainy reason—thereby contributing to the creation of perennial rivers.

United States Environmental Protection Agency (EPA) defines watershed as 'the area of land where all of the water that is under it or drains off, it goes into the same place.' John Wesley Powell, scientist geographer, put it best when he said that a watershed is 'that area of land, a bounded hydrologic system, within which all living things are inextricably linked by their common water course and where, as humans settled, simple logic demanded that they become part of a community.'[88] A watershed could also be referred to as a geo-hydrological unit with a common drainage point.[89] The Department of Conservation, State of California, USA, defines watershed management as 'the process of creating and implementing plans, programs, and projects to sustain and enhance watershed functions that provide the goods, services, and values desired by the community affected by conditions within a watershed boundary.'[90] Watershed management aims to increase and sustain the needs of the community that is part of the watershed. An effective watershed management programme takes into consideration the hydrology, biology, geology, and sociology of the watershed.

Indigenous Water Conservation Systems in India

India is the third largest dam builder in the world, with more than 5000 dams in India. While this has helped in increased power generation and irrigation facilities, it has also resulted in dissection of rivers into isolated reservoirs and blocking of water flow in the rivers. While the country is still discussing about 'Environmental Flows' (also referred to as E-Flows, which means the amount of water and flow that should be left in the river from source to sea so that it supports its ecosystem, the dependent livelihoods and the values the river provides to humans and other organisms), an exploration indicates the existence of a number of indigenous water conservation systems in India (see Table 4.11 for a timeline that speaks about the evolution of water harvesting in India).

---

88 http://water.epa.gov/type/watersheds/whatis.cfm, last accessed on 22 February 2013.
89 http://www.orissawatershed.org/Faq.php, last accessed on 22 February 2013.
90 http://www.conservation.ca.gov/dlrp/wp/Documents/California%20Watershed%20Program.pdf, last accessed on 22 February 2013.

TABLE 4.11[91] Water harvesting timeline in ancient and medieval India

3rd millennium BC	Dams built of stone rubble were found in Baluchistan and Kutch.
3000–1500 BC	Indus-Sarasvati civilization had several reservoirs to collect rainwater runoff. Each house had an individual well.
321–291 BC	Archeological evidence for dams, lakes, and irrigation systems in the time of Chandragupta Maurya's rule.
3rd century BC	Kautilya's Arthasastra mentions irrigation using water-harvesting systems.
1st century BC	Sringaverapura near Allahabad had a sophisticated water-harvesting system using the floodwaters of the Ganges.
2nd century AD	Grand Anicut or Kallanai built by Karikala Chola across the river Cauvery to divert water for irrigation is still functional.
11th century AD	King Bhoja of Bhopal built the largest artificial lake (65,000 acres) in India fed by streams and springs.
12th century AD	Rajatarangini by Kalhana describes a well-maintained irrigation system in Kashmir.

In the southern part of the country, every village had a minimum of two water bodies accessible to all public—one meant for human usage and the other for cattle and birds. The practice of harvesting rainwater dates back to Vedic times when the need to create water sources that would remain both clean and provide in plenty was recognized. Wells were dug in the cities of the Indus-Sarasvati valley by 3000 BC. The 'Great Bath', one of the structures of the Indus Valley civilization, was possibly a water storage tank. The Indus Valley civilization was also known for excellent systems of water drainage. Dholavira, located in Kachchh district of Gujarat and one of the archaeological sites belonging to the Indus Valley civilization, had a sophisticated water conservation system with channels and reservoirs, the earliest found anywhere in the world. The city also had storm water drains. The inhabitants of Dholavira created sixteen or more such reservoirs (see Fig. 4.6).

Oorani Oorani is the name given to a dug out tank or a pond that harvests rainwater and stores it. They are found in rural areas of South India, especially Tamilnadu, and these structures could be man-made. Oorani could be square, circular or rectangular and are usually dug to a depth of 2–5 metres below the ground level. The size of the Oorani is decided by the number of people accessing the Oorani and their water needs. Water in Oorani was collected from the surface run-off rain water and also sub-surface flow.

Tankas Tankas are traditional water harvesting systems found in places such as Dwarka, Bikaner, etc. They are underground tanks built under the house or in the

---

91 http://cpreec.org/pubbook-traditional.htm, last accessed on 26 April 2012, Used with permission from C.P.R. Environmental Education Centre, Chennai.

FIG. 4.6[92] Water reservoir at Dholavira

courtyard. The water collected in Tankas are used mainly for drinking. To keep the water in the Tanka clean, a small pot filled with lime (as a disinfectant) is put inside the Tankas. At the bottom of the Tanka, there is a slope which leads to a 2 X 2 feet area. The water is collected from here. This area falls below the opening in the ground and people draw water though this opening.

Kunds Kund is a covered underground tank found in the arid regions of Western Rajasthan. The first known construction of a Kund in the region was done by Raja Sursingh, during the year 1607 AD. However, there is a possibility that Kunds were in existence prior to that too. Kund is a circular underground well. It has a saucer-shaped catchment area with a slope towards the centre where the well is located. Most of these wells/pits have a dome-shaped cover or a lid to protect the water from the debris. This makes the Kund look like an upturned cup kept on top of saucer. Water is drawn out from a Kund with the aid of a bucket (see the two images in Fig. 4.7)

Construction of the tank, usually circular, is done with lime plaster or cement. Disinfectants like lime and ash are used on the sides of the well pit. Wire meshes are kept across the water-inlets to prevent the entry of debris, reptiles, etc., in to water. The size of the Kund (diameter, depth, and catchment areas) is decided by the needs of the community. The catchment size varies from 20 sq. m to 2 hectare. A two hectare

---

92 Photo by Jitaditya Narzary, used with permission. Image Source: http://travellingslacker.com/2014/03/dholavira-bricks-of-oblivion/, last accessed on 3 August 2014.

FIG. 4.7[93] Kund in Rajasthan

catchment area with a 2–3 per cent slope will suffice for a Kund of 200 cubic metres capacity. The catchment area was prepared from locally available materials. The surface vegetation was removed, a smooth slope towards the tank was created and this catchment area was lined with silt. The area was made semi-impermeable with *murrum* till the surface was compacted.

Khadin These are water harvesting structures, found in western Rajasthan, to stop the surface run-off during monsoon. These structures are earthen embankments, 100–300 metres, with spillways to allow the flow and drainage of excess water. These embankments are built below a plateau or gravelly uplands. The upland catchment area could be 15 times the area of a Khadin. The harvested rainwater is kept within the Khadin area throughout the monsoon period. As the water percolates down, this land is used for crop production.

93 Used with permission from Center for Science and Environment (CSE), a public interest research and advocacy organization based at New Delhi..

Vaav/Bawdi/Barav   These are the wells in which water can be stored and is reached by a series of descending steps (see Fig. 4.8). Though most common in western part of India, these step-wells are found across the country. The first rock-cut step wells in India predates to 200–400 AD. Similar to step-wells were the stepped ponds, which were built near a temple. Step wells and stepped ponds more or less had the same purpose. Stepped ponds were illuminated by the sun/moon, whereas step wells more or less were less visible from surface. A major reason for the breakdown of this traditional system is the pressure of centralization and agricultural intensification.

FIG. 4.8[94] Chand Baori, a step-well located at Abhaneri village, near Jaipur, Rajasthan. Built in the 9th century, this well is 100 feet deep, and has 3500 steps in 13 storeys.

Some of the advantages of traditional water harvesting system were that they use eco-friendly materials and practices focusing on water conservation. The traditional water harvesting system also promotes social cohesion and self-reliance. Many of them require only low monetary costs during construction as the local materials available in the villages are used for construction. Traditional water harvesting systems are also community driven with the construction and day-to-day management usually done by people within the community. Many temples in India are known for having temple tanks and temple ponds which used to act as store-houses of water (see Fig. 4.9).

94 Photo by Ramon, used with permission. Image Source: https://www.flickr.com/photos/sitomon/7338326518/in/photostream/, last accessed on 2 August 2014.

FIG. 4.9[95] The Ananthapura lake temple, Kasaragod, Kerala

Water Harvesting Techniques

The following table (Table 4.12) lists some of the water harvesting systems in India, their location, and the ecological zone.

TABLE 4.12[96] Water harvesting systems in India

Eco-zone	Traditional water harvesting systems	Description	Region
Trans-Himalayan Region	Zing	Tanks for collecting water from melted ice	Ladakh
Western Himalayas	Kul	Water channels in mountain areas	Jammu and Himachal Pradesh
	Naula	Small ponds	Uttaranchal

(Contd)

---

95 Photo by Manoj Ravindran, Image Source: https://commons.wikimedia.org/wiki/File:Ananthapura_lake_temple_-_kasargod.JPG, last accessed on 4 August 2014.

96 http://cpreec.org/pubbook-traditional.htm, last accessed on 26 April 2012, Used with permission from C.P.R. Environmental Education Centre, Chennai.

TABLE 4.12 (*Contd*)

Eco-zone	Traditional water harvesting systems	Description	Region
	Kuhl	Headwall across a ravine to divert water from a natural stream for irrigation	Himachal Pradesh
	Khatri	Chambers carved in hard rock for storing water	Himachal Pradesh
Eastern Himalayas	Apatani	Terraced plots connected by inlet and outlet channels	Arunachal Pradesh
Northeastern Hill Ranges	Zabo	Impounding run-off	Nagaland
	Cheo-oziihi	Channels from rivers	Nagaland
	Bamboo drip irrigation	Water from streams in the hills is brought to the plains via bamboo pipes for drip irrigation	Meghalaya
Brahmaputra Valley	Dongs	Ponds	Assam
	Dungs/jampois	Small irrigation canals linking rice fields and a stream	West Bengal
Indo-Gangetic Plain	Ahar-pynes	Embanked catchment basin and channels	South Bihar
	Bengal's inundation channels	Inundation canals	West Bengal
	Dighis	Small square or circular reservoir fed by canals from rivers	Delhi
	Baolis	Step wells	Delhi
Thar Desert	Kunds/kundis	Underground storage	West Rajasthan
	Kuis/beris	Deep pits near tanks	West Rajasthan
	Baoris/bers	Community wells	Rajasthan
	Jhalaras	Tank	Rajasthan and Gujarat
	Nadi	Village ponds	Jodhpur, Rajasthan
	Tankas	Underground tank	Bikaner, Rajasthan
	Khadins	Embankment across lower hill slopes	Jaisalmer, West Rajasthan
	Vav/Vavdi/Baoli/Bavadi	Step wells	Gujarat and Rajasthan
	Virdas	Shallow wells	Rann of Kutch, Gujarat
	Paar	Area where water has percolated, accessed by kuis	-

(*Contd*)

Central Highlands	Talab/Bandhis	Reservoirs	Bundelkhand, Madhya Pradesh
	Saza Kuva	Open well	Mewar, East Rajasthan
	Johads	Earthen check dams	Alwar district, Rajasthan
	Naada/bandh	Stone check dam	Mewar, Thar desert
	Pat	Diversion bund across stream	Jhabua district, Madhya Pradesh
	Rapat	Percolation tank	Rajasthan
	Chandela tank	Tank	Rajasthan
	Bundela tank	Tank	Rajasthan
Eastern Highlands	Katas/Mundas/ Bandhas	Earthen embankments across drainage lines	Orissa, and Madhya Pradesh
Deccan Plateau	Cheruvu	Reservoirs to store runoff	Chitoor and Cuddapah districts of Andhra Pradesh
	Kohli tanks	Tanks	Maharashtra
	Bhandaras	Check dams	Maharashtra
	Phad	Check dams and canals	North western Maharashtra
	Kere	Series of tanks	Central Karnataka
	Ramtek Model	Intricate network of groundwater and surface water bodies, connected through surface and underground canals	Ramtek, Maharashtra
Western Ghats	Surangam	Horizontal well	Kasargode, Kerala
Western Coastal Plains	Virdas	Shallow wells	Rann of Kutch, Gujarat
Eastern Ghats	Korambu	Temporary wall of brushwood, grass, and mud laid across channels to raise the level of water	Kerala
Eastern Coastal Plains	Yeri	Tank	Tamilnadu
	Ooranis	Pond	Tamilnadu
The Islands	Jackwells	Bamboo pipes are used to lead water into shallow pits	Great Nicobar Island

LAND MANAGEMENT

Land management involves development of land resources, driven by the needs of the growing human population. This could also include agriculture. To ensure sustainability, human needs on land are assessed in the context of its impact on water, bio-diversity, ecological processes, etc. Irresponsible land management can result in degradation.

Land Degradation, Desertification, and Soil Erosion

The loss of the productive capability of the soil is referred to as land degradation. Land degradation forces people, who are dependent on land resources, to search for new settlements. Land degradation could be caused due to a number of reasons and few are as follows

- Urbanization, due to industries and human settlements
- Soil pollution and nutrient imbalance, caused by increased use of pesticides and fertilizers
- Soil erosion, caused by wind and rainfall
- Water logging and salination
- Landslides

Another process through which the productive potential of land is lost is through desertification. Desertification is primarily characterized by the loss of the vegetation in the area. Other characteristics could typically involve depletion of ground water, salination of the soil, and soil erosion. While deserts are usually formed by natural phenomena, it could also be caused due to human-induced activities like deforestation, mining and quarrying, and overgrazing. Recommended remedies include replanting the area with drought tolerant plants.

Soil erosion is caused by natural elements like wind and rainfall, or through human-induced actions. Wind can carry top soil and can also cause sand dunes. In addition to rainfall, melting of snow can also remove the top soil. Over-grazing of cattle removes the vegetational cover protecting the soil, thereby aggravating the possibility of soil erosion. The major negative effect of soil erosion is the loss of fertility, as the fertile top soil gets carried away. Soil erosion can be controlled by:

(a) Afforestation and reforestation (See Fig. 4.10)
(b) Structures that arrest the flow of water–ponds, reservoirs, etc.
(c) Contour farming

FIG. 4.10 A board in front of a residence indicating the gifting of the flowers of Kannikonna (golden shower tree) and Kannikonna tree saplings on the occassion of Vishu, a festival that mandates the inclusion of Kannikonna flowers during the celebration

CHAPTER SUMMARY

- India has a unique situation when it comes to energy management. Despite having 40 crore people living without access to electricity, electricity shortage in the country is estimated at 25–35 GW.
- Renewable energy sources refers to those energy sources that last for a relatively longer period of time, like thousands of years, unlike non-renewable energy sources that deplete in probably decades or centuries.
- Alternate energy sources like solar, wind, tidal, and biomass do not produce emissions like fossil fuel industries and they are natural sources for generation.
- Solar energy is considered to be an abundant form of energy. One hour of solar irradiation on this planet is enough to power humanity's energy needs for 2020.
- The generation cost for wind energy would be ₹3.50–3.60 per Kwh while for coal it should be ₹4.00 per Kwh. Almost 30 per cent of electricity demand in TN is met by wind energy.
- It has been estimated that India has a potential of generating about 8000 MW tidal energy.
- Biomass refers to organic materials that could be used for generating energy through their usage as a fuel. It could also refer to biodegradable wastes.
- Compressed natural gas (CNG) is considered a cleaner fuel as it emits lesser amount of pollutants like carbon dioxide, carbon monoxide, sulphur oxides, nitrogen oxides, and particulate matter, in comparison with other fuels like petrol.
- One of the ways through which an attempt is made to dispose waste is by burning them. This is known as incineration and involves the combustion of organic substances that are part of the waste materials.
- Due to poor practices in harvesting, storage, and transportation, as well as market and consumer wastage, it is estimated that 30–50 per cent (or 1.2–2 billion tonnes) of all food produced never reaches a human stomach.
- Reduction in food wastage will result in more efficient and effective usage of land, water, and energy.
- Modern agriculture practices persuaded the construction of big dams. Construction of big dams and the resulting flood irrigation gave an option for food producers to shift to crops that require high usage of water content.
- Fertilizer could be of organic and inorganic nature. However, the usage of synthetic fertilizers has become increasingly prevalent that one associates fertilizers to synthetic fertilizers. Pesticides have been known for causing harm to the environment and human health.
- Mineral resources are the abiotic natural resources that exist in the world. Metals such as gold, copper, tin, etc., are derived from these mineral resources.
- It is estimated that the livelihood of almost 1.6 billion people depends on the forests. Up to 80 per cent of the population in developing countries depends on non-timber forest products for economic subsistence and for nutrition.
- Deforestation is the removal of a forest or trees from a land, which is converted to non-forest uses that may include farms, ranches, and urban use.
- Water footprint is the volume of water used for a product/service that is consumed. This is measured in water volume consumed (evaporated) and/or polluted.
- Blue water footprint is the volume of freshwater that evaporated from surface water and ground water.
- Green water footprint is the volume of water evaporated from rainwater stored in the soil as soil moisture.
- Grey water footprint is the volume of polluted water associated with the production. It is estimated as the volume of water required to

dilute pollutants to maintain the water quality at or above the agreed water quality standards.

- Rainwater harvesting includes the techniques and processes of accumulating and storing rainwater for future use.
- The Department of Conservation, State of California, USA, defines watershed management as 'the process of creating and implementing plans, programs, and projects to sustain and enhance watershed functions that provide the goods, services, and values desired by the community affected by conditions within a watershed boundary'.
- Oorani is the name given to a dug out tank or a pond that harvests rainwater and stores it. They are found in rural areas of South India, especially Tamilnadu, and these structures could be man-made.
- Tankas are traditional water harvesting systems found in places like Dwarka, Bikaner, etc. They are undergound tanks built under the house or in the courtyard.

- Kund is a covered underground tank found in the arid regions of Western Rajasthan. Kund is a circular underground well. It has a saucer-shaped catchment area with a slope towards the centre where the well is located.
- Khadin are water-harvesting structures to stop the surface run-off during monsoon. These structures are earthen embankments, with spillways to allow the flow and drainage of excess water.
- Vaav/Bawdi/Barav are the wells in which water can be stored and is reached by a series of descending steps.
- The loss of the productive capability of the soil is referred to as land degradation. Land degradation forces people, who are dependent on land resources, to search for new settlements.

KEYWORDS

Biomass	Mineral resources
Compressed natural gas	Modern agriculture
Deforestation	Oorani
Energy efficiency	Renewable and non-renewable energy sources
Environmental flow (e-Flow)	Solar energy
Forest resources	Tankas
Fossil fuel	Tidal energy
Khadin	Vaav/Bawdi/Barav
Kund	Water footprint
Land management	Wind energy

EXERCISES

Multiple-choice Questions

1. _____ refers to those energy sources that last for a relatively longer period of time, rely on naturally existing energy flows, and their usage is non-depleting or they get replaced at a rate faster than their usage.
   (a) Renewable energy sources
   (b) Non-renewable energy sources
   (c) Biomass
   (d) Tidal energy

2. _____ refers to organic materials that could be used for generating energy through their usage as a fuel. It could also refer to biodegradable wastes.
   (a) Renewable energy sources
   (b) Non-renewable energy sources
   (c) Biomass
   (d) Tidal energy

3. _____ is considered a cleaner fuel as it emits lesser amount of pollutants like carbon dioxide, carbon monoxide, sulphur oxides, nitrogen oxides, and particulate matter, in comparison with other fuels like petrol.
   (a) Compressed natural gas
   (b) Biomass
   (c) Tidal Energy
   (d) Fossil Fuel

4. _____ are the abiotic natural resources that exist in the world. Metals such as gold, copper, tin, etc., are derived from these resources.
   (a) Mineral resources
   (b) Energy resources
   (c) Water resources
   (d) Forest resources

5. _____ is the removal of a forest or trees from a land, which is converted to non-forest uses that may include farms, ranches, and urban use.
   (a) Deforestation
   (b) Afforestation
   (c) Soil erosion
   (d) Drought

6. _____ is the volume of water used for a product/service that is consumed. This is measured in water volume consumed (evaporated) and/or polluted.
   (a) Water footprint
   (b) Carbon footprint
   (c) Ecological footprint
   (d) Flood

7. _____ is the volume of freshwater that evaporated from surface water and ground water.
   (a) Blue footprint
   (b) Green footprint
   (c) Grey footprint
   (d) Black footprint

8. _____ is the volume of water evaporated from rainwater stored in the soil as soil moisture.
   (a) Blue footprint
   (b) Green footprint
   (c) Grey footprint
   (d) Black footprint

9. _____ is the volume of polluted water associated with the production. It is estimated as the volume of water required to dilute pollutants to maintain the water quality at or above the agreed water quality standards.
   (a) Blue footprint
   (b) Green footprint
   (c) Grey footprint
   (d) Black footprint

10. _____ includes the techniques and processes of accumulating and storing rainwater for future use and is a cost-effective way of raising the water table.
    (a) Rainwater harvesting
    (b) Green footprint
    (c) Grey footprint
    (d) Black footprint

11. Rainwater harvesting structures has

_____

(a) catchment area
(b) rainwater collection device
(c) conveyance system
(d) all of these

12. _____ refers to the area of land where all of the water that is under it or drains off of it and goes into the same place.
(a) Watershed
(b) Dam
(c) Drought
(d) Flood

13. _____ means the amount of water and flow that should be left in the river from source to sea so that it supports its ecosystem, the dependent livelihoods, and the values the river provides to humans and other organisms.

(a) Environmental flows
(b) Rain water harvesting
(c) Footprint
(d) Watershed

14. _____ is referred to as the loss of the productive capability of the soil.
(a) Land degradation
(b) Salination
(c) Desertification
(d) Soil Erosion

15. _____ is primarily characterized by the loss of the vegetation in the area.
(a) Land degradation
(b) Salination
(c) Desertification
(d) Soil erosion

Short Answer Questions

1. Write short notes on renewable and non-renewable energy sources.
2. Enlist the steps that could be undertaken to reduce the wastage of food.
3. Mention the name of five rivers that runs dry due to exploitation of its water.
4. Write short notes on Oorani, Tankas, Kund, Khadin, and Vaav/Bawdi/Barav.
5. What are the results of deforestation?
6. List out any 10 organizations in USA that uses only electricity made from renewable energy sources.
7. What are the targets of Phase II and Phase III of the Jawaharlal Nehru National Solar Mission?
8. Define land degradation.
9. Write a note on the control of soil erosion.

Long Answer Questions

1. Differentiate between energy efficiency and energy intensity.
2. What is a 'waste-to-energy' energy? Is it a highly recommended option? What is the expert opinion and recommendations about a waste-to-energy project? (One may also refer to

Chapter 7 to have a comprehensive view about this concept).
3. What are the negative effects of using synthetic fertilizers and pesticides? Why is it important to have a healthy population of bees in this world?

Reflective Question

1. Consider that the entire history of planet Earth is compressed into a 24 hour timeline. Find out (from the internet) at what minute of this 24 hours timeline did human beings appear on the planet. Then ponder on this question—how appropriate is it for human beings to exploit resources that was created millions of years prior to the human emergence on this planet? At an individual level, what can you do to consume only what you need, and not what you desire?

Take-home Activities

1. Visit FreeRice.com and explore how you can contribute to reducing world hunger.
2. After reading through the section on water harvesting, which are the techniques that you feel can be customized to be implemented as a water-harvesting technique at your home?

Recommended Books

1. Stephanie Kaza, *Mindfully Green: A Personal and Spiritual Guide to Whole Earth Thinking*, Shambhala, 2008.
2. Gita Kavarana, Sushmita Sengupta, *Catch Water Where It Falls - Toolkit on Urban Rainwater Harvesting*, Centre for Science and Environment New Delhi.
3. Suresh Kumar Rohilla, Deblina Dwivedi, *Reinvent, Recycle, Reuse - Toolkit on Decentralised Wastewater Management*, Centre for Science and Environment, New Delhi.

Recommended Documentaries/Movies

1. Among Giants. Rainhouse Cinema, 2011 (This documentary is available for free viewing at http://www.globalonenessproject.org/library/films/among-giants). Duration: 13 minutes.
2. Anupam Mishra: The Ancient Ingenuity of Water Harvesting, November 2009 (This documentary is available for free viewing at http://www.ted.com/talks/anupam_mishra_the_ancient_ingenuity_of_water_harvesting). Duration: 17 minutes

Answers to Mutiple-choice Questions:

1(a)   2(c)   3(a)   4(a)   5(a)   6(a)   7(a)   8(b)   9(c)   10(a)   11(d)   12(a)   13(a)   14(a)   15(c)

5

BUSINESS AND SUSTAINABILITY

After reading the chapter, the reader will be able to understand the following:

- Why business can exist only in the context of environmental sustainability
- How sustainability practices of business organizations is not just good for the planet, but contributes to the well-being of the businesses also
- Practices and methods that could lead us to a path of sustainable development
- Eco-labelling and sustainability certifications

The purpose of business is to make the world a better place for our children. I do NOT think that the business of business is business. You can say that the purpose is to make a profit, but it must be an ethical profit, profiting the employees and the communities they are in, making products that are worthwhile and that do not harm the world. Only sustainable businesses that care for people, the planet, and profit will survive.

I declined a lot of jobs before accepting the position of COO at the museum. A multinational pharmaceutical company asked me to work for them, but I said, no thank you. They produce a lot of things that I don't think are good. A grand casino asked me to be on their board, and I said no, it is not going to be in my portfolio. I will only work for a company that has good products that make the world a better place. The idea is that the product itself has to be worthwhile; it has to be in alignment with my spiritual view of life, which is caring for and being responsible for the earth and its inhabitants.

Carol Franklin,
Former Head-Human Resources,
Swiss Re Insurance, Switzerland,
and Former CEO, World-Wide
Fund for Nature (WWF), Switzerland[1]

1 http://www.globaldharma.org/Files%20-%20Adobe%20Acrobat/SBL/All%20Interviews%20Purpose%20of%20Business.pdf, Accessed on June 13, 2013. Quotations extracted from the public knowledge-base of the "Spiritual Based Leadership Research Programme" are © 2006 by the Global Dharma Center (GDC). GDC retains the copyright to all excerpts from this knowledge-base.

ECONOMY—'A WHOLLY OWNED SUBSIDIARY OF THE NATURAL ENVIRONMENT'[2]

Joss Tantram, Partner, Terrafiniti LLP, a company that offers consulting services focused on sustainability and CSR, says, 'This is a potentially catastrophic category error, the environment is not a sub category of the economy, rather, the reverse is true.'[3] The idea that business operations are a wholly owned subsidiary of the natural environment (see Fig. 5.1) and a change in the natural environment will have a significant impact on the business has found empirical support. A study done by two researchers at University of New Hampshire concluded that 'a failure to address the challenge of climate change' will result in tough times for businesses related to winter tourism. Shrinking number of winter tourists will directly affect industries related to skiing, snowboarding, and snowmobile. It will also affect the revenues of supportive businesses including food and beverage outlets, lodging, stores, and shops. The analysis estimated that the winter tourism industry in USA had a loss of $1 billion and 27,000 fewer jobs through the past one decade, driven by reduced snowfall patterns and resulting changes in the outdoor habits of Americans.[4] 'Without a stable climate, our industry, our jobs, the economies of mountain communities everywhere, and the valued lifestyle of winter will be gone,' says Chris Steinkamp, executive director, Protect our Winters, a US-based not-for-profit organization that engages with the winter sports community.[5] More than 100 ski resorts in USA signed a climate declaration, which asks for a bipartisan effort in tackling climate change and states that tackling climate change is 'simply the right thing to do'.[6]

SUSTAINABLE DEVELOPMENT AND ITS BACKGROUND—BRUNDTLAND COMMISSION AND RIO SUMMIT

In the 1980s, a growing need was felt to harmonize the increasing prosperity, to be in harmony with nature. While economic growth was happening, it also resulted in environmental degradation. In 1983, Javier Pérez de Cuéllar, the UN Secretary General, asked Gro Harlem Brundtland, the Prime Minister of Norway, to create an organization that focuses on developmental and environmental issues. This organization was referred to as the Brundtland Commission, or, the World Commission on Environment and Development (WCED). The commission released a report, 'Our Common Future' that became famous for the definition it gave for sustainable development—'development that

2 From a speech given by Timothy Worth, the US Undersecretary of State for Global Affairs, at a World Bank conference on ethics and development (1997). As quoted by Debra and William Miller at http://www.globaldharma.org/Files%20-%20Adobe%20Acrobat/SBL/Spirituality.%20Emerging%20Context%20for%20Bus.%20Ldrship%20UPDATED%20Oct08.pdf, last accessed on 2 October 2012.

3 http://www.guardian.co.uk/sustainable-business/blog/pricing-natural-capital-weighing-dog, last accessed on 1 October 2012.

4 http://www.nrdc.org/media/2012/121206.asp, last accessed on 12 December 2012.

5 http://www.nrdc.org/media/2012/121206.asp, last accessed on 11 June 2013.

6 http://www.ceres.org/bicep/climate-declaration, last accessed on 11 June 2013.

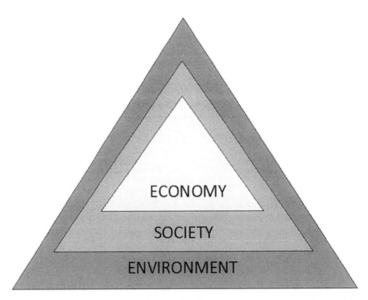

FIG. 5.1   The diagram indicates the relationship between economy, society, and natural environment, where both economy and society are subsets of the natural environment

meets the needs of the present without compromising the ability of future generations to meet their own needs'[7],[8]. The commission states that the idea of sustainable development contains two key concepts[9]:

- the concept of 'needs', in particular the essential needs of the world's poor, to which overriding priority should be given; and
- the idea of limitations imposed by the state of technology and social organization on the environment's ability to meet present and future needs.

Sustainable development communicates that our current consumption patterns should not turn out to be a burden for future generations. Through various chapters of this textbook, the reader would be able to understand how our current development paradigm is closely linked to the notion of unhindered economic growth, and how this has caused imbalances to the planet and its communities. Firms have been trying to reduce their negative impact on the planet. However, this has its limitations. 'Using less fuel or producing less waste today does not, unfortunately, erase the products of last year's less-efficient practices; nor does it make up for the increase in output that, efficiencies

---

7 http://www.un-documents.net/ocf-02.htm, last accessed on 4 July 2014.
8 http://www.un.org/esa/sustdev/csd/csd15/media/backgrounder_brundtland.pdf, last accessed on 4 July 2014.
9 http://www.un-documents.net/ocf-02.htm, last accessed on 4 July 2014.

notwithstanding, must accompany a company's expansion... As a result, the world is more unsustainable now than in 1972 in spite of the sustainability programs of firms worldwide,' says John R. Ehrenfeld in *MIT Sloan Management Review*.[10] Unsustainability is driven by economic growth and our consumption driven lifestyle that makes significant demands on the planet.

The objectives of sustainable development are as follows:
- To enhance the well-being of all life forms of this Universe, not just of human beings
- To delink the conventional notion of how growth is linked to development
- To focus on growth and development that incorporates practices and processes that are friendly to the planet and its communities
- To explore possibilities of developing and ascertaining optimum size for communities and organizations, including for-profit companies

In 1992, The United Nations Conference on Environment and Development (UNCED) (also referred as Rio Summit, Rio Conference, and Earth Summit) happened in Rio de Janeiro with participation from 172 governments. This conference resulted in (a) Rio Declaration on Environment and Development—a declaration with 27 principles aimed to guide sustainable development across the world, (b) Agenda 21—a non-binding action plan regarding sustainable development, and (c) Forest Principles—a non-legally binding recommendation plan aimed towards the conservation and sustainable development of forestry. The conference also witnessed legally binding agreements opened for signature. They were: (a) Convention on Biological Diversity, (b) Framework Convention on Climate Change (UNFCCC), and (c) United Nations Convention to Combat Desertification.

The Business Case for Sustainability

Going green is not just about being responsible. There is a strong business case for incorporating sustainability practices in an organization. Poor environmental performance can increase costs as companies have to engage in compliance problems and waste management. This will result in decreased returns to investors of the company. Customers, both as voters and as buyers of products and services, have a significant impact on environmental policy. According to a *USA Today*/Gallup Poll conducted in March 2007, more than 8 in 10 Americans consider that a company's environmental record should be an important factor in deciding whether to buy its products.

Pollution is often a form of economic waste, says Micheal Porter, Professor, Harvard Business School, in an article in *Harvard Business Review*.[11] In an interview with *Forbes* magazine, Porter says, 'What we find is most pollution is fundamentally waste; it's

10 http://sloanreview.mit.edu/article/sustainability-redefined-setting-a-goal-of-a-flourishing-world/, last accessed on 11 March 2014.
11 Porter, Michael E, Claas van der Linde 1995, Green and Competitive: Ending the Stalemate, *Harvard Business Review*, September-October 1995.

wasted resources, it's the ineffective use of technology, it's the wasteful use of water and in fact the more environmentally efficient you are the more profit you get. Now there may be a transitional period of investment where you do have to invest, but it's like any other investment. If you invest in improving your technology, closed looping your processes, recycling your materials, and taking unnecessary hazardous materials out of your product, lo and behold, you're now more efficient and more productive.'[12] Retail industry in India will agree to this, and believes that being environment-friendly do pay monetary dividends for the company.[13] Porter is also of the opinion that 'Strict environmental regulations do not inevitably hinder competitive advantage against foreign rivals; indeed, they often enhance it.'[14]

Studies[15] have explored the connection between the environmental performance of the firms and their effectiveness in improving the financial indicators. There is evidence and acknowledgment of the materiality of environmental, social, and governance (ESG) factors and its influence in driving business strategy.[16] A meta-analysis of 52 studies indicated that, 'corporate virtue in the form of social responsibility and, to a lesser extent, environmental responsibility is likely to pay off...'[17] In a research paper, 'Can Environmental Factors Improve Stock Selection?', Gluck and Becker supported 'the assertion that sensitivity to environmental issues, particularly for the extreme performers, may enhance returns of an active strategy over time.'[18] In a study 'The Economic Value of Corporate Eco-Efficiency', the researchers reported that 'eco-efficiency relates positively to operating performance and market value' and suggested that company managers do not face a trade-off between eco-efficiency and financial performance, and that investors can use environmental information for investment decisions.[19] Researchers have also compared stock market returns of top ranking companies in Newsweek Green Rankings 2009 with the stock market returns given by the broad market. This ranking list had 500 companies. Table 5.1 indicates the average market returns, in %, for various years, generated by the various segments and also the average market returns generated by various broad market indices.

12 http://www.forbes.com/sites/karlmoore/2011/04/04/harvards-michael-porter-on-how-business-can-recapture-its-reputation/, last accessed on 3 July 2014.

13 http://www.thehindubusinessline.com/economy/retailers-find-going-green-can-save-money-too/article5012919.ece, last accessed on 4 July 2014.

14 http://www.isc.hbs.edu/research-areas/Pages/environmental-quality.aspx, last accessed on 3 July 2014.

15 Dowell, G, S Hart, B Yeung, 'Do Corporate Environmental Standards Create or Destroy Market Value?', *Management Science*, 2000.

16 Asset Management Working Group (AMWG), the United Nations Environment Programme Finance Initiative (UNEP FI), and Mercer, *Demystifying Responsible Investment Performance; A Review of Key Academic and Broker Research on ESG Factors*, 2007.

17 Orlitzky, Marc, Frank L Schmidt, Sara L Rynes, 'Corporate Social and Financial Performance: A Meta-Analysis', *Organization Studies*, Vol. 24, Edn 3, March 2003, pp. 403–441.

18 http://papers.ssrn.com/sol3/papers.cfm?abstract_id=1585933, last accessed on 3 July 2014.

19 Guenster, N, R Bauer, J Derwall, K Koedijk, 'The Economic Value of Corporate Eco-Efficiency', *European Financial Management*, Vol. 17, Edn. 4, 2011, pp. 679–704.

TABLE 5.1 Average market returns of companies over the years

Returns (%)	Year 1	Year 2	Year 3	Year 4	Year 5
Companies ranked 1–50	15.39	34.57	58.71	35.08	26.86
Companies ranked 51–100	16.03	30.8	56.94	31.98	24.73
Companies ranked 101–150	38.85	43.4	89.6	53.67	43.74
Companies ranked 151–200	26.29	48.2	93.38	56.09	46.08
Companies ranked 201–250	22.95	40.1	75.68	46.27	33.49
Companies ranked 1–250	23.84	39.48	74.94	44.53	34.95
Dow Jones Industrials	1.3	12.58	34.9	7.52	-4.55
Dow Jones Composite	11.45	24.41	45.75	27.33	9.46
S&P 500	7.16	16.71	35.11	6.89	-5.72
NYSE Composite	13.29	26.23	50.48	19.38	5.06
NASDAQ Composite	9.65	16.48	39.04	13.42	11.29
Wilshire 5000	9.64	19.76	39.32	12.28	-0.09
Russell 3000	9.25	19.07	37.72	10.37	-2.36

The findings indicated that the selected ranking segments outperformed all the broad market indices such as Dow Jones Industrials, Dow Jones Composite, S&P 500, NYSE Composite, NASDAQ Composite, Dow Jones Wilshire, and Russell 3000, thereby suggesting that companies that follow green practices need not lag behind broad market indices when it comes to generating stock market returns. The research also concluded that 'there may be a strong possibility that engaging in corporate green practices can increase the stock market returns. The stock market rewarded corporations engaged in green practices, and thus investors who applied a buy-and-hold strategy would have increased their portfolio value by investing in stocks of corporations that engage in green practices. These results also imply that the top management of a company can alleviate their concerns that responsible green practices leads to worse stock market performance.'[20]

As part of the year 2006 Global 100 sustainability ranking, Innovest Venture Partners, a sustainability research firm found that the financial returns generated by stocks of those companies that occupy top slots in sustainability ranking 2006 outperformed other stocks (indicated through MSCI World Index). On back testing, it was found that the stocks of Global 100 sustainable companies outperformed MSCI world index by 13.46 per cent, 5.47 per cent, and 7.11 per cent during a one-year, three-year, and five-year period respectively.

STRATEGIES FOR SUSTAINABLE DEVELOPMENT

'*If we're going to talk about transport, I would say that the great city is not the one that has highways, but one where a child on a tricycle or bicycle can go safely everywhere.*'[21]

Enrique Peñalosa Londoño, Former Mayor of Bogota, Colombia.

20 Sankar RN, Vaishnavi Krishnan, *3rd International Conference on Integrating Spirituality and Organizational Leadership*, Haridwar, conducted by IIT Roorkee, Gurukula Kangri Vishwavidyalaya and ISOL Foundation, 1–5 February 2011.

Integrating Environmental Sustainability into Core Business Practices

There existed a notion that sustainability related endeavours are peripheral to the business processes of a company. One of the dominant thoughts in the world of business used to be, 'Make money. Once you have a significant surplus, do philanthropy, if you wish.' However, there were always organizations for whom social and environmental responsibility and love for the creation was part of their process DNA. Organizations such as Toms of Maine (http://www.tomsofmaine.com/home), Ben & Jerry's (http://www.benjerry.com/), Krya (http://krya.in/), GoodSearch (http://www.goodsearch.com/), Ecosia (http://www.ecosia.org/), FabIndia (http://www.fabindia.com/), Interface (http://www.interfaceglobal.com), Ecologin (http://ecologin.org/), Ethicus (http://www.ethicus.in/, and http://www.appachicotton.com/), etc., have embodied these values in varying degrees. For these companies, sustainability parameters are not just peripheral to their business processes, but are core to the company's decision-making processes. Integrating sustainability into a company's business practices also has other benefits. A study done in France found that employees who work in environment-friendly firms are more likely to work uncompensated overtime hours, and feel more useful and equitably recognized at work.[22]

Corporate social responsibility (CSR) is not just about how a company shares its profit with the society, it is also about how the company generates its revenue from the society!

Through the years, we find that many of the more recognized companies are integrating sustainability related parameters into their business processes. Table 5.2 cites some of these examples, indicating that AkzoNobel have incorporated corporate environmental strategy, while PUMA has introduced environmental accounting as a business practice.

TABLE 5.2[23] Integrated environmental sustainability parameters used by companies

Corporate strategy	AkzoNobel
Corporate accounting	PUMA, The Dow Chemical Company
Project siting and development	Shell, The Walt Disney Company
Environmental and social impact assessments (ESIAs)	BP
Land management	Lafarge, Mead Westvaco

(Contd)

21 http://www.itdp.org/news/enrique-penalosa-urges-san-francisco, last accessed on 5 March 2013.

22 Joseph Lanfranchia, Sanja Pekovicb, How green is my firm? Workers' attitudes and behaviors towards job in environmentally-related firms, Ecological Economics, Volume 100, April 2014, Pages 16–29; Also available at http://www.sciencedirect.com/science/article/pii/S0921800914000044, Accessed on March 1, 2014.

23 'Private Sector Uptake of Ecosystem Services Concepts and Frameworks: The Current State of Play', BSR, March 2013; Also available at http://www.bsr.org/reports/BSR_Private_Sector_Uptake_Ecosystem_Services.pdf, last accessed on 28 August 2013.

Payments for ecosystem services	Rio Tinto, Vittel (Nestlé Waters), Goldman Sachs
Supply chain management	British American Tobacco
Corporate performance reporting	Weyerhaeuser
Corporate environmental management	Coca-Cola, Hitachi
Risk assessment	Anglo American, EDP, Rabobank
Stakeholder engagement	Holcim
External collaboration and partnerships	Dow and The Nature Conservancy, American Electric Power and the Wildlife Habitat Council

Extended Producer Responsibility

Extended producer responsibility or EPR is a mandate making the manufacturer of the product responsible for the entire life-cycle of the product, including post-consumer usage. This mandate has an objective of decreasing the total environmental impact of a product, and includes take-back, recycling, and disposal.

Planned obsolescence, which is an industrial design practice where a product is designed with a limited shelf life, has resulted in easy disposals and waste (Fig. 5.2 shows a cartoon on 'Planned obsolescence'). This is beneficial for a company as the consumer has to buy the newer update, either from the same company or its competitor, who may also follow planned obsolescence practices. One of the examples that could be considered as planned obsolescence could be the release of the iPhone line of smart-phones by Apple Inc. The original iPhone, iPhone 3G, iPhone 3GS, iPhone 4, iPhone 4S, iPhone 5 were released in the year 2007, 2008, 2009, 2010, 2011, iPhone 5C and 5S, and iPhone 6 and 6 Plus 2012, 2013, and 2014 respectively. In countries like India, while some of these phones may get down-cycled (conversion into something of lower quality), some of them become e-waste in landfills, and adds to the toxicity of the planet. With EPR, manufacturers take responsibility for recycling or disposal of such wastage. For example, Nokia India has set up 1400+ recycling points across India where one can drop old cell-phones and accessories of any brand for recycling.

Some of the attributes of EPR are as follows:

• EPR encourages manufacturers to design products that are environmentally-friendly. This is because the responsibility of managing the products after end-of-life rests with the manufacturer. As the costs related to take-back, recycling/disposal are internalized, manufacturers will be prompted to design products that are long-lasting, reused, recyclable, and have less materials usage. Speaking about the general reluctance to reuse or recycle plastic based materials, Carl

'If we're going to talk about transport, I would say that the great city is not the one that has highways, but one where a child on a tricycle or bicycle can go safely everywhere.'
Enrique Peñalosa Londoño, Former Mayor of Bogota, Colombia.

Safina, a marine biologist, the founding president of the Blue Ocean Institute and a research professor at Stony Brook University, says, 'It's too cheap to recycle because the makers and sellers don't pay the costs of disposal. As with many "cheap" things, the price reflects only the fact that the sellers privatize their profits and socialize the costs. Many things priced cheap are really rather costly.'[24] If EPR are instituted, the companies may also be prompted to incentivize consumers to recycle.

- It relieves local governments from the efforts given for private waste management, which usually is funded by public money.

- With increasing funding from companies, these practices may promote new innovations in recycling related technologies and processes.

- From an economic perspective, an EPR initiative tends to correct an existing anomaly, by shifting the product's price to also include the waste management cost. As products start reflecting their true costs, the consumer will bear the cost of its disposal, and not the non-consumer.

- Job creation in areas related to recovery, reuse, and recycling.

FIG. 5.2 Planned obsolescence (of children)

24 http://e360.yale.edu/feature/carl_safina_gyre_tons_of_trash_covers_shores_alaska/2668/, last accessed on 3 July 2013.

A cartoon by Joe Mohr that indicates the link between childhood obesity and consumption of sugary drinks.[25]

Poverty Alleviation and Bottom of Pyramid Models

Bottom of Pyramid (BoP) is a term popularized by CK Prahalad, Professor, Corporate Strategy, Ross School of Business, University of Michigan through *The Fortune at the Bottom of the Pyramid*, a book that spoke about successful organizations such as Aravind Eye Hospitals and Jaipur Rugs that provided goods and services to the poorest people of the world. During the period April 2013 to March 2014, Aravind Eye Hospitals conducted a total of 3,78,035 surgeries out of which 85,935 were done free of charge (23 per cent) and 101, 908 were done at a subsidized cost (27 per cent).[26]

In the context of Economics, bottom of pyramid refers to the population that lives on less than US$2.5 a day. This is also the poorest and largest socio-economic group. In an article previously written on the same theme, Prahalad and Stuart L Hart, Professor, Strategic Management, Kenan-Flagler Business School, University of North Carolina, convey the idea that contrary to perception 'that the poor cannot participate in the global market economy',[27] 'the real source of market promise is not the wealthy few in the developing world, or even the emerging middle-income consumers: It is the billions of aspiring poor who are joining the market economy for the first time.'[28]

Cleaner Production

As per the United Nations Environment Programme (UNEP), '"Cleaner Production" is the continuous application of an integrated preventative environmental strategy to processes, products, and services to increase efficiency and reduce risks to humans and the environment.'[29] Cleaner Production encompasses the following:

- Good housekeeping—preventing leaks and spills and proper maintenance
- Change of input material—Replacing hazardous/non-renewable materials with non-hazardous/less hazardous/renewable materials and/or by materials with a longer service life-time
- Improving process control
- Technology upgradation—Upgrading production equipment and processes to improve efficiency, reduce waste, and emissions
- Recovery and reuse of waste materials

25 Image Source: http://joemohrtoons.com/2013/05/01/planned-obsolescence-of-children/, last accessed on 19 June 2013. Used with permission.
26 http://www.aravind.org/downloads/AECS Report201314.pdf, last accessed on 4 March 2015.
27 http://www.stuartlhart.com/sites/stuartlhart.com/files/Prahalad_Hart_2001_SB.pdf, last accessed on 13 June 2013.
28 http://www.stuartlhart.com/sites/stuartlhart.com/files/Prahalad_Hart_2001_SB.pdf, last accessed on 13 June 2013.
29 http://www.unido.org/what-we-do/environment/resource-efficient-and-low-carbon-industrial-production/cp/cleaner-production.html, last accessed on 11 May 2013.

Cradle to Cradle Design and Sustainable Products and Services

In *Ecology of Commerce*, Paul Hawken visions a transformed economy that runs on 'solar income' such as sunlight, biomass, wind-power, etc., as opposed to 'solar wealth' like fossil fuels. In that economy, wastes produced from one production process becomes input for another. Cradle to Cradle (C2C) design is a bio-mimetic approach popularized by Michael Braungart, a chemist from Germany and William McDonough, an architect from USA. This approach was outlined in their book, '*Cradle to Cradle: Remaking the Way We Make Things*'. In this approach to design of systems, materials involved in industrial/commercial production are viewed as nutrients circulating in healthy, safe metabolisms. This phrase was coined by Water R. Stahel in the 1970s. In the C2C model, all materials used in an industrial/commercial process are seen as either technical or biological nutrients. Non-toxic, non-harmful, and synthetic materials that have no harmful effects on the natural environment fall under technical nutrients. They can be used again instead of being 'downcycled' to lesser products, finally becoming waste. Biological nutrients are materials that are organic in character. Once used, they can be disposed in any natural environment without harming the natural environment. These organic wastes also provide food for smaller life forms during decomposition.

Products that meet the C2C certification program parameters given the C2C certification. This is awarded at five levels—basic, bronze, silver, gold, and platinum. Certifying a product as C2C is based on the product meeting the requirements for a given level across five categories, which are[30]

- Material health—Making products out of materials that are safe and healthy for humans and the environment
- Material reutilization—Designing products so all materials can be re-used by nature or industry
- Renewable energy and carbon management—Assembling and manufacturing products with renewable and non-polluting energy
- Water stewardship—Making products in ways that protect and enrich water supplies
- Social fairness—Treating all the people involved in the product manufacturing process in socially responsible ways

The C2C model often lowers the financial cost of systems. An example is the redesign of the Ford River Rouge Complex by William McDonough. It is said that Ford saved $35,000,000 on

ASDA, a supermarket chain with retail outlets in more than 550 locations in UK, entered into a partnership with Fareshare, a UK based charitable organization working to relieve food poverty, to distribute leftover chilled surplus food stock.

---

30 http://c2ccertified.org/product_certification/c2ccertified_product_standard, last accessed on 8 March 2013, Used with permission.

mechanical treatment plants by planting native grasses (sedum) on assembly plant roofs that resulted in cleansing of rain water which also moderated the internal temperature of the building. The roof is part of a rainwater treatment system designed to clean 20 billion gallons of rainwater, annually. The greened 10 acre roof decreased the energy cost by 7 per cent and improved air quality by 40 per cent.

Earlier, as part of eco-friendly manufacturing practices, the objective was to reduce the amount of pollution or harm created to the planet and people—the objective was not complete elimination of pollution. Practices like C2C Design aims at zero-harm for the planet. Though businesses have not been completely successful in implementing this philosophy across their business value chain, there have been a number of initiatives that could be considered path-breaking. An example could be the initiative from Nike to reuse the worn-out shoes to provide cushion in basketball, volleyball, and tennis courts. It is also used in Nike apparels and in shoes like Nike Air Jordan XX3.

Bio-mimicry

As per the Centre for Biomimetics, University of Reading, bio-mimicry or bio-mimetics refers to the abstraction of good design from nature. The processes and models followed by nature are observed, and they are replicated in human endeavours, primarily meant to solve a human need. This design process works on the conviction that nature already has time-tested solutions that can provide answers to many of the problems, businesses are grappling with. For example,

- Heliotropism displayed by certain flowers[31] (the pattern of flowers tracking the direction of sun)—Designing an array of solar cells based on this pattern of Heliotropism.
- Honeycomb geometry—A honeycomb structure provides minimal density. Such structures provide maximum functionality with minimal weight and minimizing the amount of quality and amount of material. This idea could be used to increase the efficiency and effectiveness of people practices in organizations. Re-aligning and joining together undervalued assets, people, and services that could create path-breaking functions and endeavours.

Green Product Design—Environmental Responsibility and Economic Viability

Designing green products will entail looking into the entire product life cycle (PLC) of a product with the objective of reducing the negative impact of a product on the planet and also on the health of living beings, including human beings. Such a design process aims to improve the efficiency and effectiveness though the entire life cycle—from the

---

31 http://www.youtube.com/watch?v=3MYJEm99MYQ, last accessed on 11 May 2013.

'An advanced city is not a place
where the poor move about in
cars, rather it's where even the rich
use public transportation.'
Enrique Peñalosa Londoño, Former
Mayor of Bogota, Colombia.

sourcing and usage of raw materials to post-purchase behaviour of the consumer. Green product design can also be referred to as green design, eco-design, or design for environment. Green product design normally involves system thinking, a perspective that looks into the whole, rather than in fragmentation.

Green product design will look into the following points:

Sourcing of raw materials that are recyclable, recycled, and have no toxicity   '...trend of replacing traditional materials with sustainable alternatives is something that's emerging across almost all industries...' says John Viera, Director of Sustainable Business Strategies, Ford Motor Company.[32] PepsiCo, in March 2011, announced the launch of the world's first PET plastic bottle made entirely from plant-based, fully renewable resources and is 100 per cent recyclable. This will go for pilot production in 2012. At Ford Motor Company, soy-based foam is used to fill seats and headliners in Ford automobiles, instead of using the conventional petroleum-based plastics. For carpet insulation, the company used old blue jeans. For storage bins and door panels, wheat straw was used while recycled soda pop bottles contributed to making carpets and fabrics. All these ensured that almost 95 per cent of the materials used in Ford vehicles were recyclable.

Creating durable and multi-use products   Unlike the conventional product design trends, many of which promote a disposable culture, a green product design aims to create products that are durable and can be used multiple times through upgrades or minor improvements. For example, a computer manufacturer that designs a computer system allowing for future upgradation can be considered to have a better green product design as compared to a computer manufacturer who promotes a use-and-throw culture. A number of Apple iPhone users disposed the older version product to purchase the newer version product as soon as the newest version product enters the market. A manufacturer who allows for future upgradation is practicing environmental responsibility as the consumer need not buy the future upgrades on a frequent basis, thereby saving on the resources and the environmental impact these products will have.

Design for minimal energy and resource requirement   The manufacturing and usage of the product should result in the consumption of minimum energy and resource requirement. Energy efficiency is one of the important aspects of green design.

---

32 http://www.greenbiz.com/blog/2011/08/16/rethinking-green-products-re-imagining-your-inputs, last accessed on 3 October 2011.

End-of-life recycling and reuse capability Designers will try to focus on sustainable design principles such as C2C design and bio-mimicry to ensure complete and constant reuse of materials in closed loops.

Facilitating sharing of resources Shifting from a mode that is privately owned to a sharing mode. For example, instead of creating a situation where people use personal automobiles for transportation, one may go for public transportation, car-sharing services, etc.

Emotionally durable designs Increasing the quality of relationship between people and the products they use can result in reducing consumption and waste of resources.

In certain occasions, environmental responsibility and economic viability can be in opposite poles, while in certain times, they function together. For example, usage of high quality ingredients in a food item will result in a higher pricing. However, shifting to a higher standard collective alternative may result in lower cost, as could be in the case of a high quality Mass Rapid Transport System (MRTS), instead of using a private vehicle.

Green Vehicles and Electric Mobility

'An advanced city is not a place where the poor move about in cars, rather it's where even the rich use public transportation.'[33] says Enrique Peñalosa Londoño, Former Mayor of Bogota, Colombia.

With increasing emissions of the harmful carbon dioxide, depletion of fossil fuels, and the emerging demand for alternative transportation needs, green transportation has been in increasing focus. A report by Navigant Research[34] indicates that the sales of plug-in electric vehicles, in USA, will have a compounded annual growth rate (CAGR) of 18.6 per cent between 2013 and 2022. Globally, by 2020, the sale of Hybrid electric vehicles (HEVs) is expected to double its share of the global light duty vehicle sales (to 4 per cent from 2 per cent). By 2020, sales of plug-in electric vehicles will reach 3 million vehicles, a three per cent share of the global light-duty vehicle market.[35] Though emission targets for gasoline burning automobiles are becoming more stringent, a quantum shift is required in transportation paradigm if emissions are to be curbed significantly. There has been much discussion and research into vehicles that do not emit any polluting emissions, also referred to as zero emission vehicles (see Fig. 5.3 depicting a cartoon on zero emission vehicles).

---

33 http://anarchogeek.com/2012/09/21/translating-tweet-goes-viral/, last accessed on 5 March 2013.

34 http://www.navigantresearch.com/newsroom/california-new-york-washington-and-florida-will-lead-the-united-states-in-plug-in-electric-vehicle-sales-through-2022, last accessed on 19 October 2013.

35 http://www.navigantresearch.com/research/electric-vehicle-market-forecasts, last accessed on 19 October 2013.

FIG. 5.3[36] A cartoon by Joe Mohr on zero emission vehicles

One of the options assessed as part of green mobility is public transportation, primarily driven by electric mobility. Experts have considered electric based transportation as 'the only feasible and market-ready technology for zero-emission vehicles.'[37] A successful electric mobility paradigm can emerge if there is a supportive environment. A supportive environment can be created if there is improvement in the battery technologies, automobile manufacturers producing electric versions of the vehicles, and support from the government. Government can provide incentives for research and development into alternate technologies like electric mobility. The government can also increase fuel-efficiency targets, discourage carbon dioxide emitting transportation systems, and reduce fossil fuel subsidies. Media has reported that subsidies given by rich countries for fossil-fuels are five times that of climate aid given by them to help developing nations reduce emissions and mitigate the negative effects of climate change. Bloomberg, quoting Oil Change International, a Washington based campaign group, says, 'In 2011, 22 industrialized nations paid $58.7 billion in subsidies to the oil, coal, and gas industries, and to consumers of the fuels, compared with climate-aid flows of $11.2 billion.'[38] The government could also aid in developing a charging infrastructure for electric vehicles of all kinds.

Green Buildings and Natural Buildings

Organic architecture is increasingly in the news. Organic architecture is a design approach that attempts a harmony between the human dwelling and the natural environment.

---

36 Image Source: http://joemohrtoons.com/2013/02/14/hank-d-and-the-bee-zero-emissions-vehicles/, last accessed on 19 June 2013. Used with permission.

37 Berger, Roland 2011,*Green Growth, Green Profit: How Green Transformation Boosts Business*, Palgrave Macmillan, 2011

38 http://www.bloomberg.com/news/2012-12-03/fossil-fuel-subsidies-of-rich-nations-are-five-times-climate-aid.html, last accessed on 21 December 2012.

In 2014, P.K. Sreenivasan from Vasthukam Organic Architects constructed a series of eco-friendly houses in a tribal village. The process used materials available in the locality and almost half of the construction costs were given as wages to the tribals. Experiments are on to explore alternate mechanisms and resources to design and construct human habitats. This includes green buildings and natural buildings.

Green Buildings

As per Environment Protection Agency (EPA), a green building is one 'whose construction and lifetime of operation assure the healthiest possible environment while representing the most efficient and least disruptive use of land, water, energy, and resources.'[39] Estimates indicate that buildings consume approximately 40 per cent of global energy and are responsible for 30 per cent of global greenhouse gas emissions.[40] The building sector consumes three billion tonnes of raw material on an annual basis.[41]

The building industry can deliver cost savings, create green jobs, and improve local economies. A report by Confederation of Indian Industry (CII), *Energy Efficiency in Building Design and Construction*[42] states that the energy saving potential for a green building can be as high as 40–50 per cent if efficiency measures are incorporated in design state, and it could be 20–25 per cent for an existing building that goes for retrofitting. A green building uses less energy, water, and natural resources. It uses design principles such as day-lighting (the use of natural resources to supplement or replace artificial lighting) and green roofing. Researchers have found that 'The integration of green roofs in urban spatial planning strategies has great potential to enable higher connectivity among green spaces.'[43] Green buildings generate less waste and provide a healthy living environment for the occupant. Other benefits mentioned for green buildings include operational cost savings and high rental or capital value for owners. In the commercial real estate sector, it has been found that buildings with a green rating generate a rental rate that is three per cent higher per square foot. A 16 per cent premium in sales price is also noted for green buildings. In the residential real estate market, a green labelled home gives a nine per cent sales price premium.[44] Green buildings also provide better working conditions within the building.

---

39 http://www.epa.gov/statelocalclimate/documents/pdf/12_8_what_is_green_GGGC.pdf, last accessed on 30 September 2013.

40 http://www.unep.org/sbci/pdfs/UNEP_SBCI_Call_to_action_final.pdf, last accessed on 23 June 2012.

41 http://www.unep.org/sbci/pdfs/BuildingsandClimateChange.pdf, last accessed on 23 June 2012.

42 http%3a//www.igbc.in%3a9080/site/mmbase/attachments/43046/Energy_efficiency.pdf, last accessed on 29 April 2012.

43 Braaker, Sonja, Jaboury Ghazoul, Martin K. Obrist, and Marco Moretti,' Habitat connectivity shapes urban arthropod communities : the key role of green roofs, *Ecology*, Vol. 95, No. 4 : 1010-1021, http://dx.doi.org/10.1890/13-0705.1. Abstract availabe at http://www.esajournals.org/doi/abs/10.1890/13-0705.1?af=R&, last accessed on 4 October 2013.

44 http://www.greenbiz.com/blog/2013/01/04/value-green-labels-real-estate-market, last accessed on 8 January 2013.

There are a number of green building rating systems in the world. Two major green building rating systems prevalent in India are 'Leadership in Energy and Environmental Design' (LEED) India (see Fig. 5.4 for an image of a green building), which is administered by the Indian Green Building Council (IGBC) and Green Rating for Integrated Habitat Assessment (GRIHA) developed by TERI (The Energy and Research Institute). These independent, third-party verification systems ensure that a project engages in the highest green related practices and performance measures.

The LEED India rating system has the following five components:

1. Sustainable sites
2. Water efficiency
3. Energy and atmosphere
4. Materials and resources
5. Indoor environmental quality

In addition to these five components, design measures not covered under any of these heads are included under a category titled 'innovation and design process'. Buildings can earn credits under these segments. The more the credits earned, the better the green rating.

FIG. 5.4[45] Suzlon, a wind turbine supplier, has its corporate campus at Pune. It's 'One Earth' campus is 100 per cent powered by renewable energy and the building in the photo is LEED Platinum rated building.

45 Photo: Suzlon (www.suzlon.com). Used with permission.

The highest level of rating is LEED Platinum, followed by LEED Gold, LEED Silver, and LEED certified building. Table 5.3 gives the details for the certification for a residential unit.

Credits earned from a LEED rated green building can be traded in the carbon market. LEED Platinum certified green buildings are energy efficient, utilize renewable energy, conserve and recycle water, and preserve the ecosystem around them. A benefit cost analysis study[47] done by Jones Lang Lasalle (JLL) on a LEED-Gold certified green building indicated that the payback period for the cost premium incurred was 2–3 years. The earlier mentioned CII report states, 'The incremental cost incurred for achieving energy efficiency is 5–8 per cent vis-à-vis conventional design cost and can have an attractive payback period of 2–4 years' (see Tables 5.4 and 5.5). As green buildings incur a premium, one common question is about the payback period. 'Since this question is asked often, most green building professionals will simply state that most green buildings have an added cost of 5–15 per cent (compared to a conventional building) and that the payback period is usually 3–5 years. While this is true in many cases, I personally believe the cost of going green is relative and cannot be accurately quantified,' says Yusuf Turab, Managing Director, YT Enterprises, and also an IGBC accredited professional and a LEED green associate.

TABLE 5.3[46] LEED India certification for a residential building

Ratings	Credits required for an individual residential unit	Credits required for a multi-dwelling residential unit
LEED Certified	38–44	50–59
LEED Silver	45–51	60–69
LEEED Gold	52–59	70–79
LEED Platinum	60–75	80–100

TABLE 5.4[48] Monitoring of energy savings in three LEED Platinum rated buildings

Building	Built-up area (sq.ft)	Consumption of conventional building (kWh)	Consumption of LEED designed building (kWh)	Reduction (%)	Annual energy savings (in Lakhs)
Wipro Technologies, Gurgaon	1,75,000	48,00,000	31,00,000	40	102
ITC Green Centre, Gurgaon	1,70,000	35,00,000	20,00,000	45	90
CII Godrej GBC, Hyderabad	20,000	3,50,000	1,30,000	63	9

46 https://online.igbc.in/igbc/redirectHtml.htm?redVal=showGreenHomesnosign#CertificationLevels, last accessed on 3 July 2014.

47 http://www.joneslanglasalle.com/ResearchLevel1/research_greenomics_cost_efficiency_of_green_buildings_in_india.pdf, last accessed on 29 April 2012

48 http://cii.in/WebCMS/Upload/Mr%20S%20Raghupathy.pdf, last accessed on 6 October 2013. Used with permission from Confedaration of Indian Industry (CII).

TABLE 5.5[49] Payback period for green buildings

Building	Year awarded	Built-in area (sq. ft)	Rating achieved	increase in cost	Payback
Technopolis, Kolkata	2006	72,000	Gold	6%	3 years
Spectral Services Consultants Office, Noida	2007	15,000	Platinum	8%	4 years
HITAM, Hyderabad	2007	78,000	Silver	2%	3 years

TERI's GRIHA Rating System

Green Rating for Integrated Habitat Assessment (GRIHA) is the national green building rating system and acts as integrating platform for various national building codes. Endorsed by Ministry of New and Renewable Energy (MNRE), this code provides a rating of up to five stars for green buildings based on 34 criteria that takes into consideration health and well-being, materials and resources used, water efficiency, energy efficiency, and usage of renewable energy, sustainable site planning, and solid waste management.

'Green building promoted in India must be affordable. If solutions are not for all, they are not necessarily green… Climate specific passive comfort strategies should be promoted and encouraged to reduce reliance on energy for cooling, heating as well as lighting. The focus would be not on new materials, but using old materials in new ways with an aim to reduce the dependence on industrial manufactured materials like cement and steel…Ideally, technologies that employ a significant proportion of unskilled labour would be further beneficial for Indian society which is in rapid transition,' says[50] Anupama Kundoo, who teaches architecture at the University of Queensland, Brisbane.

ITC Hotels became the first hotel chain in the world that had all its eight luxury properties LEED Platinum certified. All ITC luxury hotels—ITC Maurya, New Delhi, ITC Maratha, Mumbai, ITC Grand Central, Mumbai, ITC Sonar, Kolkata, ITC Windsor, Bengaluru, ITC Gardenia, Bengaluru, ITC Kakatiya, Hyderabad, and ITC Mughal, Agra—have been awarded the highest green building standards by US Green Building Council (USGBC) or by Indian Green Building Council (IGBC) for practicing energy, water, and waste management efficiency.

Natural Buildings—Tools and Techniques

While LEED, GRIHA, etc., mostly incorporate latest technologies, there is another style of sustainable architecture—natural buildings. The following are the attributes related to natural buildings:

• Natural building includes a variety of building techniques that focus on creating sustainable buildings which minimize their negative ecological impact. Natural buildings incorporate traditional forms of architecture

---

49 http://cii.in/WebCMS/Upload/Mr%20S%20Raghupathy.pdf, last accessed on 6 October 2013. Used with permission from Confedaration of Indian Industry (CII).

50 Kundoo, Anupama 2012, Sustainable urban development and affordability, *The Hindu Survey of the Environment 2012*.

and construction based on the goal of using abundantly and locally available, renewable, reused, recyclable, recycled, and renewable materials. Clay, sand, wood, straw, bamboo, and rock are some of the materials used in natural buildings.

- As compared to green buildings, natural buildings provide a heightened focus on architectural design that should be in semblance with the natural environment. Respect and sensitivity to the local natural area and landscape are guiding values, and thus minimal disruption is caused to the existing landscape.
- While there is a strong need to lessen the environmental impact of buildings, care is given to ensure comfort, healthy living environment, aesthetics, and indoor air quality.
- Natural building tends to rely on human labour, more than technology. It celebrates human craft.
- Natural buildings focused on reduction in energy consumption during the construction and usage. Energy is also generated from renewable sources.

Adobe   Adobe are bricks made by mixing clay and sand, along with water. To this mixture, chopped straw or other fibres may be added. The mixture can be poured into moulds and dried, or can be pressed into blocks. Adobe has good thermal mass and thus is slow to transmit heat or cold. Building structures made of adobe are some of the most durable. However, they are prone to seismic activities.

Cob   Cob is also made from clay, sand, straw, and water, almost similar to adobe. In adobe-based construction, adobe bricks are made, dried, and then construction is done. In cob-based construction, the buildings are constructed while the mixture is wet and they are sculpted into monolithic structures or wall.

Cob structures are known to be fireproof, earthquake resistant, and inexpensive. Cob structures are created bottom up and uses no forms, bricks or wooden framework. Once the cob structure is built, its outer surface is trimmed to give perfect shape. The wall of the building will be of 1-2 feet thickness in a cob. Cob is suitable for rainy areas also. The lifespan of cob is much higher than adobe. While construction of a cob building is labour intensive, it provides the benefit of flexibility in conversion to any form. Cob-like mixes are also used as plaster and fillers in other natural buildings.

Rammed earth   It is a technique used to make walls of a building using soil, chalk, lime, and gravel. If machinery is not used, their construction is labour-intensive. This technique is simple and involves compressing of a damp mixture of the earlier mentioned materials into a frame or a mould. The frame is made of wood to act as a mould that gives shape and dimension to the wall. The damp mixture is poured into the frame to a depth of approximately 25 cm and then compressed to 50 per cent of its original height. A ramming pole was used for this compression. Once this is done, the next round of damp mixture is poured. Gradually, the wall is built to the top of the frame. Rammed earth technique is similar to cob——the uniqueness being that rammed earth uses wooden frames or moulds to keep the size of the walls exact. Rammed earth technique has been in use since 5000 BC. The by-products of this process are bio-degradable. Rammed earth is termite resistant, non-toxic, and fireproof.

Straw bale   In this building method, bales of straw, wheat, rice, oats, and rye, are stacked together on the foundation of the building. The bales are tied together and then they are plastered with a lime or clay mixture (see Fig. 5.5).

Wattle and daub   Wattle and daub is a construction technique used for making walls. Wattle is a lattice of wooden or bamboo strips. This wattle is covered and plastered (daub) with a sticky mixture made of clay, sand, water, and straw. Wattle and daub was being used 6000 years back.

Sod roof   Sod roof is the roof of a building that is partially or completely covered with sod, a type of grass. The roof is usually made of the bark of birch trees and this bark provides the water-tight element. These roofs are usually found in Scandinavian countries.

Earthbags   Earthbags are formed by mixing clay and sand, and packing them into bags. They are formed into a wall.

FIG. 5.5[51] A straw bale-based construction in progress

---

51 Photo by Philipp Schmidt J, Image Source: http://www.flickr.com/photos/43686844@N00/418679778, last accessed on 3 July 2014. Used with permission.

Papercrete   Papercrete is a plastering material formed from pulp made from newspapers, magazines, and other publications, and is mixed with clay or cement.

Cordwood   In this technique, short and round pieces of firewood are used.

Slipstraw   Loose straw is coated with a mixture of clay and water, which is mixed to the consistency of paint. This mixture is compressed to form walls.

Compressed earth block   This is made with soil and clay.

Other techniques include timber frame, stone, bamboo, and earthen floors.

Some of the organizations/architects involved in using indigenous, green, sustainable, and aesthetic methods of construction in India include the following:

- Vasthukam, The Organic Architects (http://www.vasthukamarchitects.com/gallery.aspx)
- G Shankar and Habitat Technology Group (http://habitatonweb.com/wp/)
- COSTFORD, inspired by Laurie Baker (http://www.costford.com/index.htm)
- Eugene Pandala (http://eugenepandala.com/Eugene_pandala/HOME.html)
- Dr Chandrasekhar Hariharan, ZED Habitats (http://www.zed.in/)
- Chitra Vishwanath (http://www.inika.com/chitra/)
- Mistry Architects (http://mistrys.com/)
- KrishnaRao Jaisim (http://www.jaisimfountainhead.in/)
- Sanjay Prakash (http://sanjayprakash.co.in/)
- Abhikram Architects (http://www.abhikram.com/home.php)
- Inspiration (http://inspire-india.com/index.html)
- Good Earth (http://www.goodearthhomes.net/)
- Rare Earth (http://www.rareearthdevelopers.com/index.html)
- Anupama Kundoo (http://anupamakundoo.com/)
- Castelino & Marchese (http://castelinomarchese.com/)

Green Investing/Socially Responsible Investing

Socially responsible investing (SRI) is an investment strategy that considers financial returns, social good, and environmental impacts while making an investment. Green investing could be considered a subset of SRI. SRI is broader in focus as compared to green investing. The investments can be considered to be green investments if the following hold true:

- it does not make negative impacts on the environment
- it makes a negative environmental impact that is significantly less than the negative environmental impacts of other similar projects
- it adds to the ecological well-being

Green investors invest in businesses that do not pollute the environment or minimize the pollution, businesses that are sustainable in the long run and are involved eco-friendly business practises. Green investing focuses on investment in projects that contribute not just to economic well-being, but also to the well-being of the society and also the planet.

The eco-task force (ETF) of Territorial Army and the Delhi Government has been successful in transforming a degraded land to an urban forestry initiative by planting native tree saplings and rejuvenating the grasslands. The Deramandi urban foresty project is the only project from India accepted by the UN Framework Climate Change (UNFCC) Clean Development Mechanism (CDM), making it an eligible project for carbon credit trading in the international market.

Green investments can be in the form of green shares, green bonds, green funds, green deposits, etc. By investing in equity of a company that engages in sustainable development, an investor can be said to own a green share. Banks collect money from public and channelize it/lend it to those who are looking for money. Banks that run green deposits lend the money only to those projects/businesses that are ecologically friendly. The bank will not channelize that money to businesses/practices that cause harm to the ecology. Some of the mutual funds offer fund offerings that are green. For example, ABN Amro launched India's first ecologically responsible fund with the launch of 'ABN Amro Sustainable Development Fund' in March 2007. The investment objective of the fund was 'to generate long-term capital growth from an actively managed portfolio of equity and equity related securities primarily of the socially responsible companies focusing on sustainable development. The scheme will aim to identify investment opportunities in companies across all ranges of market-capitalization, defined as *Socially Responsible Companies*.'[52]

The fund managers of such mutual funds invest only on those companies that are rated high in their ecology friendly practices. They will screen for companies that are environment friendly and screen against companies that are harming the environment. These decisions are taken based on ascertaining whether the company practices sustainability reporting/triple bottom line reporting, whether the company is listed on sustainability indices like Dow Jones Sustainability Index (DJSI), rated high on various green rankings etc. DJSI is the first global index to track the performance of companies that operate on long-term sustainable principles.

Some of the key performance indicators used to ascertain the greenness of a company includes energy efficiency, deployment of renewable energy sources, sector-specific KPIs which apply to certain sectors, CO_2 emissions, NO and SO emissions, waste, environmental compatibility, and end-of-lifecycle impact.

As part of managing a green portfolio, the fund managers may adopt various investing strategies. This could be negative screening, divestment, shareholder activism, shareholder engagement, and positive investment.

- *Negative screening* is the process of excluding certain securities from investment consideration based on green factors. Companies involved in the manufacturing of nuclear weapons/nuclear energy, tobacco, fossil fuel, animal testing (for non-medical purposes), factory farming, genetically modified organisms (GMOs), agricultural pesticides, etc., may be excluded from the list of companies where the fund management will invest.

---

52 www.moneycontrol.com/pdffiles/abn-sustain.pdf, last accessed on 13 April 2012.

- Contrary to negative screening is *positive investment*. As part of positive investment, investment will be made on companies that have a high positive social/environmental impact. This would typically be companies involved in alternative energy, eco-friendly products, green technology, organic/natural food supply, water solutions, sustainable development, community investment, recycling technologies, air-pollution control, and pollution.
- *Divestment* will include removal of stocks from a portfolio based on environmental considerations. For example, if a company's negligence results in a serious health hazard or environmental destruction, such a company is divested from the portfolio.
- As part of *shareholder activism* and *shareholder engagement*, the investors try to initiate conversations with the management on environmental issues. These conversations could be on environmental issues related to tar sands, coal ash, sustainable procurement, chemicals in packaging, adopting comprehensive sustainability reporting, and sustainable agriculture. An example of a successful proxy filing was done by 'As You Sow' (www.asyousow.org), a leader practitioner of shareholder advocacy in USA, along with Calvert Asset Management Company Inc. , and Trillium Asset Management, both known for the socially responsible investment or asset management practices. They filed a resolution in 2009 against the low sustainability commitments of IDACORP, an Idaho based Energy Company. They got 52 per cent support from shareholders. IDACORP committed to reduce their emissions by 10–15 per cent by 2013 and also launched wind-energy projects, and began research into solar generation.

Carbon Offsetting and Carbon Neutrality

Carbon offsetting is the process of reducing and eliminating the emissions of carbon dioxide or greenhouse gases, by investing in renewable technologies or restoring ecosystems, in order to compensate for the production of carbon dioxide or greenhouse gases made by an individual or an organization. Carbon offsetting process aims to attempt carbon neutrality, where the net emissions of an individual or an organization reaches zero. In this process, the primary focus is on reducing emissions (also see 'Role of an Individual in Conservation of Natural Resources and In Preventing Pollution' in Chapter 9). When it is not possible to reach a net zero level with these attempts, individuals or organizations funds projects elsewhere that result in reduction of carbon dioxide or greenhouse gas emissions. An organization purchasing one tonne of carbon dioxide equivalent (CO_2e) emissions results in the reduction of one tonne of CO_2e from the atmosphere, or, elimination of one tonne of CO_2e from the atmosphere that would have got created otherwise.

Carbon offsetting projects can be varied. Some of these are investments in: (a) planting and nurturing trees, (b) energy-efficiency projects in buildings, transportation, and power plants, and (c) protecting existing forests. In addition to protection of ecology, carbon offsetting projects also create opportunities for employment, technology transfer, and community development.

Google has been carbon neutral since 2007. In 2010, Google's carbon dioxide emissions came to 1,457,982 metric tons.[53] Google's calculation of carbon footprint took into account emissions from its vehicles, employee commuting, electricity, and other fuels that power its data centres and offices, business travel, data centre construction, server manufacturing, and other emissions. Annual assessments are verified by a third party service provider. The company adopted a three-pronged plan to be carbon-neutral:

- Reducing energy consumption by focusing on operational efficiency.
- Maximizing usage of on-campus use of renewable energy sources and purchasing clean energy from outside to power its offices and data centres.
- For those emissions that the company is unable to eliminate, Google purchased carbon offsets.

Google states, 'We see carbon offsets not as a permanent solution, but rather as a temporary tool that allows us to take full responsibility for our impact today. When considering an offset project, we carefully examine the project's environmental integrity, its ability to be monitored and verified, and ensure that the carbon savings of the project are real and additional to what would have happened without our investment.'[54]

It is important to ensure that carbon offsetting projects results in meeting the emissions targets that has been claimed, creation of the project do not result in additional emissions elsewhere, and also communicates that the offsetting project would not have happened but for the offsetting investment. Once the offsetting investment is made, the project should not be resold in the market. There are various standards that validate the quality of an offsetting project. Some of them are (a) verified carbon standard (http://www.v-c-s.org/), (b) clean development mechanism (http://cdm. unfccc.int/index.html), and (c) gold standard (http://www.goldstandard.org/).

There are criticisms against carbon offsetting projects as an environmental solution. Offsetting projects may result in organizations and individuals attempting to reduce emission by adopting easily available methods that do not require long-term commitment. For example, it is easier to buy an offset rather than bringing about a lifestyle change or a change in the business process (shifting to a low-carbon diet, or shifting to a green fleet of vehicles that supports the supply chain of the organization). Offset thus distracts individuals and organizations from taking decisions that are important and require long-term commitment.

Climate Registry

The Climate Registry, based in Los Angeles, California, is a non-profit organization that collaborates among the states of North America to track the greenhouse gas (GHG) emissions of businesses, municipalities, etc. The registry has the mandate to calculate, verify, and publicly report GHG emissions into a singly registry. The registry has helped the

---

53 http://www.google.com/green/the-big-picture.html#/intro/infographics-1, last accessed on 29 December 2011.
54 http://www.google.com/green/operations/neutral-as-switzerland.html, last accessed on 29 December 2011.

On 13 December 2011, Toronto-Dominion Bank, based in Toronto, Canada, and its subsidiaries, collectively known as TD Bank Group (TD), announced that its North American operations will become paper neutral by the end of 2012. The company plans to reduce the amount of paper it uses (20 per cent by 2015—an amount equal to approximately 300,000,000 sheets of typical office paper) by enhancing paperless banking options and introducing a forest conservation program to offset the paper it uses despite the planned reductions. Earlier, in 2010, TD became the first North American based bank to be carbon neutral.

various states of USA in the standardization of best practices while reporting GHG emissions.

GREEN BUSINESSES AND THEIR GROWTH

Emerging economies, which are also growing in terms of population, will focus on lifting people out of poverty. However, these countries may have to chart a new path of growth and development as compared to the path chosen by the developed nations of the world. For the first time in the history of the world, in 2009, more than half of the world's population was living in the cities. The number of megacities, a metropolitan area that has a population higher than 10 million people, amounted to 20 megacities, in 2011. Many of these megacities, including cities such as Tokyo, Guangzhou, Jakarta, Seoul, Shanghai, Mexico City, Delhi, New York City, São Paulo, Karachi, Mumbai, and Manila have a population that exceeds 20 million people.

Urbanization creates pressure in available infrastructure, housing, power and water supply, sewage, and waste disposal. Countries with a significantly high population of youth (for example, India and Saudi Arabia) will have to create housing infrastructure for this group. Creating an environment for building air-conditioned homes for this booming population will be impractical and unsustainable. More than 90 per cent of all water requirements in Abu Dhabi are met by desalinizing seawater. An increase in population and migration to cities makes it imperative for the development of sustainable products and technologies. This could include products and services that cater to the needs of clean drinking water and products and service that improve the quality of life while reducing the consumption of energy.

Green businesses can help in addressing some of the challenges created by the changes in business environment. Those businesses that provide alternatives to energy-intense housing practices (think about a power gulping air conditioner) will have a global market opportunity. This could involve businesses that contribute to the usage of renewable energy, improving energy efficiency, municipal waste management, emission management, sea-water desalination plants, energy efficient public transportation systems, construction companies engaged in eco-friendly and low cost construction, and more. Estimates by Roland Berger,[55] a Munich, Germany-based strategy consulting firm, indicates that the global market for green business may reach more than €3.2 trillion by 2020.[56] Roland Berger believes that there are six lead markets in the green business sector, and following is their estimated market size in 2010.[57]

---

55 www.rolandberger.com, last accessed on 9 February 2015.

The European Environment Agency has reported that European Union (EU) is very close to meeting one of its 2020 objectives of reducing its greenhouse gas emissions by 20 per cent, from the base year of 1990. By 2013, EU has already reduced its emission by 18 per cent.

- Environmentally friendly power generation and storage—€210 billion
- Energy efficiency—€630 billion
- Material efficiency—€130 billion
- Waste management and recycling—€40 billion
- Sustainable water management—€425 billion
- Sustainable mobility—€220 billion

The growth in green business is clearly perceivable. Between 2000 and 2010, the number of hybrid electric car models increased from two to 30. LEED rated buildings in the same period increased from three to 8000. Investments in renewable energy increase to $257 billion, almost double the figure as that in 2007. As of June 2012, Khosla Ventures, the venture capital firm founded by Vinod Khosla, co-founder, Sun Microsystems, has invested in almost 50 clean technology start-up that operates in distributed generation, electrical efficiency, mechanical efficiency, batteries, advanced hydrocarbons, cellulosic alcohol, advanced carbohydrates, building materials, plastics and chemicals, utility scale generation, and agriculture. Roland Berger estimates that green business will have a compounded annual growth rate (CAGR) of 6.5 per cent until 2020.

Globalization has created opportunity for green businesses from emerging economies to be leaders of the world. Suzlon, a wind power company from Pune, India, has become the fifth largest wind turbine manufacturer (by cumulative installed capacity) in the world, and Yingli Solar from Boading, China, becomes one of the largest solar PV module manufacturers in the world. It has been noted that countries that adopt clean energy and clean technology also tends to produce companies that enjoy global leadership in this field. Europe had progressive policies in adopting wind energy for power production. As per IHS Emerging Energy Research, of the top ten wind turbine manufacturers by annual installed capacity, four of them were from Europe (Vestas, Gamesa, Enercon, Siemens Wind Power), four were from China (Goldwind, China Guodian Corporation, Sinovel, Ming Yang), and one each from US and India (GE Energy and Suzlon Group).[58]

In addition to providing labour intensive services like waste management and recycling, environmental services and green businesses can also include ecological friendly power generation and storage, energy and material efficiency, sustainable mobility solutions, and water management. The factors driving the growth of green business can be classified into two:

- External trends such as increasing population, change in demographics, climate change, urbanization, and globalization

56 Berger, Roland 2011,*Green Growth, Green Profit: How Green Transformation Boosts Business*, Palgrave Macmillan, 2011
57 Berger, Roland 2011,*Green Growth, Green Profit: How Green Transformation Boosts Business*, Palgrave Macmillan, 2011
58 http://www.rechargenews.com/wind/article1295534.ece, last accessed on 22 December 2012.

- Perceivable shift in the way human beings are relating to the universe

Two decades ago, the United States was making more than 40 per cent of the solar technology sold worldwide. Today it's just over 5 per cent. In contrast, China increased its share of the global solar market from 6 to an impressive 54 per cent. While some may attribute this to the low-cost production that China has been known for, it need not be true. A study by Roland Berger Strategy Consultants among Germany's green technology market have found that availability of skilled workers and strong product demand are the two most important factors when selecting a location for manufacturing. It was also found that countries outside Germany that value-add to German green technology products have similar labour costs.

Brand Strategy and Sustainability

As part of a 2013 Meaningful Brands study (involving 1,34,000 people in 23 countries) conducted by Havas Media to observe how humans connect with global brands, found that majority of the people worldwide is not bothered if 73 per cent of brands disappeared tomorrow.[59] In a survey conducted by AC Nielsen[60] in 2011, more than half of the participants mentioned that the following sustainable practices will have an impact on the environment.

- Energy-efficient products or appliances (86 per cent)
- Products in recyclable packaging (79 per cent)
- Organic products (70 per cent)
- Products brought from a farmer's market (66 per cent)
- Ethically produced or grown products (62 per cent)
- Products with little or no packaging (53 per cent)
- Products that have not travelled long distances to get to the store (53 per cent)

In the survey, nine out of ten Indians indicated that they were concerned with air and water pollution, and eight out of ten Indians considered climate change as an important environmental issue. While consumers are becoming more aware of environmental issues, marketers note that the social conscience need not get converted to making a purchase of eco-friendly products. This survey indicated that 44 per cent of respondents are willing to purchase eco-friendly products even if it is expensive, and a similar number would switch over to eco-friendly products if the price is on par with competitive products.

The young people coming into the workforce are driven by a desire to have a career that makes a difference.

This preference, which the potential customers are indicating, has an impact on the way marketers position the brand. This positioning is not just for a product/service, it could also be for an entire organization. If an organization is seen as a sustainable and caring organization, more

---

59 http://www.havasmedia.com/meaningful-brands/meaningful-brands-global-infographic, last accessed on 6 August 2014.
60 http://in.nielsen.com/news/20110828.shtml, last accessed on 27 October 2011.

number of people will apply to the organization as potential employees. 'The young people coming into the workforce are driven by a desire to have a career that makes a difference... Jeffrey Immelt at GE says that their ecomagination campaign has done amazing things for their recruiting efforts. When BP first announced that climate change was real in 1997, one of the internal drivers of that was recognizing that they were having a tough time recruiting the best and brightest because no one wanted to work in the oil industry at that time,' says Andrew Hoffman, Professor, Ross School of Business, University of Michigan.[61] The 2013 Meaningful Brands study found that the top 20 per cent of brands in the 'Meaningful Brands' study outperformed the stock market by 120 per cent.[62] Therefore there are linkages between the sustainability practices of a company and its brand strategy.

In a study done by CSRHub, an aggregator of global CSR information and Brand Finance, a brand valuation consultancy, it was found that there is correlation between corporate social responsibility (CSR) endeavours of a company and its brand strength (see Fig. 5.6 for a graphical representation).[63] A unique find that emerged from this study is that the correlation strength between brand strength of a company to its CSR doubled in the year 2012, as compared to the average of the past four years, a possible indication that environmental and social factors, as a driver of business success, has reached a critical mass.[64]

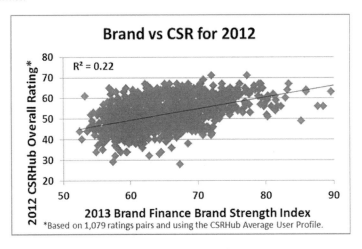

FIG. 5.6[65] Brand vs CSR for 2012

61 http://www.interbrand.com/en/best-global-brands/Best-Global-Green-Brands/2013/interviews/andrew-hoffman-michigan.aspx, last accessed on13 June 2013.

62 http://www.havasmedia.com/meaningful-brands/meaningful-brands-global-infographic, last accessed on 13 June 2013.

63 http://www.csrhub.com/blog/2013/06/there-is-a-strong-link-between-brand-strength-and-sustainability.html, last accessed on 23 June 2013.

64 http://www.triplepundit.com/2013/06/new-insights-correlation-between-csr-brand-strength/, last accessed on 23 June 2013.

65 Image Source: 'There is a Strong Link Between Brand Strength and Sustainability' by Bahar Gidwani, co-founder and CEO, CSRHub (http://www.csrhub.com). Used with permission; http://www.csrhub.com/blog/2013/06/there-is-a-strong-link-between-brand-strength-and-sustainability.html, last accessed on 2 April 2012.

This study indicates that organizational practices that amount to stakeholder sustainability (employees, society, environment, etc.) and not just shareholder sustainability are contributing to brand strength. Therefore, an executive aiming at improving brand strength also needs to focus on improving performance in the parameters of sustainability.

Green Marketing and Greenwashing

American Marketing Association has given three definitions[66] to green marketing—from a retailing perspective, from a social marketing perspective, and from an environment perspective. Those definitions are as follows:

- Green marketing is the marketing of products that are presumed to be environmentally safe.
- The development and marketing of products designed to minimize negative effects on the physical environment or to improve its quality.
- The efforts by organizations to produce, promote, package, and reclaim products in a manner that is sensitive or responsive to ecological concerns.

Proponents of green marketing believe that potential consumers acknowledge the green characteristic of the product or service as a benefit and will prefer to buy the product or service which is greener. Indeed, innumerable research studies[67,68,69,70,71,72,73,74] have indicated that possibility. What has been inconclusive is the amount that consumers will be willing to pay extra for green products/services, if asked to do so.

Why Green Marketing?

With increasing population, and increasing human consumption, the demand on natural resources is going up. Infinite growth and infinite consumption cannot happen in a planet with finite resources. Therefore optimal usage of resources becomes important. People are also becoming more aware of issues related to social and environmental concerns. In such a context, it gives an opportunity for marketers to communicate sustainable practices and green initiatives of a company as the company's unique sales propositions. When consumers start purchasing products and services of companies that are green,

---

66 http://www.marketingpower.com/_layouts/Dictionary.aspx?dLetter=G, last accessed on 2 April 2012.

67 http://www.allbusiness.com/marketing-advertising/market-research-analysis-market/8518289-1.html, last accessed on 2 April 2012.

68 http://www.clickgreen.org.uk/research/trends/122115-75-of-consumers-say-they-prefer-sustainable-food.html, last accessed on 2 April 2012.

69 http://www.megameeting.com/news/Green-Conferencing-News/Study-finds-consumers-prefer-green-businesses,-such-as-those-that-use-videoconferencing-19899823.html, last accessed on 2 April 2012.

70 http://www.abiresearch.com/press/1501-Nearly+Half+of+US+Consumers+Would+Choose+a+%E2%80%9CGreen%E2%80%9D+Handset+At+the+Right+Price, last accessed on 2 April 2012.

71 http://risnews.edgl.com/retail-trends/Consumers-Prefer-Seeing-Green–Want-Retailers-to-Avoid-Greenwashing38640, last accessed on 2 April 2012.

72 http://energyboom.com/transportation/worldwide-survey-shows-60-consumers-would-prefer-buy-green-cars, last accessed on 2 April 2012.

73 http://www.ecoelectrons.com/consumers-prefer-to-do-business-with-companies-that-have-sustainable-initiatives/index.html, last accessed on 2 April 2012.

74 http://www.greenecoservices.com/60-of-consumers-prefer-restaurants-that-recycle/, last accessed on 2 April 2012.

sustainability becomes a competitive advantage for the company. Major corporations of the world have incorporated sustainability into their strategic plans. For example,

- Wal-Mart has three 'simple and straightforward' goals. They are:
  - To be supplied 100 per cent by renewable energy
  - To create zero waste
  - To sell products that sustain people and the environment
- Unilever has three goals to be achieved by 2020:
  - Halve the environmental footprint of their products
  - Help more than 1 billion people take action to improve their health and well-being
  - Source 100 per cent of their agricultural raw materials sustainably
- Interface Carpets has been on a 'Mission Zero' goal. This goal indicates that from year 2020, the company will have zero negative impact on the natural environment. All its business processes will be in harmony with the natural environment.

Green marketing tries to communicate some of the benefits associated with green products/services and the benefits may include the following:

Performance, efficiency, and cost effectiveness   Many of the green products are also energy efficient than the conventional and prevalent products. Though the initial investment may be a little higher than the conventional pricing, they are cost-effective and in the long run they bring in a surplus. An example is LEED rated green buildings. Another example is the LED lamps, which is better than CFL lamps and incandescent bulbs. The improved performance helps these products to command a premium price in the market.

Health and safety   Citizens are aware that their food is being burdened with pesticides, chemicals, hormones, preservatives, etc., that is causing imbalance in the body, especially among pregnant women, children, and the elderly. This has resulted in people looking forward to food that is organic and healthy. Producers of organic food communicate this benefit to the citizens. For example, industry estimates are that the consumer demand for organic food is growing in India[75] and will continue to do so 30–50 per cent annually in the coming years.[76]

Symbolism, status, and positioning   Green products are associated as icons of status. The person who drives a Toyota Prius is considered a flag bearer of sustainability initiatives in the society. Ethicus, a premium textile brand from Coimbatore, promotes themselves as 'India's first ethical fashion brand'. ITC communicates 'responsible luxury' by telling the consumer that all its hotel properties under the luxury/premium segment have been LEED platinum rated and is the first in the world to do so. Kerala Tourism has been positioning the state as 'God's own country' with green (see Fig. 5.7) and heritage as its themes.

75 http://business.outlookindia.com/printarticle.aspx?279652, last accessed on 27 April 2012.
76 http://www.businessworld.in/businessworld/businessworld/content/Green-Quotient-Your-Life.html, last accessed on 27 April 2012.

FIG. 5.7[77] An elevated walk-through near Thenmala forest region, Agasthyamala Biosphere Reserve, Kerala

77 Photo by Jayadeep R, licensed under public domain via Wikimedia Commons. Image source: https://commons. wikimedia.org/wiki/File:Thenmala_Adventure_Zone.jpg#mediaviewer/File:Thenmala_Adventure_Zone.jpg, last accessed on 6 August 2014.

Convenience Some of the green products offer ease of convenient usage. LED lamps require infrequent replacement as compared to incandescent bulbs, LED lamps also have fewer breakages as compared to incandescent bulbs.

Green marketing, if done without sincerity, is greenwashing. The following are some of the definitions of greenwashing:

- Disinformation disseminated by an organization so as to present an environmentally responsible public image (Oxford English Dictionary)[78]
- An unjustified appropriation of environmental virtue by a company, an industry, a government, a politician, or even a non-government organization to create a pro-environmental image, sell a product or a policy, or to try and rehabilitate their standing with the public and decision makers after being embroiled in controversy (SourceWatch)[79]
- A superficial or insincere display of concern for the environment that is shown by an organization (Dictionary.com)[80]

When an organization promotes its sustainable practices, without having accreditations/recommendations from a respectable external source, there is a good possibility that it may be a greenwashing practice. When a company spends more time, money, and energy to promote their environmental programs rather than to run and improve those programs, it could be an example of greenwashing.

There are various ways in which greenwashing could be done. Some organizations call themselves 'environment friendly', and claim their products to be 'made from natural products', etc. However, they do not communicate to the citizens the reasons on why those products/services are environmental friendly. The marketers may also create some labels and logos that look official, professionally neutral, and third party certified. However, in actuality, that may not be so. Companies sponsor and promote associations, who in turn certify products/services of those companies. There are also companies that mislead the consumers stating some green credentials. However, the company may not have the green credential. For example, a company may claim to be 'Rain Forest Alliance' certified, while it may not be so. Companies may also make irrelevant claims like 'CFC-free'. This cannot be communicated as a differentiator as the usage of CFC has been banned by law.

GREEN RANKINGS

Green rankings have emerged to be popular with the growing need to understand the green practices and green character of a company. While these rankings were organization-specific, there were occasional studies that looked into the green character of a region/country. The green rankings helped consumers to channelize their money

---

78 http://oxforddictionaries.com/definition/greenwash, last accessed on 5 April 2012.
79 http://www.sourcewatch.org/index.php?title=Greenwashing, last accessed on 5 April 2012.
80 http://dictionary.reference.com/browse/greenwash, last accessed on 5 April 2012.

to purchase only products and services made by companies that follow sustainability practices. Such rankings also helped people to decide on their career preferences with a company.

In July 2011, GreenBiz.com reported that there were 108 sustainability ratings, a climb from 21 in 2011. This clearly indicates that sustainability indexes are going mainstream. Newsweek, starting 2009, has come out with its 'Green Rankings' rating 500 largest companies listed in USA, which has not extended to another study that ascertains the greenness of the 500 largest companies of the world. Interbrand, a leading branding consultancy firm comes out with its annual 'Best Global Green Brands' study. ClimateCounts.org rates companies on their commitment to reduce global warming. The organization issues a scorecard[81] for companies in 16 sectors and ranks them under four categories—stuck, starting, striding, and soaring.

National Geographic comes out with 'Green Guides' that helps a consumer choose the greenest product in a category. In 2008, National Geographic Magazine also started the Greendex survey on the theme of 'global consumer choice and the environment'. The 2008 and 2009 Greendex results were based on survey feedback from 14 countries. In 2010 and 2012, responses were collected from 17 countries. In 2012, survey responses were collected from 17,000 consumers from the 17 countries of Argentina, Australia, Brazil, Canada, China, France, Germany, Great Britain, Hungary, India, Japan, Mexico, Russia, South Korea, Spain, Sweden, and the United States (see Table 5.6 for details about Greendex ranking between 2008 and 2012).

TABLE 5.6 Greendex ranking between 2008 and 2012

	Rank 1	Rank 2	Rank 3	Rank 4	Rank 5
2008	Brazil	India	China	Mexico	Hungary
2009	India	Brazil	China	Argentina and South Korea	
2010	India	Brazil	China	Mexico	Argentina
2012	India	China	Brazil	Hungary and South Korea	

ECO-LABELS AND ENVIRONMENTALLY PREFERRED PURCHASING

'I've worked in an economy that rewards someone who saves the lives of others on a battle-field with a medal, rewards a great teacher with thank-you notes from parents, but rewards those who can detect the mispricing of securities with sums reaching into the billions,' says Warren Buffet, the famous investor, and CEO and Chairman of Berkshire Hathaway.[82] Similar incongruence exists in the marketplace too. A visit to GoodGuide.com, a website that enables consumers to receive information on the health,

81 http://www.climatecounts.org/pdf/CC_2012_FinalScores.pdf, last accessed on 3 July 2014.
82 http://money.cnn.com/2010/06/15/news/newsmakers/Warren_Buffett_Pledge_Letter.fortune/, last accessed on 4 November 2013.

environmental, and social impacts of a product, will reveal that products that are popular in the marketplace need not be leaders in social and environmental responsibility. Eco-labels attempts to correct this variance by giving credence to a product/company that respects environmental and social responsibility.

Eco-labels or green labels are labelling systems that indicate that ecological considerations have been given due importance during the life cycle (sourcing of the raw material, manufacture, and after-sales of the product) of a product/service. Products that are certified by eco-labels are less polluting, are recyclable or biodegradable, and contribute to a reduction in the usage of natural resources as compared to that of other products offered in the market. For a consumer, a product's association with an eco-label is an indication that it is environmentally more progressive among similar products. Eco-labels can be a voluntary, third-party certification or it could be informative self-declaration claims (see Fig. 5.8). As could be expected, third party certifications based on multiple criteria are more respected by the stakeholders as compared to self-declaration claims. In certain cases, the criteria could be set by third party while the assessment could be done by the company itself.

FIG. 5.8 Mulching on the tree saplings planted as part of the Miyawaki method based rapid afforestation programme at the outbound training center of PSG Institute of Management, Coimbatore, the first green certified business school in India. As part of this programme, 300 native tree saplings were planted in an area of 1000 square feet.

There are also labels that are mandated by the government. An example is the labelling program of Bureau of Energy Efficiency (BEE)[83], Ministry of Power, Government of India, has drawn ideas from the EPA Energy Star Labelling. The star labelling of BEE ranges from one to five. The more the number of stars in the label, the more energy efficient the product is. BEE labelling is mandatory for some product categories while voluntary for other categories. Currently, BEE label covers frost free refrigerators, direct cool refrigerators, fluorescent lamps, air conditioners, distribution transformers, induction motors, pump sets, ceiling fans, LPG stoves, electric geysers, colour televisions, washing machines, and notebook computers/laptops.

In 2007, the practice of adding carbon footprint labels to food and other products started in United Kingdom. Carbon footprint labels identified the quantity of carbon dioxide emissions associated with the manufacture and transportation of products. In the same year, Tesco, a retailing company from UK, said that it would put carbon labels in all the products that it sells. It has been found[84] that the major benefit of carbon labelling is the process that goes into the creation of such a label—as it helps a company to identify areas that offer the potential to reduce emissions. Companies like Tesco estimates that its supply chain produces ten times emission as compared to the emissions due to the company's operations. Walmart believes that 90 per cent of the emissions associated with its products are from its supply chain that consisted of more than 120,000 companies.

Some products also try to incorporate 'Use-Phase' emissions to their products. Use-Phase emission refers to emissions that are created during the consumption or usage of the product. For example, Levis Strauss, while doing a life cycle analysis for its famous 501 jeans, found that 57 per cent of the emissions associated with the product were related to the way the jeans were washed—in warm water and machine dried. The company found that if washed in cold water and sun-dried, the Use-Phase emissions of its 501 jeans could be reduced by 90 per cent.

Environmental labelling schemes are emerging across the globe. Ministry of Economy, Trade, and Industry (METI), Japan, has recommended product category rules for 53 products. South Korea has a 'CooL label'. Other countries that have environmental labels focusing on carbon emissions include Thailand, Canada, Switzerland, Sweden, etc. In 2010, France passed Grenelle 2, a mandatory environmental labelling law. France is planning to broaden the labelling standards by incorporating data related to a product's water footprint and impact on biodiversity.

There has been a growing demand, especially from businesses, for standardization of various carbon footprinting labels existing across the world. ISO 14067, designed by International Organization for Standardization is expected to finalize in 2012, and GHG Protocol designed by World Resources Institute and World Business Council for Sustainable Development, is expected to be released in September 2011.

---

83 http://beeindia.in/

84 Upham, Paul, and Mercedes Bleda 2009, *Carbon Labelling: Public Perceptions of the Debate*, Tyndall Centre for Climate Change Research, University of Manchester, England, 2009; http://www.fcrn.org.uk/sites/default/files/Tyndall%20carbon%20label%20report.pdf, last accessed on 29 April 2012.

Table 5.7 lists a few of the eco-labels and their logos with details.

TABLE 5.7[85] Some eco-labels and their logos

Eco-labelling endeavors	Logo
Certified B Corporation—In USA, a benefit corporation is a for-profit legal corporate entity that needs to consider social and environmental impact during their decision making processes. The purpose of the organization is the benefit of all stakeholders rather than only the shareholders. A Certified B Corporation is a certification provided by B-Lab, a non-profit organization that ascertains the overall social and environmental impact of the organization is to be certified, and mandates the organization to achieve a certain minimum score on these areas. Weblink: http://www.bcorporation.net/	**Certified** (B) **Corporation** bcorporation.net
Cradle to Cradle Certified™—This certification is given by the Cradle to Cradle Products Innovation Institute. It is a quality standard based on Cradle to Cradle® design principles. The certification is multi-attribute and requires a commitment to continuous improvement as manufacturers raise their certification levels from Basic to Bronze, Silver, Gold and finally Platinum. Weblink: http://www.c2cCertified.org/	CERTIFIED cradle to cradle PRODUCTS PROGRAM
Ecocert—Ecocert certifies organic agricultural products. Though this organization was started in France in 1991, it has offices across the world, with India operations starting in 2002. Ecocert certifies operations in nearly 80 countries. Weblink: http://www.ecocert.com/en	ECO CERT®
Ecomark—This was launched by Government of India in the year 1991. However, this label failed to take off in the Indian market.	
EPA Energy Star Labeling—The Environmental Protection Agency (EPA) of US government came out with Energy Star labels that indicated that products that carried the Energy Star label have met specific energy efficiency guidelines suggested by the US EPA. Weblink: http://www.energystar.gov/	energy ★ ENERGY STAR

(Contd)

---

85 The logos used here belong to the respective organizations and are used here with permission or available in the public domain. This is for educational purposes only.

TABLE 5.7 (*Contd*)

Eco-labelling endeavors	Logo
Fairtrade—Fairtrade is an international trading partnership operating with the objective to help marginalized producers and workers by guaranteeing them with fair prices and usually above market prices for goods. Faritrade establishes a direct trade between consumers and producers and favours, practices that are environmentally and economically sustainable. This certification is meant for products that meet environmental, labour, and developmental standards set by Fairtrade International and audited by the independent company FLO-CERT. There are minimum requirements that all producer organizations must meet and the producer organizations also need to demonstrate certain improvements over time. Weblink: http://www.fairtrade.net/	
Forest Stewardship Council (FSC) Certification—This label is given for forest products that are responsibly harvested and are from verifiable sources. There are two types of FSC certificate, the first one is Forest Management (FM) certificate which is applied by forest companies that would like to follow suit the FSC standards. The second type of certification is FSC Chain-of-Custody (COC) certification, which is applied by companies that are processing the FSC certified materials (including packaging material) and would like to pass down the FSC claims (e.g. processors, traders, and manufacturers). The COC certificate will involve audits of the companies to ensure it has the capacity to maintain the supply chain. Weblink: https://ic.fsc.org/	
Green Signal—Green Signal is India's first sustainability eco-label, based on a life-cycle perspective (from cradle to grave). This label has been incubated by Centre for Innovation, Incubation and Entrepreneurship (CIIE) at the Indian Institute of Management, Ahmedabad (IIM-A). Weblink: http://cbalance.in/	
GoodWeave—The GoodWeave label is given to rugs as an assurance that no child labour was used in the making of the rug. To earn the GoodWeave label, rug exporters in producing countries and importers in consumer countries must be licensed under the GoodWeave certification program and sign a legaly binding contract to adhere to GoodWeave's no-child-labour standard, and allow unannounced random inspections by independent GoodWeave inspectors. GoodWeave's certification standard has included other environmental and social criteria, guided by ISEAL's Codes of Good Practice. Each producer will work with GoodWeave to develop a plan for improving working conditions and mitigating environmental impacts over time. Web link: http://www.goodweave.org/about/child_labor_free_rugs	

(Contd)

TABLE 5.7 (*Contd*)

Eco-labelling endeavors	Logo
Leaping Bunny—The Leaping Bunny logo is given by the Coalition for Consumer Information on Cosmetics in the United States and Canada and by Cruelty Free International in the European Union, which certifies that a product was not tested on animals. Weblink: http://www.leapingbunny.org/	
LEED Certified—Details of LEED certification has been provided elsewhere in the book. Weblink: http://in.usgbc.org/leed#certification	
Marine Stewardship Council—The Marine Stewardship Council (MSC) is an international non-profit organization working to transform the global seafood market to a sustainable basis. The MSC runs the only certification and eco-labelling programme for wild-capture fisheries consistent with the ISEAL Code of Good Practice for Setting Social and Environmental Standards and the United Nations Food and Agricultural Organization (UN FAO) Guidelines for the eco-labelling of Fish and Fishery Products from Marine Capture Fisheries. These guidelines are based upon the UN FAO Code of Conduct for Responsible Fishing. Over 230 fisheries globally were certified to the MSC standard of sustainability by June 2014. For more information, visit http://www.msc.org	
Rainforest Alliance Certified Farms—Farms that meet social, economic, and environmental criteria as laid down by Sustainable Action Network (SAN), a coalition of non-profit conservation organizations, are certified. More than 100 types of crops that include cocoa, coffee, fruits, tea, vegetables, ferns, and cut flowers can be certified. Weblink: http://www.rainforest-alliance.org/certification-verification	

(Contd)

USDA Organic—In USA, the US Department of Agriculture (USDA), through the National Organic Programme (NOP), is responsible for administering and enforcing the regulatory framework governing organic food. The 'USDA Organic' seal is given to those products that meet the requirements stipulated by the NOP. NOP primarily covers food products, though it also covers non-food products. Weblink: http://www.ams.usda.gov/AMSv1.0/NOPFAQsHowCertified

Vegetarian Mark—In India, the green dot symbol on the left indicates vegetarian food, while the brown dot symbol on the right indicates non-vegetarian food. This is used in packaged food products.

WindMade—This is a label given to products or organizations that uses electricity generated from wind and other renewable sources. For products to labeled as 'WindMade', at least 75% of the total electricity used during its manufacturing life cycle (from extraction of raw materials till the product leave the factory gate), has to be generated from wind and other renewable sources. Organizations that procure and use a minimum of 25% of its electricity from wind electricity as part can also use 'WindMade' labels for their operations. The 'WindMade' label will communicate the consumption of electricity generated from wind energy and other renewable sources. Weblink: http://www.windmade.org/

SUSTAINABILITY/ENVIRONMENTAL REPORTING STANDARDS AND CERTIFICATIONS

Increased public demand for corporate accountability, governmental regulations, need for international cooperation in promoting sustainability practices, and leadership initiatives from the industry to improvise their sustainability practices have contributed to the emergence of guidelines and codes related to sustainability reporting. The nature of these reporting standards is varied.

Triple Bottom Line Reporting

As per Global Reporting Initiative (GRI), a sustainability report is an organizational report that gives information about economic, environmental, social, and governance performance.[86] To release sustainability reports, an organization has to create a reporting

---

86 https://www.globalreporting.org/information/sustainability-reporting/Pages/default.aspx, last accessed on 29 May 2012.

cycle that ensures the collection of data from the organization on a consistent basis. The term 'sustainability reporting' is also used synonymously with triple bottom line reporting (financial, environmental, and social parameters).

Sustainability disclosure helps business organizations to identify opportunities caused by change in demographics and also mitigate negative impacts caused by issues like climate change and loss of biodiversity. Sustainability reporting helps investors, and observers like analysts to gain knowledge about the company's outlook and performance related to long-term health of the company and the company's approaches to changing business environment. This helps the investors to decide on the companies that are capable of meeting long-term risks posed to the company and they may want such companies as their preferred investment destinations. With senior management having relevant data on growing the long-term values of the company, the company soon is in a position to manage long-term risks. For example, if the senior management of companies such as PepsiCo and The Coca-Cola Company are aware of the falling ground water supply in areas they operate, they will look for more effective water management practices. Disclosure also helps the company to build trust with consumers and civil society. An organization that adds to the well-being of the society and communicates the data to the society is building trust among its stakeholders. As the company becomes transparent in its operations, consumers and citizens can ascertain how the company's operations are impacting the society and how better/worse the company is performing vis-à-vis its peers.

Sustainability Reporting Milestones

Table 5.8 lists some of the important developments in the area of sustainability reporting.

TABLE 5.8 Crucial developments in sustainability reporting

1989	CERES Principles published.
2000	Launch of UN Global Compact (UNGC) Principles.
2006	GRI G3 Guidelines and Principles of Responsible Investment (PRI) supported by UN launched.
2007	Guideline on fulfilling social responsibility practices by state owned enterprises in China.
2008	Carbon Disclosure Project (CDP) publishes emission data for 1550 of the world's largest companies.
2009	Securities and Exchange Commission (SEC) of USA tries to incorporate Environmental, Social, and Governance (ESG) in the filings that companies has to make to SEC.
2010	SEC releases interpretive guidance on disclosure related to climate change. ISO 26000, an international standard giving guidance on social responsibility, launched.
2011	5th update to the OECD Guidelines for Multinational Enterprises.
2013	GRI G4 Guidelines launched.
2013	Companies Act in India makes CSR spending mandatory—CSR mandatory for 'All companies with turnover of Rs 1,000 crore and more, or a net worth of ₹500 crore and more, or net profit of ₹5 crore and more will have to spend at least two percent of their three-year average profit every year on CSR activity.'

Sustainability Reporting Initiatives

Global Reporting Initiative

The *Global Reporting Initiative* (GRI) is one of the recognized global standards for sustainability reporting. GRI has developed a framework, which enables organizations to measure and report economic, environmental, social, and governance performance. G4 guidelines were released in mid-2013. The GRI guidelines are continuously developed through a multi-stakeholder consensus approach.

UN Global Compact

The *UN Global Compact* (UNGC) is a UN driven principle based framework for organizations that are committed to align their operations with 10 principles in the areas of human rights, labour, the environment, and anti-corruption. Two of the major objectives of the Global Compact are to mainstream the ten principles in business activities throughout the globe and to catalyse actions in support of broader UN goals like the Millennium Development Goals (MDGs).[87] Organizations adhering to the Global Compact have to incorporate transparency and accountability through submitting an annual Communication on Progress (COP) to the stakeholders. COP should have a description of the actions undertaken by the company to implement the ten principles, and a measurement of outcomes.

Ten principles of UNGC   The UNGC's ten principles in the areas of human rights, labour, the environment, and anti-corruption enjoy universal consensus and are derived from:

- The Universal Declaration of Human Rights
- The International Labour Organization's Declaration on Fundamental Principles and Rights at Work
- The Rio Declaration on Environment and Development
- The United Nations Convention Against Corruption

The UNGC asks companies to embrace, support, and enact, within their sphere of influence, a set of core values in the areas of human rights, labour standards, the environment, and anti-corruption (see Table 5.9).

UN Principles for Responsible Investment

UN Principles for Responsible Investment (UNPRI) is a voluntary initiative of certain investors in partnership with the UNEP Finance Initiative and the UNGC. These principles help the investors in integrating Environmental, Social, and Governance (ESG) issues into investment decisions. Adherents to UNPRI have to mandatorily give their responses to a reporting framework. While individual responses were kept confidential, signatories were encouraged to publish their full responses on the UNPRI

---

87 http://www.unglobalcompact.org/AboutTheGC/index.html, last accessed on 29 May 2012.

TABLE 5.9[88] Ten principles of UNGC

Human rights	Principle 1: Businesses should support and respect the protection of internationally proclaimed human rights; and
	Principle 2: make sure that they are not complicit in human rights abuses.
Labour	Principle 3: Businesses should uphold the freedom of association and the effective recognition of the right to collective bargaining;
	Principle 4: the elimination of all forms of forced and compulsory labour;
	Principle 5: the effective abolition of child labour; and
	Principle 6: the elimination of discrimination in respect of employment and occupation.
Environment	Principle 7: Businesses should support a precautionary approach to environmental challenges;
	Principle 8: undertake initiatives to promote greater environmental responsibility; and
	Principle 9: encourage the development and diffusion of environmentally friendly technologies.
Anti-corruption	Principle 10: Businesses should work against corruption in all its forms, including extortion and bribery.

website. UNPRI website also released the aggregated results. In 2012, UNPRI came out with an updated reporting framework.

Principles of responsible investment[89]   As institutional investors, we have a duty to act in the best long-term interests of our beneficiaries. In this fiduciary role, we believe that environmental, social, and corporate governance (ESG) issues can affect the performance of investment portfolios (to varying degrees across companies, sectors, regions, asset classes, and through time). We also recognize that by applying these principles investors may align better with broader objectives of society. Therefore, we commit to the following when consistent with our fiduciary responsibilities (see Table 5.10):

TABLE 5.10 Six principles of UNPRI

Principle1	We will incorporate ESG issues into investment analysis and decision-making processes.
	Possible actions:
	a. Address ESG issues in investment policy statements
	b. Support development of ESG-related tools, metrics, and analyses
	c. Assess the capabilities of internal investment managers to incorporate ESG issues
	d. Assess the capabilities of external investment managers to incorporate ESG issues
	e. Ask investment service providers (such as financial analysts, consultants, brokers, research firms, or rating companies) to integrate ESG factors into evolving research and analysis
	f. Encourage academic and other research on this theme
	g. Advocate ESG training for investment professionals

(Contd)

88 http://www.unglobalcompact.org/AboutTheGC/TheTewnPrinciples/index.html, last accessed on 30 May 2012. Used with permission.

89 http://www.unpri.org/principles/, last accessed on 8 May 2014. Used with permission.

Principle 2	We will be active owners and incorporate ESG issues into our ownership policies and practices.
	Possible actions:
	a. Develop and disclose an active ownership policy consistent with the Principles
	b. Exercise voting rights or monitor compliance with voting policy (if outsourced)
	c. Develop an engagement capability (either directly or through outsourcing)
	d. Participate in the development of policy, regulation, and standard setting (such as promoting and protecting shareholder rights)
	e. File shareholder resolutions consistent with long-term ESG considerations
	f. Engage with companies on ESG issues
	g. Participate in collaborative engagement initiatives
	h. Ask investment managers to undertake and report on ESG-related engagement
Principle 3	We will seek appropriate disclosure on ESG issues by the entities in which we invest.
	Possible actions:
	a. Ask for standardized reporting on ESG issues (using tools such as the Global Reporting Initiative)
	b. Ask for ESG issues to be integrated within annual financial reports
	c. Ask for information from companies regarding adoption of/adherence to relevant norms, standards, codes of conduct, or international initiatives (like the UNGC)
	d. Support shareholder initiatives and resolutions promoting ESG disclosure
Principle 4	We will promote acceptance and implementation of the Principles within the investment industry.
	Possible actions:
	a. Include Principles-related requirements in requests for proposals (RFPs)
	b. Align investment mandates, monitoring procedures, performance indicators, and incentive structures accordingly (for example, ensure investment management processes reflect long-term time horizons when appropriate)
	c. Communicate ESG expectations to investment service providers
	d. Revisit relationships with service providers that fail to meet ESG expectations
	e. Support the development of tools for benchmarking ESG integration
	f. Support regulatory or policy developments that enable implementation of the Principles
Principle 5	We will work together to enhance our effectiveness in implementing the Principles.
	Possible actions:
	a. Support/participate in networks and information platforms to share tools, pool resources, and make use of investor reporting as a source of learning
	b. Collectively address relevant emerging issues
	c. Develop or support appropriate collaborative initiatives
Principle 6	We will each report on our activities and progress towards implementing the Principles.
	Possible actions:
	a. Disclose how ESG issues are integrated within investment practices
	b. Disclose active ownership activities (voting, engagement, and/or policy dialogue)
	c. Disclose what is required from service providers in relation to the Principles

(Contd)

TABLE 5.10 (*Contd*)

> d. Communicate with beneficiaries about ESG issues and the Principles
> e. Report on progress and/or achievements relating to the Principles using a 'Comply or Explain' approach (requires signatories to report on how they implement the Principles, or provide an explanation where they do not comply with them)
> f. Seek to determine the impact of the Principles
> g. Make use of reporting to raise awareness among a broader group of stakeholders

TABLE 5.11[90] Total return for Global 500, CDLI, and CPLI 2011

	Global 500	CDLI	CPLI
Total return % ($) from January 2005 to May 2011	42.71%	82.44%	85.72%

Carbon Disclosure Project

The Carbon Disclosure Project (CDP), a UK-based organization, works with companies and shareholders to reduce the business risks posed by climate change by asking 6,000 of the world's largest companies to disclose greenhouse gas emissions, their climate strategies, and energy use. A response request from the companies would seek to elicit (a) the views of the company on the risks and opportunities that climate change presents to business, (b) accounting of greenhouse gas emissions, (c) strategy adopted by the company to reduce emissions, and (d) corporate governance practices related to climate change. Companies with the highest disclosure scores are listed in Carbon Disclosure Leadership Index (CDLI). From the list of leading companies of CDLI, CDP further assesses and ranks a company's performance in contributing to climate change mitigation, adaptation, and transparency. Leaders in this ranking are listed in Carbon Performance Leadership Index (CPLI). It has been found that companies in the 2011 CDLI and CPLI provide approximately double the average total return of the Global 500 between January 2005 and May 2011 (see Table 5.11). This suggests a strong correlation between higher financial performance and good climate change disclosure and performance.

OECD guidelines for MNEs

The Organization for Economic Co-operation and Development (OECD) guidelines for Multinational Enterprises (MNEs) are part of the OECD Declaration on International Investment and Multinational Enterprises. The guidelines provide voluntary principles and standards for responsible business conduct of multi-national enterprises operating in or from countries adhered to the declaration. Under Section III on 'Disclosure', the declaration state, 'Enterprises are also encouraged to apply high quality standards for non-financial information including environmental and social reporting where they exist. The standards or policies under which both financial and non-financial information

90 https://www.cdproject.net/CDPResults/CDP-G500-2011-Report.pdf, last accessed on 1 December 2011.

are compiled and published should be reported.'[91] The guidelines cover areas such as Employment and Industrial Relations, Environment, Combating Bribery, Consumer Interests, Science and Technology, Competition, and Taxation.

Ceres Principles

Ceres is a not-for-profit network consisting of investors, environmental organizations, and other interest group that aims to address sustainability related challenges. The Ceres 10 point codes of corporate environmental ideals are to be publicly endorsed by the companies adhering to the principles. Following are the Ceres Principles.[92]

Protection of the biosphere We will reduce and make continual progress toward eliminating the release of any substance that may cause environmental damage to the air, water, or the earth or its inhabitants. We will safeguard all habitats affected by our operations and will protect open spaces and wilderness, while preserving biodiversity.

Sustainable use of natural resources We will make sustainable use of renewable natural resources, such as water, soils, and forests. We will conserve non-renewable natural resources through efficient use and careful planning.

Reduction and disposal of wastes We will reduce and where possible eliminate waste through source reduction and recycling. All waste will be handled and disposed of through safe and responsible methods.

Energy conservation We will conserve energy and improve the energy efficiency of our internal operations and of the goods and services we sell. We will make every effort to use environmentally safe and sustainable energy sources.

Risk reduction We will strive to minimize the environmental, health, and safety risks to our employees and the communities in which we operate through safe technologies, facilities, and operating procedures, and by being prepared for emergencies.

Safe products and services We will reduce and where possible eliminate the use, manufacture, or sale of products and services that cause environmental damage or health or safety hazards. We will inform our customers of the environmental impacts of our products or services and try to correct unsafe use.

Environmental restoration We will promptly and responsibly correct conditions we have caused that endanger health, safety, or the environment. To the extent feasible, we will redress injuries we have caused to persons or damage we have caused to the environment and will restore the environment.

Informing the public We will inform in a timely manner everyone who may be affected by conditions caused by our company that might endanger health, safety, or the environment. We will regularly seek advice and counsel through dialogue with persons in communities near our facilities. We will not take any action against employees for reporting dangerous incidents or conditions to management or to appropriate authorities.

---

91 http://www.oecd.org/dataoecd/56/36/1922428.pdf, last accessed on 30 May 2012.
92 http://www.ceres.org/about-us/our-history/ceres-principles, Used with permission, last accessed on 30 May 2012.

Management commitment   We will implement these Principles and sustain a process that ensures that the Board of Directors and Chief Executive Officer are fully informed about pertinent environmental issues and are fully responsible for environmental policy. In selecting our Board of Directors, we will consider demonstrated environmental commitment as a factor.

Audits and reports   We will conduct an annual self-evaluation of our progress in implementing these Principles. We will support the timely creation of generally accepted environmental audit procedures. We will annually complete the Ceres Report, which will be made available to the public.

SA8000 Standard

The *SA8000 standard* is an auditable social certification standard aiming for decent work conditions that protect the basic human rights of workers. The standard is based on the conventions of International Labour Organization (ILO), the United Nations Convention on the Rights of the Child, the Universal Declaration of Human Rights, and various national laws. This compliance's standard focus is on eight elements: (a) child labour, (b) forced and compulsory labour, (c) health and safety, (d) freedom of association and right to collective bargaining, (e) discrimination, (f) disciplinary practices, (g) working hours, and (h) remuneration.

International Organization for Standardization

The *International Organization for Standardization (ISO)* is an international standard setting body who has developed more than 17,500 standards. Some of the popular standards developed by ISO related to sustainability includes ISO 14000 series of standards on environmental management, as indicated in Table 5.12. ISO 14000 series of standards from the perspective of a Plan, Do, Check, Act (PDCA) perspective is indicated in Table 5.13.[93]

TABLE 5.12 Overview of ISO 14000 standards

ISO 14001:2004 ISO 14004:2004	Environmental management systems
ISO 14005	Phased implementation of an environmental management system to facilitate the take-up of EMS by small and medium enterprises (SMEs).
ISO 14006	Eco-design
ISO 14020	Environmental labelling and declaration
ISO 14031	Evaluating environmental performance
ISO 14033	Guidelines for compiling and communicating quantitative environmental information.
ISO 14040	Principles and conduct of life cycle assessment (LCA)
ISO 14045	Principles and requirements for eco-efficiency assessment

---

93 http://www.iso.org/iso/theiso14000family_2009.pdf, last accessed on 12 April 2014. Used with permission, copyright remains with ISO.

ISO 14051	General principles and framework of material flow cost accounting (MFCA)
ISO 14063	Guidelines on environmental communication
ISO 14064 part 1, 2, 3	GHG accounting and verification
ISO 14065	Requirement to accredit organizations undertaking GHG validation using ISO 14064 or other relevant standards
ISO 14066	Competency requirements for GHG validators and verifiers
ISO 14067	Carbon footprint of products
ISO 14089	Carbon footprint of products, services, and supply chain

TABLE 5.13 ISO 14000 according to the PDCA cycle

PLAN	DO	CHECK	ACT
Environmental management system implementation	Conduct life cycle assessment and manage environmental aspects	Conduct audits and evaluate environmental performance	Communicate and use environmental declarations and claims
ISO 14050:2009 Environmental management—Vocabulary	ISO 14040:2006 Environmental management—Life cycle assessment—Principles and framework	ISO 14015:2001 Environmental management—Environmental assessment of sites and organizations (EASO)	ISO 14020:2000 Environmental labels and declarations—General principles
ISO 14001:2004 Environmental management systems—Requirements with guidance for use	ISO 14044:2006 Environmental management—Life cycle assessment—Requirements and guidelines	ISO 14031:1999 Environmental management—Environmental performance evaluation—Guidelines	ISO14021:1999 Environmental labels and declarations—Self-declared environmental claims (Type II environmental labelling)
ISO 14004:2004 Environmental management systems—General guidelines on principles, systems, and support techniques	ISO/TR 14047:2003 Environmental management—Life cycle impact assessment—Examples of application of ISO 14042	ISO 19011:2002 Guidelines for quality and/or environmental management systems auditing	ISO 14024:1999 Environmental labels and declarations—Type I environmental labelling—Principles and procedures
ISO/DIS 14005 Environmental management systems—Guidelines for the phased implementation of an environmental management system, including the use of environmental performance evaluation	ISO/TS 14048:2002 Environmental management—Life cycle assessment—Data documentation format		ISO 14025:2006 Environmental labels and declarations—Type III environmental declarations—Principles and procedures

(Contd)

TABLE 5.13 (*Contd*)

			ISO/AWI 14033 Environmental management—Quantitative environmental information—Guidelines and examples

Address environmental aspects in products and product standard		**Evaluate greenhouse gas performance**	
ISO Guide 64:2008 Guide for addressing environmental issues in product standards	ISO/TR 14049:2000 Environmental management—Life cycle assessment—Examples of application of ISO 14041 to goal and scope definition and inventory analysis	ISO 14064-3:2006 Greenhouse gases—Part 3: Specification with guidance for the validation and verification of greenhouse gas assertions	ISO 14063:2006 Environmental management—Environmental communication—Guidelines and examples
ISO/CD 14006 Environmental management systems—Guidelines on eco-design	ISO/CD 14051 Environmental management—Material flow cost accounting – General principles and framework	ISO 14065:2007 Greenhouse gases—Requirements for greenhouse gas validation and verification bodies for use in accreditation or other forms of recognition	
	ISO/WD 14045 Eco-efficiency assessment—Principles and requirements		
	Manage greenhouse gases		
ISO/TR 14062:2002 Environmental management—Integrating environmental aspects into product design and development	ISO 14064-1:2006 Greenhouse gases—Part 1: Specification with guidance at the organization level for quantification and reporting of greenhouse gas emissions and removals	ISO/CD 14066 Greenhouse gases—Competency requirements for greenhouse gas validators and verifiers document	

(*Contd*)

ISO 14064-2:2006 Greenhouse gases—Part 2 : Specification with guidance at the project level for quantification, monitoring, and reporting of greenhouse gas emission reductions or removal enhancements		
ISO/WD 14067-1 Carbon footprint of products—Part 1: Quantification ISO/WD 14067-2 Carbon footprint of products—Part 2: Communication		
ISO/AWI 14069 GHG—Quantification and reporting of GHG emissions for organizations (Carbon footprint of organization)—Guidance for the application of ISO 14064-1		

In addition to these, ISO 26000 is related to social responsibility. However, unlike other standards, ISO 26000 only provide guidance, rather than requirements. Other standards that are in some way related to sustainability practices could also include ISO 9000 series on quality management, ISO 31000 standard on risk management, ISO 22000 on food safety management, ISO 50001 on Energy management, and ISO 24510 standards on water supply and treatment services.

AA1000 AccountAbility Principles Standard

AA1000 AccountAbility Principles Standard (AA1000APS) issued by the UK-based AccountAbility 'provides a framework for an organization to identify, prioritize, and respond to its sustainability challenges.'[94]94 http://www.accountability.org/standards/index.html, Accessed on April 5, 2013. These principles are based on the three parameters of inclusivity, materiality, and responsiveness. The process also establishes goals and standards through which the organization's performance in these three criteria can be measured.

---

94 http://www.accountability.org/standards/index.html, Accessed on April 5, 2013.

Extractive Industries Transparency Initiative

The objective of Extractive Industries Transparency Initiative (EITI) is to increase transparency in transactions between governments and companies within extractive industries. This coalition of governments, for-profit, and not-for-profit organizations, requires regular public disclosure of payment transactions made by companies to governments and revenues received by the governments from these companies. As of April 2013, there were 32 countries that have produced EITI reports, which are published by the countries implementing the EITI standard. These reports disclose the revenues from extraction of the country's natural resources. Payments made to the government by the companies in the form of taxes, royalties, etc., are reported and the government reports its receipts. An independent reconciler reconciles these two reports.

CHAPTER SUMMARY

- Extended producer responsibility (EPR) is a mandate making the manufacturer of the product responsible for the entire life cycle of the product, including post-consumer usage.
- Cleaner production is the continuous application of an integrated preventative environmental strategy to processes, products, and services to increase efficiency, and reduce risks to humans and the environment.
- Cradle to Cradle (C2C) design is a bio-mimetic approach popularized by Michael Braungart. In this approach to design of systems, materials involved in industrial/commercial production are viewed as nutrients circulating in healthy, safe metabolisms. The categories are material health, material reutilization, renewable energy and carbon management, water stewardship, and social fairness.
- Bio-mimicry or bio-mimetics refers to the abstraction of good design from nature. The processes and models followed by nature are observed, and they are replicated in human endeavours, primarily meant to solve a human need.
- Green building refers to a structure and using process that is environmentally responsible and resource-efficient throughout a building's life-cycle: from siting to design, construction, operation, maintenance, renovation, and demolition.

- LEED is a green building rating system. LEED India rating system has five components (a) sustainable sites, (b) water efficiency, (c) energy and atmosphere, (d) materials and resources, and (e) indoor environmental quality. Green Rating for Integrated Habitat Assessment (GRIHA) is the national green building rating system and acts as an integrating platform for various national building codes.
- Some of the techniques/tools involved in making natural buildings include adobe, cob, rammed earth, straw bale, wattle and daub, sod roof, earth bags, papercrete, cordwood, slip straw, and compressed earth block.
- Socially responsible investing (SRI) is an investment strategy that considers financial returns, social good, and environmental impacts while making an investment. As part of managing a green portfolio, the fund managers may adopt various investing strategies. This could be negative screening, divestment, shareholder activism, shareholder engagement, and positive investment.
- Green marketing is the marketing of products that are presumed to be environmentally safe. Green marketing tries to communicate some of the benefits associated with green products/service. Green marketing, if done without sincerity, is referred to as greenwashing.

- Eco-labels or green labels are labelling systems that indicate that ecological considerations have been given due importance during the life cycle (sourcing of the raw material, manufacture, and after-sales of the product) of a product/service.
- As per Global Reporting Initiative (GRI), a sustainability report is an organizational report that gives information about economic, environmental, social, and governance performance. Some of the other sustainability reporting Initiatives are The UN Global Compact (UNGC), UN Principles for Responsible Investment (UNPRI), Carbon Disclosure Project, OECD guidelines for MNEs, Ceres Principles, the SA8000 standard, International Organization for Standardization (ISO), and AA1000 AccountAbility Principles Standard (AA1000APS).

KEYWORDS

- Agenda 21
- Bio-mimicry
- Bio-degradable
- Bottom of pyramid
- Brundtland Commission
- Carbon footprint
- Carbon disclosure project
- Carbon Offsetting
- Certified B Corporation
- CFC
- Cradle -to-cradle design
- Downcycling
- Extended producer responsibility
- Earth summit
- Ecocert
- Ecomark
- Energy Star
- Ecomagination
- Fairtrade
- Forest Stewardship Council Certification
- Forest principles
- Green marketing

- Greenwashing
- Green guide
- Green Signal
- Green investing
- GRIHA rating system
- Green building
- Heliotropism
- India Organic
- Leaping Bunny
- Marine Stewardship Council
- Mulching
- Natural building
- Obsolescence
- Product life cycle
- Rainforest Alliance
- Stewardship
- Sea-water desalination
- Sustainable site
- Stakeholder engagement
- Urbanization
- USDA Organic

EXERCISES

Multiple-choice Questions

1. Cleaner production does not encompass the following:
   (a) Replacement of old parts by new parts
   (b) Good housekeeping
   (c) Change of input material
   (d) Technology upgradation

2. Which of the following is not a component for LEED India rating system?
   (a) Energy and atmosphere
   (b) Indoor environmental quality
   (c) Outdoor environmental quality
   (d) Materials and resources

3. Which of the following are some of the definitions of green washing?
   (a) Disinformation disseminated by an organization so as to present an environmentally responsible public image
   (b) An unjustified appropriation of environmental virtue by a company, an industry, a government, a politician or even a non-government organization to create a pro-environmental image, sell a product or a policy, or to try and rehabilitate their standing with the public and decision makers after being embroiled in controversy
   (c) A superficial or insincere display of concern for the environment that is shown by an organization
   (d) All of these

4. Who does the star certification on energy efficiency for electrical appliances manufactured and sold in India?
   (a) Bureau of Indian Standards
   (b) Bureau of Energy Efficiency
   (c) Environmental Protection Agency
   (d) Ecocert

5. This is India's first sustainability eco-label, based on a life cycle perspective (from cradle to grave). This label has been incubated by Centre for Innovation, Incubation and Entrepreneurship (CIIE) at the Indian Institute of Management, Ahmedabad (IIM-A):
   (a) Green Signal
   (b) Ecomark
   (c) LEED Certified
   (d) India Organic

6. In the Cradle to Cradle (C2C) model, (1) all materials used in an industrial/commercial processes are seen as either technical or biological nutrients. (2) In this approach to design of systems, materials involved in industrial/commercial production are viewed as nutrients circulating in healthy, safe metabolisms. Which of the following is true?
   (a) (1)
   (b) (2)
   (c) Neither (1) nor (2)
   (d) Both (1) and (2)

7. As part of managing a green portfolio, the fund managers may adopt various investing strategies. Which of the following is not one of those strategies?
   (a) Negative screening
   (b) Neutral screening
   (c) Positive investment
   (d) Shareholder activism

8. This natural building technique involves compressing of a damp mixture of soil, chalk, lime, and gravel into a frame or a mould. The frame is made of wood to act as a mould that gives shape and dimension to the wall:
   (a) Rammed earth
   (b) Adobe
   (c) Cob
   (d) Straw bale

9. This is a plastering material formed from pulp made from newspapers, magazines, and other publications, and is mixed with clay or cement:
   (a) Papercrete
   (b) Earthbags
   (c) Cordwood
   (d) Compressed earth block

Short Answer Questions

1. Explain bio-mimicry with example.
2. Give two examples of green product designs.
3. Write short note on green vehicles and electric mobility.
4. What are the strategies of green portfolio?
5. What is green marketing and why is it important?
6. What is meant by green washing?
7. What are the major eco-label certifications?

Long Answer Questions

1. Explain cradle to cradle (C2C) design, its uses and importance, with example.
2. What are the objectives of sustainable development?
3. What are the different techniques of making natural buildings? Explain each of them.
4. Detail the significance of socially responsible investing/green investment.
5. Write a note on climate change strategies.
6. Explain about green business and its growth.
7. Write about green marketing and its importance in the present business scenario.
8. What are the salient features of Green Product Design?
9. Elaborate the different sustainability reporting standards and certificates.
10. Detail the different sustainability reporting initiatives.
11. Explain the Ceres principles.
12. Discuss 'the business case for sustainability'.

Reflective Question

1. On a daily/weekly/monthly/annual basis you and your family is spending money to purchase various products and services. List down various ways through which you can ensure that this spending of money is ethical, socially and environmentally responsible, and contribute to the well-being of all.

Web Readings

1. Websites of companies/organizations that operate with a green business model:
   Krya (a company that makes natural detergent powder)—http://krya.in
   Ecologin (experience based alternate tourism service provider)—http://ecologin.org
   Ecosia (a websearch site that gives 80 percent of its revenues to a rainforest protection program)—http://www.ecosia.org
   Grow-Trees (a gifting site where you can plant trees for various occasions)—http://www.grow-trees.com
   Ethicus (India's first ethical and sustainable fashion brand)—http://www.ethicus.in/ and http://www.appachicotton.com

2. List of eco-labels:
   http://www.ecolabelindex.com/ecolabels/
3. Organizations that report on developments related to environmental and social sustainability and green businesses:
   Environmental Leader, http://www.environmentalleader.com
   Green Biz, http://www.greenbiz.com
   Triple Pundit, http://www.triplepundit.com
4. About green buildings:
   India Green Building Council (IGBC) LEED Reference Guide - http://www.igbc.in/site/igbc/abrid.jsp
   US Green Building Council - www.usgbc.org

5. About socially responsible investing (SRI):
   Social Investment Forum, www.socialinvest.org
   Investors Circle, www.investorscircle.net
6. Organizations engaged in green consulting:
   cBalance, http://cbalance.in/
   The Natural Step, http://www.naturalstep.ca
   Terrafiniti, http://www.terrafiniti.com

7. Non-profit organizations/associations that
   promote dialogues about sustainability in
   business and industry:
   Network for Business Sustainability, http://nbs.net/
   BSR Network, http://www.bsr.org/
   World Business Council for Sustainable Development,
   http://www.wbcsd.org/home.aspx

Recommended Books

1. Paul Hawken, *Blessed Unrest: How the Largest
   Movement in the World Came into Being and Why No
   One Saw It Coming*, Penguin USA, 2007

2. Peter Pruzan, Kirsten Pruzan Mikkelsen, *Leading
   with Wisdom: Spiritual-based Leadership in Business*,
   Sage Response, 2008

Recommended Documentaries/Movies

1. Who Killed the Electric Car. Dir. Chris Paine.
   Sony Pictures Classics, 2006.
2. The Dark Side of Chocolate. Dirs. Miki
   Mistrati, U. Roberto Romano. Bastard Film &
   TV, 2010. (This documentary is available for
   free viewing at https://www.youtube.com/
   watch?v=7Vfbv6hNeng). Duration: 46 minutes.

3. William McDonough: Cradle to Cradle design
   (This talk is available for free viewing at http://
   www.ted.com/talks/william_mcdonough_
   on_cradle_to_cradle_design and https://
   www.youtube.com/watch?v=IoRjz8iTVoo).
   Duration: 22 minutes.

Answers to Mutiple-choice Questions:
1(a)   2(c)   3(d)   4(b)   5(a)   6(d)   7(b)   8(a)   9(a)

6

PROCESSES, TOOLS, AND STANDARDS FOR ENVIRONMENTAL MANAGEMENT

Today our world is changing faster than ever before—economic, geopolitical, and environmental challenges abound. However, taking shortcuts is not the pathway to achieving sustainable competitive advantage, nor is it an avenue toward satisfying customers. In times such as these, a company must invest in the key ingredients of profitability: its people, communities, and the environment.[1]

Warren Buffet, Chairman and CEO, Berkshire Hathaway, sustainability report of Johns Manville (a Berkshire Hathaway company), which manufactures building materials.

After reading the chapter, the reader will be able to understand the following:

- Instituting an environmental management system in an organization and the benefits of the same
- Various environmental impact measurement tools and their role in assessing environmental impacts
- Methods of ecosystem valuation and how they help in stakeholder communication
- Interpreting sustainability reports

INTRODUCTION

Environmental management refers to the approach, functions, and practices undertaken to conserve and enhance the health of the natural world. By exploring the interaction between humans and natural environment, environmental management attempts to conserve natural resources for future generations, not just of human beings, but all species of the planet. In an organization, environmental management helps the organization to comply with environmental rules and regulations. In the more progressive organizations, environmental management can help in embedding sustainability into the core values, practices, and strategy of the organization.

ENVIRONMENTAL MANAGEMENT SYSTEM

Organizations achieve their environmental objectives with the help of an environmental management system (EMS). EMS is a systematic integration of various practices adopted by the

---

1 http://www.jm.com/sustainability/2011JMSustainabilityReport.pdf, last accessed on 19 April 2012.

organization to achieve its environmental objectives. As per United States Environmental Protection Agency (USEPA), EMS is a set of processes and practices that enables
an organization to reduce its environmental impacts and increase its operating efficiency.[2]
EMS is comprehensive, focusses on documentation, and reports on performance
parameters. One of the popular EMS standards is the ISO 14001. EMS can adopt a
plan, do, check, action (PDCA) cycle (see Fig. 6.1), popularized by W Edwards Deming[3].
The *Planning* phase would detail the objectives that the organization plans to achieve as
part of their EMS. *Doing* is the implementation phase where initiatives to achieve the
objectives are put in practice. *Checking* involves ascertaining and assessment of the results,
while *action* involves incorporating the feedback into the processes and attempting to
refine and improvise the process.

The following are some of the key aspects of an EMS:

- Developing an environmental policy
- Understanding compliance and legal requirements
- Establishing objectives and targets
- Allocating roles and responsibilities
- Communication and documentation
- Creating emergency response measures
- Monitoring and tracking performance
- Taking corrective actions and review

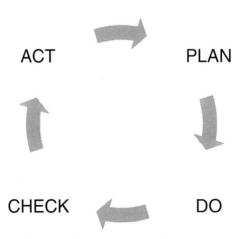

FIG. 6.1 Plan, do, check, action cycle

---

2 http://epa.gov/ems/, last accessed on 14 June 2014.

3 *Note*: An American statistician known for his work with Japanese companies in improving their quality and productivity
   standards after World War II.

EMS not only helps the organization in achieving environmental compliance, but also helps in improving the efficiency and effectiveness of the business practices for the following reasons:

- Brings clarity to the goals and the mode of achieving them—This involves creating standards that meet compliance norms, without which the organization can attract regulatory hurdles, fines, and public resentment. If the organization goes a step further and incorporates sustainability parameters, it could result in increased monetary gains for the company, through waste reduction and new sources of revenue generation. Such practices can also improve the brand mileage of the company as an 'environmentally friendly' organization among the public. It can also help in boosting employee morale.
- Training, responsibility allocation, and accountability—Charting out goals helps in defining the skill sets an organization requires, in order to achieve them. Training people helps in accomplishing those goals. Assigning responsibility and role allocation brings about clarity of purpose among employees.
- Allocation of resources—It optimizes the distribution and usage of resources.
- Reporting, assessment, and continuous improvement—EMS is an opportunity to develop performance reporting standards. A mature reporting standard can give the management of an organization both an overview and detailing of the health of an organization's processes.
- Respect among clients, peers, and customers—An EMS certification is a communication to the society that the organization demonstrates compliance, and possibly, sets higher standards for its supply chain and operational practices, and thus is reliable.

Environmental Risk Management

Organizations, as part of their daily operations, can cause environmental impacts. Environmental risk management (ERM) processes help to evolve a framework to evaluate the environmental risks associated with a proposed policy/plan/programme. In an ERM process, the following steps could be involved:

- Problem formulation—This would involve (a) defining the spatial (related to geography) and temporal boundaries (related to time) of the problem, (b) documenting areas of constraints, uncertainty, and assumptions, and (c) developing the source-pathway-receptor linkages (linkages between sources of hazard, pathways through which these hazards impacts the receptors). For example, if one is ascertaining risk management related to floods, the source could be strong rainfall, receptors could be people and infrastructure, and pathways could be inadequate urban drainage.
- Risk assessment—It helps in ascertaining the probability of an event and the magnitude of the consequences on the receptors.

- Selection of the risk management practice—This involves ascertaining the advantages and disadvantages of the risk management options. Some of the methodologies adopted could include cost benefit analysis, trade-off analysis, and multi-criteria analysis.
- Implementation of the risk management practice.

Environmental Design Management

Environmental design management is a process through which the design practices are used to meet environmental standards and improvement in environmental quality. The environmental requirements are incorporated at the stage of the design itself. GE's 'Ecomagination Treasure Hunts' is a process that identifies opportunities of energy savings, waste and emission reduction, and conservation of natural resources. During this process, GE uses cross-functional teams for this process. Teams having 4–6 members may focus on energy sources (solar, steam, natural gas, thermal, and coal), geographic areas (manufacturing plant A, and manufacturing plant B), operational processes (dyeing, and knitting), or types of equipment used (printers, air conditioners, and lighting). To provide an appropriate perspective to the team members about all stages of energy usage—non-productive, start-up, productive, and break—the treasure hunt begins on Sunday mid-day and ends Tuesday afternoon. More than 300 treasure hunts have been conducted at GE resulting in the company identifying more than 6,50,000 million tons of carbon dioxide reduction opportunities and $150 million in energy savings. This process has also resulted in GE reducing its energy intensity by 37 percent.[4]

Backcasting

Backcasting is the process of visualising a desirable future scenario and then working backwards to the present, by creating policies and practices, which will create that desirable future. The question that drives this creation is, 'What do we need to do today to reach that successful outcome?'[5] It is about 'beginning with an end in mind'. Backcasting is used for resource management practices, management of water and energy, urban and infrastructure planning, and more.

The natural step, a network of non-profit organizations that promotes education, dialogue, and innovative solutions related to sustainable development, has designed four sustainability principles[6] while engaging in backcasting, which are as follows:

- Reduce and eventually eliminate our contribution to the systematic accumulation of materials from the earth's crust. This means substituting use of

---

4 http://files.ecomagination.com/wp-content/uploads/2010/07/Treasure_Hunt_FAQs_071110.pdf, last accessed on 5 October 2011.
5 http://www.naturalstep.org/backcasting, last accessed on 2 March 2013.
6 http://www.naturalstep.ca/sites/default/files/planning-for-sustainability.pdf, last accessed on 31 December 2014. Used with permission.

certain minerals that are scarce in nature with others that are abundant, using all mined materials efficiently, and systematically reducing our dependence on fossil fuels.

- Reduce and eliminate our contribution to the systematic accumulation of substances produced by society. This means systematically substituting certain persistent and unnatural compounds with ones that are normally abundant or break down more easily in nature and using all substances produced by the society efficiently.

- Reduce and eliminate our contribution to the ongoing physical degradation of nature. This means drawing resources only from well-managed ecosystems, systematically pursuing the most productive and efficient use of those resources and land, and exercising caution in all kinds of modifications of nature, such as over-harvesting and the introduction of invasive species.

- Reduce and eliminate our contribution to conditions that systematically undermine people's ability to meet their basic needs. This means offering products and services and changing practices, suppliers, and business models to those that ensure that human rights are respected, income-making barriers are removed, safe and healthy work environments are provided, and living conditions allow local communities to meet the needs of the citizens.

INDUSTRIAL ECOLOGY AND TOOLS FOR MEASURING ENVIRONMENTAL IMPACTS

Industrial ecology (IE) is the study of the flow of material and energy through human activities (including industrial activities) and its effect on the environment. IE aims to design systems with the understanding that industrial processes are part of a natural system and these processes can be designed in a way that has similarities with the natural environment, in order to have optimal utilization of resources and respect for the sustainability of the whole process and its components. Towards the achievement of these goals, the process aims to close the loops—a process where waste of one industry can be used as a raw material by another. IE adopts a systems thinking approach.

Network for Business Sustainability,[7] a not-for-profit sustainability organization, has identified some of the methods/tools used for assessing environment related impacts (see Table 6.1). The recording of environmental impacts is usually calculated as a measurement or as a value. A measurement determines the magnitude of a quantity while valuation assigns a monetary value to an impact. For example, we can calculate the carbon dioxide emissions per hour from an automobile (measurement), while valuation may refer to the health cost that the society will incur due to the inhalation of polluted air. As indicated by the aforementioned example, these two recordings need not be mutually exclusive.

---

7 www.nbs.net

TABLE 6.1[8] Methods/Tools used to measure environmental impacts

S. no.	Measurement-based methods/tools	Applications
1.	Balanced scorecard approach	To evaluate environmental, social, and financial measures
2.	Carbon footprint	To determine the total amount of carbon dioxide an organization is linked to
3.	Destination environmental scorecard	To evaluate the environmental performance of small and medium sized hotel operations
4.	Ecological footprint	To compare established operations in different locations
5.	Environmental evaluation matrix	To appraise the environmental impacts of projects
6.	Environmental management system modelling	To evaluate the management of an organization's environmental programs
7.	Epstein Roy framework	To determine how to modify environmental, social, and financial performance
8.	Genuine wealth accounting model	To evaluate environmental, social, and financial measures
9.	Green globes design	To improve the sustainability and environmental performance of commercial buildings
10.	Green productivity index	To integrate environmental protection into corporate performance
11.	Life cycle analysis	To evaluate the environmental and social damages related to a specific service or product
12.	Lowell centre hierarchy	To evaluate environmental, social, and financial measures
13.	Materials flow analysis	To evaluate the flow of a material through a firm and its affected ecosystems
14.	Responsive business scorecard	To integrate stakeholder demands into environmental, social, and financial goals
15.	Whole life value	To integrate stakeholder values with a life cycle analysis of a product or project
S. no.	Valuation-based methods/tools	Applications
1.	Cost-benefit analysis	To weigh the benefits of a new project, program, or product with its costs
2.	Ecosystem service valuation	To determine the value of a new construction project on undeveloped land

(Contd)

8 http://nbs.net/wp-content/uploads/NBS-Systematic-Review-Impacts1.pdf, last accessed on 2 October 2013. Used with permission.

S. no.	Valuation-based methods/tools	Applications
3.	Environmental input-output model	To determine the total economic, social, and environmental value of a product or service
4.	Sustainable value added	To increase company efficiency while considering all environmental and social impacts
5.	Triple bottom line reporting	To determine the total economic, social, and environmental value of an organization

Network for business sustainability found that only seven of the aforementioned twenty were studied in both academic and practitioner settings. The seven were balanced scorecard approach, carbon footprint, ecological footprint, ecosystem service valuation, life cycle analysis, sustainability value added, and triple bottom line. The study found that life cycle analysis was the most commonly used tool, followed by ecological footprint, balanced scorecard, environmental management system modelling, environmental input-output model, and ecosystem service valuation. While the popular tool among academics was life cycle analysis, practitioners preferred ecosystem service valuation, life cycle analysis, and the ecological footprint. Another finding of the study was that the balanced scorecard approach, life cycle analysis, environmental management system modelling, and the ecological footprint were the major tools used to measure an organization's environmental performance. To study the environmental performance of a specific product or event, life cycle analysis was the popular tool. Ecological footprint was used to measure the impacts of geographical region. Ecosystem service valuation was the most common tool used to study ecosystems.

Ecological Footprint

The ecological footprint (environmental footprint/eco-footprint) is a measurement that compares human demands on the planet with the planet's capability to regenerate the required demands. The measurement indicates the area of ecologically productive land and water required to support human demands like food, energy resources, housing demands, and assimilation of wastes with prevailing technology. The measurement of both ecological footprint and bio-capacity is usually done in global hectares (gha). In 2008, as per the *Living Planet Report*, the Earth's total biocapacity was 12.0 billion gha (1.8 gha/individual) while humanity's ecological footprint was 18.2 billion gha (2.7 gha/individual), clearly indicating that the sustainable limits had been breached. As per the *Living Planet Report 2012*, if all of the human beings lived like an average human being living in USA, four more planet Earths would be required to meet the demand of people.[9]

Assessment is done to identify whether a region/country's ecological footprint is higher than its biocapacity. A region whose footprint is smaller than its biocapacity has an ecological reserve and is thus considered to be an ecological creditor. For example,

---

9 http://awsassets.panda.org/downloads/lpr_2012_summary_booklet_final.pdf, last accessed on 13 May 2014.

Bolivia's per capita footprint is only 2.6 gha, while it has a per capita biocapacity of 18 gha.[10] A region whose ecological footprint exceeds its biocapacity has an ecological deficit, and is referred to as an ecological debtor. For example, UAE has a biocapacity of 0.6 gha only, though its ecological footprint is 8.4 gha.[11] Most of the countries are now exceeding their biocapacities and have an ecological deficit. Globally, there is an ecological deficit, and this is referred to as an ecological overshoot. Global Footprint Network states that, for 2006, humanity was using ecological services 1.4 times faster than the planet can renew these services.

Ecological footprint was originally conceptualized by Mathis Wackernagel and his Ph.D guide Professor William Rees at the University of British Columbia in Vancouver, Canada, in 1990–1994. In recent times, the calculation of ecological footprint takes into consideration the need for reserving a portion of the earth's resources for non-human species. Organizations like Redefining Progress and Global Footprint Network have been working to improve the methodology for calculating ecological footprint. The three drivers of ecological footprint are: a) population growth, b) consumption of products/ services by an individual, and c) footprint intensity (the efficiency rate at which natural resources are converted to goods/services).

Living Planet Report 2012 indicates that many countries that ranked high on the human development index also have a high ecological footprint. Such a proposition, where development has to be accompanied by a higher ecological footprint, is an unsustainable proposition. One of the goals of development could be improving the human well-being without having a high ecological footprint.

Earth Overshoot Day

Earth Overshoot Day is that day of the year when the demands made by the human population for that year exceed the capacity of the planet for that year. Earth Overshoot Day, also known as Ecological Debt Day, was developed and popularized by New Economics Foundation (http://www.neweconomics.org) and Global Footprint Network (http://www.footprintnetwork.org). It was in the mid-1970s that demands made by human beings started exceeding the production and sustenance capability of the planet. The following is a list of when the Earth Overshoot Day was observed during the past few years.

2013: August 20
2012: August 22
2003: September 22
1993: October 21

In 2013, human species consumed in less than nine months what the planet takes 12 months to produce. This also means that the human species are now borrowing ('overdraft') from the resources that are kept for future generations. The above table

---

10 http://awsassets.panda.org/downloads/lpr_2012_summary_booklet_final.pdf, last accessed on 13 May 2014.
11 http://awsassets.panda.org/downloads/lpr_2012_summary_booklet_final.pdf, last accessed on 13 May 2014.

also indicates that the overshoot day has been moving ahead every year, as the demand made by the human species is continuously increasing on the planet. Global Footprint Network indicates that the Earth Overshoot Day has been advancing almost three days every year, since 2001.[12]

Carbon Footprint and Carbon Dioxide Equivalent

Carbon footprint is a measure of an individual's impact on the planet in terms of the amount of greenhouse gases (GHG) produced due to the lifestyle of the individual. Carbon footprint is measured in units of carbon dioxide equivalent (CO_2e). Emissions of greenhouse gases are usually expressed with CO_2e, which is used as a common metric. Most greenhouse gases have a higher global warming potential (GWP) as compared to carbon dioxide. CO_2e of a particular gas indicates the impact this particular gas has in terms of the amount of carbon dioxide that would be required to create an equivalent amount of global warming. For example, methane has a higher global warming potential as compared to CO_2, and on a hundred year timespan, one tonne of methane will cause the same amount of global warming as that of 25 tonnes of carbon dioxide (see Table 6.2 for CO_2e of various GHGs).

Direct/Indirect Emissions and Scope 1/Scope 2/Scope 3 Emissions

Carbon emissions can be direct or indirect. Direct emissions are those that can be controlled or owned by organizations that is reporting the emissions. Indirect emissions are also caused by the operations of the organization that is reporting the emissions, yet, these emissions occur at locations/processes that are not owned or controlled by the reporting organization. All the emissions are categorized under Scope 1, Scope 2, and Scope 3 emissions.

TABLE 6.2[13] GWP of some greenhouse gases on different timespans, in comparison with CO_2

Name of the GHG	On a 20 year times pan	On a 100 year times pan	On a 500 year times pan
Methane	72	25	7.6
Nitrous oxide	289	298	153
Carbon tetrachloride	2700	1400	435
Methyl bromide	17	5	1
Methyl chloroform	506	146	45
Sulphur hexafluoride	16,300	22,800	32,600
Nitrogen trifluoride	12,300	17,200	20,700

---

12 http://www.footprintnetwork.org/en/index.php/gfn/page/earth_overshoot_day/, last accessed on 29 August 2013.
13 http://www.ipcc.ch/publications_and_data/ar4/wg1/en/ch2s2-10-2.html, last accessed on 13 May 2014.

Scope 1 emissions are the direct GHG emissions from sources owned or controlled by the organization. This could include emissions from the on-site burning of fossil fuels, emissions from organization owned vehicles, etc.

Scope 2 emissions refer to the indirect emissions resulting from the activities done off-site and purchased by the organization (generation of electricity, steam, heating, and cooling) and also the transmission and distribution (T&D) losses associated with the usage of chilled water, steam, and hot water by the reporting organization.

Scope 3 emissions are indirect emissions generated not at the locations or processes owned or controlled by the organization, but related to the activities of the organization. Scope 3 emissions include emissions associated with employee travel, contracted solid waste disposal, contracted wastewater treatment, vendor supply chains, outsourced activities, site remediation activities, leased space, and T&D losses associated with purchased electricity.

Value Chain Carbon Footprint

Value chain carbon footprint measures the emissions of an organization across its value chain, both upstream and downstream activities, and the emissions are categorized across an organization's value chain.

Life Cycle Analysis

Life cycle analysis (LCA), also referred to as life cycle assessment, cradle-to-grave analysis, and ecobalance, looks into the cumulative social and environmental impact caused by a product or service, through the entire life cycle of a product's life—from raw material extraction, manufacturing, distribution and retail, usage and maintenance, disposal, and recycling and waste management. Joel Makower, Chairman and Executive Editor, GreenBiz Inc., defines LCA as, 'a process of measuring the environmental impacts associated with all the stages of a product's life from raw materials to the end of its useful life'.[14]

During LCA, assessment is done on damages caused due to aspects like greenhouse gases, soil acidification, water pollution, ozone depletion, and habitat destruction. LCA procedures are part of ISO 14000 environmental standards. It is important to analyse the impact of a product in order to select measures that should be taken to increase environmental sustainability. The following are the different functional aspects that could be taken into consideration while doing a LCA (see Fig. 6.2):

- Research and development
- Packaging development

---

14 http://www.greenbiz.com/blog/2013/01/14/tom-gloria-and-life-cycle-lca?page=full, last accessed on 17 January 2013.

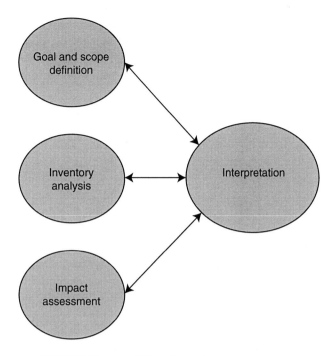

FIG 6.2[15] Phases of life cycle analysis

- Supplier activities (sourcing of raw materials and shipment)
- Production/manufacturing
- Distribution
- Retail
- Consumption
- Disposal

The preliminary step to LCA involves 'goal and scope definition', which involves defining and describing the product or process, establishing the boundaries of the system, and assessment perspectives.

- Reasons and goals vary on why an organization decides to conduct an LCA. Some examples are to select a product/process that have the least impact on the environment or the technology that will cause the least impact on the environment, etc.
- During this phase, the researcher determines the type of information required to communicate to the stakeholders.
- The type of information required corresponds to the defined study parameter. The study parameters are defined by the questions that decision makers care about.

15 Image Source: http://en.wikipedia.org/wiki/File:PhasesOfLifeCycleAnalysis.png, last accessed on 1 August 2011.

- The required specificity of the information to be collected will be based on LCA objectives and scope. It could be product/process specific or generic to an industry.
- Determination of data organization and result presentation is decided. Studies may require the creation of a common functional unit so that products across different categories can be compared.
- While LCA means studying the entire lifecycle, in certain instances only certain stages are studied.

Following goal and scope definition, 'inventory analysis' is done and this involves identifying and quantifying the inputs, wastes, emissions, and co-products associated with the life cycle chain. During this phase, the inputs and outputs of the system are mapped. A plan for data collection is developed and the data is collected. This is followed by evaluation of the results.

The next step includes the 'impact assessment' of the inventory items. This includes the following phases:

Identification of categories Identifying categories that cause environmental impacts and defining those categories. Some of the impact categories include global warming, eutrophication, acidification, ozone depletion, resource depletion, land use, and water use.

Classification of categories Classifying categories for the purpose of inventory analysis. For example, release of effluents to toxicity.

Characterization modelling and normalization Assessing the impacts of inventory on categories. Through the use of characterization factors, also referred to as equivalency factors, results of inventory analysis are converted to representative indicators. During this phase, characterization factors translate inventory inputs to directly comparable impact indicators. Through the process of normalization, indicator data can be compared across impact categories. For example, the impact of carbon dioxide and methane on global warming.

Grouping of indicators It is done based on parameters like characteristics (emission type) or location (global, regional, and local).

Weighting Emphasis is given to those parameters that are perceived to be most important and have relevant potential impacts. The weighting should also reflect the objectives of the study.

Evaluation and reporting of results This stage involves the verification of the accuracy of the results.

L'Oréal group, one of the leading cosmetic brands in the world, while estimating its carbon footprint[16] for eight product categories (that included a shampoo, a hair-dye, a lipstick, etc.), found that raw materials accounted for 12 per cent of the carbon footprint of the entire life cycle. This raw materials phase included all phases in the life of the raw material (including mining of a mineral, processing, packaging, shipment, use, and end of life disposal), packaging contributed 14 per cent, and 2 per cent came from services such

---

16 http://loreal.com/_en/_ww/pdf/LOREAL_RDD_2008.pdf, last accessed on 11 February 2013.

In 2012, the Government of India passed the Companies Bill, which suggested that every company, which has a net worth of ₹ 500 crore or more, OR a turnover of ₹ 1000 crore or more, OR a net profit of ₹ 5 crore or more should spend at least 2 percent of average net profits of the company in the previous three preceding financial years, in nine broad areas that encompass a lot of endeavours related to social and environmental responsibility.

as software, insurance, surveys, and others. Cumulatively, supply chain related activities contributed to approximately 28 per cent, production accounted for about 5 per cent, and distribution accounted for 7 percent of the company's carbon footprint. The company found that a staggering 58 per cent of the company's total carbon footprint was from consumer use and this was being significantly contributed by the products that are used with hot water (shampoos, conditioners, etc.). The disposal/end-of-life phase was estimated to contribute 2 per cent. This indicated that L'Oréal could create the highest environmental advantage by focussing on reducing/eliminating the amount of water used during the application of shampoos or conditioners, as this phase had the larger share of carbon footprint.

Therefore, LCA helps an organization collect and compile inputs and outputs related to energy, material, and environmental related aspects. This information helps an organization in choosing the least ecologically and socially impactful product/processes while creating its goods and services.

In 1969, Coca-Cola Company did an LCA to find which variety of beverage containers had the least negative effect on the environment. This is considered to be the first LCA study.[17] Most LCAs are simplified LCAs, as, in practicality, an organization may find it easier to assess the aspects that are directly related to a product or service and not to those aspects in the extremes of the value chain.

Ecosystem Services and Valuation

Visit any temple in rural India, and there is a good possibility that one will see one or many banyan trees. Banyan tree is known for its extensive branches, it's evergreen nature, the shade it provides, and its oxygen producing capability. Banyan tree is the national tree of India, and has derived its name from *bania* (trader) who utilized the shade provided by the banyan trees to conduct their businesses under. The following is a hymn to the Ashwatha Vruksha (banyan tree).

> *Moolatho brahma roopaaya madhyatho vishnu roopine*
> *Agratha shiva roopaaya vrukhsa raajaaya the namaha*

This translates to, 'My salutations to the king of trees, whose root is the form of Brahma, the centre is the form of Lord Vishnu, and top is the form of Lord Shiva.' Married women used to worship banyan tree to lead a long and happy married life. The existence of these practices indicate that they were based on the idea of the importance of ecosystem and its services to human beings, and the interdependence of various species.

---

17 http://www.umich.edu/~nppcpub/resources/compendia/CORPpdfs/CORPlca.pdf, http://link.springer.com/article/10.1007%2FBF02978624#page-1, http://www.epa.gov/nrmrl/std/lca/pdfs/chapter1_frontmatter_lca101.pdf, last accessed on 31 December 2014.

The term ecosystem services has become popular in the mid-2000s, especially after the release of the Millennium Ecosystem Assessment of 2005.

Ecosystem services are the processes by which the natural environment creates an environment that sustains life on earth. Ecosystem services are those services that contribute directly to life, such as the dispersal of seeds for flora reproduction or a conservation area that supplies both recreation to humans and a habitat for animals. Most often we take these services for granted. The following are some such examples and attempts to maintain them:

- Mississippi river valley had natural flood protection systems. These natural services were destroyed when the adjacent wetlands were drained and channels were altered. When the 1993 flood occurred, it resulted in property damages resulting in twelve billion dollars—a result of the inability of the valley to lessen the impacts of high volumes of water.
- More than 1,00,000 species, including bats, bees, birds, butterflies, flies, and moths provide free pollination services. One-third of the human food comes from plants pollinated by wind pollinators.
- About 80 per cent of the global population relies on natural medicinal products. Of the leading 150 prescription drugs used in USA, 118 prescription drugs originate from natural sources {74 per cent from plants, 18 per cent from fungi, 5 per cent from bacteria, and 3 per cent from one vertebrate (snake species)}.
- The people of Kuhan, a village located in the district of Kangra, Himachal Pradesh, India, has constructed a check dam on Gulana Khad, a creek that flowed through the village. The construction of this check dam resulted in crop production going up by six times and thus enabling the villagers to grow more vegetables and fruits. However, this dam was soon filled with silt due to the soil erosion happening upstream. The people of Kuhan entered into a co-operative agreement with the people of Ooch, the village that existed upstream. As part of the agreement, the villagers of Ooch was to cease their practice of grazing for eight years in their four-hectare common land that caused soil erosion and accumulation of silt in the dam. Instead Ooch villagers planted tree saplings bearing fruit and fodder in their land. They also planted elephant grass and bamboo. For engaging in these services, the villagers of Kuhan paid for the tree saplings.
- After examining the restorative effect of natural views on surgical patients in a suburban Pennsylvania hospital in USA, researchers summarized that '...in comparison with the wall view group, the patients with the tree view had shorter post-operative hospital stays, had fewer negative evaluative comments from nurses, took fewer moderate and strong analgesic doses, and had slightly lower scores for minor post-surgical complications.'[18]

---

18 http://mdc.mo.gov/sites/default/files/resources/2012/10/ulrich.pdf, last accessed on 3 February 2013.

- In the Keoladeo National Park, located in Bharatpur, at Rajashtan, India, the park management decided to incorporate an entrance fee to ensure scaling down of public access for using the national park for their morning workouts. The morning workouts undertaken by the public inside the national park were at times noisy and were affecting the birds and other wildlife in the wetland areas of that park, which was also a World Heritage site. The local population protested against the decision and demanded that the national park be reopened for their daily exercises. This is an example indicating that people also use ecosystem services for their recreation, tourism, and aesthetic appreciation.[19]

Classification of Ecosystem Services

Provisioning services refers to services obtained from ecosystems that sustain human life. Regulating services refers to benefits derived by humankind from regulation of ecosystem processes. Cultural services include the nonmaterial benefits derived by human beings from ecosystems. Supporting services are the services necessary for the creation and sustenance of all other ecosystem services. Following are few indicative examples of ecosystem services.

TABLE 6.3 Classification of ecosystem services

Provisioning services	Regulating services	Cultural services
Food	Micro and macro climate regulation	Aesthetic and inspirational
Fresh Water	Regulation of erosion, flood, and storms	Cultural heritage
Fibre	Biological/natural control of pests	Recreation and eco-tourism
Biochemicals and dyes	Purification and regulation of air and water	Educational
Fuelwood	Detoxification and decomposition of wastes	Religious
Medicinal resources	Regulation of natural disturbances	Spiritual
	Disease regulation	
	Protection from the sun's ultraviolet rays	
	Supporting services	
	Seed dispersal	
	Biodiversity maintenance	
	Plant pollination	
	Nursery function	
	Nutrient cycling	
	Soil formation	

---

19 http://www.teebweb.org/media/2013/10/Discounts-on-entrance-fees....pdf, last accessed on 13 May 2014.

Ecosystem service valuation assigns monetary value to ecosystem services and tries to measure how important ecosystem services are to humans. '...description of these (intangible ecosystem services) values can hardly convince policymakers and planners, as most of them are conventionally trained or driven by the financial aspects, that too the immediate gains. Therefore, there is a need felt for converting the ecosystem service values into economic values,'[20] states V.S. Vijayan, former Chairman, Kerala State Biodiversity Board, Founder-Trustee, Salim Ali Foundation, while explaining the rationale of assigning monetary values for ecosystem services. However, ecosystem valuation and accounting for natural capital had its critics too. Joss Tantram, Partner, Terrafiniti LLP, a company that offers consulting services focussed on sustainability and CSR, says, '...we don't need to know in dollars, pounds or renminbi how valuable natural capital and natural productivity is in order to tell us that we should behave more sustainably. We should already know that because of the manifest global impacts produced by our current industrial and economic models.'[21]

Ecosystem service valuation methods incorporate market values and non-market values. Market values are values that are directly available based on a market transaction, for example, the cost of paddy produced from a particular region or the cost of electricity from a wind power source. Non-market values are values that are neither directly available nor easy to calculate. Placing values on the ecosystem services can help in determining how the ecosystem services values will change as a consequence of a project. Calculation of ecosystem services will result in a total economic value. The ecosystem services valuation process is extensive, thorough, in-depth, and requires time and resources. Researchers may use different methods to do valuation and comparison between multiple valuation studies may not be possible (see Table 6.4 and 6.5).

TABLE 6.4 Different valuation methods

Valuation method	Description	Example
Contingent valuation method/ willingness-to-pay method/ willingness-to-accept method	Value of an ecosystem service is ascertained by asking people their willingness to pay for a change in environmental quality/good/service.	'Would you be willing to pay ₹100 monthly from your pocket money for creating and maintaining a 1 sq. km. area of lush green park near your home?'
Choice experiment method/choice modelling method	Value attributed for a change in a particular good or service. Involves assessing the preference of the respondent for various options, typically three or four.	'Would you be willing to pay: (1) ₹100 monthly from your pocket money for creating and maintaining a 1 sq. km. area of lush green park near your home? (2) ₹200 monthly from your pocket money for creating and maintaining a 2 sq. km area of lush green park near your home? (3) ₹300 rupees from your pocket money for creating and maintaining a 3 sq.km. area of lush green park near your home? (4) Maintaining status quo. No cost, no park.'

(Contd)

20 Vijayan, VS 2012, Turning wetlands into badlands, *The Hindu Survey of the Environment 2012*.
21 http://www.guardian.co.uk/sustainable-business/blog/pricing-natural-capital-weighing-dog, last accessed on 1 October 2012.

Travel cost method	Value to attend a specific event—costs associated with a specific trip; costs that they would not have spent normally. It could be regarded as the price of access to the site.	Costs of attending a conference/meeting in another city instead of being at the office. The costs may include air travel, boarding and lodging fee, fee associated with the conference/meeting, domestic travel, related expenses, etc. This method could also be used for ascertaining the value of a recreational site. The recreationists are surveyed and asked questions about the number of trips they take and their travel cost to the site (see Fig. 6.3).
Hedonic pricing method	Value of an environmental amenity, calculated in association with an environmental uniqueness provided by a house, building, or property.	To determine the value of a sea view, one can find out the difference between the value of purchasing a house overlooking the sea and another identical house that is not facing the sea. The researcher could also compare the difference in prices among sea facing and non-sea facing rooms of a hotel. An employee may choose to work in a city with clean air and water, though the salary may be lesser, as compared to working in a city where salary is higher, yet the air and water is polluted. The monetary value that is foregone by the employee by this choice could be the environmental valuation.
Benefit transfer or value transfer method	Valuing an ecosystem service using secondary data due to time/budget constraints. Results of a study pertaining to one project area are transferred to a study pertaining to a different, yet similar project area.	A researcher estimating the value of a carbon sequestration services offered by one wildlife sanctuary may use the carbon sequestration values offered by another similar wildlife sanctuary.
Avoided cost method and replacement cost method	Value of services provided by ecosystem that we do not pay for as those services are being provided by the ecosystem. Replacement cost indicates the value incurred to replace the ecosystem service with a human created product/service.	Trees provide the oxygen that human beings require for breathing. If the trees are not there, then human beings will have to create oxygen producing devices. Value for that device will be considered to be the ecosystem value. Another example is the cool breeze provided by wind. Purchase, installation, and maintenance value of an air-conditioner and electricity costs associated with its usage could be considered as the ecosystem value here. Cost of fertilizers and manpower associated with its usage could be the ecosystem value offered by worms that provide nutrients.
Restoration cost method	Value of services provided by an ecosystem to restore itself to its original state, following a disturbance.	A water body like a river or sea has an innate ability to dilute the effluents/pollutants discharged into the water body. However, major disturbances like the Deepwater Horizon oil spill or the Gulf War oil spill would require human intervention to clean up the area. The cost incurred to restore an ecosystem prior to its natural state would be the restoration cost.

(Contd)

TABLE 6.4 *(Contd)*

Valuation method	Description	Example
Factor income method	Value of services provided by an ecosystem that enhances the value of other ecosystem services.	An acre of crop area may produce more mangoes if their flowers are pollinated well by bees and other pollinating agents. Factor income is the difference between the income generated if the flowers were pollinated by pollinating agents resulting in more mangoes and when the flowers were not pollinated by pollinating agents.
Dose response method	Value of services provided by an ecosystem that maintain optimal productivity by humans, plants, and animals.	The physiological response of humans, plants, and animals depends on the conducive ecosystem. With the stress of pollution there will be changes in farm outputs, human production, etc. The loss of the crop output could be used as the value provided by the ecosystem.

FIG. 6.3[22]   View from Abra del Acay, Argentina. How much extra effort, energy, and money would you be willing to give, to enjoy a view like this?

---

22 Photo by Jason Hollinger, used with permission. Image source: https://www.flickr.com/photos/7147684@N03/898091771, last accessed on 7 August 2014.

TABLE 6.5[23]   Estimates of monetary values of some of the ecosystem services offered by some of the biomes of earth

	Provisioning services	Regulating services	Habitat services	Cultural services	Total
Open oceans	22	62			**84**
Coral reefs	20,892	33,640	56,137	1,084,809	**11,95,478**
Coastal systems	7549	30,451	164	41,416	**79,580**
Coastal wetlands	8289	1,35,361	68,795	2904	**2,15,349**
Inland wetlands	9709	23,018	3471	8399	**44,597**
Rivers and lakes	5776	4978		2733	**13,487**
Tropical forests	9384	7135	5277	1426	**23,222**
Temperate and boreal forests	1736	456	2575	96	**4863**
Woodlands	862	1088			**1950**
Grasslands	715	2067	298	11	**3091**

Note: Maximum values are taken, $/ha/year-2007

Ecosystem Services Provided by Rainforests

The rainforests of the world provide a number of ecosystem services. Forests provide livelihood to 1.6 billion people.[24] In addition, rainforests also offers belongingness, heritage value, and is of cultural and spiritual significance to human beings. Forests are also home to two-thirds of all plants and animals living on land, and are the most diverse terrestrial ecosystems.[25] Rainforests are biologically rich. Dr Thomas E Lovejoy, Professor, George Mason University, who also holds the Biodiversity Chair, Heinz Centre for Science, Economics, and Environment, mentions 'Whereas a New England forest may have 20 or 30 species of trees at most and a coniferous forest may have only one or two tree species, a 25 hectare plot near Camp 41[26] in the Amazon has 295 species of trees. A single tree in Peru has more ant species than all of the United Kingdom. And the Amazon River system has 3000 species of fish—more than the entire North Atlantic.'[27] These species in rainforests could provide clue to the creation of new medicines.[28]

'The Amazon region produces half its own rainfall through the moisture it releases into the atmosphere.'

23 http://www.teebweb.org/Portals/25/Documents/DO%20%20Chapter%205%20Appendix%20C.pdf, last accessed on 29 September 2012. This data has been made available in the public domain by TEEB.

24 http://www.unep.org/yearbook/2011/pdfs/emerging_perspectives_on_forests_biodiversity.pdf, last accessed on 6 December 2012.

25 http://www.unep.org/yearbook/2011/pdfs/emerging_perspectives_on_forests_biodiversity.pdf, last accessed on 6 December 2012.

26 *Note*: Camp 41 is a research camp near the Brazilian city of Manus.

27 http://www.paradiseearth.com/richness.html, last accessed on 6 December 2012.

28 http://www.paradiseearth.com/daily.html, last accessed on 31 December 2014.

Many of the rainforests receive very few nutrient input from outside. These rainforests recycles the nutrients they themselves have created. If the tree cover of these rainforests is removed, the nutrients would be lost and the forests would not survive. Many of the rainforests are located in areas that have clay-like soils and are acidic in nature. This soil is low in nutrients and cannot sustain life. The trees and plants of these regions provide the organic material, and they also prevent the nutrients from being washed away during rains.

Rainforests in the Amazon region and Congo facilitates the creation of rainfall in the surrounding areas that sustains on agriculture. It has been noted that 'the Amazon produces half its own rainfall through the moisture it releases into the atmosphere.'[29] If the rain creating trees are eliminated in the Amazonian region, then the rainfall will reduce which will in turn destroy the remaining trees. 'Moisture is brought in on westward winds from the Atlantic and then recycles as it moves toward the Andes.[30] Rain that falls on the forest evaporates off the forest's complex surfaces and is transpired by the leaves, so that it returns to the air mass and can form the basis for rain farther to the west. …when the moisture recycled across the Amazon basin reaches the high wall of the Andes it is deflected. A significant portion goes south and provides important rainfall for south central Brazil and northern Argentina. So the newly recognized Amazon rain machine is making a vital contribution to the Brazilian economy through its benefits to agro-industry and some hydroelectric facilities,' says Thomas Lovejoy, Chief Biodiversity Adviser to the President of the World Bank, Senior Advisor to the President of the United Nations Foundation, and President of the Heinz Center for Science, Economics, and the Environment.[31] While in India, the Western Ghats is the source of water for the entire Peninsular India. The region has almost 4000 species of flowering plants, many of which are endemic to the region.[32]

A research article published in *Nature*, in 1997, states that the ecosystem services could range between $16 trillion–54 trillion per year.[33] To put this in perspective, India's GDP in 2011, as per World Bank estimates, was only $1.848 trillion.

Application of Ecosystem Services in Business and Industry
Ecosystem services find a number of applications in the industrial world, as listed in Table 6.6:

29 http://environment.nationalgeographic.com/environment/habitats/last-of-amazon/, last accessed on 5 December 2012.
30 *Note:* The longest continental mountain range in the world and extends through Venezuela, Colombia, Ecuador, Peru, Bolivia, Chile, and Argentina.
31 http://www.paradiseearth.com/services.html, last accessed on 6 December 2012.
32 http://envfor.nic.in/sites/default/files/HLWG-Report-Part-1_0.pdf, last accessed on 14 May 2014.
33 http://www.nature.com/nature/journal/v387/n6630/abs/387253a0.html, last accessed on 15 April 2013.

TABLE 6.6 Applications of ecosystem services

Real estate management	1. Assess 'idle' lands in terms of what ecosystem services exist and can be restored, with conservation value used to communicate the value that can be realized. 2. Prioritize selection of lands for restoration and assess how to efficiently allocate resources.
Corporate finance	Factor ecosystem services opportunities and risks into decisions about potential mergers, acquisitions, major investments, and new project development.
Corporate strategy	1. Define and embody environmental leadership by applying an ecosystem services approach and conducting an assessment of impacts and dependencies. 2. Support brand value and differentiate from competitors.
Supply chain management	1. Assess potential for supply chain disruption due to future changes in flows of ecosystem services, as a result of climate change, or land management practices on adjacent lands. 2. Analyse parts of the supply chain to identify quantifiable impacts and dependencies on ecosystem services.
Product life cycle assessment (LCA)	Assess how life cycle stages could affect biodiversity and ecosystem services.

Note: This table is originally published in a March 2013 report 'Private Sector Uptake of Ecosystem Services Concepts and Frameworks: The Current State of Play' by BSR, a global business network and consultancy focussed on sustainability. Please visit www.bsr.org for more information. Table used with permission.[34]

Ecosystem Valuation in Business and Industry

Ecosystem valuation has its application in business and industry. An offshoot of ecosystem valuation is corporate ecosystem valuation (CEV), a process that uses ecosystem valuation to make informed business decisions. The following are the ways CEV can help a company:

- By ascertaining the environmental risks associated with the business of a company, for many times ecology related risks are not taken into consideration in conventional approaches to business planning and analysis.
- Finding out the most appropriate long-term usage of a company's land holdings.
- Helping the company to choose a mitigation measure that will help the company to avoid paying disproportionate costs.
- Giving a direction to the company in choosing the investment option that will provide not just financial surplus, but societal and environmental surplus too.

---

34 www.bsr.org/reports/BSR_Private_Sector_Uptake_Ecosystem_Services.pdf, last accessed on 28 August 2013. Used with permission.

- As a metric to convince government and regulators to change towards progressive rules and guidelines, which will help companies that are sensitive to environmental and societal concerns.
- Helping a company to be future ready, with more stringent environmental regulations companies will need to adhere to higher benchmarks in operating practices. For example, vehicle emission norms and fuel efficiency norms are becoming increasingly tougher. A CEV can help the company to predict the direction of new environmental regulations and thus be ready when the regulations are operationalized.

Benefit-cost Analysis or Cost-benefit Analysis

The most common application of ecosystem valuation is a benefit-cost analysis. This analysis compares benefits and costs to society of policies, programs, or actions to protect or restore ecosystems. It can also measure the gain or loss to ecosystem/society from a policy or action. The analysis determines whether society, as a whole, will enhance/ degrade its well-being if the policy or action is implemented. As a part of benefit-cost analysis, a single policy or action may be evaluated, or several policies or programs may be compared to determine which one provides the greatest net economic benefits. The analysis requires identifying, enumerating, and evaluating all of the measurable benefits and costs. The analysis focusses on quantifiable economic values. Even environmental services are quantified. Since it focusses only on quantifiable economic benefits, the analysis may not be the most environmentally preferred option. Usually when decisions are required to be made, a benefit-cost analysis is only one of the instruments used to aid in decision-making. The decision could also be made based on other information and other influencing factors.

The benefit-cost analysis is conducted in four steps. The following is the explanation of the process with an example of an upgrade of a sewage treatment plant.

- Specification and description of policy or action to be taken. The need/reason for which this policy/action is introduced can also be included as a part of this phase.
- Information related to location, timing/duration, and stakeholders associated with the project, who will be affected by the policy or action, is assessed. The first step is to specify and describe the policy or action to be evaluated, while the second step is to include information such as its location, timing, duration, and the people who will be affected. For example, if the benefit-cost analysis is for an upgrade of a sewage treatment plant, information would be collected on the area the plant serves (the panchayats/municipalities, etc.), identifying the sources from where the sewage will be collected, discharge points, life span of the proposed plant, and time span for completion of the project.
- The next step is to describe and quantify the effects of the policy or program that will lead to benefits and costs to society. For example, information is collected

on the annual maintenance costs, expected improvement in water quality, and how the improvement is expected to benefit people and other living beings. Ecosystem valuation methods could be used at this level.

• Comparison of benefits and costs are done now. As many of the benefits and costs occur over many years, the present value of those benefits and costs are carried out, usually, with the tool of 'discount rating'. For example, if the upgrade of the sewage plant would be functional for 15 years, benefits and costs associated with each of those 15 years are discounted to their present values. If the net present value is positive, then the project could be considered to be worthwhile in terms of economic efficiency.

Pollution control can result in two benefits—market benefits and nonmarket benefits. Market benefits include those benefits that can directly be measured in terms of monetary value. For example, cleaning up of a polluted river may result in rise in tourism related endeavours that generate revenue, like boating in the river. Nonmarket benefits comes under three categories—use value, option value, and existence value. Use value indicates the value associated with people using that resource more usefully and effectively. Cleaning up of a polluted river may result in people using the river water for drinking, swimming, washing, etc., without paying for those services. Option value is the value associated to preserve the option that a particular resource may prove valuable in the future. An environmental resource will have option value if the future benefit of the resource's yield is uncertain and depletion of the resource is effectively irreversible.[35] Existence value is the value attributed to an entity just for its continued existence. For example, a sparrow may not have use value or option value directly associated with it. However, many citizens will be willing to pay an annual amount for the conservation of this species on the planet.

What could be the value of a tree?

Find out first:
1. *What is the cost of an oxygen cylinder?*
2. *How many days does an oxygen cylinder provide oxygen for you?*
3. *How much oxygen does a tree provide?*

An analysis was conducted by International Institute for Applied Systems Analysis in Austria (IIASA),[36] ascertaining the economic impact of delaying measures, to reduce carbon dioxide emissions by 2020. This study, conducted for the Doha Climate Summit, found that such a delay would increase the costs to $25 trillion from $20 trillion. If suitable action is not taken immediately, there will be a 25 per cent increase in cost.[37] On 8 March 2011, the European Commission unveiled a roadmap of transforming the European Union (EU) into a low-carbon growth path. Their intention was to reduce greenhouse gas emissions of

35 Goodstein, Eban S., *Economics and the Environment*, Wiley, 2011.

36 A Laxenburg, Austria-based organization that 'conducts policy-oriented research into problems of a global nature that are too large or too complex to be solved by a single country or academic discipline.'

37 http://www.independent.co.uk/environment/climate-change/fiddling-while-rome-burns–the-3trn-cost-of-climate-delay-8449863.html, last accessed on 10 February 2013.

1990 levels by 80–95 per cent by 2050. Economic modelling underlying the roadmap indicated that to achieve this objective a reduction in the order of 40 per cent should be achieved by 2030 and by 60 per cent by 2040. In order to achieve this, over the next four decades EU needs to invest an additional €270 billion or 1.5 per cent of its GDP annually, on average. The commission stated such investments would result in additional job creation for 1.5 million people by 2020. The commission also estimated a saving of €175–320 billion annually on fuel costs over the next four decades and decreased expenditure on air pollution control systems and healthcare (less pollution thus less respiratory diseases) that could result in a savings of up to €88 billion a year (see Fig. 6.4).

Stakeholder Analysis

Stakeholder analysis identifies the clusters of individuals/groups that are likely to be impacted by the implementation of a proposed plan or action. This analysis facilitates the process of nullifying any negative impact on the stakeholders as part of the implementation of the plan/action.

Total Value Chain Analysis

Total value chain analysis refers to the process of describing the activities that link together to add to the value of the business. First assessment is made about the contribution that each part makes to the overall values of the business. This is followed by the assessment of the potential that each part/activity has towards adding to the

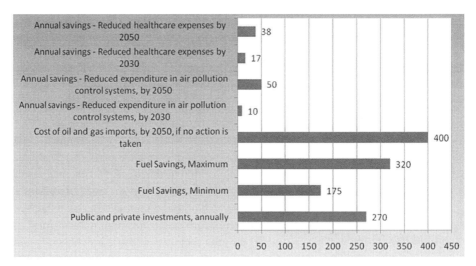

FIG. 6.4[38] Cost-benefit analysis of EU 2050 emission reduction roadmap in billion euros

---

38 http://eur-lex.europa.eu/LexUriServ/LexUriServ.do?uri=CELEX:52011DC0112:EN:NOT, data can be reused as stated in their copyright notice http://eur-lex.europa.eu/content/legal-notice/legal-notice.html, lastaccessed on 27 October 2011.

value of the business. An application of total value chain analysis in environmental management could be when a company is asking/encouraging its supply chain partners to engage in sustainability approaches. In October 2011, Microsoft started a pilot project asking its suppliers to release sustainability reports as per Global Reporting Initiative (GRI) standards from 2013 onwards.

EROEI—Energy Returned on Energy Invested

Energy returned on energy invested (EROEI) is the ratio between energy that is received from an energy source and the energy that is given as an input to gain that. As technologies advance, it has been found that EROEI also improves. However, as the availability of the resource becomes scarce, it requires more energy to tap that resource and then EROEI decreases. When the EROEI of an energy source falls down below one, or is equal to one, the energy source can no longer be considered a viable source of energy. Initial investments are required for constructing energy production facilities. Expenditure also needs to be monitored for regular maintenance and operations. One of the parameters taken into consideration while determining investment in a potential energy source is the energy payback period. Energy payback period refers to the estimated time required to recover the initial amount of energy invested to build up the potential energy source. If the energy payback period is less, then better the investment.

Carbon Rating

A carbon rating could have multiple meanings:
   (a) Carbon ratings are used to communicate the overall quality of an emission reduction project.
   (b) Carbon rating are used as a label in products, including fast-moving consumer goods (FMCG), to indicate the carbon emissions associated with the whole/ partial life cycle of the product that is sold.
The carbon ratings accorded to a product or a project depends on the methodology adopted by the ratings giver to accord the rating.

ENVIRONMENTAL IMPACT ASSESSMENT AND AUDITING

Environmental impact assessment (EIA) helps to address the environmental consequences of a proposed action. This assessment helps the decision maker make informed choices on whether they should proceed with the proposed action or not. The International Association for Impact Assessment (IAIA) has defined EIA as 'The process of identifying, predicting, evaluating, and mitigating the biophysical, social, and other relevant effects of development proposals prior to major decisions being taken and commitments made.'[39] The following objectives are considered by IAIA for conducting an EIA:

---

39 http://www.iaia.org/publicdocuments/special-publications/Principles%20of%20IA_web.pdf, last accessed on 1 April 2013.

- To ensure that environmental considerations are explicitly addressed and incorporated in the development of decision making process.
- To anticipate and avoid, minimize or offset the adverse significant biophysical, social, and other relevant effects of development proposals.
- To protect the productivity and capacity of natural systems and the ecological processes which maintain its functions.
- To promote development that is sustainable and optimizes the resource use and management opportunities.

Following the EIA, if the decision is made to proceed with the proposed plan/project, it is usually a practice to conduct an environmental audit, after the culmination of the project.

The Government of India EIA Notification 2006 states that environmental clearance process for new projects will comprise of four stages—screening, scoping, public consultation, and appraisal. The *screening* stage determines whether the project requires further environmental studies including the preparation of an EIA report. *Scoping* involves projects that require further studies. As part of scoping, a detailed 'terms of reference' are drawn to address relevant environmental concerns in preparation of the EIA report. *Public consultation* process ascertains the concerns of people who are affected by the environmental impact of the project. *Appraisal* involves scrutiny of application, EIA report, outcome of the public consultation hearing, etc., in order to grant or reject permission for environmental clearance of the project.

CHECKLISTS FOR APPLYING ENVIRONMENTAL CLEARANCE

As part of the EIA notification, the Ministry of Environment and Forests (MoEF), Government of India, has issued the following checklists[40] for applying for environmental clearance.

General Checklist

(a) Construction, operation, or decommissioning of the project involving actions, which will cause physical changes in the locality (topography, land use, changes in water bodies, etc.)

Information/checklist confirmation	Yes/ no	Details thereof [41] with source of information data
Permanent or temporary change in land use, land cover, or topography including increase in intensity of land use (with respect to local land use plan)		
Clearance of existing land, vegetation, and buildings?		

(Contd)

---

40 http://www.moef.nic.in/sites/default/files/so1533_4.pdf, last accessed on 16 June 2014.
41 *Note*:with approximate quantities/rates, wherever possible

(Contd)

Creation of new land uses?		
Pre-construction investigations, for example, bore houses, soil testing?		
Construction works?		
Demolition works?		
Temporary sites used for construction works or housing of construction workers?		
Above ground buildings, structures, or earthworks including linear structures, cut and fill, or excavations		
Underground works including mining or tunnelling?		
Reclamation works?		
Dredging?		
Offshore structures?		
Production and manufacturing processes?		
Facilities for storage of goods or materials?		
Facilities for treatment or disposal of solid waste or liquid effluents?		
Facilities for long-term housing of operational workers?		
New road, rail or sea traffic during construction or operation?		
New road, rail, air, waterborne, or other transport infrastructure including new or altered routes, and stations, ports, airports, etc.?		
Closure or diversion of existing transport routes or infrastructure leading to changes in traffic movements?		
New or diverted transmission lines or pipelines?		
Impoundment, damming, culverting, realignment, or other changes to the hydrology of watercourses or aquifers?		
Stream crossings?		
Abstraction or transfers of water from ground or surface waters?		
Changes in water bodies or the land surface affecting drainage or run-off?		
Transport of personnel or materials for construction, operation, or decommissioning?		
Long-term dismantling, decommissioning, or restoration works?		
Ongoing activity during decommissioning which could have an impact on the environment?		
Influx of people to an area in either temporarily or permanently?		

(Contd)

Information/checklist confirmation	Yes/no	Details thereof [41] with source of information data
Introduction of alien species?		
Loss of native species or genetic diversity?		
Any other actions?		

(b)   Use of natural resources for construction or operation of the project (such as land, water, materials, or energy, especially any resources which are non-renewable or in short supply)

Information/checklist confirmation	Yes/no	Details thereof (with approximate quantities/rates, wherever possible) with source of information data
Land especially undeveloped or agricultural land (ha)		
Water (expected source and competing users) unit: KLD		
Minerals (MT)		
Construction material—stone, aggregates, and sand/soil (expected source—MT)		
Forests and timber (source—MT)		
Energy including electricity and fuels (source and competing users), unit: fuel (MT), energy (MW)		
Any other natural resources (use appropriate standard units)		

(c)   Use, storage, transport, handling, or production of substances or materials, which could be harmful to human health or the environment or raise concerns about actual or perceived risks to human health

Information/checklist confirmation	Yes/no	Details there of [42] with source of information data
Use of substances or materials, which are hazardous (as per MSIHC rules) to human health or the environment (flora, fauna, and water supplies)		
Changes in occurrence of disease or affect disease vectors (e.g., insect or water borne diseases)		
Affect the welfare of people, for example by changing living conditions?		
Vulnerable groups of people who could be affected by the project, for example hospital patients, children, the elderly, etc.		
Any other causes		

---

42 *Note:* with approximate quantities/rates, wherever possible

(d) Production of solid wastes during construction or operation or decommissioning (MT/month)

Information/checklist confirmation	Yes/no	Details there of[43] with source of information data
Spoil, overburden, or mine wastes		
Municipal waste (domestic and/or commercial wastes)		
Hazardous wastes (as per Hazardous Waste Management and Handling Rules)		
Other industrial process wastes		
Surplus product		
Sewage sludge or other sludge from effluent treatment		
Construction or demolition wastes		
Redundant machinery or equipment		
Contaminated soils or other materials		
Agricultural wastes		
Other solid wastes		

(e) Release of pollutants or any hazardous, toxic, or noxious substances to air (Kg/hr)

Information/checklist confirmation	Yes/no	Details there of[44] with source of information data
Emissions from combustion of fossil fuels from stationary or mobile sources		
Emissions from production processes		
Emissions from materials handling including storage or transport		
Emissions from construction activities including plant and equipment		
Dust or odours from handling of materials including construction materials, sewage, and waste		
Emissions from incineration of waste		
Emissions from burning of waste in open air (e.g., slash materials, and construction debris)		
Emissions from any other sources		

---

43 *Note*: with approximate quantities/rates, wherever possible
44 *Note*: with approximate quantities/rates, wherever possible

(f)   Generation of noise and vibration, and emissions of light and heat

Information/checklist confirmation	Yes/no	Details thereof[45] with source of information data
From operation of equipment, for example, engines, ventilation plant, and crushers		
From industrial or similar processes		
From construction or demolition		
From blasting or piling		
From construction or operational traffic		
From lighting or cooling systems		
From any other sources		

(g)   Risks of contamination of land or water from release of pollutants into the ground or into sewers, surface waters, groundwater, coastal waters, or the sea

Information/checklist confirmation	Yes/no	Details there of[46] with source of information data
From handling, storage, use, or spillage of hazardous materials		
From discharge of sewage or other effluents to water or the land (expected mode and place of discharge)		
By deposition of pollutants emitted to air into the land or into water		
From any other sources		
Is there a risk of long-term build-up of pollutants in the environment from these sources?		

(h)   Risk of accidents during construction or operation of the project, which could affect human health or the environment

Information/checklist confirmation	Yes/no	Details there of[47] with source of information data
From explosions, spillages, fires, etc., from storage, handling, use or production of hazardous substances		
From any other causes		
Could the project be affected by natural disasters causing environmental damage (e.g., floods, earthquakes, landslides, cloudburst, etc.)?		

---

45 *Note*: with approximate quantities/rates, wherever possible
46 *Note*: with approximate quantities/rates, wherever possible
47 *Note*: with approximate quantities/rates, wherever possible

(i) Factors which should be considered (such as consequential development) which could lead to environmental effects or the potential for cumulative impacts with other existing or planned activities in the locality

Information/checklist confirmation	Yes/ no	Details there of [48] with source of information data
Lead to development of supporting cities, ancillary development or development stimulated by the project which could have impact on the environment, for example: • supporting infrastructure (roads, power supply, waste or • wastewater treatment, etc.) • housing development • extractive industries • supply industries • other		
Lead to after-use of the site, which could have an impact on the environment		
Set a precedent for later developments		
Have cumulative effects due to proximity to other existing or planned projects with similar effects		

(j) Environmental sensitivity

Areas	Name/identity	Aerial distance (within 15 km.) proposed project location boundary
Areas protected under international conventions, national or local legislation for their ecological, landscape, cultural, or other related value		
Areas which are important or sensitive for ecological reasons—Wetlands, watercourses or other water bodies, coastal zone, biospheres, mountains, and forests		
Areas used by protected, important or sensitive species of flora or fauna for breeding, nesting, foraging, resting, over wintering, and migration		
Inland, coastal, marine, or underground waters		
State and national boundaries		
Routes or facilities used by the public for access to recreation or other tourist and pilgrim areas		

---

48 *Note*: with approximate quantities/rates, wherever possible

Defence installations		
Densely populated or buil-tup area		
Areas occupied by sensitive man made land uses (hospitals, schools, places of worship, and community facilities)		
Areas containing important, high quality or scarce resources (ground water resources, surface resources, forestry, agriculture, fisheries, tourism, and minerals)		
Areas already subjected to pollution or environmental damage (those where existing legal environmental standards are exceeded)		
Areas susceptible to natural hazard which could cause the project to present environmental problems (earthquakes, subsidence, landslides, erosion, flooding, or extreme or adverse climatic conditions)		

(k)   Proposed terms of reference for EIA studies

Checklist of Environmental Impacts (Only for Construction Projects)[49]

1.   **Land environment**

1.1.   Will the existing land use get significantly altered from the project that is not consistent with the surroundings? Proposed land use must conform to the approved master plan/development plan of the area. Change of land use if any and the statutory approval from the competent authority be submitted. Attach maps of (i) site location, (ii) surrounding features of the proposed site (within 500 meters), and (iii) the site (indicating levels and contours) to appropriate scales. If not available, attach only conceptual plans.

1.2.   List out all the major project requirements in terms of the land area, built-up area, water consumption, power requirement, connectivity, community facilities, parking needs, etc.

1.3.   What are the likely impacts of the proposed activity on the existing facilities adjacent to the proposed site (such as open spaces, community facilities, details of the existing land use, and disturbance to the local ecology)?

1.4.   Will there be any significant land disturbance resulting in erosion, subsidence, and instability? Details of soil type, slope analysis, vulnerability to subsidence, seismicity, etc., may be given.

---

49 http://www.moef.nic.in/sites/default/files/so1533_4.pdf, last accessed on 16 June 2014.

1.5. Will the proposal involve alteration of natural drainage systems? Give details on a contour map showing the natural drainage near the proposed project site.

1.6. What are the quantities of earthwork involved in the construction activity— cutting, filling, reclamation, etc. Give details of the quantities of earthwork involved, transport of fill materials from outside the site, etc.

1.7. Give details regarding water supply, waste handling, etc., during the construction period.

1.8. Will the low-lying areas and wetlands get altered? Provide details of how low-lying and wetlands are getting modified from the proposed activity.

1.9. Whether construction debris and waste during construction cause health hazard? Give quantities of various types of wastes generated during construction including the construction labour and the means of disposal.

2. Water environment

2.1. Give the total quantity of water requirement for the proposed project with the breakup of requirements for various uses. How will the water requirement be met? State the sources and quantities and furnish a water balance statement.

2.2. What is the capacity (dependable flow or yield) of the proposed source of water?

2.3. What is the quality of water required, in case, the supply is not from a municipal source? Provide physical, chemical, and biological characteristics with class of water quality.

2.4. How much of the water requirement can be met from the recycling of treated wastewater? Give the details of quantities, sources, and usage.

2.5. Will there be diversion of water from other users? Please assess the impacts of the project on other existing uses and quantities of consumption.

2.6. What is the incremental pollution load from wastewater generated from the proposed activity? Give details of the quantities and composition of wastewater generated from the proposed activity.

2.7. Give details of the water requirements met from water harvesting. and furnish details of the facilities created.

2.8. What would be the impact of the land use changes occurring due to the proposed project on the runoff characteristics (quantitative as well as qualitative) of the area in the post construction phase on a long-term basis? Would it aggravate the problems of flooding or water logging in any way?

2.9. What are the impacts of the proposal on the ground water? Will there be tapping of ground water? Give the details of ground water table, recharging capacity, and approvals obtained from competent authority, if any.

2.10. What precautions/measures are taken to prevent the runoff from construction activities polluting land and aquifers? Give details of quantities and the measures taken to avoid the adverse impacts.

2.11. How is the storm water from within the site managed? State the provisions made to avoid flooding of the area and details of the drainage facilities provided along with a site layout indicating the contour levels.

2.12. Will the deployment of construction labourers particularly in the peak period lead to unsanitary conditions around the project site? Justify with proper explanation.

2.13. What on-site facilities are provided for the collection, treatment, and safe disposal of sewage? Give details of the quantities of wastewater generation, treatment capacities with technology, and facilities for recycling and disposal.

2.14. Give details of dual plumbing system if treated waste is used for flushing of toilets or for any other use.

3. Vegetation

3.1. Is there any threat of the project to the biodiversity? Give a description of the local ecosystem with its unique features, if any.

3.2. Will the construction involve extensive clearing or modification of vegetation? Provide a detailed account of the trees and vegetation affected by the project.

3.3. What are the measures proposed to be taken to minimize the likely impacts on important site features? Give details of proposal for tree plantation, landscaping, creation of water bodies, etc., along with a layout plan to an appropriate scale.

4. Fauna

4.1. Is there likely to be any displacement of fauna—both terrestrial and aquatic—or creation of barriers for their movement? Provide the details.

4.2. Any direct or indirect impacts on the avifauna of the area? Provide the details.

4.3. Prescribe measures such as corridors, fish ladders to mitigate adverse impacts on fauna.

5. Air environment

5.1. Will the project increase atmospheric concentration of gases and result in heat islands? Give details of the background air quality levels with predicted values based on dispersion models taking into account the increased traffic generation as a result of the proposed constructions.

5.2. What are the impacts on generation of dust, smoke, odorous fumes, or other hazardous gases? Give details in relation to all the meteorological parameters.

5.3. Will the proposal create shortage of parking space for vehicles? Furnish details of the present level of transport infrastructure and measures proposed for improvement including the traffic management at the entry and exit to the project site.

5.4.   Provide details of the movement patterns with internal roads, bicycle tracks, pedestrian pathways, footpaths, etc., with areas under each category.

5.5.   Will there be significant increase in traffic noise and vibrations? Give details of the sources and the measures proposed for mitigation of the above.

5.6.   What will be the impact of DG sets and other equipment on noise levels, and vibration, and ambient air quality around the project site? Provide the details.

6.   Aesthetics

6.1.   Will the proposed constructions in any way result in the obstruction of a view, scenic amenity, or landscapes? Are these considerations taken into account by the proponents?

6.2.   Will there be any adverse impacts from new constructions on the existing structures? What are the considerations taken into account?

6.3.   Whether there are any local considerations of urban form and urban design influencing the design criteria? They may be explicitly spelt out.

6.4.   Are there any anthropological or archaeological sites or artefacts nearby? State if any other significant features in the vicinity of the proposed site have been considered.

7.   Socio-economic aspects

7.1.   Will the proposal result in any changes to the demographic structure of local population? Provide the details.

7.2.   Give details of the existing social infrastructure around the proposed project.

7.3.   Will the project cause adverse effects on local communities, disturbance to sacred sites, or other cultural values? What are the safeguards proposed?

8.   Building materials

8.1.   May involve the use of building materials with high-embodied energy. Are the construction materials produced with energy efficient processes? Give details of energy conservation measures in the selection of building materials and their energy efficiency.

8.2.   Transport and handling of materials during construction may result in pollution, noise, and public nuisance. What measures are taken to minimize the impacts?

8.3.   Are recycled materials used in roads and structures? State the extent of savings achieved.

8.4.   Give details of the methods of collection, segregation, and disposal of the garbage generated during the operation phases of the project.

9.   Energy conservation

9.1.   Give details of the power requirements, source of supply, backup source, etc. What is the energy consumption assumed per square foot of built-up area? How have you tried to minimize energy consumption?

9.2. What type and capacity of power backup do you plan to provide?

9.3. What are the characteristics of the glass you plan to use? Provide specifications of its characteristics related to both short wave and long wave radiation.

9.4. What passive solar architectural features are being used in the building? Illustrate the applications made in the proposed project.

9.5. Does the layout of streets and buildings maximize the potential for solar energy devices? Have you considered the use of street lighting, emergency lighting, and solar hot water systems for use in the building complex? Substantiate with details.

9.6. Is shading effectively used to reduce cooling/heating loads? What principles have been used to maximize the shading of walls on the east, the west, and the roof? How much energy saving has been effected?

9.7. Do the structures use energy-efficient space conditioning, lighting, and mechanical systems? Provide the technical details. Provide details of the transformers and motor efficiencies, lighting intensity, and air conditioning load assumptions. Are you using CFC and HCFC free chillers? Provide specifications.

9.8. What are the likely effects of the building activity in altering the micro-climates? Provide a self-assessment on the likely impacts of the proposed construction on creation of heat island and inversion effects?

9.9. What are the thermal characteristics of the building envelope on (a) roof, (b) external walls, and (c) fenestration? Give details of the material used and the U-values or the R-values of the individual components.

9.10. What precautions and safety measures are proposed against fire hazards? Furnish details of the emergency plans.

9.11. If you are using glass as wall material, provide details and specifications including emissivity and thermal characteristics.

9.12. What is the rate of air infiltration into the building? Provide details of how you are mitigating the effects of infiltration.

9.13. To what extent the non-conventional energy technologies are utilized in the overall energy consumption? Provide details of the renewable energy technologies used.

10. Environment management plan

The environment management plan would consist of all mitigation measures for each item wise activity to be undertaken during the construction, operation, and the entire life cycle to minimize adverse environmental impacts as a result of the activities of the project. It would also delineate the environmental monitoring plan for compliance of various environmental regulations. It will state the steps to be taken in the case of emergency such as accidents at the site including fire.

Structure of EIA document[50]

	EIA structure	Contents
1	Introduction	• Purpose of the report • Identification of project and project proponent • Brief description of nature, size, location of the project, and its importance to the country/region • Scope of the study—details of regulatory scoping carried out (as per terms of reference)
2	Project description	Condensed description of those aspects of the project (based on project feasibility study), likely to cause environmental effects. Details should be provided to give clear picture of the following: • Type of project • Need for the project • Location (maps showing general location, specific location, project boundary, and project site layout) • Size or magnitude of operation (including associated activities required by or for the project) • Proposed schedule for approval and implementation • Technology and process description • Project description, including drawings showing project layout, components of project, etc. Schematic representations of the feasibility drawings which give information important for EIA purpose • Description of mitigation measures incorporated into the project to meet environmental standards, environmental operating conditions, or other EIA requirements (as required by the scope) • Assessment of new and untested technology for the risk of technological failure
3	Description of the environment	• Study area, period, components, and methodology • Establishment of baseline for valued environmental components, as identified in the scope • Base maps of all environmental components
4	Anticipated environmental impacts and mitigation measures	• Details of investigated environmental impacts due to project location, possible accidents, project design, project construction, regular operations, final decommissioning, or rehabilitation of a completed project • Measures for minimizing and/or offsetting adverse impacts identified • Irreversible and irretrievable commitments of environmental components • Assessment of significance of impacts (criteria for determining significance and assigning significance) • Mitigation measures

(Contd)

50 http://www.moef.nic.in/sites/default/files/so1533_4.pdf, last accessed on 16 June 2014.

(Contd)

5	Analysis of alternatives (technology and site)	In case, the scoping exercise results in need for alternatives: • Description of each alternative • Summary of adverse impacts of each alternative • Mitigation measures proposed for each alternative • Selection of alternative
6	Environmental monitoring program	• Technical aspects of monitoring the effectiveness of mitigation measures (including measurement methodologies, frequency, location, data analysis, reporting schedules, emergency procedures, detailed budget, and procurement schedules)
7	Additional studies	• Public consultation • Risk assessment • Social impact assessment. Resettlement and rehabilitation (R&R) action plans
8	Project Benefits	• Improvements in the physical infrastructure • Improvements in the social infrastructure • Employment potential—skilled, semi-skilled, and unskilled • Other tangible benefits
9	Environmental cost benefit analysis	If recommended at the scoping stage
10	EMP	• Description of the administrative aspects of ensuring that mitigated measures are implemented and their effectiveness monitored, after approval of the EIA
11	Summary and conclusion (this will constitute the summary of the EIA report)	• Overall justification for implementation of the project • Explanation of how adverse effects have been mitigated
12	Disclosure of consultants engaged	The names of the consultants engaged with their brief resume and nature of consultancy rendered

Environmental Auditing

Environmental audit refers to the review and evaluation of an organization's operations and processes to assess environmental compliance and gaps in implementation of environmental policies. The audit may also recommend corrective measures. Audits will compare the current operational standards with the norms prescribed by a statutory body or regulations prescribed at an international, national, state, and local governance levels (see Chapter 5 for details on ISO standards—ISO 14000 series of standards). Environmental audits also help in improving business process efficiency, as the management will be having information on areas that it can focus on to improve its efficiency. Information is gathered through direct visit to the area of operation, document reviews, and interviews with the stakeholders.

ENVIRONMENTAL DECISION MAKING

The following are some issues that could be considered as a part of environmental decision making process:

What are the goals of the participants and stakeholders?

- Extent of involvement of participants and stakeholders to the decision
- Issues being negotiated, the process adopted, and the tools used to aid the decision making process
- What are the facilitating factors and constraining factors?
- Impact on decision making

Sustainability Reporting Best Practice Questions

There are certain guiding questions that indicate the best practices during the process of sustainability reporting. The following table (see Table 6.7) has been reprinted with permission from *Sustainability reporting best practice questions* produced by Terrafiniti LLP,[51] which provides the guidelines for sustainability reporting.

TABLE 6.7 Guidelines for best practices of sustainability reporting

System/methodology/approach	Does management of sustainability:
Sustainability reporting presents a narrative report on the management of sustainability within an organization. As such it should be clear from a report that the company takes a strategic and systematic approach towards management and reporting. The use of formal and informal management system approaches and the use of reporting guidance are therefore essential aspects of best practice.	• utilize a formal environmental management system (e.g., ISO 14001, EMAS), or an informal systematic approach (e.g., use of UN Global Compact)? • utilize a recognized sustainability reporting approach (e.g., Global Reporting Initiative)? • mention external, independent indicators of commitment/performance (e.g., ethos institute indicators, principles from ISO 26000)?
Leadership and stakeholders Sustainability should be managed as part of normal business practice, alongside any other business priority. To put it simply, if something is important to you, then it should be treated as such. In addition, increasing importance and value is being given to the role that stakeholders can play in identifying key environmental and social priorities, and in enhancing the value of your sustainability activities.	• Does the report have a statement from the Chairman and/or CEO? • Does management identify the contribution of sustainability to overall business strategy? • Is there a clear description of company sustainability vision and values? • Is stakeholder engagement a clear part of the sustainability management approach? • Is there a clear description of the stakeholder engagement process?

(Contd)

51 www.terrafiniti.com. *Sustainability reporting best practice questions*, Terrafiniti LLP, a Guildford, UK, last accessed on 31 January 2014.

TABLE 6.7 *(Contd)*

Governance Disclosure of governance processes (how management takes place) and especially sustainability governance are an essential part of a good report. Such information provides an indicator of the importance that the company places on such issues and also the extent of embedding of environmental priorities within overall business priorities.	• Is there a clear description of how sustainability is managed within the company? • Are overall sustainability governance structures clear? • Is there a clear description of identified stakeholder issues? • Are there dedicated structures to support sustainability?
Focus—material issues Sustainability management, and therefore reporting, should focus primarily upon those environmental and social issues and impacts that are most relevant and significant (material) for the company and its stakeholders. Therefore, the material issues focussed upon should be those most closely aligned with the delivery of core business and not those associated with peripheral or 'good news' stories.	• Is there a clear process for the identification of material/business relevant sustainability issues? • Is the identification of material sustainability issues integrated into: (a) risk management? (b) governance processes?
Performance and continuous improvement Reporting should be able to tell an evolving story. How has a company progressed against its stated aims and objectives, and how is its performance improving? The disclosure of clear objectives and targets, alongside the disclosure of performance, whether positive or negative, allows the company to communicate its commitment clearly to investors, employees, and wider stakeholders. Comparison with sector best practice is also a useful way of demonstrating progress/the distance still to travel.	• Does the report explain how long-term objectives are identified? For example, is there a clear link between the way the issues are identified and managed with the set objectives? • Is the year-on-year performance disclosed? • Is performance against stakeholder identified issues specifically disclosed year-on-year? • Is performance data normalized as well as absolute (e.g., CO_2 production given as a total tonnage and as tones per unit of production/turnover)? • Does the report note performance of the company relative to sector best practice?
Openness—telling the whole story Transparency and accountability are key themes in sustainability and reporting should reflect this. Not only through communicating practice across the whole organization, but also in discussing and acknowledging the wider implications of social and environmental trends for the organization's strategy, policy, and marketplace over time. It is through such analysis and disclosure that an organization can really create value through sustainability; by interpreting, understanding, and communicating the implications of social and environmental trends.	• Does the report give its reader a comprehensive picture of a whole organization? • Do the given case studies focus on material issues? • Are difficult issues openly discussed? • Are the implications of 'big picture' trends and issues discussed?

(Contd)

TABLE 6.7 *(Contd)*

Third party statements, assurance, and verification An independent third party assurance statement is considered to be a fundamental requirement for good practice in reporting. Assurance statements can cover 'softer' content including policies, governance structures, and processes in addition to the assurance of hard data. In addition, feedback from assurance providers can provide a useful dialogue on continuous improvement.	• Does the report have an independent statement which comments on the quality/veracity of the contents of the report? • Does the statement use a recognized formal assurance methodology, for example, AA 1000 AS, ISAE 3000, or COS 3410N? • Does the statement comment on previous performance indicate key future issues for consideration?

How to Read a Sustainability Report

The following is an article *'How to Read a Sustainability Report: Five tips to help you make sense of the next sustainability report you read'*, authored by Marc Gunther and published in Ensia.[52]

Corporate sustainability reports have been around since... well, it's hard to say. The first report may have been published by 'companies in the chemical industry with serious image problems' in the 1980s, or by Ben & Jerry's in 1989 or Shell in 1997. No matter—since then, more than 10,000 companies have published more than 50,000 reports, according to CorporateRegister.com, which maintains a searchable database of reports.

But who really reads them? As a reporter who covers business and sustainability, I do. Maybe you do, too—as an employee, investor, researcher, or activist.

Here, then, are five tips to help you make sense of the next report that lands on your desk or arrives via email. They were developed with help from Steve Lydenberg of Domini Social Investments—the principal author of *How to Read a Corporate Social Responsibility Report*, an excellent 2010 study from the Boston College Center for Corporate Citizenship—and Bill Baue, a consultant and leader of the Sustainability Context Group, an organization working to improve corporate reporting.

Pay attention to what's in the report—and what's left out   Lots of companies fill their sustainability reports with anecdotes, but these are often off point. Chevron's 2012 corporate responsibility report says a Chevron executive in Angola is part of 'a team that protects endangered turtles that come ashore to breed, dig sandy nests, and lay their eggs on the beaches at Chevron's Malongo oil production facilities.' And we learn that the company has partnered with the Wildlife Conservation Society to 'introduce passive acoustic monitoring in the south Atlantic Ocean to assess humpback whale breeding activity' as it explores for oil.

---

52 http://ensia.com/voices/how-to-read-a-sustainability-report/, last accessed on 31 January 2014. Under the terms of Creative Commons' Attribution-NoDerivs 3.0 Unported license-Ensia enables the reader to share-to copy, distribute, and transmit the work, and to make commercial use of the work.

That's nice, but environmentalists will want to understand what the giant oil company (2012 revenues: $234 billion) is doing about climate change, if anything. Figuring that out from the report is hard, if not impossible. Chevron reports that its 2012 emissions from operations were 56.3 million metric tons of CO_2 equivalent, down by about 3.5 million metric tons from 2011, and below its goal of 60.5 million metric tons. That sounds like progress. But you have to read the footnotes to learn that the decline was largely caused by the sale of one refinery in Alaska and 'decreased production' from a second refinery in Richmond, Calif., where an August 2012 fire sent thousands of people to hospitals and later led Chevron to pay $2 million in fines and restitution.

What's more, emissions from operations account for only part of Chevron's impact. The company's report says, 'combustion of our products resulted in emissions of approximately 364 million metric tons of CO_2 in 2012, approximately 8 percent less than the 396 million metric tons emitted in 2011.' Why the decline? Is the fact that people are burning less gas and oil good for the planet but bad for Chevron? The report doesn't explain.

More importantly, is Chevron trying to move away from fossil fuels and develop cleaner forms of energy? It doesn't seem to be, since the word 'renewable' appears nowhere in the body of the report.

Follow the (big) money   A good sustainability report should focus on those company activities that have the greatest impact. So, for example, what matters most in the financial services industry is not paper consumption, LEED-certified work spaces or direct greenhouse gas emissions, but lending and investment practices. Citi's most recent report says it opened 23 LEED-certified branches in 2012—a data point that is hard to put into context (since the report doesn't say how many branches the company operates) and not very meaningful, in any event. What we want to know about Wall Street is how the big banks are taking environmental issues into account in their lending and investments. 'No other industry has as much ability to affect the environmental and social practices of other industries as financial services does,' says Lydenberg.

Bank of America (BA) tackles the big question better than most. In its report, BA says it has committed $70 billion over 16 years to 'address global climate change and demands on natural resources,' and it describes the goal as 'the largest among our peers.' That's helpful. The bank also tallies where the first $21 billion of its climate-friendly financing has gone. To its credit, BA also tries to explain why it does business with the coal industry in the face of criticism from environmental groups. 'If large financial institutions were to unilaterally discontinue financing the coal industry, it would have negative consequences for the US and global economies,' the BA report says. The bank also notes, helpfully, that it supports government policies to tax or regulate carbon emissions.

Like most banks, however, BA doesn't provide an accounting of its loans to or investments in fossil fuel companies. (According to Rainforest Action Network, BA finances Coal India, one of the world's biggest coal mining companies, which has displaced forest communities and destroyed critical tiger habitat.) How do BA's investments in fossil fuels, which aggravate climate change, compare to the $70 billion it has pledged to finance, in part, climate solutions? Is the bank making the climate crisis better or worse? Good luck finding out.

Think about context   When trying to understand a company's impact on climate or energy usage or water, a single number or two won't help. You'll need to look at absolute numbers (how much energy did the company use, in total), normalized numbers (adjusting for acquisitions or divestitures), and numbers that reflect energy or water intensity (how much was used per unit of product or dollar of revenues). These numbers only become meaningful when they are accompanied by year-over-year comparisons, or when set against previous goals. You can be confident that most companies present their data in the most favourable light.

The concept of context-based sustainability is designed, in part, to cut through obfuscations and generate meaningful sustainability goals and targets. The idea is elegant: companies should measure their impacts against science-based sustainability thresholds and resource limits. Is Coca-Cola only using its fair share of the water supply in India? What should Ford's carbon reduction target be? These aren't easy questions, but Baue and Mark McElroy of the Center for Sustainable Organizations—leading advocates of context-based sustainability—says, 'answers can be found'. Companies, for example, could for reporting purposes be allocated a share of greenhouse gas emissions based on their contributions to gross national product; they would then set emissions reduction targets that are deep enough to meet global climate goals, and report on their progress against those targets.

Several companies are experimenting with context-based sustainability, including the Vermont dairy company Cabot Creamery Cooperative, EMC, and Mars. British Telecom (BT) has developed a methodology to determine its share of GHG emissions, as has the California software company Autodesk, which makes its tool, called C-FACT (Corporate Finance Approach to Climate-Stabilizing Targets), available for free.

Read more than one report at a time   How many glasses of water does it take to brew a gallon of beer? I have no idea either, so reading that New Belgium, a Colorado brewing company, wants to reduce its water use per barrel to 3.5 to 1 by 2015 doesn't tell me much. In 2011, the ratio was 4.22 to 1.

New Belgium has a well-deserved reputation for sustainability but when it comes to water, the brewer lags behind its bigger competitors. MillerCoors' latest sustainability reports says it achieved an average water-to-beer ratio of 3.82 to 1 across its major breweries, while the world's biggest beer company, Anheuser-Busch InBev, does even better, reporting a water-to-beer production ratio of 3.5 to 1.

Reading the Coca-Cola and PepsiCo reports side by side is more enlightening than reading one at a time. The same is with UPS and FedEx. But be aware that peer-to-peer comparisons are inexact. New Belgium explains that a practice called 'dry hopping' has increased the water intensity in the brewing process. A bottle of Fat Tire is not the same as a Bud or a Coors Light, as any beer drinker knows.

Look for all the news that's fit to print   Good sustainability reporting, above all, needs to be credible. It's not easy to decide whether to trust what a company is telling us, but one sign is whether companies deliver the bad news along with the good. In the Chevron report, the refinery fire in Richmond, as well as a fire on an offshore oil-drilling rig near Nigeria, gets only a passing mention. 'These incidents do not reflect the expectations we have of ourselves,' the report says. We should hope not.

By contrast, Gap has been more willing than most companies to air its dirty linen (pun intended). The company has been forthcoming about what it calls 'the severity of worker safety issues in Bangladesh' since 2010. When it comes to the environment, the company is clear about where it will exert its influence—over its supply chain and its own operations—and where it will leave the problems for others to solve.

At the end of the day, the most important thing to know about corporate sustainability reports may be that they almost inevitably raise more questions than they answer. A report cannot, by itself, be relied upon to explain a company's environmental impact. It's a useful starting point, at best.

CHAPTER SUMMARY

- The process of environmental risk management involves, (a) problem formulation, (b) risk assessment, (c) selection of the risk management practice, and (d) implementation of the risk management practice.
- Environmental design management process identifies opportunities of energy savings, waste and emission reduction, and conservation of natural resources.
- Backcasting is the process of visualising a desirable future scenario and then working backwards to the present, by creating policies and practices, which will create that desirable future.
- Ecological footprint compares human demands on the planet with the planet's capability to regenerate the required demands. Three of the drivers of ecological footprint are (a) population growth, (b) consumption of products/services by an individual, and (c) footprint intensity (the efficiency rate at which natural resources are converted to goods/services).
- Carbon footprint is the measure of an individual's impact on the planet in terms of the amount of greenhouse gases produced due to the lifestyle of the individual, in units of carbon dioxide.
- Life cycle analysis (LCA) looks into the cumulative social and environmental impact caused by a

product or service, through the entire life cycle of a product's life. 'Goal and scope definition' and 'inventory analysis' are the steps involved in LCA.
- Ecosystem services and valuation is the process by which the natural environment creates an environment that sustains life on earth. Ecosystem services are those services that contribute directly to life.
- Ecosystem services are classified into provisioning services, regulating services, cultural services, and supporting services. Provisioning services refers to services obtained from ecosystems that sustain human life. Regulating services refers to benefits derived by humankind from regulation of ecosystem processes. Cultural services include the nonmaterial benefits derived by human beings from ecosystems. Supporting services are the services necessary for the creation and sustenance of all other ecosystem services.
- Corporate ecosystem valuation (CEV) is a process, which uses ecosystem valuation to make informed business decisions.
- Energy returned on energy invested (EROEI) is 'the ratio of the amount of usable energy acquired from a particular energy resource to the amount of energy expended to obtain that energy resource'.

- Carbon ratings are used to communicate the overall quality of an emission reduction project; or carbon rating are used as a label in products, including fast moving consumer goods (FMCG), to indicate the carbon emissions associated with the whole/partial life cycle of the product that is sold.
- Benefit-cost analysis or cost-benefit analysis is an analysis that compares benefits and costs to society of policies, programs, or actions to protect or restore ecosystems. It could also measure the gain or loss to ecosystem/society from a policy or action.
- Stakeholder analysis identifies the clusters of individuals/groups, which are likely to be impacted by the implementation of a proposed plan or action.

- Total value chain analysis refers to the process of describing the activities that link together to add to the value of the business.
- Environmental impact assessment and auditing (EIA) is the process of identifying, predicting, evaluating, and mitigating the biophysical, social, and other relevant effects of development proposals prior to major decisions being taken and commitments made.
- Environmental audit refers to the review and evaluation of an organization's operations and processes to assess environmental compliance and gaps in implementation of environmental policies.

KEYWORDS

- Avoided cost method
- Backcasting
- Benefit-cost analysis
- Bio-capacity
- Carbon footprint
- Choice modelling method
- Contingent valuation method
- Cost-benefit analysis
- Cradle to grave analysis
- Destination environmental scorecard
- Dose response method
- Ecological debtor
- Ecological footprint
- Ecological overshoot
- Ecosystem service valuation
- Energy payback period
- Environmental design management
- Environmental input-output model
- Environmental management system modelling
- Epstein Roy framework

- Factor income method
- Footprint intensity
- Genuine wealth accounting model
- Green globes design
- Greenhouse gas
- Green productivity index
- Hedonic pricing method
- Life cycle analysis
- Lowell center hierarchy
- Materials flow analysis
- Nutrient cycling
- Responsive business scorecard
- Restoration cost method
- Soil acidification
- Stakeholder analysis
- Sustainability report
- Sustainable value added
- Triple bottom line reporting
- Whole life value

EXERCISES

Multiple-choice Questions

1. Which step of environment risk management process involves ascertaining the advantages and disadvantages of the risk management options?
   (a) Problem formulation
   (b) Risk assessment
   (c) Selection of the risk management practice
   (d) Implementation of the risk management practice

2. GE's ecomagination treasure hunt is a process that identifies opportunities of _____
   (a) Energy savings
   (b) Waste and emission reduction
   (c) Conservation of natural resources
   (d) All of these

3. Carbon footprint is about:
   (a) Determining the total amount of carbon dioxide an organization is linked to
   (b) Evaluate the environmental performance of small and medium sized hotel operations
   (c) Evaluating the management of an organization's environmental programs
   (d) Determining how to modify environmental, social, and financial performance of an organization

4. A region that has its ecological footprint exceeding its bio-capacity has an ecological deficit and is referred to as an _____
   (a) Ecological creditor
   (b) Ecological debtor
   (c) Ecological surplus
   (d) Ecological defect

5. Increasing ecological footprint is driven by
   _____
   (a) Population growth
   (b) Consumption of products/services by an individual
   (c) Footprint intensity
   (d) All these

6. Provisioning services provided by ecosystem services refer to

   (a) Services obtained from ecosystems that sustain human life
   (b) Benefits derived by humankind from regulation of ecosystem processes
   (c) The nonmaterial benefits derived by human beings from ecosystems
   (d) The services necessary for the creation and sustenance of all other ecosystem services

7. Which of the following statements is not true for EROEI?
   (a) EROEI is the ratio of the amount of usable energy acquired from a particular energy resource to the amount of energy expended to obtain that energy resource.
   (b) When the EROEI of a resource is less than or equal to one, that energy source becomes an 'energy sink', and can be used as a primary source of energy.
   (c) The lesser the energy payback period, the better the investment.
   (d) Energy payback period refers to the estimated time required to recover the initial amount of energy invested to construct the source.

8. Read the following two statements:
   (1) Carbon ratings are used to communicate the overall quality of an emission reduction project.
   (2) Carbon rating are used as a label in products, including fast moving consumer goods (FMCG), to indicate the carbon emissions associated with the whole/partial life cycle of the product that is sold.
   Which of the above two statements are correct?
   (a) Both
   (b) Neither
   (c) Only (1)
   (d) Only (2)

9. What is the unit of measurement of ecological footprint?
   (a) Kilometers/miles
   (b) Watt/joule
   (c) Acres/hectares
   (d) Kilogram
10. In which ecosystem services valuation method is the expenses related to attend a specific event or price to access a site taken into consideration:
    (a) Hedonic pricing method
    (b) Travel cost method
    (c) Contingent valuation method
    (d) Value transfer method

Short Answer Questions

1. What is meant by life cycle analysis?
2. What are the different phases that have to be considered while doing life cycle analysis?
3. Classify the ecosystem services with examples.
4. What are the corporate applications of ecosystem services?
5. What is corporate ecosystem valuation and how it can help a company?
6. Explain EROEI.
7. What is meant by carbon rating?
8. Explain the following: stakeholder analysis and total value chain analysis.
9. Explain EIA.
10. What is environmental auditing?
11. What is meant by triple bottom-line reporting?
12. What is ISO?

Long Answer Questions

1. What is meant by ecological footprint? What is its significance? How is it different from carbon footprint?
2. What is environmental risk management? Elaborate the process of environmental risk management.
3. What is meant by backcasting? Explain the sustainability principles as laid out by 'the natural step' while engaging in backcasting.
4. Elaborate the various tools of industrial ecology.
5. Explain the process of life cycle analysis with the steps. What are the different phases of life cycle analysis?
6. What is ecosystem service? Explain with the example of ecosystem services provided by rainforests.
7. Explain the different types of valuation methods for ecosystem services.
8. What is benefit-cost analysis? Explain the process with steps and example.

Reflective Question

1. You would have noticed that the societal trend is to put concrete/pavements/tiles, etc., all over the ground, that we are unable to see much of mud ground nowadays. This stops the seepage of water into the ground, and therefore water level in wells and ponds go down. Trees, too, do not receive enough water for their sustenance.
   (a) What are the possible reasons for this dysfunctional trend
   (b) Would you suggest any alternatives?

Take-home Activity

1. Select any natural ecosystem near your educational institution—this could be a natural water tank, a wetland, a mountain, etc. Find out the value of that natural ecosystem through any of ecosystem services valuation techniques.

Web Readings

1. Find out your ecological footprint by taking the following quizzes: http://myfootprint.org/en/ http://www.footprintnetwork.org/en/index. php/GFN/page/calculators/ http://www.naturalcapitalproject.org/
2. Case-studies connecting the ecosystem services and their economic significance: http://www. teebweb.org/resources/case-studies/
3. For a detailed write-up on life cycle analysis: http://www.epa.gov/nrmrl/std/lca/pdfs/ chapter4lca101.pdf

Recommended Book

1. Daniel Goleman, *Ecological Intelligence: How Knowing the Hidden Impacts of What We Buy Can Change Everything*, Allen Lane, 2009.

Recommended Documentaries/Movies

1. Talk by Pavan Sukhdev, 'What is the World Worth? Putting Nature on the Balance Sheet', 2010. This talk is available for free viewing at http://www.abc.net.au/tv/bigideas/ stories/2010/08/24/2989069.htm and also at YouTube on https://www.youtube.com/ watch?v=0n7lY3iYQ3s, duration: 1 hour, 17 minutes.
2. Toyota Prius Life Cycle Assessment, this clipping is available for free viewing at https:// www.youtube.com/watch?v=CVa4GBze3tU, duration: 5 minutes

Answers to Mutiple-choice Questions:
1(c)   2(d)   3(a)   4(b)   5(d)   6(a)   7(b)   8(a)   9(c)   10(b)

7

WASTE MANAGEMENT SYSTEMS AND PRACTICES

After studying this chapter, the reader will be able to understand the following:

- Reasons for the generation of waste and its characteristics
- Steps involved in waste management
- Governmental directives on e-waste management and municipal solid waste management
- Types of waste disposal practices and their advantages and/or disadvantages

Most of us allow our lives to be shaped and defined by models that stress scarcity, competition, and individualism. We live in housing that accentuates our personal space more than community space, making it hard for our neighbours to even know when we are in need, let alone help us, and vice versa. We throw excess food into the garbage in one part of the country and even our town, while people go hungry in another. Our market economy convinces us that what is most scarce is most valuable, and traps us into believing that what we need most is only available at the mall.[1]

Excerpt from the *Living Oneness: Restoring Wholeness in a Fragmented World*, a study guide released by 'A Global Oneness Project'.

INTRODUCTION

Many citizens, including nature-lovers and trekkers, are of the opinion that it is important to keep regions of pristine natural beauty out of bounds for human beings and transportation facilities to such regions should not be developed. While this may sound archaic and anti-developmental, history has proven that facilitating convenient travel has resulted in much ecological misadventure. Facilitating convenience in transportation results in an increased number of people travelling, and increased waste creation in these regions. An example is Sabarimala, a holy place considered to be the abode of Lord Ayyappan. The temple, located in the Western Ghats region of southern Kerala, India, is surrounded by mountains and forests. However, with easier transportation facilities, and with the purpose of visiting Sabarimala as another item in the 'to-do' lists, millions of people

---

1 http://www.globalonenessproject.org/sites/default/files/education/resources/livingonenessstudyguide.pdf, last accessed on 28 May 2013. Used with permission.

started visiting this temple, resulting in an enormous amount of waste being collected at Sabarimala and the river Pamba being polluted, thereby eroding the pristine environs of this region. Though the governmental authorities have banned the use of plastic in Sabarimala, a huge influx of devotees has resulted in the creation of waste dumps consisting of plastic bottles, plastic covers, plastic wrappers, silver foils, etc. In recent times, attempts have been made by groups of devotees to promote eco-friendly pilgrimages and the 'Clean Sabarimala' (http://www.cleansabarimala.com) campaign is one of them. This campaign promotes the use of biodegradable paper covers instead of plastic covers, avoiding products made from synthetic chemicals, the dumping of water bottles, candles, and balloons as part of the river worship ritual (*Pamba Vilakku*), not dumping dhotis and towels in the river, and promoting the use of biodegradable plates during *Annadaanam*.

Waste generation in Sabarimala is replicated in other pilgrimage sites of India too, be it Haridwar or Vrindavan. The Sabarimala example also illustrates the typical constructs behind waste creation increasing population, increased ease and access to fulfilment of desire, constraints faced by governmental agencies in implementation of rules and guidelines to reduce waste generation, and preference for comfort vis-à-vis responsibility.

Wastes are materials that are discarded, intended to be discarded, or required to be discarded. Article 2.1 of the Basel Convention, an international treaty to reduce the international movement of hazardous waste, states 'wastes are substances or objects which are disposed of or are required to be disposed of by the provisions of national law.'[2] Synonyms for waste include rubbish, trash, refuse, garbage, junk, and litter.

CONSUMERISM AND WASTE PRODUCTS

Consumerism is a societal mind-set that focuses on the purchase of goods and services in much larger amounts, despite being detrimental to the well-being of the purchaser and the society. From purchasing goods and services to satisfy a need, the process of consumption gradually becomes a pre-occupation, and could also become an addiction. As consumption increases, the amount of unused materials and waste materials also increases (see Fig. 7.1).

GENERATION AND CHARACTERISTICS OF WASTE

Waste can be generated from any of the following economic activities, among others:
- Manufacturing
- Mining and quarrying
- Construction
- Electricity, gas, steam, and air conditioning supply
- Agriculture and forestry

---

2 http://www.basel.int/Portals/4/Basel%20Convention/docs/pub/metologicalguidee.pdf, last accessed on 10 April 2013.

FIG. 7.1[3] A 'Buy Nothing Day' campaign image from Adbusters. This campaign criticizes unrestrained consumption and focuses on starting a commitment to consume less, and produce less waste.

- Water treatment
- Sectors like chemicals and fertilizers, pharmaceuticals, and electronics
- Household or domestic waste

As per the US Environmental Protection Agency (EPA)[4], waste can be considered hazardous if it exhibits one of the following four characteristics:

Ignitability Wastes that are spontaneously combustive and have a flash point of less than 60° Celsius.

Corrosivity Acids or bases that have the capability to corrode metal containers (with pH $\leq$ 2 or $\geq$ 12.5).

Reactivity Materials that are unstable under normal conditions, which can cause explosions, toxic fumes, gases, or vapours when heated, compressed, or mixed with water.

Toxicity Wastes that are harmful when ingested or absorbed.

---

3 Image Source: http://www.adbusters.org/sites/default/files/downloads/jpgs/BND-yellow.jpg, last accessed on 31 December 2014; Used with permission.

4 Made available in the public domain, not copyrighted.

TYPES OF WASTE

Understanding the nature of waste can be of help in effective waste management practices. Depending on the waste management objectives, waste can be classified under various categories. This textbook has adopted a general classification, as follows:

Solid Waste

As per the New York State Department of Environmental Conservation, solid wastes are 'discarded (abandoned or considered waste-like) materials. Solid wastes can be solid, liquid, semi-solid, or containerized gaseous material.'[5] The waste management practice that involves the management of solid waste is referred to as solid waste management. It has also been noted that the definition of solid waste management can be expansive and it includes other than solid wastes.[6]

Details of solid waste management can be found under the section 'Integrated Waste Management'.

Industrial Waste

Industrial waste is also referred to as institutional waste or commercial waste. The waste that is produced by institutional or commercial establishments contributes significantly to the amount of solid waste. Industrial wastewater is also considered as a part of industrial waste. Examples of industrial waste include cafeteria garbage, waste ink, sludge from refining processes, scrap metals, oil, solvents, chemicals, wood, and scrap lumber, etc. Some of the industrial waste such as dry cleaning fluids and embalming fluids include carcinogens/suspected carcinogens.

Construction and Demolition Waste

One of the constituents of industrial waste includes the construction and demolition (C&D) waste. This is the debris that is generated as part of the construction, demolition, and renovation of buildings, roads, and bridges. As per the definition of *Municipal Solid Wastes (Management and Handling) Rules*, 2000, C&D waste means the waste from building materials debris and rubble resulting from construction, re-modelling, repair, and demolition operations.[7] Some of the C&D materials include:
- Asphalt, sourced from roads and roofing
- Bricks
- Building components like doors, windows, and plumbing fixtures
- Concrete
- Debris from clearing sites—rock and gravel, trees, stumps, etc.

---

5 http://www.dec.ny.gov/chemical/8732.html, last accessed on 1 January 2014.
6 http://curiosity.discovery.com/question/solid-waste-management-controlling-pollution, lasy accessed on 1 January 2014.
7 http://www.envfor.nic.in/legis/hsm/mswmhr.html, last accessed on 21 July 2014.

- Glass
- Gypsum
- Metals
- Plastics
- Wood, sourced from buildings

Some of the C&D materials can be bulky and heavy.

Special Wastes

As per US EPA, certain wastes are considered as special wastes, and they are listed as follows:

- Cement kiln dust (CKD)—CKD is the waste removed from cement kiln exhaust gas. This is fine-grained and has high alkaline content.
- Mining waste—Mining wastes include waste generated during the extraction, beneficiation, and processing of minerals.
- Oil and gas drilling muds and oil production brines—These are wastes generated during the exploration and production of petroleum and geothermal energy.
- Phosphate rock mining, beneficiation, and processing waste.
- Uranium waste
- Utility waste (i.e., fossil fuel combustion waste)

Hazardous Waste: Management and Treatment

Hazardous waste could involve waste from paints and solvents, automotive wastes (used motor oil, antifreeze, etc.), pesticides, waste that contains mercury, electronic waste (also referred to as e-waste), caustics/cleaning agents, refrigerant containing appliances, aerosols, and propane cylinders, specialty batteries, radioactive waste, ammunition, etc. India's Environmental Protection Act (1986) defines a hazardous substance as any substance or preparation that by reason of its chemical or physicochemical properties, or handling, is liable to cause harm to human beings, other living creatures, plant, micro-organism, property, or the environment.

Popular Mechanics writes, '...the United States produces some 2.25 million tons of e-waste each year, and only about 18 per cent of that is recycled.'[8] It has been estimated that India generates almost 4,00,000 tonnes of e-waste on an annual basis. However, only 19,000 tons are recycled—less than 5 per cent. The Center for Science and Environment (CSE) states that India generates 3,50,000 tons of e-waste and 50,000 tons are imported to the country. In August 2012, the European Union updated its waste electrical and electronic equipment directive, requiring that from 2016, each of its member states should collect a minimum of 45 per cent of electronic equipment sold for approved recycling or disposal. The directive also mentions that the collection level should increase to 65 per cent by 2019.

---

8 http://www.popularmechanics.com/science/environment/recycling/changing-e-waste-recycling-landscape, last accessed on 20 October 2011.

Hazardous waste is normally stored for a period of time prior to its treatment or disposal. The following are some of the ways in which it is stored:

- Containers such as tanker trucks, railroad cars, buckets, bags, and test tubes.
- Tanks made of non-earthenware materials like steel, plastic, fiberglass, and concrete.
- Completely enclosed structures, also known as containment buildings.
- Open waste piles, designed and kept in such a way that the leachate from the waste does not contaminate surface/ground water supplies.
- Surface impoundments that are man-made or are naturally existing topographical depressions.

Hazardous waste may be disposed in landfills, surface impoundments, waste piles, land treatment units, injection wells, and geologic repositories such as salt dome formations, salt bed formations, underground mines, and underground caves.

WASTE MANAGEMENT—COLLECTION, STORAGE, TRANSPORT, AND DISPOSAL

Waste management refers to the process of collection, transport, storage, and disposal of waste materials. Monitoring these activities is also a part of the waste management process. Waste collection involves the transfer of waste material from the point of use and disposal to landfill/recycling plants. Wastes are segregated based on the nature of the waste matter (see Fig. 7.2). In many places, waste is deposited in open spaces and is loaded manually in traditional trucks. It has been found that waste collection, storage, and transportation has not been effective due to the following reasons:

FIG. 7.2[9] Four separate waste bins for glass bottles, plastic bottles, newspapers and magazines, and drinks' cans

---

9 Photo by Calum Hutchinson. Licensed under public domain via Wikimedia Commons. Image source: https://commons.wikimedia.org/wiki/File:Aber_Recycling.jpg#mediaviewer/File:Aber_Recycling.jpg, last accessed on 6 August 2014.

In 2014, Tata Global Beverages Limited (formerly Tata Tea Limited), joined the Tea 2030 partnership. The partnership will focus on (a) sustainable production that benefits the communities and the natural environment where tea is cultivated, (b) engaging consumers so that they demand more sustainable tea, and (c) providing values to all players in the supply chain. Other members of this alliance include Unilever, Rainforest Alliance, Fairtrade International, Yorkshire Tea, Finlays, the Ethical Tea Partnership, and IDH Sustainable Trade Initiative.

(a) Irregular removal of waste

(b) Irregular transportation due to the limited number of specialized vehicles needed for collection and transportation of waste

(c) Open transportation of waste resulting in nuisance

India is witnessing the emergence of a number of waste management ventures operating on social entrepreneurship models, and some of these ventures are driven by youngsters. These include GreenBhoomi (operating in Coimbatore, http://www.greenbhoomi.com) and Kuppathotti (operating in Bangalore and Chennai, http://kuppathotti.com). Such organizations have attempted to increase the effectiveness of waste collection, storage, and transportation.

Waste Disposal Practices

Waste treatment and disposal includes the process of changing the waste characteristics (physical, chemical, and biological) to minimize its threat to the environment. Some of the waste disposal practices involve the following:

- Landfill
- Incineration and energy recovery
- Recycling
- Biological reprocessing

Landfill

The act of burying waste is referred to as landfilling. Landfills are dumping grounds and are one of the common methods of waste management, though it cannot be considered the most effective method of waste management. In the process of landfilling, wastes that are acceptable as per the waste acceptance criteria are layered on the ground and compacted. This is done with the help of a bulldozer to reduce the size of the waste. It is followed by a layering that may include soil, chipped wood, and other materials. Landfill also has its disadvantages. This practice can pollute the groundwater and surface-water through leakage. Other damages are soil contamination, bad odour, and a place for inhabitation for disease causing organisms like flies and rodents.

Incineration and Energy Recovery

Incineration is a waste disposal practice that involves the burning of waste materials. It is also referred to as thermal treatment. Organic substances in the material are burned at high temperatures. Following the process, residues of ash may be formed due to the presence of inorganic materials. Burning also results in the formation of a number of gases and steam that could be released into the atmosphere, after they are removed from polluting particulate matter. Heat, a resultant of burning, is used in many cases to generate electricity. While incineration is recommended as a safe disposal option for many waste materials like medical waste from hospitals, it is not considered to be an effective waste management process as compared to 'Reduce, Recycle, Repair'. There have been concerns about the pollutant gases that are released after burning of the materials. The emissions from an incinerator, if not cleaned, will include particulate matter, heavy metals, dioxins, furans, sulphur dioxide, methane, hydrochloric acid, and more. Environmental organizations like 'Friends of the Earth' have stated that 'when materials are destroyed in incinerators, huge amounts of energy are required to replace them'. Thus, preference is given to waste segregation at source. The organization also states that 'the toxic substances in our waste do not disappear, and as the chimney technology improves, reducing hazards emitted to the air, the levels of toxins left behind in the incinerator ash increases. This ash then has to be sent to landfills, where it is a toxic time bomb for future generations'.[10] Dr Paul Connett, Professor of Chemistry, St Lawrence University, Canton, New York, states, 'It is impossible to convert thousands of tonnes of trash into nothing. The message to the industry is this—If we can't reuse it, if we can't recycle it, we can't compost it, you should not be making it.'[11] Attempts have been made to generate electrical energy from incinerators. Electricity produced through incinerators has been found to create less pollution as compared to the coal-fired power plants.

Recycling

Recycling is the process of collecting, sorting, and reprocessing old and used material into usable new raw materials. As per EPA, recycling is the process of collecting and processing materials that would otherwise be thrown away as trash and turning them into new products (see Fig. 7.3).[12] The products that can be collected and removed from the solid waste stream so that it can be used for manufacturing another product are referred to as recyclable products. Many for-profit companies are looking forward to a 'Zero Waste' operation. This means that the company aims to eliminate the creation of waste materials in a product life cycle by conserving and recovering all resources. Recycling is considered to be an advantageous option because of the following reasons:

(a) Prevents useful materials being dumped into a landfill
(b) Stops the extraction and consumption of fresh raw materials
(c) Reduces pollution
(d) Reduces emission of greenhouse gases
(e) Creates green jobs
(f) Conserves resources for future generations

10 http://web.archive.org/web/20071007232207/http://www.foe.co.uk/resource/briefings/main_uk_directives.pdf, last accessed on 23 October 2013.
11 http://www.youtube.com/watch?v=XB5iOtxlpCs, last accessed on 23 October 2013.
12 http://www2.epa.gov/recycle/recycling-basics, last accessed on 26 October 2013.

FIG. 7.3[13] Old car tyres, used as seats, an example from Thailand

(a), (b), and (c) contribute to cleaner air, water, and land, and therefore better health for all.

Recycling is done through various ways. One of the most popular methods is the kerbside collection/curbside collection done in urban and suburban areas. In this method, the households keep the segregated waste in different containers, and the contents of these containers are collected by the local authorities. The collected materials are sent to a recovery facility where they are sorted, cleaned, and processed into materials that can be used as raw materials again.

Recycling is not just a mechanical process. It also has a human value and is about emotional identification. Philip Gröning, the director of the documentary 'Into Great Silence', was living with the Carthusian monks at the Grande Chartreuse monastery in the French Alps. While sharing one of the incidents during his stay at the monastery, he says, '...I remember that I once threw something away; I don't recall what. The tailor immediately came looking for me to ask me why I had done that. Did I have no respect for the fact that this had once been made through the work of someone's hands? Why did I think this was worthless? This has nothing to do with thriftiness, but

---

13 Photo by User:Mattes—Own work. Licensed under public domain via Wikimedia Commons. Image source: https://commons.wikimedia.org/wiki/File:Car_tires_as_seats_in_Thailand.JPG#mediaviewer/File:Car_tires_as_seats_in_Thailand.JPG, last accessed on 27 October 2013.

with care. The care with which one deals with everything here: with things, with time, with oneself, with the soul.'[14]

Biological Reprocessing and Recovery of Biological Conversion Products: Biogas and Compost

Many waste materials like manure, sewage, municipal waste, green waste, and plant material have organic components. Breaking down these organic components in the absence of oxygen produces a gas typically referred to as biogas. This gas is used for cooking, heating purposes, and also to produce heat and electricity. Organizations like SKG Sangha (http://www.skgsangha.org/) have been engaged in the practice of developing biogas plants, including those that fit a domestic household, and have installed more than a lakh biogas plants with sizes ranging from 25 to 1000 cubic metre gas per day. BIOTECH (http://www.biotech-india.org/) is another popular organization engaged in the process of setting up of biogas plants of various sizes. It has been estimated that the costs incurred for setting up a biogas installation in an average family will give them their payback in three years just from savings from the use of LPG[15]. Setting up biogas plants reduces health risks through the removal of waste material, and can also be used to generate electricity. Cooking with biogas, instead of wood or related materials, can reduce the incidence of respiratory complaints, eye problems, and headaches.[16]

Compost is the decomposed organic matter that is rich in nutrients. As per the definition of Municipal Solid Wastes (Management and Handling) Rules, 2000, composting means a controlled process involving microbial decomposition of organic matter.[17] One can use food waste, vegetable scraps, fallen leaves, weeds, wood chips, grass, etc., as materials available for compost. Decomposition of anything is a natural process, and composting involves the intervention of human beings in enhancing and accelerating the process of this decay. The time duration for decomposition may be weeks or months. Dairy and meat products are not recommended for composting in small piles as they attract rodents and other pests. Compost is therefore used as a medium in which plants can flourish. Compost is rarely used alone. It is usually mixed along with soil, coir, peat, etc.

Composting results in the reuse of organic waste, which otherwise would have gone to a landfill. Compost is rich in nutrients and thus enriches soil, thereby eliminating or reducing the need of additional manure. Daily Dump, a Bangalore-based organization has been promoting Composting (http://dailydump.org/about) at household levels and provides solutions and services towards the same. This organization also conducts a one-day 'trash trail' tour detailing the waste management supply-chain in Bangalore.

---

14 http://www.zeitgeistfilms.com/films/intogreatsilence/intogreatsilence.presskit.pdf, last accessed on 27 April 2010.
15 http://www.ashden.org/files/BIOTECH%20full_0.pdf, last accessed on 21 July 2014.
16 http://www.ashden.org/files/SKG%20full.pdf, last accessed on 21 July 2014.
17 http://www.envfor.nic.in/legis/hsm/mswmhr.html, last accessed on 21 July 2014.

Mosaic (https://joinmosaic.com/), Abundance Generation (https://www.abundancegeneration.com/), and crowdEnergy (https://www.crowdener.gy/) are companies that facilitate crowd funding in renewable energy projects, thereby helping individual investors to directly invest in renewable energy projects.

Take-back Programs, Individual Producer Responsibility, and Collective Producer Responsibility

Communities and governments across the world have started instituting waste management regulations that include collection, treatment, and recycling. Take-back regulations ask the manufacturer of a product to collect back the end-of-life products.

A company engaged in a take-back program may partner with another organization or do the take-back activity by itself. Collection of the used products could be done at (a) service centres of the company, (b) various retail outlets—for example, Acer, an electronics and computer company, allows its US customers to drop their old products in Best Buy, a retail chain. Acer makes a payment to Best Buy for collecting, transporting, and recycling these products, (c) specific recycling locations, (d) home collection—customers of Wipro can call the company and ask them to collect the e-waste,[18] (e) companies also operate a mail-back program where the customers can send the used products to the companies through mail. In the USA, Dell has partnered with FedEx for transporting the Dell products.

The take-back programs are related to Extended Producer Responsibility (EPR). E-waste (Management and Handling) Rules 2011, defines EPR as the responsibility of any producer or electrical or electronic equipment, for their products beyond manufacturing until environmentally sound management of their end-of-life products.[19] EPR can be segmented as Collective Producer Responsibility (CPR) and Individual Producer Responsibility (IPR). CPR involves the collection of waste produced by all manufacturers. In this practice, several manufacturers would be sharing the same recycling infrastructure. The costs incurred to collect and recycle these wastes are shared amongst the various manufacturers. It has been said that this sharing of expenses is based on the market-share of the manufacturer, and not on the amount of waste belonging to each brand or on the recyclability of the product.[20] CPR has the potential to give misguided signals to the manufacturers, as the manufacturers do not know the cost they are incurring in the waste collection and recycling process. When manufacturers knows the costs they are incurring, it would act as a financial incentive in designing more durable and recyclable products.

IPR incentivizes producers to take responsibility for their products during its end-of-life period. While IPR does not demand that the producer collect the waste products

---

18 http://www.wiprogreentech.com/individual_producer_responsibility.html, last accessed on 6 November 2013.
19 http://www.moef.nic.in/downloads/rules-and-regulations/1035e_eng.pdf, last accessed on 21 July 2014.
20 http://www.greenpeace.org/international/en/campaigns/toxics/electronics/philips/individual-producer-responsibi/, last accessed on 10 November 2013.

The US Army has piloted a project to have five of its defense installations/ bases to be Net Zero Energy, five installations to be Net Zero Waste, five installations to be Net Zero Water, and one defense installation to meet all these criteria by 2020. Net Zero Energy base is a base that produces as much renewable energy consumed by that base. Net Zero Water base refers to a base that captures/repurposes/recharges an amount of water that is equal to or greater than the water the base has consumed. A Net Zero Waste installation reduce/reuse/ recovers waste stream, and aims for a zero landfill. The US Army base in Fort Bliss has aimed for a Net Zero Energy, Net Zero Water and Net Zero Waste by 2020. One of the endeavors undertaken by Fort Bliss is to have a solar farm in their base— the largest for a military base.

manufactured only by them, it does put a responsibility on the manufacturer to find out the costs incurred to recycle the waste they have produced and differentiate those costs from the costs incurred to recycle the waste produced by another manufacturer. The manufacturer has to finance the recycling cost of their products.

Urban Waste Management

'The city's commons belong to everyone and so do its streets. The proportion of people using the footpath to the proportion of people on cars on the streets are a good indicator of how the land intended for common transport is to be divided in general, with adjustment space for specific situations. But has anyone heard of footpath-widening as opposed to road-widening? What is especially ironic is how the shrinking, unmaintained footpath has become lower priority in the urban development discourse.'[21]

Garga Chatterjee, columnist, *Down to Earth* magazine

Causes, Effects, and Control Measures

Urban living is generally becoming more extractive of the resources from the villages and semi-urban areas surrounding them, and generates an enormous amount of wastage. The electricity that powers the city and the food and water that sustain the city are usually generated and sourced from regions outside the city. In addition to this extraction, the city also dumps its waste in areas outside the city. The World Bank states that 'The overall goal of urban solid waste management is to collect, treat, and dispose of solid wastes generated by all urban population groups in an environmentally and socially satisfactory manner using the most economical means available.'[22] One of the prime requirements in waste management is to stop looking at waste as waste, and instead look at waste as something from which value added products can be created. ITC's recycling program, 'Wealth out of Waste', collects recyclable waste from companies and institutions, and converts these waste materials into products from which the company can generate revenue.

Increase in generation of urban waste is driven by the economic growth in the cities. This results in:

a) Increased disposable income and consumption patterns

b) Increased business activity and consumption patterns

21   http://www.downtoearth.org.in/content/hope-jaywalkers, last accessed on 12 October 2013.

22   http://web.worldbank.org/WBSITE/EXTERNAL/TOPICS/EXTURBANDEVELOPMENT/EXTUSWM/0,, menuPK:463847~pagePK:149018~piPK:149093~theSitePK:463841,00.html, last accessed on 14 February 2014.

Increased consumption patterns results in an increase in the production of waste. Industrialization also results in the increased production of toxic wastes.

The following points regarding the waste management practices are discovered by the local governments:

- Availability of land for disposal practices becomes scarce.
- With disposal lands located far away, vehicles that carry waste have to travel longer, and thus, there is increased expenditure for managing the fleet.
- With an increase in traffic congestion in towns/cities, the productivity of the vehicles used in waste management also decreases.
- Expansion of cities also results in population influx to the city from other areas. Municipal corporations have to cater to the increasing human population, to whom they provide their services.
- Non-collection of waste, lack of maintenance in waste management equipment and transportation, and lack of waste management services to an ever-increasing population, soon becomes the norm.
- Unmanaged waste can result in clogged drains, unhealthy conditions, seepage of waste material into sources of drinking water supply, pollution of food systems, and more.

A number of control measures can be instituted as part of urban waste management. Normally, in the context of waste management, we discuss the 4R's—Reduce, Reuse, Recycle, and Recover (see the next section for details). It is important, that we add one more R to it and make it into 5R's—REFUSE, Reduce, Reuse, Recycle, and Recover. Refusal to purchase and consume that which is not needed is of primary importance in creating a zero-waste society.

Municipal Corporations and City Waste Management

Municipal corporations or local governments of the areas are usually responsible for providing waste management services in the city. With increasing costs and complexity involved in waste management, local governments have to involve a number of stakeholders thereby necessitating a multi-pronged approach towards waste management.

> Normally, we discuss about the 4R's—Reduce, Reuse, Recycle, and Recover. It is important, that we add one more R to it and make it into 5R's —REFUSE, Reduce, Reuse, Recycle, and Recover. Refusal to purchase that which is not needed and refusal to consume that which is not needed is of primary importance in creating a zero-waste society.

The following are some of the interventions that municipal corporations can undertake/facilitate:

- Promoting optimum technology that requires the consumption of low energy rather than high-energy consumption solutions. Solutions should focus on product life cycle rather than end-of-the-pipe solutions.
- Giving focus towards waste minimization.
- Create opportunities for community participation.
- Communicating the benefits of waste minimization and recovery.

- Promoting landscaping that focuses on mulched gardens and trees, rather than manicured unnatural lawns, which consumes a lot of water.
- Promote, acknowledge, and reward resource recovery practices.
- Changing product designs so that
  - consumption of raw material resources is reduced.
  - durability of the product increases.
- Promoting cleaner production practices.
- Ensure compliance to waste reduction practices through strict enforcement.
- Initiating greener practices in government procuring.
- Starting and sustaining fairs that promote 'share economy'—where citizens can share their used goods and items with others, free of cost.

Public Private Partnership (PPP)—Example 1

In 2008, Kanpur Nagar Nigam (KNN), after a competitive bidding process, awarded A2Z Infrastructure Pvt. Ltd., a BOOT (Build, Own, Operate, and Transfer) contract to process and dispose the solid waste of the city. In the second half of 2010, the company was also awarded the contract for collection and transportation of municipal solid waste, for a period of 30 years.[23] With the award of the contract, the company was given the entire gamut of solid waste management—door-to-door collection, transportation, processing, disposal, and generation of electricity.

Waste was collected from 8,50,000 households and the quantity amounted to approximately 1500 tonnes on a daily basis. Collection of garbage was done 'door-to-door' by 'Safai Mitras' who used protective masks and hand-gloves. Some of the Safai Mitras were former rag pickers and were provided with social security and health benefits. Households and industry had to pay a monthly user fee and these were set by KNN and collected by A2Z.[24] The garbage was collected in bins attached to rickshaws. The waste collected in these bins were later unloaded into trucks that had refuse compactors. Each truck was able to carry the load of 40-50 bins. All trucks included in garbage transportation were tracked through GPS.

The plant of A2Z infrastructure was located in the Panki area of Kanpur. The land that holds the plant was provided for free by the Kanpur Municipal Corporation on a lease of 30 years. The Central Government, Kanpur Municipal Corporation, and A2Z Infrastructure invested 50 per cent, 30 per cent, and 20 per cent of the cost respectively, in establishing the plant. The plant area had a tipping platform, facilities for pre-segregation, composting, plastic segregation, briquette manufacturing, a RDF (Refuse Derived Fuel) unit, and a secured landfill. The project was an Integrated Resource Recovery Facility (IRRF), and derived various products/derivatives from the garbage, including compost, material for producing interlocking tiles, and production of Refuse Driven Fuel (RDF) from which 15 MW of electricity is produced using Circulating

---

23 http://www.indiaprwire.com/pressrelease/environmental-services/2010102065758.htm, last accessed on 21 July 2014.

24 http://archive.indianexpress.com/story-print/978894/, last accessed on 21 July 2014.

Fluidised Bed Combustion (CFBC) technology. This project has also resulted in the production of 150 tonnes of compost on a daily basis and this was marketed under the name 'Vasundhara'. Due to the segregation and treatment at site, less than 10 per cent of the waste collection went to the sanitary landfill.[25] This public private partnership (PPP) also resulted in the creation of the first municipal solid waste to power project in India.

Example 2

In 2000, the Chennai Corporation, after a global tender, selected CES Onyx to manage the collection of solid waste in three zones of the city (Triplicane, Kodambakkam, and Adyar). Waste from these three zones represented approximately one-third of the total waste collection from the city. With this decision, Chennai became the first city in India to opt for a private partnership in solid waste management. The bid was allotted to the company at a price (₹648 per tonne) that was lower than the prevalent operational costs (estimated at ₹1050 per tonne) of the corporation of Chennai. Bins were kept at various locations and these were emptied by the agency at least once a day. The agency used compactors that were able to handle garbage of 7–8 tonnes. The collected garbage was transported to the Perungudi dumping grounds. The company had a training department to train all the employees of the company and the litter collectors were trained in collecting and disposing the waste without touching it. A report in the The Hindu mentions, 'The private operator recruited over 2000 workers, trained them in modern garbage clearance, provided them with uniform and safety gear, and brought about a scientific way of garbage clearance.'[26]

INTEGRATED WASTE MANAGEMENT

For managing waste, many methods are adopted. The following image (see Fig. 7.4) indicates the preference given to various waste management methods:

Source reduction It is about waste reduction. Source reduction practices can include reusing, donating, and redesigning products to use fewer resources (for example, reduction in packaging material, eliminating toxic components in the products, etc.). Reducing the demand for new materials and reusing is the most preferred method of waste management. Buying used items, using products that use less number of packaging, preferring to purchase reusable over disposable items, repairing of products and reusing them, and sharing of items, are some of the ways through which source reduction could be done.

Recycling and composting It has been explained in earlier sections.

Energy recovery It involves converting waste materials to energy, in the form of heat or electricity. Some of the methods through which this is done include combustion, gasification, anaerobic digestion, etc.

---

25 http://www.cseindia.org/userfiles/kanpur_municipal_corporation.pdf, last accessed on 21 July 2014.
26 http://www.hindu.com/2007/02/25/stories/2007022518870300.htm, last accessed on 19 July 2014.

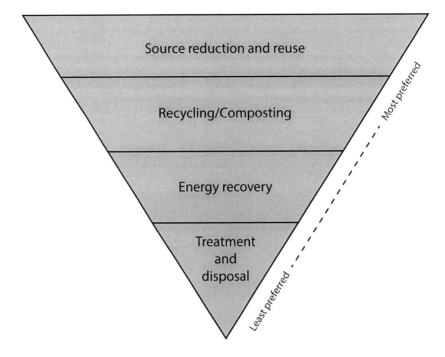

FIG. 7.4 Degree of preference of different waste management methods

Treatment and disposal   It is the least preferred method as it is the most harmful to the environment. Much of the waste is treated to make it less harmful and then released to nature. A common method of disposal is to dump the waste into a landfill.

Integrated waste management (IWM) employs the complementary uses of the waste management practices cited aforementioned.

It is estimated that the USA wastes approximately 40 per cent of its food produced.[27] In India, in the Food Corporation of India storage facilities, 1,94,502 metric tonnes of food grains was wasted between 2005 and March 2013.[28] An Indian Council of Agricultural Research (ICAR) study indicates that post-harvest losses for pulses ranged between 3.4 per cent and 5 per cent of the production, for oil seeds the range was 2.2 per cent and 9 per cent, and for fruits, it ranged between 4.2 per cent and 13.9 per cent of the production.[29] The most preferred route is to avoid generation of food waste. This could be done through avoiding over-production and usage of food. If there is surplus food, it could be distributed to organizations that redistribute food or food products to people

27 http://www.greenbiz.com/blog/2013/08/01/massachusetts-businesses-ahead-ban-food-waste,last accessed on 8 August 2013.

28 http://www.thehindu.com/news/national/fci-admits-194-lakh-mt-foodgrain-wasted-between-200513/article5680994.ece, last accessed on 22 July 2014.

29 http://www.ciphet.in/upload/file/PHL%2020092.pdf, last accessed on 22 July 2014.

who are needy such as some organizations such as food banks, shelters, etc. Some of the excess food may be unfit for human consumption, but may be fit for animal consumption. In such cases, the food could be utilized for animal consumption. Food waste that cannot be used by humans and animals can be sent for producing compost or can be used as resource material for producing heat or electricity. Disposal should be the least preferred method.

POLICIES ON WASTE MANAGEMENT

Increased generation of waste has necessitated the formulation of policy guidelines and laws that result in effective waste management. Two of the important directional guidelines for waste management in India are discussed in this section.

E-waste (Management and Handling) Rules, 2011[30]

Some of the salient features of the aforementioned rules, notified by Ministry of Environment and Forests (MoEF) on 12 May 2011 and came into effect on 1 May 2012 are as follows:

The producer of electrical and electronic equipment shall be responsible for:

(a) the collection of e-waste generated during the manufacture of electrical and electronic equipment, and channelizing it for recycling or disposal.

(b) the collection of e-waste generated from the 'end of life' of their products in line with the principle of 'extended producer responsibility' and to ensure that such e-wastes are channelized to registered dismantler or recycler. Producer shall ensure collection and channelization by authorizing collection agencies.

(c) the setting up of collection centers or take back systems either individually or collectively.

(d) financing and organizing a system to meet the costs involved in the environmentally sound management of e-waste generated from the 'end of life' of its own products and historical waste available on the date from which these rules come into force. The financing arrangement of such a system shall be transparent. The producer may choose to establish such a system either individually or by joining a collective scheme.

(e) providing contact details such as address, telephone numbers/helpline number of authorized collection centers to consumer(s) or bulk consumer(s) so as to facilitate return of used electrical and electronic equipment.

(f) creating awareness through publications, advertisements, posters, or by any other means of communication and information booklets accompanying the equipment, with regard to—

- information on hazardous constituents
- information on hazards of improper handling, accidental breakage, damage, and/or improper recycling of e-waste

---

30 http://www.moef.nic.in/downloads/rules-and-regulations/1035e_eng.pdf, last accessed on 21 July 2014.

- instructions for handling the equipment after its use, along with the 'Do's and Don'ts'
- affixing a visible, legible, and indelible symbol on the products or information booklets to prevent e-waste from being dropped in garbage bins containing waste destined for disposal

(g) obtaining an authorization from the concerned authority.

(h) maintaining records of the e-waste handled and make such records available for scrutiny.

(i) filing annual returns on or before the 30th day of June following the financial year to which that return relates.

Every dismantler shall:

(a) obtain authorization and registration.

(b) ensure that no damage is caused to the environment during storage and transportation of e-waste.

(c) ensure that the dismantling processes do not have any adverse effect on the health and the environment.

(d) ensure that the facility and dismantling processes are in accordance with the standards or guidelines published by the Central Pollution Control Board from time to time.

(e) ensure that dismantled e-waste are segregated and sent to the registered recycling facilities for recovery of materials.

(f) ensure that non-recyclable/non-recoverable components are sent to authorized treatment storage and disposal facilities.

(g) file a return with State Pollution Control Board (SPCB).

(h) Not process any e-waste for recovery or refining of materials, unless he is registered with SPCB as a recycler for refining and recovery of materials.

As per the E-waste (Management and Handling) Rules, 2011, 'e-waste' means waste electrical and electronic equipment, whole or in part or rejects from their manufacturing and repair process, which are intended to be discarded.[31]

Toxics Link (http://www.toxicslink.org), a not-for-profit organization working in the area related to research and advocacy related to toxics pollution, and also campaigned for governmental regulation on e-waste, states, 'The rule explicitly places responsibility in the hands of the manufacturers to address both upstream and downstream issues that necessitate series of action on part of the manufacturers. The role of regulators is also of critical importance as they set the rule into motion and create conditions for the rule to be effective and to ensure high levels of compliance.'

In 2014, the NGO came out with a report 'Time to Reboot'[32] to evaluate the effectiveness of the E-waste (Management and Handling) Rules, 2011. As part of this

---

31 http://www.moef.nic.in/downloads/rules-and-regulations/1035e_eng.pdf, last accessed on 21 July 2014.
32 http://toxicslink.org/docs/Time-to-Reboot.pdf, last accessed on 21 July 2014.

report, Toxics Link attempted to assess and rate the manufacturers on the take-back practices introduced by them. Following the evaluation of 50 brands across multiple parameters, the NGO rated these organization under four categories—good, fair, not so good, and bad. The leading seven brands that were top ranked for its e-waste management practices were:

1. Onida
2. Intex Technologies, Lenovo, and Nokia
3. Canon India, Panasonic India, and Sansui India

These seven manufacturers provided adequate information on the website related to e-waste take-back, had a take-back policy, and had set up collection points where customers can drop their used hardware.

Municipal Solid Wastes (Management and Handling) Rules, 2000

Municipal Solid Wastes (Management and Handling) Rules, 2000, was noted for assigning responsibility to the municipal authority on waste management. The rules mentioned, 'Every municipal authority shall, within the territorial area of the municipality, be responsible for the implementation of the provisions of these rules, and for any infrastructure development for collection, storage, segregation, transportation, processing, and disposal of municipal solid wastes.'[33] Table 7.1 provides the compliance criteria involved in the collection, segregation, transportation, processing, and disposal of solid wastes.

TABLE 7.1[34] Management of municipal solid wastes

Parameters	Compliance criteria
Collection of municipal solid wastes	1. Littering of municipal solid waste shall be prohibited in cities, towns, and in urban areas notified by the State Governments. To prohibit littering and facilitate compliance, the following steps shall be taken by the municipal authority, namely: (i) Organising house-to-house collection of municipal solid wastes through any of the methods, like community bin collection (central bin), house-to-house collection, collection on regular pre-informed timings and scheduling by using bell ringing of musical vehicle (without exceeding permissible noise levels). (ii) Devising collection of waste from slums and squatter areas or localities including hotels, restaurants, office complexes, and commercial areas. (iii) Wastes from slaughter houses, meat and fish markets, fruits and vegetable markets, which are biodegradable in nature, shall be managed to make use of such wastes.

(Contd)

---

33 http://www.envfor.nic.in/legis/hsm/mswmhr.html, last accessed on 21 July 2014.
34 Adapted from http://www.envfor.nic.in/legis/hsm/mswmhr.html, last accessed on 21 July 2014.

TABLE 7.1 *(Contd)*

Parameters	Compliance criteria
	(iv) Bio-medical wastes and industrial wastes shall not be mixed with municipal solid wastes and such wastes shall follow the rules separately specified for the purpose.
	(v) Collected waste from residential and other areas shall be transferred to community bin by hand-driven containerized carts or other small vehicles.
	(vi) Horticultural and construction or demolition wastes or debris shall be separately collected and disposed off following proper norms. Similarly, wastes generated at dairies shall be regulated in accordance with the State laws.
	(vii) Waste (garbage and dry leaves) shall not be burnt.
	(viii) Stray animals shall not be allowed to move around waste storage facilities or at any other place in the city or town and shall be managed in accordance with the State laws.
	2. The municipal authority shall notify waste collection schedule and the likely method to be adopted for public benefit in a city or town.
	3. It shall be the responsibility of generator of wastes to avoid littering and ensure delivery of wastes in accordance with the collection and segregation system to be notified by the municipal authority.
Segregation of municipal solid wastes	In order to encourage the citizens, municipal authority shall organize awareness programmes for segregation of wastes and shall promote recycling or reuse of segregated materials. The municipal authority shall undertake phased programme to ensure community participation in waste segregation. For this purpose, regular meetings at quarterly intervals shall be arranged by the municipal authorities with representatives of local resident welfare associations and non-governmental organizations.
Storage of municipal solid wastes	Municipal authorities shall establish and maintain storage facilities in such a manner that they do not create unhygienic and insanitary conditions around it. Following criteria shall be taken into account while establishing and maintaining storage facilities, namely:
	(i) Storage facilities shall be created and established by taking into account quantities of waste generation in a given area and the population densities. A storage facility shall be so placed that it is accessible to users.
	(ii) Storage facilities to be set up by municipal authorities or any other agency shall be so designed that wastes stored are not exposed to open atmosphere and shall be aesthetically acceptable and user-friendly.

	(iii) Storage facilities or bins shall have easy-to-operate design for handling, transfer, and transportation of waste. Bins for storage of biodegradable wastes shall be painted green, those for storage of recyclable wastes shall be printed white, and those for storage of other wastes shall be printed black.
	(iv) Manual handling of waste shall be prohibited. If unavoidable due to constraints, manual handling shall be carried out under proper precaution with due care for safety of workers.
Transportation of municipal solid wastes	Vehicles used for transportation of wastes shall be covered. Waste should not be visible to public, nor exposed to open environment preventing their scattering. The following criteria shall be met, namely: (i) The storage facilities set up by municipal authorities shall be daily attended for clearing of wastes. The bins or containers wherever placed shall be cleaned before they start overflowing. (ii) Transportation vehicles shall be so designed that multiple handling of wastes, prior to final disposal, is avoided.
Processing of municipal solid wastes	Municipal authorities shall adopt suitable technology or combination of such technologies to make use of wastes so as to minimize burden on landfill. Following criteria shall be adopted, namely: (i) The biodegradable wastes shall be processed by composting, vermicomposting, anaerobic digestion, or any other appropriate biological processing for stabilization of wastes. (ii) Mixed waste containing recoverable resources shall follow the route of recycling. Incineration with or without energy recovery including palletization can also be used for processing wastes in specific cases. Municipal authority or the operator of a facility wishing to use other state-of-the-art technologies shall approach the Central Pollution Control Board to get the standards laid down before applying for grant of authorization.
Disposal of municipal solid wastes	Land filling shall be restricted to non-biodegradable, inert waste, and other waste that are not suitable either for recycling or for biological processing. Land filling shall also be carried out for residues of waste processing facilities as well as pre-processing rejects from waste processing facilities. Land filling of mixed waste shall be avoided unless the same is found unsuitable for waste processing. Under unavoidable circumstances or till installation of alternate facilities, land-filling shall be done following proper norms.

CHAPTER SUMMARY

- Consumerism is a societal mind-set that focuses on purchase of increasing quantities of goods and services in spite of their harmful effects on the purchaser and society.

- Waste is generated from economic activities like manufacturing, mining and quarrying, construction, electricity, gas, steam, air condition supply, agriculture and forestry, and households.

- Waste is hazardous if it exhibits one of the four characteristics: ignitability, corrosivity, reactivity, and toxicity.

- Waste management is the process of collection, transport, storage, disposal of waste materials, and the monitoring of these activities.

- Hazardous waste involves waste from paints and solvents, pesticides, automotive waste, e-waste, caustic/cleaning agents, refrigerants, specialty batteries, radioactive waste, ammunition, etc.

- According to Popular Mechanics, '...the United States produces some 2.25 million tons of e-waste each year, and only about 18 per cent of that is recycled.' It has been estimated that India generates almost 4,00,000 tonnes of e-waste on an annual basis. However, only 19,000 tons are recycled—less than 5 per cent.

- Hazardous waste is stored in containers, tanks made up of non-earthenware material, containment buildings, open waste piles, and surface impoundments.

- Hazardous waste may be disposed in landfills, surface impoundments, waste piles, land treatment units, injection wells, and geologic repositories.

- Landfill, incineration and energy recovery, recycling, and biological reprocessing are some of the waste disposal practices commonly followed.

- Landfill is the practice of burying the waste in dump lands, compaction of it through aid of a bulldozer to reduce its size and finally layering it.

- Electricity produced through incineration, which is the practice of burning waste materials, results in less pollution in comparison to coal-fired power plants.

- Recycling is an advantageous waste management practice as it prevents useful materials being dumped into a landfill, stops the extraction and consumption of fresh raw materials, reduces pollution and greenhouse gases, and conserves resources for future generations.

- Recycling is more than a mere mechanical process, but it is about human value and identification. Philip Gröning, the director of the documentary 'Into Great Silence' after having lived with the Carthusians monks at the Grande Chartreuse monastery in the French Alps, said, 'I remember that I once threw something away; I don't recall what. The tailor immediately came looking for me to ask me why I had done that. Did I have no respect for the fact that this had once been made through the work of someone's hands? Why did I think this was worthless? This has nothing to do with thriftiness, but with care. The care with which one deals with everything here: with things, with time, with oneself, with the soul.'

- Composting, rich in nutrients and derived from food waste, vegetable scraps, fallen leaves, weeds, wood chips, grass, etc., enriches the soil and eliminates the need for using additional manure.

- Communities and governments across the world have started instituting waste management regulation that includes collection, treatment, and recycling.

- A company engaging in a take-back program, through partnership with another organization or by itself, collects used products from service centres, retail outlets, recycling locations, homes of the customers, mail-back programs, etc.

- Extended producer responsibility (EPR), an extension of take-back programs can be categorized into two: Individual Producer Responsibility (IPR) and Collective Producer Responsibility (CPR).
- According to the New York State Department of Environmental Conservation, any discarded, abandoned or waste-like materials are referred to as solid waste. This includes solid, liquid, semi-solid or containerized gaseous material, industrial waste like asphalt, bricks, building components, concrete, debris, glass, gypsum, metals, plastics, wood, etc.
- Urban dwelling results in enormous amount of wastage. As cities expand and the number of people migrating to and living in cities increase, waste management and control becomes complex.
- When it comes to waste management, along with the 4R's (Reduce, Reuse, Recycle, and Recovery), the incorporation of an additional R—REFUSAL to purchase that which is not necessary, and REFUSAL to consume that which is not needed— is of primary importance in creating a zero-waste society.

- The local governments that are responsible for providing waste management services in the cities can undertake a lot of intervention measures to facilitate waste management. These include: promoting optimum technology that consumes less energy, focusing on waste minimization, creating opportunities for community participation, promoting landscaping that focuses on mulched gardens and trees rather than manicured unnatural lawns, changing the product design so that consumption of raw materials is reduced and durability of the product increases, ensuring compliance to waste reduction practices through strict enforcement, initiating greener practices in government procuring, and starting and sustaining fairs that promote 'shared economy'.
- Integrated waste management employs the complementary use of the waste management practices:
  Source reduction and reuse, recycling or composting, energy recovery, treatment and disposal, are the commonly used waste management methods. Among these, treatment and disposal is the least preferred as it causes most harm to the environment.

KEYWORDS

- Biological reprocessing
- BOOT (Build, Own, Operate, and Transfer)
- Collective producer responsibility (CPR)
- Consumerism
- Energy recovery
- E-Waste (Management and Handling) Rules, 2011
- Hazardous waste
- Incineration
- Individual producer responsibility (IPR)
- Integrated waste management (IWM)

- Landfill
- Municipal Solid Wastes (Management and Handling) Rules, 2000
- Public private partnership (PPP)
- Recycling
- Take-back programs
- Toxics link
- 4Rs
- 5Rs

EXERCISES

Multiple-choice Questions

1. What is the societal mind-set that focuses on purchase of goods in greater amount in spite of the harmful effects it may cause?
   (a) Consumerism
   (b) Socialism
   (c) Capitalism
   (d) Mixed-economy

2. How many tonnes of e-waste does India generate annually, according to the Center for Science and Environment?
   (a) 3,00,000
   (b) 3,50,000
   (c) 4,00,000
   (d) 2,00,000

3. Incineration is recommended as a safe disposal option for which type of waste?
   (a) Medical waste
   (b) Hazardous waste
   (c) Automotive waste
   (d) e-waste

4. What is the method that prevents useful materials from being dumped into landfills, stops the consumption of fresh raw materials and reduces pollution?
   (a) Recycling
   (b) Waste collection
   (c) Compaction
   (d) Energy recovery

5. Which of the following is rich in nutrients and enriches the soil, eliminating the need to add additional manure?

   (a) Compost
   (b) Biogas
   (c) Pesticides
   (d) Organic phosphates

6. What is the take-back program by which end-of-life products are collected from customers by all the manufacturers who produced the product?
   (a) Individual producer responsibility
   (b) Collective producer responsibility
   (c) Extended producer responsibility
   (d) None of these

7. What is the economy in which citizens can share their used goods and items with others free of cost?
   (a) Shared economy
   (b) Capitalist economy
   (c) Mixed economy
   (d) None of these

8. What is the least preferred waste management method?
   (a) Source reduction and reuse
   (b) Recycling and composting
   (c) Energy recovery
   (d) Treatment and disposal

9. Which of the following is the most preferred way of food waste management?
   (a) Avoiding generation of food waste
   (b) Feeding people in need
   (c) Feeding livestock
   (d) Creating compost and energy

Short Answer Questions

1. What are the activities that lead to the generation of waste?
2. What are the characteristics for waste to be considered hazardous?
3. Define waste management.
4. How does waste collection cause harm to the others?

5. State the reasons why waste collection, management, and transportation have not been effective.
6. Define hazardous substance as laid down by the Environmental Protection Act of 1986.
7. What are the ways in which hazardous waste is stored before it is disposed?

8. Name some waste disposal practices.
9. Define compaction.
10. Explain incineration or waste treatment.
11. State the reasons as to why waste recycling is a better option of waste management in comparison to other techniques.
12. What is compost?
13. Define solid waste management.
14. What is industrial waste?

15. State some of the construction and demolition waste (C&D) generated as a result of construction of buildings, roads, and bridges.
16. What is special waste? Give a few examples.
17. What is the ultimate goal of urban solid waste management?
18. Define source reduction.
19. Define zero waste.

Long Answer Questions

1. Explain how and why 'recycling' is not only an effective means of waste management, but is also considered to have a human value.
2. What are the challenges faced by the local government when it comes to waste management? Suggest the control measures that can be taken, with a specific reference on the 5R's (Refuse, Reduce, Reuse, Recycle, and Recover).

3. State the intervention measures that the municipal corporations can undertake to facilitate waste management in the city.
4. What are the different waste management methods? Explain why treatment and disposal is the least preferred method to waste management and elaborate on integrated waste management.

Reflective Question

1. Collect all the dry waste that your house generates for a week. Segregate them.
   (a) What are the various ways in which you can reuse and recycle them?
   (b) Who is responsible for this waste—the producer (manufacturer) or the consumer? Is it the producer who uses such material;

   the consumer who purchases such product; or the government that allows such practices to continue?
   (c) What are your ideas on minimising such waste production, and increasing reusing and recycling?

Take-home Activities

1. Find out the amount of waste generation that happens in your campus/ home. Brainstorm (a) ways through which this waste generation could be reduced and (b) how does this waste generation can contribute to greenhouse gas emissions?

2. Read through the webpage that details about the 'trash trail' tour conducted by Bangalore-based 'Daily Dump' detailing the supply chain of waste management practices in Bangalore (http://dailydump.org/trash-trail, as accessed on December 31, 2014). Design a similar single day tour for your own city/ town.

Web Reading

1. A free online game on recycling, designed by US EPA—http://www.epa.gov/recyclecity/gameintro. htm

Recommended Book

1. Pathak, Bindheshwar, *The Road to Freedom: A Sociological Study on the Abolition of Scavenging in India*, Motilal Banarsidass, 2000.

Recommended Documentaries/Movies

1. Minus One Project of Samsung Printers, 2012 (This short clipping is available for free viewing at https://www.youtube.com/ watch?v=KThJoYt4ml8), Duration: 2 minutes.
2. Story of Bottled Water (This documentary is available for free viewing at http:// storyofstuff.org/movies/story-of-bottled- water/ and https://www.youtube.com/ watch?v=Se12y9hSOM0), Duration: 8 minutes.
3. Story of Electronics (This documentary is available for free viewing at http://storyofstuff. org/movies/story-of-electronics/ and https:// www.youtube.com/watch?v=sW_7i6T_H78), Duration: 8 minutes.

Answers to Mutiple-choice Questions:

1(a)   2(b)   3(a)   4(a)   5(a)   6(b)   7(a)   8(d)   9(a)

8

BIODIVERSITY

When we try to pick out anything by itself we find that it is bound fast by a thousand invisible cords that cannot be broken, to everything in the universe.[1]

John Muir, a naturalist, author, and an advocate of preservation of wilderness in the United States.

After studying this chapter, the reader will be able to understand the following:
- Importance and value of biodiversity
- Aichi Biodiversity Targets
- Management of various ecosystems
- Critically endangered species of India and the IUCN red-list

INTRODUCTION

As per the UN Convention on Biological Diversity (CBD), *biological diversity* means the variability among living organisms from all sources including, inter alia, terrestrial, marine, and other aquatic ecosystems, and the ecological complexes of which they are part; this includes diversity within species, between species, and of ecosystems[2]. Biodiversity is the quantity in the variety of all forms of life in a given natural environment. It is these diverse biological resources that sustain the human civilization. Constituents of biodiversity provide food and fibre to human beings. Bacteria and microbes transform many waste products into usable products, insect population pollinates crops and flowers, and coastlines are protected by coral reefs and mangroves. However, habitat destruction and species loss is happening at an unprecedented scale in recent times (Fig. 8.1).

Biodiversity makes life possible. It provides services that may not be directly perceivable. An example could be the role played by insects in food production. Though cereals such as rice and wheat are not dependent on animal pollination (as they are wind-pollinated), about 46 of the 100 crops

---

1 http://www.sierraclub.org/john_muir_exhibit/writings/misquotes.aspx, last accessed on 10 July 2013.
2 http://www.cbd.int/convention/articles/default.shtml?a=cbd-02, last accessed on 28 June 2014.

FIG 8.1[3] Deforestation in Amazon rainforest

The photo indicates a 'fish-bone' pattern in forest destruction. Increased road-building in forests can contribute to destruction of forests.

In 2011, Sprint Corporation, a telecommunications company, based in Overland Park, USA, came out with its zero e-waste goal to collect 100 per cent of its electronic waste for reuse and recycling by 2017. The company, by then, also plans to collect 90 per cent of all phones sold for reuse or recycling.

directly used for human food are dependent on insect pollination. Productivity of pulses, fruits, and vegetables are dependent on the pollinators. Bees, butterflies, moths, flies, bats, and birds help pollinate the crops. Bees pollinate more than 400 crops in the world. In the tropical region, honeybees and some of the species of stingless bees contribute to half of the pollination provided by animals. Animal pollination improves the production of 70 per cent of tropical plants. The total economic value of pollination worldwide, as of 2005, amounted to €153 billion, which

3 *Amazonie deforestation*,licensed under public domain via Wikimedia Commons, https://commons.wikimedia.org/wiki/File:Amazonie_deforestation.jpg#mediaviewer/File:Amazonie_deforestation.jpg, last accessed on 16 May 2013.

represented 9.5 per cent of the value of the world agricultural production used for human food.[4]

During the inauguration of the High Level Segment of the 11th Conference of Parties (COP) to the Convention on Biological Diversity (CBD) in 2012, at Hyderabad, the Prime Minister of India remarked, 'Our approach in protecting and promoting biodiversity has been guided by the belief that all three objectives of the Convention on Biological Diversity, namely, conservation, sustainable use, and sharing of benefits from the utilization of genetic resources, should receive adequate and equal focus. This approach is the basis of India's Biological Diversity Act of 2002. The 2008 National Biodiversity Action Plan further identifies specific action points by various government agencies.'[5] As part of this conference, India pledged USD 50 million to strengthen the institutional mechanism for biodiversity conservation in India.

GENETIC, SPECIES, AND ECOSYSTEM DIVERSITY

Biological variety has typically been identified at three levels—genetic diversity, species diversity, and ecosystem diversity. The following is the description of the three levels as provided by the United Nations Environment Programme[6]

- Genetic diversity is all the different genes contained in all the living species, including individual plants, animals, fungi, and microorganisms.
- Species diversity is all the different species, as well as the differences within and between different species.
- Ecosystem diversity is all the different habitats, biological communities, and ecological processes, as well as variation within individual ecosystems.

Value of Biodiversity: Consumptive Use, Productive Use, Social, Ethical, Aesthetic, and Option Values

The value of biodiversity can be put in two different perspectives—anthropocentric and intrinsic. Anthropocentric perspective is based on the idea of how biodiversity is valuable to human beings (see Table 8.1). Intrinsic perspective is based on respect and reverence of life. Satish Kumar, Editor-in-Chief, Resurgence Magazine (a magazine considered as the artistic and spiritual voice of the green movement in United Kingdom) states that a tree is good in itself, not just because of the utility of a tree to humans as it gives oxygen, firewood, flowers, or fruits. He says, 'Tree has intrinsic value. River has a right to flow unpolluted, uncontaminated, and undammed.'[7] Biodiversity also provides services that could be directly measurable and also values that cannot be measured directly.

4 Gallai, Nicola, Jean-Michel Salles, Josef Settele, and Bernard E. Vaissière, Economic valuation of the vulnerability of world agriculture confronted with pollinator decline, Ecological Economics, vol 68, issue 3, 2009, pp. 810-821.
5 http://www.cbd.int/doc/speech/2012/sp-2012-10-16-cop11-hls-in-pm-en.pdf, last accessed on 4 June 2014.
6 www.unep.org/wed/2010/english/PDF/BIODIVERSITY_FACTSHEET.pdf, last accessed on 16 May 2013.
7 http://www.bigpicture.tv/?id=3117, last accessed on 24 March 2012.

TABLE 8.1 Anthropocentric values of biodiversity

Direct values	Indirect values
Consumptive use values	Social, cultural, and religious values
Productive use values	Ethical values
	Aesthetic values
	Optional values
	Environmental service values

Direct Values of Biodiversity

Direct values can be further classified into consumptive use values and productive use values. Consumptive use values typically include food, fuel, and medicinal resources, consumed locally and are not sold. People cultivate for themselves—'living off the land'. They use fuel wood and organic materials (biomass) for their daily sustenance. Many medicines, especially in practices like Ayurveda, are sourced directly from nature (see Table 8.2). As per Foundation for Revitalization of Local Health Traditions (FRLHT), almost 85 per cent of the known and recorded medicinal plant diversity of India is from the forest and wild habitats. As per FRLHT, more than 6000 species of plants are used for various healthcare requirements, an implication that almost 40 per cent of the plant diversity in India is used as medicinal plants. Ved and Goraya (2007)[8] note that 82 per cent of the high consumption botanical products (with a trade of more than 100 MT annually), are from wild sources.

TABLE 8.2 Some important herbs with significant healthcare functions

Bhumyamalaki, Long Pepper, Chirayata	Improves liver functions
Ashwagandha, Amla, Tulsi	Improves immunity
Brahmi, Sweet Flag, Jyotishmati	Improves brain functions
Arjuna, Guggul, Brahmakamal	Improves heart functions
Bael, Chebulic Myrobalan	Improves alimentary canal functions
Gokshura, Boerrhavia, Crataeva	Improves functioning of the urinary system
Turmeric, Licorice	Improves functioning of the respiratory tract
Tamalpatra, Bitter Gourd, Jamun	Improves functioning of the pancreas
Ashwagandha, Monkey bean	Improves the functioning of men's reproductive system
Shatavari, Hibiscus, Ashoka	Improves functioning of women's reproductive system

---

8 Ved, D.K., G.S.Goraya, *Demand and Supply of Medicinal Plants in India*, NMPB, New Delhi and FRLHT, Bangalore, India, 2007.

The value that is assigned to goods harvested from the environment that are marketed/traded are referred to as productive use values. This will include timber and non-timber forest produces, natural pesticides, marine products, fibres such as cotton, fruits, and vegetables, etc. Some species of the nature also act as blueprints for medicines. It has been noted that more than half of the new medicines introduced during the past 25 years comes from nature.[9] Medicines can have its base in almost all living forms in the planet—insects, plants, animals, microbes, marine life, etc. Researchers have suggested conservation of plant species, as they could potentially be medicine producing species.[10] Some of the medicines derived from nature as a source is listed in Table 8.3.

TABLE 8.3 List of medicines derived from nature

Amrubicin	Anidulafungin	Apomorphine	Artemotil	Atropine
Aztreonam	Biapenem	Bivalirudin	Bleomycin	Bromelain
Caffeine	Colchicine	Camphor	Capsaicin	Caspofungin
Cefditoren	Cocaine	Codeine	Codinaeopsin	Dronabinol
Daptomycin	Digitoxin	Dimethyltryptamine	Doripenem	Fumagillin
Ergotamine	Ertapenem	Everolimus	Exenatide	Ixabepilone
Galantamine	Glaziovine	Gossypol	Indicine N-oxide	Methylnaltrexone
L-Dopa	Lisdexamfetamine	Menthol	Mescaline	Mycophenolate
Micafungin	Miglustat	Monocrotaline	Morphine	Penicillin
Nitisinone	Orlistat	Paclitaxel	Papain	Retapamulin
Phenethylamine	Pimecrolimus	Quinine	Reserpine	Taxol
Romidepsin	Rosuvastatin	Scopolamine	Spiruchostatins	Tiotropium
Telavancin	Telithromycin	Temsirolimus	Tigecycline	
Trabectedin	Vinblastine	Ziconotide	Zotarolimus	

Indirect Values of Biodiversity

Indirect values of biodiversity can be further classified into social, cultural, and religious values, ethical values, aesthetic values, option values, and environment service values.

- Social, cultural, and religious values—Many species are considered holy and are venerated. Similarly, many geographical locations and landscapes are considered sacred. These are also detailed in the second chapter 'Spiritual Perspectives on Environment'.

---

9   http://www.livescience.com/14016-natural-products-nih.html, last accessed on 16 June 2013.

10 Ibrahim, Mohamed Ali, MinKyun Na, Joonseok Oh, Raymond F. Schinazi, Tami R. McBrayer, Tony Whitaker, Robert J. Doerksen, David J. Newman, Louis G. Zachos, and Mark T. Hamann, *Significance of endangered and threatened plant natural products in the control of human disease*, proceedings of the National Academy of Sciences, 2013 doi: 10.1073/pnas.1311528110; http://www.pnas.org/content/early/2013/09/27/1311528110, last accessed on 10 October 2013.

- Ethical values—Ethical values are similar to the intrinsic values of biodiversity. The ethical value indicates that each species has a moral right to exist on this planet, and access to the bounty of this planet is not just the prerogative of human beings. Ethical value is related to the importance of protecting all forms of life on earth.
- Aesthetic values—Biodiversity contributes to the beauty that we appreciate in nature. Undisturbed natural landscapes provide a visual appeal to the human mind. It also helps in promoting eco-tourism.
- Option values—Those potentials of biodiversity that could provide benefits for future generation are referred to as option values. Many aspects related to biodiversity are unknown or unexplored, and could prove to be an aid in improving the well-being of the generations of the future.
- Environment service values—These are the value of the services provided by biodiversity. A detailed classification of the same is provided in Chapter 6 under the topic 'Ecosystem Services and Valuation'.

BIODIVERSITY AT GLOBAL, NATIONAL, AND LOCAL LEVELS

Biodiversity of a region depends on a number of parameters including climatic conditions such as temperature and precipitation, characteristics, altitude, and the presence and population of various species. Rainforests are known to have higher rates of biodiversity. 'Life on land today is as much as 25 times as diverse as life in the sea,' says *Geological Journal*[11]. The diversity of species of Earth is estimated to range between 2 million and 100 million. One study indicated that it could be approximately 8.7 million, and 'some 86 per cent of the species on Earth, and 91 per cent in the ocean, still await description'.[12]

Bio-geographical Classification of India

As per the Wildlife Institute of India, India has been divided into ten different zones, with each zone having multiple provinces, as follows (see Fig. 8.2 and Table 8.4):

India as a Mega-diversity Nation

Why is the great voice of India silent?
Is India lost in quest of its own soul? Is India asleep?
No, India is awake in the toil of the plough man
And the housewife over her woodfire;
India is awake in the tears and laughter of her poor.

---

11 Benton, Michael J., Biodiversity on land and in the sea, *Geological Journal*, July-Dec 2001, Vol. 36, Issue 3-4, pp. 211-230.

12 Mora, Camilo, Derek P. Tittensor, Sina Adl, Alastair G.B.Simpson, Boris Worm, How Many Species Are There on Earth and in the Ocean?PLoS Biol 9(8): e1001127, 23 August 2011, DOI:10.1371/journal.pbio.1001127.

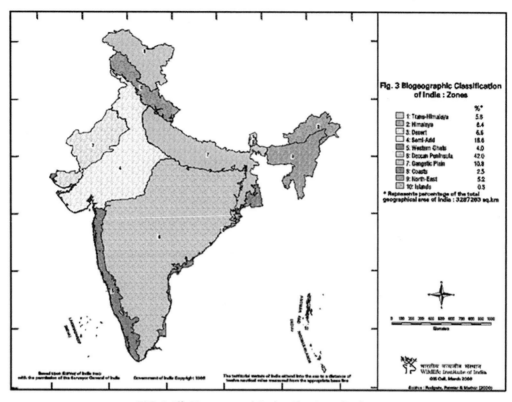

FIG. 8.2[13] Bio-geographic classification of India

Source: Rodgers, Panwar, and Mathur (2000)/Wildlife Institute of India

TABLE 8.4 Classification of India and its percentage geographical area

Classifications and provinces	% of the total geographical area of India
1a. Trans-Himalayas - Ladakh mountains	3.3%
1b. Trans-Himalayas - Tibetan plateau	2.3%
2a. Himalaya - North-west Himalaya	2.1%
2b. Himalaya - West Himalaya	1.6%
2c. Himalaya - Central Himalaya	0.2%
2d. Himalaya - East Himalaya	2.5%
3a. Desert – Thar	5.4%
3b. Desert – Kutch	1.1%

(Contd)

---

13 Materials hosted in the website can be reproduced. For more details, http://wiienvis.nic.in/Content/Copyright_166.aspx

TABLE 8.4 *(Contd)*

Classifications and provinces	% of the total geographical area of India
4a. Semi-arid - Punjab Plains	3.7%
4b. Semi-arid - Gujarat Rajputana	12.9%
5a. Western Ghats - Malabar Plains	2.0%
5b. Western Ghats - Western Ghats mountains	2.0%
6a. Deccan Peninsula - Central Highlands	7.3%
6b. Deccan Peninsula - Chota Nagpur	5.4%
6c. Deccan Peninsula - Eastern Highlands	6.3%
6d. Deccan Peninsula - Central Plateau	12.3%
6e. Deccan Peninsula - Deccan South	10.4%
7a. Gangetic Plain - Upper Gangetic Plain	6.3%
7b. Gangetic Plain - Lower Gangetic Plain	4.5%
8a. Coasts - West Coast	0.6%
8b. Coasts - East Coast	1.9%
8c. Coasts – Lakshadweep	>0.1%
9a. North-East - Brahmaputra valley	2.0%
9b. North-East - North-East hills	3.2%
10a. Islands – Andamans	0.2%
10b. Islands – Nicobars	0.1%

For India's soul, wealth is her poverty,
Her spirit of quiet independence,
Her dedication to truth,
For her voice comes from deep within,
The one true God who manifests
in every stone and tree
And lives in the heart's mind![14]

—Bulu Imam, tribal art conservationist

Norman Myers, a UK-based environmentalist, has been influential in popularising the concept of biodiversity hotspots and mega-diverse nations. Pondering about conserving the maximum number of species at the least cost, Myers and co-researchers wrote, in a seminal article published in *Nature*[15], 'One way is to identify *biodiversity hotspots* where exceptional concentrations of endemic species are undergoing exceptional loss of habitat. As many as 44 per cent of all species of vascular plants and 35 per cent of all species in four vertebrate groups are confined to 25 hotspots comprising only 1.4 per cent of the land surface of the Earth. This opens the way for a "silver bullet" strategy

---

14 http://lifepositive.com/earth-crusader/, last accessed on 6 May 2014. Used with permission.
15 Myers,Norman, Russell A.Mittermeier, Cristina G.Mittermeier, Gustavo A.B.da Fonseca, Jennifer Kent, Biodiversity hotspots for conservation priorities, Nature 403, pp. 853-858, February 2000. Summary of the article also available at http://www.nature.com/nature/journal/v403/n6772/full/403853a0.html

on the part of conservation planners, focusing on these hotspots in proportion to their share of the world's species at risk.' These hotspots (detailed in the following section) are located in different regions of the world. In order to conserve a hotspot area, Myers recommended focusing on 'mega diversity' countries. A mega diversity country was defined as a country 'that either (a) contains 20,000 higher plant species or, in the case of a country with fewer than 20,000 but more than 10,000 such species, atl east 5000 endemics; or (b) contains at least 2000 species of higher vertebrates (mammals and birds), or 200 such species as endemics.'[16]About 17 nations were identified as mega-diverse countries, and they encompassed 60-70 per cent of all global biodiversity. These are the countries that are extremely bio-diverse and sustains majority of the species on the planet. India is one amongst those countries, along with Australia, Brazil, China, Colombia, Democratic Republic of Congo, Ecuador, Indonesia, Madagascar, Malaysia, Mexico, Papua New Guinea, Peru, Philippines, South Africa, United States, and Venezuela. Around 6–12 per cent of the world's species are found in India.[17]

Hotspots of Biodiversity

A biodiversity hotspot is an ecologically diverse region that is also facing significant threat of habitat loss, climate loss, and species loss. Worldwide 25 sites are recognized as hotspots of biodiversity, with nine sites to be possibly included. While these 25 hotspots sustain high number of endemic species, supporting almost 60 per cent of the plant, bird, mammal, reptile, and amphibian species, their combined area covers only 2.3 per cent of Earth's land surface. The 34 regions, distributed geographically, are listed in the following table (see Table 8.5).

THREATS TO BIODIVERSITY

There are significant amount of threats faced by biodiversity. 'Losing a species to extinction is like tearing a page out of sacred scripture... God is revealed to us in nature... so each species lost denies us a unique opportunity to know and praise God,' says Calvin DeWitt, a Christian evangelical leader and also a Professor at Nelson Institute for Environmental Studies, University of Wisconsin-Madison.[18] Following are some of the threats to biodiversity.
- Habitat loss and destruction
- Poaching of wildlife and man-wildlife conflicts
- Exploitation of natural resources
- Invasive species
- Climate change, pollution, and contamination

16 Myers, Norman, Hotspots, *Encyclopedia of Biodiversity*, Vol 3, pp. 371-381, 2001.
17 http://www.biodiversityofindia.org/, last accessed on 19 June 2013.
18 http://livinggreenmag.com/2014/04/17/people-solutions/earth-day-save-the-wild-before-its-gone/, last accessed on 18 April 2014.

TABLE 8.5 Hotspots of biodiversity in the world

North and Central America	Europe and Central Asia	South-east Asia and Asia-Pacific
California Floristic Province	Caucasus	Vietnam
Caribbean Islands	Irano-Anatolian	East Melanesian Islands
Madrean pine-oak woodlands	Mediterranean Basin	New Caledonia
Mesoamerica	Mountains of Central Asia	New Zealand
South Asia	**Africa**	Philippines
Eastern Himalaya	Maputaland-Pondoland-Albany	Polynesia-Micronesia
Indo-Burma and Myanmar	Madagascar and the Indian Ocean Islands	Southwest Australia
Western Ghats	Horn of Africa	Sundaland
Sri Lanka	Guinean Forests of West Africa	Wallacea
East Asia	Cape Floristic Region	**South America**
Japan	Coastal Forests of Eastern Africa	Atlantic Forest
Mountains of Southwest China	Eastern Afromontane	Cerrado
		Chilean Winter Rainfall-Valdivian Forests
		Tumbes-Choco-Magdalena
		Tropical Andes

Habitat Loss and Destruction

Human activity aimed at the generation and extraction of natural resources, urbanization, overfishing, and agriculture results in natural habitats being unable to support the species that are prevalent there. This process is referred to as habitat destruction. Habitat loss has been identified as the main threat to 85 per cent of all the species in the IUCN Red List of Threatened Species (also referred to as the IUCN Red List or Red Data List, http://www.iucnredlist.org/), the most comprehensive inventory of the global conservation status of biological species. The construction of roads, dams, water diversion, agricultural activities, (see Fig. 8.3), and other activities done in the name of development results in the fragmentation of the habitat. This also affects the migration patterns of migratory species.

The IUCN's Polar Bear Specialist Group have stated that of the 19 polar bear sub-populations in the Arctic region, only one is increasing, eight are declining, three are stable, and there is insufficient data for the remaining seven sub-populations.[21] As wildlife disappears, local ecological knowledge has been found to disappear too. 'Younger people today cannot experience the sights and sounds of forest animals that their parents grew up with and, consequently, knowledge of these species is passing from cultural memory,' says a research paper.[22]

FIG. 8.3[19] Tea plantation in Ooty

Many of the areas that have monoculture plantations (like tea, palm, eucalyptus, etc.,) have been created by destroying forests. Such monoculture plantations are referred to as 'Green Deserts'. Guadalupe Rodríguez, a member of the Germany-based Rainforest Rescue, says 'Monoculture forests tend to be seen as a good thing, because they are green and pretty. But if you approach them, you won't hear a single bird, because there is nothing there, just silence... A monoculture forest is almost like a stone quarry. In tropical rainforests, by contrast, you hear animals, water flowing, because they are full of life.'[20]

19 'Tea gardens ooty' by Challiyan at ml.wikipedia - transferred from ml.wikipedia by user:Sreejithk2000 using CommonsHelper. Licensed under public domain via Wikimedia Commons - https://commons.wikimedia.org/wiki/File:Tea_gardens_ooty.JPG#mediaviewer/File:Tea_gardens_ooty.JPG, last accessed on 4 August 2014.

20 http://www.theguardian.com/environment/2011/sep/26/monoculture-forests-africa-south-america, last accessed on 13 August 2013.

21 http://pbsg.npolar.no/en/status/status-table.html, last accessed on 10 February2013.

22 Kai,Zhang, Teoh Shu Woan, Li Jie, Eben Goodale, Kaoru Kitajima, Robert Bagchi, Rhett D.Harrison 2014, Shifting Baselines on a Tropical Forest Frontier: Extirpations Drive Declines in Local Ecological Knowledge, PLoS One 9(1), 2014; http://www.plosone.org/article/info%3Adoi%2F10.1371%2Fjournal.pone.0086598, last accessed on 21 February 2014.

Poaching of Wildlife and Human–Wildlife Conflicts

Poaching involves a number of practices, some of the prominent being, hunting down an animal illegally, using illegal means to kill an animal, and selling the animals for a profit. At least four leopards are poached every week in India.[23] In 2012, 72 tigers were found dead, and the first half of 2013 witnessed the death of almost 44 tigers, and many of these deaths are attributed to poaching.[24] As per a World Wide Fund for Nature (WWF) report cited in BBC, the global illegal trade in wildlife is $19 billion a year.[25] Almost two-thirds of the elephants in Africa have been killed due to poaching for ivory.[26] In contrast to what is commonly thought, poaching could also be related to flora. Poaching has resulted in the decrease of the population of many rare species (see Fig. 8.4).

Wildlife trafficking is not just an environmental problem. In May 2013, the African Development Bank came with the Marrakech declaration to combat wildlife trafficking, which stated, 'The violence and damage now threaten peace and the rule of law, as well as the revenue many African countries earn from tourism and other wildlife uses; some of the poorest and most vulnerable communities that depend on wildlife for their livelihoods suffer... wildlife trafficking thwarts governments' efforts to stop other illicit trades, such as arms and drugs. It fuels organized crime and corruption, and compromises regional security.'[27] It has been reported that terrorist organizations also generate funds from illegal wildlife trafficking.[28] Drug trafficking has also been reported to increase deforestation.[29] Traffickers prefer to engage with forest lands due to its sparse population and lack of monitoring by law enforcement authorities. Trees are felled to build roads and to set up landing strips for planes. As per TRAFFIC, a wildlife trade monitoring network, 'Wildlife and forest crime often overlaps with other criminal activities, including illicit trade in arms, corruption and money laundering. Left unaddressed, wildlife and forest crime can facilitate the growth of other organized crime, and hinder governments' ability to halt other illicit activities.'[30]

---

23 http://www.wwfindia.org/news_facts/?9520/South-Asia-steps-up-investigative-efforts-against-wildlife-crime-and-illicit-trade-in-tigers, last accessed on 12 August 2013.

24 http://www.tigernet.nic.in/Alluser/Map2.0.aspx, last accessed on 12 August 2013.

25 http://www.bbc.co.uk/news/science-environment-20679454, last accessed on 18 May 2013.

26 http://www.theguardian.com/environment/2013/mar/05/two-thirds-forest-elephants-killed, last accessed on 28 December 2013.

27 http://www.afdb.org/fileadmin/uploads/afdb/Documents/Generic-Documents/The%20Marrakech%20Declaration%20-%20A%2010-Point%20Action%20Plan%20to%20Combat%20Illicit%20Wildlife%20Trafficking.pdf, last accessed on 28 December 2013.

28 http://www.independent.co.uk/news/world/africa/illegal-ivory-trade-funds-alshabaabs-terrorist-attacks-8861315.html, last accessed on 28 December 2013.

29 http://conservationmagazine.org/2014/02/disturbing-link-cocaine-deforestation/, last accessed on 19 February 2014.

30 www.traffic.org/non-traffic/CCPCJ-brief.pdf, last accessed on 28 May 2014.

FIG. 8.4[31] Martha, the last passenger pigeon

Passenger pigeons were one of the most populated species in the Americas, especially during the period when Europeans arrived there. Their extinction has been attributed to hunting and habitat destruction.

Exploitation of Natural Resources

Changes in the consumption pattern of human beings are considered a significant factor in the exploitation of natural resources. Raw materials for increased consumption have to come from the planet. This is primarily done through extraction of minerals and

---

31 Photo by Enno Meyer, Image source: http://archive.org/stream/publishedfigures00shuf#page/466/mode/2up, licensed under public domain via Wikimedia Commons - https://commons.wikimedia.org/wiki/File:Martha_last_passenger_pigeon_1914.jpg#mediaviewer/File:Martha_last_passenger_pigeon_1914.jpg, last accessed on 18 May 2013.

increased production of agro-produce. In most cases, both these practices destroy/ alter natural ecosystems, thereby affecting the biodiversity of the planet. As per United Nations Environment Programme, deforestation continues at the rate of 13 million hectares of forest on an annual basis.[32] This is roughly equal to the size of Portugal or Greece or the state of Tamilnadu or Chhattisgarh in India. This is also equivalent to the destruction of a land area equivalent to a football field, every second of the day (see Fig. 8.5). Palm Oil, a commonly used ingredient in many of the consumer goods ranging from chocolates, cosmetics, and also in bio-fuels, has resulted in the destruction of the tropical rainforests of Malaysia and Indonesia where these forest areas are cleared for palm oil plantations. 'Since the 1970s, the area planted with oil palm in Indonesia has grown over 30-fold

FIG. 8.5[35] A football field in Mexico City

Every second, forest area equivalent to the area of a football field is eliminated

32 http://www.unep.org/forests/AboutForests/tabid/29845/Default.aspx, last accessed on 20 May 2013.

to almost 12,000 square miles. In Malaysia, the area devoted to oil palm has increased 12-fold to 13,500 square miles,' says a report by Center of Science in Public Interest, a Washington-based advocacy organization.[33] The report also states that the demand for the oil is going to increase. Unhindered consumption has also resulted in man trying to explore minerals in deep sea. This affects the balance of the living beings present in the sea. The 2010 Deepwater Horizon oil spill, which resulted in the accidental release of 4.9 million barrels of crude oil to the sea, has been described as the 'worst environmental disaster the US has faced'.[34]

Invasive Species

A living organism not native to an ecosystem, that harms the indigenous organisms are considered invasive species. Many invasive species has a quick growth and reproduction rate, and aggressively competes with the native species for food and nutrients, resulting in the death of the native species. Water Hyacinth, a native of Brazil, is now in many countries, including India, and in the process has colonized water bodies. Invasive species need not necessarily be species from another country; they can be from within the country.

Climate Change, Pollution, and Contamination

One of the species significantly affected by climate change is fire corals. On contact with fire coral, one usually gets a burning sensation. It is believed that this coral is possibly extinct in India, though it is still found in Indonesia, Gulf of Chiriquí, Panama Pacific Province, etc. Impact of climate change on flora and fauna has been dealt with in various chapters of the textbook, including Chapter 3. Pollution and contamination has also affected the biodiversity. For example, the report 'Critically Endangered Animal Species of India,' released by Ministry of Environment and Forests, Government of India, in 2011, states that the population of three species of vultures: white-backed vulture (*Gyps africanus*), slender-billed vulture (*Gyps tenuirostris*), and long-billed vulture (*Gyps indicus*) has declined by 99%. The report states, 'A major threat to vultures is the painkiller diclofenac used by veterinarians to treat cattle. When vultures consume these carcasses, diclofenac enters their system, but they are unable to metabolize it. Accumulation of diclofenac results in gout-like symptoms such as neck-drooping, ultimately leading to death.'[36] Usage of the chemical DDT has caused significant harm to species in land, water, and air. Water pollution has resulted in the reduction of fish population, including fish-kill, which is caused by reduction of oxygen in water.

---

35 Photo by David Mark, copyright free image (released under CC0). Image Source: http://pixabay.com/en/mexico-city-soccer-football-field-92973/, last accessed on 6 August 2014.

36 http://www.moef.nic.in/downloads/public-information/critically_endangered_booklet.pdf, last accessed on 19 May 2013.

33 http://www.cspinet.org/new/pdf/palm_oil_final_5-27-05.pdf, last accessed on 28 May 2014.

34 http://www.bbc.co.uk/news/10194335, last accessed on 20 May 2013.

The Indian Agricultural Research Institute (IARI), New Delhi, has made the following predictions[37] with reference to the production of wheat and rice:

Wheat production

- About a 2°C in temperature reduced potential grain yields in most places.
- In sub-tropical environments the decrease in potential wheat yields ranged from 1.5 to 5.8 per cent, while in tropical areas, the decrease was relatively higher, suggesting that warmer regions can expect greater crop losses.

Rice production

- An increase of 2–4°C is predicted to result in a reduction in yields.
- Eastern regions are predicted to be most impacted by increased temperatures and decreased radiation, resulting in relatively fewer grains and shorter grain filling durations.
- By contrast, potential reductions in yields due to increased temperatures in Northern India are predicted to be offset by higher radiation, lessening the impacts of climate change.

CONSERVATION OF BIODIVERSITY

Conservation can be done in two ways—in-situ and ex-situ. In-situ conservation is on-site conservation while ex-situ conservation is off-site conservation. In-situ conservation refers to the conservation done in the species' natural ecosystems, like protection of wildlife habitats. Ex-situ conservation involves relocating an endangered species outside its natural habitat to a place where it can be regenerated, such as the creation of botanical gardens and zoological parks. There have also been native techniques aimed to conserve biodiversity. In the ancestral homes, a portion of the land was kept aside untouched and these patches of land gradually became micro-forests. According to Jahnavi G Pai and M Soubadra Dey, Ashoka Trust for Research in Ecology and Environment (ATREE), Bangalore, 'Traditional methods of agriculture maintained a wild patch within farming landscapes. Such existing patches can be declared as biodiversity heritage sites and farmers can be compensated for any loss that they might incur from non-availability of such land for cultivation.'[38]

Conservation Status of a Species and the IUCN Red List

International Union for Conservation of Nature (IUCN) has released a Red List of Threatened Species[39], the world's most comprehensive inventory on the conservation status of plant and animal species. The Red List aims to 'provide information and analyses on the status, trends, and threats to species in order to inform and catalyse action

---

37 http://agricoop.nic.in/Climatechange/ccr/india-climate-6-agriculture.pdf, last accessed on 6 August 2014.
38 Pai, Jahnavi G., M Soubadra Devi, 'Forgotten pollinators, forsaken food security', *The Hindu Survey of the Environment*, 2012.
39 http://www.iucnredlist.org, last accessed on 18 June 2013.

for biodiversity conservation'.[40] Conservation status of a group of organisms indicates the extent to which the population of the group is prevalent and the likelihood of the group becoming extinct. Species are classified into nine groups taking into consideration criteria such as rate of decline, population size, area of geographic distribution, and degree of population and distribution fragmentation. All the nine groups are listed in Table 8.6.

TABLE 8.6 Classification of species

Extinct (EX)—No known individuals remaining. It is proven beyond reasonable doubt, through exhaustive surveys over a time frame that failed to record a member of the species.	Extinct in the Wild (EW)— Known to be alive only in captivity, or as a naturalized population outside its historic range.	Critically Endangered (CR)— Extremely high risk of extinction in the wild.
Endangered (EN)—High risk of extinction in the wild.	Vulnerable (VU)—High risk of endangerment in the wild.	Near Threatened (NT)—Likely to become endangered in the near future.
Least Concern (LC)—Lowest risk. Does not qualify for a higher risk category. Widespread and abundant species are included in this category.	Data Deficient (DD)—Not enough data to make an assessment of its risk of extinction.	Not Evaluated (NE)—Has not yet been evaluated against any criteria.

IUCN has a network of more than 9000 experts from various fields who form part of the Species Survival Commission (SSC), which provide information to IUCN on biodiversity conservation, role of ecosystem services, and the role of species. This information helps in the formation of the IUCN Red List. The SSC also provides scientific inputs to various governmental and conservation organizations, and helps in supporting the implementation of multilateral environmental agreements. There are 130 specialist groups, Red List Authorities, and task groups.

Aichi Biodiversity Targets

As part of the 'Conference of the Parties' of the CBD, held in October 2010, in Nagoya, Japan, a strategic plan for biodiversity was adopted, and these were known as the Aichi Biodiversity Targets.[41]

Strategic goal A   Address the underlying causes of biodiversity loss by mainstreaming biodiversity across government and society

- Target 1: By 2020, at the latest, people should be aware of the values of biodiversity and the steps they can take to conserve and use it sustainably.
- Target 2: By 2020, at the latest, biodiversity values should be integrated into national and local development, poverty reduction strategies and planning processes, and should be incorporated into national accounting accordingly, and reporting systems.

---

40 http://www.iucnredlist.org/about/red-list-overview, last accessed on 18 June 2013.
41 http://www.cbd.int/sp/targets/, last accessed on 16 May 2013. Used with permission.

The 'Apollo Lunar Landing Legacy Act' is a bill filed in US Congress that aims to create a national park in the surface of the moon where Apollo lunar missions have landed. The bill aims to protect the spots where Apollo 11 through 17 missions landed, and also the artifacts the 12 astronauts who landed on the moon left behind.

- Target 3: By 2020, at the latest, incentives, including subsidies, that are harmful to biodiversity are eliminated, phased out, or reformed in order to minimize or avoid negative impacts, and positive incentives for the conservation and sustainable use of biodiversity are developed and applied, consistent, and in harmony with the convention and other relevant international obligations taking into account national socio economic conditions.
- Target 4: By 2020, at the latest, Governments, businesses, and stakeholders at all levels should be taking steps to achieve or implement plans for sustainable production and consumption, and keep the impacts of use of natural resources well within safe ecological limits.

Strategic goal B Reduce the direct pressures on biodiversity and promote sustainable use
- Target 5: By 2020, the rate of loss of all natural habitats, including forests, should be at least halved and wherever feasible brought close to zero, and degradation and fragmentation reduced significantly.
- Target 6: By 2020, all fish and invertebrate stocks and aquatic plants should be managed and harvested sustainably, legally, and by applying approaches based on the ecosystem , such that overfishing is avoided, recovery plans, and measures are in place for all depleted species, and therefore fisheries have no significant adverse impacts on threatened species and vulnerable ecosystems, and the impacts of fisheries on stocks, species, and ecosystems are within safe ecological limits.
- Target 7: By 2020, areas under agriculture, aquaculture, and forestry are managed sustainably, ensuring conservation of biodiversity.
- Target 8: By 2020, pollution, including from excess nutrients, is brought to levels that are not detrimental to ecosystem function and biodiversity.
- Target 9: By 2020, invasive alien species and pathways are identified and prioritized, priority species are controlled or eradicated, and measures are in place to manage pathways to prevent their introduction and establishment.
- Target 10: By 2015, the multiple anthropogenic pressures on coral reefs, and other vulnerable ecosystems impacted by climate change or ocean acidification are minimized, so as to maintain their integrity and functioning.

Strategic goal C To improve the status of biodiversity by safeguarding ecosystems, species, and genetic diversity
- Target 11: By 2020, at least 17 per cent of terrestrial and inland water, and 10 per cent of coastal and marine areas, especially areas of particular importance for biodiversity and ecosystem services, are conserved through effective and

equitably managed, ecologically representative, and well-connected systems of protected areas and other effective area-based conservation measures, and integrated into the wider landscapes and seascapes.

- Target 12: By 2020, the extinction of known threatened species is prevented and their conservation status, particularly of those most in decline, is improved and sustained.
- Target 13: By 2020, the genetic diversity of cultivated plants and farmed, and domesticated animals and of wild relatives, including other socio-economically as well as culturally valuable species, is maintained, and strategies developed and implemented for minimizing genetic erosion and safeguarding their genetic diversity.

Strategic goal D   Enhance the benefits to all from biodiversity and ecosystem services

- Target 14: By 2020, ecosystems that provide essential services, including services related to water, contribute to health, livelihoods, and well-being, are restored and safeguarded, taking into account the needs of women, indigenous and local communities, and the poor and vulnerable.
- Target 15: By 2020, ecosystem resilience and the contribution of biodiversity to carbon stocks is enhanced, through conservation and restoration, including restoration of at least 15 per cent of degraded ecosystems, thereby contributing to climate change mitigation and adaptation, and to combating desertification.
- Target 16: By 2015, the Nagoya Protocol on Access to Genetic Resources and the Fair and Equitable Sharing of Benefits Arising from their Utilization is in force and operational, consistent with national legislation.

Strategic goal E Enhance implementation through participatory planning, knowledge management, and capacity building

- Target 17: By 2015, each party should have developed, adopted a policy instrument, and commenced implementing an effective, participatory, and updated national biodiversity strategy and action plan.
- Target 18: By 2020, the traditional knowledge, innovations, and practices of indigenous and local communities relevant for the conservation and sustainable use of biodiversity, and their customary use of biological resources, are respected, subject to national legislation and relevant international obligations, fully integrated and reflected in the implementation of the convention with the full and effective participation of indigenous and local communities, at all relevant levels.
- Target 19: By 2020, knowledge, the science base, and technologies relating to biodiversity, its values, functioning, status and trends, and the consequences of its loss, are improved, widely shared and transferred, and applied.
- Target 20: By 2020, at the latest, the mobilization of financial resources for effectively implementing the Strategic Plan for Biodiversity 2011-2020 from all sources, and in accordance with the consolidated and agreed process in

the Strategy for Resource Mobilization, should increase substantially from the current levels. This target will be subject to changes contingent to resource need assessments to be developed and reported by parties.

Endangered and Endemic Species of India

As per the list released by Ministry of Environment and Forests, Government of India,[42] the following are classified as 'Critically Endangered' species of India:

Birds   Jerdon's Courser, Forest Owlet, White-bellied Heron, White-backed Vulture, Slender-billed Vulture, Long-billed Vulture, Red-headed Vulture, Bengal Florican, Himalayan Quail, Pink-headed Duck, Sociable Lapwing, Spoon Billed Sandpiper, and Siberian Crane.

Mammals   Pygmy Hog, Andaman White-toothed Shrew, Jenkin's Andaman Spiny Shrew, Nicobar White-tailed Shrew, Kondana Rat, Large Rock Rat or Elvira Rat, Namdapha Flying Squirrel, Malabar Civet, Sumatran Rhinoceros, and Javan Rhinoceros.

Reptiles   Gharial, Hawksbill Turtle, Leatherback Turtle, Four-toed River Terrapin or River Terrapin, Red-crowned Roofed Turtle or the Bengal Roof Turtle, and Sispara Day Gecko.

Amphibians   Anamalai Flying Frog, Gundia Indian Frog, Kerala Indian Frog, Charles Darwin's Frog, Kottigehar Bubble-nest Frog, Amboli Bush Frog, Chalazodes Bubble-Nest Frog, Small Bush Frog, Green-eyed Bush Frog, Griet Bush Frog, Kaikatt's Bush Frog, Mark's Bush Frog, Munnar Bush Frog, Large Ponmudi Bush Frog, Resplendent Shrub Frog, Sacred Grove Bush Frog, Sushil's Bush Frog, Shillong Bubble-nest Frog, and Tiger Toad.

Fish   Pondicherry Shark, Ganges Shark, Knife-tooth Sawfish, Large-tooth Sawfish, and Long-comb Sawfish or Narrow-snout Sawfish.

Spiders   Rameshwaram Ornamental or Rameshwaram Parachute Spider, Gooty Tarantula, and Metallic Tarantula or Peacock Tarantula.

In addition to these 'Critically Endangered' species, there are a number of species listed under the 'Endangered' category (see Fig. 8.6).

ECOSYSTEM MANAGEMENT

As per UNEP, ecosystems management is an approach to natural resource management that focuses on sustaining ecosystems to meet both ecological and human needs in the future.[43] The following are some other definitions of ecosystems management.

---

42 http://www.moef.nic.in/downloads/public-information/critically_endangered_booklet.pdf, last accessed on 19 May 2013.

43 http://www.unep.org/ecosystemmanagement/Introduction/tabid/293/language/en-US/Default.aspx, last accessed on 18 June 2014.

FIG. 8.6[44] Endangered species Nilgiri Tahr

Nilgiri Tahr is endemic to the Nilgiri Hills and the southern portion of the Western Ghats, India. It is an endangered species.

---

44 Photo by Sreeraj PS. Used with permission. 'Nilgiri Tahr Adult' by Sreeraj PS aka Ezhuttukari - Own work. LICENSED under Creative Commons Attribution-Share Alike 3.0 via Wikimedia Commons - https://commons.wikimedia.org/wiki/File:Nilgiri_Tahr_Adult.jpg#mediaviewer/File:Nilgiri_Tahr_Adult.jpg, last accessed on 11 February 2013.

- The careful and skilful use of ecological, economic, social, and managerial principles in managing ecosystems to produce, restore, or sustain ecosystem integrity and desired conditions, uses, products, values, and services over the long term.[45]
- To restore and maintain the health, sustainability, and biological diversity of ecosystems while supporting sustainable economies and communities.[46]
- The application of ecological and social information, options, and constraints to achieve desired social benefits within a defined geographic area and over a specified period.[47]

Forests and Woodlands

Forests are regions with a high density of trees. Woodlands are low-density forests and are characterized by an abundance of sunlight. Woodlands can also be transition phases/ zones between grasslands or deserts and forests. The Indian Forest Act of 1927 does not provide a definition to forests. As per the Supreme Court order dated 12.12.1996, the term 'Forest' encompasses the definition in the dictionary. As per Forest Survey of India (FSI), while 'Forest Cover' in India refers to all lands more than one hectare in area with a tree canopy density of more than 10 per cent, 'Forest Area' refers to all the geographic areas recorded as 'Forests' in government records. FSI's State of the Forest Report (SFR) 2011 states that 'Forest Area' denotes the legal status of the land, whereas 'Forest Cover' indicates the presence of trees on any land irrespective of their ownership.[48] Definition of forests, as per FSI, also includes plantations of eucalyptus, rubber, tea, and coffee, which, by their nature of mono-cropping, do not promote biodiversity. 'Forest Area' consists of 'Reserved Forests' and 'Protected Forests'. SFR 2013 has adopted the following forest classification system.[49]

- Very dense forests (VDF) are those lands with tree canopy density of 70 per cent and above.
- Moderately dense forests (MDF) are those lands with tree canopy density of 40 per cent and more but less than70 per cent.
- Open forests (OF) are those lands with tree canopy density of 10 per cent and more but less than 40 per cent.

45 Overbay, James C. 1992, *Ecosystem management, Proceedings of the national workshop: Taking an Ecological Approach to Management*, Department of Agriculture, US Forest Service, WO-WSA-3, Washington, DC, 1992, pp. 3-15.

46 United States Environmental Protection Agency 1994, *Integrated ecosystem protection research program: a conceptual plan*, Working Draft, 1994, pp. 89.

47 Lackey, Robert T. 1998, Seven pillars of ecosystem management, *Landscape and Urban Planning*, vol. 40(1/3), 1998, pp. 21-30.

48 http://fsi.org.in/cover_2011/chapter1.pdf, last accessed on 3 June 2014.

49 http://fsi.org.in/cover_2013/sfr_forest_cover.pdf, last accessed on 3 June 2014.

- Scrub (not considered as forests), are degraded forest lands with canopy density less than 10 per cent.

Areas not included in these four categories were referred to as non-forests. SFR 2013 states that VDF, MDF, and ODF cover 2.54 per cent, 9.70 per cent, 8.99 per cent of India's total land area, thereby constituting approximately 21.23per cent of India's total area, whilescrubs constituted 1.26 per cent of India's land area.

As per UNEP, forests cover one-third of the earth's land mass. Almost 1.6 billion people depend on forests for their livelihood. As per the definition given by Food and Agricultural Organization (FAO) of the United Nations, forest includes 'a minimum threshold for the height of trees (5 m), at least 10 per cent crown cover (canopy density determined by estimating the area of ground shaded by the crown of the trees) and a minimum forest area size (0.5 hectares)'.[50]Almost 30 per cent of the land area of the Earth is covered by forests (approximately 4 billion hectares).[51]

Forest Management and Wildlife Management

Forest management is a branch of forestry, and deals with the protection and regulation of forests. Forest management can be based on the need for conservation or economics, or a balance between these two needs. In 2012, Costa Rica, a country in the American continent, banned recreational hunting and abolished zoos. Costa Rica also started promoting responsible tourism (see Fig. 8.7). Managing forests according to the principles of sustainable development will result in sustainable forest management.

Though there are a number of forest classification systems, a uniform classification standard is yet to evolve. Table 8.7 indicates the classification as per WWF, which is also used by UNEP's World Conservation Monitoring Centre (WCMC)[52]. As per the WWF Eco-region analysis, there are 14 biomes and 825 eco-regions that reflect the vegetation cover as it would have been 500 years earlier. Further, these biomes are classified on whether they are forests or not.

Wildlife management tries to find the balance between the needs of the wildlife and the needs of people. Conservation of wildlife is an important aspect of wildlife management and aims to halt the loss in biodiversity. Wildlife management also involves the process of keeping wild species at desirable and optimum levels, as determined by wildlife administrators. Wildlife management can be classified into

---

50 http://www.grida.no/_res/site/file/publications/vital_forest_graphics.pdf, last accessed on 26 June 2013.
51 http://www.grida.no/_res/site/file/publications/vital_forest_graphics.pdf, last accessed on 26 June 2013.
52 Global Ecological Forest Classification and Forest Protected Area Gap Analysis 2009, http://ia600505. us.archive.org/8/items/globalecological08schm/globalecological08schm.pdf, last accessed on 14 May 2014.

FIG. 8.7 [53] Arenal Volcano National Park, Costa Rica

Costa Rica plans to become the first carbon-neutral country by 2021. The New Economics Foundation (NEF), a London based research foundation, ranked Costa Rica top most in its 2009 Happy Planet Index, and again in 2012. The NEF also ranked Costa Rica in 2009 as the greenest country in the world. Costa Rica also does not have an army.

TABLE 8.7 Types of forests as per WWF Eco-region analysis

Biome name	Number of eco-regions	Forest
Tropical and subtropical moist broadleaf forest	231	Yes
Tropical and subtropical dry broadleaf forests	54	Yes
Tropical and subtropical coniferous forests	17	Yes
Temperate broadleaf and mixed forests	84	Yes
Temperate coniferous forest	53	Yes
Boreal forests/Taiga	28	Yes
Mediterranean forests, woodlands, and shrub	39	Yes

(Contd)

53 Photo by Ben Haeringer, used with permission. Image Source: https://www.flickr.com/photos/benhaeringer/5679161858, last accessed on 4 August 2014.

Mangroves	19	Yes
Tropical and subtropical grasslands, savannas, and shrublands	49	No
Temperate grasslands, savannas, and shrublands	43	No
Flooded grasslands and savannas	25	No
Montane grasslands and shrublands	50	No
Tundra	37	No
Desert and Xeric shrublands	96	No

segments—manipulative management and custodial management. Manipulative management of wildlife includes acting on a species population to increase or decrease its numbers by direct means or through indirect means like altering the food supply for the population, changing the habitat, changing the predator population, and disease control. These could be done when the population of a species moves to extreme levels—high or low. Custodial management is primarily done when the population of species is reduced to negligible levels, which has to be prevented or protected from external influences.

Project Tiger is one of the popular examples of wildlife management endeavours undertaken by Government of India. A century ago India had several thousands of tigers. However, the first tiger census conducted in 1972 found that the population of tigers dwindled to approximately 1,800, driven by hunting of the animal. The tiger census conducted in 2006, based on a new methodology, estimated the tiger population in India to be only 1,411. As part of the 'Project Tiger' plan, tiger reserves were created and each reserve designed wildlife management plans based on certain principles such as (a) removal of human interference and biotic disturbance from the core area of the tiger reserves, (b) rationalization of activities in the buffer zone of the reserve, and (c) facilitating recovery of the ecosystem to its natural state.

Rainforests, Deforestation, and Afforestation

Rainforests are forest regions receiving high amount of rainfall with a minimum amount of rainfall of 1750–2000 mm (68–78 inches) (See Fig 8.8). It has been observed that rainforests have four layers—(a) forest floor, (b) understory layer, which have plants with large leaves, so that they can capture whatever little sunlight that falls down to this region, (c) canopy layer, the primary layer of the forest that casts a shadow on the forest floor and understory layer, and is characterized by leaves and branches, and (d) emergent layer, created by the upper portion of the tallest evergreen trees.

The process of growing a forest or a thick patch of trees in an area where there was no prior forest is considered to be afforestation. Reforestation, in contrast, refers to the creation of a forest where there was prior existence of a forest cover. This could happen naturally or through artificial means. Deforestation has also been explained in Chapter 4.

FIG. 8.8[54] Gambia river flowing through Senegal's Niokolo-Koba National Park
This national park is listed among the UNESCO list of World Heritage in Danger. Developed countries subsidize over-fishing to the account of almost $35 billion on an annual basis, through fossil fuel subsidies and vessel buybacks. This amount could be channelized to protect more land and oceans.

Wetlands and Mangroves

Wetlands are ecosystems characterized by saturation of water on a land area. Swamps, marshes, and mangroves are a few of the wetland categories. The vegetation and soil at the wetlands store water, filter sediments, and removes pollutants from fresh water supplies. The wetlands stabilize the shorelines by reducing erosion and storm surges associated with rising sea levels.[55] Coastal wetlands in forested ecosystems are known for reducing storm surges and wind energy during cyclones/hurricanes/storms. This helps in reducing damage to life and property. Degradation of these coastal wetlands reduces the capacity of wetlands to provide these ecosystem services. This results in an increase in the risk of living and working in coastal landscapes.[56] In the 1990s, in Thailand,

---

54 Image source: https://commons.wikimedia.org/wiki/File:River_gambia_Niokolokoba_National_Park.gif, last accessed on 4 August 2014. Image available in the public domain.

55 Daily, G.C., P.A. Matson, and P.M. Vitousek 1997. Ecosystem services supplied by soil, *Nature's Services: Societal Dependence on Natural Ecosystems*, G.C. Daily (ed.), Island Press, Washington, DC.; Mitsch, W.J. and J.G. Gosselink 2000. Wetlands, John Wiley and Sons, New York, NY.

56 Twilley, Robert R., Coastal Wetlands and Global climate change: Gulf Coast Wetland Sustainability in a Changing Climate, December 2007;http://www.c2es.org/docUploads/Regional-Impacts-Gulf.pdf, last accessed on 19 December 2011.

The total ecosystem service values of the wetlands in India, including the rain-fed paddy area, comes to ₹ 124 lakh crores.

a number of coastal mangrove swamps were converted to shrimp farms. With no mangroves to cushion the storm surges, the country faced billions of dollars' worth of damage during the ocean storm surges of 2011. Wetlands also act as life support systems for many species. In rural regions, wetlands sustained water levels in the ponds and tanks used for drinking. V S Vijayan, Former Chairman, Kerala State Biodiversity Board, and Founder-Trustee, Salim Ali Foundation, says, '...wetlands have become the first casualty for every so called "development" project, from bus stands, shopping malls, IT industries, commercial flats, villas, convention halls, and even liquor shops and funeral grounds.'[57]

The following are the reasons for the loss of wetlands.

    a. Encroachment of wetlands for 'development' projects including commercial building complexes, educational institutions, and industrial units

    b. Usage of wetlands for dumping of waste and sewage

    c. Conversion of wetlands for commercial farming and cash-crops

    d. Run-off of water loaded with pesticides, fertilizers, and industrial effluents, into wetlands

Vijayan continues, 'The recent assessment of The Economics of Ecosystems and Biodiversity (TEEB) 2010 considering 22 ecosystem services, estimates the annual average wetland values at ₹ 22,24,350/ha, which makes the ecosystem service values for the entire wetlands in the country (105,64,899 ha), around ₹ 23 lakh crores, annually; almost one-and-a-half times more than the total expenditure in Union Budget for 2012–2013. If the monetary values of the ecosystem services of coral reefs and coastal wetlands are also taken together, the total annual estimated value of the Indian wetlands would come to ₹ 75.04 lakh crores; more than five times that of the Union budget for 2012–13 (₹ 14,90,925 crore) and, eight times more than the revenue receipt—₹ 9,35,685 crores! Since the rain-fed paddy ecosystem is also considered as wetlands, the ecosystem service values of the same come to ₹ 49 lakh crores (considering the rain-fed paddy area to be approximately 22 million ha). Therefore, the total ecosystem service values of the wetlands in India, including the rain-fed paddy area comes to ₹ 124 lakh crores (to put this in perspective, India's nominal GDP would be approximately 100 lakh crores). It is pertinent to note that this wealth, that too annual wealth, is coming from just 4.6% of our land area. It is further to be noted that this estimate is not made for the Indian wetlands, but is an estimate from the studies conducted on various wetlands in the world and it is only an average value. However, since our wetlands are much more complex, the values will be many times more, and certainly will not be less.'[58]

---

57 Vijayan, V.S. Turning wetlands into badlands, The Hindu, Survey of the Environment 2012, 2012.
58 Vijayan, V.S. Turning wetlands into badlands, The Hindu, Survey of the Environment 2012, 2012.

Wildlife and its Protection

The practice of protecting endangered flora and fauna and the natural habitats to which these species belong to are referred to as wildlife conservation. As per International Union for Conservation of Nature (IUCN), 'a protected area is a clearly defined geographical space, recognized, dedicated, and managed, through legal or other effective means, to achieve the long-term conservation of nature with associated ecosystem services and cultural values'.[59] As per IUCN, protected areas could fall under categories like national parks, wilderness areas, community conserved areas, nature reserves, and so on. As per IUCN, the following are the six categories for protected areas.[60]

Ia: Strict Nature Reserve

Strict nature reserves are protected from all except for light human use in order to preserve complete geology and geomorphic features of the region and their biodiversity, which is often dense and restricted exclusively for scientific monitoring, study, or education. Being in such preserved environments, strict nature reserves can be used as an indicator of external human influence, which can be increasingly difficult to guard against as climate and air pollution can potentially penetrate protected boundary areas. Occasionally strict nature reserves are of spiritual significance to surrounding communities in which case the people are generally allowed to continue the practice of their faith and may be directly involved in the area's conservation and management objectives, though perpetual human intervention would more suitably be allocated to categories IV or V.

Ib: Wilderness Area

Generally larger than strict nature reserves, the main objectives of these areas is to provide an environment in which biodiversity and ecosystem processes (including evolution) are allowed to flourish or experience restoration if it was disturbed by human activity earlier. Human use is limited, often allowing only those who are willing to travel of their own accord rather than via established touristic activities. Wilderness areas can be classified as such only if they are devoid of modern infrastructure, although they allow human activity to the level of sustaining indigenous groups living wilderness-based lifestyles.

II: National Park

Similar to the objectives of wilderness areas, national parks provide protection for functioning ecosystems, but tend to be more lenient with human visitation and the supporting infrastructure. National parks are managed in a way that may contribute to local economies by promoting educational and recreational tourism at a scale that will not reduce the effectiveness of conservation efforts. The surrounding areas of a national

---

59 http://cms.iucn.org/about/work/programmes/gpap_home/pas_gpap/, last accessed on 14 July 2013.
60 UNEP-WCMC, http://www.unep-wcmc.org/iucn-protected-area-management-categories_591.html, last accessed on 14 July 2013. Used with permission.

park may be for consumptive or non-consumptive use, but should nevertheless act as a barrier for the defence of the protected area's native species and communities to enable them to remain sustainable in the long term.

III: Natural Monument or Feature

These are comparatively smaller areas that are specifically allocated to protect a natural monument and its surrounding habitats. Natural monuments or features can be natural in totality, or include elements that have been influenced or introduced by humans. The latter should hold biodiversity associations or could otherwise be classified as a historical or spiritual site, though this distinction can be quite difficult to ascertain. The classification then falls into two subcategories, those in which the biodiversity in uniquely related to the conditions of the natural feature, and those in which the current levels of biodiversity are dependent on the presence of the sacred sites that have created an essentially modified ecosystem. Natural monuments or features have a high cultural or spiritual value which can be utilized to gain support for conservation challenges.

VI: Habitat/Species Management Area

Habitat/species management areas focus on more specific areas of conservation in correlation to an identifiable species or habitat that requires continuous protection. These protected areas will be sufficiently controlled to ensure the maintenance, conservation, and restoration of particular species and habitats—possibly through traditional means—and public education of such areas is widely encouraged as part of the management objectives. Habitat or species management areas may exist as a fraction of a wider ecosystem or protected area and may require varying levels of active intervention including—but not limited to—the prevention of poaching, creation of artificial habitats, halting natural succession, and supplementary feeding practices.

V: Protected Landscape/Seascape

Protected landscapes and seascapes cover entire bodies of land or ocean which engages a range of for-profit activities within the management plan. The main objective is to safeguard regions that have built up a 'distinct character' in regards to their ecological, biological, cultural, or scenic value. Protected landscapes and seascapes allow a higher level of sustainable interaction with surrounding communities (such as traditional agricultural and forestry systems) and should represent an integral balance between people and nature. Protected landscapes and seascapes are one of the more flexible categories and may be able to accommodate contemporary developments like ecotourism whilst maintaining historical agro-biodiversity and aquatic biodiversity management practices.

VI: Protected Area with Sustainable Use of Natural Resources

Category VI is a more encompassing classification that is based on a mutually beneficial relationship between nature conservation and the sustainable management of natural resources in accordance with the livelihoods of surrounding communities. A wide range of socio-economic factors are taken into consideration in creating local, regional, and national approaches to the use of natural resources. Though human involvement is a large factor in the management of these protected areas, developments are not allowed for wide-scale industrial production. These areas would be particularly suitable to vast areas that already have a low level of human occupation that has had little or no negative impact on the environmental health of the region, as a proportion of the land mass is expected to remain in its natural condition—a regulation to be enforced on a national level, and usually with specificity to each protected area. Governance has to be developed to adapt to the diverse and possibly growing range of interests that arise from the production of sustainable natural resources.

In India, protection of biodiversity is carried through protected areas such as Tiger Reserves, Biosphere Reserves, Elephant Reserves, Ramsar Wetland sites, and World Heritage sites. These are referred to as the 'Conservation Areas' of India, as per the Wildlife Institute of India. The protected areas of India include its national parks, wildlife sanctuaries, conservation reserves, and community reserves (see Table 8.9).

TABLE 8.9[61] Number of protected areas of India

	Number	Area	% of geographical area
National Parks (NPs)	102	40075 km²	1.22 %
Wildlife Sanctuaries (WLSs)	528	125295.30 km²	3.81%
Conservation Reserves (CRs)	57	2017.94km²	0.06 %
Community Reserves	4	20.69 km²	0.0 %
Protected Areas (PAs)	**691**	**167408.29 km²**	**5.09 %**

In addition to officials involved in wildlife protection, the help of locals are also taken into account during the process of wildlife conservation. For example, in Kenya, a lion protection program named 'Lion Guardians' took the help of Ilmurran, who are the traditional warriors of the region, to convince members of their communities not to kill lions who were harmed by the community members in retaliation to the lions killing the livestock belonging to the community.[62]

The following are some of the non-governmental organizations (NGOs) and research institutions engaged in wildlife conservation and research.

61 http://wiienvis.nic.in/Database/Protected_Area_854.aspx, last accessed on 4 December 2014.

62 Hazzah, Leela, Stephanie Dolrenry, Lisa Naughton, Charles T.T.Edwards, Ogeto Mwebi, Fiachra Kearney, Laurence Frank, Efficacy of Two Lion Conservation Programs in Maasailand, Kenya, Conservation Biology, 2014; http://onlinelibrary.wiley.com/doi/10.1111/cobi.12244/abstract, last accessed on 19 February 2014.

Bombay Natural History Society (http://bnhs.org)

Greenpeace India (http://www.greenpeace.org/india/en)

Wildlife First (http://www.wildlifefirst.info)

Wildlife Protection Society of India (WPSI, http://www.wpsi-india.org)

World Wide Fund for Nature-India (WWF, http://www.wwfindia.org)

The following are some of the conservation research institutions.

Ashoka Trust for Research in Ecology and Environment (ATREE, http://www .atree.org/)

Wildlife Trust of India (WTI, http://www.wti.org.in)

Nature Conservation Foundation (NCF, http://www.ncf-india.org)

Institutions that offer programs in conservation include the Wildlife Institute of India (WII, http://www.wii.gov.in) and the National Centre for Biological Sciences (NCBS, http://www.ncbs.res.in/).

Wildlife Conservation in India

India has 102 national parks, 520 wildlife sanctuaries, 57 conservation reserves, and four community reserves. About 5.02% of India's geographical area is considered to be protected areas.[63] The country also has six world heritage sites (under natural properties category), these are listed in Table 8.10.[64]

TABLE 8.10 List of India's world heritage sites under natural properties category

Name of world heritage site	State location	Area (hectares)
Kaziranaga National Park	Assam	42,996
Keoladeo National Park	Rajasthan	2,873
Manas Wildlife Sanctuary	Assam	39,100
Nanda Devi and Valley of Flowers National Park	Uttarakhand	71,783
Sundarbans National Park	West Bengal	133,010
Western Ghats	Maharashtra, Goa, Karnataka, Tamil Nadu, and Kerala	795,315
Great Himalayan National Park Conservation Area	Himachal Pradesh	90,540

Project Tiger, aimed at conserving the population of Bengal Tigers and its natural habitat, is administered by the National Tiger Conservation Authority. Starting with nine reserves in 1973-74, the number of tiger reserves has by now risen to 41. The following is the list of tiger reserves in India (see Table 8.11)[65]

63 http://wiienvis.nic.in/Database/Protected_Area_854.aspx, last accessed on 8 July 2013.
64 http://whc.unesco.org/en/list, last accessed on 10 July 2013.
65 http://wiienvis.nic.in/Database/Tiger_Reserve_Database_7850.aspx, Accessed on July 11, 2013.

TABLE 8.11 List of tiger reserves in India

Name of Project Tiger reserve	State	Total area (sq. km)
Achanakmar	Chattisgarh	914
Anamalai	Tamil Nadu	1480
Bandhavgarh	Madhya Pradesh	1598
Bandipur	Karnataka	1456
Bhadra	Karnataka	1064
Biligiri Ranganatha Temple	Karnataka	575
Buxa	West Bengal	758
Corbett	Uttarakhand	1288
Dampa	Mizoram	988
Dandeli-Anshi	Karnataka	1098
Dudhwa	Uttar Pradesh	2202
Indravati	Chhattishgarh	2799
Kalakad-Mundanthurai	Tamil Nadu	1602
Kanha	Madhya Pradesh	2052
Kawal	Telengana	2019
Kaziranga	Assam	1174
Manas	Assam	3151
Melghat	Maharashtra	2769
Mudumalai	Tamil Nadu	689
Nagarahole	Karnataka	1206
Nagarjunsagar Srisailam	Andhra Pradesh and Telengana	5908
Namdapha	Arunachal Pradesh	2053
Nameri	Assam	344
Pakke	Arunachal Pradesh	1198
Palamau	Jharkhand	1130
Panna	Madhya Pradesh	1579
Parambikulam	Kerala	644
Pench	Maharashtra	741
Pench	Madhya Pradesh	1180
Periyar	Kerala	925
Ranthambhore	Rajasthan	1411
Sahyadri	Maharashtra	1166
Sanjay-Dubri	Madhya Pradesh	1675
Satkosia	Odisha	964
Satpura	Madhya Pradesh	2133

(Contd)

Sariska	Rajasthan	1213
Similipal	Odisha	2750
Sunderbans	West Bengal	2585
Tadoba-Andhari	Maharashtra	1728
Udanti-Sitanadi	Chattisgarh	1843
Valmiki	Bihar	899
Total Area (sq. km)		**63879**

Project Elephant provides financial and technical support to states for management of wild Asian Elephants. The following is the list of elephant reserves (see Table 8.12).

TABLE 8.12 List of elephant reserves

Elephant range	Elephant reserve
East-Central Landscape (South-West Bengal-Jharkhand-Odisha)	Mayurjharna, Singhbhum, Mayurbhanj, Mahanadi, Sambalpur, Baitami, South Orissa, Lemru,and Badalkhol - Tamorpingla
Kameng-Sonitpur Landscape (Arunachal - Assam)	Kameng and Sonitpur
Eastern-South Bank Landscape (Assam-Arunachal)	Dihing-Patkai and South Arunachal
Kaziranga-Karbi Anglong-Intanki Landscape (Assam-Nagaland)	Kaziranga-Karbi Anglong, Dhansiri-Lungding, and Intanki
North Bengal - Greater Manas Landscape (Assam - West Bengal)	Chirang-Ripu and Eastern Dooars
Meghalaya Landscape (Meghalaya)	Garo Hills and Khasi-hills
Brahmagiri-Nilgiri-Eastern Ghat Landscape (Karnataka-Kerala-Tamilnadu-Andhra)	Mysore, Wayanad, Nilgiri, Rayala, Nilambur, and Coimbatore
Anamalai-Nelliampathy-High Range Landscape (Tamilnadu-Kerala)	Anamalai and Anamudi
Periyar-Agasthyamalai Landscape (Kerala-Tamilnadu)	Periyar and Srivilliputhur
North-Western Landscape (Uttarakhand-Uttar Pradesh)	Shivalik and Uttar Pradesh

As part of the Man and the Biosphere Programme (MAB), UNESCO established the World Network of Biosphere Reserves. Biosphere Reserves aims to achieve conservation, development, and logistic support. As per UNESCO, one of the characteristic of a Biosphere Reserve is 'Outpacing traditional confined conservation zones, through appropriate zoning schemes combining core protected areas with zones where sustainable development is fostered by local dwellers and enterprises with often highly innovative and participative governance systems.'[66] The following are the Biosphere Reserves listed in India (see Table 8.13):

---

66 http://www.unesco.org/new/en/natural-sciences/environment/ecological-sciences/biosphere-reserves/main-characteristics/, last accessed on 11 July 2013.

TABLE 8.13 List of biosphere reserves in India

Biosphere reserve	Area (sq. km)	State
Achanakmar-Amarkantak	3835.51 (Core 551.55; Buffer 3283.86)	Madhya Pradesh and Chhattisgarh
Agasthyamalai(Refer Fig. 8.9)	1828	Kerala
Cold Desert	7770	Himachal Pradesh
Dehang – Dibang	5111.50	Arunachal Pradesh
Dibru Saikhowa	765 (Core 340; Buffer 425)	Assam
Great Nicobar	885 (Core 705; Buffer 180)	Andaman and Nicobar
Gulf of Mannar	10,500	Tamilnadu
Kachchh	12,454	Gujarat
Khangchendzonga	2619.92	Sikkim
Manas	2837	Assam
Nanda Devi	5860.69	Uttarakhand
Nilgiri	5520	Tamilnadu, Kerala, and Karnataka
Nokrek	820	Meghalaya
Pachmarhi	4926	Madhya Pradesh
Seshachalam Hills	4755.997	Andhra Pradesh
Simlipal	4374	Orissa
Sunderbans	9630	West Bengal
Panna	2998.98	Madhya Pradesh

Wasteland Reclamation

Due to the increasing use and abuse of land resources, land may become unsuitable for any productive purposes. Wasteland could be classified as (a) barren and uncultivable wasteland and (b) cultivable wasteland. Wasteland could be reclaimed in a number of ways. For example, in eight villages in the district of Sirsa in Haryana, farmers were planting trees such as Jund, Eucalyptus, Sheesham, Beri, Dates, and other cash crops to convert a wasteland. This wasteland restoration project was also the first project in India to be approved under Clean Development Mechanism (CDM). In addition to planting of trees, other methods used for wasteland reclamation include construction of water channels/bunds etc., for proper management of water resources in these areas.

PEOPLE'S BIODIVERSITY REGISTER

It was in 1995 that People's Biodiversity Register (PBR) was initiated by the Foundation for the Revitalization of Local Health Traditions (FRLHT), Bangalore. As part of the Biodiversity Conservation Prioritization programme, Indian Institute of Science (IISc) coordinated the activities of PBR at 52 sites, located in eight states of India. The objective

FIG. 8.9[67] Ottakkal Lookout, Agasthyamalai Biosphere Reserve, Kerala

of PBR was to create a grass-root level information system on biodiversity resources. The register was also meant to document and support claims of local communities and individuals about their knowledge on biodiversity resources and their use. The Biological Diversity Act of 2002 stipulated the setting up of a Biodiversity Management Committee (BMC) by every local body. The act states that 'The main function of the BMC is to prepare People's Biodiversity Register in consultation with local people. The Register shall contain comprehensive information on the availability and knowledge of local biological resources, their medicinal use, or any other use.'[68]

The following are the processes in PBR publication, as per the revised 2013 guidelines issued by National Biodiversity Authority.[69]

---

67 'Ottackal look out' Original uploader was Akhilan at ml.wikipedia-Transferred from ml.wikipedia, transfer was stated to be made by User:Akhilan. Licensed under Public domain via Wikimedia Commons - https://commons.wikimedia.org/wiki/File:Ottackal_look_out.jpg#mediaviewer/File:Ottackal_look_out.jpg, last accessed on 7 August 2014.
68 http://nbaindia.org/uploaded/Model_PBR.pdf, last accessed on 18 June 2014.
69 http://nbaindia.org/uploaded/Model_PBR.pdf, last accessed on 18 June 2014.

- Formation of Biodiversity Management Committee (BMC)
- Sensitization of the public about the study, survey, and possible management
- Training of members in identification and collection of data on biological resources and traditional knowledge
- Collection of data—Data collections includes review of literature on the natural resources of the districts, Participatory Rural Appraisal (PRAs) at village level, household interviews, individual interviews with village leaders and knowledgeable individuals, household heads, key actors of the panchayat raj institutions, NGOs, and direct field observations
- Analysis and validation of data in consultation with technical support group and BMC
- Preparation of People's Biodiversity Register (PBR)
- Computerization of information and resources

The process of creating PBRs has been initiated all over India. Table 8.14 indicates the number of PBRs documented across India, as of May 2014.[70]

TABLE 8.14 Number of PBRs documented in India

State	Number of PBRs documented
Andhra Pradesh	17
Arunachal Pradesh	-
Gujarat	81
Himachal Pradesh	-
Jharkhand	11
Karnataka	267
Kerala	596
Madhya Pradesh	741
Manipur	3
Mizoram	2
Tripura	60
Uttar Pradesh	6
Uttarakhand	13
West Bengal	66

---

70 http://nbaindia.org/content/105/30//pbr.html, last accessed on 18 June 2014.

CHAPTER SUMMARY

- Biodiversity is defined as the variability among living organisms from all sources and the ecological complexes of which they are part.
- Biological variety has typically been identified at three levels – genetic diversity, species diversity, and ecosystem diversity. Genetic diversity is all the different genes contained in all the living species, including individual plants, animals, fungi, and microorganisms. Species diversity is all the different species, as well as the differences within and between different species. Ecosystem diversity is all the different habitats, biological communities, and ecological processes, as well as variations within individual ecosystems.
- The value of biodiversity can be put in two different perspectives–anthropocentric perspective and intrinsic perspective. Anthropocentric perspective is based on the idea of how biodiversity is valuable to human beings, while intrinsic perspective is based on respect and reverence of life, and not from the perspective of whether it is valuable to human beings or not.
- A biodiversity hotspot is a region, while being ecologically diverse, is also facing significant threat of habitat loss, climate loss, and species loss.
- Some of the threats to biodiversity include (a) Habitat loss and destruction, (b) Poaching of wildlife and man-wildlife conflicts, (c) Exploitation of natural resources, (d) Invasive species, and (e) Other factors such as climate change, pollution and contamination.
- As per United Nations Environment Programme, deforestation continues at the rate of 13 million hectares of forest on an annual basis. This is roughly equal to the size of Portugal or Greece or the state of Tamilnadu or Chhattisgarh in India. This is also equivalent to the destruction of a land area equivalent to a football field, every second of the day.
- In-situ conservation refers to the conservation done in the species' natural ecosystems, such as protection of wildlife habitats. Ex-situ conservation involves relocating an endangered species outside its natural habitat to a place where it can be regenerated, such as the creation of botanical gardens and safari parks.
- As per the IUCN Red List, species are classified into nine groups—extinct (EX), extinct in the wild (EW), critically endangered (CR), endangered (EN), vulnerable (VU), near threatened (NT), least concern (LC), data deficient (DD), and not evaluated (NE).
- Rainforests are forest regions receiving high amount of rainfall, and are observed to have four layers —(a) Forest floor, (b) Understory layer, (c) Canopy layer, and (d) Emergent layer.
- The process of growing a forest or a thick patch of trees in an area where there was no prior forest is considered to be afforestation. Reforestation, in contrast, refers to the creation of a forest where there was prior existence of a forest cover.
- The total ecosystem service values of the wetlands in India, including the rain-fed paddy area, totals to ₹124 lakh crores. To put this in perspective, India's nominal GDP would be approximately 100 lakh crores.

KEYWORDS

- Aesthetic values
- Aichi Biodiversity Target
- Biodiversity
- Biodiversity hotspot
- Consumptive use value
- Economic value of pollination
- Ecosystem diversity
- Environment service values
- Endangered species
- Ethical values
- Ex-situ conservation
- Forest management
- Genetic diversity
- Green deserts
- Habitat loss and destruction
- Invasive species

- In-situ conservation
- IUCN Red List
- Mangroves
- Monoculture plantations
- Option values
- Productive use value
- Poaching
- Project elephant
- Project Tiger
- Species diversity
- Value of biodiversity
- Wildlife trafficking
- Wildlife management
- Wetlands
- Wasteland reclamation

EXERCISES

Multiple-choice Questions

1. _____ refers to all the different genes contained in all the living species, including individual plants, animals, fungi, and microorganisms.
   (a) Genetic diversity
   (b) Species diversity
   (c) Ecosystem diversity
   (d) Biodiversity

2. _____ perspective is based on the idea of how biodiversity is valuable to human beings.
   (a) Anthropocentric
   (b) Intrinsic
   (c) Bio-centric
   (d) None of the these

3. A _____ is a region, while being ecologically diverse, is also facing significant threat of habitat loss, climate loss, and species loss.

   (a) habitat
   (b) biodiversity hotspot
   (c) ecosystem diversity
   (d) genetic diversity

4. A living organism not native to an ecosystem and harms the indigenous organisms are considered _____
   (a) invasive species
   (b) endangered species
   (c) parasite
   (d) vulnerable species

5. _____ is a branch of forestry, and deals with the protection and regulation of forests.
   (a) Forest management
   (b) Wildlife management
   (c) Biodiversity management
   (d) Ecosystem management

6. The process of growing a forest or a thick patch of trees in an area where there was no prior forest is considered to be _____
   (a) reforestation
   (b) afforestation
   (c) deforestation
   (d) habitation

7. _____ refers to the creation of a forest where there was prior existence of a forest cover.
   (a) Reforestation
   (b) Afforestation
   (c) Deforestation
   (d) Habitation

8. _____ are regions with a high density of trees.
   (a) Forests
   (b) Woodlands
   (c) Wilderness area
   (d) Habitat

9. _____ are low-density forests.
   (a) Forests
   (b) Woodlands
   (c) Wilderness area
   (d) Habitat

10. _____ focus on more specific areas of conservation in correlation to an identifiable species or habitat that requires continuous protection.
   (a) Protected landscapes and seascapes
   (b) Habitat/species management areas
   (c) Natural monuments or features
   (d) Biodiversity management

Short Answer Questions

1. Explain levels of biological variety.
2. What is a hotspot region?
3. What are the types of conservation?
4. List some critically endangered animals in India.
5. What is forest management?
6. What is wildlife management and explain its significance?
7. What are the levels of a rainforest?
8. What is the difference between forests and wetlands?
9. What are the six categories of protected areas?
10. List out some of the non-governmental organizations (NGOs) and research institutions engaged in wildlife conservation.
11. What is wasteland reclamation?
12. What are the kinds of wasteland reclamation?
13. What are the nine groups of threatened species released by IUCN?

Long Answer Questions

1. Explain different threats to biodiversity. Amongst the various threats, which threat do you consider to be the most significant threat for India in the next 50 years, and why do you think so?

2. As per IUCN, what are the six categories for protected areas?

Reflective Question

1. You must have heard that many rivers are drying up.
   a) List out the reasons on why the rivers are dying.
   b) How have you contributed to that process directly or indirectly?
   c) What can you do to ensure that you do not contribute to such a process?
   d) What can you do to ensure the well-being of a river and its living beings?

2. List down activities that you would like your Panchayat/MLA/MP should take up to promote eco-friendliness in the society? How can you contribute to those activities?

Take-home Activities

1. List out NGOs and research institutions, that are located within a 50 kilometre radius of your locality, and is engaged in activities related to conservation, environmental management etc. Volunteer at least 50 hours with one of those NGOs or research institutions.
2. Assume that the government authorities have asked you to redesign your city/town/village. While reflecting on this, you tried to bring in a stakeholder perspective. You started thinking from the perspectives of myriad life forms.

What additional facilities would you bring to your city/town/village, if you were redesigning your city/town/village from the perspective of:
- A 10-year-old child
- A blind man
- An old lady
- A squirrel
- A sparrow
- An elephant
- A banyan tree

Web Reading

1. Magazines that write and report on ecology, nature, and environment:
   (a) Sanctuary Magazine, http://www.sanctuaryasia.com
   (b) Down to Earth Magazine, http://www.downtoearth.org.in
   (c) National Geographic Magazine, http://ngm.nationalgeographic.com

Recommended Book

1. Bill McKibben, Eaarth: Making a Life on a Tough New Planet, Henry Holt and Company, 2010.

Recommended Documentaries/Movies

1. *GREEN: a film.* Dir. Patrick Rouxel. Green Planet Films, 2009 (This documentary is available for free viewing at http://www.greenthefilm.com/ and http://www.youtube.com/watch?v=-WNgoqBGw4Y). Duration: 47 minutes.
2. How your T-shirt can make a difference (This documentary is available for free viewing at https://www.youtube.com/watch?v=xEExMcjSkwA). Duration: 2 minutes.
3. Knowing how to Nurture Ourselves (This documentary is available for free viewing at http://www.globalonenessproject.org/library/films/knowing-how-nurture-ourselves and https://www.youtube.com/watch?v=I9wllerqtEQ). Duration: 4 minutes.
4. Millet Madness (This clipping is available for free viewing at https://www.youtube.com/watch?v=LojLTEWTXN0). Duration: 5 minutes.

Answers to Mutiple-choice Questions:
  1(a)   2(a)   3(b)   4(a)   5(a)   6(b)   7(a)   8(a)   9(b)   10(b)

9

ENVIRONMENTAL ETHICS

After reading the chapter, the reader will be able to understand the following:

- The way ecocentrism focuses on the inherent and intrinsic value of all species
- International environmental legal instruments such as Earth Charter, Akwé: Kon voluntary guidelines, and the Tkarihwaié:ri code of ethical conduct
- Emergence of ethical consumerism, sustainability-based shareholder resolutions, and Locavorism
- Different methods and techniques through which citizens can contribute to the care and protection of planet Earth

There is a great lesson I've learned from nature, from the birds, the insects, from the ecosystems: The awareness that everything has a reason to exist in nature, nothing is redundant; nothing is insignificant. A spider is as important as a dragonfly, an insect, a bird, a mammal, or a huge tree. Perhaps a tiny plant has a specific and important function that makes it important as a giant tree. This is the awareness that everything has its purpose and nothing is insignificant because everything has its own value.

Juan Manuel Carrion
Biologist and ornithologist, studied
and painted birds for over 30 years.[1]

ANTHROPOCENTRISM AND ECOCENTRISM

Anthropocentrism is based on the idea of human beings being the central and most important species in the universe. This idea results in human beings being given a higher status than that of every other species in nature or assessment of its reality. This perspective, in the context of compassion and care for all, can result in mutual co-existence. A letter (Caritas in Veritate, No. 48) sent by Pope Benedict XVI states, 'The environment is God's gift to everyone, and in our use of it we have a responsibility towards the poor, towards future generations, and towards humanity as a whole.'[2] However, this perspective is rarely kept mindful and meaningful in our daily acts of life, resulting in humans abusing and inflicting violence on all

---

1 http://www.globalonenessproject.org/sites/default/files/education/resources/livingonenessstudyguide.pdf, last accessed on 18 July 2013.

2 http://www.vatican.va/holy_father/benedict_xvi/encyclicals/documents/hf_ben-xvi_enc_20090629_caritas-in-veritate_en.html, last accessed on 6 March 2014.

life and non-life forms. The perspective of looking at all non-human forms as commodities of consumption results in extraction of resources, in a way that is not sustainable (see Fig. 9.1) and is decreasing bio capacity.

Anthropocentrism is considered to be one of the reasons why humans consider dominating other species of the planet. As per the Anthropocentric philosophy protection of non-human life forms are based on the utility they provide to the human beings. Ecocentrism denotes a nature-centred perspective, where humans are only one of the species amongst the many species on the planet. When decision-making related to political, economic, and social policies are done, this perspective of all species having their own intrinsic value helps in the creation of a society that respects all creations.

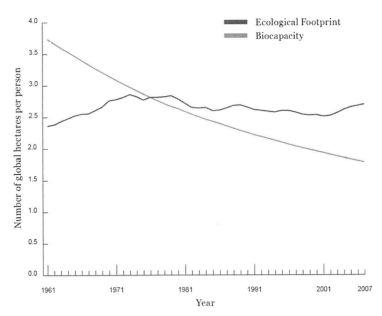

Changes in the Ecological Footprint and global biocapacity available per person between 1961 and 2007.
The total biocapacity available per person has declined with increasing population (Global Footprint Network, 2010)

FIG. 9.1[3] Changes in the ecological footprint and global biocapacity available per person

EARTH CHARTER

Earth Charter,[4] an international declaration, endorsed by more than 4500 organizations, works towards the creation of a just, sustainable, and peaceful global society. Following is the final text of the Earth Charter that was approved and launched in 2000 after a multi-year worldwide consultation process.

---

3 Living Planet Report 2010, http://awsassets.panda.org/downloads/wwf_lpr2010_lr_en.pdf, last accessed on 9 October 2013. Used with permission.
4 http://www.earthcharterinaction.org/content/pages/Read-the-Charter.html, last accessed on 20 July 2013. Used with permission.

Preamble

We stand at a critical moment in Earth's history, a time when humanity must choose its future. As the world becomes increasingly interdependent and fragile, the future at once holds great peril and great promise. To move forward we must recognize that in the midst of a magnificent diversity of cultures and life forms we are one human family and one Earth community with a common destiny. We must join together to bring forth a sustainable global society founded on respect for nature, universal human rights, economic justice, and a culture of peace. Towards this end, it is imperative that we, the people of Earth, declare our responsibility to one another, to the greater community of life, and to future generations.

Earth, Our Home

Humanity is part of a vast evolving universe. Earth, our home, is alive with a unique community of life. The forces of nature make existence a demanding and uncertain adventure, but Earth has provided the conditions essential to life's evolution. The resilience of the community of life and the well-being of humanity depend upon preserving a healthy biosphere with all its ecological systems, a rich variety of plants and animals, fertile soils, pure waters, and clean air. The global environment with its finite resources is a common concern of all people. The protection of Earth's vitality, diversity, and beauty, is a sacred trust.

The Global Situation

The dominant patterns of production and consumption are causing environmental devastation, the depletion of resources, and a massive extinction of species. Communities are being undermined. The benefits of development are not shared equitably and the gap between rich and poor is widening. Injustice, poverty, ignorance, and violent conflict are widespread and the cause of great suffering. An unprecedented rise in human population has overburdened ecological and social systems. The foundations of global security are threatened. These trends are perilous—but not inevitable.

The Challenges Ahead

The choice is ours: form a global partnership to care for Earth and one another or risk the destruction of ourselves and the diversity of life. Fundamental changes are needed in our values, institutions, and ways of living. We must realize that when basic needs have been met, human development is primarily about being more, not having more. We have the knowledge and technology to provide for all and to reduce our impacts on the environment. The emergence of a global civil society is creating new opportunities to build a democratic and humane world. Our environmental, economic, political, social, and spiritual challenges are interconnected, and together we can forge inclusive solutions.

Universal Responsibility

To realize these aspirations, we must decide to live with a sense of universal responsibility, identifying ourselves with the whole Earth community as well as our local communities. We are at once citizens of different nations and of one world in which the local and global are linked. Everyone shares responsibility for the present and future well-being of the human family and the larger living world. The spirit of human solidarity and kinship with all life is strengthened when we live with reverence for the mystery of being, gratitude for the gift of life, and humility regarding the human place in nature.

We urgently need a shared vision of basic values to provide an ethical foundation for the emerging world community. Therefore, together in hope we affirm the following interdependent principles for a sustainable way of life as a common standard by which the conduct of all individuals, organizations, businesses, governments, and transnational institutions is to be guided and assessed.

Principles

I. Respect and care for the community of life

1. Respect Earth and life in all its diversity.
   a. Recognize that all beings are interdependent and every form of life has value regardless of its worth to human beings.
   b. Affirm faith in the inherent dignity of all human beings and in the intellectual, artistic, ethical, and spiritual potential of humanity.
2. Care for the community of life with understanding, compassion, and love.
   a. Accept that with the right to own, manage, and use natural resources comes the duty to prevent environmental harm and to protect the rights of people.
   b. Affirm that with increased freedom, knowledge, and power comes increased responsibility to promote the common good.
3. Build democratic societies that are just, participatory, sustainable, and peaceful.
   a. Ensure that communities at all levels guarantee human rights and fundamental freedoms and provide everyone an opportunity to realize his or her full potential.
   b. Promote social and economic justice, enabling all to achieve a secure and meaningful livelihood that is ecologically responsible.
4. Secure Earth's bounty and beauty for present and future generations.
   a. Recognize that the freedom of action of each generation is qualified by the needs of future generations.
   b. Transmit to future generations the values, traditions, and institutions that support the long-term flourishing of Earth's human and ecological communities.

In order to fulfil these four broad commitments, it is necessary to:

II. Ecological integrity

5. Protect and restore the integrity of Earth's ecological systems, with special concern for biological diversity and the natural processes that sustain life.

   a. Adopt at all levels sustainable development plans and regulations that make environmental conservation and rehabilitation integral to all development initiatives.

   b. Establish and safeguard viable nature and biosphere reserves, including wild lands and marine areas, to protect Earth's life support systems, maintain biodiversity, and preserve our natural heritage.

   c. Promote the recovery of endangered species and ecosystems.

   d. Control and eradicate non-native or genetically modified organisms harmful to native species and the environment, and prevent introduction of such harmful organisms.

   e. Manage the use of renewable resources such as water, soil, forest products, and marine life in ways that do not exceed rates of regeneration and that protect the health of ecosystems.

   f. Manage the extraction and use of non-renewable resources such as minerals and fossil fuels in ways that minimize depletion and cause no serious environmental damage.

6. Prevent harm as the best method of environmental protection and, when knowledge is limited, apply a precautionary approach.

   a. Take action to avoid the possibility of serious or irreversible environmental harm even when scientific knowledge is incomplete or inconclusive.

   b. Place the burden of proof on those who argue that a proposed activity will not cause significant harm, and make the responsible parties liable for environmental harm.

   c. Ensure that decision making addresses the cumulative, long-term, indirect, long distance, and global consequences of human activities.

   d. Prevent pollution of any part of the environment and allow no build-up of radioactive, toxic, or other hazardous substances.

   e. Avoid military activities damaging to the environment.

7. Adopt patterns of production, consumption, and reproduction that safeguard Earth's regenerative capacities, human rights, and community well-being.

   a. Reduce, reuse, and recycle the materials used in production and consumption systems, and ensure that residual waste can be assimilated by ecological systems.

   b. Act with restraint and efficiency when using energy, and rely increasingly on renewable energy sources such as solar and wind.

c. Promote the development, adoption, and equitable transfer of environmentally sound technologies.

     d. Internalize the full environmental and social costs of goods and services in the selling price, and enable consumers to identify products that meet the highest social and environmental standards.

     e. Ensure universal access to health care that fosters reproductive health and responsible reproduction.

     f. Adopt lifestyles that emphasize the quality of life and material sufficiency in a finite world.

8. Advance the study of ecological sustainability and promote the open exchange and wide application of the knowledge acquired.

     a. Support international scientific and technical cooperation on sustainability, with special attention to the needs of developing nations.

     b. Recognize and preserve the traditional knowledge and spiritual wisdom in all cultures that contribute to environmental protection and human well-being.

     c. Ensure that information of vital importance to human health and environmental protection, including genetic information, remains available in the public domain.

III. Social and economic justice

9. Eradicate poverty as an ethical, social, and environmental imperative.

     a. Guarantee the right to potable water, clean air, food security, uncontaminated soil, shelter, and safe sanitation, allocating the national and international resources required.

     b. Empower every human being with the education and resources to secure a sustainable livelihood and provide social security and safety nets for those who are unable to support themselves.

     c. Recognize the ignored, protect the vulnerable, serve those who suffer, and enable them to develop their capacities and to pursue their aspirations.

10. Ensure that economic activities and institutions at all levels promote human development in an equitable and sustainable manner.

     a. Promote the equitable distribution of wealth within nations and among nations.

     b. Enhance the intellectual, financial, technical, and social resources of developing nations, and relieve them of onerous international debt.

     c. Ensure that all trade supports sustainable resource use, environmental protection, and progressive labour standards.

     d. Require multinational corporations and international financial organizations to act transparently in the public good, and hold them accountable for the consequences of their activities.

11. Affirm gender equality and equity as prerequisites to sustainable development and ensure universal access to education, health care, and economic opportunity.
   a. Secure the human rights of women and girls and end all violence against them.
   b. Promote the active participation of women in all aspects of economic, political, civil, social, and cultural life as full and equal partners, decision makers, leaders, and beneficiaries.
   c. Strengthen families and ensure the safety and loving nurture of all family members.
12. Uphold the right of all, without discrimination, to a natural and social environment supportive of human dignity, bodily health, and spiritual well-being, with special attention to the rights of indigenous peoples and minorities.
   a. Eliminate discrimination in all its forms, such as that based on race, colour, sex, sexual orientation, religion, language, and national, ethnic or social origin.
   b. Affirm the right of indigenous people to their spirituality, knowledge, lands and resources, and to their related practice of sustainable livelihoods.
   c. Honour and support the young people of our communities, enabling them to fulfil their essential role in creating sustainable societies.
   d. Protect and restore outstanding places of cultural and spiritual significance.

IV. Democracy, non-violence, and peace

13. Strengthen democratic institutions at all levels, and provide transparency and accountability in governance, inclusive participation in decision making, and access to justice.
   a. Uphold the right of everyone to receive clear and timely information on environmental matters and all development plans and activities which are likely to affect them or in which they have an interest.
   b. Support local, regional, and global civil society, and promote the meaningful participation of all interested individuals and organizations in decision making.
   c. Protect the rights to freedom of opinion, expression, peaceful assembly, association, and dissent.
   d. Institute effective and efficient access to administrative and independent judicial procedures, including remedies and redress for environmental harm and the threat of such harm.
   e. Eliminate corruption in all public and private institutions.

f. Strengthen local communities, enabling them to care for their environments, and assign environmental responsibilities to the levels of government where they can be carried out most effectively.

14. Integrate into formal education and life-long learning the knowledge, values, and skills needed for a sustainable way of life.

     a. Provide all, especially children and youth, with educational opportunities that empower them to contribute actively to sustainable development.

     b. Promote the contribution of the arts and humanities as well as the sciences in sustainability education.

     c. Enhance the role of the mass media in raising awareness of ecological and social challenges.

     d. Recognize the importance of moral and spiritual education for sustainable living.

15. Treat all living beings with respect and consideration.

     a. Prevent cruelty to animals kept in human societies and protect them from suffering.

     b. Protect wild animals from methods of hunting, trapping, and fishing that cause extreme, prolonged, or avoidable suffering.

     c. Avoid or eliminate to the full extent possible the taking or destruction of non-targeted species.

16. Promote a culture of tolerance, nonviolence, and peace.

     a. Encourage and support mutual understanding, solidarity, and cooperation among all people and within and among nations.

     b. Implement comprehensive strategies to prevent violent conflict and use collaborative problem solving to manage and resolve environmental conflicts and other disputes.

     c. Demilitarize national security systems to the level of a non-provocative defence posture, and convert military resources to peaceful purposes, including ecological restoration.

     d. Eliminate nuclear, biological, and toxic weapons, and other weapons of mass destruction.

     e. Ensure that the use of orbital and outer space supports environmental protection and peace.

     f. Recognize that peace is the wholeness created by right relationships with oneself, other persons, other cultures, other life, Earth, and the larger whole of which all are a part.

The Way Forward

As never before in history, common destiny beckons us to seek a new beginning. Such renewal is the promise of these Earth Charter principles. To fulfil this promise, we must commit ourselves to adopt and promote the values and objectives of the Charter.

This requires a change of mind and heart. It requires a new sense of global interdependence and universal responsibility. We must imaginatively develop and apply the vision of a sustainable way of life locally, nationally, regionally, and globally. Our cultural diversity is a precious heritage and different cultures will find their own distinctive ways to realize the vision. We must deepen and expand the global dialogue that generated the Earth Charter, for we have much to learn from the ongoing collaborative search for truth and wisdom.

Life often involves tensions between important values. This can mean difficult choices. However, we must find ways to harmonize diversity with unity, the exercise of freedom with the common good, short-term objectives with long-term goals. Every individual, family, organization, and community has a vital role to play. The arts, sciences, religions, educational institutions, media, businesses, nongovernmental organizations, and governments are all called to offer creative leadership. The partnership of government, civil society, and businesses is essential for effective governance.

In order to build a sustainable global community, the nations of the world must renew their commitment to the United Nations, fulfil their obligations under existing international agreements, and support the implementation of Earth Charter principles with an international legally binding instrument on environment and development.

Let ours be a time remembered for the awakening of a new reverence for life, the firm resolve to achieve sustainability, the quickening of the struggle for justice and peace, and the joyful celebration of life.

ROLE OF CONSUMERS AND INVESTORS IN MAKING BUSINESSES SUSTAINABLE

The 2012 Edelman goodpurpose study[5] indicated that emerging markets like India would drive the market for sustainable and socially responsible products. Sentiments about social causes are generally stronger in emerging markets than in matured markets. While 37 per cent of respondents from developed countries mentioned that they

---

5 http://www.scribd.com/doc/90411623/Executive-Summary-2012-Edelman-goodpurpose%C2%AE-Study, last accessed on 7 May 2012.

purchased a product associated with a cause at least once a month, the percentage was higher at 62 per cent for respondents from emerging economies. Overall, 73 per cent of the respondents said that they would switch brand if a different brand of the same quality supported a good cause. Also 53 per cent of the respondents indicated that social purpose is the most important factor in choosing a brand among its peers, when quality and price are the same.

In a study conducted by Yale University and George Mason University in 2013[6], with reference to the US consumer market, it was found that 28 per cent of the Americans, in the past one year, have rewarded companies that took steps to reduce global warming by purchasing the products of those companies. Almost 21 per cent of the Americans also mentioned that, during the past one year they have punished companies who opposed steps to reduce global warming by not purchasing the products of those companies. The study also mentioned that, at least four in ten Americans said that, during the past one year, they 'often' or 'occasionally' purchased food grown or produced locally (69 per cent) or organic food (42 per cent). Consumers by taking decisions to purchase products and services from companies that are socially responsible, environmentally-friendly, and health-friendly, are giving business to companies that follows higher standards of moral and responsible behaviour, thereby increasing the revenues and profits of such companies. The data related to the existence of the ethical consumerism in the UK is shown in Table 9.1[7]. The data is from the Ethical Consumer Markets Reports 2012, produced by the Co-operative Group.

TABLE 9.1 Ethical consumerism in the UK, 2000–2011

Units in UK£ million	2000	2010	2011	% growth (2010-11)
Ethical Food and Drink				
Organic	605	1,527	1,500	−1.77
Fairtrade	33	1,017	1,262	24.09
Rainforest Alliance	–	1,198	1,346	12.35
Free range eggs	182	497	526	5.84
Free range poultry	44	252	266	5.56
Farmers' markets	142	220	220	0.00
Vegetarian products	479	787	800	1.65
Freedom foods	–	127	149	17.32
Sustainatxtle fish	–	222	292	31.53
Boycotts	587	1,084	1,113	2.68
Sub-total	**2,072**	**6,931**	**7,474**	**7.83**

(Contd)

6 http://environment.yale.edu/climate-communication/files/Behavior-April-2013.pdf, last accessed on 20 July 2013.

7 http://www.co-operative.coop/PageFiles/416561607/Ethical-Consumerism-Report-2011.pdf, last accessed on 12 August 2013. Used with permission.

Green home			
Energy efficient electrical appliances	229	2,069	2,045	−1.16
Energy efficient txtoilers	214	2,332	2,375	1.84
Micro-generation	–	248	958	286.29
Energy efficient light bulbs	12	44	48	9.09
Ethical cleaning products	3	42	42	0.00
Sustainable timber and paper	629	1,655	1,706	3.08
Green energy	–	352	378	7.39
Rechargeable batteries	5	34	33	−2.94
Buying for reuse– household products	759	823	819	−0.49
Green funerals	–	7	8	14.29
Sub-total	**1,851**	**7,606**	**8,412**	**10.60**
Eco-travel and transport			
Responsible tour operators	73	182	188	3.30
Environmental tourist attractions	2	19	20	5.26
Green cars	4	846	1,088	28.61
Bicycles (new)	348	698	650	−6.88
Boycotts	112	1,068	1,198	12.17
Subtotal	**539**	**2813**	**3,144**	**11.77**
Ethical personal products			
Ethical clothing	5	177	150	−15.25
Ethical cosmetics	175	528	566	7.20
Charity shops	141	350	389	11.14
Buying for reuse – clothing	218	321	330	2.80
Boycotts	174	333	346	3.90
Real nappies	–	5	5	0.00
Subtotal	**713**	**1,714**	**1,786**	**4.20**
Community			
Local shopping	1,620	2,330	2,368	1.63
Charitable donations	2,764	3,040	3,125	2.81
Subtotal	**4,384**	**5,370**	**5,493**	**2.30**
Ethical money			
Sub-total	**6,483**	**20,666**	**20,893**	**1.10**
GRAND TOTAL	**16,042**	**45,100**	**47,202**	**4.66**

Bhutan aims to be a zero emission nation, and visions its capital city, Thimphu, to be a 'clean electric' city. As part of that vision, the country has partnered with Nissan to supply electric cars and install quick charging points across the country.

As can be inferred from this table that the markets for ethical products are generally on an increase. The report also suggests that this growth is primarily driven by enlightened businesses, regulatory intervention and ethical consumers.

The previous two decades have also seen a trend of investors demanding senior management of publicly listed companies to demonstrate higher standards of socially and environmentally responsible behaviour. In its 2012 report on Sustainable and Responsible Investing Trends in the United States,[8] the United States Forum for Sustainable and Responsible Investment (US-SIF) has mentioned that the overall total of socially responsible investing (SRI) assets in 2012 is $3.74 trillion, while it was $3.06 trillion in 2010 (an increase of 22 per cent in two years). This also included $1.54 trillion held by more than 200 institutional investors/money managers that filed or co-filed shareholder resolutions on environmental, social or governance (ESG) issues.

Shareholder Resolutions

Shareholder resolutions are non-binding proposals submitted by the shareholders of a publicly listed company for a vote, in the company's annual meeting. In the US, shareholder resolutions are filed in areas related to corporate governance, executive compensation, and social and environmental responsibility issues including areas such as global warming, use of toxicants like tobacco, human rights, and animal welfare. Filing a shareholder resolution will result in that resolution being included in the management proxy circular and this is submitted for a vote at the company's annual general meeting (AGM). Companies normally tend to prefer the removal of such resolutions from the AGM agenda, and thus engage in a dialogue with those who filed the resolution. This may result in the company management adopting some of the changes requested by the person who filed the resolution. The following are certain circumstances under which resolutions could be withdrawn:

- The company agrees to significantly adopt the suggestion or demand made through the resolution, even before reaching the resolution it reaches the voting stage.
- The company agrees to make partial adoption of the suggestions/demands made through the resolution and is willing to conduct dialogue between the organization or the person who filed the resolution and the decision making personnel in the company.
- The company gives evidence to prove that it is already dealing with the issues raised by the resolution.

---

8 http://www.ussif.org/files/Publications/12_Trends_Exec_Summary.pdf, last accessed on 22 July 2013.

If the company does not agree to a dialogue, then the resolution goes for voting in the AGM. Prior to the AGM, the organization/person who filed the resolution issues a proxy alert that challenges the response given by the company and also gives additional reasons on why investors should support the resolution. Due to various reasons, including the conventional practice that most investors vote with the management without even considering the merits of the case, these resolutions rarely win the majority support. However, in a number of cases, the company management realizes that shareholder concern about a sustainability related issue is building up, and the issue raised through the resolution could be an opportunity for the company to create a long-term competitive advantage.

Some of the impacts of the shareholder resolutions filed in various companies in 2013 are given in Table 9.2. The details were tracked by CERES, a network of investors, companies, and public interest groups that promote sustainability leadership.[9]

TABLE 9.2 Shareholder resolution of various companies in year 2013

Name of the company	Resolution summary	Filer	Status
Alpha Natural Resources, Inc.	Climate Risk Report	Unitarian Universalist Association of Congregations	Vote: 18%
Amazon.com Inc.	Climate Risk Report	Calvert Asset Management Company, Inc.	Withdrawn; Company will address
Ameren Corporation	Report on energy efficiency and renewable energy	New York State Comptroller	Vote: 11%
Ameren Corporation	Set goals to reduce water use and thermal impacts	As You Sow	Withdrawn; Company will address
Berkshire Hathaway Inc.	Greenhouse gas emissions reduction goals	Newground Social Investment	Vote: 8.8%
Cabot Oil & Gas Corporation	Curtail toxicity of fracking fluids	New York State Comptroller	Withdrawn; Company will address
Cameron International Corporation	Sustainability Report	Calvert Asset Management Company, Inc.	Withdrawn; Company will address
Caterpillar Inc.	Executive compensation linked to ESG	The Nathan Cummings Foundation	Vote: 7.1%
CF Industries Holdings, Inc.	Sustainability report including energy efficiency	Presbyterian Church (USA)	Vote: 67%
Chevron Corporation	Hydraulic fracturing impacts	Sisters of St Francis of Philadelphia	Vote: 30.2%

(Contd)

---

9 http://www.ceres.org/investor-network/resolutions, last accessed on 22 July 2013. Used with permission.

TABLE 9.2 *(Contd)*

Name of the company	Resolution summary	Filer	Status
Chevron Corporation	Independent board members with environmental expertise	New York State Comptroller	Vote: 21.7%
Chubb Corporation	Sustainability report including ESG performance	First Affirmative Financial Network, LLC	Vote: 32.2%
Church & Dwight Co. Inc.	Palm oil policy	Province of St. Joseph, Capuchin Order	Withdrawn; Company will address
Cincinnati Financial Corp.	Sustainability report including systemic risk reduction from climate change	Miller/Howard Investments, Inc.	Vote: 28%
Citrix Systems, Inc.	Energy use management report	California State Teachers' Retirement System	Withdrawn; Company will address
Cleco Corporation	Sustainability report including ESG performance and water risk analysis	Calvert Asset Management Company, Inc.	Vote: 45.6%
Coach, Inc.	Sustainability report	Unitarian Universalist Association of Congregations	Filed
Coherent Inc.	Sustainability report including ESG performance and GHG goals	Walden Asset Management	Withdrawn; Company will address
ConocoPhillips	Greenhouse gas emissions reduction goals	Presbyterian Church (USA)	Vote: 29.4%
CONSOL Energy Inc.	Report on fossil fuel reserve risks to company and society	As You Sow	Vote: 19.7%
Continental Resources Inc.	Set goals to reduce or eliminate natural gas flaring	Mercy Investment Services, Inc.	Withdrawn; Ongoing dialogue
Cousins Properties, Inc.	Sustainability report including GHG emissions, ESG impacts, water and worker safety	Laborers' International Union of North America	Filed
CR Bard Inc.	Sustainability report including ESG performance and GHG goals	Walden Asset Management	Vote: 34.9%
Darden Restaurants, Inc.	Adopt and implement a comprehensive sustainable palm oil policy	Sisters of the Presentation of the Blessed Virgin Mary	Filed
Dean Foods Company	Adopt and implement a comprehensive sustainable palm oil policy	Sisters of St Francis of Dubuque, Iowa	Withdrawn; Company will address

(Contd)

Denbury Resources Inc.	Board commitment to oversight of environmental and social matters	Calvert Asset Management Company, Inc.	Withdrawn; Company will address
Dominion Resources, Inc.	Energy efficiency report and goals	Elena Baum	Omitted
Dominion Resources, Inc.	Biomass power plant decommissioning	Mary Booth	Omitted
Dominion Resources, Inc.	Report addressing long-term price stability of natural gas	Ivy Main	Omitted
Dominion Resources, Inc.	Mountain top removal impacts	Bernice Schoenbaum	Vote: 6.9%
Dominion Resources, Inc.	Executive compensation linked to ESG	Ruth Amundsen	Vote: 7.1%
Dominion Resources, Inc.	Climate risk report including financial impacts from extreme weather	Pam Morgan	Vote: 22.6%
Dominion Resources, Inc	Offshore-wind development report	Robert Vanderhye	Omitted
Dominion Resources, Inc.	Report on energy efficiency and renewable energy	Presbyterian Church (USA)	Omitted
DTE Energy Co.	Report on energy efficiency and renewable energy	New York State Comptroller	Withdrawn; Company will address
Dun & Bradstreet Corp.	Energy use management report	California State Teachers' Retirement System	Withdrawn; Company will address
Dunkin' Brands	Palm oil sourcing	New York State Comptroller	Withdrawn; Company will address
Electronic Arts Inc.	Energy use management report	California State Teachers' Retirement System	Withdrawn; Company will address
EMC Corporation	Suppliers to issue sustainability reports	New York City Office of the Comptroller	Withdrawn; Company will address
Emerson Electric Co.	Sustainability report including ESG performance and GHG goals	Walden Asset Management	Vote: 37.6%
Empire District Electric Company	Report on cost effective energy efficiency resources	James Evans	Vote: 13.9%
EOG Resources, Inc.	Hydraulic fracturing impacts	Green Century Capital Management	Withdrawn; Company will address
Equity Residential	Sustainability report	New York City Office of the Comptroller	Vote: 42%
Estee Lauder Companies Inc.	Palm oil policy	Sisters of St Francis of Assisi	Filed

(Contd)

TABLE 9.2 *(Contd)*

Name of the company	Resolution summary	Filer	Status
Exxon Mobil Corporation	Climate risk report including financial impacts from extreme weather	The Christopher Reynolds Foundation	Omitted
Exxon Mobil Corporation	Hydraulic fracturing impacts	New York City Office of the Comptroller	Vote: 30.2%
Exxon Mobil Corporation	Adopt quantitative GHG goals for products and operations	Tri-State Coalition for Responsible Investment	Vote: 26.7%
FirstEnergy Corp.	Report on energy efficiency and renewable energy	New York State Comptroller	Omitted
FirstEnergy Corp.	Set goals to reduce water risk	As You Sow	Omitted
Fiserv, Inc.	Energy use management report	California State Teachers' Retirement System	Withdrawn; Company will address
FLIR Systems, Inc.	Energy use management report	California State Teachers' Retirement System	Omitted
Fossil, Inc.	Supply chain environmental impacts report	Calvert Asset Management Company, Inc.	Vote: 29%
Freeport-McMoRan Copper & Gold Inc.	Independent board member with environmental expertise	New York State Comptroller	Filed
Gap Inc.	Suppliers to issue sustainability reports	New York City Office of the Comptroller	Withdrawn; Company will address
Gentex Corporation	Sustainability report including ESG performance and GHG goals	Walden Asset Management	Vote: 36.2%
Health Management Associates, Inc.	Sustainability report	Calvert Asset Management Company, Inc.	Vote: 31.4%
Home Depot, Inc.	Storm water management policy	David Brook	Vote: 4.4%
International Business Machines Corp.	Suppliers to issue sustainability reports	New York City Office of the Comptroller	No Vote For Technical Reasons
International Business Machines Corp.	Set company-wide renewable energy targets	Green Century Capital Management	Withdrawn; Company will address
JP Morgan Chase & Co.	Report assessing climate risk from financed emissions	Boston Common Asset Management, LLC	Filed
Kimco Realty Corporation	Sustainability report	New York City Office of the Comptroller	Withdrawn; Company will address

(Contd)

Kohl's Corp.	Suppliers to issue sustainability reports	Laborers' International Union of North America	Withdrawn; Company will address
Kroger Co.	Report on feasibility of taking responsibility for post-consumer packaging	As You Sow	Vote: 12.5%
Kroger Co.	Adopt and implement a comprehensive sustainable palm oil policy	Sisters of the Presentation of the Blessed Virgin Mary	Vote; Company will address
Lifepoint Hospitals Inc.	Sustainability report	Calvert Asset Management Company, Inc.	Withdrawn; Company will address
Lowe's Companies Inc.	Board commitment to oversight of environmental and social matters	Calvert Asset Management Company, Inc.	Withdrawn; Company will address
Men's Wearhouse	Sustainability report	Trillium Asset Management	Filed
Molycorp, Inc.	Sustainability report including water risk mitigation	Mercy Investment Services, Inc.	Withdrawn; Ongoing dialogue
Mondelez International, Inc.	Report on feasibility of taking responsibility for post-consumer packaging	As You Sow	Vote: 9.5%
Mondelez International, Inc.	Deforestation impact and risk mitigation report	Domini Social Investments LLC	Omitted
Monsanto Co.	Water Risk Report	Midwest Coalition for Responsible Investment	Withdrawn; Company will address
Motorola Solutions, Inc.	Suppliers to issue sustainability reports	New York City Office of the Comptroller	Vote: 6.1%
Nabors Industries Ltd.	Sustainability report including ESG performance, greenhouse gas reductions, and water usage	Appleseed Fund	No vote for technical reasons
Newfield Exploration Co.	Independent board member with environmental expertise	New York State Comptroller	Vote: 5.1%
Nike Inc.	Suppliers to issue sustainability reports	New York City Office of the Comptroller	Filed
ONEOK Inc.	Fugitive methane report	Trillium Asset Management	Vote: 38.2%
Pioneer Natural Resources Co.	Report describing environmental and social challenges and opportunities associated with hydraulic fracturing	Calvert Asset Management Company, Inc.	Vote: 41.7%
PNC Financial Services Group Inc.	Report assessing climate risk from financed emissions	Boston Common Asset Management, LLC	Vote: 22.8%

(Contd)

TABLE 9.2 *(Contd)*

Name of the company	Resolution summary	Filer	Status
Public Storage	Energy efficiency goals	Calvert Asset Management Company, Inc.	Withdrawn; Company will address
Ralcorp Holdings Inc.	Water risk report	Calvert Asset Management Company, Inc.	No vote for technical reasons
Ralph Lauren Corporation	Sustainability report	New York State Comptroller	Withdrawn; Company will address
Range Resources Corporation	Report including measuring, mitigating, and disclosing methane emissions	Trillium Asset Management	Vote: 21.7%
Range Resources Corporation	Board commitment to oversight of environmental and social matters	Calvert Asset Management Company, Inc.	Withdrawn; Company will address
Rockwood Holdings, Inc.	Energy efficiency goals	Wesleyan University	Omitted
Roper Industries Inc.	Sustainability report including energy efficiency	Presbyterian Church (USA)	Withdrawn; Company will address
Scana Corp.	Report on energy efficiency and renewable energy	New York State Comptroller	Withdrawn; Ongoing dialogue
Simpson Manufacturing Co., Inc.	Sustainability report including greenhouse gas reduction goals	Walden Asset Management	Vote: 33.1%
SL Green Realty Corporation	Sustainability report	New York City Office of the Comptroller	Withdrawn; Company will address
Spectra Energy Corp.	Report on measurement, mitigation, and discloser of methane emissions	Trillium Asset Management	Vote: 35.4%
Starbucks Corporation	Palm oil policy	Green Century Capital Management	Withdrawn; Company will address
Starwood Hotels & Resorts Worldwide Inc.	Sustainability report	Trillium Asset Management	Withdrawn; Ongoing dialogue
Stryker Corp.	Greenhouse gas emissions reduction goals	Walden Asset Management	Withdrawn; Company will address
Target Corp.	Suppliers to issue sustainability reports	New York City Office of the Comptroller	Withdrawn; Company will address
Texas Instruments Inc.	Suppliers to issue sustainability reports	New York City Office of the Comptroller	Withdrawn; Company will address
Transocean Ltd.	Independent board member with environmental expertise	New York State Comptroller	No vote for technical reasons
Ultra Petroleum Corp.	Hydraulic fracturing impacts	Green Century Capital Management	Withdrawn; Company will address

(Contd)

United Parcel Service, Inc.	Board commitment to oversight of environmental and social matters	Calvert Asset Management Company, Inc	Withdrawn; Company will address
Walter Energy, Inc.	Energy use management report	California State Teachers' Retirement System	Withdrawn; Company will address
Westinghouse Air Brake Technologies Corporation	Sustainability report including ESG performance and GHG goals	Walden Asset Management	Withdrawn; Company will address
Whole Foods Market, Inc.	Report on feasibility of taking responsibility for post-consumer packaging	As You Sow	Vote: 7.4%
Yum! Brands, Inc.	Comprehensive sustainable palm oil policy	Trillium Asset Management	Withdrawn; Ongoing dialogue
Yum! Brands, Inc.	Adopt a comprehensive on-premises recycling strategy for food and beverage packaging	As You Sow	Withdrawn; Ongoing dialogue

EQUITABLE USE OF RESOURCES FOR SUSTAINABLE LIFESTYLES

> *'My mother always wore khadi (Indian homespun cotton fabric). When we wanted nylon she said: "I'll buy you nylon. But you know, if you buy nylon, some industrialist will get another Mercedes, and if you buy khadi, some woman's chulha (kitchen fire) will get lit. You decide".'*[10]

Vandana Shiva, Founder, Navdanya, an organization that promotes seed saving, biodiversity conservation, and organic farming.

'Indian tradition regards the Earth as a Goddess, Bhudevi; her consort, Vishnu, the supreme divinity, incarnates from age to age to relieve her of the burden of demonic forces—sometimes of humanity itself. This he does out of love for the earth, his companion... Earth is as sacred as Heaven, since she is our mother - not a dead heap of "natural resources".'

The National Environment Policy states, 'It is recognized that maintaining a healthy environment is not the state's responsibility alone, but also that of every citizen. A spirit of partnership should thus be realized throughout the spectrum of environmental management in the country. While the state must galvanize its efforts, there should also be recognition by each individual—natural or institutional, of its responsibility towards maintaining and enhancing the quality of the environment.' A few of the commonly advocated sustainability steps include stabilization of population growth, achievement of food security, adoption, promotion of clean technology, conservation of bio-diversity, and living a life that is in harmony with the nature.

---

10 http://www.lifepositive.com/body/nature/environmental.asp, last accessed on 28 May 2013.

There is something more fundamental that men of wisdom are calling attention to. Sadhguru Jaggi Vasudev, Founder—Isha Foundation, which launched a green project endeavour titled 'Project Greenhands' that facilitated the planting of more than two crore tree saplings, says, 'We are looking at the planet as a commodity. We are not looking at it as a source of our life, which is a serious, serious mistake and an extremely crass way of existence. So, if you look at your mother as a delivery system for you, it's a very gross way of existence. If you look at the planet as commodity, it's a very gross way of existence. It's time this is conveyed to the children of the planet because they are the future generations and if that has to happen, then this generation has to get it too first. It has to spread the message (that) it's very, very important.'[11] In *Indian Culture and India's Future*[12], Michel Danino mentions, 'Indian tradition regards the Earth as a Goddess, Bhudevi; her consort, Vishnu, the supreme divinity, incarnates from age to age to relieve her of the burden of demonic forces—sometimes of humanity itself. This he does out of love for the Earth, his companion. Sita, his wife when he is Rama, means furrow, and in the end she returned to the earth whence she had come. Shiva, too, is bound to the earth through Parvati, daughter of Himavat or the Himalayas. Earth and Heaven are therefore inseparable: "Heaven is my father; my mother is this vast earth, my close kin," says the Rig Veda. Earth is as sacred as Heaven, since she is our mother—not a dead heap of "natural resources". Nature, rather than an adversary to be conquered and despoiled, is our best defence: "Blue Water, open space, hills, and thick forests constitute a fortress," proclaims Valluvar in the *Kural* (verse 742). Rivers from Ganga to Sarasvati and Kaveri are goddesses (the Brahmaputra, of course, is a rare God among them), mountains from the Himalayas to the Vindhyas are Gods. The whole of nature is felt to be pervaded with the divine Spirit.'

Role of an Individual in the Conservation of Natural Resources and in Preventing Pollution

What are the ways through which you can serve the environment?

1. Pray. Pray for the well-being of all—living and non-living.
2. Keep yourself updated about environmental issues. This will also help you to be a source of information to others.
3. Indians were known for 'Simple Living and Noble Thinking'. Be a true citizen of this glorious land.
4. Use less paper. While taking print-outs, use both sides of the paper. Use recycled paper wherever possible.
5. Plant and nurture as many trees as possible. Plant saplings of the trees native to the region. The vegetation will capture most of the dust from the road before it reaches the building. Research studies have indicated that the existence of roadside trees could result in more than 50 per cent reduction in particulate

---

11 http://www.ecowalkthetalk.com/blog/2012/09/01/sadhguru-jaggi-vasudev-project-green-hands-and-tree-planting-in-tamil-nadu/, last accessed on 1 October 2012.
12 DK Printworld, New Delhi, 2011.

matter concentration inside the roadside houses.[13] Plant tree saplings on the birthday of your near and dear ones. And more importantly, nurture them. Plant tree saplings on sacred occasions and festivals.

6. Searching in the internet? Use web-search sites like http://www.ecosia.org and http://goodsearch.com—these are websites that donate almost 50 per cent of its revenues to endeavours that contribute to the greater common good.

7. Switch off, not just unwanted lights, fans, and electrical appliances—but also demotivating discussions.

8. Why go to the gym/fitness centre in the second floor by taking the lift/elevator, which consumes electricity? Walking up the stairs is a healthy exercise. One can also go for a walk in the outdoors.

9. While bathing, use the shower, instead of the bathtub. It is still better to use a mug and a bucket.

10. While gifting, make meaningful gifts. You may give a gift certificate that sponsors tree planting, bird nests, supports environmental initiatives, promote animal care, and more.

11. Carry reusable cloth bags while going shopping.

12. Build a rainwater harvesting system in your house.

13. Use energy-efficient lighting. Use low-energy compact fluorescent bulbs, or LED lamps.

14. Learn about the trees, animals, and birds that exist in your area.

15. Engage in responsible purchasing. Purchase of fur, corals, ivory, tiger nails, etc., negatively affect the lives of animals and ecology.

16. In Indian tradition, the river has been considered to be a place of worship. Do not throw garbage into the river or other water bodies. The river sustains life for millions of life forms.

17. Protect the river banks by planting vegetation on the banks of rivers. This will also improve the quality of the water by reducing the run-off of water from the ground to the rivers.

18. Prefer public transport over private motor vehicles. While travelling to common destinations, share one vehicle instead of everyone taking their individual vehicles. Prefer bicycles over motorcycles. Walk to the grocery shop. (see Fig. 9.2)

19. Unplug chargers and other electronic devices when not in use.

20. Why take receipts at ATMs? Have you noticed the amount of paper receipts lying in waste bins at ATM kiosks? Now, think about the amount of garbage created on a daily basis across the globe due to these receipts.

---

13 Barbara A. Maher, Imad A. M. Ahmed, Brian Davison, Vassil Karloukovski, Robert Clarke, Impact of Roadside Tree Lines on Indoor Concentrations of Traffic-Derived Particulate Matter, Environmental Science & Technology, November 11, 2013, DOI: 10.1021/es404363m. Also available at: http://pubs.acs.org/doi/abs/10.1021/es404363m, Accessed on November 28, 2013.

FIG. 9.2[14] Use public transport over private motor vehicles

21. Do as many financial transactions as possible online. Pay insurance premium through the internet. Prefer online funds transfer, rather than sending a DD/ cheque. Opt for e-statements rather than monthly statements delivered by post.

22. Maximize the use of natural light. Paint walls in light colours to brighten rooms. Keep window curtains open during the day to let in sunlight and air.

23. It is challenging for any business organization to go green (even if they want to), unless they have an incentive to do so. And we can provide that incentive. Vote with your wallet. While making purchases, purchase from organizations that are known for their environmental and social sustainability practices.

24. Suits and ties reduce the possibility of natural air conditioning for the body, especially in countries like India, which has a tropical climate. Avoid them if you are confident without them. Allow the fresh healthy natural air to flow in as much as possible at work place and also at home, rather than switching on the air-conditioning system. If you are using the A/C—remember that even adjusting the temperature by 1° Celsius contributes to saving a lot of energy. Why put on a three piece suit and then switch on the air conditioner, which requires loads of power to run?

---

14 This image is an adapted work from the photo by Martin M, used with permission. Image source: https://www.flickr. com/photos/43423301@N07/3998449040, last accessed on 4 August 2014.

25. Use electrical appliances that have higher energy star ratings.

26. Like to procrastinate? Procrastinate while taking printouts. Whenever taking printouts, use both sides of paper. Use recycled paper. Prefer a manufacturer who uses eco-friendly methods while making paper.

27. Visualize how consuming less can make our life more light and stress free—practice 'Ceilings on Desires'.

28. Wash your clothes yourself. Sun dry clothes, rather than using the dryer in the washing machine. This saves energy and money, in addition to giving a good exercise to the body.

29. Increase the proportion of fresh fruits and vegetables, preferably those that are produced locally, in your diet. Buying locally produced foods helps the local economy and also cuts down on the fossil fuel usage due to limited transportation.

30. Create a vegetable garden in your home.

31. Explore options of incorporating organic food in the daily diet. While the cost of organic food may be higher, organic food does not contain pesticide residues. It also supports farmers who practice farming without the usage of pesticides and fertilizers. Citing tests done by US Food and Drug Administration (FDA), a press release by Environmental Working Group (EWG)[15] suggested the existence of 'superbugs' or antibiotic resistant bacteria in a high percentage of meat available in American supermarkets—81 per cent of raw ground turkey, 55 per cent of raw ground beef, and 39 per cent of raw chicken parts were infected with these microbes.

32. Promote natural farming and organic farming. Buy organic textiles.

33. Eat as you need. Ask who is hungry—the stomach or the tongue? Discriminate between need and want.

34. Be a vegetarian.

35. Reduce the dependence on refrigerator. Eat freshly prepared food. As the food, so the mind.

36. Watch less of TV. This saves energy and money, and reduces furthering the unsettling of our mind.

37. Carry a cloth bag from home, while shopping for grocery, vegetables and fruits (and maybe everything else too).

38. Reduce, Reuse, and Recycle. Recycle/give away your old mobile phones. Mobile phones have toxic substances, and throwing away the phone will cause harm to all.

39. Gift one's text books/journals/study materials to juniors/libraries.

40. Refill ball point pens, rather than buying a new disposable pen. It may only be a gain of 50 paise, but this action will result in less wastage.

---

15 http://www.ewg.org/release/superbugs-invade-america-s-supermarket-meat, last accessed on 28 December 20

41. Unsubscribe from public/group e-mailing lists if you are not reading those e-mails. Data and server farms are heavy consumers of electric power.

42. Walk more, fly less. Airline emissions melts the Polar Ice. Walking ensures health for our heart, so that it can melt on hearing the update that Polar Bear will soon lose its habitat.

43. Watch environmental documentaries and movies like 'Home' and 'An Inconvenient Truth'.

44. While taking a bath, usage of a bucket and mug, instead of a bathtub, saves substantial water. While shaving, remember to turn off the tap. This saves water too.

45. Let us make our pilgrimages green. Lord Ayyappa was at home, in the company of forest and animals. Lord Shiva was at home, in the company of the serene environs of Kailash. Now Sabarimala and Kailash are ecologically affected regions.

46. Sustain wetlands. Recreate wetlands. Wetlands play a significant role in water conservation, purification, and supporting birds.

47. Go solar. Go wind. Use renewable energy as much as possible. Campaign with your government to increase investments in renewables.

48. Harvest rainwater. Dig pits in ground. Collect rainwater falling in roofs.

49. Spend your free time in service activities that benefit nature and all of its creation.

50. Use water filters, rather than bottled water.

51. Teach basics on waste management to the larger community. Sort garbage into three waste bins—for (a) paper, (b) plastics and metals, and (c) organic waste.

52. Create and engage in community endeavours that serve the planet—clean-up days, participating in Earth Day, World Environment Day, Earth Hour, and World Water Day celebrations. You can clean the beach, rivers and river banks, pull the nails plunged to trees, and more.

53. For public functions like weddings, use natural materials such as earthen cups and leaf plates.

54. Fix dripping taps. Repair pipes that are broken or leaking.

55. Carry your own plates and mugs while going to a cafeteria. Refuse plastic or styrofoam plates and cups.

56. If you are not shutting down your computer, at least leave it in standby/hibernation mode. The highest energy savings emerges if you are shutting down your computer system. Do not run a screensaver.

57. Electronic equipment's continue to use power even after they are switched off. There are possibilities of further energy savings, if these equipment's are disconnected from the power source, or the switch at the power source is switched off.

58. Invest in technological solutions like video conferencing that can reduce the amount of employee travel.

59. At your office, initiate a 'green purchasing' policy. Make it a policy to source office requirements from ecologically friendly service providers.

60. Plan the purposes of your trips and list them out—include several errands in one trip.

61. Many of the purchases are done with an attempt to impress or please people to gain attention, to feel loved or rewarded. Ask yourself whether it is an absolute necessity.

62. While constructing home, use recycled building materials and indigenous technologies. Search on the internet for more details about sustainable buildings, green buildings, and natural buildings. It has been found that usage of sustainable building technologies can reduce the cost of the building without any reduction in the quality of the building. Use only paints that are natural. Alternatively, one may use paints with low Volatile Organic Content (VOC). As a general rule, paints with low VOC do not have odour.

63. Vote for political parties who aim for the well-being of all, including the earth and all its inhabitants, not just human beings.

64. Wherever possible, develop the habit of using reusable items. We may be using disposable items only once. However, each of those items requires raw materials, time, money, and energy for its production. Also, these disposable items do not disappear after our usage. It becomes waste, ends up in landfills, and can pollute the society.

65. Visit GoodGuide.com to ascertain the health, environmental and social responsibility associated with a product or service that you plan to purchase.

In 2011, DuPont achieved zero landfill status in its Building Innovations business by following the 3R principles of Reducing, Reusing, and Recycling manufacturing byproducts and waste at the manufacturing sites of DuPont. Through a three-year initiative, Dupont eliminated its annual landfill wastage of 81 million pounds to zero. Some of the waste materials have been converted to filler replacement in concrete, road sub-base material, landscape stones, animal bedding, adhesives, worm bedding or energy.

66. During travel, carry water from home. As far as possible, avoid purchasing bottled drinking water. While you may be purchasing drinking water, along with water comes the plastic container, which is disposed.

67. Engage in waste segregation at home and at office. Keep different bins for different wastes. Vegetable waste can be used to create compost.

68. Learn how to compost and practice composting.

69. Include and practice REFUSE, before the 4Rs of Reduce, Reuse, Recycle, and Recover, and make them into 5Rs (see Fig. 9.3). Refuse your life to be flooded with too many gadgets and goods. Refuse the invasion of advertising driven ethics in your life.

Can you think about any more ideas that can be added to this list? If yes, do email the author of the textbook. If the idea can be presented to the readers, we will publish the idea in the next edition of this textbook.

FIG. 9.3 The 5R's

Locavorism

Locavorism is a term that refers to the practice of having food that is produced locally. Due to modern trends in food production and consumption, food is travelling hundreds of miles before it reaches the plate, thus significantly contributing to pollution. For example, the food consumed in Illinois, USA, travels an average of 1500 miles between the farming of the food materials and the final consumption.[16] Some of the food materials make trans-national journeys. India imports food products from around the globe. Sugar and sugar confectionary are imported from countries such as Brazil, Thailand, Guatemala, and Spain. Dried vegetables are imported from Canada, USA, and Australia. Cashew nuts are imported from Benin, and dates from Afghanistan. Grapes are imported from Mexico and Peru. Oranges are imported from Spain. Such long-distance travel results in excessive carbon emissions and also creates a need for excessive packaging.

People who prefer to eat locally grown food are referred to as localvores or locavores. It is a collaborative effort to build more locally based, self-reliant food economies—one in which sustainable food production, processing, distribution, and consumption is integrated to enhance the economic, environmental, and social health of a particular place.[17] A locavore prefers to consume food that is produced locally—within a limited radius of 50 or 100 miles.

Benefits of Locavorism and its Criticisms

- Locally grown food is fresh as it is consumed almost immediately after harvest.
- The need for usage of chemical preservatives and irradiation to increase shelf-life is reduced or eliminated. Elimination of preservatives and antibiotics contributes in safeguarding one's health.
- In India, it is observed that the prices of food products available in the weekly fairs are lower than what that is available in major retail stores.

---

16 http://www.greenbiz.com/blog/2011/10/19/how-responsible-investing-can-change-food-system, last accessed on 20 October 2011

17 Feenstra, Gail 2002, Creating space for sustainable food systems: lessons from the field, *Agriculture and Human Values*, Vol 19, No. 2, 2002, pp. 99–106.

In the mid-2000s, *Mathrubhumi*, one of the leading Malayalam dailies, refused to take any advertisement from the multi-national cola companies, in an act of solidarity with the ongoing citizens' protest against exploitation of groundwater resources by the cola companies at Plachimada, Palakkad, Kerala. While this has resulted in significant loss of advertisement revenue for *Mathrubhumi*, it continued to maintain its bold stand against such exploitation. *Mathrubhumi* also filed with a ₹50 lakh defamation suit by a cola company, a case which was later dismissed by a sub-court in Kochi.

- In a farmers market, farmers/producers sell directly to consumers. Such practice avoids the need of middleman. This helps the farmer/producer to receive a higher price for their produce.
  - The practice of buying vegetable, groceries, etc., from the farmers market also strengthens local economies by protecting small farms, local jobs, and local shops.
  - Purchase of local food also helps in the preservation of indigenous varieties of seeds/crops and farming practices.
  - Sourcing locally result in lesser food miles, a term used to measure the distance travelled by food from the time of production to that of consumption.
  - As the farmer receives a decent income, the incentive to sell or convert farmland becomes less attractive.
  - You can purchase what you like to purchase, rather than someone making you want to purchase. Local businesses create new products based on the needs as mentioned and suggested by local citizens, unlike national megastores who sell products based on a national marketing and sales plan.

However, many of the benefits associated with consumption of local food go away, when the local food is produced under industrial conditions. The limitation of food miles is that it indicates only the distance travelled. Beans grown in Kenya and transported to UK will have food miles significantly higher as compared to beans grown in UK itself. However, beans grown in UK use manual labour and cow-dung as manure. On the contrary, agriculture in UK could use significantly higher fertilizers that have petroleum as their source, and the fields could be ploughed by tractors that burn diesel. 'Driving 6.5 miles to buy your shopping emits more carbon than flying a pack of Kenyan green beans to the UK,' said Gareth Thomas, Minister for Trade and Development, UK.[18]

Unsustainable Dietary Habits

Commenting on the increasing prevalence of obesity among global population, *The Economist* writes, 'Two-thirds of American adults are overweight... Alarmingly, 36 per cent of adults and 17 per cent of children are not just overweight but obese...

18 http://www.guardian.co.uk/environment/2008/mar/23/food.ethicalliving, last accessed on 28 October 2012.
19 http://www.economist.com/news/special-report/21568065-world-getting-wider-says-charlotte-howard-what-can-be-done-about-it-big, last accessed on 20 December 2012.

if current trend continues by 2030 nearly half of American adults could be obese…
in Britain, 25 per cent of all women are obese, with men following close behind at
24 per cent. Czech men take the European biscuit: 30 per cent are obese.'[19] Obesity
has negative impacts on the society. It can affect the mental health of an individual
and increases the risk of an individual being affected by diseases such as diabetes,
heart disease, strokes, and some kinds of cancers. It also hinders the productivity of
employees. In 2005, $190.2 billion (20.6 per cent of all medical expenditures) was spent
on obesity related illnesses.[20] With increased personal income, indulgence, and waste
may also increase. 'Greater wealth means that bicycles are abandoned for motorbikes
and cars, and work in the fields is swapped for sitting at desk. In rich countries the share
of the population that gets insufficient exercise is more than twice as high as in poor
ones…. Families can afford to eat more food of all kinds, and particularly those high in
fat and sugar. Mothers spend more time at work and less time cooking. Food companies
push their products harder,' comments *The Economist*. In Mexico, unreliable drinking
water supply and smart marketing by Coca-Cola company have resulted in making the
country the world's leading consumer of Coca-Cola beverage products—the average
adult consumed 675 servings in 2010 (see Table 9.3). The worldwide average was 89.
The Economist adds, 'All big food companies are working hard to sell more products
to more of the world. Many unhealthy products are very profitable.'[21] For 2011, the
worldwide average servings of Coca-Cola beverage products increased to 92 and Mexico
topped the list again, with a serving of 728.[22] In 2011, sparkling beverages of Coca-
Cola Company (Coca-Cola, Diet Coke, Fanta, Thums Up, Sprite, etc.), represented
approximately 75 per cent of global sales, in terms of unit case volume for 2011. Sales
of trademark Coca-Cola beverages accounted for approximately half of the worldwide
unit case volume for 2011.[23] Mexico is also a country that has one of the highest levels
of obesity in the world.[24, 25] An editorial in the *New England Journal of Medicine* says,
'The increase in consumption of sugar sweetened beverages among both adults and
children in the United States and other countries is considered a potential contributor to
the obesity pandemic…Unlike carbohydrates with high fibre content, sugar sweetened
beverages are nutrient-poor and are often associated with consumption of salty foods
and fast foods. An emerging association between the increased consumption of sugar
sweetened beverages and chronic diseases such as type 2 diabetes, hypertension, and
coronary heart disease is a major concern.'[26]

20 Cawley, John, Chad Meyerhoeferd 2012, The medical care costs of obesity: An instrumental variables approach,
    Journal of Health Economics, Vol 31, Issue 1, January 2012, pp. 219–230.
21 http://www.economist.com/news/special-report/21568064-food-companies-play-ambivalent-part-fight-against-
    flab-food-thought, last accessed on 24 December 2012.
22 http://www.coca-colacompany.com/annual-review/2011/pdf/TCCC_2011_Annual_Review.pdf, last accessed on
    24 December 2012.
23 10-K filing made by Coca-Cola company for year 2011
24 http://www.telegraph.co.uk/expat/expatnews/7128022/Mexico-has-record-childhood-obesity.html, last accessed
    on 25 December 2012.
25 http://www.economist.com/node/17314636, last accessed on 25 December 2012.
26 http://myeloma.org/pdfs/NEJM-Calories-From-Soft-Drinks.pdf, last accessed on 24 January 2013.

TABLE 9.3[27] Per capita consumption of Coca-Cola beverage products in 2010, based on US 8 fluid ounces of a finished beverage

Servings per capita per annum	Country
11	India
12	Mali
13	Indonesia
15	Pakistan
28	Nigeria
34	China
40	Kenya
54	Egypt
69	Russia
69	South Korea
89	Average worldwide
94	Thailand
125	Colombia
139	Italy
143	France
144	Philippines
159	Turkey
178	Japan
179	Germany
193	Peru
204	Great Britain
221	Bolivia
229	Brazil
236	Canada
254	South Africa
255	Austria
284	Spain
318	Argentina
319	Australia
394	United States
445	Chile
675	Mexico

27 http://assets.coca-colacompany.com/ba/22/39fae0564dcda20c694be368b8cf/TCCC_2010_Annual_Review_Per_Capita_Consumption.pdf, last accessed on 24 December 2012.

Food Miles and Slow Food Movement

In modern times, food produced travels thousands of miles before reaching the hands of the consumer. The distance travelled by food, from its source of production, till it reaches the consumer, is referred to as 'food miles'. As 'food miles' related to a food product increases, the carbon emission associated with the food also increases. It has been found that there has been a 25 per cent increase in the 'food miles', between 1980 and 2007. The Sunday Times[28] reported, 'Scottish prawns are being hand-shelled in China, Atlantic haddock caught off Scotland is being prepared in Poland, and Welsh cockles are being sent to Holland to be put in jars before going on sale in Britain.' The article further states, 'Traidcraft coffee, sold at Sainsbury's, is made from beans grown in Bukoba, Tanzania. Once the coffee is cultivated, it is driven 656 miles to Dar-es-Salaam, and then shipped 3,250 miles to Vijayawada in India where it is packed. The coffee is loaded back on the ships and transported another 5,000 miles to Southampton. It is then driven 330 miles to Gateshead and is finally driven to Leeds for distribution to Sainsbury's stores.' Similarly, nuts produced in Bolivia (in South America) are packed in Italy and then taken to Britain. The following is an excerpt from *Living Oneness: Restoring Wholeness in a Fragmented World*, a study guide released by 'A Global Oneness Project'.[29]

> *In a worldview of separation, we can use food just like we use other natural resources. We take it from nature, and commodify it as an abstract component of our economic system. When we treat food this way, we create items to eat, but they do not remind us of our relationship with nature, or offer a way to be fed by life's essential nourishment. The co-modification of food emphasizes food as objects of our desire, rather than an entryway into a supportive life system.*
>
> *A Twinkie does not resemble food in its natural state, not does a bag of Cheetos. These are contrived 'things,' not nourishing food, and as we ingest them we distance ourselves from our own bodies, which do not benefit from such 'things'. But the more we force the body to try, the more we transform it into a thing itself.*
>
> *We eat 'junk food' all the time—but if we understood that we are what we eat, would we want to consume, and become, 'junk'?*
>
> *Carlo Petrini, founder of Slow Food, an international non-profit supporting healthy local food production and enjoyment, illustrates the mind-boggling absurdity of living in a culture that supports the production and consumption of low quality food: 'Publicity has convinced us to eat worse food so we can consume other things. So now we're at this absurd figure where underwear costs more than food…'*

28 http://www.timesonline.co.uk/tol/news/uk/article1813836.ece, last accessed on 31 October 2011.

29 http://www.globalonenessproject.org/sites/default/files/education/resources/livingonenessstudyguide.pdf, last accessed on 28 May 2013. Used with permission.

In contrast to the emergence of Fast Food culture nowadays, the 'Slow Food Movement' emerged as part of the 'Slow Movement' that explored possibilities of slowing down life's pace. 'Slow Movement' included experiments such as 'Slow Cities' (Cittaslow), 'Slow Living', 'Slow Travel', and 'Slow Design'. Slow Food Movement strives to promote food that is fresh, flavoursome, seasonal, and part of the local culture. It advocates a food production and consumption system that does not harm the environment, animal welfare, and planet Earth. It also aims to provide food at fair accessible prices for consumers, under fair conditions, and pay for small-scale producers. Slow Food organization 'opposes the standardization of taste and culture, and the unrestrained power of the food industry multinationals and industrial agriculture.'[30] The organization aims to achieve its objectives by undertaking:

MC Mehta, a lawyer in the Supreme Court of India, is known for pioneering environmental activism through legal means. Often termed as the 'One Man Enviro-legal Brigade', he has filed a series of Public Interest Litigations (PILs) at the Supreme Court of India. He is known for filing litigations related to saving the Taj Mahal and 255 other historic monuments within the Taj trapezium from environmental pollution, vehicular pollution across India, illegal mining, pollution of the water flowing in River Ganga and Yamuna, pollution of water by tanneries, groundwater pollution at Rajasthan, and creating awareness among the public and students about environmental issues. Through his non-profit NGO, the 'MC Mehta Environmental Foundation', Mehta creates awareness about environmental issues among the general public, and also trains people on areas related to environmental law and environmental policy frameworks.

- Projects related to food and taste education—This is done through tours of local farms or producers, school gardens, guided tastings, knowledge exchange between older generations and young people, practical workshops, and dinners with producers.
- Protecting food biodiversity and traditions—This is done through recovering traditional processing methods, safeguarding native and local breeds, cataloguing and promoting foods related to specific communities and cultures, creating food gardens in schools, villages, and urban fringe areas, and adding narrative labels in products that will communicate the story of the food (information related to area of origin, techniques used for farming and processing, varieties and breeds associated with the food product, practice adopted for animal welfare and preservation, etc.)
- Creating networks—To improve the prevailing food system, Slow Food organization started the Terra Madre network, which brings together many stakeholders in a food system, such as small-scale farmers, breeders, fishers, and food artisans with academics, chefs, consumers, and youth. These communities are defined by a place of origin and focus on local economy. Under the Terra Madre network, more than 2,000 such communities have been found. Slow Food

---

30 http://www.slowfood.com/international/2/our-philosophy, last accessed on 29 July 2013.

Organization also creates markets where the small-scale producers and farmers can sell their product directly to consumers.

ROLE OF NGOS

World Bank defines non-governmental organizations (NGOs) as private organizations that pursue activities to relieve suffering, promote the interests of the poor, protect the environment, provide basic social services, or undertake community development.[31] As per this World Bank document, NGOs are categorized into (a) Operational NGOs and (b) Advocacy NGOs. The purpose of operational NGOs is the design and implementation of development related projects while Advocacy NGOs are those that promote a specific cause and tries to influence policies and practices. Operational NGOs can be classified into: (a) Community-based organizations, (b) National organizations, and (c) International organizations.

Paul Hawken, an entrepreneur and author, writes that the member countries of the UN peacekeeping nations spends 2000 times the amount of money on war-making, as compared to UN peacekeeping efforts. He also noted that four of the five countries of the UN Security Council (that has the veto power over all UN resolutions)—USA, UK, France, and Russia—are the top weapon dealers of the world.[32] While that sounds like meeting a wall, Hawken adds, 'What I see are ordinary and some-not so-ordinary individuals willing to confront despair, power, and incalculable odds in an attempt to restore some semblance of grace, justice, and beauty to this world.'[33] He says this in the context of the non-profit groups and community organizations that works towards benefitting the people and the planet (see Fig. 9.4—a promotional campaign by Mozilla Firefox).

Some corporations may find it difficult to embrace corporate social responsibility endeavours due to a number of reasons, one of them being a lack of competence in the area. In such situations, the NGOs can prove to be an effective partner. The corporation and the NGO can complement their roles. There have been news reports[34,35] that public sector units like Coal India, for year 2011–12, were able to spend only ₹82 crore from the allotted ₹553.33 crore for social responsibility endeavours. For 2010–11, the

31 http://www-wds.worldbank.org/external/default/WDSContentServer/WDSP/IB/1995/03/01/000009265_3961
    219103437/Rendered/PDF/multi_page.pdf, last accessed on 24 August 2013.
32 Hawken, Paul 2007, *Blessed Unrest: How the Largest Movement in the World Came into Being and Why No One Saw It Coming*, New York: Viking Press, 2007.
33 Hawken, Paul 2007, *Blessed Unrest: How the Largest Movement in the World Came into Being and Why No One Saw It Coming*, New York: Viking Press, 2007.
34 http://articles.economictimes.indiatimes.com/2013-04-23/news/38763257_1_csr-activities-csr-projects-crore, last accessed on 25 August 2013.
35 http://www.indiacsr.in/en/?p=10606, last accessed on 25 August 2013.

FIG. 9.4[36] An advertisement by Mozilla

company spent only ₹108.4 crore instead of the budget allocation of ₹262.2 crore. Under-utilization of CSR funds has happened during 2007–08, 2008–09, and 2009–10. Effective NGOs has the possibility to change such situations and work towards the global good.

GREEN GOVERNANCE

In a message on Earth Day, Sadhguru Jaggi Vasudev, Founder, Isha Foundation, mentioned, 'How audacious that we can even think that we will allot a day for the earth!

---

36 Photo by Henrik Moltke, image released under Creative Commons Attributions 2.0 Generic Licence, Used with permission, Image source: http://gondwanaland.com/mlog/2011/12/22/mozilla-money-freedom/, This is an adapted version of the original picture available at https://www.flickr.com/photos/henrikmoltke/5587199796, by Henrlk Moltke, last accessed on 12 August 2013.

Both day and night happen only because of the revolutions of the earth. Our very body is an extract from this planet. Everything that we are is earth. For the human beings who have forgotten that they have just temporarily come out of the womb of this earth and that they will one day be sucked back into this earth, for them, this day is a reminder that you are a part of this earth. If humanity has to live for a long time, you have to think like the earth, act like the earth, and be the earth, because that is what you are.'[37]

Many indigenous and local communities have very intimate relationships with biological resources, and this has been recognized by the international community, in the preamble to the Convention of Biological Diversity.

Convention of Biological Diversity

Convention of Biological Diversity is an internationally legally binding treaty with the goals of conservation of biodiversity, sustainable use of its components, and fair and equitable sharing of benefits arising from genetic resources. The cultures of these communities and their traditional knowledge have been closely rooted in their enviroment. They have also used biodiversity in their region in a sustainable way for thousands of years. There was concern among these communities that developments proposed to take place on their areas may have potential long-term negative impacts on their livelihoods and traditional knowledge. Parties to the convention agreed to respect, preserve, and maintain traditional knowledge relevant for the conservation and sustainable use of biological diversity, and to promote its wider application. The following are two of the guidelines adopted by the parties to the convention.

Akwé: Kon Guidelines

Akwé: Kon[38] guidelines[39] are voluntary guidelines for the conduct of cultural, environmental, and social impact assessments regarding developments proposed to take place on, or which are likely to impact on, sacred sites and on lands and waters traditionally occupied or used by indigenous and local communities. These were developed by the secretariat of the convention on biological diversity. Akwé: Kon refers to a Mohawk term that means 'everything in creation'. The following is the suggested ten-step process for impact assessment of proposed development as a guideline.[40]

   1. Notification and public consultation of the proposed development by the proponent.

---

37 http://blog.ishafoundation.org/masters-words/the-state-of-the-planet/, last accessed on 28 April 2012.

38 Pronounced "agway-goo". The term was provided by the Kahnawake community located near Montreal, Canada, where the guidelines were negotiated.

39 Secretariat of the Convention on Biological Diversity (2004).Akwé: Kon Voluntary Guidelines for the Conduct of Cultural, Environmental and Social Impact Assessment regarding Developments Proposed to Take Place on, or which are Likely to Impact on, Sacred Sites and on Lands and Waters Traditionally Occupied or Used by Indigenous and Local Communities Montreal, 25p. (CBD Guidelines Series). Permission allowed for reproduction/ duplication that involves educational purpose.

40 http://www.cbd.int/doc/publications/akwe-brochure-en.pdf, last accessed on 28 April 2012.

2. Identification of indigenous and local communities and relevant stakeholders likely to be affected by the proposed development.

3. Establishment of effective mechanisms for indigenous and local community participation, including for the participation of women, the youth, the elderly, and other vulnerable groups, in the impact assessment processes.

4. Establishment of an agreed process for recording the views and concerns of the members of the indigenous or local community whose interests are likely to be impacted by a proposed development.

5. Establishment of a process whereby local and indigenous communities may have the option to accept or oppose a proposed development that may impact on their community.

6. Identification and provision of sufficient human, financial, technical, and legal resources for effective indigenous and local community participation in all phases of impact assessment procedures.

7. Establishment of an environmental management or monitoring plan (EMP), including contingency plans regarding possible adverse cultural, environmental, and social impacts resulting from a proposed development.

8. Identification of actors responsible for liability, redress, insurance, and compensation.

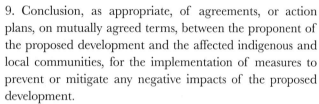

Interface Inc., in partnership with Zoological Society of London, has created Net-Works, an organization through which Interface will collect old fishing nets from 26 villages in Danajon Bank, one of the world's six double barrier reefs. Due to unsustainable fishing practices and dumping of old fishing nets (that can circle the earth 1.5 times, if laid out end to end), Danajon Bank has become one of the most degraded coral reefs of the world. Interface plans to recycle the old nets into new carpet fibers.

9. Conclusion, as appropriate, of agreements, or action plans, on mutually agreed terms, between the proponent of the proposed development and the affected indigenous and local communities, for the implementation of measures to prevent or mitigate any negative impacts of the proposed development.

10. Establishment of a review and appeals process.

Tkarihwaié:ri Code Of Ethical Conduct

The Tkarihwaié:ri[41] code of ethical conduct is to ensure respect for the cultural and intellectual heritage of indigenous and local communities relevant to the conservation and sustainable use of biological diversity. The ethical principles that guide the Tkarihwaié:ri code are as follows:[42]

Respect for existing settlements This principle recognizes the importance of mutually agreed settlements or

41 The word "Tkarihwaie:ri" is a Mohawk term meaning "the proper way". The term was provided by the Elders of the Mohawk Community of Kahnawake. The Mohawk are the traditional custodians of the area of Montreal where the code was negotiated.

42 Secretariat of the Convention on Biological Diversity grants permission to reproduce/ duplicate the Tkarihwaié:ri code of ethical conduct, if the reproduction is meant for educational purposes. The comprehensive document that details this code of conduct can be found at http://www.cbd.int/traditional/code/ethicalconduct-brochure-en.pdf

agreements at national level that exist in many countries, and that respect should be applied to such arrangements at all times.

Intellectual property   Community and individual concerns over, and claims to, cultural and intellectual property relevant to traditional knowledge, innovations, and practices related to the conservation and sustainable use of biodiversity should be acknowledged and addressed in the negotiation with indigenous and local communities, prior to starting activities/interactions.

Non-discrimination   The ethics and guidelines for all activities/interactions should be non-discriminatory, taking into account affirmative action, particularly in relation to gender, disadvantaged groups, and representation.

Transparency/full disclosure   Indigenous and local communities should be adequately informed in advance, about the nature, scope, and purpose of any proposed activities/interactions carried out by others that may involve the use of their traditional knowledge, innovations, and practices related to the conservation and sustainable use of biodiversity, occurring on or likely to impact on, sacred sites and on lands and waters traditionally occupied or used by indigenous and local communities. This information should be provided in a manner that takes into consideration and actively engages with the body of knowledge and cultural practices of indigenous and local communities.

Prior informed consent and/or approval and involvement   Any activities/interactions related to traditional knowledge associated with the conservation and sustainable use of biological diversity, occurring on or likely to impact on sacred sites and on lands and waters traditionally occupied or used by indigenous and local communities and impacting upon specific groups, should be carried out with the prior informed consent and/or approval and involvement of indigenous and local communities. Such consent or approval should not be coerced, forced or manipulated.

Inter-cultural respect   Traditional knowledge should be respected as a legitimate expression of the culture, traditions, and experience of indigenous and local communities and as part of the plurality of existing knowledge systems. It is highly desirable that those interacting with indigenous and local communities respect the integrity, morality, and spirituality of the cultures, traditions, and relationships of indigenous and local communities and avoid the imposition of external concepts, standards, and value judgments, in inter-cultural dialogue. Respect for cultural heritage, ceremonial, and sacred sites, as well as sacred species, and secret and sacred knowledge ought to be given specific consideration in any activities/interactions.

Safeguarding collective or individual ownership   The resources and knowledge of indigenous and local communities can be collectively or individually owned. Those interacting with indigenous and local communities should seek to understand the balance of collective and individual rights and obligations. The right of indigenous and local communities to safeguard, collectively or otherwise, their cultural and intellectual heritage, tangible and intangible, should be respected.

Fair and equitable sharing of benefits   Indigenous and local communities ought to receive fair and equitable benefits for their contribution to activities/interactions related to biodiversity and associated traditional knowledge proposed to take place on, or which are likely to impact on, sacred sites, and lands and waters traditionally occupied or used by indigenous and local communities. Benefit-sharing should be regarded as a way of strengthening indigenous and local communities and promoting the objectives of the Convention on Biological Diversity and ought to be equitable within and among relevant groups, taking into account relevant community-level procedures.

Protection   Proposed activities/interactions within the mandate of the Convention should make reasonable efforts to protect and enhance the relationships of affected indigenous and local communities with the environment and thereby promote the objectives of the Convention.

Precautionary approach   This principle reaffirms the precautionary approach contained in principle 15 of the Rio Declaration on Environment and Development and in the preamble to the Convention on Biological Diversity. The prediction and assessment of potential harms to biological diversity should include local criteria and indicators, and should fully involve the relevant indigenous and local communities.

CHAPTER SUMMARY

- Anthropocentrism is based on the idea of human beings as the species that is the central and most important in the universe. Ecocentrism denotes a nature-centred perspective, where humans are only one of the species amongst the many species on the planet.

- In the US, shareholder resolutions are filed in areas related to corporate governance, executive compensation, and social and environmental responsibility issues including areas like such as warming, use of toxicants like tobacco, human rights, and animal welfare. Filing a shareholder resolution will result in that resolution being included in the management proxy circular and this is submitted for a vote at the company's annual general meeting (AGM). Companies normally tend to prefer the removal of such resolutions from the AGM agenda, and thus engage in a dialogue with those who filed the resolution.

- Locavorism is a term that refers to the practice of having food that is produced locally. People who prefer to eat locally grown food are referred to as localvores or locavores. It is a collaborative

effort to build more locally based, self-reliant food economies—one in which sustainable food production, processing, distribution, and consumption is integrated to enhance the economic, environmental and social health of a particular place. A locavore prefers to consume food that is produced locally—within a limited radius of 50 or 100 miles.

- The distance travelled by food, from its source of production, till it reaches the consumer, is referred to as 'food miles'. As 'food miles' related to a food produce increases, the carbon emission associated with the food also increases. It has been found that there has been a 25 per cent increase in the 'food miles' between 1980 and 2007.

- Slow food movement strives to promote food that is fresh, flavoursome, seasonal, and part of the local culture. It advocates a food production and consumption system that does not harm the environment, animal welfare, and planet Earth. It also aims to provide food at fair accessible prices for consumers and fair conditions and pay for small-scale producers. Slow food organization

'opposes the standardization of taste and culture, and the unrestrained power of the food industry multinationals and industrial agriculture.'
- Non-Governmental Organizations (NGOs) as private organizations that pursue activities to relieve suffering, promote the interests of the poor, protect the environment, provide basic social services, or undertake community development.
- Convention of Biological Diversity is an internationally legally binding treaty with the goals of conservation of biodiversity, sustainable use of its components and fair and equitable sharing of benefits arising from genetic resources.

- Akwé: Kon guidelines are voluntary guidelines for the conduct of cultural, environmental and social impact assessments regarding developments proposed to take place on, or which are likely to impact on, sacred sites and on lands and waters traditionally occupied or used by indigenous and local communities.
- The Tkarihwaié:ri code of ethical conduct is to ensure respect for the cultural and intellectual heritage of indigenous and local communities relevant to the conservation and sustainable use of biological diversity.

KEYWORDS

- Akwé: Kon guidelines
- Anthropocentrism
- Convention of biological diversity
- Ecocentrism
- Locavorism, food miles

- Non-governmental organizations (NGOs)
- Shareholder resolutions
- Slow food movement
- The earth charter
- Tkarihwaié:ri code of ethical conduct

EXERCISES

Multiple-choice Questions

1. The Earth Charter, an international declaration work towards the purpose of creating a _____.
   (a) just, sustainable and peaceful global society.
   (b) world where people can easily exploit the natural resources.
   (c) world that can easily harness peace.
   (d) society that will safeguard animals.
2. Which tradition regards Earth as goddess?
   (a) Islam
   (b) Sikhism
   (c) Christianity
   (d) Hinduism

3. What does the term Locavorism refer to?
   (a) Food that is produced locally
   (b) Hot spicy food
   (c) Red meat
   (d) A meal consisting of Burger and Soda
4. The distance travelled by food, from its source of production, till it reaches the consumer, is referred to as _____.
   (a) food miles
   (b) sourcing
   (c) food travel
   (d) carbon trading
5. Convention of Biological diversity was instrumental in creating the _____.

(a) Akwé: Kon
(b) human
(c) Tkarihwaié:ri code of ethical conduct
(d) CSR

6. Tkarihwaié:ri code of ethical conduct stands for
_____
(a) respect for cultural local communities related to biodiversity
(b) for endangered species
(c) conservation of wildlife
(d) none of these

7. Recognizing that all beings are interdependent and every life form has value regardless of its worth to human beings, comes under which responsibility of the earth charter?
(a) Ecological integrity
(b) Respect and care for the community of life
(c) Social and economic justice
(d) Democracy, non- violence and peace

8. According to the Edelman goodpurpose study (2012) what is the most important factor in choosing a brand among peers, when quality and price are the same?
(a) Social purpose
(b) Brand image
(c) Advertisements
(d) Recommendation

9. What are the experiments conducted under slow movement?
(a) Slow cities
(b) Slow living
(c) Slow travel
(d) All of these

10. Which is the country that has the highest level of obesity and also known for high consumption of carbonated drinks?
(a) Spain
(b) Mexico
(c) America
(d) India

11. 'Not every venture is about capital' is the promotional campaign of which of the following web browsers?
(a) Internet Explorer
(b) Google chrome
(c) Mozilla Firefox
(d) None of these

12. What does the term *Akwe: Kon* refer to?
(a) Everything in creation
(b) Living in harmony
(c) Protecting mother earth
(d) Preventing pollution

Short Answer Questions

1. Write a note about the Earth Charter.
2. What role can a consumer and investor play in making a business sustainable?
3. List at least 5 roles an individual must play in conservation of natural resources and preventing pollution.
4. In 2011, which company achieved zero landfill status by following the 3R's?
5. What is Locavorism? Explain with 2 examples.
6. Mention some of the important features of the National Environmental policy.
7. Define food miles.
8. What are the objectives of the slow food organization?
9. Define NGOs. What are the two types of NGOs?
10. What are the two guidelines adopted by the parties of the Convention of Biological Diversity in recognition of the intimate relationship that indigenous and local communities have with biological resources?

Long Answer Questions

1. Explain the principles followed under 'Social and Economic Justice' for sustainable way of life as per the 'Earth Charter'.
2. Mention some of the benefits and criticism related to Locavorism. Give some ideas on promoting Locavorism.
3. Comment on the prevalent unsustainable dietary habits and give your ideas on incorporating sustainability practices in dietary habits.
4. What is 'Food Miles'? How is 'Slow Food Movement' different from 'Food Miles' and what are its objectives?
5. What is the Convention on Biodiversity? Briefly explain the two guidelines adopted by the convention.
6. State the four broad categories under 'Respect and care for the community of life' of the Earth charter and describe in brief as to what should be done in order to fulfill these broad commitments.
7. What are shareholder resolutions? Elaborate on (a) the areas related to shareholder resolution, (b) the process of filing, withdrawal, and approval of shareholder resolution by a company, and (c) how companies use it to create competitive advantage.
8. What are the roles that an individual can engage in to conserve the natural resources and environment? State 15 ways by which an individual can serve the environment.
9. Explain the role that can be played by NGOs in implementing CSR activities of a company.
10. What are the ten principles spelt out in the Akwe: Kon guidelines?
11. What are the ethical principles that guide the Tkarihwaie:ri code of ethical conduct?

Reflective Questions

1. Be aware of your breathing. Can you feel your last breath? Where did it come from? Before sustaining you with this breath, whom did it sustain prior to that? After you breathe out, where it will go? Whom it will sustain?
2. Think about the food that you ate during your last meal. Where did it come from? Can you think about the entities involved in the preparation of that food? It is only people, or are there entities beyond people?
3. This question is related to bringing your conscience and values into your purchase decisions. Read the questions below:
   (a) List out few products/services that you bought recently (in the previous few weeks).
   (b) Which of the following factors most influenced your purchase?
      (i) **Advertising**—Encouragement from a company to buy its product
      (ii) **Appearance**—How a product looks
      (iii) **Brand loyalty**—You have commitment to a certain brand and continue to buy this brand repeatedly
      (iv) **Location of origin**—The place where the product was made
      (v) **Durability**—How long the product lasts
      (vi) **Environmental impact**—
         1. Environmental impact caused during the life-cycle of the product—Sourcing of raw materials, manufacturing of the product, distribution and retailing of the product, consumption of the product, and recycling of the product
         2. Environment-friendly actions undertaken by the manufacturer of the product

(vii) **Social/People/Labour impact**—
3. Impact caused during the life cycle of the product—Sourcing of raw materials, manufacturing of the product, distribution and retailing of the product, consumption of the product, and recycling of the product
4. Environment-friendly actions undertaken by the manufacturer of the product

(viii) **Popularity and peer influence**—Bought and used by many people

(ix) **Price**—The cost of something

(x) **Product warranty/guarantee**—A promise from a company to repair/replace something that breaks

(xi) **Recommendation**—Someone you know encouraged you to buy a product that he/she uses

(c) Do you think that this is a good reason to buy a product? If not, how will you purchase differently in the future?

(d) Now pick up any three values from the 35 values given in the following list, which are deeply held by your heart.

Paropakara (Helpfulness)	Daya (Kindness)	Samyama (Self-control)	Vaastavata (Authenticity)	Gyana/Jnana (Awareness)
Maanan (Respect)	Sathya (Truth)	Seva (Selfless service)	Prema (Love)	Dharma (Character)
Dheeratha (Fortitude)	Kshama (Forgiveness)	Saralata (Simplicity)	Sama-cittatwam (Equanimity)	Sthairyam (Perseverance)
Karuna (Compassion)	Dheeratha (Courage)	Ahinsa (Non-violence)	Saumyata (Gentleness)	Upasana (Devotion)
Maitri (Friendship)	Mahanubhavata (Generosity)	Krutajnata (Gratitude)	Vinaya (Humility)	Tyaaga (Sacrifice)
Arjavam (Rectitude)	Atma-visvasa (Self-confidence)	Abhaya (Fearlessness)	Bhratrutva (Brotherhood)	Shanthi (Peace)
Trupti (Satisfaction)	Atma-abhimana (Self-respect)	Viswasa (Trust)	Ekatwa (Unity)	Vijnana (Wisdom)
Sankalpa (Determination)	Anahankara (Absence of self-importance)	Shaucham (Inner and outer purity)	Janma-mrityu-jara-vyadhi-duhkha-dosanudarshanam (Knowledge of the limitations of birth, death, old age, illness, and pain)	Vairagyam (Detached involvement)
Pratibha (Creativity)	Sraddha (Attentive faith)	Samarpan (Dedication)	Tulyatva (Equality)	Svatantrata (Freedom)

(e) How would you bring those deeply held values to action during your purchase decisions?

Take-home Activity

1. Plant a minimum of five tree saplings and inspire another person to plant a tree sapling. You can plant tree saplings at public/private spaces (places of worship, educational institutions,

government offices, on the side of roads, hostels, playgrounds, home, etc.). Saplings of native trees are to be planted. Let there be diversity in the tree saplings that you choose. You can have a mix of different type of trees (such as a fruit giving tree, a shade giving tree, a flower bearing tree, medicinal tree, trees that have religious significance, trees that are of benefit for animals and other plants, trees that exist for centuries etc.). As we all know, a baby needs to be nurtured after given birth. Hence, nurturing the saplings are as important as planting the saplings. The tree sapling needs to be planted at a location where you can water it regularly. If the tree sapling is planted in areas where there is a possibility that the sapling may be destroyed, a tree guard should be used.

Web Readings

1.   Green NGOs
   (a) Project Greenhands—http://www.projectgreenhands.org
   (b) Nature Forever—http://natureforever.org/
   (c) Greenpeace—http://www.greenpeace.org/india/en/
   (d) WWF India—http://www.wwfindia.org/

Recommended Books

1.   Aldo Leopold, *A Sand County Almanac*, Oxford University Press, 1963.

2.   Satish Kumar, *You Are, Therefore I Am: A Declaration of Dependence*, Green Books, 2002.

Recommended Documentaries/Movies

1.   Shaped by Hand. Dirs. Elias Koch, Arron Wilder. (This documentary is available for free viewing at http://www.globalonenessproject.org/library/films/shaped-hand), Duration: 4 minutes.

2.   Spitian: A Short Documentary (This documentary is available for free viewing at https://www.youtube.com/watch?v=BX2BYL0qnP4). Duration: 9 minutes.

3.   The Slow Poisoning of India, The Energy and Resources Insitute (TERI) (This documentary is available for free viewing at https://www.youtube.com/watch?v=_WvoB2gRJbE). Duration: 26 minutes.

Answers to Mutiple-choice Questions:
1(a)   2(d)   3(a)   4(a)   5(a)   6(a)   7(b)   8(a)   9(d)   10(b)   11(c)   12(a)

10 ENVIRONMENTAL LAWS, POLICIES, AND TREATIES

Aakashasya Sthithiryavad
yaavangca jagat sthithi:
Taavanmama sthithirbhooya
Jagad-dukhani nighnatha:

(For as long as space endures, and for as long as living beings remain, until then may I too abide, to dispel the misery of the world.)

Shantideva, an 8th-century Buddhist monk and scholar who studied at Nalanda University

After studying the chapter, the reader will be able to understand the following:
- Evolution of environmental laws in India
- Laws and guidelines related to conservation of natural ecosystems
- Various international agreements and laws related to conservation
- How Ecuador and Bolivia have given specific legal rights to planet Earth

INTRODUCTION

Reverence towards Earth and the diversity of creation that inhabit this planet has been embedded in many indigenous cultures, including India (see Chapter 2). Amongst other thoughts, the culture of India supported the idea of seeing God in a stone, and also facilitated the journey of an individual to experientially realising this. In addition to Hinduism, oriental religions like Buddhism and Jainism also evoked reverence towards the nature and its creation (see Fig. 10.1). King Ashoka (304BC–232BC) from the Mauryan Empire, who embraced Buddhism, relinquished the habit of hunting animals, a practice that is continued by some even now. An edict on the fifth pillar of the seven pillar edicts, states that King Ashoka declared many animals and birds to be protected.[1] This included mynas, parrots, geese, wild ducks, bats, queen ants, boneless fish, tortoise, porcupines, squirrels, deer, bulls, wild, and domestic pigeon. It was forbidden to kill goats and sheep who are nurturing their young ones or is at a stage of milking

---

1 http://www.buddhanet.net/pdf_file/edicts-asoka6.pdf, last accessed on 23 July 2014.

their young ones.[2] Restrictions were also placed in the killing and selling of fishes and animals, and forests were not to be burnt for killing living beings or without valid reasons.[3] Therefore, philosophical ideas and spiritual experiences had a significant role to play in the way life in India. The idea of *Vasudhaiva Kutumbakam*—the world as one family, encompassed all forms, living and non-living.

It was in the twentieth century that the need and purpose of environmental laws were being acknowledged by the international community, primarily driven by objective knowledge about the negative impacts that human beings are having on this planet. A uniqueness about environmental laws across the world is their similarity in basic principles and objectives. 'Environmental lawyers speak a universal legal, scientific, and ethical language. The reason is simple: the institutional problems that give rise to environmental degradation, pollution, and the loss of biodiversity are basically similar throughout the world and variations in response come more at the enforcement rather than at the legislative level,' says Dan Tarlock, Professor of Law and Co-Director, Program in Environmental and Energy Law, Chicago-Kent College of Law, USA.[4]

FIG. 10.1[5] A statue of Gautama, the Buddha, at Tawang Monastery, Arunachal Pradesh, India. The diversity of life forms is represented around the statue.

---

2 http://www.sdstate.edu/projectsouthasia/upload/Ashokan-Pillar-Edicts.pdf, last accessed on 23 July 2014.
3 http://www.katinkahesselink.net/tibet/asoka1b.html, last accessed on 23 July 2014.
4 http://www.eolss.net/Sample-Chapters/C04/E4-21-01.pdf, last accessed on 23 July 2014.
5 Photo and (c): Y Giridhar Appaji Nag, giridhar@appaji.net, used with permission. Image Source: https://secure.flickr.com/photos/appaji/285878126/in/set-72157594444077629, last accessed on 20 August 2014.

One of the earliest environmental protection laws in modern India was 'The Elephants Preservation Act, 1879', which forbid the killing and capture of wild elephants. The oldest federal environmental law in the United States is the 'The Rivers and Harbors Appropriation Act of 1899', a law that made it a misdemeanour to dump waste matter into navigable waters.[6] However, it was only in the 1960s and later, that the creation of environmental rules and guidelines gained strength internationally. It has been found that almost 500 national climate laws have been passed in 66 countries since 1997. This has been a steep increase from almost 50 laws in 2000.[7] Following are some of the major environmental legislations that have come into effect in India.[8]

CHRONOLOGY OF ENVIRONMENTAL LAWS IN INDIA

General

1986   *The Environment (Protection) Act* authorizes the central government to protect and improve environmental quality, control, and reduce pollution from all sources, and prohibit or restrict the setting and/or operation of any industrial facility on environmental grounds.

1986   *The Environment (Protection) Rules* lays down procedures for setting standards of emission or discharge of environmental pollutants.

1989   The objective of *Hazardous Waste (Management and Handling) Rules* is to control the generation, collection, treatment, import, storage, and handling of hazardous waste.

1989   *The Manufacture, Storage, and Import of Hazardous Rules* define the terms used in this context, and sets up an authority to inspect, once a year, the industrial activity connected with hazardous chemicals and isolated storage facilities.

1989   *The Manufacture, Use, Import, Export, and Storage of Hazardous Micro-organisms/ Genetically Engineered Organisms or Cells Rules* were introduced with a view to protect the environment, nature, and health, in connection with the application of gene technology and microorganisms.

1991   *The Public Liability Insurance Act and Rules and Amendment, 1992* was drawn up to provide for public liability insurance for the purpose of providing immediate relief to the persons affected by accident while handling any hazardous substance.

1995   *The National Environmental Tribunal Act* has been created to award compensation for damages to persons, property, and the environment arising from any activity involving hazardous substances.

---

6 http://www.law.cornell.edu/uscode/text/33/407, last accessed on 23 July 2014.

7 Nachmany, M, S Fankhauser, T Townshend, M Collins, T Landesman, A Matthews, C Pavese, K Rietig, P Schleifer, J Setzer 2014. *The GLOBE Climate Legislation Study: A Review of Climate Change Legislation in 66 Countries*, Fourth Edition. London: GLOBE International and the Grantham Research Institute, London School of Economics. Report meant for free circulation; http://www.globeinternational.org/news/item/climate-legislation-study-online-app.

8 http://edugreen.teri.res.in/explore/laws.htm, last accessed on 29 July 2013. Used with permission from The Energy and Resources Institute (TERI).

The Whanganui River in New Zealand was granted a legal personhood by the government of New Zealand in 2012, as part of a settlement between the Maori iwi, a group of indigenous Polynesian people in New Zealand. The agreement recognizes the status of a river as 'Te Awa Tupua' (an integrated living whole from the mountains to sea).

1997 *The National Environment Appellate Authority Act* has been created to hear appeals with respect to restrictions of areas in which classes of industries etc., are carried out or prescribed subject to certain safeguards under the EPA.

1998 *The Biomedical waste (Management and Handling) Rules* is a legal binding on the health care institutions to streamline the process of proper handling of hospital waste such as segregation, disposal, collection, and treatment.

1999 *The Environment (Siting for Industrial Projects) Rules, 1999* lay down detailed provisions relating to areas to be avoided for siting of industries, precautionary measures to be taken for site selecting as also the aspects of environmental protection which should have been incorporated during the implementation of the industrial development projects.

2000 *The Municipal Solid Wastes (Management and Handling) Rules, 2000* apply to every municipal authority responsible for the collection, segregation, storage, transportation, processing, and disposal of municipal solid wastes.

2000 *The Ozone Depleting Substances (Regulation and Control) Rules* have been laid down for the regulation of production and consumption of ozone depleting substances.

2001 *The Batteries (Management and Handling) Rules, 2001* rules shall apply to every manufacturer, importer, re-conditioner, assembler, dealer, auctioneer, consumer, and bulk consumer involved in the manufacture, processing, sale, purchase, and use of batteries or components so as to regulate and ensure the environmentally safe disposal of used batteries.

2002 *The Noise Pollution (Regulation and Control) (Amendment) Rules* lay down such terms and conditions as are necessary to reduce noise pollution, permit use of loud speakers or public address systems during night hours (between 10:00 p.m. to 12:00 midnight) on or during any cultural or religious festive occasion.

2002 *The Biological Diversity Act* is an act to provide for the conservation of biological diversity, sustainable use of its components and fair and equitable sharing of the benefits arising out of the use of biological resources and knowledge associated with it.

2010 *The National Green Tribunal Act* enables the creation of special tribunal towards effective and expeditious disposal of cases related to environmental protection and conservation.

Forests and Wildlife

1927 *The Indian Forest Act and Amendment, 1984,* is one of the many surviving colonial statutes. It was enacted to 'consolidate the law related to forest, the transit of forest produce, and the duty leviable on timber and other forest produce'.

1972   *The Wildlife Protection Act, Rules 1972* and *Amendment 1991* provides for the protection of birds and animals and for all matters that are connected to it whether be it their habitat or the waterhole or the forests that sustain them.

1980   *The Forest (Conservation) Act and Rules, 1981*, provides for the protection of and the conservation of the forests.

Water

1882   *The Easement Act* allows private rights to use a resource that is, groundwater, by viewing it as an attachment to the land. It also states that all surface water belongs to the state and is a state property.

1897   *The Indian Fisheries Act* establishes two sets of penal offences whereby the government can sue any person who uses dynamite or other explosive substance in any way (whether coastal or inland) with intent to catch or destroy any fish or poisonous fish in order to kill.

1956   *The River Boards Act* enables the states to enrol the central government in setting up an Advisory River Board to resolve issues in inter-state cooperation.

1970   *The Merchant Shipping Act* aims to deal with waste arising from ships along the coastal areas within a specified radius.

1974   *The Water (Prevention and Control of Pollution) Act* establishes an institutional structure for preventing and abating water pollution. It establishes standards for water quality and effluent. Polluting industries must seek permission to discharge waste into effluent bodies. The CPCB (Central Pollution Control Board) was constituted under this act.

1977   *The Water (Prevention and Control of Pollution) Cess Act* provides for the levy and collection of cess or fees on water consuming industries and local authorities.

1978   *The Water (Prevention and Control of Pollution) Cess Rules* contains the standard definitions and indicate the kind of and location of meters that every consumer of water is required to affix.

1991   *The Coastal Regulation Zone Notification* puts regulations on various activities, including construction, are regulated. It gives some protection to the backwaters and estuaries.

Air

As per a World Bank report titled 'Diagnostic Assessment of Select Environmental Challenges in India', and released in July 2013, the annual cost due to environmental degradation is ₹3.75 trillion, which is approximately 5.7 per cent of India's GDP in 2009.

1948   *The Factories Act and Amendment in 1987* was the first to express concern for the working environment of the workers. The amendment of 1987 has sharpened its environmental focus and expanded its application to hazardous processes.

1981   *The Air (Prevention and Control of Pollution) Act* provides for the control and abatement of air pollution. It entrusts the power of enforcing this act to the CPCB.

1982   *The Air (Prevention and Control of Pollution) Rules* defines the procedures of the meetings of the Boards and the powers entrusted to them.

1982 *The Atomic Energy Act* deals with the radioactive waste.

1987 *The Air (Prevention and Control of Pollution) Amendment Act* empowers the central and state pollution control boards to meet with grave emergencies of air pollution.

1988 *The Motor Vehicles Act* states that all hazardous waste is to be properly packaged, labelled, and transported.

DOMESTIC LAWS

Environmental Protection Act

Environmental Protection Act of 1986 indicated that the Central Government 'have the power to take all such measures as it deems necessary or expedient for the purpose of protecting and improving the quality of the environment and preventing controlling and abating environmental pollution.' The law outlines

- creating a nationwide programme for the prevention, control, and abatement of environmental pollution
- setting standards on environmental quality, discharge of pollutants, and emissions
- restriction of areas in which any industries can operate
- creating and examining procedures and safeguards for the prevention of accidents and handling of hazardous substances
- carrying out investigations, research, and dissemination of information in areas related to environment

Air (Prevention and Control of Pollution) Act

This legislation was enacted in 1981, and later amended in 1987, to prevent and control air pollution. The act provided for the establishment of Boards that were conferred with the power of preventing, controlling, and abatement of air pollution. Through this act, the existing Central Board for the Prevention and Control of Water Pollution, constituted under the Water (Prevention and Control of Pollution) Act, 1974, was entrusted with the functions of the Central Board for the Prevention and Control of Air Pollution. Similarly, the existing state boards for the prevention and control of water pollution were exercised with the powers to perform the functions related to the state board for the prevention and control of air pollution.

B9 Shipping, an Ireland-based shipping company, has started work on a demonstration vessel, which will be powered by a wind-based sail propulsion system and an engine powered by liquid bio-methane produced from municipal waste. The company states that the wind powered sail system is expected to provide 60 per cent of the vessel's thrust.

Water (Prevention and Control of Pollution) Act

Through this act, the central government constituted a central board that was empowered with powers related to the prevention and control of water pollution. Similarly, the state governments were to appoint state boards that were empowered with powers related to the prevention and control of water pollution at state levels. The act also provided for the constitution of a joint board between two or more state governments or by the central government and one or more state governments. The boards constituted as part of this act were to play the role of advising the governments on matters concerning the prevention and control of water pollution. These boards were also to provide technical assistance, guidance, investigations and research, conduct training programmes, organize mass media programmes, collect and publish statistical data, etc., that could result in the prevention and control of water pollution.

Wild Life Protection Act

The Wild Life (Protection) Act, 1972 focused on the prohibition of hunting wild animals and prohibition of picking and uprooting of specified plants. However, exceptions were granted under special circumstances (for example, an animal has become dangerous to human life, or is disabled or diseased beyond recovery). The central government recommended the constitution of the Central Zoo Authority, which has to stipulate the minimum standards for housing and care for animals in the zoo, monitor the maintenance of these standards, and identifying endangered animals for the purpose of captive breeding. An important clause of the act is that 'No person shall tease, molest, injure or feed any animal or cause disturbance to the animals by noise or otherwise, or litter the grounds in a zoo.'[9]

Wild animals will be the property of the government and killing, molesting or teasing a wild animal will be considered a crime. No person is allowed to sell, offer for sale or transport wild animals, without written permission from Chief Wildlife Warden or the authorized officer.

The act authorized the government to appoint a Wildlife Advisory Board, Directors, Assistant Directors, Chief Wildlife Wardens, Wildlife Wardens, and other officers and employees who can carry out the objectives related to this act.

Forest Conservation Act

The salient features of the *Forest Act 1980* are as follows:

The act instituted a 'Restriction on the de-reservation of forests or use of forest land for non-forest purpose'.[10, 11] The act barred the state governments from dereserving any forest area and using the forest land for any non-forest purpose, unless with the prior approval of the central government. The act also recommended the government to constitute a forest advisory committee that can advise the government.

---

9 http://www.moef.nic.in/legis/wildlife/wildlife1c4a.html, last accessed on 4 September 2013.

10 http://nbaindia.org/uploaded/Biodiversityindia/Legal/22.%20Forest%20%28Conservation%29%20Act,%20 1980.pdf, last accessed on 29 September 2013.

11 http://www.envfor.nic.in/legis/forest/forest2.html, last accessed on 29 September 2013.

CLEARANCE/PERMISSIONS FOR ESTABLISHING INDUSTRY

The clearances and permissions required for establishing industrial units remain varied. There are region specific laws like *The Kerala Conservation of Paddy Land and Wetland Act, 2008* which forbids the owner of paddy land to convert paddy lands.[12] One can also find industry specific guidelines—for example, mining projects, pesticide units, bulk drugs, etc. Governmental authorities can also provide unique guidelines in certain clusters like special economic zones (SEZs). However, in general, industries need to receive a 'consent to establish' certificate (popularly known as 'No Objection Certificate') and clearances from the State Pollution Control Boards (SPCBs) or Ministry of Environment and Forests (MoEF), Government of India. Industrial units, on completion of the project and after meeting the norms related to maintaining environmental standards, needs to get the consent and authorization from the SPCBs or its regional offices.

ISSUES INVOLVED IN ENFORCEMENT OF ENVIRONMENTAL LEGISLATION

Concern over loss of organizational competitiveness   It is said that environmental regulations will result in the organization requiring to make extra investment and this will increase the cost of the production. While, costs can go up, it can also result in cost savings due to energy efficiency. Strict environmental regulations encourage innovations and induce efficiency. Michael Porter, Professor, Harvard Business School, says, '...properly designed environmental standards can trigger innovation that may partially or more than fully offset the costs of complying with them. Such "innovation offsets", as we call them, can not only lower the net cost of meeting environmental regulations, but can even lead to absolute advantages over firms in foreign countries not subject to similar regulations. Innovation offsets will be common because reducing pollution is often coincident with improving the productivity with which resources are used. In short, firms can actually benefit from properly crafted environmental regulations that are more stringent (or are imposed earlier) than those faced by their competitors in other countries. By stimulating innovation, strict environmental regulations can actually enhance competitiveness.'[13] In January 2011, the Chennai High Court directed the dyeing and processing units in Tirupur textile cluster in Tamilnadu to shut its operations due to the extreme pollution they were creating on Noyyal River for decades. This closure was expected to create a significant negative impact on the textile industry. However, this order also created a situation where the industry could innovate. In two years, Tirupur became the first textile cluster in India to meet zero liquid discharge (ZLD) norms.[14]

12 http://keralalawsect.org/acts/Act2008/act28_2008/index.html, last accessed on 23 July 2014.

13 Porter, Michael E, Claas van der Linde, Toward a New Conception of the Environment-Competitiveness Relationship, *Journal of Economic Perspectives*, Vol 9, Number 4, Fall 1995, pp. 97-118.

14 http://www.business-standard.com/article/economy-policy/tirupur-textile-units-achieve-zero-liquid-discharge-112120702031_1.html, last accessed on 22 April 2013.

The Supreme Court of India has played an active role in helping the citizens in alleviating the problems caused by pollution and also in directing the governmental authorities to take actions to protect the environment. Some of the notable interventions of the Supreme Court include cases related to Ratlam Municipality, the Delhi gas leak, quarrying in Dehradun, Endosulfan pesticide issue, relocation of hazardous industries from the National Capital Region (NCR), conversion of diesel powered buses in Delhi to CNG, illegal mining in the states of Karnataka, Odisha, Jharkhand, and in the Shivalik ranges of the Himalayas, Kanpur tanneries and pollution of River Ganga, and saving the Taj Mahal and other historical and cultural monuments at Agra.

During the period of two years, sixteen common effluent treatment plants (CETP) that covered 420 dyeing units were set up that met ZLD norms.[15]

Concern over loss of jobs Strict environmental regulations sometimes result in the loss of jobs. However, it has also been found that new jobs are created in pollution abatement and innovative processes.[16] 'The job creation and the job destruction roughly cancel each other out,'[17] says Richard Morgenstern, researcher with Resources for the Future.[18] Richard Morgenstern, in 2002, co-published a study which stated, '…it is possible that both employers and employees may overstate the job destructive aspects of environmental regulation and understate its job creation potential'.[19]

Concern over loss of productivity In a study done by Booth School of Business, University of Chicago, it was found that clean air regulations introduced in USA cost the country approximately $21 billion per year in lost productivity. However, the study also found that these regulations resulted in improved health, reduced infant mortality, and increased property values. Therefore, these regulations created a benefit of more than $100 billion.[20]

Prevalence of corruption among enforcement agencies Management and utilization of natural resources is considered as one of the three major contributors to black money in India. The country has witnessed a series of scandals related to corruption in the area of natural resource management. This is also one of the major sources attributed to black money generation in India. Amongst these scams, the one that was most glaring was the corruption in the allocation of coal fields, referred to as the Coalgate scam.

---

15 http://www.thehindu.com/todays-paper/tp-national/tp-tamilnadu/closure-of-dyeing-units-hardly-hits-knitwear-industry/article4352176.ece, last accessed on 22 April 2013.

16 http://www.businessweek.com/magazine/regulations-create-jobs-too-02092012.html, last accessed on 22 April 2013.

17 http://www.businessweek.com/magazine/regulations-create-jobs-too-02092012.html, last accessed on 22 April 2013.

18 A Washington-based not-for-profit organization that researches into issues related to environment and energy, through economics.

19 Morgenstern, Richard D, William A Pizer, Jhih-Shyang Shih 2002, Jobs versus the Environment: An Industry-level Perspective, *Resources for the Future*, June 2000; http://www.globalurban.org/Jobs_vs_the_Environment.pdf, last accessed on 22 April 2013.

20 http://www.forbes.com/sites/jeffmcmahon/2012/02/27/clean-air-regulations-cost-us-21-billion-per-year-economist/, last accessed on 22 April 2013.

PUBLIC INTEREST LITIGATIONS

There have been increasing number of citizen driven movements against the degradation of their life support systems—it could be civic movements in the city (see Fig. 10.2) or protests against nuclear power plants, as happened in Koodankulam, Tamilnadu. Public interest litigations (PILs) are legal instruments through which the interest of the public can be protected. In addition to the aggrieved party, the case can be taken up by the court itself or by a third party. It is noted that PILs have been able to bring the courts to the disadvantaged sections of the society.[21] Examples of PILs related to the areas of environmental management and ecology included defacing of rocks through advertisements, protection of Taj Mahal from nearby refineries, pollution of rivers, relocation of industries from Delhi, making the buses of Delhi run with the environment-friendly fuel, smoking in public places, and more.

FIG. 10.2[22] Protest against tree felling in Bangalore

INTERNATIONAL AGREEMENTS, LAWS, AND TREATIES

Nature is beyond geographic boundaries. The effects of manipulating nature are also felt in regions beyond the boundaries. Environmental actions, including mitigation of environmental fall-outs require international cooperation. There is a growing recognition about the need for trans-boundary research, sharing of global best practices, the need for joint actions, and a growing consensus to commit towards international guidelines.

---

21 http://unpan1.un.org/intradoc/groups/public/documents/apcity/unpan047384.pdf, last accessed on 12 March 2014.

22 Photo by Kiran Jonnalagadda, used with permission. Image Source: https://www.flickr.com/photos/jace/3451196468, last accessed on 5 August 2014.

International Agreements and Laws

Montreal Protocol

Montreal Protocol, also referred to as 'The Montreal Protocol on Substances that Deplete the Ozone Layer' is a treaty aimed at the protection of ozone layer by phasing out substances that cause ozone depletion. Ozone depletion refers to a steady decline of 4 per cent per decade in total volume of ozone in Earth's stratosphere (the ozone layer) and a decrease in stratospheric ozone over Earth's Polar Regions (ozone hole). The destruction of ozone is caused by manmade halocarbon refrigerants like CFCs, freons, and halons. The ozone layer prevents the passage of the most harmful wavelengths of ultraviolet light through the Earth's atmosphere. Increased UV exposure may result in an increase in skin cancer and cataract, reduction of plankton populations in the ocean's photic zone, and damage to plant kingdom. The treaty, opened for signature in 1987, has now been ratified by 196 states. Montreal Protocol has resulted in a decrease in the atmospheric burden of ozone-depleting substances and there are signs of ozone recovery.[23] If the agreement is adhered to, the ozone layer is expected to recover by 2050.

United Nations Framework Convention on Climate Change

The United Nations Framework Convention on Climate Change (UNFCCC or FCCC) is an international environmental treaty produced at the Earth Summit, Rio de Janeiro, 1992. UNFCCC focuses on stabilizing the concentration of greenhouse gases in the atmosphere at a level that would prevent dangerous interference with the climate system.[24] Two focus areas of UNFCCC include the mitigation aspects and also the adaptation aspects.

International assistance to developing countries to support adaptation process is done through funding, technology transfer, and capacity building. Some of the funding opportunities available include the Global Environment Facility (GEF) Trust Fund, the GEF managed Least Developed Countries Fund (LDCF), the GEF managed Special Climate Change Fund (SCCF), and The Adaptation Fund (AF) managed by the Adaptation Fund Board (AFD) and the Green Climate Fund (GCF).

Garuda Stotra (Prayer to Garuda/ Eagle)

Kumkumaankitha Varnaaya
Kundenthu Dhavalaayacha
Vishnuvaahana Roopaaya
Pakshi Raajayathe Namaha

The one who adorns the colour of saffron, the one who shines like the fair moon, the one who is the vehicle of Lord Vishnu, Salutations to you, Garuda, the King of the Bird Kingdom.

Kyoto Protocol and Clean Development Mechanism

Kyoto Protocol is the principal update to the UNFCCC. Kyoto Protocol was initially adopted in Kyoto, Japan, in 1997, as part of the UNFCCC held there in the same year. The protocol entered into force in 2005. As part of the protocol, 37 countries, also referred to as 'Annex I countries'

---

23 http://www.esrl.noaa.gov/csd/assessments/ozone/2006/report.html, last accessed on 31 August 2011.
24 http://newsroom.unfccc.int/about/, last accessed on 12 August 2014.

agreed to cut their emissions by 5.2 per cent from their emissions level in 1990. Emissions trading and Clean Development Mechanism (CDM) was part of Kyoto Protocol. CDM supported projects that reduced emissions and purpose of CDM was to support developing countries in their efforts of emission reduction. In a report titled 'Benefits of the Clean Development Mechanism 2012', released by United Nations Framework Convention on Climate Change, it was stated, 'The CDM was designed to meet two objectives, namely to help Annex I parties (most of the developed countries) to cost-effectively meet part of their emission reduction targets under the Kyoto protocol and to assist non-Annex I parties in achieving sustainable development. While CDM projects create certified emission reductions (CERs) that project participants can sell to Annex I parties to help them meet their Kyoto Protocol targets, they can also provide complementary benefits to non-Annex I parties such as new investment, the transfer of climate-friendly technologies and knowledge, the improvement of livelihoods and skills, job creation, and increased economic activity.'[25]

Some of the attributes of CDM are as follows:[26]

- An international investment mechanism
- Created incentives for investment in clean technologies in developing countries
- Generated investment worth almost $215 billion towards the developing countries
- Operationalized over 200 quality-assured methodologies that have been used to globally reduce emissions, monitor them, and effectively price carbon

TABLE 10.1[27] Estimated revenue from the sale of CERs at primary market prices (US$ million)

	2007	2008	2009	2010	2011	Total
India	5	822	227	106	396	1,555
Worldwide	177	3,154	1,676	1,325	3,251	9,583
% of India's share	2.82	26.06	13.54	8.00	12.18	16.23

TABLE 10.2[28] Estimated revenue from the sale of CERs at secondary market prices (US$ million)

	2007	2008	2009	2010	2011	Total
India	9	1,249	297	147	526	2,228
Worldwide	298	4,795	2,192	1,841	4,324	13,451
% of India's share	3.02	26.05	13.55	7.98	12.16	16.56

25 http://cdm.unfccc.int/about/dev_ben/ABC_2012.pdf, last accessed on 7 February 2013.

26 http://cdm.unfccc.int/about/dev_ben/CDM-Benefits-2012.pdf, last accessed on 7 February 2013.

27 Data sourced from http://cdm.unfccc.int/about/dev_ben/CDM-Benefits-2012.pdf, last accessed on 7 February 2013.

28 Data sourced from http://cdm.unfccc.int/about/dev_ben/CDM-Benefits-2012.pdf, last accessed on 7 February 2013.

As can be noted from tables 10.1 and 10.2, India has significantly benefited from the existence of CDM. It is said that CDM has lost its relevance today. This is due to the fall in the price of CER and uncertainty regarding the continuation of CDM. However, it has also been stated that till an alternative global trading mechanism emerges to replace CDM, it is worthwhile to continue with the existing practice that has an experience and learning of ten years.[29]

Ramsar Convention on Wetlands

The Ramsar Convention on Wetlands, also referred to as 'The Convention on Wetlands of International Importance', is an intergovernmental treaty that seeks to promote conservation and sustainable utilization of wetlands. The treaty uses a broad definition for wetlands and includes 'lakes and rivers, swamps and marshes, wet grasslands and peatlands, oases, estuaries, deltas and tidal flats, near-shore marine areas, mangroves and coral reefs, and human-made sites such as fish ponds, rice paddies, reservoirs, and salt pans.'[30] As of July 2013, the number of contracting parties under the convention include 168, the number of sites designated for the list of wetlands of international importance are 2,131 and the total surface area of designated sites are 205,490,520 hectares. Some of the sites in India designated under the Ramsar wetland conservation are listed in Table 10.3.

TABLE 10.3[31] List of Ramsar sites in India

Name of site	Location
Ashtamudi Wetlands	Kerala
Bhitarkanika Mangroves	Orissa
Bhoj Wetlands	Madhya Pradesh
Chandra Taal	Himachal Pradesh
Chilika Lake	Orissa
Deepor Beel	Assam
East Calcutta Wetlands	West Bengal
Harike Wetland	Punjab
Hokera Wetland	Jammu and Kashmir
Kanjli Wetland	Punjab
Keoladeo National Park	Rajasthan
Kolleru Lake	Andhra Pradesh

(Contd)

---

29 http://cdkn.org/2012/10/safeguarding-the-clean-development-mechanism-will-benefit-southern-and-northern-nations-alike/, last accessed on 13 August 2014.
30 http://www.ramsar.org, last accessed on 10 July 2013.
31 Adapted from http://www.ramsar.org/pdf/sitelist.pdf, last accessed on 13 August 2014.

TABLE 10.3 *(Contd)*

Name of site	Location
Loktak Lake	Manipur
Nalsarovar Bird Sanctuary	Gujarat
Point Calimere Wildlife and Bird Sanctuary	Tamilnadu
Pong Dam Lake	Himachal Pradesh
Renuka Wetland	Himachal Pradesh
Ropar	Punjab
Rudrasagar Lake	Tripura
Sambhar Lake	Rajasthan
Sasthamkotta Lake	Kerala
Surinsar-Mansar Lakes	Jammu and Kashmir
Tsomoriri	Jammu and Kashmir
Upper Ganga River (Brijghat to Narora Stretch)	Uttar Pradesh
Vembanad-Kol Wetland	Kerala
Wular Lake	Jammu and Kashmir

United Nations Convention on the Law of the Sea

The United Nations Convention on the Law of the Sea (UNCLOS), an international treaty signed and concluded in 1982, outlines the rights and responsibilities of various nations/states regarding the usage and protection of the oceans and its natural resources. The treaty entered into force in 1994. UNCLOS mentioned that the area at or beneath the seabed are the common heritage of mankind (Article 136).[32] It was also mentioned that the activities in this area be carried out for the benefit of mankind as a whole (Article 140), and is used exclusively for peaceful purposes (Article 141). Article 145 spoke about ensuring effective protection for the marine environment in this area from harmful activities. UNCLOS also established the International Seabed Authority, through which the parties to the convention administered the resources of the seabed.

The Basel Convention

'The Basel Convention on the Control of Trans-boundary Movements of Hazardous Wastes and their Disposal' entered into force in 1992. This treaty aimed at minimizing the generation of wastes, treating wastes as near as possible to where they were generated, and reducing international movements of hazardous wastes.

The Convention on Biological Diversity

The Convention on Biological Diversity (CBD) is a multilateral treaty with three main objectives of (a) conserving biological diversity, (b) sustainable use of the components of biodiversity, and (c) fair and equitable sharing of the benefits from the usage of genetic resources. The treaty entered into force in 1993, and has contributed to the development

---

32 http://www.un.org/Depts/los/convention_agreements/texts/unclos/unclos_e.pdf, last accessed on 23 July 2014.

of national strategies towards the conservation and sustainable usage of biodiversity. Aichi Biodiversity targets (see Chapter 1) is an important component of CBD.

The United Nations Convention to Combat Desertification

The United Nations Convention to Combat Desertification (UNCCD) is an international legal framework linking environment and development to land management, especially in dry lands. The convention focuses on reversing desertification, mitigating the effects of droughts, and also to improve the living conditions of people living in the dry lands. The treaty entered into force in 1996.

The Convention on Migratory Species

The Convention on Migratory Species (CMS), also referred to as the Convention on the Conservation of Migratory Species of Wild Animals or Bonn Convention, 'aims to conserve terrestrial, aquatic, and avian migratory species throughout their range'.[33] The treaty entered into force in 1983. Agreements under CMS may range from legally binding treaties to Memoranda of Understanding (MoU). For example, the first MoU to be concluded was focused on conserving the Siberian crane. India was one among the 11 nations to be part of this MoU (see Fig. 10.3) to know the migratory route taken by Siberian crane.

FIG. 10.3[34] Migratory path undertaken by Siberian crane. Those Siberian cranes that used to take the Western/Central Asian flyway no longer arrives at the Keoladeo National Park, Bharatpur, Rajasthan. The last sighting of the bird was in 2002.

---

33 http://www.cms.int/en, last accessed on 11 August 2014.
34 Photo by Shyamal, licensed under public domain via Wikimedia Commons. Image source: http://commons. wikimedia.org/wiki/File:SiberianCrane.svg#mediaviewer/File:SiberianCrane.svg, last accessed on 12 August 2014.

The Convention on International Trade in Endangered Species of Wild Fauna and Flora

The Convention on International Trade in Endangered Species of Wild Fauna and Flora (CITES) aims to 'ensure that international trade in specimens of wild animals and plants does not threaten their survival'[35]. This treaty, also known as the Washington Convention, entered into force in 1975 wherein 180 countries were part of this treaty. CITES implements certain controls in international trade related to certain species. CITES has listed approximately 5,600 species of animals and 30,000 species of plants against exploitation. Introduction, export, import, and re-export of species listed in CITES' list, requires a license from a management authority, usually a governmental organization. This organization, based in each country that is party to the treaty, is also advised by a scientific authority who is appointed to advise the management authority on the implication of the trade on these species. Depending on the threat assessment to the species, decisions related to trade on that species is made.

Global Developments

In India, it is said that a person who takes to the path of spiritual knowledge, opens the door of salvation to seven generations before, and seven generations after, in the family. In ancient cultures, there is a concept of making decisions only after assessing the impact it will have seven generations from now. Such qualitative and expansive thoughts guided decision-making and living. There have been attempts to recognize the importance of nature as an entity that has a unique legal existence. Ecuador's 'Rights of Nature' and Bolivia's 'Law of the Rights of Mother Earth' are two examples in this direction.

Ecuador and Rights of Nature

In 2008, Ecuador, a country in South America, became the first country to incorporate rights of nature in the country's constitution. The country's constitution includes a chapter addressing Rights for Nature. Following are the chapter details.[36]

> **Article 1**   Nature or Pachamama, where life is reproduced and exists, has the right to exist, persist, maintain, and regenerate its vital cycles, structure, functions, and its processes in evolution.
>
> Every person, people, community or nationality, will be able to demand the recognitions of rights for nature before the public organisms. The application and interpretation of these rights will follow the related principles established in the constitution.

---

35 http://www.cites.org/eng/disc/what.php, last accessed on 11 August 2014.
36 http://www.rightsofmotherearth.com/ecuador-rights-nature/, last accessed on 6 July 2012. Used with permission.

Bolivia has passed the 'Law of the Rights of Mother Earth' which gives specific rights to Mother Earth, thereby giving a legal identity to a natural system.

The state will motivate natural and juridical persons as well as collectives to protect nature; it will promote respect towards all the elements that form an ecosystem.

Article 2   Nature has the right to an integral restoration. This integral restoration is independent of the obligation on natural and juridical persons or the state to indemnify the people and the collectives that depend on the natural systems.

In the cases of severe or permanent environmental impact, including the ones caused by the exploitation on non-renewable natural resources, the state will establish the most efficient mechanisms for the restoration, and will adopt the adequate measures to eliminate or mitigate the harmful environmental consequences.

Article 3   The state will apply precaution and restriction measures in all the activities that can lead to the extinction of species, the destruction of the ecosystems or the permanent alteration of the natural cycles.

The introduction of organisms and organic and inorganic material that can alter in a definitive way the national genetic patrimony is prohibited.

Article 4   The persons, people, communities, and nationalities will have the right to benefit from the environment and form natural wealth that will allow well-being.

The environmental services cannot be appropriated; its production, provision, use, and exploitation, will be regulated by the state.

'Public organisms' in Article 1 means the courts and government agencies, i.e., the people of Ecuador would be able to take action to enforce nature rights if the government did not do so.

In March 2011, Richard Frederick Wheeler and Eleanor Geer Huddle won a case against the provincial government of Loja, Ecuador, in favour of Nature, specifically, Vilcabamba river, on which large quantities of rocks and other debris were deposited as part of the Vilcabamba-Quinara road widening project. Road widening project and the resulting dumping decreased the width of the river to half and thus doubled the speed of the flow, creating risk of floods for riverside populations. The court upheld the injunction and halted the road widening project.

Bolivia and the 'Law of the Rights of Mother Earth'

Bolivia, through 2010–12, passed the 'Law of the Rights of Mother Earth' which gives specific rights to Mother Earth (defined as '...the dynamic living system formed by the indivisible community of all life systems and living beings whom are interrelated,

FIG. 10.4 A road-sign near Coonoor, Nilgiris[37] indicating the need to respect the 'Right of Way' for elephants. In a study done in France, it was found that birds adjusted their flight distance depending on the speed limits of the roads, possibly to reduce their collision risks and decrease their own mortality. The pertinent question remains—Who is invading whose habitat—animals, birds and reptiles invading the habitat of human beings OR human beings invading the habitat of other species?[38]

interdependent, and complementary, which share a common destiny') and the following are the seven specific entitled rights.

To life To maintain the integrity of life systems and natural processes that sustain those systems, and also the right to maintain the capacities and conditions for their renewal and regeneration

---

37 Photo by Eric Herrmann, used with permission. Image Source: http://cyclingtheworldforbirds.blogspot.in, last accessed on 5 August 2014.

38 Legagneux, Pierre, Simon Ducatez 2013, European birds adjust their flight initiation distance to road speed limits, *Biology Letters*, October 2013, Vol. 9, No. 5; http://rsbl.royalsocietypublishing.org/content/9/5/20130417.

To the diversity of life To preserve the differentiation and variety of beings that create Mother Earth, without genetically altering, or artificially modifying their structures, in a manner that threatens their existence, functioning, and potential

To water To preserve the functionality of water cycles, the quality, and composition of water, to sustain life systems and their protection against pollution, for renewal of the life of Mother Earth and all its components

To clean air To preserve the quality and composition of air for sustaining life systems, their protection from pollution, for renewal of the life of Mother Earth and all its components

To equilibrium To maintain or restore the inter-relation, interdependence, complementarity, and functionality of the components of Mother Earth, in a balanced way for the continuation of its cycles and the renewal of its processes

To restoration To restore life systems affected by direct or indirect human activities in a timely and effective manner

To pollution-free living To preserve Mother Earth free of pollution, toxic, and radioactive waste generated by human activities

This law gives a legal identity to a natural system. This will empower citizens, on behalf of Mother Earth, to engage in legal actions against individuals and organizations that infringe on the integrity of Mother Earth. This is also considered a shift from an anthropocentric perspective to an earth-community perspective. Commenting on this development, *Huffington Post* remarked, 'Bolivians have long revered the *Pachamama*, Andean goddess of Mother Earth, and the law is said to be greatly inspired by resurgence in the indigenous belief that the deity is central to all life. As Vice President Alvaro Garcia Linera said when describing the measure, "Earth is the mother of all...the harmony [between man and nature] must be preserved as a guarantee of its regeneration."'[39] A reader commented on this article, 'Light years ahead of us. Bravo, Bolivia.'[40]

---

39 http://www.huffingtonpost.com/2011/04/13/bolivias-law-of-mother-earth_n_848966.html, last accessed on 24 June 2012.

40 http://www.huffingtonpost.com/2011/04/13/bolivias-law-of-mother-earth_n_848966.html, last accessed on 24 June 2012.

CHAPTER SUMMARY

- *Environmental Protection Act of 1986* indicated that the Central Government 'have the power to take all such measures as it deems necessary or expedient for the purpose of protecting and improving the quality of the environment and preventing controlling and abating environmental pollution'.
- *Air (Prevention and Control of Pollution) Act* provided for the establishment of Boards that were conferred with the power of preventing, controlling, and abatement of air pollution.
- *The Wild Life (Protection) Act, 1972* focused on the prohibition of hunting wild animals, and prohibition of picking and uprooting of specified plants.

- *The Forest Act 1980* instituted a 'Restriction on the de-reservation of forests or use of forest land for non-forest purpose'.
- Montreal Protocol is a treaty aimed at the protection of ozone layer by phasing out substances that cause ozone depletion.
- The United Nations Framework Convention on Climate Change (UNFCCC) focuses on stabilizing the concentration of greenhouse gases in the atmosphere at a level that would prevent dangerous interference with the climate system.
- In 2008, Ecuador, a country in South America, became the first country to incorporate rights of nature in the country's constitution.

KEYWORDS

- Air (Prevention and Control of Pollution) Act
- Clean development mechanism (CDM)
- Environmental Protection Act of 1986
- Ecuador and rights of nature
- Forest Conservation Act 1980
- Kyoto Protocol
- Montreal Protocol
- Ramsar Convention on Wetlands
- The Basel Convention on the Control of Transboundary Movements of Hazardous Waste and their Disposal

- The Convention on Migratory Species (CMS)
- The Convention on International Trade in Endangered Species of Wild Fauna and Flora (CITES)
- The United Nations Convention on the Law of the Sea (UNCLOS)
- The United Nations Framework Convention on Climate Change (UNFCCC)
- The United Nations Convention to Combat Desertification (UNCCD)
- The Wild Life (Protection) Act 1972
- Water (Prevention and Control of Pollution) Act

EXERCISES
Multiple-choice Questions

1. What does the National Green Tribunal Act of 2010 aims to achieve?
   (a) Effective and expeditious disposal of the cases related to environmental protection and conservation.
   (b) Faster Environmental Impact Assessment of

   power projects.
   (c) Acting as a consultant for green NGOs, industry and the government.
   (d) Setting up of green tribunes in every state of India.

2. In which year was The National Environmental Tribunal Act created?
   (a) 1990
   (b) 2000
   (c) 1995
   (d) 1992
3. Ramsar Convention is related to which of the following ecosystems?
   (a) Rainforests
   (b) Wetlands
   (c) Deserts
   (d) Oceans
4. Who is the Andean Goddess for Mother Earth?
   (a) Gayathri
   (b) Athena
   (c) Pachamama
   (d) Gaia
5. Which act provides for the 'protection of birds and animals and for all matters that are connected to it whether it is their habitat or the waterhole or the forests that sustain them'?
   (a) The Wildlife Protection Act
   (b) The Forest (Conservation) Act
   (c) The Indian Forest Act
   (d) All of these
6. When was the last sighting of the Siberian crane in Keoladeo National Park, Bharatpur, Rajasthan?
   (a) 2002
   (b) 2003
   (c) 2004
   (d) 2005
7. What does the Montreal Protocol aim at?
   (a) Protection of ozone layer
   (b) Biodiversity
   (c) Organic farming
   (d) Green buildings
8. Bolivia became the centre of world attention by passing which act in year 2010-2012?
   (a) Law of the Rights of Mother Earth
   (b) The Forest (Conservation) Act
   (c) Conservation of Bolivian Forests
   (d) The Act to protect Siberian Crane
9. Among the following, what are the attributes of CDM?
   (a) An international investment mechanism
   (b) Created incentives for investment in clean technologies in developing countries
   (c) Both A and B
   (d) None
10. Which was the first country to incorporate rights of nature in its constitution?
    (a) Ecuador
    (b) India
    (c) USA
    (d) Japan

Short Answer Questions

1. Write short notes on Air (Prevention and Control of Pollution) Act?
2. Explain Wildlife Protection Act.
3. What is Montreal Protocol?
4. What is the difference between CMS and CDM?
5. Expand the following:
   (a) UNFCCC
   (b) CITES
   (c) CBD
   (d) UNCLOS

Long Answer Questions

1. Write notes on some of the major environmental legislations that have come into effect in India.
2. What are the issues involved in enforcement of environmental legislation?

3. Write short notes on UNFCCC and UNCLOS.
4. What is meant by 'Rights of Nature'? Give an example.

5. What is the 'Law of the Rights of Mother Earth'?, Write down the seven specific rights.

Reflective Question

1. You are given an opportunity to improvize on India's constitution by adding specific rights for Planet Earth and Nature (similar to how human beings have been given rights). What all rights would you include?

Recommended Books

1. Vandana Shiva, *Biopiracy: The Plunder of Nature and Knowledge*, South End Press, 1999.
2. Patrick Curry, *Ecological Ethics: An Introduction*, Polity Press, 2005.

3. David Suzuki, Holly Dressel, *Good News for a Change: How Everyday People are Helping the Planet*, Greystone Books, 2003.

Recommended Documentary/Movie

1. Seeds of Freedom (This documentary is available for free viewing at http://www.seedsoffreedom.info/watch-the-film/watch-the-film-english/ and https://www.youtube.com/watch?v=C-bK8X2s1kI) Duration: 30 minutes.

Answers to Mutiple-choice Questions:
1(a)   2(c)   3(b)   4(c)   5(a)   6(a)   7(a)   8(a)   9(c)   10(a)

11

ENVIRONMENTAL ECONOMICS AND GREEN ECONOMY

If we are to end gross disparity and poverty, reduce rampant climate change and species extinction, avoid massive depletion and destruction of resources, and pre-empt the resulting overshoot and collapse of societies, we must go well beyond simplistic indicators such as the gross domestic product that have today become the grossest mismeasures of progress.[1]

Ashok Khosla, President, International
Union for Conservation of Nature;
Co-President, Club of Rome

After studying this chapter, the reader will be able to understand the following:

- The difference between environmental and ecological economics
- How the practice of externalization is hiding the actual environmental and social costs of a product or service
- The debate over the ineffectiveness of conventional growth indicators like GDP, and the emergence of alternative indicators such as GPI and GNH
- Required operational and regulatory changes in financial markets and economy to promote sustainable development

ENVIRONMENTAL ECONOMICS

Environmental economics offers numerous techniques for placing an economic value on environmental effects, based on generalized market transactions that may be real (health cost due to pollution) or imaginary (what people might be willing to pay for an environmental benefit or accept for its loss, if the benefits were actually traded). The global economy is built on the health of ecosystems. If monsoon fails in India, it will affect the revenue of major companies like Hindustan Unilever. If there is a good monsoon, the farmers will have good yields of agricultural produces, resulting in affordable income to purchase products and services from these companies. It is nature's reward, through crops, fish, timber, and other commodities that sustain Indian economy. Agriculture and allied sectors accounted for 15.7 per cent of India's GDP in 2009–10, employed 52.1 per cent of the total workforce, and contributed 10.2 per cent in total exports.[2]

---

1 http://www.beyond-gdp.eu/key_quotes.html, last accessed on 8 May 2012.
2 *Economic Survey 2009–10*, Ministry of Finance, Government of India, p. 179.

Professor Arif A. Waqif, Former Dean, School of Management Studies, University of Hyderabad, states[3] that economic development means 'transformation of natural and environmental resources into goods and services to meet our needs and wants'. Utilization of environmental resources (ER) and services depends on quality and stock of environmental resources. The stock depends on rate of regeneration (RoR) and rate of utilization (RoU).

Stock (S) = RoR – RoU
When RoU > RoR = Depletion
Quality of stock (QoS) = Rate of assimilation (RoA) – rate of waste generation (RoWG)
When RoWG > RoA = Pollution or degradation

Increasing or rising pollution or degradation results in increased private and social costs. Bad sanitation and water pollution has cost India 6 per cent of its national income.[4] Costs incurred by direct users are referred to as private costs while those incurred by third parties are referred to as social costs. Social costs can happen across time and space. For example, destruction of a forest land for a residential gated 'green and verdant' community may result in the drinking water supply of a city getting affected some months later. This is because the destruction of forests results in decreased water seepage to the underground, increased soil erosion, fall in the water table downstream, and less availability of water supply in the tail-pipe.

Quantified value of pollution and/or degradation (resulting in both private and social costs) is referred to as damage costs (DC). Costs incurred to manage pollution and degradation at 'sustainable' levels is referred to as total containment costs (TCC).

Total environmental cost (TEC) = Total damage cost + total containment cost

Sustainability and Enhanceability

Sustainability occurs when rate of utilization is at par with rate of regeneration, and when assimilation is at par with rate of pollution, that is,

RoU = RoR and RoA = RoP

For example, in the imaginary village of Paani Panchayat, a new bottled water manufacturing company was set up. The villagers soon found out that their bore wells were running dry. The borewells also started giving salt-water. The villagers understood that if this continues, life will be miserable. Earlier, it was just the villagers, now the new company too was extracting water from the bore wells. Also, in the name of comfort and modernization, with people putting concrete pavement on the ground, even the possibility of water seeping into the ground got reduced. Following discussions and meetings, people of the village came to the conclusion that they should engage

3 In a session delivered for MBA students of the University (Batch 2002-04).
4 'Shoots, greens and leaves', *The Economist*, 24 June 2012, Vol. 403, Number 8789.

in water harvesting measures. The villagers collectively agreed to promote open green spaces, open wells, water tanks, and wetlands. The company was willing to contribute significantly to these water harvesting measures, not just in this village, but also in the surrounding villages. The company assured the village council that they will draw the amount of water that could be replenished through these water harvesting measures. With this commitment, the company became merit-worthy with its claim of engaging in sustainability practices.

Enhanceability occurs when utilization is less than regeneration, and when pollution is less than assimilation, that is,

RoU < RoR and RoP < RoA

For example, in the imaginary village of Aam Rajya, there was a grove consisting of 20 mango trees, which produced delicious mangoes. The villagers' consumption came primarily from the mangoes that fell down, though sometimes, they did pluck a few mangoes from the trees. The villagers allowed mangoes to ripen on the trees so that birds and insects could also consume these mangoes. Such a harmonious existence resulted in the gradual increase of biodiversity of the region. Though almost two-thirds of the foods eaten by these villagers were raw vegetables and fruits, they did cook some food items. While the villagers used natural ingredients for cooking, the waste was thrown in the nearby river, thereby polluting it. However, as these wastes were biodegradable, it was eaten by the fish in the rivers and soon the river ecosystem was able to return to its pristine nature.

ECOLOGICAL ECONOMICS AND GREEN ECONOMY

Environmental economics and ecological economics have been considered as two different schools of thought. Ecological economics considers economy as a subsystem of the ecosystem and emphasizes on preserving natural capital while environmental economics is related to the economic analysis of the natural environment. Ecological economics emphasizes strong sustainability.

As per United Nations Environment Programme (UNEP), green economy is a development model that results in 'improved human well-being and social equity, while significantly reducing environmental risks and ecological scarcities'. Green economy aims for a low carbon, resource efficient, and socially inclusive economic paradigm. Green economy calculates the economic value of natural capital and ecosystem services. This valuation influences policy decisions. Pavan Sukhdev, Founder-CEO of GIST Advisory, an environmental consulting firm and former Managing Director—Global Markets Division, Deutsche Bank, cites[5] an example of how valuation influences policy decision. He says,

---

5 Talk given at the Sydney Opera House, Sydney, on 3 August 2010. The session was conducted by Centre for Policy Development (CPD), Sydney, Australia. The transcript of the talk can be accessed at http://cpd.org.au/2010/08/pavan-sukhdev-sydney-lecture-transcript/, last accessed on 27 September 2012. CPD content is published under a Creative Commons Licence with attribution, as is indicated at http://cpd.org.au/about/media-centre/

'I want to give a small example of this. Small, because it is a locational, very specific example. This comes from South Thailand. This is about a shrimp farm which arose from a mangrove. And, in fact, this applies to a specific area in South Thailand. So, economically the logic was very clear. Shrimp farms, worth $9600 per hectare, and if you leave the forest as it is, the mangrove forest, then that's only providing you with something like $600 per hectare, based on the fuel wood that is extracted from there by the local community. Economic choice, very obvious. Convert the mangrove to a shrimp farm. But, hang on, if you also look at the subsidies that the local government, the Thailand government, provides to the shrimp farm, well, that's $8,000. But if you subtract that, we're talking about not such a huge comparison—$1,200 vs $600. But, hang on, that's not the end of the story. Because having the mangrove there means that you actually have a massive store of protection from storms and cyclones as they get more frequent, especially with climate change. And not only that but as a result of the shrimp farm, typically in three to five years, you end up having to just reconstruct the whole area because salination and the deposition of chemicals has basically destroyed that land. So you need to redo the whole area. That costs money. It costs about $10,000. And the value, you can work it out, of the mangrove protecting the area that you've got along the coastline in terms of local communities, their housing and their livelihoods, that can be measured in terms of areas which had mangroves and those which didn't, how much cyclonic damage they suffered versus the others. And that works out to something like $12,000. Now look at the trade-off choice. And this is the whole point that if you look at public wealth and include that in your trade-off decisions, you get to a completely different answer than if you simply looked at private profits and worked your trade-off choice on that basis. In fact you get the opposite answer. You get conservation as the right economic choice and not conversion.'

EXTERNALIZATION

Externalization is drawn from the word 'external', which pertains to something that is outside. Externalization is about pushing something outside its boundary. It is a generic term that could be applied in several contexts. In economics, an externality is an effect of an action, resulting in a cost or a benefit, incurred by a party who was unrelated in exercising the choice resulting from that action. Benefits are referred to as positive externalities while costs are referred to as negative externalities. In the context of a company, negative externalization refers to a situation where the company externalizes its costs onto society and the environment, and does not take responsibility and ownership of these costs. Cost externalization can be done spatially and temporally. Spatial externalization refers to the ways in which costs are transferred to other entities in the present time period, while temporal externalization refers to the ways in which costs are transferred from the present time period to that of the future.

An example indicating the effect of positive externalization could be benefits accrued by patients from the design of ultra-lightweight prosthetic foot support, as a spin-off

On 10 April 2012, FedEx Express, one of the leading transportation companies of the world, announced that transportation emissions associated with its iconic FedEx envelopes will be carbon neutral. FedEx envelopes, widely used for document shipping, were already made from 100 per cent recycled content, and are also 100 per cent recyclable. More than 200 million FedEx envelopes are transported across the world annually. The company will calculate its annual carbon emissions from the shipment of all global FedEx envelopes. Offsetting of these emissions will be done by investing in low carbon development or conservation projects.

from India's missile programme. If this foot support was designed by a for-profit enterprise, it could have incurred cost in research and development. In an activity generating positive externality, social benefit is higher than private benefit, and in an activity generating negative externality social cost is higher than private cost. This is the reason why companies are incentivized to move towards creation of negative externalities. From an economist's point of view, market systems generate pollution because natural inputs (such as air and water) that are also inputs into the production of goods and services are 'underpriced'.[6] As per *Guide to Corporate Ecosystem Valuation: A framework for improving corporate decision-making*, a report by World Business Council for Sustainable Development (WBCSD),[7] environmental externalities include externalities to ecosystems and ecosystem services, but they also include impacts upon people, buildings, infrastructure, and other economic activities (e.g., from air emissions).

Examples of Negative Spatial Externalization

The following are some examples of negative spatial externalization:

- Cost incurred by the society for disposing plastic waste, created by irresponsible behaviour of consumers—While it is the responsibility of the manufacturer and the consumer of the plastic cover to spend for the disposal of plastic cover, this cost in reality is externalized to the society, who pays for the same.

- Costs incurred by local community due to pollution of a river, caused by the release of harmful effluents from industries—The effluents affect the health of the local community, when they use the river water for their daily usage, and they incur costs of health check-ups. The government may subsidize their healthcare. So though the responsibility for these costs is with the polluter, this cost is externalized to the local community/society/government that actually incur the cost.

- Costs incurred by a pedestrian due to respiratory troubles arising from inhaling polluted air, caused by increasing vehicular traffic (see Fig. 11.1 showing a glimpse of traffic in Kolkata in 1945)—Though the responsibility of causing the air emission lies with the owner/user/manufacturer of the vehicles, the costs are externalized to the pedestrian who does not use any vehicle.

---

6 Goodstein, Eban S., *Economics and the Environment*, Wiley, 2011.
7 http://www.wbcsd.org/work-program/ecosystems/cev.aspx, last accessed on 29 May 2013.

FIG. 11.1[8] Traffic in Kolkata, in 1945. Increasing usage of private vehicles resulted in pedestrians and cyclists being deprived of their mode for travel. They also bear the brunt of pollution caused by others. Inefficient usage of private vehicles (fewer people travelling in the vehicle, as compared to its full capacity) also takes up disproportionate space on the road as compared to public transportation.

Examples of Negative Temporal Externalization

The following are some examples of negative temporal externalization:

- Lack of appropriate recycling of waste materials results in the accumulation of waste and causes a problem for the future, thus externalizing the costs to future generations, who are not responsible for these emissions. The future generation will have to incur costs to clean up this waste.
- Unabated release of carbon dioxide emissions will result in climate change, which will affect future generations. The costs are thus externalized to a future time period.

---

8 Photo by Claude Waddell, 'Traffic1945'-http://oldsite.library.upenn.edu/etext/sasia/calcutta1947/, licensed under public domain via Wikimedia Commons— https://commons.wikimedia.org/wiki/File:KolkataTraffic1945. jpg#mediaviewer/File:KolkataTraffic1945.jpg, last accessed on 8 August 2014.

- Over-consumption resulting in depletion of natural resources will result in future generation incurring a cost to explore new resources. Excessive water usage may even cause conflicts (social cost) among societies.

Cost of Pollution

Accounting for externalities is one of the methods suggested by sustainability thinkers to shift business to the path of sustainability.[9] Many of the resources used by for-profit corporations for their existence—mineral wealth available in sea, land, water, trees, etc.,—is available free of cost. Assigning an economic value to these resources can help citizens ascertain the role that a for-profit corporation needs to play in the society. 'If companies had to pay for the full environmental costs of their activities, they would have lost 41 cents out of every (US) $1 earned in 2010... The external environmental costs of 11 key industry sectors rose by almost 50 per cent between 2002 and 2010, from $566 billion to $854 billion,' stated Yvo de Boer, Former Executive Director, United Nations Framework Convention on Climate Change (UNFCCC).[10] Corporate externalities, the unaccounted costs to society due to the 'business as usual' practices, are an estimated US$ four trillion annually.[11] To put this in perspective, India's GDP in 2011, as per World Bank estimates, is only US$1.848 trillion.

The following are two examples related to the costs of pollution.

- A study by Harvard Medical School that compiled a 'Full Cost Accounting for the Life Cycle of Coal' stated that 'life cycle effects of coal and the waste stream generated are costing the US public a third to over one-half of a trillion dollars annually'. The study also says that the estimates are conservative. The paper[12] states, 'yearly and cumulative costs stemming from the aerosolized, solid, and water pollutants associated with the mining, processing, transport, and combustion of coal affect individuals, families, communities, ecological integrity, and the global climate. The economic implications go far beyond the prices we pay for electricity. Our comprehensive review finds that the best estimate for the total economically quantifiable costs, based on a conservative weighting of many of the study findings,

Trucost Plc, a sustainability consulting firm has found that a platinum ring costing $650 would increase to $689 (a 6 per cent increase in costs), and a gold ring costing $150 would increase to $210 (a 40 per cent increase in costs), if the total costs of environmental impacts are taken into account.

---

9 http://www.islandpress.org/dms/ip/press/Sukhdev_brochure/sukhdev_brochure.pdf, last accessed on 8 October 2012.

10 http://www.triplepundit.com/2012/04/brazils-wealth-grew-3-indias-9-1990-2008-according-new-inclusive-wealth-indicator/, last accessed on 28 October 2012.

11 http://www.guardian.co.uk/sustainable-business/corporate-models-green-economy, last accessed on 15 April 2013.

12 Epstein, Paul R, Jonathan J Buonocore, Kevin Eckerle, Michael Hendryx, Benjamin M Stout III, Richard Heinberg, Richard W Clapp, Beverly May, Nancy L Reinhart, Melissa M Ahern, Samir K Doshi, and Leslie Glustrom 2011, Full cost accounting for the life cycle of coal in "Ecological Economics Reviews," Robert Costanza, Karin Limburg, and Ida Kubiszewski, Eds, *Ann. NY Acad. Sci.* Vol. 1219, pp. 73–98, February 2011.

amount to some US$345.3 billion, adding close to 17.8¢/kWh of electricity generated from coal. The low estimate is US$175 billion, or over 9¢/kWh, while the true monetizable costs could be as much as the upper bounds of US$523.3 billion, adding close to 26.89¢/kWh. These and the more difficult to quantify externalities are borne by the general public.' The paper continues to add that these figures do not represent the full societal and environmental burden of coal, and lists a number of omissions that should ideally be included in the costs. The paper states, 'The true ecological and health costs of coal are thus far greater than the numbers suggest. Accounting for the many external costs over the life cycle for coal-derived electricity conservatively doubles to triples the price of coal per kWh of electricity generated.'

- Trucost Plc,[13] a sustainability consulting firm, states that the 'direct and supply chain environmental costs of S&P 500 retail companies totalled almost $22 billion.' The research also said that the costs associated with food and beverage companies were $68.68 billion. This $69 billion constituted of water usage ($38.3 billion), land and water pollutants ($12billion), greenhouse gas (GHG) emissions ($10.3billion), other air pollutants ($7.6billion), and waste ($0.4billion).[14]

TRUE COST ECONOMICS

There has been increasing demand to internalize the negative externalities. Adbusters, a Canada-based NGO, known for starting the 'Occupy Wall Street' movement was one among them. They popularized the term *True Cost Economics*, which has now entered into mainstream discussion. Investopedia defines True Cost Economics as 'an economic model that seeks to include the cost of negative externalities into the pricings of goods and services.'[15] As per the World Bank, governments around the globe subsidize environmentally and economically harmful activities worth about $1.2 trillion a year—$500 billion on fossil fuels, $300 billion on cheap or free water, $400 billion on fishing and farm subsidies.[16] While not all the money spent here are wasteful expenditure, such subsidies result in misuse of the resources. Farmers in China overuse fertilizers because the government has made them so cheap, resulting in fertilizer run-off to nearby rivers and lakes. Many in India use water inefficiently as it is available at very low cost. Channelizing the fossil fuel subsidies to renewable energy research can result in a more secure future. Understanding the true cost of a product/service, would aid in improved decision making. Trucost Plc, states that, if nature charged for

13 http://www.trucost.com/
14 http://www.greenbiz.com/blog/2013/02/05/true-cost-s-p-500, last accessed on 21 February 2013.
15 http://www.investopedia.com/terms/t/truecosteconomics.asp, last accessed on 13 May 2013.
16 Shoots, greens and leaves, *The Economist*, 24 June 2012, Vol. 403, Number 8789.

its services, the actual cost of a desktop would be approximately 6 per cent higher than the retail price, while the actual cost of a laptop would be 14 per cent higher than the retail price.[17] Similarly, it was found that a platinum ring costing $650 would increase to $689 (a 6 per cent increase in costs), and a gold ring costing $150 would increase to $210 (a 40 per cent increase in costs), if the total costs of environmental impacts are taken into account.

RESPONSES TO MARKET FAILURES

Market mechanism is meant to allocate limited resources effectively. However, there are times when markets fail to allocate resources that achieve socially efficient levels of output.

Common Types of Market Failures in the Context of Sustainability

Some of the common types of market failures relevant to sustainable development are as follows:

Creation of externalities (see previous sections)   Negative externalities result in the market producing a larger quantity of that good/service, than what is socially desirable. Positive externalities may result in the underproduction of that good/service.

Tragedy of commons   When there are common resources, the tendency is to exploit it to its fullest for personal gain, if everyone acts only for their own self-interest. This eventually leads to societal tragedies. Overfishing from the oceans and over-extraction of ground water are two examples of 'tragedy of commons'.

Missing markets and incomplete markets   Certain goods/services would never be produced and sustained in the market. Companies that could cater to the need of public services, such as, waste management and recycling, may fail to form.

Monopoly/duopoly/oligopoly power   Markets may create few service providers who exert significant influence on the society. As they turn out to be the only/few service providers, it would be difficult for the society to control their vested interests. They can enter into collusive pricing. These service providers also have significant clout that they influence public dialogues and decision making. For example, in USA, 'The Repeal Big Oil Tax Subsidies Act', would have resulted in the elimination of $2.4 billion in annual tax deduction for five of the major oil companies—BP, Exxon, Chevron, Shell, and ConocoPhilips. This bill was defeated in the US senate twice, in 2011 and 2012.[18,19]

---

17 http://www.greenbiz.com/blog/2012/10/03/true-cost-personal-computers, last accessed on 5 October 2012.

18 http://priceofoil.org/content/uploads/2012/05/FIN.USCapitolSubsidyGraphicFlyer.pdf, last accessed on 19 June 2014.

19 http://www.opencongress.org/bill/s2204-112/show, last accessed on 18 June 2014.

Responses to Market Failures

The following are the most suggested responses to market failures, in the context of sustainable development:

- Command and control regulation
- Incentives and taxes
- Cap and trade mechanisms
- Direct governmental involvement

Command and Control Regulation

For the purpose of environmental degradation, economists have asked the government to engage in command-and-control regulations. This is a direct regulatory approach enforced through legislation to set environmental standards. The following are some of the regulatory options that are included:

- Standards and targets for electricity boards/utilities to produce and purchase renewable energy.
- Creating regulatory frameworks for emissions trading.
- Asking public sector units to invest in sourcing clean energy.
- Improving the technology performance standards, such as, emission norms and efficiency norms for vehicles. For example, Government of India introduced the India 2000 emission norms, based on Euro I standards, in 2000. Gradually, the government mandated that, by 2010, all new four wheeled vehicles should meet Bharat III emission standards and 13 major cities in India should meet Bharat IV emission norms.
- The government could create regulations to increase efficiency standards for fuel combustion equipment, lighting, and power. This would include asking the industries to incorporate technologies that will reduce the release of greenhouse emissions to the atmosphere. It can include asking manufacturers to meet energy efficient design standards. From 2010, Bureau of Energy Efficiency (BEE), a statutory body under Ministry of Power, Government of India, made the BEE star labelling mandatory for frost free refrigerator, air-conditioner, tubular fluorescent lamp, and distribution transformer. The labelling was voluntary when it was introduced in 2006.
- Providing exclusive lanes for cyclists, pedestrians, and vehicles of public mass transportation, while building roads.
- Replacing GDP as the indicator of development with alternative indicators such as Genuine Progress Indicator (GPI), Gross National Happiness (GNH), Happy Planet Index (HPI), etc.
- Setting up of air quality standards and water quality standards.
- There have been calls for increased regulation in advertising. While system change consultants like Frank Dixon has argued for the prohibition of western

style advertising,[20] sustainability experts like Pawan Sukhdev has commented that 'Advertising is the single biggest driver of excessive demand' with advertising focusing on the need to purchase more than what is needed. A more sustainable method, Sukhdev argues, is taking a life cycle approach, advertising how long a product will last, where its materials come from, how to properly dispose of, and recycle it.

- In 2003, the state government of Tamil Nadu, made rainwater harvesting mandatory for every building in the state. An example at an international level could be the new emission regulations announced by International Maritime Organization on mandatory regulations to reduce greenhouse gases (GHGs) to take effect from 1 January 2013. In the initial phase (2015-19), ships will be required to have a fuel efficiency improvement of 10 per cent. The efficiency standard would be improved every five years. It is expected that the new rules will result in a 25-30 per cent emission reduction by 2030, as compared to the average efficiency for ships that were built between 1999 and 2009.

When such regulations are not followed, the legal authorities are empowered to take actions. In 2011, the Madras High Court ruled to shut down 752 dyeing and bleaching units in Tirupur for failing to conform to zero discharge of effluents and releasing toxic effluents into the Noyyal River which killed the river's ecosystem and made farming impossible.

Incentives and Taxes

It has also been suggested that the government agencies should promote incentive-based regulation. Positive externalities could result in the market producing a smaller quantity than what is socially desirable. Subsidies, grants, and tax credits could create a situation where the market starts producing goods/services that are necessary for social welfare. An example could be that of the financial incentives announced by the Ministry of New and Renewable Energy (MNRE), Government of India in 2010. It was a 20 per cent incentive on the ex-factory price of electric vehicles till the end of financial year 2011–12. To promote wind energy, MNRE has facilitated concession on import duty for components of wind electric generators, excise duty exemption to manufacturers, and a 10 year tax holiday on income incurred from wind energy projects. Government of India is also supporting Generation Based Incentives (GBIs), accelerated depreciation, preferential tariffs, and interest and capital subsidies.

In 2003, in the city of London, a congestion pricing scheme was introduced whereby vehicles were charged for driving into central London congestion zone on weekdays between 7 AM and 6 PM. The charge was £10 (approximately ₹1,000)[21] daily, with

---

20 http://www.globalsystemchange.com/GSC/Articles_files/GNH%20Bhutan%202-4.pdf, last accessed on 28 October 2012.

21 http://www.tfl.gov.uk/modes/driving/congestion-charge/paying-the-congestion-charge, last accessed on 11 May 2014.

£65–£195 (₹6,500–19,500)[22] levied as a fine for non-compliance. This resulted in a 21 per cent reduction in the traffic entering the congestion zone, providing revenue earning of £123 million in 2006–2007.[23] Significant percentage of this revenue could be used for transportation improvements in the city, especially public transportation infrastructure.

As part of incorporating incentives and taxes for creating a green infrastructure, the government could offer the following:

- Subsidies for promoting green technologies.
- Giving tax reduction for renewable energy production and purchases by companies.
- Providing research grants to educational institution to develop green technologies.
- Implementing energy taxes, and carbon taxes.
- Increasing taxes on resource usage.
- Removing environmentally harmful subsidies (an example could be providing free electricity and subsidized motor pumps to a large-scale 'farmer' for irrigation, resulting in reckless extraction, and usage of underground water sources).

There have been suggestions that, to promote sustainable operations, companies should also be taxed for the common resources that they take from the planet. For example, mining companies should be taxed for the quantity of minerals that they mine from earth, rather than taxing them for their profits. Another example is about taxing companies for the quantity of water they collect.

Polluter pays principle   Trucost, in a report[24] has stated that in 2009 primary production (agriculture, forestry, fisheries, mining, oil and gas exploration, and utilities) and primary processing (cement, steel, pulp and paper, and petrochemicals) are costing the economy approximately $7.3 trillion a year. As per the report, the social and environmental costs of water usage could amount to $1.9 trillion per year. Many a times, the costs are not paid by the emitting source. Firms may choose not to pay for the pollutants as managing pollution may result in additional costs. However, what is cheapest for the firm is not always cheapest for society as a whole. As per 'polluter pays principle' (PPP), price of a good or a service should fully reflect its total cost of production, including the cost of all the resources used. In this process, polluters internalize the externalities. The aim of PPP is to integrate the use of environment into the economic sphere through the use of price signals and the use of economic instruments such as pollution taxes, charges, and permits. The marginal cost of pollution reduction is equal to the marginal cost of the damage caused by such pollution. Addressing the fourth international conference on Gross National Happiness at Bhutan, Ronald Colman, Executive Director, GPI Atlantic, an organization that is creating a well-being indicator

22 http://www.tfl.gov.uk/modes/driving/congestion-charge/penalties-and-enforcement?intcmp=2067, last accessed on 11 May 2014.
23 http://www.tfl.gov.uk/cdn/static/cms/documents/fifth-annual-impacts-monitoring-report-2007-07-07.pdf, last accessed on 11 May 2014.
24 http://www.teebforbusiness.org/how/natural-capital-risk.html, last accessed on 17 October 2013.

for the Canadian province of Nova Scotia, says, 'Nothing changes people's behaviour like price signals. All the preaching about greenhouse gas emissions and energy conservation and all the good energy efficiency and climate change indicators in the world didn't tempt North Americans to switch away from their gas-guzzling SUVs (sports utility vehicles). But a doubling of oil prices very quickly stopped the SUV lust in its tracks and created an overnight demand for small fuel-efficient cars that the market could not meet.'[25]

Pigovian tax and pollution taxes   To correct negative externalities, governments can levy a *Pigovian tax*. When there are negative externalities, the social/environmental costs are not included in the process/product cost, and this may lead to over-consumption of the product/service. Named after economist Arthur Pigou, Pigovian taxes try to correct this inefficient market outcome. Economists try to peg a Pigovian tax as a sum equivalent to the cost of the negative externality. Pigovian tax operates on the basis of PPP. Regulatory bodies and governmental authorities also administer pollution taxes. Some of the examples of pollution taxes are:

- Germany introduced an eco-tax for energy consumption through electricity and petroleum. This tax has lesser or no tax for energy produced from efficient conventional energy power plants or renewable sources.
- Car registration taxes in Finland, Netherlands, Portugal, and Spain are lower for environment-friendly and energy-efficient cars.
- In July 2011, Australia announced a carbon tax plan, to be implemented in July 2012, to tax the 500 largest polluting companies in Australia. The country has set a tax of A\$23 per ton of carbon emissions. Australia will raise the price of carbon emission 2.5 per cent every year until 2015. Post 2015, the scheme will become an emission trading scheme.

'Nothing changes people's behaviour like price signals. All the preaching about greenhouse gas emissions and energy conservation and all the good energy efficiency and climate change indicators in the world didn't tempt North Americans to switch away from their gas-guzzling SUVs. But a doubling of oil prices very quickly stopped the SUV lust in its tracks and created an overnight demand for small fuel-efficient cars that the market could not meet.'

- In February 2010, India announced a tax of ₹50 on every tonne production of coal. Revenue generated through this tax is expected to be channelized to the development of clean energy. Through the years the tax has been on an increase, and in budget 2015, the tax has reached ₹200.
- In 2013, the International Civil Aviation Organization (ICAO) decided to regulate global carbon emissions from aviation, through a mandatory emissions trading programme that will start in 2020. However, this has been considered to be a 'too little, too late' plan, in the context of European Union (EU) attempting to include non-European airlines that are flying from/to European region, in its already existing Emission Trading Scheme (ETS) for European airlines.

25 http://www.bhutanstudies.org.bt/pubFiles/1.GNH4.pdf, last accessed on 13 May 2012.

Cap and Trade Mechanisms

One of the market-based approaches applied to control pollution was referred to as emissions trading where economic incentives were provided for achieving emission reductions. In this approach, a limit or cap was set on the amount of pollution that could be emitted by a region/country. This limit or cap is enforced by a governmental/quasi-governmental authority. Emissions cap is the limit placed on an organization or a country regarding the amount of greenhouse gases that the organization or country can release.

From this amount of allowed pollution, a firm needs to buy emission permits equivalent to their emissions. Emission permit allows a firm to emit a specific amount of pollutant. Firms that release emissions beyond the permitted level will have to buy emission permits from those firms that pollute less than what is permitted for them. This buying/selling of permits is referred to as emission trading. If it is related to carbon dioxide emission, it is referred to as carbon trading.

Carbon trading can thus be:

- a trading system designed to offset carbon emissions caused by individuals, organizations, and countries.
- an exchange of carbon credits that happens between two parties.
- a process that entails an organization or a region to acquire the right to pollute.

The practice of trading carbon credits developed after the Kyoto Protocol of 1997, which planned to reduce the carbon dioxide emissions in the atmosphere. What is implied in this trading is that a buyer is paying for the right to pollute more, while the seller of the emission permit gets rewarded for reduced emissions. This trading is also referred to as cap-and-trade.

There are variations in the ways in which a cap-and-trade scheme is operated. Usually, cap or limits are made stringent over time in line with a regional/national emissions reductions target. There are systems where a portion of the traded permits are retired every time a transaction happens. There are systems where not-for-profit groups (like environmental NGOs) can also participate in the trade. They can purchase and retire permits. With this, the number of available permits goes down, thereby driving up the price of the remainder permits. As the organization is forced to spend higher amounts of money to purchase permits, it is expected, the organization will soon start focusing on implementing energy efficiency, renewable energy, etc.

A criticism related to cap-and-trade is that such offsets may not result in emission reductions. Organizations may continue to purchase permits without focusing on environmental sustainability and low-carbon business practices. Critics mention that carbon trading allows companies to exceed their emission cap and the net result of

In 2012, Mexico passed a climate change bill that set a target of generating 35 per cent of its energy from clean energy sources by 2024, and to halve its carbon emissions by 2050, from 2000 levels. In the same year, South Korea passed a bill that establishes a cap-and-trade emissions trade program that will begin in 2015.

carbon offsetting is only the moving of emissions from one location to another (usually from developed and emerging economies to third world countries) without any net reduction in emission production.

PAT and REC Mechanisms

Two market based mechanisms in India that focuses on improving energy efficiency and promoting the use of renewable energy is emission trading is the 'Perform, Achieve, and Trade' (PAT) mechanism and the 'Renewable Energy Certificate' (REC) mechanism.

In 2012, Government of India, as part of the National Mission for Enhanced Energy Efficiency (NMEEE) launched the PAT scheme. This market based mechanism focuses on improving energy efficiency of 478 units, in the sectors of aluminium, cement, chlor-alkali, fertilizer, iron and steel, pulp and paper, textiles, and thermal power. These units, referred to as 'Designated Customers' (DCs), are given Specific Energy Consumption (SEC) targets that are to be achieved during a three year period. Those who achieve the target, and thus achieve a positive surplus, can trade the surplus with those units who were unable to achieve their targets. This trading happens through Energy Saving Certificates (ESCerts). Unlike traditional cap-and-trade schemes, India's PAT scheme focuses on energy limits that are based on energy intensity rather than absolute caps. The units under this scheme, is expected to improve their energy efficiency by 1–2 per cent annually.

As part of the Indian Electricity Act 2003, the State Electricity Regulatory Commissions (SERCs) demanded the power companies to source a percentage of their total power from renewable energy sources. These targets were referred to as Renewable Purchase Obligations (RPOs). Different states had different RPOs. If the power companies were unable to meet the RPOs, they could compensate the same by buying Renewable Energy Certificates (RECs) from the market. A power producer can sell one REC for one MWh (or 1000 kWh) of energy generated from renewable sources.

Direct Governmental Involvement

There are a number of ways through which government can directly respond to market failures. The following are some of them:

- Investing in green businesses, incubating in green businesses, and running green businesses
- Coaching and mentoring green entrepreneurs to take their products/services to markets
- Facilitating and leading green technologies to market
- By being a leading purchaser of sustainable/green technologies, goods, and services. Governmental organizations and public sector units should use their procurement practices for promoting sustainability objectives

'I also don't like saying that growth is the problem, because for most people, growth is really positive. You love it when your grandchildren grow, your love grows, your flowers grow. We should not bless what we're doing now with the term 'growth'. We should call it what it is, an economy of waste and destruction.'

• Promote public transport as compared to private transport through increased investments in mass transit transportation options
• Increasing R&D spending on developing greener technologies
• Increasing investment in R&D on renewable energy sources such as wind, solar, tidal, biomass, etc.
• By providing feed-in tariffs
• Setting up organizations that (a) regularly ascertain and update economic value to ecosystem services and biodiversity, (b) release regular updates on non-conventional development indicators like GPI, GNH, Green GDP, etc.

The following are some of the best practices in transportation that required significant government investments:

• Indian cities such as Ahmedabad, Delhi, and Jaipur have Bus Rapid Transit (BRT) systems with segregated lanes for them. These BRTs are high-capacity public-transit systems with its own right of way and high frequency services.
• Delhi Metro, a rapid rail transit system serving the National Capital Region (NCR) of India, is estimated to carry approximately 16 lakh people every day.[26]

CLUB OF ROME AND LIMITS TO GROWTH

Founded in 1968, Club of Rome (http://www.clubofrome.org) is an informal association whose members 'share a common concern for the future of humanity and the planet.'[27] Club of Rome generated public attention in 1972 when it released *The Limits of Growth*, a book that tried to explore the consequences of unhindered economic and population growth, in the context of the existence of finite resources. It predicted that the world would be witnessing an economic and societal collage by the 21st century, and the economic and population growth go unchecked. There is also a school of thought that believes that equating growth with planetary degradation is unfair. While on a conversation, Frances Moore Lappé, author of *Diet for a Small Planet* and *Hope's Edge* and a recipient of the Right Livelihood Award, says, 'I also don't like saying that growth is the problem, because for most people, growth is really positive. You love it when your grandchildren grow, your love grows, your flowers grow. We should not bless what we're doing now with the term 'growth'. We should call it what it is, an economy of waste and destruction.'[28]

26 http://www.delhimetrorail.com/press_reldetails.aspx?id=JUVWaUlI0G0lld, last accessed on 28 June 2011.
27 http://www.clubofrome.org/?p=324, last accessed on 14 May 2013.
28 http://www.ecoliteracy.org/essays/hope-what-we-become-action-frances-moore-lappe-and-fritjof-capra-conversation, last accessed on 13 September 2013.

DEVELOPMENT INDICES AND ALTERNATIVE GROWTH INDICATORS

'Viewing the development of country only in terms of GDP is not right. The actual meaning of GDP has become Greed Driven Plunder of the country because only this has become the driving force for the country's development,' said Rajendra K Pachauri, former Chairman, Intergovernmental Panel on Climate Change (IPCC).[29] Similar voices are raised by many across the globe drawing attention to the idea that many of the popular growth indicators fail to be indicators of human and societal well-being.

Economists themselves have indicated that an issue with economic think-tanks and society is their obsession with 'GDP growth' as the all-important measure of success. In 1968, the political economist Bertrand de Jouvenel mentioned that 'because national accounts are based on financial transactions they account nothing for Nature, to which (we) don't owe anything in terms of payments but to which we owe everything in terms of livelihood.'[30] As we are communicated with the idea that 'Only that which is measured, gets managed well', it is important that our conventional economic compass that is faulty must be refined and redefined to incorporate the role of natural capital.

Criticism against using GDP as a development indicator stemmed from the fact that GDP is only a measure of monetary value. GDP does not incorporate value to goods and services that have not been incorporated with a price. For example, social service done by an individual or an organization without charging a fee is not accounted for GDP. This would indicate that if a nation has higher levels of service attitude, there could be a possibility that the GDP may be low (in an idealistic world like 'Ramarajya', most of the professional services are expected to be offered without cost, with an attitude of serving others). Interestingly, all the house-holding services engaged by women are also not accounted, on a monetary basis. Of course, there will be valid suggestions that we need not connect everything to monetary value. The idea is that GDP is not the indicator that decision makers should be obsessed with as GDP does not measure well-being. It also does not reveal economic inequality concerns. Scholars have indicated that rising income is clearly correlated with increased life satisfaction only up to around the median income level.[31] It is also documented that rich people are not much happier than middle-class people.[32,33,34] Therefore, the idea that GDP 'should' be the primary

29 'Climate change affects the poor most', *The Hindu*, Coimbatore, 12 March 2011; http://www.hindu.com/2011/03/12/stories/2011031250620200.htm, last accessed on 20 March 2011.

30 http://pavansukhdev.com/2011/04/05/%E2%80%9Cto-make-poverty-history-make-nature-the-future%E2%80%9D/, last accessed on 25 May 2011.

31 Goodstein, Eban S 2011, *Economics and the Environment*, Wiley, 2011.

32 Easterlin, Richard, 'Does economic growth improve the human lot? Some empirical evidence', *Nations and households in economic growth: Essays in Honor of Moses Abramovitz*, edited by Paul A David and Melvin W Reder, New York: Academic Press, 1974.

33 Layard, Richard 2005, *Happiness: Lessons from a new science*, Penguin Press, New York, 2005.

34 Kahneman, Daniel, Alan B. Krueger, Developments in the measurement of subjective well-being, *Journal of Economic Perspectives*, Vol. 20, pt. (1), pp. 3–24, 2006.

indicator to measure a society's well-being is an incomplete and ignorant argument, especially when GDP is reported to be synonymous with progress. Joseph Stiglitz, the economist who won Nobel Prize in 2001, has been quoted as saying, 'No one would look just at a firm's revenues to assess how well it was doing. Far more relevant is the balance sheet, which shows assets and liability. That is also true for a country.'[35]

An interesting finding was revealed by the 'Inclusive Wealth Indicator' (IWI) project of United Nations University-International Human Development Program's (UNU-IHDP). Their 'Inclusive Wealth Report' (IWR) attempted to measure natural, human, manufactured, and social forms of capital. One of their reports indicated that, the wealth of Brazil and India, as measured by GDP per capita, increased 34 per cent and 120 per cent between 1990 and 2008, respectively. However, during the same period, the natural capital of Brazil and India declined by 46 per cent and 31 per cent respectively, Brazil's IWI rose just 3 per cent and India's rose 9 per cent over the period.[36]

Pondering on the ineffectiveness of many metrics that we use as unquestioned fundamentals of finance and economics, Pavan Sukhdev, Founder–CEO of GIST Advisory, an environmental consulting firm and former Managing Director—Global Markets Division, Deutsche Bank, wrote, 'Our tendency to discount future benefits compared with today's (benefits) discriminates against future generations. Using a discount rate of 4 per cent (most studies use between 3 per cent and 5 per cent) arithmetically amounts to saying that we value and will trade off a benefit to our own grandchild, 50 years hence, at one-seventh of its value to us today. Furthermore, our use of indicators which are not weighted for poverty discriminates against the poor. We may dismiss ecosystem services as only "10-20 per cent of GDP", but they are actually "50-90 per cent of the GDP of the poor". These are all ethical choices that we make, not economic choices. Economics is mere weaponry—the direction in which we shoot is an ethical choice.'[37]

Dr Pablo Muñoz, Scientific Director at UNU-IHDP's 'Inclusive Wealth Indicator' project states, 'Until the yardsticks which society uses to evaluate progress are changed to capture elements of long-term sustainability, the planet and its people will continue to suffer under the weight of short-term growth policies.'[38] There have been attempts to develop alternate indicators that are more meaningful. Two of the indicators that attempt to measure well-being are the GPI and GNH. These indicators try to measure a broad range of social development indicators including education levels, life expectancy, poverty, and unemployment rate. These indicators also try to incorporate aspects of environmental well-being by looking into environmental pollution and waste, and state

35 http://www.beyond-gdp.eu/key_quotes.html, last accessed on 8 May 2012.
36 http://www.ihdp.unu.edu/article/read/iwr, last accessed on 29 October 2012.
37 http://pavansukhdev.com/2011/04/05/%E2%80%9Cto-make-poverty-history-make-nature-the-future%E2%80%9D/, last accessed on 25 May 2011.
38 http://www.triplepundit.com/2012/04/brazils-wealth-grew-3-indias-9-1990-2008-according-new-inclusive-wealth-indicator/, last accessed on 28 October 2012.

of natural resources. Aspects related to human well-being are given due importance with focus on quality of an individual's life in relation to their family, job, etc.

Genuine Progress Indicator

GPI tries to ascertain whether the economic growth of the country has resulted in adding to the well-being of the people in the country. This indicator tries to distinguish between worthwhile growth and a growth that erodes a decline in the quality of life. Many of the factors that contribute to the growth of the GDP have potential harmful effects. Therefore the benefits come along with costs. The following are some of the costs incurred:

- Cost of pollution
- Cost associated with environmental hazards—ozone depletion, acid rain, etc.
- Cost of resource depletion
- Cost of crime
- Cost of family breakdown
- Loss of wetland and similar life sustaining ecosystems
- Loss of farmland
- Loss of leisure time

GPI takes into account these costs and losses, during the process of calculating the GPI. It is stated that a comparison between GDP and GPI could be considered as the comparison between the gross profit of a company and the net profit of a company. Net profit is derived by subtracting the costs from the gross profit. Similarly, GPI is derived by subtracting costs related to crime, pollution, etc. The GPI would thus touch zero, if the financial costs associated with environmental hazards, pollution, crime, resource depletion, etc., equals the financial gains made in the production of goods and services, all other factors being constant. GPI is still evolving and thus there are no standard practices that need to be followed while developing a GPI. When the US state of Maryland started measuring its GPI, 26 indicators were used (see Table 11.1):[39]

TABLE 11.1 Parameters used to measure GPI in the US state of Maryland

Economic indicators	Environmental indicators	Social indicators
Personal consumption expenditures	Cost of water pollution	Value of housework
Income inequality	Cost of air pollution	Cost of family changes
Adjusted personal consumption	Cost of noise pollution	Cost of crime
Services of consumer durables	Cost of net wetlands change	Cost of personal pollution abatement
Cost of consumer durables	Cost of net farmland change	Value of volunteer work
Cost of underemployment	Cost of net forest cover change	Cost of lost leisure time

(Contd)

39 http://www.green.maryland.gov/mdgpi/indicators.asp, last accessed on 9 May 2012.

TABLE 11.1 *(Contd)*

Economic indicators	Environmental indicators	Social indicators
Net capital investment	Cost of climate change	Value of higher education
	Cost of ozone depletion	Services of highways and streets
	Cost of non-renewable energy resource depletion	Cost of commuting
		Cost of motor vehicle crashes

If another region is planning to develop GPI, it may not be necessary for them to use the same 26 indicators that were used by Maryland. The parameters could differ based on local considerations and needs. In the Canadian province of Nova Scotia, the parameters used are as listed in Table 11.2.

TABLE 11.2 Parameters used to measure GPI in Nova Scotia, Canada

Time use	Living standards	Natural capital	Human impact on the environment	Human and social capital
Value of civic and voluntary work	Income and its distribution	Soils and agriculture	Solid waste	Population health
Value of unpaid housework and child care	Financial security— debt and assets	Forests	Ecological footprint	Costs of crime
Value of leisure time	Economic security index	Fisheries and marine resources	Greenhouse gas emissions	Educational attainment
Paid work hours		Energy	Transportation	
		Air		
		Water		

Gross National Happiness[40]

Gross national happiness (GNH) was designed as an indicator that measures quality of life or social progress. This indicator has been associated with Bhutan. The term GNH was coined by the Bhutanese King Jigme Singye Wangchuck, whose intention was to build an economy that would serve Bhutan's culture founded on Buddhist spiritual values. GNH is based on the promotion of sustainable development, preservation, and promotion of cultural values, conservation of natural environment, and establishment of good governance. GNH guides Bhutan's five year planning process and all other economic/development plans for the country. In most countries, a proposed industrial project has to do an environmental impact assessment (EIA). Similarly, the proposed developmental policies and programmes in Bhutan should undertake a GNH review.

---

40 **Note**: The section on Gross National Happiness has been written with the help of R Shyaam prasadh, a research scholar at IIT Chennai. He can be reached at shyaam.sishil@gmail.com.

Though GNH has its origins in Buddhist ethos and Bhutan, this is an indicator that could be adopted in other parts of the globe too.

After 1972, as more countries riveted their economies on substantial expansion of materialistic aspect, the then Kingdom of Bhutan looked for, through public action, to inflate the well-being and true happiness of its people. It was one of the last countries to allow the introduction of television, which happened only in 1999. The goal of GNH was first enunciated by the Fourth King, His Majesty Jigme Singye Wangchuck. He reposes on the legacy of Bhutan's government since the 1729 legal code by Zhabdrung Rimpoche, which dates from the unification of Bhutan. The legal code stated that 'if the government cannot bring into existence happiness (dekidk) for its people, there is no purport for the government to exist'. Article 9 of Bhutans' Constitutions states, "the State shall strive to promote those conditions that enable the successful pursuit of Gross National Happiness. GNH at its core comprises a set of values that promote collective happiness as the end value of any development strategy.

GNH might be keyed out as:

Holistic   Recognizing all vistas of people's needs of spiritual, material, physical, and social

Balanced   Accentuation of balanced progress towards the attributes of GNH

Collective   Reckoning happiness to be an all-encompassing collective phenomenon

Sustainable   Pursuing wellbeing for both current and future generations

Equitable   Achieving reasonable and equitable distributed level of well-being

Investopedia states that 'GNH attempts to measure the sum total not only of economic output, but also of net environmental impacts, the spiritual, and cultural growth of citizens, mental and physical health, and the strength of the corporate and political systems.' GNH had been designed to create both material and spiritual development.

The GNH Index renders the government and others to increase GNH in two ways. It can either increase the percentage of people who are happy or decrease the insufficient conditions of people who are not yet happy. GNH in Bhutan is multi-dimensional and it interiorizes responsibility and other concerning motivations explicitly. The 'four pillars of GNH', are: (a) sustainable and equitable socio-economic development; (b) environmental conservation; (c) the preservation and promotion of culture; and (d) good governance. Subsequently, nine dimensions of GNH were identified that specify the four pillars. The nine dimensions were selected on normative grounds and map more specifically the key areas of GNH. The dimensions are: psychological well-being, health, education, cultural diversity and resilience, time used, good governance, community vitality, living standard, and ecological diversity, and resilience.

Construction of GNH index   The GNH Index is based on a survey of 7,142 people, which was completed in all 20 districts of Bhutan in the year 2010 and is representative by rural and urban area, and by districts or Dzongkhags. The survey was initiated by the Centre for Bhutan Studies (CBS). The survey included all nine domains and gave innovative insights into happiness. The process is too complex due to intensive data, perplexed with the attainment of perfection. In a state of measuring the 9 domains of GNH, 33 indicators have been selected according to 5 different criteria (see Table 11.3).

TABLE 11.3 GNH indicators in Bhutan

Domain	Indicators	Weight	Domain	Indicators	Weight
(1) Psychological well-being	Life satisfaction	33.00%	(5) Time-used	Work	50.00%
	Positive emotions	17.00%		Sleep	50.00%
	Negative emotions	17.00%	(6) Good governance	Political participation	40.00%
	Spirituality	33.00%		Services	40.00%
(2) Health	Self-reported health	10.00%		Government performance	10.00%
	Healthy days	30.00%		Fundamental rights	10.00%
	Disability	30.00%	(7) Community vitality	Donation (time and money)	30.00%
	Mental health	30.00%		Safety	30.00%
(3) Education	Literacy	30.00%		Community relationship	20.00%
	Schooling	30.00%		Family	20.00%
	Knowledge	20.00%	(8) Ecological diversity and resilience	Wildlife damage	40.00%
	Value	20.00%		Urban issues	40.00%
(4) Cultural diversity and resilience	Zorig chusum skills (thirteen arts and crafts)	30.00%		Responsibility towards environment	10.00%
	Cultural participation	30.00%		Ecological issues	10.00%
	Speak native language	20.00%	(9) Living standard	Per capita income	33.00%
	Driglam namzha (etiquette)	20.00%		Assets	33.00%
				Housing	33.00%

The GNH Index is created from two numbers namely (a) % of people who are happy, and (b) intensity of sufficiency among those who are not-yet-happy. The GNH Index formulae can be written GNH = 1 - (Hn × A), where Hn is the percentage of not-yet-happy people [Hn = (1 - Hh), where Hh stands for percentage of happy people] and A is the intensity of sufficiency among those who are not-yet-happy. In 2010, the percentage of people who were happy was 40.9 per cent, and those not-so-happy were 59.1 per cent. The intensity of sufficiency amongst those who were not yet happy is 43.4 per cent. For 2010, the GNH index had been calculated as = 1 - (0.591 × 0.434) = 0.743.

NATURAL CAPITAL

As part of the United Nations Conference on Sustainable Development or Rio+20 Earth summit, a collective of 39 banks, investors, and insurers together with more than 50 countries made a collective call for natural capital valuation and accounting, termed as 'Natural Capital Declaration'. The group stated that 'Natural capital comprises Earth's natural assets (soil, air, water, flora, and fauna), and the ecosystem services resulting from them, which make human life possible. Ecosystem goods and services from natural capital are worth trillions of US dollars per year and constitute food, fibre, water, health, energy, climate security, and other essential services for everyone (see Fig. 11.2). Neither these services, nor the stock of natural capital that provides them, are adequately valued compared to social and financial capital. Despite being fundamental to our well-being, their daily use remains almost undetected within our economic system. Using natural capital this way is not sustainable. The private sector, governments, all of us, must increasingly understand and account for our use of natural capital and recognize the true cost of economic growth and sustaining human well-being today and into the future.'[41] The group suggested the importance to internalize environmental costs, and suggested ways to engage in this.

In April 2010, Caribou Coffee announced its decision that it will source all its beans from farms certified sustainable by Rainforest Alliance, a New York based non-governmental organization, which works in biodiversity conservation and promotion of sustainable business. By January 2012, Caribou Coffee, had become the second largest coffeehouse in US, announced that it was the first major coffee company in US to source all its coffee and espresso beans from farms that are certified sustainable by the Rainforest Alliance.

The Economics of Ecosystems and Biodiversity (TEEB) was a study launched in 2007 aimed at drawing attention to the global economic benefits of biodiversity and to highlight the growing costs of biodiversity loss and ecosystem degradation. As per TEEB, there is a natural capital loss of $2–4 billion on an annual basis.[42] The study also tries to establish an objective global standard basis for natural capital accounting. TEEB launched the 'Bank of Natural Capital'[43] an educational initiative to communicate its findings to people. 'By assigning a value to these services (ecosystem services) flowing from nature to people, the global economy can start to account for the costs of biodiversity loss as well as reward the benefits that nature provides. This will help protect the natural world for future generations,' said Pavan Sukhdev, Study Leader, TEEB (also Founder-CEO of GIST Advisory, an environmental consulting firm, former Managing Director—Global Markets Division, Deutsche Bank).[44]

41 http://www.naturalcapitaldeclaration.org/the-declaration/, last accessed on 24 August 2012.

42 http://www.unep.org/civil-society/Portals/59/Documents/publications/UNEP_GEI.pdf, last accessed on 27 September 2012.

43 http://bankofnaturalcapital.com

44 http://pavansukhdev.com/2011/04/05/%E2%80%9Cto-make-poverty-history-make-nature-the-future%E2%80%9D/, last accessed on 25 May 2011.

45 http://envfor.nic.in/downloads/public-information/2011-02-23%20Press%20Brief%20-%20TEEB%20India.pdf, last accessed on 20 June 2014.

On 18 February 2011, India launched a study[45] to evaluate its natural capital and ecosystem services. This was done in collaboration with 'The Economics of Ecosystems and Biodiversity' (TEEB) study. The study plans to develop a framework for green national accounts that the country can implement by 2015.

Richard Mattison, CEO, Trucost, a company that provides research services on corporate environmental efficiency, says, 'Companies can use natural capital valuation as a tool to embed natural resource considerations within everyday product and procurement decision making alongside other considerations such as cost and quality.'[46] Trucost did an analysis to find out the cost of three common food products (cheese, breakfast cereal, and fruit juice), wherein the environmental costs are also taken into consideration. The analysis resulted in the conclusion that a block of cheese, breakfast cereal, and fruit juice should cost 18 per cent, 16 per cent, and 6 per cent higher respectively as compared to their retailing price. Mattison continues, 'Over time, it will be possible to redefine how and where products are made in order to optimize value chains for natural capital... An understanding of natural capital risks can lead to changes in design—for example is it possible to substitute water intensive raw materials to reduce natural capital risk?'[47]

FIG. 11.2[48] Photo of a waterway in Kollam (Quilon), Kerala, taken somewhere between 1895 and 1905. Nature provides us means and amenities of transportation like waterways and materials to make boats while manmade construction of such means and amenities comes at exorbitant cost.

46 www.greenbiz.com/blog/2012/08/09/true-cost-food?page=full, last accessed on 15 August 2012.

47 www.greenbiz.com/blog/2012/08/09/true-cost-food?page=full, last accessed on 15 August 2012.

48 Photo by Zacharias D'Cruz, licensed under public domain via Wikimedia Commons. Image source: https://commons.wikimedia.org/wiki/File:General_view_north_from_the_bridge,_Quilon.jpg#mediaviewer/File:General_view_north_from_the_bridge, last accessed on 7 August 2014.

ROLE OF INCENTIVES IN ENFORCING ENVIRONMENTAL QUALITY

On 19 October 2011, a group of 285 investors/investing firms that represented assets of more than $20 trillion released a statement urging the governments and international policy makers to make new and meaningful steps in the fight against climate change. This statement, referred to as the '2011 Global Investor Statement on Climate Change' mentioned,

> *'Those countries that succeed in attracting private capital into low-carbon growth areas such as cleaner and renewable energy, energy efficiency, and decarbonisation will enjoy multiple benefits, including new jobs, new businesses, new research and technology innovation, more resilient and secure energy systems, and, ultimately, more sustainable economies. Private investment can and must play a critical role in addressing the risks and opportunities posed by climate change. However, private sector investment will only flow at the scale and pace necessary if it is supported by clear, credible, and long-term domestic and international policy frameworks— "investment-grade climate change and energy policies"—that shift the balance in favour of low-carbon investment opportunities.*'[49]

This statement indicates that regions and nations can benefit from the changing business environments if they are willing to act. Incentives are not just financial incentives. The business community is also looking forward to credible policy frameworks that shift the balance in favour of low-carbon investment opportunities.

Reducing Emissions from Deforestation and Degradation

Reducing emissions from deforestation and degradation (REDD) is a series of initiatives aimed at reducing deforestation, which causes approximately 20 per cent of global carbon emissions. During the evolution of REDD, there have been various proposals. The following are the proposals that were chosen to be included:

- Reducing emissions related to deforestation (RED)[50,51]
- Reducing emissions related to deforestation and degradation (REDD)
- Reducing emissions related to deforestation, degradation, and enhancement (REDD+)

While these proposals are not financial incentives per se, these proposals also aim to create a financial value for the carbon stored in forests. This is done by providing incentives to engage in conservation in sustainable management of forests and also for enhancing quality and the expanse of forest cover. Funding for REDD is expected to come from financing schemes resulting from international negotiations and from national government programmes. It is estimated that REDD+ related financial flows for greenhouse gas emission reductions could reach $30 billion on an annual

---

49 http://www.ceres.org/files/press-files/2011-global-investor-statement-on-climate-change/official-2011-global-investor-statement-on-climate-change, last accessed on 26 October 2011.

50 http://www.cbd.int/doc/meetings/for/wscbredd-apac-01/other/wscbredd-apac-01-cifor-en.pdf, last accessed on 20 June 2014.

51 http://theredddesk.org/what-is-redd, last accessed on 20 June 2014.

As part of the International Coastal Cleanup Day, Method (a San Francisco based cleaning products company) partnered with beach cleanup volunteers and organizations to collect the plastic trash collected from the oceans and to recycle them to new packaging materials.

basis.[52] The program conceptualizes improvement in livelihood and food security. Ministry of Environment and Forests, Government of India, estimates that 'a REDD+ programme for India could provide capture of more than 1 billion tonnes of additional CO_2 over the next three decades and provide more than US$ three billion as carbon service incentives under REDD+.'[53]

There are a number of initiatives that assist countries in engaging in REDD+ activities. This includes the United Nations Programme on Reducing Emissions from Deforestation and Forest Degradation (UN-REDD Programme), Forest Carbon Partnership Facility (FCPF) of World Bank, International Climate and Forest Initiative (ICFI) from Norway, Australia's International Forest Carbon Initiative (IFCI), and the Collaborative Partnership on Forests (CPF).

Reduction in emissions, also referred to as 'avoided deforestation', is quantified as credits and could be sold/traded in an international carbon market. International funds set up to provide financial compensation for conservation measure could use these credits to provide compensation for conserving forests. The following are some of the challenges associated with REDD schemes:

- Measure the value of the carbon bearing potential of a forest area
- Payment mechanisms
- Funding mechanisms
- Accountability for incentive payments

Payments for Ecosystem Services (PES)

Food and Agricultural Organization of the United Nations (FAO)[54] refers to Payments for Ecosystem Services (PES)[55] as 'an economic instrument designed to provide incentives to land users, on behalf of service beneficiaries, for agricultural land, coastal, or marine management practices, that are expected to result in continued or improved service provision, so a specific user or society will benefit more broadly.' One of the attributes of PES is that it maintains 'a flow of a specified ecosystem "service"—such as clean water, biodiversity habitat, or carbon sequestration capabilities—in exchange for something of economic value.'[56] As per Centre for International Forestry Research (CIFOR)[57], a PES scheme is[58]

52　http://www.un-redd.org/aboutredd/tabid/582/default.aspx, last accessed on 15 May 2013.

53　http://envfor.nic.in/downloads/public-information/REDD-report.pdf, last accessed on 15 May 2013.

54　Headquartered in Rome, Italy, FAO is an agency of United Nations that works to remove hunger from the world.

55　Headquartered in Rome, Italy, FAO is an agency of United Nations that works to remove hunger from the world.

56　http://www.unep.org/pdf/PaymentsForEcosystemServices_en.pdf, last accessed on 3 October 2012.

57　A non-profit profit organization based at Bogor, Indonesia, that does research related to the usage and management of forests in less-developed countries.

58　http://www.cifor.org/pes/_ref/about/index.htm, last accessed on 3 October 2012.

- a voluntary transaction in which
- a well-defined environmental service (ES), or a form of land use likely to secure that service,
- is bought by at least one ES buyer
- from a minimum of one ES provider,
- if and only if the provider continues to supply that service (conditionality).

PES causes a benefit to occur where it would not have otherwise. PES in relation to water is shown in Table 11.4.

TABLE 11.4 [59]   Examples of PES in services related to water

	Ecological service provided	Supplier	Buyer	Instruments	Intended impacts on forests	Payment
Self-organized private deals	France: Perrier Vittel's payments for water quality					
	Quality drinking water	Upstream dairy farmers and forest landholders	A bottler of natural mineral water	Payments by bottler to upstream landowners for improved agricultural practices and reforestation of sensitive filtration zones	Reforestation but little impact because program focuses on agriculture	Vittel pays each farm about $230 per hectare per year for seven years. The company spent an average of $155,000 per farm or a total of $3.8 million.
	Costa Rica: FONAFIFO and hydroelectric utilities payments for watershed services					
	Regularity of water flow for hydroelectricity generation	Private upstream owners of forestland	Private hydroelectric utilities, Government of Costa Rica and local NGO	Payments made by utility company via a local NGO to landowners; payments supplemented by government funds	Increased forest cover on private land; expansion of forests through protection and regeneration	Landowners who protect their forests receive $45/ha/yr; those who sustainably manage their forests receive $70/ha/yr, and those who reforest their land receive $116/ha/yr.

(Contd)

59 http://www.unep.org/pdf/PaymentsForEcosystemServices_en.pdf, last accessed on 3 October 2012; Reproduction allowed for educational purposes.

TABLE 11.4 *(Contd)*

	Ecological service provided	Supplier	Buyer	Instruments	Intended impacts on forests	Payment
	Colombia: Associations of irrigators' payments (Cauca River)					
	Improvements of base flows and reduction of sedimentation in irrigation canals	Upstream forest landowners	Association of irrigators; government agencies	Voluntary payments by associations to government agencies to private upstream landowners; purchase by agency of lands	Reforestation, erosion control, springs and waterways protection, and development of watershed communities	Association members voluntarily pay a water use fee of $1.5-2/litre on top of an already existing water access fee of $0.5/litre.
Trading Schemes	United States: Nutrient trading					
	Improved water quality	Point source polluters discharging below allowable level; non-point source polluters reducing their pollution	Polluting sources with discharge above allowable level	Trading of marketable nutrient reduction credits among industrial and agricultural polluting sources	Limited impact on forests— mainly the establishment of trees in riparian areas	Incentive payments of $5 to $10 per acre
	Australia: Irrigators financing of upstream reforestation					
	Reduction of water salinity	State Forests of New South Wales (NSW)	An association of irrigation farmers	Water transpiration credits earned by State Forests for reforestation and sold to irrigators	Large-scale reforestation, including planting of desalination plants, trees, and other deep rooted perennial vegetation	Irrigators pay $40/ha per year for 10 years to the State Forests of NSW, a government agency that uses the revenues to reforest on private and public lands, keeping the forest management rights.

As per PES, the following are the various methods of delivering the payments:
- Direct monetary payment to an individual/community
- Indirect monetary payment to the individual/community—This could be in the form of financial support to build a service that benefits the community, like a school of a medical service facility. Compensation could be given to community forest management organizations to protect or regenerate forest areas. The community organization is then given financial benefits that could be distributed among the community.
- In-kind payments—This could be technical resources, tools for skill-building, tools for improving livelihood opportunities, etc.

How Payment for Ecosystem Services Can Benefit Poor

It is said that poverty could result in environmental degradation, as poor may start over-utilizing the natural resources. If they can be incentivized to adopt ecologically-friendly methods of using natural resources, it will result in both poverty reduction and reduced harm to the environment. Farmers engaged in small-scale farming are among the poorer groups of the society, and are potential service providers. PES can include opportunities that provide employment to the involved people through creation of livelihood opportunities that enable sustainable biodiversity management. Examples could be creation of tree nurseries and community based forest enterprises, and initiatives like 'pay per tree' wherein individual tree growers are rewarded, on a per tree basis, for the carbon sequestering service offered by the tree. Farmers engaged in farming on the slopes of the upper watersheds could be incentivized to protect the watersheds. Other forms of PES could include providing increased opportunities to the service provider in decision making processes and recognition of their rights to land and its resources like forests, water, and grass.

NEED FOR REGULATORY AND OPERATIONAL CHANGES IN FINANCIAL MARKETS AND ECONOMY

Incentivizing long-term investing The focus of financial markets on short-termism creates instability. The demand for immediate economic gains pressures top management of an organization to focus on short-term value creation while neglecting long-term value creation. Short-term value creation almost always focuses on maximum possible extraction. Long-term value creation can happen only when an organization takes into consideration sustainability related factors. In an article in *The Wall Street Journal*,[60] Al Gore, Former vice president of the United States, and David Blood, Managing Partner, Generation Investment Management, states, '...companies could issue securities that offer investors financial rewards for holding onto shares for a certain number of years. This would attract long-term investors with patient capital and would facilitate both long-term value creation in companies and stability in financial markets.'

---

60 Gore, Al, and David Blood, 'A Manifesto for Sustainable Capitalism', *The Wall Street Journal*, 14 December 2011, Also available at http://online.wsj.com/article/SB10001424052970203430404577092682864215896.html#printMode, last accessed on 15 May 2013.

Rethinking quarterly reporting   Too much focus on the quarterly earning calendar creates a business environment of short-term focus. Putting a stop on practices like quarterly earnings guidance could encourage long-term focus. Some leading companies such as Unilever, Coca-Cola, and Google have already stopped the practice of issuing quarterly earnings guidance. It is believed that the time and attention a company spends in providing earnings guidance could be better spend on paying focus to business fundamentals.

Making integrated reporting mandatory   Along with the regular reporting of financial indicators, it is important that a company reports its non-financial performance parameters. The information revealed by many companies about their environmental and social performance and impacts are way too little. 'Many (consumers) would like the choice between Coke or Pepsi, Apple or Samsung, Lego or Playmobil to be based on more than just aesthetics and branding. Since companies are not currently required to measure (let alone disclose) their broader footprint, they are able to veil most of the information about how their products are produced,' says Corp2020.com.[61] Increased sustainability related information will help the consumer to make more informed choices.

Resource taxation   A shift in the logic of taxation, from taxing a company based on the profits they earn, to taxing a company for the resource extraction and resource usage done from the planet.

---

61 http://www.corp2020.com/disclosing-externalities.html, last accessed on 15 May 2013.

CHAPTER SUMMARY

- Economic development means 'transformation of natural and environmental resources into goods and services to meet our needs and wants'. Utilization of environmental resources (ER) and services depends on quality and stock of environmental resources. The stock depends on rate of regeneration (RoR) and rate of utilization (RoU).
- Stock (S) = RoR − RoU
- RoU > RoR = Depletion (D)
- Quality of stock (QoS) = Rate of assimilation (RoA) − Rate of waste generation (RoWG)
- RoWG > RoA = Pollution (P) or degradation (D)
- Increasing or rising pollution or degradation results in increased private and social costs. Costs incurred by direct users are referred to as private costs while those incurred by third parties are referred to as social costs. Social costs can happen across time and space.
- Quantified value of pollution and/or degradation (resulting in both private and social costs) is referred to as damage costs (DC). Costs incurred to manage pollution and degradation at 'sustainable' levels is referred to as total containment costs (TCC).
- Total environmental cost (TEC) = Total damage cost + Total containment cost
- Sustainability occurs when rate of utilization is at par with rate of regeneration, and when assimilation is at par with rate of pollution OR RoU = RoR, RoA = RoP
- Enhancability occurs when utilization is less than regeneration, and when pollution is less than assimilation OR RoU<RoR, RoP<RoA
- Ecological economics considers ecosystem as a subsystem of the ecosystem and has an emphasis on preserving natural capital while environmental economics is related to the economic analysis of the natural environment. Ecological economics emphasizes strong sustainability.

- As per United Nations Environment Programme (UNEP), green economy is a development model that results in 'improved human well-being and social equity, while significantly reducing environmental risks and ecological scarcities'. Green economy aims for a low carbon, resource efficient, and socially inclusive economic paradigm. Green economy calculates the economic value of natural capital and ecosystem services.
- Externalization means to put something outside of its original borders. In economics, an externality is a cost or benefit, not transmitted through prices, incurred by a party who did not agree to the action causing the cost or benefit. Benefits are referred to as positive (temporal) externalities while costs are referred to as negative (spatial) externalities. In an activity generating positive externality, social benefit is higher than private benefit, and in an activity generating negative externality, social cost is higher than private cost.
- True Cost Economics is an economic model that seeks to include the cost of negative externalities into the pricings of goods and services.
- Some of the common types of market failures relevant to sustainable development are: (a) creation of externalities, (b) tragedy of commons, (c) missing markets and incomplete market, and (d) monopoly/duopoly/oligopoly power. Some of the responses to these market failures are (a) command and control regulation, (b) incentives and taxes, (c) cap and trade mechanisms, and (d) direct governmental involvement.

- GDP is only a measure of monetary value. GDP does not incorporate value to goods and services that have not been incorporated with a price.
- Genuine progress indicator (GPI) tries to ascertain whether the economic growth of the country has resulted in adding to the well-being of the people of the country.
- Gross national happiness (GNH) was designed as indicator that measures quality of life or social progress.
- Natural capital comprises Earth's natural assets (soil, air, water, flora, and fauna), and the ecosystem services resulting from them, which make human life possible. Ecosystem goods and services from natural capital are worth trillions of US dollars per year and constitute food, fibre, water, health, energy, climate security, and other essential services for everyone.
- Reducing Emissions from Deforestation and Degradation (REDD) is a series of initiatives that uses financial incentives to reduce deforestation, which causes approximately 20 per cent of global carbon emissions.
- Payments for Ecosystem Services (PES) is 'an economic instrument designed to provide incentives to land users, on behalf of service beneficiaries, for agricultural land, coastal, or marine management practices, that are expected to result in continued or improved service provision, so a specific user or society will benefit more broadly.'

KEYWORDS

- Assimilation
- Biodiversity management
- Cap and trade mechanism
- Designated customers (DCs)
- Ecological economics
- Enhanceability

- Environmental economics
- Energy saving certificates (ESCerts)
- Externalization
- Green economy
- Green national accounts
- Genuine progress indicator (GPI)

- Gross national happiness (GNH)
- Missing markets and incomplete markets
- Negative externalization
- Natural capital
- Perform, achieve, and trade (PAT) mechanism
- Pigovian tax
- Positive externality
- Polluter pays principle (PPP)
- Rate of regeneration (RoR)
- Rate of utilization (RoU)

- Resource taxation
- Renewable energy certificate (REC)
- REDD+
- Renewable purchase obligations (RPOs)
- Sustainability
- True Cost Economics
- Tragedy of commons
- The Economics of Ecosystems and Biodiversity (TEEB)

EXERCISES

Multiple-choice Questions

1. Costs incurred by direct users are referred to as private costs while those incurred by _____ parties are referred to as social costs.
   (a) second
   (b) third
   (c) indirect
   (d) private

2. Total environmental cost (TEC) =
   (a) Total damage cost − total containment cost
   (b) Total social cost + total private cost
   (c) Total damage cost + total containment cost
   (d) Total social cost − total private cost

3. Sustainability occurs when
   (a) rate of utilization (RoU) is on par with rate of regeneration (RoR)
   (b) assimilation is on par with rate of pollution
   (c) either A or B
   (d) neither A nor B

4. What is the development model that results in 'improved human well-being and social equity, while significantly reducing environmental risks and ecological scarcities'?
   (a) Green economy
   (b) Social economy
   (c) Neo-classical economics
   (d) Semi-classical economics

5. What will be zero if the financial costs of crime and pollution equal the financial gains in production of goods and services, all other factors being constant?
   (a) Gross domestic product
   (b) Genuine progress indicator
   (c) Gross national happiness
   (d) Natural capital

6. Natural capital comprises of
   (a) earth's natural assets and liabilities
   (b) global financial assets
   (c) earth's natural assets
   (d) all of these

7. Enrique Penalosa, Mayor (1998-2001), Bogata, Columbia, was driven by an economic philosophy that aims at
   (a) an increase in national capital
   (b) an increase in natural capital
   (c) fostering economic sustenance
   (d) fostering human happiness

8. Over-fishing from the oceans and over-extraction of ground water are two examples of
   (a) tragedy of commons
   (b) sustainable enterprises
   (c) missing markets and incomplete markets
   (d) all of these

Short Answer Questions

1. Write about externalities, positive and negative, with suitable examples.
2. What is True Cost Economics? How will assigning a true cost influence a purchase decision?
3. Write briefly about polluter pays principle (PPP).
4. What are the criticisms against using GDP as a development indicator?
5. Define natural capital.
6. Give an introduction to the concept of payments for ecosystem services (PES).
7. What is the difference between ecological and environmental economics?

Long Answer Questions

1. Explain market failures and responses.
2. Write about Reducing Emissions from Deforestation and Degradation (REDD).
3. Discuss about Genuine Progress Indicator (GPI) and Gross National Happiness (GNH), and how these indicators are considered to be better indicators of well-being as compared to indicators like Gross Domestic Product (GDP).

Reflective Question

1. Which is your favourite political party?
   (a) Find out their policies on social and environmental responsibility?
   (b) What can you do to take your favourite political party towards a higher level of social and environmental responsibility?
   (c) What suggestion would you give to your favourite political party to create a green economy?

Take-home Activity

1. Map out the 'Genuine Progress Indicator' for your district, state, or country.

Web Readings

1. About 'Payments for Ecosystem Services': http://www.unep.org/pdf/PaymentsForEcosystemServices_en.pdf
2. About ecosystem valuation:
   (a) Essentials of ecosystem valuation http://www.ecosystemvaluation.org/essentials.htm
   (b) Valuing ecosystem services: Toward better environmental decision-making http://www.nap.edu/openbook.php?isbn=030909318X
   (c) Ecosystem goods and services series: Valuation 101 http://www.worldchanging.com/archives//006048.html
   (d) Coastal capital: Economic valuation of coastal ecosystems in the caribbean http://www.wri.org/project/valuation-caribbean-reefs

3. Measuring prosperity in Maryland through Genuine Progress Indicator http://www.thesolutionsjournal.com/node/1070

4. About Gross National Happiness http://www.grossnationalhappiness.com/multimedia/

Web Video Link

1. 'Putting a value on Nature' (a) In this TED talk, Pavan Sukhdev, speaks about putting a value on nature http://www.youtube.com/watch?v=A-QpKiU-NHo (17 minutes) (b) Pavan Sukhdev's talk at Centre for Policy Development, Sydney http://www.youtube.com/watch?v=0n7lY3iYQ3s (1 hour, 18 minutes)

Recommended Book

1. E.F. Schumacher, *Small Is Beautiful: A Study of Economics as if People Mattered*, Random House, 1973.

Recommended Documentary/Movie

1. *Bogota: Building a Sustainable City*, PBS e2 series (This documentary is available for free viewing at https://www.youtube.com/watch?v=IjhMQM8eaVY) Duration: 26 minutes.

Online Game

1. An internet-based game developed by BBC where you play the role of the President of the European Nations with the objective of tackling climate change while remaining popular among people to retain your role. http://www.gamesforchange.org/play/climate-challenge/

12 CASE STUDIES AND CASELETS

CASE STUDIES

1. The story of Ethicus—India's first ethical fashion brand
2. Walmart's environmental strategy
3. Making sustainability a strategy: The case of interface
4. Compensation for watershed services at Los Negros, Bolivia
5. Radiant Clothing: Communicating the value of an environment-based strategy
6. Project GreenHands

CASELETS

1. Arogyapacha and Jeevani
2. East Kolkata Wetlands
3. Narmada Bachao Andolan and the Sardar Sarovar Dam project
4. Examples of sustainable transportation: Green Tomato Cars, Nextbike, TransMilenio, Delhi Metro, and Nature Air
5. The Natural Step
6. Siachen Peace Park

CASE STUDY 1

THE STORY OF ETHICUS—INDIA'S FIRST ETHICAL FASHION BRAND[1]

" *We have got this big problem with our lifestyle, which is not eco-friendly. Ethicus is not just about the fabric, it is not just about organic cotton, it is about a new kind of lifestyle. The very process is organic. In my tenure, I've been focusing on socially and environmentally responsible designs. Ethicus was very much related to this ideology, they are socially and environment ally responsible, and is an ideal company that way. I visited their entire set up and it was very encouraging.* "

Rahul Mishra, Fashion Designer, explaining
his association with Ethicus

" *Once it happened that my entire cotton stock was up in flames, probably a sabotage. I was seeing fire all around, and people were trying to extinguish the fire. I did not know what to do and started walking, just like that, without direction. Soon I reached the top of a nearby hill. Then while looking down, it dawned on me that whatever I thought as big and important, all looked so tiny and trivial… The purpose of Ethicus is to sow the seeds of change by sharing our own experience on transformation and innovation. I'm only paying back my debts. One of the learnings I had in my life is that whenever I did something only for me, it failed, it had been disastrous. Whatever successes I had, it happened when I went beyond the narrowly defined goals and aspirations. There are some subtle things which we miss, because we think from the head. There are also possibilities from the heart, which is connected to consciousness, which is connected to the Totality…* "

Mani Chinnaswamy, Managing Partner,
Appachi Cotton and Co-Founder, Ethicus

---

1 *Note:* This case is prepared as the basis for group discussion rather than to illustrate either effective or ineffective handling of a situation. Unless mentioned otherwise, all quotations used in this case study were derived through primary research. All characters in the case are real. The case is authored by Ajith Sankar R N, with the help of Karthik G. The case author is thankful to Mrs Vijayalakshmi Chinnaswamy and Mr Mani Chinnaswamy (Co-founders, Ethicus) for the energy, time, and resources that they shared with the case author. The author is also thankful to others who shared their perspectives about Ethicus. This case is dedicated to Sri Sathya Sai Baba, who had a vision of a world wherein education is offered with love and discipline, and free of cost. In line with that vision, this case study is released to the public domain, free of cost. The author holds the copyright to the case study. Feel free to reproduce, distribute, publish, and transmit this case study in any form, by any means, including photocopying, recording, or other electronic or mechanical methods provided that (1) no text or photographs are altered; (2) the copyright, acknowledgement, gratitude clauses are included. This case was originally published by the author in the *Journal of Values Based Leadership*, Valparaiso University, Vol. V, Issue I, Winter/Spring 2012.

Ethicus, launched in September 2009, in Mumbai, was the first ethical fashion brand in India. The brand was launched by Appachi Cotton, a textile company based at Pollachi, Tamilnadu, India. The products made under the Ethicus brand name were made out of organic cotton, natural and eco-friendly dyes, and ethical silk. The Ethicus products were handcrafted using traditional weaving techniques on revived jacquard handlooms of the Pollachi region. The initiative drew positive responses from stakeholders such as media, customers, employees, and even peers. The brand is yet to make any profit. The founders, who expressed their deeply held spiritual and ethical values through their business practices, believed that the brand had to be incubated for another 3–5 years for it to be able to make any profit, and had a stoic belief that everything will go well with the brand.

APPACHI COTTON AND INTEGRATED COTTON CONTRACT FARMING

Appachi Cotton is a three-generation old cotton business; it was founded in 1948 by L. Mariappa, initially, as a cotton ginning business. This business was inherited by Vijayalakshmi Nachiar (Vijayalakshmi) and Mani Chinnaswamy (Mani), a wife-husband duo. Mani was the grandson of Mariappa. Vijayalakshmi had a master's degree in textiles from SNDT Mumbai, while Mani had a master's degree in business administration from Philadelphia College of Textiles and Science (Philadelphia University), USA. In continuance with the business inheritance, Mani bought cotton from farmers, converted it to cotton bales, and supplied them to textile mills.

Mani pioneered the 'Integrated Cotton Contract Farming' (ICCF). During the 1990s, there was a spate of farmer suicides in India. While industrialization was driving India, farmers were in distress. As Mani had been in the cotton business for many years, he was aware of the hardships a farmer faced. 'I am also living off him (cotton farmer). The money that I have made is because of his hardwork. But, what is it that I've done…, in terms of giving back to the society?' These thoughts used to continually be on his mind. It was in 1999 that Mani got a forward contract from Lakshmi Mills, a textile company based at Coimbatore, to supply 1000 bales of cotton to them. He travelled across India to find farmers who could supply him with cotton on a consistent basis. While travelling, Mani came to Mundgod, a town in the Uttara Kannada district in Karnataka, India, which is the largest Buddhist settlement in India. There, he saw Tibetan monks bring their products to the town for sale. He entered into a discussion with them and found that they followed a co-operative society model, and these co-operative societies more or less acted as the government for them. He was very inspired by the model of administration followed by the Tibetan Administrative Offices, and thus, in 2000, started ICCF.[2]

---

2 In 1959, Jawaharlal Nehru, the then Indian Prime Minister, gave permission for Tibetan refugees to settle at various regions across India.

Through ICCF, Mani brought together the seed producer, farmer, ginner, spinning industry, and the government. In this model, consolidation of farmlands was done, and the small and marginal farmers were provided with resources, technologies, and finances. As the industry was working in concert with the farmer, it cultivated cotton as per the needs of the textile mill. The farmer was provided with assured marketing tie-up and also financial support from financial institutions. The ginner/spinner became the Coordinating Agency (CA), and acted as the bridge between the farmers, the input suppliers, financial institutions offering banking and insurance services, textile mills, and the government. The ICCF model also helped Appachi Cotton receive a consistent supply of cotton. However, there were changes in the political environment, and election manifestos spoke about political parties promising to waive off bank loans taken by farmers. Soon, the farmers started wilful defaulting. In 2004–05, financial institutions took a retreat from this model and Mani also followed in due course of time.

NOTE ON TEXTILE INDUSTRY

As per the Government of India Economic Survey 2010, India maintained a 6.7 per cent GDP growth in 2008–09, despite the financial crisis in 2007–10 that shook the world. The growth rate was 7.4 per cent in 2009–10. Economic Survey 2011 predicted that growth rate for 2010–11 would be 8.6, and also projected growth rate for 2011–12 at 9 per cent. Goldman Sachs predicted that 'middle class growth in India will accelerate throughout this decade' and 'as the middle class grows, consumption becomes more discretionary'.[3] In 2009, Goldman Sachs predicted that India will grow at an average growth rate of 6.5 per cent, 6.4 per cent, 6.6 per cent, and 5.8 per cent during the decades 2011–20, 2021–30, 2031–40, and 2041–50 respectively[4] (see Exhibit 12.1 for indicators related to trends that influence textile industry in India).

According to the 2009–10 annual report released by the Ministry of Textiles, Government of India, the Indian textile industry contributed approximately 4 per cent to India's GDP, 17 per cent to the country's export earnings, and 14 per cent to industrial production. The sector also provided direct employment for more than 35 million people, thereby being the second largest employment provider in India, after agriculture. As per the Ministry of Textiles, Government of India, India's textile industry, domestic and exports combined, is expected to grow from US$70 billion in 2011 to US$220 billion by 2020.[5] Technopak, a consulting firm, indicated[6] that India's export potential in textiles and apparels would be US$44 billion by 2015 and US$80 billion by 2020. They also suggested that India's domestic market in textiles and apparels would be US$89

3 http://www2.goldmansachs.com/ideas/brics/brics-decade-doc.pdf, last accessed on 28 June 2011.

4 http://www2.goldmansachs.com/ideas/brics/brics-at-8/BRICS-doc.pdf, last accessed on 18 June 2011.

5 http://articles.economictimes.indiatimes.com/2011-02-02/news/28426670_1_textiles-industry-textiles-and-clothing-bn-industry, last accessed on 7 June 2011.

6 Presentation at World Textile Conference, 6 May 2011.

billion by 2015 and US$140 billion by 2020. Reports[7] also indicate that some of the leading apparel exporters of the country are focusing more on the domestic market. '… with the domestic market growing at 15–20 per cent, even the larger, organized apparel exporters are increasing their presence within the country,' said Rahul Mehta, President of the Clothing Manufacturers' Association of India (CMAI).[8] For the five years ending in FY 2011, the top ten textile companies in India, in terms of revenues, charted a compounded annual growth rate of 23 per cent.[9]

Cotton was one of the major raw materials for the textile industry in India. India has the largest cotton cultivation area in the world, at 9 million hectares and constitutes 25 per cent of the world's total cotton cultivation area. It is the second largest cotton producing nation in the world (after China), with a production of 2,40,00,000 (480 pound) bales.[10] It is also the second largest exporter of cotton (after United States).

The Ministry of Textiles states that cultivation area of Bt cotton (genetically modified cotton or GM cotton) in 2008–09 increased by 7 per cent at 68.18 lakh (6.818 million) from the previous year. In 2008–09, area under Bt cotton occupied 73 per cent of the total acreage of 93.73 lakh (9.373 million) hectare under cotton cultivation.[11] Another report,[12] released by the International Service for the Acquisition of Agri-Biotech Applications (ISAAA),[13] stated that the usage of Bt cotton increased to 8.4 million hectares in 2009 from 50,000 hectares in 2002. According to this report, 87 per cent of the total cultivated area in India, in 2009, was under GM cotton, with 9.6 million hectares being the total cultivated area for cotton. Supporters of Bt cotton opined that this increase in usage could be attributed to a combination of increased farm income and reduced pesticide usage to control the cotton bollworm.

A report[14] by the Environmental Justice Foundation[15] and Pesticide Action Network, UK[16] indicated that cultivation of cotton was responsible for the release of 16 per cent of insecticides in the world, despite covering only 2.5 per cent of world's cultivated land. Cotton cultivation consumed more insecticides than any other crop. Organic Trade Association[17] stated that 25 per cent of the world's insecticides and 10 per cent

---

7 http://businessstandard.com/india/news/domestic-market-beckons-garment-exporters/436139/, last accessed on 7 June 2011.

8 CMAI, based at Mumbai, is an association representing more than 20,000 companies from the Indian apparel industry.

9 http://articles.economictimes.indiatimes.com/2011-05-23/news/29574073_1_textile-industry-tufs-technology-upgradation-fund-scheme/2, last accessed on 20 June 2011.

10 http://www.cotton.org/econ/cropinfo/cropdata/rankings.cfm, last accessed on 31 May 2011.

11 http://texmin.nic.in/sector/note_cotton.pdf, last accessed on 31 May 2011.

12 http://www.isaaa.org/resources/publications/briefs/41/executivesummary/default.asp, last accessed on 31 May 2011.

13 http://www.isaaa.org/default.asp, last accessed on 31 May 2011.

14 http://www.ejfoundation.org/pdf/the_deadly_chemicals_in_cotton.pdf, last accessed on 4 June 2011.

15 *Note*: A UK-based charity that campaigns for human dignity and environmental issues.

16 *Note*: Pesticide Action Network is coaltion of more than 600 NGOs and individuals from more than 90 countries.

17 *Note*: A North American association of organic businesses.

of pesticides were used for cotton cultivation. In India, more than 3000 tonnes of Endosulfan was used for cotton cultivation.[18] Farmers lacked protective gear while using the hazardous pesticides. The report indicated serious health symptoms in many Indian farmers who were exposed to pesticides while growing cotton. 'With no less than 99 per cent of the world's cotton farmers living in the developing world, the pesticides are applied in fields where illiteracy is high and safety awareness is low, putting both the environment and lives at risk. The dangers faced by poor illiterate children and farmers to keep our clothes cheap, is unacceptable,' said Steve Trent, Director, Environmental Justice Foundation.[19]

India was also the leading producer of organic cotton. The 'Organic Cotton Market Report 2009'[20] stated that there had been a 35 per cent increase in the sales of organic cotton apparel and home textile products worldwide and it touched US$4.3 billion in 2009. 'Today, only 0.15 per cent of the world's cotton is guaranteed to be pesticide-free. This means that the majority of the cotton we wear is likely to have contributed to the poisoning of lives and the environment in some of the world's most vulnerable communities. If the fashion industry is truly concerned about its impact in this world, then it needs to clean up its act and demand organic cotton,' said Linda Craig, Director of Pesticide Action Network, UK.[21]

India has also been the second largest producer of silk in the world, after China. Some organizations also came out with Ahimsa Silk—a process through which silk is made without killing silk worms. The word 'Ahimsa' stands for non-violence. The main producers of Ahimsa silk are Andhra Pradesh State Handloom Weavers' Cooperative Society,[22] based at Hyderabad, and Ahimsa Peace Silk Pvt Ltd, based at Pune.

EVOLUTION OF ETHICUS

'Think about the thousands of artisans India has. If they are not revived, the craft will die.'

Prasad Bidappa, Fashion designer and choreographer,
while launching Ethicus at Mumbai.[23]

While the ICCF model lost its steam, Mani did not want the linkages to meet with death. He started enquiring whether farmers would require marketing support. Mani said, 'We went to Karnataka... The region that I chose was Kabini.[24] It's all in the forest periphery

---

18 *Note*: Photographs related to the ill-effects of using Endosulfan in cashew farming in Kerala, India can be found at http://www.endosulphanvictims.org/gallery.htm. The images may be gory.

19 http://www.ejfoundation.org/page324.html, last accessed on 4 June 2011.

20 *Note*: Released by Organic Exchange in May 2010.

21 http://www.ejfoundation.org/page324.html, last accessed on 4 June 2011.

22 http://www.ahimsasilks.com, last accessed on ....

23 Shree, Shilpa, 'Talk fashion, think environment', http://www.mydigitalfc.com/leisure-writing/talk-fashion-think-environment-119, 29 September 2009, last accessed on 7 December 2010.

24 *Note*: Kabini, in Karnataka, is a popular wildlife destinations.

of Nagarhole,[25] Bandipur, etc. This is also an elephant corridor. The farmers have given way for the dam to be built there and the farmers are settled on the banks of the dam where they were growing crops. Cotton is a crop that elephants do not like. So the farmer is forced to grow a mono-crop of cotton every season. After the fertility of the soil is gone, the farmer pumps more fertilizers so that the crop is sustainable. But the fertilizer runs off to the Kabini dam, contaminating the surrounding. This is where I needed to reinvent.' Mani thus started moving to wards organic farming of cotton, in 2004. During the process of manufacturing cotton, chemical fertilizers or pesticides were not used.

The engagement with ICCF and travels to farmlands across India gave Mani inputs on various aspects of farming. In 2004–05, Mani converted their 25-acre vanilla farm into an organic farm. In a few years, he understood that this was a 'total disaster', due to the mono-cropping practice. During this period, Mani and Vijayalakshmi got an input on growing food for themselves, without utilizing pesticides and chemical fertilizers. Therefore, they started growing coconut, vegetables, paddy, etc., in their farm. This was one experience that helped Mani and Vijayalakshmi form their journey of creating a sustainable enterprise dealing with organic cotton.

'We thought we needed a healthy lifestyle for doing ethical business. So we had to bring about a change in our business. We stopped dealing with regular cotton, which was cultivated using pesticides as it clashed with our ideology,' said Vijayalakshmi.[26] This was in 2007. 'We were doing pretty well—about 40 crores turnover, and it was a conscious decision to stop my conventional business and totally get into organic cotton business.' During that period, the organic business of the company only contributed to 10 per cent of the revenues of Appachi Cotton. Mani and Vijayalakshmi converted the enterprise into a 100 per cent organic firm, and their cotton products were termed as Appachi Eco-logic Cotton.

The organic cotton yields were lesser than conventional cotton in the initial years as the chemical fertilizers were no longer used. It was expected that the land will take three–five years to revitalize. 'It's difficult until the farm reaches a balance, until it sheds the chemicals it has and is ready to take care of itself. Once that happens, around the fifth year, it becomes cheaper to grow organic cotton and its productivity is comparable to, if not higher than, normal cotton,' said Balaji, brother of Mani.[27]

In 2006, the company associated itself with an organic farmers group named 'Savayava Krushikara Sangha', which was incubated by the Mysore Resettlement and Development Agency (MYRADA)[28], and partnered with them in the organic certification

---

25 *Note*: Nagarhole National Park is located 94 km from Mysore in Karnataka, South India. It is located to the north-west of Bandipur National Park. It is spread between Kodagu district and Mysore district, and Kabini reservoir separates the two districts.

26 Vipin, Manu, 'The organic revolution in fashion', http://expressbuzz.com/entertainment/fashion/the-organic-revolution-in-fashion/197589.html, 13 August 2010, last accessed on 28 November 2010.

27 Srinivasan, Sriram, 'Seeking organic growth', Outlook Magazine, 9 August 2008, http://business.outlookindia.com/article.aspx?101363, last accessed on 28 November 2010.

28 *Note*: MYRADA has experience in rural credit programmes in Southern India. It also works in areas related to Micro-watersheds, Forestry, and Resettlement.

process. The process was called 'SKS Appachi Eco-Logic', and was certified organic by IMO Control, a Switzerland-based certified agency.

During this period of transition/conversion from a fertilizer-driven production to organic cultivation, Appachi Cotton paid the farmers a premium of 10 per cent from the prevalent market price. 'We kept paying contract farmers during that time. You have to raise a couple of crops before your cotton meets certification standards,' said Mani.[29] In 2009, Control Union (formerly SKAL) from Netherlands had offered the Global Organic Textile Standards (GOTS) certification for the textile production of Appachi. In 2007, IMO Control, certified Appachi's farm and ginning operations.

While the company started sourcing and stock-piling organic cotton, there was a dilemma about the course the company should take in the changed paradigm. 'Two years we were toying with the idea of what to do…,' said Mani. He was not keen on supplying all the organic cotton to textile mills. Mani believed that every player in the textile value chain has to have his own individual identity and respect. He did not have the desire to sell the cotton into the conventional market as it would be an exact replica of what their family had been practicing. 'Mani would always crib, that the conventional cotton value chain was a thankless operation. The ginner never appreciated what the farmer did, the mill owners never appreciated what the ginner did, the fabric people never appreciated what the mills did, the retailers never appreciated what the fabric people did, and finally the end customer never even cared to recognize what the farmer, ginner, mill owner, fabric producer or the retailer did. One can understand from above, why he was so adamant not to sell the cotton to the conventional operators,' mentioned Vijayalakshmi. Initially he thought about exporting this cotton. However, the cotton yarn produced from this cotton was too exclusive for the foreign buyers to absorb. Their preference was in the 30–40 count while the cotton produced by Mani had a count of 100–120. Vijayalakshmi understood that what they were having was one of the most exclusive yarns in the organic world. She said, 'I knew at the very moment, the right utilization for them—in the handlooms. Traditionally, Indian handloom weavers have been used to handling very fine cotton yarns for over centuries.' Mani further added that Ethicus was the creative vision of Vijayalakshmi.

They met with Sally Holkar from 'Women Weave', Mumbai, who was instrumental in reviving the Maheshwari sarees from the state of Madhya Pradesh. With the help of Sally Holkar, they delivered their yarns to the weavers in North India. However, the time taken to deliver the fabric was about six months, which was challenging for Mani, whose cotton stock situation was on an upward spiral with more farmers joining the organic movement in Kabini. 'There was a big learning for me in the above episode. In our pursuit to get anything done, we at times take quick emotional decisions that are

29 Umachandran, Shalini, Swati Anand, 'Slip into a shirt, save the earth', 23 October 2010, http://timesofindia. indiatimes.com/life-style/fashion/trends/Slip-into-a-shirt-save-the-earth-/articleshow/6180590.cms, last accessed on 28 November 2010.

not necessarily practical. And we keep pursuing it, even after we may realize that it is not a long-term solution. In that process, we fail to recognize/realize the opportunities that lay hidden in our vicinity… Nature has its own mechanism, it gives you a long rope to work things out yourself, and when it realizes that you are wandering too much away from your destined path, it gives you a tug and makes you realize your chosen path. We wandered aimlessly, in creating our value chain, but the 'tug' came 6 months later. Whenever we had our foreign friends visit us, we have been taking them around our villages around Pollachi, showing them the occupation—particularly the handloom weaving of Pollachi. Never once did it occur to us that we should utilize the services of our local weavers to covert our yarns into fabrics,' reminisces Vijayalakshmi. Pollachi, the town from where they were operating, and the villages nearby, used to be home for thousands of handloom weavers and they used very fine cotton, which was similar to the cotton that Appachi was stocking. For a year, Vijayalakshmi and Mani visited people and places requesting the conversion of their cotton to yarns, but the effort was in vain. Then, the duo discovered that in Chennimalai, a panchayat town in Erode district in the state of Tamil Nadu, 2800 looms were dismantled and piled up in a godown, and were kept for sale. Some of the looms were made of 50 year-old wood. 'It was a really pathetic sight. What is happening to our heritage? This is something which we should be proud of, and sustain.' They selected 42 looms, brought it to Pollachi, refurbished the looms (see Exhibit 12.2 for photographs of these looms) and brought in weavers.

Vijayalakshmi and Mani also set up a design and weaving studio. 'If a designer wants to design something we have the whole set up ready over there. We have an in-house person who can recreate the design on computer. Since the entire design development happens under one roof, there is no way that it can be copied or made a sample of, ensuring that designs are in safe hands,' added Vijayalakshmi.[30] Ethicus assured the designers that their design will not be replicated till it was released in the market. At Appachi Cotton, each loom was product specific—there were looms that weaved only bed linen, or curtains, or materials for salwar kameezes. Such a process ensured that cloth was not wasted. In addition to natural/vegetable dyes, the company also used other organically certified dyes—the dyes that did not have heavy metals, were azo-free,[31] and met compliance norms. 'Natural dyes are more expensive…,' explained Vijayalakshmi.[32]

Two per cent of the proceeds from the sale of Ethicus branded goods was diverted to educating a weaver's child. The children of weavers were given free education at Nachiar Vidyalayam (www.nachiarvidyalayam.org), a school run by Appachi Cotton. In India, traditional crafts and professions, like weaving and farming, were no longer popular. The community members who were engaged in these professions did not show interest in the

---

30 Shree, Shilpa, 'Talk fashion, think environment', http://www.mydigitalfc.com/leisure-writing/talk-fashion-think-environment-119, 29 September 2009, last accessed on 7 December 2010.

31 *Note*: Azo dyes may be mutagenic, carcinogenic, allergic, and are not biodegradable.

32 Meera S, 'Organic is the way to go', 20 June 2010, http://www.hindu.com/rp/2010/06/20/stories/2010062050020100.htm, last accessed on 28 November 2010.

next generation continuing with these professions. 'In many of the villages, youngsters are sacrificing their traditional knowledge because they are paid more for working in other sectors,' said Mani.[33] 'These are hard jobs with poor returns. Neither farmers nor weavers want their children to follow them into the profession, but if we lose their skills, we lose an important part of our heritage,' said Mani.[34] 'While India is growing, the heritage sector is going out, because there is not enough young weavers anymore. When India is arriving, I want the farmer and my weaver to arrive,' mentioned Mani. Mani started a community college at Nachiar Vidyalayam. The community college was run in association with the Indira Gandhi National Open University (IGNOU), New Delhi. He continued, 'I am trying to educate my weaver's child through the community college that is run in my school. We are giving training in apparel design, embroidery, etc., and they do not have to go back to the loom. If one girl is educated as a textile designer, she will sustain the whole village, the whole cluster. That is what we are trying to do in inclusive growth.' In addition to the regular curriculum, Nachiar Vidyalayam also taught traditional art forms like Mallakhamb, the ancient Indian art of pole gymnastics. The school also integrated dance, drama, music, yoga, and karate into its curriculum. 'We are building our own curriculum of weaving, hand spinning, and even designing. So youngsters from the weaver community can become designers rather than weavers, and they can sustain the future generation,' said Mani.[35] The school and community college also provided environmental education and values, thereby empowering future generations to respect the environment. 'If living and working conditions are made attractive enough, the next generation will also take up weaving. Weaving is in their blood. With training and exposure they can make a viable living out of it,' said Vijayalakshmi.[36]

Going organic ensured the promotion of sustainable agriculture in the Pollachi and Kabini region, which otherwise could have adopted the cultivation of genetically modified cotton. 'Is Bt cotton necessary everywhere? There are not many studies assessing how Bt cotton has impacted the flora and fauna of the region. We should at least have a minimum buffer zone of 20 km outside the wildlife region where permission is not given for the usage of Bt cotton. There is a possibility that Bt may affect the food-chain of elephants,' cautioned Mani. The Eco-logic program initiated by Appachi Cotton encouraged the farmers to grow traditional varieties of cotton like Suvin. 'India had more than 1000 varieties of cotton,' said Mani. The company had also entered into a tie-up with University of Agricultural Sciences, Dharwad,[37] to maintain a gene bank for

33 Srinivasan, Sriram, 'Seeking organic growth', Outlook Magazine, 9 August 2008, http://business.outlookindia.com/article.aspx?101363, last accessed on 28 November 2010.

34 Umachandran, Shalini, Swati Anand, 'Slip into a shirt, save the earth', 23 October 2010, http://timesofindia.indiatimes.com/life-style/fashion/trends/Slip-into-a-shirt-save-the-earth-/articleshow/6180590.cms, last accessed on 28 November 2010.

35 Vipin, Manu, 'The organic revolution in fashion', http://expressbuzz.com/entertainment/fashion/the-organic-revolution-in-fashion/197589.html, 13 August 2010, last accessed on 28 November 2010.

36 Srinivasan, Pankaja, 'Common Threads, uncommon people', The Hindu, 23 January 2010, http://www.hindu.com/mp/2010/01/23/stories/2010012353510600.htm, last accessed on 28 November 2010.

conserving many of the indigenous seeds. 'I can say unequivocally that my farmers are the real winners. Their quality of life has improved. With a healthy farm environment, there is much less sickness, and yields have improved,' said Mani,[38] who believed that India's tradition had been rooted in organic farming. In 2011, the company had a tie-up with 185 cotton farmers who grew organic cotton in approximately 444 hectares.

The organization adopted the fair trade philosophy. 'I pay above the minimum wages to my employees, no child labour is involved, farmers are paid a premium over the market price while purchasing cotton, and the processes are environment-friendly. Effluent discharge is treated,' said Mani. 'The weavers traditionally work their looms in the cramped confines of their homes all day. But, here in a well ventilated, clean and bright environment, they have a chance to move out of their homes and work for fixed hours,' said Mani.[39] Appachi Cotton employed 35 people exclusively for Ethicus—25 in handloom and 10 at the garment unit. Appachi Cotton employed another 35–40 people for its EcoLogic cotton, which was mainly exported, as the extra-long staple cotton[40], This had a huge international demand. Appachi Cotton adopted the 'Slow Fiber' movement, akin to the 'Slow Food' movement,[41] and also conducted workshops on this theme for people taking the 'Cotton Trail' (see next paragraph). Under the Ethicus brand, Appachi Cotton also sold products made from 'Ahimsa Silk', for silk manufactured without killing silk worms. 'There are some segments of people who've stopped wearing silk for religious reasons or sentiments. We have created Ahmisa Silk for them,' explained Vijayalakshmi, who herself belongs to the Jain[42] community.

'Cotton Trail', a 12-day journey between Kabini and Pollachi, was started to communicate the essence of what Ethicus stood for. The trail covered those regions closely associated with the creation of Ethicus products, starting from the farming of organic cotton, the raw material used in Ethicus products. The trail traced its path from the Kabini Elephant corridor to the foothills of the Anaimalai Tiger Reserve, and shared its borders with the states of Tamilnadu, Karnataka, and Kerala (see Exhibit 12.3 for a map of this trail and itinerary). The trail covered locations like Bangalore, Mysore, Kabini, Pollachi, and Anaimalai. This trail was a retro experience, starting with the city life in Bangalore, going back 300 years to experience the Indian royalty as expressed in the palaces of Mysore, covering visits to organic farmlands and pristine forest regions, and getting an introduction to spirituality.

---

37 *Note*: Located in Karnataka, India.

38 Chari, Pushpa, 'Going Organic', http://www.hindu.com/fr/2010/06/25/stories/2010062550900100.htm, 25 June 2010, last accessed on 28 November 2010.

39 Srinivasan, Pankaja, 'Common Threads, uncommon people', The Hindu, 23 January 2010, http://www.hindu.com/mp/2010/01/23/stories/2010012353510600.htm, last accessed on 28 November 2010.

40 *Note*: Also known as Pima cotton, Egyptian cotton, etc. Extra staple cotton has a staple length of 1-3/8" or more.

41 *Note*: This is an international movement founded by Carlo Petrini in 1986 that strives to preserve traditional and regional cuisine and is considered an alternative to fast food. It encourages food characteristic of the local ecosystem. 'Slow Fiber' movement is considered to be a 'thoughtful approach of textile making and textile design'. For more details, refer http://shiboriorg.wordpress.com/projects/slow-fiber/

42 *Note*: Jainism is a religion that prescribes pacifism and a path of non-violence towards all living beings.

'Of late, there have been a lot of questions raised by international buyers about certification integrity issues in India. Their apprehensions are genuine, as some projects in India were blacklisted for their fraudulent organic claims. The concept of cotton trail started when our clients, who happened to be Italians, wanted to check (the authenticity of) our claims. We told the clients, "Forget the certificates, talk to the farmer, see what he is doing, and then you believe it."' This assessment journey soon became a structured trail when word of mouth communication aroused interest in people. Hence, the cotton trail was started. Ethicus had entered into the promotion of this cotton trail, and made investments in a tour website, had tie-ups with foreign tour operators, conducted test tours for tour operators, and was involved in other related promotional material. The project will break even in three years if cotton trail can bring in 5 groups/year. The per person charges amounted to US$2570–3778, depending on the number of people taking the trip, with the minimum of six people in a group. One of the highlights of the tour was, 'At the end of the cotton trail our guests would have travelled the shortest footprint area recorded for high fashion textiles that measures only about 300 kilometres. And would have witnessed the only such sustainable organic model of textiles in the world.'[43]

The founders of Ethicus had been telling 'The Cotton Trail, the Eco-Logic Story' to as many people as possible. 'Their story must be told,' said Mani and Vijayalakshmi.[44] 'We will not stock up our product where the story is not told. We'll create our own ethical consumers. The people who've travelled as part of the cotton trail, they've seen the whole chain.' The partners cited the example of 14 ladies from abroad who travelled the cotton trail and then visited the Ethicus stock room and did a business of two lakh rupees, within two hours. '…It touches them, they feel affiliated to the product, and the design is appealing. We are using the cotton trail as a window of opportunity. We have a completely different perspective of marketing,' said Mani. He also added that some of these members sponsored amenities that improved the infrastructural conditions of the school run by Appachi Cotton. 'We have to create our own identity. People from abroad ask us, 'What is India and what is ethnic to the country? Also, if I replicate something done elsewhere, I am taking away jobs from that region. So we have to create something that is indigenous.'

Ethical Consumerism and Market Performance

'Both contemporary and organic, the brand is testimony to the fact that fashion can, and should be, responsible and aware. Style needs to take into account circumstances and opportunities, which is what this duo has done.'[45]

Nandhini Parthib, Principal Correspondent, India Today

---

43 http://www.asian-connections.net/news/COTTON-TRAIL-PROPOSAL.pdf, Accessed on June 23, 2011

44 Srinivasan, Pankaja, 'Common threads, uncommon people', The Hindu, 23 January 2010, http://www.hindu.com/mp/2010/01/23/stories/2010012353510600.htm, last accessed on 28 November 2010.

45 http://indiatoday.intoday.in/site/story/ethical--designs/1/104358.html, last accessed on 8 June 2011.

'Ethicus' was a combination of 'Ethics' and 'Us' (see Exhibit 12.4 for Ethicus brand logo). 'As we desired to create our own identity involving farmers, us, and the weavers, we also felt that may be the final customer is also longing for an identity in this faceless world. May be he is looking for an opportunity to establish it, by making a style statement that would amplify his belief system. So if we earnestly pursued "ethical" business practices at Appachi Cotton, we felt the need to extend the platform to the final customer. We have to help them join and share our 'ethics', as he/she is an integral part of 'us'. ETHICS and US, thus became ETHICUS,' said Vijayalakshmi. During the Mumbai launch,[46] Ethicus gave a cotton sapling to all the visitors in their exhibition. The visitors were asked to grow that cotton, harvest it, and send to Ethicus, to be gifted with an Ethicus handkerchief. Through this initiative, Ethicus wanted to communicate the challenges met by the cotton farmers during the growing of cotton. The company received more than 50 responses. The website of Ethicus[47] quoted, 'When you take home an Ethicus product, you do more than just buy a brand, you buy a cause.' 'There is a growing sense of ethical consumerism. Customers want to know the origins of the products that they are buying. And hence do their bit for the environment in whatever small way they can,' said Mani.[48] Mani felt that for a city-dweller, one of the simplest way to help the environment was to choose a product that is produced responsibly. 'By wearing organic cotton, one shows one's commitment to the environment,' mentioned Mani.[49]

Each Ethicus product had a tag that had a stamp sized photograph of the weaver. 'When we tied this, he (the weaver) had tears in his eyes. He has been doing this for many years, and nobody knew who he was in the value chain,' said Mani. In addition to the photograph, the name of the weaver and the time taken to produce the work was also mentioned in the tag. (see Exhibit 12.5 for an image of such a tag). Stakeholders were much appreciative of the concept. Pankaja Srinivasan (Pankaja), Assistant Editor, The Hindu, met Vijayalakshmi and Mani at one of the fashion shows and learnt about the organic endeavour of Appachi Cotton. She visited the Ethicus workshop at Pollachi and subsequently, did a cover story in the Hindu MetroPlus weekend edition. Pankaja said, 'I was floored by their effort to give the farmers and weavers their due recognition and make it a point to include them in the marketing of their final product. I was charmed by the tags on their products that had the picture and details of the weaver and how long he took to weave that particular product. It was great value addition to the product in my opinion. And, a great incentive and boost to the weaver who would otherwise have gone unrecognized and faceless.' Hansdak Shuchi, Textile Designer, Reid & Taylor, chose to do her four-month internship with Ethicus while she was a

---

46 *Note*: For a copy of the invitation, please access http://www.box.net/shared/tdqyl7fjqzdtpyvasasx.

47 *Note*: www.ethicus.in (one may also refer http://appachicotton.com).

48 Parthib, Nandhini, 'Ethical designs', 19 July 2010; http://indiatoday.intoday.in/site/Story/104358/SUPPLEMENTS/ethical--designs.html, last accessed on 28 November 2010.

49 S, Meera, 'Organic is the way to go', 20 June 2010, http://www.hindu.com/rp/2010/06/20/stories/2010062050020100.htm, last accessed on 28 November 2010.

textile design student at National Institute of Fashion Technology (NIFT), New Delhi. She said, 'I have always wanted to work with clusters dealing with traditional textiles as well as an organization working for causes. Ethicus is one of those organizations, which works with the traditional handlooms that I have a fascination for. It also empowers the diminishing craft of handwovens as well, as it supports the cause of green, which is most demanding in the current times.'

The products under the Ethicus brand name included sarees, stoles, skirts, jackets, kurtas, shirts, tops, scarves, duppattas, mens' garments like shirts, kurtas, knitted T-shirts, baby clothes and accessories, linen used for beds, tables, curtains, cushions, yoga mats, etc. Ethicus ventured into markets such as Mumbai, Coimbatore, Kochi, Chennai, and Hyderabad, through exhibitions. 'This is a living example of how design goes beyond boundaries; it's not just about motifs or dyes,' said Chelna Desai, a Mumbai-based fashion designer.[50] The media has given positive reviews about their products. An article in The Hindu mentioned, 'If clothing with conscience is your mantra, then the Ethicus brand should well be a part of your wardrobe. For here Ethics meets Us…'[51] Ethicus was also stocked up at fashion boutiques in Chennai, Bangalore, Hyderabad, Pune, Mumbai, Goa, New Delhi, and Kolkata. Ethicus evoked good response in exhibitions with sales charting above ₹10 lakhs (typically, sales averaged five lakhs in such exhibition of other brands). The first exhibition itself netted ₹17 lakhs. In the first year of its operations, Ethicus had a sales revenue of ₹60 lakhs. 'The customer is open to the idea of spending a little more to make a responsible choice,' said Mani.[52] However, as the company incurred significant expenses in the initial year due to brand-building expenses related to the launch of Ethicus, the brand is yet to turn in a surplus. It was the profits from Appachi Cotton that subsidized the launch of Ethicus. If the losses of Ethicus are accounted for, Appachi Cotton had a break-even in 2010.

The founders have nurtured their idea into a brand. 'We have a number of Italian designers who are interested in us. And we ourselves felt that handloom is our country's strong point, something that we need to tap into. So, instead of focusing on the export market, we nurtured it into a brand,' said Vijayalakshmi.[53] 'The customer wouldn't pay a premium on a product that looks just like a conventional textile product,' said Mani.[54] Mani and Vijayalakshmi felt that Ethicus should be a synonym for exemplary quality, and being eco-friendly was a value addition. They wanted the customers to buy Ethicus

50 'Cottoning on to design', The Times of India, Mumbai, 22 September 2009.

51 S., Priyadershini, 'Couture with a conscience', The Hindu, 11 August 2010, http://www.thehindu.com/life-and-style/fashion/article564536.ece, last accessed on 28 November 2010.

52 Umachandran, Shalini, Swati Anand, 'Slip into a shirt, save the earth', 23 October 2010, http://timesofindia.indiatimes.com/life-style/fashion/trends/Slip-into-a-shirt-save-the-earth-/articleshow/6180590.cms, last accessed on 28 November 2010.

53 Parthib, Nandhini, 'Ethical designs', 19 July 2010, http://indiatoday.intoday.in/site/Story/104358/SUPPLEMENTS/ethical--designs.html, last accessed on 28 November 2010.

54 Srinivasan, Sriram, 'Seeking organic growth', Outlook Magazine, 9 August 2008, http://business.outlookindia.com/article.aspx?101363, last accessed on 28 November 2010.

products as satisfied customers, not driven by a feeling of guilt or concern. Mani and Vijayalakshmi were of the opinion that the organic movement will not sustain if it was built on fear and guilt. While the company wanted to promote organic products, it was also focused on quality fashion. Tripti Aiyyar , one of the earliest customers of Ethicus, said to the case author, 'I liked the weaves and the colours offered by Ethicus. They seemed very Banarasi,[55] not usually seen in cotton. In addition to the fabric, I also liked the people associated with the product. I bought four or five of all the types they had.' Sanjeev Manglani, Managing Director, Kalpana, a New Delhi-based outlet focusing on saree retail, said that the customers were asking for more designs, colours, and textures in Ethicus. He also asked for thematic collections, better blouses, and better pricing.

Hisam Usman, who runs Silkworm Boutique, a Chennai-based stand-alone designer wear store for women, said that everything about Ethicus is positive. 'Thats why I have it in my store,' Said Hisam. He said that customers are curious about the product and they appreciate the designs and feel of the fabric. His store also witnessed repeat customers for Ethicus, albeit in a small number. Similar sentiments were echoed by other retailers, who displayed the newly launched Ethicus products alongside established designer labels. This included Bombay Electric and Melange (based at Mumbai), Rudraaksh (based at Pune), Amethyst and Collage (based at Chennai), and Elahi (based at Hyderabad). Nalli Silks, a chain of apparel stores based at Chennai and considered to be a synonym for quality sarees, took design and manufacturing help from Ethicus for creating a saree during the high-profile marriage of Lakshmi Venu (daughter of Venu Srinivasan, Chairman, TVS Motors) with Rohan Murthy (son of N.R. Narayana Murthy, Chairman Emeritus, Infosys Technologies).

Prabha Nagarajan, Regional Director-India, Textile Exchange (formerly Organic Exchange), said that an international non-profit organization that supports the growth of organic cotton like Ethicus is a good business model on 'how long-term partnerships can benefit all stakeholders'. She said, 'By branding organic cotton grown sustainably, by making the links to the value chain visible, and by producing innovative and beautiful handloom garments and home textiles, Mani and Viji Chinnaswamy have created something for the domestic market in India that should inspire many more.' She continued, 'Ethicus represents what they (the government) should aspire for, and include in policy. Organic does not permit Bt seeds. The GOI (Government of India) has promoted Bt cotton in such a big way that non-Bt cotton in the country is almost extinct.'

Making the Idea Viable

The current price range for Ethicus cotton sarees ranges between ₹3500 and ₹7000, while for Ahimsa Silk sarees it was between ₹8000 and ₹19,000. The sarees exhibited the highest turnover. Ethicus's target age was for the late 20s to 40s. Customers like

---

55 *Note*: Benares or Varanasi, is famous for its sarees. 'Banaras brocades and sarees' have Geographical Indication Rights

Tripti Aiyyar felt that the pricing of the products of Ethicus were slightly steep, and the company could offer more colours and textures. A similar sentiment was echoed by Pankaja, who said, 'I understand that the fact that everything is organic and so adds to the cost of the final product. Still, if the Ethicus products along with their story were accessible to a larger section of the people, maybe the awareness and the desire to support such causes may be more widespread. At the moment the products can only be bought by the high-end customers.' Appachi Cotton has now planned to start a saree range in Ethicus from as low as ₹2500. Ethicus also developed a Facebook page to communicate the developments in their organization and to receive feedback from the customers. In less than two years, the company has acquired almost 2000 fans in their Facebook page. It is also exploring possibilities of selling Ethicus products online.

'Ethicus is at their nascent stage. So they may be having difficulty in understanding markets. However, all weaknesses are windows of opportunities. They are at the right place, at the right time. They are not big, and they are not starting fashion apparel in a big way. So they can easily clear the hurdles. They can get into markets that nobody else would know about,' said Rahul Mishra (Mishra), a known fashion designer in India. Mishra believed that Appachi Cotton needs to continue to focus on their ideology, as it had been doing. He added, 'In my opinion, starting a brand is like starting a religion, it takes time. Soon, there will be followers. The founders of Ethicus need to believe in themselves. Troubles are windows of opportunities. Having troubles mean that you will be guaranteed a good future. They have to stress on their ideology, in as simplistic a way as possible. Simplicity that is visible in their product and lifestyle. Process can be complex, but the product needs to be simple.'

'Ethicus is still at a state of incubation. We are investing for the future. It will take another 3–5 years to make this venture sustainable. Brand building is a slow process and customer interest is gradually picking up,' said Mani. Out of the 42 looms at Ethicus studio, only 22 looms were utilized at a given point of time. Mani's idea was to run a business where each of those 42 looms manufactured six sarees in a month. 'Then, I would like to adopt a weaver's village, where all the weaving will be done, and this space (where weaving is currently done), will be converted to a full-fledged design studio,' added Mani. Vijayalakshmi has been focusing on ensuring that their vision gets manifested into visible and tangible results. She said, 'You cannot ride on a dream. Production planning is necessary. My brother is helping us with the business aspects of the endeavour. We have also hired a consultant, who has experience in fashion and retail, to help us out with the pricing aspects of Ethicus branded products.' More integration was brought into the company. Ginning and garmenting were done in-house while functions like spinning and processing were done with the help of other family-owned businesses. Spinning was done by Pollachi-based Ace Tex, a GOTS certified spinning unit owned by Lakshmanan, Mani's cousin. Wet processing was done by Premier Fine Fabrics Ltd, a unit of Premier Mills, a GOTS Certified unit based at Perundurai.

Values and Beliefs of the Founders

Mani remembered, 'Once my entire stock of cotton, worth 60 lakhs was up in flames. I was doomed. There was a message, "Stop, this is not for you. Turn back and go elsewhere." However, I pursued. I said, "Ok, I'll have better insurance next time!" Then I went to Madhya Pradesh and bought the entire cotton stock thinking that markets would rise and I'll be a billionaire overnight. The markets tanked. The mills refused to buy. My friends refused to buy. After stocking the cotton for a year, I sold it, at half the price. There are very subtle things that we need to keep a track of. These are messages from above. It is all in us. If we can fine-tune to that frequency, the message is very subtle, but very sure.' He believed that guidance will come and business decisions will be driven by that guidance, when an individual can fine-tune to that frequency.

Mani and Vijayalakshmi consider Vethathiri Maharishi[56] as their spiritual guide. They considered themselves to be a 'tool' in the hands of a higher power. 'How else can you explain my journey to a no-man's land in Madhya Pradesh, without my having expertize in their language, and still getting the support of 3000 farmers?' asked Mani. He continued, 'Vethathiri Maharishi was also a weaver, by profession. He used to say that our actions should not hurt anyone at the level of body or soul.' In order to create an enterprise that aligns with such an ethos, Mani and Vijayalakshmi used to work 16–18 hours every day, seven days of the week. 'Vethathiri Maharishi says, "When you eat a handful of rice from your plate, do you realize the efforts of so many people that has gone into that handful?"' said Vijayalakshmi. Ethicus was a steep learning curve for the duo. Mani believes that a business needs to be socially-conscious and should be evolved keeping the society in mind, and should not benefit by harming others. He cited the example of the dyeing industry in Tirupur region of Tamilnadu that had suffered major loses, as a large number of dyeing factories had to be shut down. This happened after a court ordered the closure of dyeing units that discharged untreated effluents to the river Noyyal, thereby killing the river's ecosystem and making farming impossible.[57, 58] Ethicus was one of the few organizations that broke that trend and continued to move forward. 'At no point in time did I have a dilemma of this business not being financially sustainable,' said Mani. As the case author bid good-bye to the partners, there was a thought in the author, "Will this enterprise be financially sustainable? If yes, it would certainly be raising the bar on how a business, especially in textiles, could be run."

---

56 *Note*: Vethathiri Maharishi had founded over 300 yoga centres around the world and was the founder-trustee of World Community Service Center.

57 *Note*: In early 2011, the Madras High Court ordered 752 dyeing and bleaching units in Tirupur to shut down for failing to conform to zero discharge of effluents and releasing toxic effluents into the Noyyal river.

58 http://www.downtoearth.org.in/content/tirupur-dyeing-units-told-close, last accessed on 2 June 2011.

Exhibit 12.1 Trends that influence Indian textile industry

	2002	2003	2004	2005	2006	2007	2008	2009
Fertilizer consumption (kg per hectare of arable land)	100.6	105.1	115.4	127.8	136.4	142.8	153.5	*
Agricultural land (%age of land area)	60.6	60.6	60.6	60.5	60.5	60.4	60.4	*
Rural population (%age of total population)	72	72	72	71	71	70	70	*
GDP per capita (current US$)	484	563	668	762	857	1105	1067	1192
CO2 emissions (metric tonnes per capita)	1.2	1.2	1.2	1.3	1.4	1.4	*	*
CO2 emissions (kilotonnes)	1,225,788	1,280,865	1,345,494	1,409,973	1,503,116	1,611,043	*	*

Source: World Bank (* indicates non-availability of data)

Exhibit 12.2 Looms used to manufacture the Ethicus line

Source: From the Facebook page of Ethicus, last accessed on 8 June 2011.

Exhibit 12.3 Map and itinerary of Cotton Trail, a 12-day journey between Kabini and Pollachi

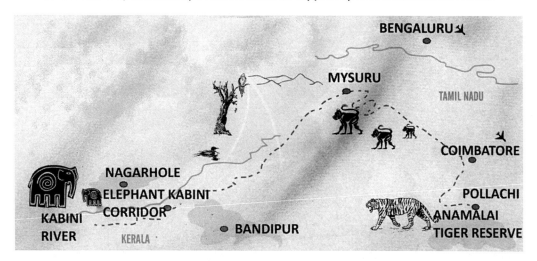

Day 1	Arrival at Bangalore, pick-up and check-in, day to explore the city
Day 2	Travel to Mysore after breakfast, visit to Mysore Palace, explore the city in the evening
Day 3, 4, and 5	Exploring Kabini Region (jungle safari, boating)
Day 6	Interaction with farmers growing organic cotton, visit to Sathyamangalam forests
Day 7	Introduction to the philosophical and spiritual teachings from India, Workshop—Introduction to organic farming
Day 8	Continuation of sessions related to the philosophical and spiritual teachings from India, visit to weaver's village
Day 9	Visiting Annamalai Tiger Reserve
Day10	Workshop on weaving techniques and handloom at Ethicus Studio, Pollachi
Day 11	Interaction with students of Nachiar Vidyalayam and return to Bangalore

Exhibit 12.4 Brand logo of Ethicus

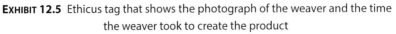

EXHIBIT 12.5 Ethicus tag that shows the photograph of the weaver and the time
the weaver took to create the product

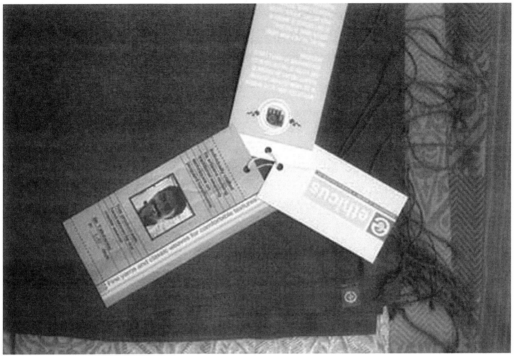

Discussion Questions

1. The case study tells that 'Ethicus is at their nascent stage. So they may be having difficulty in understanding markets....' We also understand that the brand is yet to break-even. Assess the possibilities of Ethicus becoming a winning brand.
2. What are the positive impacts the Ethicus model had on the traditional farmers and weavers?
3. What is your perspective about the leadership style and practice of the founders of Ethicus? Are they leading from a spiritual and sustainability context?

CASE STUDY 2

WALMART'S ENVIRONMENTAL STRATEGY[59]

> *I firmly believe that a company that cheats on overtime and on the age of its labour, that dumps its scraps and chemicals in our rivers, that does not pay its taxes or honour its contracts—will ultimately cheat on the quality of its products. And cheating on the quality of products is the same as cheating on customers. We will not tolerate that at Wal-Mart.*

Lee Scott, Former President and CEO, Wal-Mart Stores, Inc.[60]

Wal-Mart Stores, Inc. (also referred to as WMT, Wal-Mart, or Walmart, in the rest of the case study), branded as Walmart is an American multinational retail corporation that runs chains of large discount department stores and warehouse stores. The company is the world's largest public corporation, according to the Fortune Global 500 list in 2014, the biggest private employer in the world with over two million employees, and is the largest retailer in the world. Walmart has over 11,000 stores in 27 countries, under 55 different names. The company operates under the Walmart name in the United States, including the 50 states and Puerto Rico. It operates in Mexico as Walmart de Mexico, in the United Kingdom as Asda, in Japan as Seiyu, and in India as Best Price. In 2009, Walmart in a joint venture with Bharathi group, opened its first store in India.

A megalith corporation like WMT created a substantially large ecological footprint. Taking into consideration the influence WMT wielded and also the scale of its operations, WMT's decision to go green, as announced by Lee Scott (Scott), Former Chief Executive, WMT, was initially met with public's scepticism. However, its persistence on initiating and implementing ecologically friendly business processes seemed to have paid off. The company made cost savings through such initiatives and had been projected as one of the leading green companies by the media. WMT also found that doing the right thing resulted in improved employee morale.

COMPANY HISTORY

Sam Walton (Walton) started WMT in 1962, by opening the first store in Rogers, Arkansas, USA. The company went public in 1972 and with this fund infusion, charted a growth to operate 276 stores by the end of 1970s. In 1980, the sales revenue touched

---

59 *Note*: This case is prepared as the basis for group discussions instead of illustrating either effective or ineffective handling of a situation. This case study, written by the author of this textbook, is an improvised version of a case study published under a similar title by Asian Journal of Management Cases in 2009. The case author is thankful to Ms Dhaarani R, Ms Preethishri NM, and Mr Seshadri for their effort in sourcing data that helped in the improvisation of the case study.

60 *Note*: Announced at the Global Responsible Sourcing Initiative Summit at Beijing, China, 22 October 2008.

one billion. Table 12.1 illustrates operating results for WMT in the recent years (from 2010 to 2014).

For the fiscal year ending in 31 January 2011, Walmart reported a net income of $15.4 billion on $422 billion of revenue with a 24.7 per cent gross profit margin. The corporation's international operations accounted for $109.2 billion, or 26.1 per cent of total sales. It is the world's 18th largest public corporation, according to the Forbes Global 2000 list, and the largest public corporation, when ranked by revenue.

BACKGROUND

WMT never had a leadership position when it came to environmental initiatives. Instead, the company was encouraging conspicuous consumption, producing massive quantities of packaging waste, a 10,000 mile supply chain that is inefficient and creating water pollution due to runoff from new construction. This was in a scenario when public awareness about the destruction caused to the planet due to human intervention is on an increase. WMT had also met with sharp criticism about the way it relates to the society. The release of the documentary Wal-Mart: The High Cost of Low Price,[61] a series of lawsuits, union campaigns protesting against unfair worker treatment, and community resentment against opening of new stores, kept WMT in public focus. 'A lot of times a big company gets seriously burned in its reputation, [which is] what happened to

TABLE 12.1 Financials for Walmart between 2010 and 2014 (Amount given is in millions, except per share and unit count data)

	2010	2011	2012	2013	2014
Total revenues	$407,697	$421,395	$446,509	$468,651	$476,294
%age increase	8.1%	3.4%	6.0%	5.0%	1.6%
Gross profit margin	24.9%	24.8%	24.5%	24.3%	24.3%
Net income	14,433	15,340	15,734	16,963	15,918
Net income, diluted	3.72	4.18	4.53	5.01	4.85
Dividend per common share	1.09	1.21	1.46	1.59	1.88
Inventories	32,713	36,437	40,714	43,803	44,858
Total assets	170,407	180,782	193,406	203,105	204,751
Total units	8099	8604	9766	10408	10942

Source: 10-K Filing of Walmart

---

61 *Note*: This documentary film, released in November 2005, presents an unfavourable picture of Wal-Mart's business practices.

Wal-Mart. Although that criticism was about employment issues, not the environment, sometimes these things all go together, and you get a bad reputation that starts to hurt you,' said Eric Orts, Director, Professor—Legal Studies at Wharton School of Business.[62]

Shortly following the Katrina disaster,[63] Scott gave a speech in the month of October that came to be known as 21st Century Leadership, where he laid out three goals for WMT—'To be supplied 100 per cent by renewable energy; to create zero waste; and to sell products that sustain our resources and environment'.[64] Scott said that WMT is looking forward to being a good steward when it comes to environmental initiatives. In line with these objectives, WMT came out with specifics like cutting greenhouse emissions by 20 per cent through the following seven years, improving the supply chain by spending $500M a year to increase fuel efficiency by 25 per cent over three years and doubling the efficiency of its trucks through the next 10 years, reduction in the energy usage at its stores by 30 per cent, and a 25 per cent reduction in solid waste produced by US stores through the following three years. WMT also spoke about selling organic food that is affordable to the masses. Other initiatives announced by WMT included eliminating PVC packaging from private label brands, supporting and pursuing regulatory and policy changes that incentivizes energy efficiency and renewable energy.

However, the company also received supporters for its objectives. In July 2006, Al Gore, attended the environmental strategy meeting of an 800-member group which comprised of WMT employees, suppliers, and partners. He likened the green campaign to the Allies' righteous struggle during World War II. This meeting was also attended by Evangelical Environment Network executive director Rev Jim Ball. Following WMT's demand (along with similar demands made by GE, Shell, Exelon, Duke Energy) for a mandatory carbon cap programme from the US government, Grist Magazine, one of the popular online environmental magazine, responded to this action stating 'The heart of this monolithic retail Grinch grew three sizes that day—or so it seemed to many environmental Who's'.[65]

The company has been moving ahead with its environmental initiatives. On 25 September 2008, at the Clinton Global Initiative Annual Meeting, Walmart pledged to reduce its plastic shopping bag waste by 33 per cent per store by 2013—a 25 per cent reduction from the stores based in US and a 50 per cent reduction through the stores based in international locations. For its Chinese operations, by 2010, the company planned to launch a new store prototype which would reduce energy consumption by 40 per cent and by 30 per cent for the existing stores. Through the next two years, the

62 http://knowledge.wharton.upenn.edu/mobile/article.cfm?articleid=1653, last accessed on 10 December 2012.

63 *Note*: Hurricane Katrina, which occurred in the last week of August 2005, was the costliest and one of the five deadliest hurricanes in the history of United States. Wal-Mart believes that Hurricane Katrina was the turning point for its sustainability activities.

64 Sustainability Fact Sheet, http://Wal-martstores.com/FactsNews/FactSheets/#Sustainability, last accessed on 10 December 2012.

65 http://www.grist.org/news/maindish/2006/04/12/griscom-little/index.html, last accessed date 10 December 2012.

company also aims for a 50 per cent reduction in its water consumption. On 26 January 2009, the company said that it will reduce phosphates[66] in laundry and dish detergents in the Americas region by 70 per cent by 2011. Walmart also announced plans to reduce packaging in the Americas region by 5 per cent by the end of 2013.

STRATEGY AND LEARNING

The company has been known for its low cost pricing strategy. One of the ways in which WMT tried to ensure low prices was by making cost-effective purchases. Walmart China firmly believes in local sourcing. WMT has established partnerships with nearly 20,000 suppliers in China. Over 95 per cent of the merchandise in stores in China is sourced locally. In addition, Walmart is committed to local talent development and diversity, especially the cultivation and full utilization of female staff and executives. 'If Walmart were an individual economy, it would rank as China's eighth-biggest trading partner, ahead of Russia, Australia, and Canada,' said Thomas L Friedman in the book *The World Is Flat: A Brief History of the Twenty-first Century*. It is the supply chain management practices of WMT that helped it to be one of the leading low cost retailers.

Research and internal assessment revealed to the top management at WMT that people shopping at the retail store are looking for deals, not necessarily cheap products. The company's conclusion was that its 200 million customers belonged to three groups—people who seek low prices as they cannot afford products/services of higher cost, people with low incomes but obsessed with brand names like Kitchen Aid, and wealthier shoppers who are looking for deals. The company had already tried a repositioning exercise in early 2006 with 'look beyond the basics', but the endeavour did not give the desired results. Now WMT has taken the middle path of 'save money, live better'.

While 'save money' was always part of the WMT culture, with 'live better' it brought in an emotional component. The change in the mission statement and its environmental initiatives went together. The company wanted to ensure that the customers needed to have a guilt-free experience. The green initiatives of WMT alleviated some of the guilt feelings of the customers. It also helped the company to strengthen its own value systems.

WMT had been on a continuous learning path during the formulation and implementation of its environmental strategy. WMT had now entered an unchartered territory. However, the company embraced the uncertainty and made progress. In October 2006, Walmart and Sam's Club decided to sell 100 million compact fluorescent light (CFL) bulbs by the end of 2007. 'Like our initial environmental goals, at first, we weren't sure how we were going to achieve this—we were entering a world of the unknown. But we met our goal three months ahead of schedule… and sold nearly 137 million CFLs. We did it by changing our marketing approach and educating consumers, and in many cases lowering the prices,' said Leslie Dach, VP—Corporate

---

66 *Note*: A water pollutant

Affairs and Government Relations, WMT, in a speech to the National Retail Federation in January 2008.[67] WMT created 13 environmental sustainable value networks that comprised of environmental NGOs, suppliers, government officials, and scholars. This structure brought immense creativity to WMT's environmental initiatives, and explored options like pursuing regulatory change and raising public awareness to address systemic barriers to sustainability. 'We owe a great deal of credit for our progress to the women and men serving in these networks,' said Dach.[68]

One of the important aspects of the company's environmental strategy was to follow an organization-wide approach when it comes to environmental initiatives—be it important decisions like one of the largest solar panel purchased by the company or removing a light bulb. One of the stories shared by Dach[69] was about the suggestion made by Darrell Meyers, a WMT associate, who spotted the unnecessary glowing of light bulbs around the clock in the vending machines placed in the break rooms. Once these bulbs were removed, it resulted in a savings of more than $1 million. This money saved was channelled to 'Everyday Low Prices'[70] offered by WMT. This bottoms up approach resulted in the company getting the feedback that sustainability turned out to be one of the popular discussion topics among its associates and their families. 'Sustainability is not a separate initiative at Wal-Mart, as it is at many other firms. Sustainability is being integrated into all parts of the business,' said Frank Dixon (Dixon), former Managing Director of Research for Innovest Strategic Value Advisors, a leading sustainability research firm.

In 2013, the US Environmental Protection Agency's Green Power Partnership ranked WMT as the leading retailer for onsite generation of renewable energy in the United States. WMT kept away more than 80 per cent of their waste from landfills. As per the Global Responsibility Report 2012, WMT had been working with suppliers to incorporate the Sustainability Index into their buying decisions to make the products they sell, more environment-friendly all through the supply chain. WMT, which has been criticized for sourcing its food products from across the globe, thereby creating huge emissions, gradually improved to ensure that 10 per cent of its products sold in the US is locally grown.

Meeting Commitments

WMT had achieved success in some of their commitments. The company had become the leading seller of milk and the leading buyer of organic cotton. In May 2008, the company met the goal of transitioning its entire liquid laundry detergent category in

---

67 http://noticias.walmart.com/executive-viewpoints/making-sustainability-sustainable-lessons-weve-learned, last accessed on 8 April 2014.
68 http://noticias.walmart.com/executive-viewpoints/making-sustainability-sustainable-lessons-weve-learned, last accessed on 8 April 2014.
69 http://Wal-martstores.com/FactsNews/NewsRoom/7870.aspx, last accessed date 8 April 2014.
70 *Note*: As part of everyday low prices, companies eliminate periodic promotional discounts to offer prices that are consistently lesser than customary prices.

US to the concentrated segment—thereby meeting the pledge made at the 2007 Clinton Global Initiative Meeting. It is assessed that this commitment, within three years, will save 95 million pounds of plastic resin, more than 400 million gallons of water, and more than 125 million pounds of cardboard. On 20 November, the company announced a wind energy purchase from a Duke Energy wind farm that was expected to supply 15 per cent of WMT's total load in its 360 stores and other facilities in Texas.

In January 2008, the company opened the second generation of high-efficiency stores (HE2) which used 25 per cent less energy than the traditional Walmart supercenter. On 2 February 2009, the company announced that it had achieved more than a 25 per cent increase in efficiency within its private fleet between 2005 and 2008, by using innovative technologies, better delivery routes, and efficient loading of its trailers. This helped the company surpass one of its sustainability goals, as announced by Scott, in 2005. In line with its strategy of providing goods and services at low cost, the company tried to bring green products mainstream. In April 2008, the company launched the 'Earth Month' campaign where eco-friendly items were promoted at competitive prices. 'Wal-Mart is uniquely positioned to make sustainable choices a real option for hundreds of millions of Americans, not just the few who until now could afford to choose them,' said Kistler.[71]

The following data from the 2012 WMT sustainability report (see Table 12.2) indicates the environmental sustainability commitments given by WMT and the performance to those commitments.

TABLE 12.2 Walmart's environmental sustainability commitments and their performance

Commitment	Remarks
Reducing greenhouse gas	
To reduce greenhouse gases (GHG) emissions at stores and the distribution centres across the world by 20%, with year 2005 as the baseline.	WMT has mentioned that, in 2010, across all the countries they operate in, there was overall progress.
To eliminate 20 million metric tons of GHG emissions from global supply chain by end of 2015.	Through 2011, WMT removed more than 120,000 metric tons of GHG emissions from its supply chain. The company is also engaged in projects that have the potential to further reduce emissions by 16 million metric tons.
Energy efficiency	
With 2007 as the baseline, to improve energy efficiency in supplier factories by 20% per unit of production by the end of 2012, in the top 200 factories in China from where WMT sources directly.	WMT partnered with more than 450 factories on energy efficiency improvements, and trained them in energy efficiency measures. By the end of 2011, 148 factories achieved a 20% reduction in energy consumption.

(Contd)

---

71 'Wal-Mart Goes Green with Earth Month Campaign', *Prism Insight*, 4 April 2008.

Reducing waste	
By 2025, to eliminate landfill waste from all the stores located in US, and also Sam's Club locations.	By the end of 2011, WMT achieved a reduction rate of 80.9% in the amount of waste sent to the landfills.
By the end of 2015, with 2009 as the baseline, to reduce food waste (through throwaways) in emerging market stores by 15% and in other markets by 10%.	The company is tracking food throwaways and is developing plans for reducing throwaways.
By 2013, with 2007 as the baseline, to reduce global plastic shopping bag waste by an average of 33% per store.	In 2011, WMT reduced the plastic bag waste by 35% per store. This amounted to approximately 3.1 billion bags or 42.5 million pounds.
Sustainable food	
To increase the focus on agriculture in the Sustainability Index by engaging in a Sustainable Produce Assessment for top producers in its Global Food Sourcing network by the end of 2011.	In 2011, the company piloted the Sustainable Produce Assessment with 66 growers, covering 14 crops on four continents. This assessment examines the usage of water, energy, fertilizer, and pesticides.
By the end of 2015, for the company to use only sustainably sourced palm oil in all of the private-brand products that it sells.	In 2011, the company adopted a new palm oil procurement policy.
All seafood products sold in US to be certified as sustainable by a third party using Marine Stewardship Council (MSC), Best Aquaculture Practices (BAP) or equivalent standards. Uncertified fisheries, from whom WMT sources its products from, to develop work plans to achieve certification and report progress biannually.	In the beginning of 2012, 76% of seafood suppliers were third-party certified. An additional 8% had developed the required certification plans.
Packaging	
By 2013, with 2008 as the baseline, for the company to reduce packaging by 5% globally.	Company-wide initiatives are happening to reduce packaging and to use recycled content.
be packaging neutral globally by 2025.	The company prioritizes the use of recycled materials and returnable packaging, and works with suppliers to achieve this.
Renewable energy	
be supplied by 100% renewable energy.	Globally, the company is supplied with 22% of the total electricity and 15% of the total energy.
By 2013, with 2008 as the baseline, Walmart Mexico to reduce water usage by 20%.	The company reduced water usage by 21.3%.
Other commitments	
reduce phosphates in laundry and dish detergents in the Americas region by 70% by 2011, with 2009 as the baseline.	The company was successful in reducing the amount of phosphates in laundry and dish detergents that they sold in stores in the Americas region by 43%. Retail operations in Argentina and Brazil surpassed the 70% reduction goal. In Central America and Mexico a key supplier had made considerable

(Contd)

TABLE 12.2 *(Contd)*

Commitment	Remarks
	reductions in phosphates prior to the baseline year, and they expectd them to make another significant reduction in 2012[S30]. They continue promoting phosphate-free detergents and other alternatives that have a positive environmental impact.
By the end of 2015, for the company to sell $1 billion in food sourced from one million small and medium-sized farmers in emerging markets.	In 2011, the company developed a direct farm business model and created a blueprint for implementation in new markets.
To ensure that 95% of direct-import factories receive one of the two highest ratings in environmental and social audits.	More than 94% of direct-import factories received one of the two highest ratings.
By the end of 2015, for the company to train one million farmers and farm workers in the food supply chain, of which they expect half to be women, in emerging markets.	In progress.
By the end of 2015, for the company to raise the income of farmers they source from by10% to 15% in emerging markets.	WMT funded the University of California-Davis to develop an income scorecard to measure the income impact of its Direct Farm programs. The scorecard will provide an average income estimate. The tool is to be used in China, India, and Central America.
In the USA, by the end of 2015, and with 2009 as the baseline, for the company to double sales of locally sourced produce, accounting for 9% of all produce sold by the end of 2015.	In 2011, in the USA, there has been a 97% increase in the amount of locally sourced produces. This was more than 10% of all produce sold.
For Walmart, by the end of 2015, to expand worldwide, the existing practice of its Brazil operations sourcing beef that does not contribute to the deforestation of the Amazon rainforests.	In progress.

Greening the Supply Chain

WMT had been spending a substantial amount of energy in greening its supply chain, a strategic imperative for the company. The company outlined the goals and commitments that it expected from its suppliers. 'Achieving the goals that we lay out today is going to require a common commitment. It's going to take even stronger and deeper relationships. And it is going to take all of us working together…. We are expecting more out of ourselves at Wal-Mart, and we will also expect more out of our suppliers,'[72] said Michael T Duke (Duke), Vice-chairman, International Division, WMT (Duke became the President and Chief Executive Officer, WMT, in February 2009). WMT had been asking miners to adopt stringent social and environmental standards. Pam Mortensen, Chief buyer—Jewelry, WMT, had commented that, by 2010, 10 per cent of the gold, silver, and diamonds sourced by the company will be responsibly produced.

72 Press Release, 'Wal-Mart Announces Global Responsible Sourcing Initiative at China Summit', 22 October 2008.

One of the ways in which the company started asking right questions was pulling together top executives from its suppliers to a summit. WMT found that asking basic questions like—why the product is packaged the way it is—forced the suppliers to go reassess their operations in new ways. In 2006, WMT developed a packaging scorecard for its US operations, through which the company aimed at reducing packaging through its supply chain by 5 per cent, by 2013. The scorecard indicated the product packaging standards of suppliers based on metrics like greenhouse gas emissions, use of renewable energy during the production of packaging materials, space utilization, emissions related to the transportation of packaging materials, and product to package ratio. Suppliers received a score in each category and viewed their ratings compared to their competitors in each product category. This scorecard, in addition to helping the suppliers assess their contribution in helping WMT achieve its green goals, helped buyers make informed purchasing decisions.

WMT engaged its suppliers with new agreements that required them to certify compliance with domestic laws and regulations related to environmental and social standards. The company wanted to do this in a phased manner, starting with suppliers from China and then expanding this to all suppliers by 2011. By 2012, WMT expected its suppliers to procure 95 per cent of their production resources from institutions that receive the highest environmental and social practices.

In mid-July 2008, WMT joined the Global Forest & Trade Network (GFTN), by which the company aimed to phase out illegal and unwanted wood sources from its supply chain. 'By joining the GFTN we can further this goal by providing our customers with a reliable supply of wood products that come from responsibly managed forests,' said Matt Kistler (Kistler), Sr VP—Sustainability, WMT.[73] Indonesia, China, and Brazil, areas that WMT sources it furniture from, had been known for its illegal logging and trade. Observers pointed out that the US market has an influential role to play in protecting forests as the country has been the largest global consumer of industrial timber, pulp, and paper. WMT had been in the process of assessing where all its wood furniture was coming from. WMT committed within five years to eliminate sales of products coming from illegal and unknown sources. WMT has also said that it will stop selling wood related products that are coming from forests that are of critical importance.

Through a partnership with the Carbon Disclosure Project, WMT started a pilot project that looked into the amount of energy consumed through the supply chain, while creating seven products. This partnership, announced in September 2007, was intended to encourage suppliers to reduce their greenhouse emissions.

POLLUTION = WASTE = COST

The company had been looking for every opportunity to incorporate sustainability into every aspect of its business. In addition to being good for the environment, these initiatives saved money. By reducing the packaging size of the company's toy brand, Kid Connection, WMT saved $2.4 million annually in transportation, along with 3800 trees.

---

73 http://naturealert.blogspot.in/2008/07/wal-mart-to-ban-sales-of-wood-from.html, last accessed on 8 April 2014.

WMT believed that its pledge to reduce the shopping bag waste by one-third will eliminate plastic waste equivalent to 9 billion plastic bags per year—more than 135 million pounds of plastic waste. 'By pledging to cut its bag waste by one-third by 2013, Wal-Mart is taking a clear step forward in reducing global waste,'[74] said Gwen Ruta, VP— corporate partnerships, Environmental Defense Fund.[75] The plastic reduction effort is expected to reduce carbon dioxide emissions by 290,000 metric tons per year and reduce energy consumption of 678,000 barrels of oil. WMT also makes economic gains from this initiative. On 12 May 2008, WMT Canada announced that it will eliminate plastic packaging in the energy-saving light bulb category. The change to cardboard packaging was expected to save approximately 150,000 pounds of plastic waste every year.

ROLE OF LEADERSHIP

Observers credit the rapid progress made by WMT in achieving the green goals to the company's excellence in strategy execution and the commitment provided by the top management. 'Lee Scott has made it clear that working on sustainability projects can accelerate careers within Wal-Mart. Compensation schemes are being adjusted to provide substantial incentives for improving sustainability performance,' says Dixon.

Was it the lure of greenback that accelerated the environmental initiatives at WMT? Scott said that it was a combination of personal and business imperatives that generated an interest in sustainability factors. 'On a personal level, as you become a grandparent—I have a granddaughter—you just also become more thoughtful about what the world that she inherits, would look like' said Scott.[76]

The size of WMT enabled the creation of technologies that did not have established markets. Scott himself took interest in communicating with his peers. 'So I'm always asking, how do I work with people, whether it be Jeff Immelt at General Electric or John Browne at BP, to use our scale to help propel an industry so that the production of that technology or product is now affordable for other people? I ask, what happens to the solar-panel market if Wal-Mart makes a large commitment to solar panels?[77] What happens to the cost of compact fluorescent light bulbs or green building materials?' said Scott.[78]

In the January 2008 annual kick-off meeting speech to more than 7000 managers, Lee Scott prodded, 'What if we extended our mission of saving people money so they can live better—to save people money on energy?'[79] During this speech Scott announced

74 Press release, 'Wal-Mart Sets Goal to Reduce its Global Plastic Shopping Bag Waste by One-Third', 25 September 2008.
75 *Note*: Environmental Defense Fund, which partnered with Walmart in evolving its plastic bag reduction strategy, is a US-based non-profit environmental advocacy group.
76 Little, Amanda Griscom, 'Don't Discount Him', www.grsit.com, 12 April 2006.
77 *Note*: In May 2007, Wal-Mart announced one of the world's largest solar power purchases that will energize Wal-Mart's 22 facilities in California and Hawaii.
78 Little, Amanda Griscom, 'Don't Discount Him', www.grsit.com, 12 April 2006.

a company-wide goal to make the most energy-intensive products sold in WMT stores 25 per cent more energy efficient. 'Flat-screen TVs will be 30 per cent more efficient by 2010,' said Hank Mullany, Head-Eastern Division.[80] When Duke took over the Chief Executive Position, he added momentum to the sustainability initiatives, despite the downturn in the economy. 'These difficult economic times have led to an obvious question that a number of people have asked me: "Can Wal-Mart afford to continue to be so aggressive in sustainability?" My response has been very clear and direct: "We can't afford not to. We need to accelerate and broaden our efforts",' mentioned Duke in the 2009 Global Sustainability Report of WMT. In 2014, Doug McMillon succeeded Mike Duke as CEO. Rob Walton, Chairman, said, 'He has also shown strong leadership on environmental sustainability and a commitment to using Wal-mart's size and scale to make a difference in the lives of people, wherever they might be.'[81]

CHALLENGING THE BELIEF

Andy Ruben (Ruben), the VP—Corporate Strategy and Sustainability, WMT, said, 'You know, the biggest challenge that we've seen all the way through it has been the mindset. And what I'm talking about is, many of the opportunities that we're talking about have existed for some time. It's just the ability to see them, and look at things in a different way. And the way we're approaching this is not as a separate part of the organization that works on environment; we see it as consistent with our business and a part of the business.'[82]

In a response provided during a recording, Ruben had this to say about the criticism the company has been facing from some quarters: 'And what we have found is there are a lot of our critics out there who simply want Wal-Mart to be a better company. It's not that they are not interested in having Wal-Mart. And that type of criticism actually very productive, and we've gotten a lot of help from those people over the past year in terms of understanding, you know, the things they know a lot more about than we do. And while working with them we found great innovative solutions to things that we hadn't uncovered before.'[83]

The company had been working with some of its ardent critics. 'For Wal-Mart, it has been very hard to get some groups and individuals to sit down and talk with us. And some still won't, but it is fewer every day and now some even seek us out. It's amazing what happens when you say you want to listen and learn to have a conversation.

---

79 Press Release, 'Wal-Mart Expands Leadership On Energy Efficiency, Ethical Sourcing And Health Care', 23 January 2008.

80 Batcha, Becky, 'Wal-Mart's boss in the Northeast is pushing the company s strategy to cut costs by going green''', The Philadelphia Inquirer, 26 June 2008.

81 'Walmart Names Doug McMillon New CEO To Succeed Mike Duke', Forbes, 25 December 2014.

82 'Wal-mart to Reduce Its Environmental Footprint', http://www.loe.org/shows/shows.htm?programmeID=05-P13-00043feature 1, 25 October 2008, last accessed on 4 November 2009.

83 'Wal-mart to Reduce Its Environmental Footprint', http://www.loe.org/shows/shows.htm?programmeID=05-P13-00043feature 1, 25 October 2008, last accessed on 4 November 2009.

You start finding common ground, and people that never would have worked with you before, now become partners,' said Dach.[84]

This endeavour has won the company applauds from people. Consultants like Dixon had mentioned that WMT may be pioneering the first sustainability strategy that actually has the potential to achieve sustainability. According to Ruben, WMT had set inspirational green goals to ensure that people get out of their silos and use imagination and innovation required to meet those goals.[85] Some observers believed that the company could also gain some intangible benefits—like having a favourable public perception when it comes to opening new stores in markets where WMT was not earlier welcomed.

While cost savings had been projected as the carrot for going green, observers question to what extent this theme can be used as a sales pitch for embracing green initiatives. Americus Reed, Professor—Marketing, Wharton School of Business, said, 'The barrier to proliferation of socially responsible policies is that it's difficult to show social goodwill on the balance sheet. There is no column or item to say, "Here it is, here's the savings in dollars". That's the conundrum.'[86]

Michael T. Duke, President and CEO, said, 'Three years ago, at my first Sustainability Milestone Meeting as CEO, I pledged that we would broaden and accelerate our commitment to being a more sustainable and responsible company. I pledge that we'll continue to broaden and accelerate our commitment to environmental sustainability and beyond, in the years ahead. This is one of the most compelling reasons we have to look forward to our next 50 years at Wal-mart.'[87]

CRITICISMS

WMT had been subjected to many criticisms. Between 2005 and 2010, Walmart greenhouse gas emissions grew by 14 per cent, and the company reported that it expects its emissions to continue expanding.[88] One of the environmental sustainability objectives of Walmart was to be supplied with 100 per cent renewable energy. It has been noted that, going by the pace with which the company is moving, it may take decades to reach that objective. Another criticism was that the company's claim that investing in renewable technologies are costly, though the company made profits in billions. It was noted that retailers like Whole Foods Market, Kohl's Department Stores, Staples, Starbucks, McDonalds, and other retailers are way ahead of WMT in using renewable energy.

84 http://walmartstores.com/FactsNews/NewsRoom/7870.aspx, last accessed on 4 November 2009.

85 http://www.sustainableisgood.com/blog/2007/04/is_walmart_sust.html, last accessed on 4 November 2009.

86 http://knowledge.wharton.upenn.edu/article/its-not-easy-going-green-environmentalism-may-help-your-corporate-image-but-will-it-keep-you-in-the-black/, last accessed on 8 April 2014.

87 http://www.walmartstores.com/sites/responsibility-report/2012/messageMikeDuke.aspx, last accessed on 8 April 2014.

88 Upton, J, 2013. *Wal-mart's carbon emissions soar despite all that green talk*; also available at: http://grist.org/news/Wal-marts-carbon-emissions-soar-despite-all-that-green-talk/, last accessed on 30 March 2014.

It was also said that the company, in the name of going organic, was promoting big brands of processed foods like Rice Krispies, and Kraft Macaroni and Cheese. Though the company has committed to 'sustainable agriculture', its market power[89] has resulted in larger-scale, more industrialized food system as the company's buying power and business practices have triggered mergers among its food suppliers and processors. WMT's private-label organic milk has been criticized for coming from cows raised in factory-farm conditions. While WMT committed to double sales of locally sourced produce for its US operations, the company's distribution model favoured use of a few large suppliers, and not small farms.

The company has also been fined \$81.6 million in fines and penalties, for improper waste disposal due to the lack of an employee training program on hazardous waste management and disposal practices. A press release from EPA stated: 'hazardous wastes were either discarded improperly at the store level—including being put into municipal trash bins or, if a liquid, poured into the local sewer system—or they were improperly transported without proper safety documentation to one of six product return centres located throughout the United States.'[90] They were also criticized for the more than 1100 supercentres they added in the US since 2005, which were built on land that hadn't been developed before, including, in some cases, critical habitat for threatened and endangered species.

Discussion Questions

1. How did Wal-Mart get over the criticism of greenwashing?
2. Assess the factors that resulted in the success of Wal-Mart's green strategy.

---

89 *Note*: Walmart controls more than 50 per cent of total grocery sales in 29 metro markets.
90 http://yosemite.epa.gov/opa/admpress.nsf/2467feca6036872985257359004043d/d4628253b5e27cab85257b790
07349aa!OpenDocument, last accessed on 8 April 2014.

CASE STUDY 3

MAKING SUSTAINABILITY A STRATEGY: THE CASE OF INTERFACE[91]

Two weeks before he was due to deliver the kick-off speech at a task force meeting in August 1994, Mr Ray C Anderson (Anderson), Founder and Chairman of Interface, the global leader in carpet tile manufacturing, was sweating. The task force, comprising of representatives from all of Interface's global divisions, was meeting up for the first time to see what they were doing for the natural environment in response to growing consumer interest in that area. Jim Hartzfield, an associate in the research division, had convened the task force and insisted that Anderson make the opening speech.

In the last 21 years, by his own admission, Anderson had not seriously considered what Interface had taken from the Earth or how they were giving back. Being in the carpet tile industry, Interface's major input was petroleum. Their plants consumed huge amounts of energy to transform raw materials such as nylon and other synthetic polymers into modular carpets. Their processes resulted in waste that was sent to landfills.[92] Large transportation systems were a part of their value chain.[93] Even consumers would send the old, used, and worn carpets to landfills. Despite a lot of deliberation, Anderson had nothing better to say in his speech other than that Interface had always complied with the law.

INTERFACE—A BRIEF HISTORY

In 1969, as Director of Development, Floor Covering Division at Deering Milliken,[94] Anderson had the chance to learn about what was then a brand new product—carpet tiles. Anderson fell in love with the idea of modular carpeting and the opportunities it presented. Offices in the US were going through a phase of change where they needed to keep on upgrading their equipment to keep up with the latest technology and this implied constant rewiring and reconfiguring of the office spaces, especially the floors presenting the perfect opening for carpet tiles.

91 *Note*: This case is prepared as the basis for group discussion rather than to illustrate either effective or ineffective handling of a situation. The case is written by V D Krishnaveni, Assistant Professor, PSG Institute of Management, Coimbatore, India, with inputs from Ajith Sankar R N. The copyright for the case exists with the case writer. The case has been prepared based on secondary research. This case study is released to the public domain without cost. While the case writer holds the copyright to this case study, the reader may reproduce, distribute, publish, and transmit this case study in any form including photocopying, recording, or other electronic or mechanical methods provided that no text or figures are altered.

92 *Note*: The typical types of waste that are created during carpet production would include off-quality carpet, scrap, damaged yarn, trimmings left over after small pieces of carpet tiles have been cut out of large rolls of carpet, and so on.

93 *Note*: As per Michael Porter, Professor, Harvard Business School, value chain refers to all the activities that add value to the customer and includes everything from production to after sales service.

94 *Note*: Deering Milliken was a company that started off as a major player in the textile industry space and later moved into specialty chemical, floor covering, and performance materials sectors. In 1976, it officially changed its name to Milliken and Company.

People around Anderson were skeptical about the fact that perfectly good broadloom carpets would be cut into 18" carpet tiles and sold at around twice the price. They did not quite see the potential the new product offered; nevertheless Anderson helped Milliken bring it from the UK to the United States. In 1972, Anderson's frustrations at being passed up for a higher post six years ago and the stifling bureaucracy at Milliken made him think of starting out on his own.

Not only did Anderson have to face up to professional skeptics but even at the personal front, he did not have the support of his wife who could not understand the driving need for Anderson to want to give up a perfectly respectable job with a good pay to become an entrepreneur.

Anderson, however, did not give up on the chance to take charge of his life. He overcame legal and financial hurdles and severely strained his marriage in the process of starting a joint venture with Carpets International (CI)[95] UK in 1973. Anderson's investment was $50,000, 10 per cent of the $500,000 that CI had insisted that Anderson raise on the American side. The JV was known as Carpets International-Georgia, Inc. (with 51 per cent ownership belonging to CI and 49% with Anderson and his American investors) and had a sister company, Carpets International-Georgia (Sales) Inc. (which

EXHIBIT 12.6 Financial details of interface between 2009 and 2013

(In thousands US$, except per share data and ratios)	2013	2012	2011	2010	2009
Net sales	959,989	932,020	953,045	862,314	765,264
Cost of sales	618,880	614,841	618,303	549,184	499,078
Operating income	95,630	64,648	85,700	93,107	67,611
Income from continuing operations	48,255	22,899	38,270	10,297	15,777
Income (loss) from discontinued operations	0	(16,956)	451	(963)	(4,013)
Net income	48,255	5,943	38,721	8,283	10,918
Income from continuing operations per common share					
Basic	0.73	0.35	0.59	0.14	0.24
Diluted	0.73	0.35	0.58	0.14	0.24
Cash dividends per common share	0.11	0.09	0.08	0.04	0.01
Total assets	818,140	789,367	772,272	755,433	727,239

Source: Interface Inc. 10-K Filing for 2014

---

95 *Note*: Carpets International UK was the firm that had patented technology about carpet tile manufacturing in 1972.

handled sales and had 49 per cent ownership belonging to CI and 51% with Anderson and his American investors). The American investors who backed Anderson gave him their voting power and because of this sweat equity and his own voting share, he became an equal partner with CI. In 1982, the two companies were merged into Interface Flooring Systems, Inc. By 1987, Anderson and his American investors were able to buy out Carpet International's holdings completely.

The year 1996 saw Interface's sales exceeding $1 billion for the first time. By 1998, Interface had 29 manufacturing sites and customers in more than 110 countries. They were home to brands such as InterfaceFLOR, Heuga, Bentley, Prince Street, and FLOR. Around 40 per cent of the carpet tiles used in almost every one of the 110 countries was supplied by Interface. A series of acquisitions saw them enter the broadloom business, textiles, chemicals, and architectural products like raised access floors. By 2011, the number of employees reached 3500. It was billed by Fortune magazine as one of the 'Most Admired Companies in America'(1999) and also came up in the list of '100 Best Companies to Work For' (1998). In 2013, the company had a net income of around $48 million on sales of approximately $1 billion (see Exhibit 12.6 for financial details).

THE EPIPHANY

Moving back to 1994, Anderson knew that people did not want to hear that Interface had always complied with the law—everyone knew they were law abiding. He needed something more—something like an environmental vision. That's when he happened to chance upon the book—*The Ecology of Commerce*, by Paul Hawken.[96] By the time he was halfway through the book, Anderson knew what he had to do. He realized that the traditional way industries were run was ruinous to the Earth and that it was not sustainable. He had not just found the material for his task force meeting kick-off speech, but he even had a new vision for his company.

At the meeting, Anderson quoted Hawken liberally. He explained how the 'take-make-waste' linear system[97] followed by industries where they would take too many resources from the environment in a harmful manner, create products through processes that are highly polluting and energy-intensive, and create waste that is potentially harmful to future generations, is not sustainable. He asked the audience to make Interface a 'restorative' organization, to attain sustainability and then to go beyond sustainability and help put

---

96 *Note*: Paul Hawken is one of America's foremost authorities in the field of sustainability. He has written books and articles on the subject and also started related businesses. He is a consultant to several companies and the US Government.

97 *Note*: A linear system refers to a system where the final output does not become an input for any other process. In a cyclical system, the output of one process becomes the input of another. An example would be the carbon dioxide cycle in nature where CO_2 produced by living beings and other processes is utilized by trees which give out life supporting oxygen which in turn is utilized by living beings.

back more than what they take from the Earth. At age 60, Ray Anderson had changed from being an 'ecological plunderer' to a 'leading corporate evangelist for sustainability'.[98]

MOUNT SUSTAINABILITY AND MISSION ZERO

Very broadly, Mission Zero seeks to eliminate any negative environmental impacts by Interface by the year 2020. Sustainability was intended in all dimensions—*people, process, product, place, and profits*. Mission Zero was based on the principles of a 'consensus document' drafted by Dr Karl-Henrik Robert (Robert),[99] a Swedish oncologist and ratified by ecologists, chemists, physicists, and medical doctors. The principles state that human beings must not increase the content of substances from the Earth's crust or man-made substances in the Earth's biosphere, as this may affect the life supporting capacity of the Earth. For billions of years since its formation, the Earth has slowly absorbed all substances that are toxic to life into it, leaving a habitable biosphere; but we human beings are changing all that. We are systematically digging out substances from inside the Earth (such as fossil fuels) and polluting the planet, and fast reaching those levels beyond which they would become a hazard to all living beings. We should not reduce natural diversity and to follow these principles, we must learn to utilize resources efficiently.

Anderson likened achieving sustainability to climbing up a mountain—one that was higher than Mt Everest and one that would take a lot more effort. He called it 'Mt Sustainability' and he wanted Interface to reach its pinnacle and prove to other industries that they could do it and remain profitable at the same time.

Anderson and a global team identified seven fronts which had to be tackled to reach the summit.

1. Eliminating Waste

'...*Nothing is more basic to the argument... than the proposition that disposal of hazardous wastes is not the root problem. Rather, it is the root symptom. The critical issue is the creation of toxic wastes...*'

Paul Hawken, The Ecology of Commerce

The first thing Anderson did was to define waste. According to him, waste was any measurable cost that went into the product but did not add to customer value. Once

---

98 *Note*: As per an article in the New York Times dated 22 May 2007.
99 *Note*: Dr Karl-Henrik Robert is a cancer scientist who researched extensively on different forms of cancer. He realized that it was not just adults but also very young children who were increasingly being affected by the disease. On further analysis he realized that it was the unsustainability of our processes that were to blame for the rise in occurrences in cancer. He has co-founded 'The Natural Step'-a non-profit organization that has helped thousands of companies move towards sustainability since its inception in 1989.

waste was defined, it was easy to identify everything that fit into that definition. So, not only were scrap or bad-quality carpet considered waste but even mistakes committed by employees such as misdirected shipments constituted waste. The greenest resources were considered to be the ones that were never used. In 1998, a new addition was made to the list of wastes—fossil fuels! Interface was determined that by 2020, it would not take a single drop of oil from the planet to manufacture carpet tiles. For a company whose primary ingredient was petroleum, this was considered to be a huge commitment. Scepticism was high during InterfaceFLOR's 25th anniversary celebrations when Anderson introduced suppliers and other guests to the idea of Mission Zero 2020.

The next step was to measure waste to set up the baseline values and then come up with targets to reduce those values. A waste control programme called QUEST (Quality Utilizing Employees' Suggestions and Teamwork) was set up. Anderson believed that the best solutions would come from people who were working on the factory floor and he was right!

Suggestions poured in from all sites—dirty and damaged yarn could be used in carpet edges, green tax could be paid, trees could be planted, heat in a water supply system could be recovered by using a brass nozzle that cost less than $10 (this particular innovation saved Interface more than $10,000), huge beams could be replaced by smaller, portable creels (so that lesser thread would be wasted), and so on. Each one of these suggestions added to millions of dollars of savings for Interface over time and kept improving the efficiency of their various processes.

2. Rendering Emissions Benign

Once processes were made more efficient, the next step was to identify a list of greenhouse gases, chemical elements like dyes and softeners, trace contaminants like volatile organic compounds and other potentially harmful emissions getting out through smokestacks and effluent pipes.

A toxic chemical elimination team was created to work with suppliers to eliminate harmful chemicals upstream in the value chain. The team had to come up with ways to decrease use of CFCs, HFCs, and SARA 313[100] chemicals, and to completely eliminate volatile chlorinated chemicals. The idea was that irrespective of how lax government regulations in any country may be, all Interface plants worldwide, will comply with the most progressive environmental regulations.

Life Cycle Assessments[101] of different products was done to identify where the harm was maximum. A programme was undertaken to systematically close down smokestacks and effluent pipes. This even required redesigning some of the processes.

---

100 *Note*: A list of chemicals that require to be reported to the Environmental Protection Agency (EPA) is present in Section 313 of The Superfund Amendments and Reauthorization Act (SARA) of 1986.

101 *Note*: Life Cycle Assessment (LCA) refers to a comprehensive evaluation of the environmental impact of every stage of a product right from extraction of raw material to disposal.

The InterfaceFLOR Division in Canada is a case in point for rendering emissions benign. It completely eliminated use of any chemical on Canada's list of hazardous substances and use of process water[102] by moving away from wet printing of carpet tiles and bringing down their air emissions by 30 per cent (against 1995 baseline values). These were accomplished in the context of plant production increasing by 242 per cent. All other plants—from Maine to Europe had similar stories to tell. Three fold advantages emerged—unnecessary materials were eliminated, harmful chemicals were avoided, and processes became more efficient and cost-effective.

Another unique initiative was the voluntary buying of carbon offsets. Interface wanted its carpets to become carbon neutral even when end users were vacuuming them and generating emissions. The only way this could be achieved with the current levels of technology was to calculate the emissions that a carpet would produce from the time of manufacture to when it would be recycled and to purchase carbon credits that would offset the emissions. To this end, Interface has been spending about $2 million annually on carbon offsets.

3. Shifting to Renewable Energy

'… One statistic makes clear the demand placed on the earth by our economic system: every day the worldwide economy burns an amount of energy the planet required 10,000 days to create. Or, put another way, 27 years' worth of stored solar energy is burned and released by utilities, cars, houses, factories, and farms every 24 hours. …'

Paul Hawken, The Ecology of Commerce

All efforts were made to harness solar and wind energy. The Bentley Prince Street plant set the standard by connecting all of its solar generated electricity directly to its carpet tufting machines and selling the carpet so produced, under a new brand called Solar-Made carpet.

The InterfaceFLOR plants at LaGrange (USA), West Point (USA), Belleville (USA), Craigavon (Ireland), and Scherpenzel (The Netherlands), soon had 100 per cent of their electricity requirements met by on-site solar photovoltaic cells, Green-e-certified renewable energy credits and/or wind power. There was also a shift to newer, cleaner, and more efficient production technology. For instance, at LaGrange, methane produced in the municipal landfills was harnessed to produce energy for its operations which helped it become climate neutral.

4. Closing the Loop

Interface realized that they needed to move away from the linear system of carpet making to a cyclical process where old and worn carpets would become inputs for creating new

---

102 *Note*: Process water refers to any water that is used in the manufacturing/treatment process or other industrial processes.

carpets. It was a challenging task. Carpets contain an upper layer of yarn which could be made of nylon, wool, polypropylene, polyester or a mix of several materials. This upper layer is tufted into a polyester backed layer and there are layers of latex and vinyl plastisol holding it in place. There could also be a layer of glue holding the carpet to the floor.

Getting all these materials back from a worn carpet in a usable form seemed like a herculean task. One that Interface undertook nevertheless. Research went into the creation and production of new kinds of backing material that used lesser material, produced lesser waste, and was functionally more efficient. PVC was recycled. The tried and tested means of recovering material from worn carpets was by melting the old carpet and extruding its contents. This process required heating up to a temperature of about 400°C, which in turn required a lot of energy. A new thermoplastic process called CoolBlue was developed and it did away with such heat intensive extrusions.

A new term—negawatts—was coined. It represented all those units of electricity that never got consumed.

5. Resource Efficient Transportation

The next target was the usage of fossil fuels in the supply chain processes. Calculations revealed that sending out deliveries through rail, instead of trucks, reduced 75 per cent of BTUs[103] per ton mile. Soon, deliveries were being made through rail, ship, and river barges, which were more efficient modes of delivery, and trucks were used only in the last mile.

Research went into reducing the weight of the carpet without impairing functionality to make shipping even more efficient. Interface became a partner at the US EPA's SmartWay Transport[104] program to reduce fuel use and GHG emissions. Wide-base tyres were used (instead of multiple thin ones), aerodynamic changes were introduced in trailers, hybrid chilling systems were set up, and auxiliary power units were placed in trucks. All these small changes led to big savings. Interface's Netherlands' operations witnessed a 25 per cent decrease in shipping costs (for products bound to Italy) after the changes.

The company fleet was upgraded to cleaner and greener vehicles. Interface joined several programmes such as Trees for Travel[105] to offset carbon[106] produced through travel. Employees were given cash rewards for shifting to less polluting vehicles.

6. Sensitizing Stakeholders

Interface's stakeholders comprise its employees, customers, investors, suppliers, and just about anybody else with an interest in Interface. Interface wanted to set the industry

---

103 *Note*: A BTU refers to the amount of energy needed to raise the temperature of 1 pound of water by 1°F.

104 *Note*: The SmartWay(r) program initiated in 2004 by the EPA is a public-private collaboration to reduce emissions resulting from transportation. It incentivizes increased efficiency of the supply chain.

105 *Note*: Trees For Travel is a Dutch initiative where people and companies can offset the GHG emissions of their air travel by paying the foundation to plant and maintain forests.

106 *Note*: Carbon offsetting refers to credits gained for the reduction in emission of carbon dioxide or its equivalent in GHG.

standards when it came to sustainability—and it wanted to draw all its stakeholders into its circle of influence.

The idea was that if Interface could remain financially sound and viable while being sustainable, it would inspire others to emulate its environmental footsteps.

7. Redesigning Commerce

'…Current commercial practices are guided by the promise that we can stay the way we are, live the way we have, think the thoughts of old, and do business unburdened by real connections to cycles, climate, earth, or nature. Restorative economics challenges each of these assumptions.…'

Paul Hawken, The Ecology of Commerce

EXHIBIT 12.7[107]   Progress of the initiatives undertaken from 1996 to 2013 by interface to achieve MT sustainability

	Water usage per unit of product (gallons per square yard)	Waste to landfill from carpet factories (pounds in millions)	Renewable energy usage (%age of total energy use)	Energy user per unit of product (BTU per square yard)
1996	1.9	12.5	0%	13,827
1997	1.5	11.4	0%	12,175
1998	0.5	9.0	3%	10,962
1999	0.8	6.8	6%	13,518
2000	0.7	7.8	7%	12,834
2001	0.7	5.3	9%	12,275
2002	0.6	3.7	8%	10,397
2003	0.5	4.2	7%	9993
2004	0.5	4.4	10%	9360
2005	0.5	5.2	16%	8655
2006	0.4	5.2	19%	8339
2007	0.5	4.9	34%	8039
2008	0.5	4.8	33%	8631
2009	0.4	3.3	34%	9228
2010	0.4	3.5	34%	9232
2011	0.3	2.5	35%	8647
2012	0.4	2.0	36%	8430
2013	0.3	1.2	35%	8396

---

107 Adapted from the data available at http://www.interfaceglobal.com/Sustainability/Our-Progress/Energy.aspx, http://www.interfaceglobal.com/Sustainability/Our-Progress/Waste.aspx, and http://www.interfaceglobal.com/Sustainability/Our-Progress/Manufacturing.aspx'; last accessed on 12 August 2014.

Interface made a shift from selling products to selling services. It realized that what people wanted is not a carpet but an aesthetically appealing interior with less noise from walking, foot comfort, durability, cleanliness, and flexibility. This did not require the sale of a carpet. So, Interface embarked on a bold move to change its business model—the very core of how they were making money. Carpets were leased instead of being sold. Interface would handle carpet maintenance, take back the worn carpet after use, and replace it with something new. The Evergreen Lease was thus created.

The benefits of this new model were many. The customer got new carpet at zero capital cost and Interface had a steady supply of old carpet to feed its recycling process. Only those sections of carpets that were most worn out (usually this was only 20 per cent of the floor covering) had to be replaced, allowing the remaining carpet to be used for longer periods of time.

All these are just a few of the initiatives undertaken by Interface to reach the Mt Sustainability summit. Interface is extremely transparent with regards to its progress in different areas such as energy, climate, waste, facilities, transportation, design process, manufacturing, innovations, and culture (see Exhibit 12.7). A 2009 article published in Greenbiz gave an insight into some statistics. GHG emissions have gone down by 71 per cent as compared to 1996 values due to actual reductions and offsets. Energy consumption per unit of production is down by 44 per cent and 72 per cent of Interface's global energy needs are met by renewable energy. Three factories run completely on renewable energy. At least 24 per cent of the raw material content is recycled or bio-based. By 2010, Interface had almost achieved its goal of zero waste.

About Ray Anderson

'..Part cheerleader, part scold, part dreamer…[Anderson is] the rarest of hybrids: a born-again green industrialist..'

Fortune Magazine

Born on 28 July 1934, Anderson was the third son of William Henry Anderson and Ruth McGinty Anderson. His mother had been a teacher and was instrumental in making Ray love books. Ray's other passion was football. A football scholarship saw Ray in Georgia Tech where, after a brief stint in aeronautical engineering and textile engineering, he finally chose industrial engineering and graduated with honours in 1956. For the next 17 years he worked in different capacities at Milliken and Callaway before starting Interface.

He has received several awards and accolades for his work on sustainability. In 1996, he won the Inaugural Millenium Award from Global Green and was named Entrepreneur of the Year by Ernst and Young. He was one of Time's Heroes of the Environment in 2007. In 2010, he won the Lifetime Achievement Award from GreenLaw, the Inaugural Global Sustainability Prize from the University of Kentucky, and the Sustainability Award from the Women's Network for a Sustainable Future among many others. He was awarded 12 honorary doctorates. He died in 2011 after a prolonged battle with cancer.

The Way Forward

There are many challenges facing Interface. Not only do employees have to ensure sustainable practices in their factories but also make sure that suppliers follow sustainable practices. Interface is still relying on complex and costly inventions and innovations that are yet to materialize to move beyond the low hanging fruit in sustainability. Behavioural changes among employees and motivational levels have to be sustained, if Interface is to move to the next level.

According to Lindsay James, Director, Strategic Sustainability, InterfaceFLOR, Chicago, and Mikhail Davis, Manager, Strategic Sustainability, InterfaceFLOR, San Francisco, the biggest challenge will be to keep the efforts on track after Anderson's death. They say, 'Vision and inspiration don't appear on the balance sheet, but their absence will show up there sooner or later if we fail to pay attention…'

Discussion Questions

1. The case study speaks about 'seven fronts' that needs to be tackled to reach Mt Sustainability. Assume that you are the Chief Sustainability Officer (CSO) of the organization that you are associated with now (it could be an educational institution, for-profit company, etc.).

    (a.) What could be the possible challenges that you may face while tackling these fronts in your organization's journey towards Mt Sustainability?

    (b.) What could be the ways through which you can meet those challenges?

2. What are the possible ways through which, practicing sustainability, would have benefitted Interface? Assess this from the perspective of (a) customers, (b) employees, (c) shareholders and investors, (d) government, and (e) civil society organizations/NGOs. You are also free to collect information from sources other than those mentioned in the case study.

CASE STUDY 4

COMPENSATION FOR WATERSHED SERVICES AT LOS NEGROS, BOLIVIA[108]

People from upstream Santa Rosa and downstream Los Negros, in the Santa Cruz valley of Bolivia started a compensation-for-watershed services (CWS) scheme where the land users downstream provided compensation to upstream land owners for improved land use and water management practices. This compensation mechanism, instituted with the support of Fundacion Natura Bolivia (Natura) was in the form of beehives, apiculture training, barbed wire, and other tools that helped to compensate for the opportunity costs incurred by the upstream farmers. A number of external donors had funded the scheme to cover start-up costs, transaction costs as well as for studies, to measure the effectiveness of the scheme. The CWS enhanced livelihoods, water management, and helped in conserving forests and biodiversity. In spite of constraints like lack of trust, unclear property rights, lack of hydrological data, high costs, etc., the concept was successful and soon spread across neighbouring municipalities.

ABOUT BOLIVIA

Bolivia, a landlocked country situated in central South America, was divided into nine administrative divisions. The majority of the population of Bolivia was located in the administrative divisions of La Paz, Santa Cruz, and Cochabamba. The varied geography of Bolivia consists of the peaks of the Andes in the west, to the eastern lowlands, situated within the Amazon basin. The country's household income, in terms of the purchasing power standard, was the least in South America. Forestry and agriculture supported the small villages. While agriculture only accounted for 13.6 per cent of the country's GDP, it provided employment for 32 per cent of the country's population. However, the village economy faces problems like deforestation, soil degradation, water pollution, loss of biodiversity, and so on. Economic activities of the country included agriculture, forestry, fishing, mining, and manufacturing goods such as textiles, clothing, refined metals, and refined petroleum. The country was also rich in minerals, especially tin. The country's population was 10 million, as per 2012 census data—31 per cent of this population was from the 0-14 years age group, 63.1 per cent from the 15-64 age group while 6.1 per cent belonged to the 65 and over age group. The gender ratio of the population was 0.99 males per female.

---

108 *Note*: This case is prepared as the basis for group discussion rather than to illustrate either effective or ineffective handling of a situation. The case is written by Sayani Kaneria. The case has been prepared based on secondary research. This case study is released to the public domain without cost. While the case writer holds the copyright to this case study, the reader may reproduce, distribute, publish, and transmit this case study in any form including photocopying, recording, or other electronic or mechanical methods provided that no text or figures are altered.

Biodiversity

Bolivia consists of 4 types of biomes, 32 ecological regions, and 199 ecosystems. The country also had a number of natural reserves and parks. Bolivia had over 200,000 species of seeds, including around 1200 fern species, 1500 *marchantiophyta* and moss species, and more than 800 fungus species. There were more than 3000 species of medicinal plants and over 4000 kinds of potato. Bolivia was also considered the place of origin of chilli peppers, the peanut, the yucca, the common bean, and several species of palm. Bolivia was also the sixth most diverse country in the world with more than 2900 species that include 398 mammals. It had 1400 bird species that account for 70 per cent of the birds known to the world. There are more than 3000 types of butterflies, more than 60 domestic animals, 277 reptiles, 204 amphibians, and 635 fresh water fish.

Law of the Rights of Mother Earth

The 'Law of the Rights of Mother Earth', a Bolivian law gained global attention as one of the unique laws in the world that considers nature to have the same rights as humans. The law established the legal character of Mother Nature as 'collective subject of public interest'. The law entitled seven rights to Mother Nature and her constituent life systems, including human communities—(1) to life, (2) to the diversity of life, (3) to water, (4) to clean air, (5) to equilibrium, (6) to restoration, and (7) to live free of contamination. This law empowered citizens to sue individuals and groups as a part of 'Mother Earth' for real and alleged infringements.

ABOUT LOS NEGROS

The Los Negros Valley in the administrative division of Santa Cruz covers approximately 270 square km, thereby covering approximately 0.8 per cent of the area of Santa Cruz, which covered almost one-third of the area of Bolivia. A distance of 35 km separates the upstream Santa Rosa from the downstream Los Negros which had populations of 481 and 2970 people respectively (as of 2008). Irrigation canals provided water to the downstream Los Negros for an area equal to 1000 hectares,[109] enabling the markets of Santa Cruz and Cochabamba to get year-round supplies of carrot, lettuce, tomato, and other vegetables. Bordering the upper region of the Los Negros watershed is the 6,37,000 hectare Amboro National Park, one of the most biologically diverse areas in the world with 73 amphibian species, 145 species of mammals, and more than 800 bird species.

The Issues

The Amboro National Park and its buffer zones were threatened by illegal land invasions. Migrants belonging to Bolivian highlands entered this area for timber extraction and to clear the forest for agricultural purposes. The local communities were helpless due to

---

109 *Note*: One hectare being equal to 10,000 square metres.

unclear and unregulated property rights systems. Thus, forests were cut down, wildlife species disappeared, and the Los Negros river dried up earlier every year. Deforestation and cattle-grazing activity were affecting the region. Out of the 3000 children living in the region, almost one-sixth of them spent a significant amount of time away from school suffering from diarrhoea that was caused by drinking water contaminated by the cattle.

Dry season water flows in the Los Negros valley had halved in the last two decades. This scarcity was due to many factors such as increased water usage by upstream irrigators, inefficient water distribution system, and changes in land use causing low water supply. Many downstream land owners pointed a finger at the increasing upstream deforestation but no mechanism existed through which these farmers could influence the upstream land use decisions.

The Solution

In order to find a solution, people from upstream Santa Rosa and downstream Los Negros asked the support of Fundacion Natura Bolivia (Natura), an environmental group. Together they worked to:
- To build consensus and increase local understanding about the reasons behind the drying of Los Negros river and the reduced dry season water flows
- To assess the possible economic consequences of solving the problem

For this purpose, they conducted pilot studies in the upstream Santa Rosa and downstream Los Negros to know about the current situation in terms of the environment, infrastructure, economics, future plans, and needs. Interactions with 200 farmers (168 downstream and 32 upstream) gave inputs regarding types of land use, prices, produces from the land, cost of production, and the variation of costs according to water availability. One hectare of land with a reliable water supply was worth $6000 while a similar area of un-irrigated land was worth only $500. Natura also helped in the formation of Environment Committees in both of these regions.

The farmers expressed their interest to invest in upstream forest conservation to improve water supply. Along with Natura, they pioneered the innovative approach of solving such problems through a scheme called CWS. The project had a general objective to strengthen and consolidate the innovative community led CWS system in the Amboro National Park/Los Negros Watershed. Specifically, commencing in year 2003, the project aimed at protecting 2500 hectares of diverse cloud forest located in upstream Santa Rosa by the year 2007 through annual CWS. The start-up cost of the project, with approximately $40,000, along with running transaction costs, was provided by external donors.

Beehives and Barbed Wire

On 11 January 2003, Santa Rosa and Los Negros community agreed that the downstream water users from Los Negros would provide a compensation for upstream watershed protection in the form of one bee box for every ten hectares of water producing cloud forest, along with training in honey production. The cash equivalent of such compensation was to be about $3 a year per hectare payable upfront. For the initiation of the scheme, Natura used donation funds from the US Fish and Wildlife Service[110] for providing 60 beehives and training 5 farmers in apiculture for conserving 592 hectares of cloud forests. Natura deliberately chose to develop a dual-service Payment for Ecosystem Services (PES) scheme because the forest conservation in Santa Rosa provided several services like biodiversity support, watershed protection, carbon sequestration, pollination, etc.

Sustained support for the PES scheme required understanding of the environmental linkages. Hence in 2004, Natura started an environment education project focusing on children and teachers in six watershed communities that included Santa Rosa, Sivingal, Los Negros, Palmasola, Valle Hermoso, and Pampagrande. The organization also conducted workshops with 17 downstream farmers to discuss issues regarding water management, disposal of agrochemicals, and the promotion of an irrigator association so that problem solving can be institutionalized. Around 70 per cent of the farmers in Los Negros expressed a non-zero Willingness-To-Pay (WTP) for protecting the forest, summing up to an amount of $12,487 to $19728 (approximately 0.7 per cent to 1.1 per cent of annual household income). The Municipality of Pampagrande funded the project with more than $2000 to purchase additional bee boxes.

Interestingly, the contract renewal for the year 2006 saw requests from many Santa Rosa farmers for compensations in the form of barbed wire rather than beehives. The farmers explained that enclosing their land with barbed wire would help them strengthen their existing land claims. Also, it helped them keep their cattle away from environmentally sensitive areas. Some preferred fruit tree seedlings.

Monitoring and Compliance

The original contracts were for a year but some long term contracts (up to 10 years) had been introduced responding to demand. The payments were to be made annually

TABLE 12.3 Coverage by Natura through CWS in the years 2003–2007

Year	No. of farmers	Area enrolled
2003	5	592 hectares
2004	12	844 hectares
2005	21	1111 hectares
2006	39	2100 hectares
2007	46	2774 hectares

---

110 *Note*: The US Fish and Wildlife Service is a federal government bureau dedicated to the management of fish, wildlife, and natural habitats. This bureau works within the Department of Interior.

and the honoured contracts can be re-enrolled. A 'Project Control Team' comprising of one member from the upstream environmental committee, one member from downstream environmental committee, a field technician from Natura, and the land owner visited the parcels of land of all farmers enrolled in the program. The visit was made every 12 months and the committee assessed the parcel for effective conservation, noted down any damages, changes, and other points of interest. A report thus prepared was submitted to the Enforcement Directorate, comprising of the President of Natura and both the Presidents of the upstream and downstream environment committees. The Directorate made a final recommendation on actions to be taken against infractions.

Grading of Forests

Natura introduced a new concept in the year 2005, that some types of vegetation were more worthy of protection than others. For example, the intact cloud forests[111] and grasslands continued to receive $3 per hectare annually due to their primary importance of being a bird habitat and also water provision. The non-cloud primary forests situated at lower elevations were considered slightly less valuable for bird habitat and water provision, and hence received an amount of $2.25 per hectare annually. Using a similar logic, the mature secondary forests, or forests that are disturbed by permanent cattle grazing received $1.5 per hectare annually. This included cloud and non-cloud forests. The less important young secondary forests and disturbed grasslands received zero compensation. It was a generally well-accepted concept among all the land owners and payments were decided based on the quality of conservation and the vegetation type.

Short-term Success

Natura's short term objective of covering 2500 hectares of diverse cloud forest in upstream Santa Rosa through CWS was achieved when 46 farmers were protecting 2774 hectares by August 2007. Table 12.3 shows their progress through the years.

Scaling up to Other Municipalities

While the Municipality of Pampagrande made a second payment of $2500 in 2007, the people from Los Negros, Comarapa, and Mairana voted in favour of increasing their water tariffs by 9 per cent, 15 per cent, and 7 per cent respectively. The scheme had spread to the neighbouring municipalities of Comarapa and Mairana which protected 12000 more acres (4856 hectares) through conservation contracts. In Comarapa every $20 invested by Natura and its donors was matched by local funds of $30. This money was used to buy a beehive as compensation for the conservation of 5 acres of water producing forests for a period of five years. The concept scaled up when the governor

---

111 *Note*: As per UNEP-WCMC, cloud forests are evergreen mountain forests found in the tropical areas where local conditions cause mist and cloud to frequently come in contact with the forest vegetation. (http://www.unep-wcmc.org/tropical-montane-cloud-forest_229.html)

of the administrative division of Santa Cruz created a 1.8 million acre protected region for the conservation of the forested headwaters in the Santa Cruz valleys. The water fund concept soon spread amongst the municipalities of Moro Moro, Vallegrande, Postrervalle, Samaipata, and Pucara. Also by the year 2008, a group of irrigators in Santa Cruz valley started paying an annual amount of approximately $5 per person for the watershed services and by the year 2010, a total of 63 families were conserving 10,000 acres of land (4046 hectares).

Challenges and Solutions

The challenges faced in this process and the solutions worked out are listed in this section.

Lack of trust   There was a lack of trust among the upstream and the downstream population. However over time, the interactions between these communities helped them to slowly start building on their trust.

Unclear property rights   Lack of clear property rights and credible institutions did not guarantee contract compliance and an efficient market. Technology was used to re-enforce hand written bills of sale and purchase. The conservation plots were measured and demarcated using a hand held GPS receiver, the data of which was plotted on a land-use map based on the satellite image. The community people agreed on the usage of wire fencing, trails and signs for field demarcation.

Establishing binding contracts   The buyers and sellers co-designed the contract by themselves. For political reasons, Natura could not legally enforce compliance of the contract. Hence, Natura helped buyers and sellers draft contracts that provide locally acceptable and enforceable sanctions for non-compliance that respected local beliefs, customs, and culture.

Lack of hydrological data   It was not known how much of the reduced downstream dry season water flow was caused by increased irrigator demand upstream rather than reduced supply. Nor was it clear how much of the reduced water supply was due to factors other than land use changes, for example climate change. To deal with this problem of insufficient data, the stream depth and flow at four points in the Los Negros river, and in eight of its tributaries was regularly measured. Combined with the daily measurements, these data provided for building a hydrological baseline and monitoring scheme.

Leakage   The PES contracts were not based on the total size of the farm owned by the farmer and hence there were chances of 'on-farm leakage'. For example, upstream farmers may enroll patches of their forests which they would have not cut anyway due to its poor agricultural potential. Another leakage may be in the form of forest cutting activities being shifted to areas outside the system. The project would fail in such a case because it would not result in a net decrease in the deforestation happening in the watershed.

Permanence   PES contracts were for a maximum of 10 years. This political decision was taken to minimize land appropriation fears among the farmers. However, there had been incremental trust building and the landowners voluntarily asked for contracts with longer durations.

Landless immigrants   The immigrants in Santa Rosa who did not own any land were unable to participate in the PES scheme. A few of the PES enrolled farmers had sold the beehives to some of the immigrants who specialized in apiculture. Some of the landless immigrants were given employment to take hydrological measurements, while some others were hired as 'bee experts' who helped in managing the beehives. Some other farmers hired them for honey processing.

Efficiency of beehives compensation   When considered as a physical asset, a beehive had a monetary value of $30. The apiculture training given along was valued at $35 per participant. Yet the welfare effects were not determined by these values. The return on beekeeping was extremely dependent on the skill of the owner. Hence the most skilful beekeepers benefitted while others incurred a loss. Due to this, some PES recipients opted for alternative modes of payment.

Others issues   Benefits were provided to all the community members who could affect conservation. This may encourage migration of people to conservation areas just to take advantage of the compensation payments. The transaction costs were high in such schemes. There was also the need to avoid the perverse incentive of a responsible land owner not putting his land into permanent conservation so that he can receive annual payments.

Benefits from the Project

The following are the benefits received from this project:

Poverty alleviation   The primary beneficiaries included the Santa Rosa and Los Negros communities. While the downstream Los Negros farmers were ensured water supply for agricultural production, the members of the Santa Rosa Environment Committee upstream who belonged to the poorest economic class were also benefitted by the scheme.

Migrant invasion   The CWS model created mutual interdependence among communities and thereby resisted incursions from outside migrants or unwanted political pressures. This was very much beneficial in a country where the property rights were enforced less rigorously. Over the years, there had been no instances of migrants invading PES-enrolled land.

Preservation of forests   The scheme protected forests, conserved biodiversity, and enabled sustainable resource management while addressing problems like water pollution, channel-flow diminution, and sedimentation. Compensation in the form of beehives further enhanced the value of the forest.

Adaptability of the model   The CWS model was developed so as to adapt to the local needs with the objective of applying the idea to other watersheds, municipalities, and countries. The model provided the local water users with accurate information, transparent and fair institutional mechanisms, and appropriate incentive structures.

Donors   The scheme was successfully implemented due to help from various donors who acted as buyers of the services. Some of the donors included US Fish and Wildlife Service, Food and Health Foundation, The Conservation, The International Institute for Environment and Development, The Garfield Foundation, The United Nations

Development Program Small Grants Program, The BlueMoon Fund, The European Union, ESPA—Ecosystem Services for Poverty Alleviation, and The Municipality of Pampagrande.

Ascertaining the Effectiveness

Maria Teresa Vargas from Natura noted, 'While it all sounds great on paper, we haven't yet proven that these funds are really catalyzing new conservation in areas which otherwise would be degraded or deforested, and if local people really have received benefits that would not have occurred without the funds.'[112] In the year 2009, Natura approached Harvard's Sustainability Science Program and Vrije University, Amsterdam, to develop a program evaluation by conducting a study that could show whether direct incentives for the conservation of land and water were effective.

The experts from Harvard's Sustainability Science Programme designed an evidence-based evaluation that included statistical analysis of comparison of 130 villages in the protected area. All the 130 villages were given information about better cattle-grazing practices, alternative ways to live off forests, and the threats to watersheds. Through a simple public lottery, half of these villages were chosen at random. These 65 villages were enrolled in the payment scheme. Follow up data on the comparison between the two village groups would indicate whether the compensation paid was effective among the sites receiving payments, and also if these payments had an impact on the perceptions about the environment, local livelihoods, and local institutions. The 65 villages which were non-treated would be enrolled back into the scheme once the experiment results were acquired.

Ecosystem Services for Poverty Alleviation (ESPA) backed the project implementation until the researchers returned to the field for assessing the preliminary results of the study. Meanwhile, officials in Bolivia had designed a national strategy based on this project. Natura Bolivia helped them pilot the plan while seeking sites in the world in order to further develop the evaluation model.

Discussion Questions

1. Does CWS have scope in India? If yes, what are the areas in which CWS could be applied? Cite possible examples.
2. 'Santa Rosa and Los Negros community agreed that the downstream water users from Los Negros would provide a compensation for upstream watershed protection in the form of one bee box for every 10 hectares of water producing cloud forest, along with training in honey production.' Is it unique to provide honey bee boxes, instead of monetary payment, as compensation? Why? Will this be an effective method?

---

112 http://www.ecosystem-alliance.org/sites/default/files/documents/ARA%20Program%20Evaluation.pdf, last accessed on 23 February 2014.

CASE STUDY 5

RADIANT CLOTHING: COMMUNICATING THE VALUE OF AN ENVIRONMENT-BASED STRATEGY[113]

(A fictional case study that attempts to bring the reader's attention to Puma's endeavours related to environmental accounting)

Heather Jacobson had always been a fan of Patagonia (www.patagonia.com), a company that creates high-end outdoor clothing while at the same time caring about the environment. Being an active outdoors person herself she appreciated the quality offered by Patagonia and didn't mind paying a bit extra knowing that the company was trying to help protect the environment and outdoors that she enjoyed.

Using her outdoors passion as motivation and Patagonia as an inspiration, Heather started her own athletic apparel company three years ago—Radiant Clothing. She initially focused on athletic tops (short sleeve and long sleeve) made for the Canadian climate. This quickly expanded to include thermal underwear, pants, and jackets. From the onset, she made donations to environmental causes (10 per cent of net after-tax profit) a part of the company's practices. Her Vice President of Marketing (VPM) recently emailed her a copy of PUMA's Environmental Profit and Loss report[114] and it made her wonder if she was doing enough. Upon completing an analysis of the environmental impact along its supply chain PUMA concluded that if Planet Earth charged PUMA for the resources provided by her, the company would have had to pay €145 million. Although this analysis did not impact PUMA's financial bottom-line, it opened the company's eyes it terms of the impact of its operations on the environment. It helped Heather realize that her company was probably making a huge environmental impact.

THE COMPANY

Radiant Clothing, located in London Ontario, is a three-year-old business specializing in manufacturing a variety of athletic clothing for the 'urban adventurer'. Heather recognized that there was a growing population like her—Generation X and Y (25–50 year olds)—that, while busy working, appreciated a balanced lifestyle and didn't hesitate

---

113 *Note*: This case is written by Melissa Strom, Assistant Professor, Edwards School of Business, University of Saskatchewan, Canada and Suresh Kalagnanam, Associate Professor, Edwards School of Business, University of Saskatchewan, Canada. This case is prepared as the basis for group discussion rather than to illustrate either effective or ineffective handling of a situation. This case is dedicated to Sri Sathya Sai Baba, who visioned a world where education is offered with love and discipline, and free of cost. In line with that vision, this case study is released to the public domain, free of cost. The authors hold the copyright to the case study. Feel free to reproduce, distribute, publish, and transmit this case study in any form, by any means, including photocopying, recording, or other electronic or mechanical methods provided that the copyright, acknowledgement, and gratitude clauses are included.

114 http://about.puma.com/wp-content/themes/aboutPUMA_theme/financial-report/pdf/EPL080212final.pdf, last accessed on 14 August 2014.

to take time to explore and go on adventures and travel. They also didn't mind paying a bit more for quality and a Canadian brand name. Despite being a very young company Radiant has enjoyed a positive financial position from its first year of operations (Appendix 12.1 shows the company's latest financial statements).

ENVIRONMENT AS A CRITICAL VARIABLE

Radiant's senior management team was in the process of developing its strategic five year plan and they were sincere in wanting to emphasize the inclusion of environment as an area of strategic importance. Heather Jacobson made sure to surround herself with like-minded individuals as she was expanding the company—Allan Woo as the Chief Financial Officer (CFO) who was an avid kite-surfer who travelled to Cuba each year for the same, Sara Singh as Vice-President of Operations (VPO) who regularly travelled for rock-climbing, and Iman Ahmed as the Vice President of Marketing (VPM) who enjoyed competitive biking and running.

Heather wondered what else she could do and in what other ways she could integrate the environment into the practices of the company. Reading PUMA's report gave her several ideas and possibilities. She realized there was a spectrum of ways she could integrate—ranging from focusing on short-term goals with short term-returns such as developing environmentally friendly packaging to developing long-term goals with long-term returns such as changing production processes to reduce energy consumption. Regardless of which strategic option she chose, each would require detailed plans, such as marketing, and a strong implementation plan.

Heather convened a meeting with the senior management with the goal of presenting her ideas and to get feedback on potential impacts and ways to ensure continued success. Prior to the meeting, she sent out the PUMA report and asked the senior management to read it to help facilitate discussion.

THE MEETING

Jacobson, CEO (Jacobson) :	Thank you everyone for making it to the meeting today. I would like our business to pay more attention to the 'environment' as an important decision variable, and I have come up with a few ideas that I would like your feedback on.
Singh, VPO (Singh) :	We are on board with you Heather, but what were you thinking? Right away I am wondering if you want to change our current processes.
Ahmed, VPM (Ahmed) :	Or do you want to give out more donations each year?
Jacobson:	I am thinking bigger. I don't think we are currently doing enough. It's great that we are donating funds each year, but is it enough? Are we even making any impact? Should we

be doing more? I want to find out how we can change the company to have lesser impact on the environment and do 'greater good'?

I have three potential 'environmental positioning' ideas that I would like further thought and analysis on—the *first* is to maintain status quo, our donation of 10 per cent each year of net after tax profit. But, I would like this to be properly communicated so we have greater sales. In turn, this would allow us to donate more money. I was wondering if we could also quantify the impact of our donations. Are we doing this?

Ahmed: Not yet. We indicate on our website that we make the donations and show a list of organizations that we help each year.

Jacobson: Sounds like there is more we can do. Consumers should know when they purchase our items that a certain %age is helping in environmental causes. Perhaps it will encourage them to buy more. Is there any research on this? Do consumers buy from companies that are more environmentally or socially responsible?

Ahmed: Well… is that our goal? To generate more sales?

Jacobson: I'm not going to turn down more sales—but I'm hoping in doing so it will better the causes we are trying to support. All of us are here with this company because we love the outdoors. I don't feel we are doing enough to protect what we love. I think we need to change the objectives of the organization to better align with the mission and vision that we recently created (see Appendix 12.2). I think that we're not doing enough, especially after reading the PUMA report that Iman sent me.

As a *second* option, I was thinking we could change our inputs and manufacturing processes to be more environmentally friendly. For example, we can replace the Merano wool that we import with locally grown organic hemp and cotton. Or, we could refine our processes to capture waste water and recycle it.

Singh: Wow! 'Change the company'? We just got all of our manufacturing processes finalized with our suppliers. It sounds like what you are proposing may disrupt all of that and have dire consequences. We may no longer have a profit to donate to charities with (see Fig. 12.1 for Radiant's current processes).[115]

Jacobson:	That is short term thinking—we need to get away from that. I'm sure there is a way to work with our current suppliers, or create relationships with new ones. What about creating a concept of shared value with all our stakeholders? Is there a way to work with our suppliers so that they can lessen their environmental impact?
Woo, CFO (Woo) :	That is what PUMA indicated they did in their Environmental Profit and Loss Report. It explains in which processes it used energy, water, and produced waste as well as pollution production (see Fig. 12.2 and Appendix 12.3). It quantified the cost to the environment along its supply chain and recognized that it needed to work with suppliers to truly make a difference.
Jacobson:	Woo, you can probably use those numbers as a benchmark for assessment of options. This leads to my *third* option wherein we change the way we think about our business by fully integrating the environment into our company's culture. In my mind this means that every decision we make, we must consider its impact on the environment.
	However, regardless of which option we pursue there is a critical role for marketing and communication. Therefore, I am keen to know what Iman (Ahmed) has to say in terms of marketing and communication.
Ahmed:	Each stakeholder will require their own unique perspective in terms of marketing and communications. We have to communicate to the end consumer, but also to partners along the supply chain as well as our own internal stakeholders. Then there are various other stakeholders such as regulators and environmental groups. But based on what Heather, you, have been saying it looks like the most important stakeholder is nature which is affected by changes to the environment. Will there be an increased budget for marketing?
Jacobson:	Before we talk about budget I want ideas. How best to communicate what we are doing?
Ahmed:	Are we pursuing all the three options that you mentioned?
Jacobson:	That is what I want everyone's feedback on. Woo and Singh are to determine financial implications of the proposals

---

[115] *Note*: The production process includes a combination of manual and automated processes, some of which are outsourced. The majority of equipment is at least three years old (Radiant purchased a plant that was shut down four years ago). Raw materials are purchased from suppliers located in Asia, Europe, and North America.

	and I want you (Ahmed) to consider the marketing and communication implications.
Woo:	I realize the importance of marketing, especially given that the rest of our competition is not sitting idle. Mountain Equipment Coop (http://www.mec.ca/Main/home.jsp) publishes an accountability report for its ethical sourcing, community contributions, and how the company has 'greened' its operations. Even Columbia Sportswear (www.columbiasportswear.ca) has a link on its website which discusses the company's environmental impact. Companies such as Patagonia, Alo, and Gaiam are changing the face of how companies do business.
	I understand what you are getting at; you want to 'build the environment' into our products and processes. We have to be careful. We need to determine the best way of doing this; we must be strategic. This will cost us—are you thinking that we raise prices as well?
Jacobson:	I'm not sure. We may be able to raise prices (see Appendix 12.4 for some examples of current prices). Iman, what do you think?
Ahmed:	We have to be careful how we communicate—today's consumers are very savvy and more aware. You may have heard of the term 'greenwashing'—consumers can quickly find out which companies really are 'green' and which ones are trying to capitalize on society's concern for environmental welfare by spending a lot of money on advertising about being green, versus spending money on environmentally sound practices. We need to be transparent. Check out The Sins of Greenwashing website (http://sinsofgreenwashing.org/); if we want to start branding ourselves as a green organization we have to make serious changes and commitments. It is a big undertaking. What I mean is that Radiant should not be paying just lip service to the environment; we must actually include it as an important factor in our planning and decision making, along with other factors such as cost and quality.
Jacobson:	Absolutely.
Singh:	Clearly, we must be prepared to make trade-offs and refocus by aligning our short and long-term goals with our strategic priorities.

Ahmed:	You are absolutely right about the trade-offs. Environmental initiatives cost money and this takes away from the bottom line. But I think if we are more strategic about our marketing this doesn't have to be the case.
Woo:	Well, we cannot just hike up the price or else we'll start losing our customers. Surely we have a responsibility in terms of not charging outrageous amounts to our customers. I would like to think that we cater to more than just the wealthy few across the world.
Ahmed:	Be careful; it is often a misconception that taking on environmental initiatives costs more money. It is true in the short-term but often makes financial sense in the long-term. In addition, more people are willing to purchase from environmentally conscious companies. There are trade-offs but not as much, or as detrimental, as people think.
	Depending on how much we integrate environmentally in our policies, we will likely have to re-brand the company. We are currently positioned as a Canadian company that makes high-end athletic apparel for the outdoors. We would now want to integrate the 'green' into the branding. I don't think it will change our current customers, but it will likely open up a whole new market for us.
Woo:	And new competitors to worry about!

The meeting concluded with Jacobson reiterating the tasks laid out.

Leaving the meeting, Heather Jacobson felt very optimistic about the direction of the company. The past three years she had spent in getting the business up and running and now it was time to focus in on why the company was started in the first place. It was all about making big strides on the environmental front. However, she wondered if the move should be gradual/incremental or should there be a massive change (a major shake-up).

Meanwhile, back in her office, Iman was rethinking her decision to email the PUMA report to Jacobson. She realized that she had a big task ahead of her. She knew that she had to create several potential marketing strategies based upon how much 'environment' was integrated into the business. She would have to identify the target market, potential competitors, and methods to communicate what the company was doing and make sure value was created in return. She also realized she had to start with creating new objectives for the organization that would be included in the five-year strategic plan (see Appendix 12.5 for a sample of Radiant's current objectives).

She was also contemplating what she should be communicating. Was the end goal sales? Or, was it about educating consumers? Or, about explaining why the company was using different inputs or processes? Wouldn't that have a better long-term impact and coincide with what the company was ultimately trying to do? But, how can one do that without taking away the short-term sales?

Iman laid down her immediate tasks—she had to first think whether change should be incremental or comprehensive. One the basis of which she had to chalk out—who were the key stakeholders, what did they value, and how best to communicate to them. Also, how to make sure the communication supported the key goals of the organization which she needed to reformulate.

Discussion Questions

1. What is the value of PUMA's environmental profit and loss report for organizations such as Radiant?
2. What are the three 'environmental positioning' options that Heather Jacobson is considering? What are the pros and cons of each option? Should Radiant move gradually from one option to the next or make the transition to full integration right away?
3. Develop objectives for the three different positioning options. More specifically, develop communication and marketing related objectives.
4. What is the importance of communicating Radiant's environmental positioning to its stakeholders? Who are the most important stakeholders and how will communication differ from one stakeholder to another?
5. Assume that Radiant's senior management decides to make the transition to the third option over a five-year period. What are the implications of this decision in terms of marketing strategy?

APPENDIX 12.1

RADIANT CLOTHING'S FINANCIAL STATEMENT FOR THE YEAR 2014

RADIANT CLOTHING
INCOME STATEMENT FOR THE YEAR ENDED SEPTEMBER 30, 2014

	2014	2013
Sales	$ 42,108,394	$ 42,986,456
Cost of goods sold:		
Materials	$ 18,098,285	$ 18,983,250
Labour	$ 6,983,122	$ 7,447,641
Power & fuel	$ 845,352	$ 696,672
Other manufacturing costs	$ 2,348,719	$ 3,467,170
Gross margin	$ 13,832,916	$ 12,391,723
Operating expenses:		
Selling expenses	$ 4,327,700	$ 4,103,689
Administrative expenses	$ 5,959,236	$ 5,193,227
Income before interest, depreciation and taxes	$ 3,545,980	$ 3,094,807
Less:		
Depreciation	$ 1,091,642	$ 865,636
Interest	$ 471,528	$ 388,102
Income before taxes	$ 1,982,810	$ 1,841,068
Income tax	$ 545,273	$ 506,294
Net income	$ 1,437,537	$ 1,334,775

RADIANT CLOTHING
BALANCE SHEET AS OF SEPTEMBER 31, 2014

	2014	2013
ASSETS		
Current assets:		
Cash	$ 1,198,915	$ 658,806
Accounts receivable	$ 2,432,692	$ 2,442,450
Inventory	$ 9,326,203	$ 9,036,723
Investments, short term	$ 969,764	$ 786,007
Total current assets	$ 13,927,574	$ 12,923,986
Property and equipment:		
Land	$ 1,801,200	$ 1,801,200
Buildings and equipment, net	$ 8,335,338	$ 7,195,178
Total property and equipment	$ 10,136,538	$ 8,996,378
Total assets	$ 24,064,112	$ 21,920,365
LIABILITIES AND SHAREHOLDERS' EQUITY		
Current liabilities:		
Accounts payable	$ 3,299,540	$ 3,134,818
Current portion of long-term debt	$ 1,000,000	$ 1,000,000
Total current liabilities	$ 4,299,540	$ 4,134,818
Long-term liabilities:		
Long-term debt	$ 5,500,000	$ 4,000,000
Total long-term liabilities	$ 9,799,540	$ 8,134,818
Shareholders' Equity		
Preferred shares ($100 @ 20,000 shares)	$ 2,000,000	$ 2,000,000
Common shares ($12 par @ 500,000 shares)	$ 6,000,000	$ 6,000,000
Additional paid-in capital	$ 1,000,000	$ 1,000,000
Total paid-in capital	$ 9,000,000	$ 9,000,000
Retained earnings	$ 5,264,572	$ 4,785,547
Total shareholders' equity	$ 14,264,572	$ 13,785,547
Total liabilities and shareholders' equity	$ 24,064,112	$ 21,920,365

APPENDIX 12.2

MISSION AND VISION OF RADIANT CLOTHING

Mission

Radiant Clothing makes you a responsible outdoor explorer.

Vision

Radiant Clothing's long-term vision is to become a leader in environmental and financial sustainability.

APPENDIX 12.3

KEY FINDINGS FROM PUMA ENVIRONMENTAL PROFIT AND LOSS REPORT

Drivers of environmental impact	The impact(s)	Monetary value (millions of Euros)
Water use: Used principally in the production of agricultural products, in industrial processes.	• Water scarcity • Loss of habitat for other species • Climate change • Impacts on recreation in and around water courses	47
Greenhouse gas emissions: Arising from the burning of fossil fuels in electricity generation and transport, as well from land use conversion and cattle rearing.	• Climate change • Resulting floods/droughts/storms • Impact on crop yields	47
Land use: Converting land into buildings for production use.	• Increase in scarcity of land	37
Other air pollution: Resulting from the burning of fossil fuels as well as through the drying and processing of timber.	• Smog and acid rain • Impact on health, agriculture, and property • Acidification of waterways and soils	11
Waste: Operations and supply chain produces a variety of hazardous and non-hazardous waste	• Visually unpleasant landfills • Greenhouse gas emissions • Pollution of water courses	3
	Total	145

Source: Adapted from PUMA's Environmental Profit and Loss report (also available at http://about.puma.com/wp-content/themes/aboutPUMA_theme/financial-report/pdf/EPL080212final.pdf).

APPENDIX 12.4

PRICE LIST OF SOME OF THE CLOTHES OF RADIANT CLOTHING

Shirts		Jackets	
Women's V-neck	$59.00	Women's down sweater (zip up)	$280.00
Women's running crew neck	$56.00	Women's parka (winter coat)	$500.00
Women's tank top	$50.00	Women's thermal hoody	$250.00
Women's long sleeve	$67.00	Men's down sweater (zip up)	$280.00
Women's pullover top	$80.00	Men's parka (winter coat)	$600.00
Men's T-shirt	$47.00	Men's thermal hoody	$250.00
Men's hoody	$80.00	Pants	
Men's running shirt	$50.00	Women's khaki pants	$100.00
Men's running shirt-sleeveless	$40.00	Women's sweatpants	$90.00
		Men's khaki pants	$120.00
		Men's sweatpants	$100.00

APPENDIX 12.5

CURRENT OBJECTIVES OF RADIANT CLOTHING

Financial objective

Maintain 7 per cent growth in gross sales year after year.

Achieve 5 per cent net profit margin by 2015.

Maintain 25 per cent gross profit margin every year.

Social objective

Donate 10 per cent of net after tax income to environmental charities every year.

Raw materials

- Radiant chooses the materials that it will use in its products. Options include natural fibers (wool, silk, linen, cotton and hemp) or man made fibers (polyamide and acrylic). Radiant's products are primarily cotton-based (not organic) and merano wool.
- Radiant's raw materials come from Asia, Europe and North America.
- Environmental Considerations:
  - Man made materials often made from petrochemiclals
  - Nylon hard to recycle (30 to 40 years to decompose)
  - Chemicals and pesticides that farmers use for naturial fibres can cause harm and contamination
  - Destructiveness of intensive farm practices (wildlife)

Processing

- Processing includes dying, printing, bleaching of the raw materials
- Radiant handles 60% of its processing in house. 40% outsourced to raw material supplier.
- Environmental Considerations:
  - Dying and printing consumes vast amounts of water and chemicals
  - Energy intensive process

Manufacturing

- Manufacturing includes cutting, sewing and assembly.
- Radiant completes its manufacturing in house.
- Environmental Considerations:
  - Working conditions and pay for employees
  - Pollution caused by the factories (depending on local government requirements)
  - energy intensive process

Shipping and sales

- Radiant ships its finished products to warehouse in Missisauga. From there, product is shipped weekly to 40 retail locations across Canada to be sold (vis truck).
- Environmental Considerations:
  - Pollution from modes of transporation used

End of life cycle

- Once apparel is used, what will be the process for reclamation? Will the item be thrown away? Re-used? Recycled to make further clothing?
- Radiant has no recycling or re-using process in place.
- Environmental Considerations:
  - Landfill waste (filling fast)

FIG. 12.1 Radiant Clothing's apparel manufacturing process

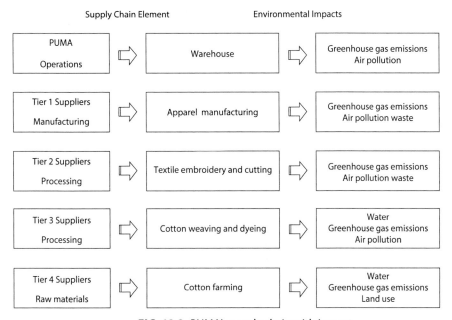

FIG. 12.2 PUMA's supply chain with impact

Note: Adapted from: http://about.puma.com/wp-content/themes/aboutPUMA_
theme/financial-report/pdf/EPL080212final.pdf

CASE STUDY 6

PROJECT GREENHANDS[116]

Trees and humans are in an intimate relationship. What they exhale, we inhale, what we exhale, they inhale. This is a constant relationship that nobody can afford to break or live without.[117]

Sadhguru Jaggi Vasudev

Project GreenHands (PGH or GreenHands) is considered to be a grassroots ecological initiative that created green consciousness among the populace of Tamilnadu (TN), a state in the Southern part of India. This initiative was planned to promote sustainable living, by planting 114 million (11.4 crore) saplings in the shortest span possible.

Planting 25,000 saplings in the Tsunami affected coastal districts of Tamil Nadu marked the beginning of the project in the year 2005. In the following year, over three days in the month of October, 256,289 people volunteered to plant 852,587 saplings in 6284 locations across 27 districts in TN, and with this initiative, GreenHands made an entry to Guinness World Records (see Annexure 12.1). By the end of 2013, Greenhands had planted 19.7 million saplings.

GreenHands worked under the aegis of Isha Foundation[118] (Isha), a non-governmental organization that worked with a mission towards the betterment of the individual, society, and the world. The success of the project had been attributed to the inspiration of Sadhguru Jaggi Vasudev (Sadhguru), partnerships with corporate organizations, non-governmental organizations (NGOs), community involvement, and a commitment shown by volunteers associated with the project. Implementation of the project had been an inspiration to many. A comment at the website of GreenHands mentioned, 'The Project GreenHands is great inspiration to the younger generation. It is great service to the humanity. The overwhelming dedication of the volunteers is to be greatly appreciated. We can surely create a greener earth." In 2010,[119] Government of India (GoI) awarded GreenHands with the Indira Gandhi Paryaavaran Puraskaar, the highest award given by GoI to individuals and organizations that have made significant and measurable contributions in the field of environment protection and improvement. In the same year, Project GreenHands won the Beyond Sport award for the category 'Sports for Environment' at a summit in Chicago, US. This award is

---

116 *Note*: This case is prepared as the basis for group discussion rather than to illustrate either effective or ineffective handling of a situation. Unless mentioned otherwise, all quotations used in this case study were derived through primary research. All characters in the case are real. The case is authored by Ajith Sankar R N. This case study is released to the public domain. While the case writer holds the copyright to this case study, the reader may reproduce, distribute, publish, and transmit this case study in any form including photocopying, recording, or other electronic or mechanical methods provided that no text or figures are altered.

117 *Note*: Quote taken from the website of Project Greenhands

118 www.ishafoundation.com

given to organizations that use sports as a tool to mobilize community for their social cause. On 5 April 2012, the Department of Environment of the Tamil Nadu State Government awarded Project GreenHands with the 'Environmental Award—2010'. On 13 July 2013, PGH was awarded the LASSIB Society Honorary Award on social responsibility for its valuable service in the field of environmental and ecological restoration.

Evolution of GreenHands

GreenHands had its root in Vanashree Eco Project, which was started in 2002 to conserve and protect the Velliangiri mountain range, where Isha Yoga Centre is located. Isha volunteers used to sow lakhs of seeds to propogate the native species in the area to revive the ecology and biodiversity of the mountains. The formal initiation of GreenHands started in 2004.

It was in December 2004 that TN, along with other Indian states, witnessed a major devastation in the coastal regions due to the Indian Ocean tsunami.[120] The lore is that the Isha volunteers, who were rehabilitating the affected people, observed that coastal areas that have enough tree cover were damaged less as compared to those areas that had less tree cover. Soon, Isha volunteers started using trees to connect with people affected by grief and tragedy. Saplings were presented in white cloths accompanied by roses, to grief struck families and they planted those saplings for their loved ones. More than 1000 saplings were thus planted. Once the project met the objective, volunteers idealized to scale up the project. 'Prodded by the project director, we then kept a plantation target of 5000 saplings. While the earlier plantation happened within residential areas, these saplings were planted within residential compounds,' mentioned Anand, a plant biologist, and a full-time volunteer of GreenHands who has been coordinating with the plantation activities since the beginning of the project. On 25 December 2005, GreenHands planted 5000 saplings in the seashores of the tsunami affected villages of Periyakuppam, Pettodai, Aiyampettai, Nayakarpettai, Thamananpettai, and Nanjalingampettai in Cuddalore district (The district collector, Gagan Dheem Singh Bedi, was the chief guest). In addition, GreenHands also planted 5000 saplings on the roadside, 5000 at villages, and 10,000 saplings at lands belonging to Panchayats.

'Isha Foundation wanted to do it large-scale. When we shared our stories of sapling plantation with other members of Isha, they chipped in. Swami Prabodha said that he will mobilize resources to plant one lakh trees. Such commitment was received from a number of people. We came to know that Sadhguru wanted to speak to the Chief Minister of Tamilnadu about this endeavour,' conveyed Anand. GreenHands soon came of age.

---

119 *Note*: For year 2008
120 *Note*: The Indian Ocean tsunami, which occurred on 26 December 2004 caused approximately 225,000 deaths in eleven countries, inundating coastal area with waves as high as 30 meters or 100 feet.

In 2006, the project entered the Guinness World Book of Records. The launch of the 2007 planting season started at Chennai, capital of TN, on Sunday, the 23rd September. In 2007, GreenHands decided to showcase some of its endeavours, and thus started focused plantation zones in seven districts. The plantation zones had been functioning with the support of corporate organizations like Suzlon and Yves Rocher. In November 2008, the TN forest department and GreenHands planted 25,000 saplings at the 22,000 reconstructed houses in TN, as part of the Tsunami Rehabilitation project.

Scope of the Probem and Design Considerations to the Response

'When I travelled around Tamil Nadu, I realized that the landscape was changing so rapidly that it would turn into a desert much before the projection of 2025. I saw thousands of palm trees with their crowns having fallen off. Palm trees can survive even in a desert but in Tamil Nadu they were losing their crowns because of the exorbitant exploitation of ground water. In Coimbatore city, about 15 years ago, one had to just dig 125–150 feet to find water for a well, and now one has to go 1400–1500 feet down to find water. Earlier the rain water was scarce, now it's in excess and so the degeneration was happening rapidly. Then as part of global warming system the southern peninsula is seeing a very excessive level of rainfall…. without vegetation, excessive rain can accelerate the desertification process because the top soil runs off.'[121]

Sadhguru

Speaking about conceptual underpinnings about the project, Ethirajulu, the concept designer for GreenHands had this to say, 'We have become an energy intensive civilization. On keen observation, we can find that what we eat is not food, but fossil fuels. The food that we eat has become poisonous, the air that we breathe is getting poisoned, and it is the same with everything that we intake. By simple, logical deduction we can conclude that man and the world has to go extinct. Man is the problem. I was into the design of structural systems. For me, a solution is built into the problem itself. If man is the problem, then man is the solution. Man's extinction is one solution. The only other solution that exists is that man has to do something about the troubles he has created for himself.' When GreenHands assessed the spread of forest cover in TN, they found that it was only 17.5 per cent, as per the data available with the forest department, while the national and global benchmark was 33 per cent.

GreenHands team assessed how many trees need to be planted to increase the green cover in TN by another 10 per cent. Therefore, the 114 million (11.4 crore) number was born. The belief was that the remaining 5–6 per cent would be done by the self-propagation capability of trees. In an interview, Sadhguru said, 'Actual statistics and practical logistics may come in the way, but the rationale is very simple —with the right kind of focus and motivation, the gap between what is needed and what is possible could be very small.' GreenHands believed that if every individual of TN can raise two saplings, which will not bring any major financial burden on the individual or the state,[122]

121 http://www.kavitachhibber.com/main/main.jsp?id=sadhguru-Dec2007

the target of 114 million can be surpassed. 'Each and every one had felt in the Isha Yoga classes that we are the parents of the entire world and the divine manifests in each and everything surrounding us,' remarked Boris Bhim A (Bhim), a part-time volunteer with GreenHands. Citing the role of GreenHands, Bhim continued, 'I could feel that I am responsible for every thing happening around me.'

Engaging Volunteers

'We wanted to make it a people's event. The project needed to be owned by volunteers. Opportunities were provided to all.' said Anand. Following are some of the ways through which GreenHands mobilized people by providing them with opportunities to:

- create awareness about the initiative (engaging the community through events, presentations, meetings and stalls, putting up posters, talking to family, friends, and corporations),
- be part of the planting process (seed sourcing, creation of nurseries, distribution, and planting of saplings), and
- supporting the project by offering resources (donations, fundraising, sponsorship, partnership, offering material resources, creation of social responsibility initiatives among corporate, etc.).

One of the attributes that attracted volunteers to GreenHands was the genuineness associated with the project. 'There is no cooking up of figures here—internally or externally. I cannot work in an organization which cooks up stories,' quipped Anand.

Processes Involved

Awareness Creation

Creation of awareness about environmental degradation was the initial step that GreenHands needed to undertake. GreenHands first communicated that trees were an essential part of our lives and not an entity distinct from us. The relationship with trees needed to be enhanced in order to enhance one's own sense of well-being. Through the years, GreenHands had been undertaking massive campaigns with the objective of taking the message across all strata of population. The part-time volunteers focused primarily on their own localities and conducted presentations, processions, video shows, games, and talent competitions for students, and nature awareness tours and hill cleaning initiatives. In the initial phases, sapling distribution was done free of cost in order to generate and attract interest towards GreenHands. However, this practice was changed. In 2014, PGH charged a minimum commitment fee of ₹5.00 for the saplings. 'In our experience we have felt that when we charge a minimum amount even if it is as less as ₹5.00 people take more responsibility and make sure they do not waste the sapling. Not just that, this contribution from general public becomes the seed money for sustenance of nursery in the ensuing year. In the earlier years, many nurseries could not

---

122 *Note*: The estimated population of Tamilnadu, as of March 2008, was 6.64 crore (66.4 million).

operate continuously because the volunteers were not able to raise funds for the nursery operations. So, we wanted to make the nursery self-sustainable. The volunteers do not have to spend time on fund raising for buying the inputs needed for the nursery,' said Archana Anand, a volunteer at PGH.

Volunteer meetings were organized to share information and learning. In cities, awareness was created through multiple media channels like newspapers, advertisement on television channels, posters, banners, hoardings, and fund-raising concerts. GreenHands also used Isha music CDs, Sadhguru's programmes on radio and TV channels, and Isha events to create awareness about the project (see Annexures 12.2, 12.3, and 12.4 for campaign related details).

In villages, volunteers did door-to-door campaigns, public announcements, and meetings. In 2007, Isha Agro Movement (IAM), a sub-project under Project GreenHands was launched to address the concerns faced by the farming community in India, especially in the context of farmer suicides that was increasingly occurring in India. This movement combined agro-forestry with organic farming practices. In addition, IAM also provided education programmes. GreenHands volunteers stayed with the villagers and met farmers. They also worked in co-ordination with organizations that were in the field trying to help the farmers. Brochures were distributed in more than 3200 villages. Isha's social outreach programmes came in handy. Isha *Gramotsavam* (village festival), an event for people belonging to 3200 villages in the state of TN, was used to promote GreenHands. The festival consisted of sports and games activities (rural olympics), rural food festival that offered more than 250 culinary preparations, rural cultural show that exhibited native art forms and handicrafts, a musical programme, and a Satsang with Sadhguru. Events like Agri-fest 2007 and 'rural olympics' promoted interest at the grassroots level.

Awareness meetings in villages were given much importance. In the meetings with villages, GreenHands communicated the importance of trees. 'The basic energy for sustenance of life on this planet is coming from the Sun. The energy transfer happened because of the existence of plants and trees. By destroying the trees, we destroyed our source of food. The kind of food we take in is very important—it is like medicine. It can nourish us or it can kill us. Self-healing capacity is there in us, it is there in nature. I am a diabetic patient since 30. For the past 25 years, I have not taken any medicines. This self-healing capability is not communicated to the humanity, probably because there is no money making possibility in human well-being,' said Ethirajulu. Awareness meetings were an on-going process and GreenHands believed that these meetings had resulted in almost 1.5 million people being aware of the project.

Decision makers, like politicians and bureaucrats, were introduced to the project by inviting them to involve in inaugural and closing ceremonies of planting and distribution of saplings. They were also given individual presentations about the project.

Nurturing and Development

'While on our visits, we saw people—be it tribals or people from other sections of the society, performing a number of rituals to bring rain. Destroying nature and then doing prayers will do no good. It was in this context that the idea of starting a nursery came about. Our nurseries started very small. We used to put 10 seeds in 10 packets daily. This initiative was more of a personal interest. It was in 2004 that nursery activities started picking up momentum,' said Swami Nagaroopa (Swami), Nursery co-coordinator, GreenHands.

GreenHands had to nurture and develop the saplings along with the awareness campaigns. The first step was sourcing healthy seeds. The selection of saplings was based primarily on two aspects: (1) quality and speed of growth, and (2) commercial value of the tree/products from the tree. For rural areas, seeds of fence trees, fruit trees, fodder trees, and timber trees were nurtured. For urban areas, avenue trees and medicinal tress were nurtured. Seeds of pioneer trees were nurtured for land development. (see Annexure 12.5 for the list of trees whose saplings were grown in GreenHands nursery).

GreenHands developed hundreds of nurseries—through sourcing of healthy seeds, creation of seed pockets and beds, distribution to planting zones—with the help of its partner organizations. GreenHands classified nurseries under four types—regional nurseries, corporate nurseries, nurseries maintained by educational institutions and centralized nurseries. Centralized nurseries were fully managed by GreenHands. Though all types of saplings were grown in centralized nurseries, the number of saplings nurtured in the first three types of nurseries was limited. The corporate nurseries were established in 2007 and centralized nurseries in 2008.

Training was given to volunteers on creating nurseries. The first nursery for GreenHands came up at Isha Foundation Centre at Velliangiri Hills, near Coimbatore. The nurseries were small, with a capacity of producing 1000–10,000 numbers of saplings. In February 2006, the first nursery outside Velliangiri Hills started. In 2007, GreenHands started nurseries that could produce 50,000 saplings. In the same year, GreenHands produced 40 lakh saplings (4 million). In 2008, it was 21 lakh (2.1 million) and in 2009, GreenHands produced 25 lakh (2.5 million) saplings and since then on an average, nearly 2.5 million saplings are produced every year in these nurseries.

During the collection of seeds, the health and maturity of mother tree was taken into consideration. Seeds from those trees that were young or old were avoided. Almost 70 per cent of the seeds were collected during April, May, and June—the months before the rainy season. Volunteers and self-help groups collected 40 per cent of the seeds for the avenue and fodder trees. The rest of the seeds were made through purchase. 'In the initial phases of the project, we did not have any contacts or money. Substantial amount of effort came from volunteers, and their mobilization was an important aspect. I was talking too much during this period,' laughed Swami. On collection of seeds, they were brought together to an area where they were cleaned, selected, packaged, and sent to appropriate nurseries.

The idea was to develop a nursery close to a planting zone in order to limit transportation as it entails transportation costs and risks damaging the saplings. GreenHands carried out a loading technique through which 8–10 layers of saplings were transported, with a maximum capacity of 10,000 to 12,000 saplings. An additional 10 per cent sapling was carried as a buffer in each truck, in order to account for any damage to the sapling or any possible replanting need. The transportation was done in a minimum of 10 days prior to the planting day, so as to account for a seasoning period.

Planting times also varied. For jack fruit, the planting had to occur within two days from the time of seed collection, while it was two months for oil seeds. In order to ensure the healthy existence of the seed, especially for those with a short time span, they were soaked in hot/cold water, or were soaked in *panchakviam*.[123] Some of the seeds were taken through anaerobic pre-germination before they were sowed in the motherbed.[124] Development of the sapling included processes like preparation and cleaning of the land, motherbed settlement, creation of Mist Chambers,[125] germination of seeds, preparation of planting pockets, transplantation of germinated seeds, nurturing in shade for two weeks with daily watering, exposure to sunlight to stimulate growth with alternate day watering, rearranging to curb root growth, weeding (3 weeks after transportation and once during subsequent 2 months), transportation, and planting. 'Growing a sapling is like growing a child. Experiencing everything as one is spirituality,' voiced Swami.

Sapling Distribution and Planting

'Of all economic activity that happens in a nation, agriculture is the most fundamental and also of paramount importance. A nation that neglects its farmers is bound to dislocate its basic life sustaining infrastructure.'[126]

Sadhguru

The mission of GreenHands is to inspire people and enable them to plant trees. GreenHands distributes saplings to third parties, who do the planting. In this model, plantation is done throughout the year. The responsibility of nurturing and monitoring the saplings that were planted are given to individuals/groups who take the onus of planting the saplings. Awareness generation was the key in the success of this model. 'Individuals and concerned groups had been approaching GreenHands as the preferred destination for saplings,' said Anand. Through this model, 1,434,382 saplings were nurtured.

---

123 An organic manure made up of cow dung, cow urine, sugar, milk and tender coconut.
124 The place where seeds are grown. The motherbed is made out of a mixture of river sand, red soil and cow dung.
125 Chambers with temperature and humidity control facilities

The other model followed by GreenHands was the Agroforestry model. These were funded projects. Explaining the Agroforestry model, Ethirajulu said, 'Soil is the basic entity that we have to protect. It takes thousands of years to create top soil. Trees play a major role in the creation of top soil; Plant trees to protect top soil. That was the origin of Project GreenHands. If soil has to be protected, it has to be done at the farmers' land. That was the beginning of Agroforestry model. Our belief is that trees can be a solution to everything. It gives back to man the connection to life that that he lost. This project is an attempt to make that connection.' The agro-forestry model was started in 2007. 'Farming is like gambling now. Farmers are concerned and insecure. Initially they had concerns that planting trees at their fields would reduce them of their income generation and the productivity of the land will go off, though the reality is otherwise. In order to alleviate farmers out of their concerns, we ask the farmers to grow the trees in the boundary. As the trees mature—it can be a fruit tree or a timber tree—it becomes like insurance. This campaign started working. This formed the basis of our agro-forestry model. We are now very clear on where trees should be planted and not planted,' mentioned Anand. Till 2012, nearly 2 million saplings had been planted through this agro-forestry model.

From 2009 onwards, GreenHands has been conducting systematic training programme on agro farming for farmers. This training, which has modules on organic/natural farming, is given by experts to volunteers who will deliver the same to the farmers.

Baseline surveys and need assessment surveys were done before plantation was done. GreenHands distributed the saplings to those with commitment towards the project. Presence of local dignitaries and popular personalities attracted attention to the project and provided awareness to people about the objective of GreenHands. These meetings were also used to encourage people to be part of this project. Planting zones were designated in areas of local support. In recent times, majority of the planting was done in these zones. The opportunity to plant the saplings were given to the volunteers of the rural community. This helped GreenHands generate enough support and commitment in those areas.

Farmlands, schools, residential areas, water catchment, and waste land areas and roadside were chosen as areas of focus. Farmlands were usually protected from invasion from cattle. Saplings of fruit trees, fodder trees, fuel trees, and timber were planted on the farmlands. Preference was given to plant the saplings on the farmlands of those farmers who showed commitment, for example, by supplying compost, sand, and vermin-compost. Tropical dry evergreen plants, which were native to TN and also drought resistant, were used in school grounds. 'Live seed banks'[127] were also created in these schools. This helped in the conservation of a number of tree species. School children looked after these plants. In addition to saplings, pitting materials were also supplied to schools by GreenHands. For residential areas, only saplings were provided by GreenHands. Pitting and planting were done by residents of these locations. It was the onus of the residents, who planted

126 *Note*: From the website of Project GreenHands
127 *Note*: Live seed banks are growing trees. They act as sources of seeds during seed collection.

fruit and medicinal saplings, to prepare protective gear for the saplings planted. To plant saplings in water catchment and waste land areas, GreenHands used paid self-help groups. Tropical dry evergreen forest species and water-tolerant species were used in the water catchment and waste land areas respectively. All resources—saplings, pitting material, and protective gear—were provided by GreenHands. Saplings of avenue trees were planted at the roadsides by the local community, with saplings, pitting material, and protective gear provided by GreenHands. (see Annexure 12.6 for the tree planting procedure criteria and methodology following while pitting and planting). Speaking about plantation on the roadside, A Murugesan, a GreenHands volunteer, who worked in Erode-based[128] KGM Softwares Pvt. Ltd said, 'It is very difficult to find place to plant trees.'

Post-plantation Care

Post-plantation care for the saplings included watering, organic manuring, pruning, replanting, and protecting the sapling from grazing animals. In water catchment areas and wasteland areas, GreenHands engaged paid self-help groups to provide this post-plantation care. In other areas, like farmland, schools, residential areas, etc., the sapling planters were responsible for ensuring post-plantation care.

Community Involvement

'In the Indian culture there are temples for trees, people worship trees; it's a very common practice. It is not a question of a custom. It came from a certain experience and understanding. It is a certain depth of experience and understanding—you understand that whatever nurtures your life is worth worshipping.'[129]

Sadhguru

It was realized that the success of the project depended on strong partnerships. The project focused on developing partnerships by energizing community, whether they were farmers, school going children, businessmen, academicians, parents, etc. Community involvement thus became the essence of the project.

GreenHands volunteers visited villages and spoke to the farmers, assessing the interest of the people there. The villagers were shown documentaries and discussions were initiated amongst the villagers. When the volunteers felt that there was sufficient commitment among the villagers who owns lands, they were initiated into the next level—integrating trees along with the prevailing crops. At the district level, a regional office was set up and this hub was used to share resources during the project period. 'The uniqueness of this project is that we are involving large number of people, common people, in planting trees. The volunteers—they are all joining because of Sadhguru. He is the heart of the project. He is like a super-hero for us. I cannot move a finger without him,' said Swami Nagarupa.

---

128 *Note*: Headquarters of Erode district in the state of Tamilnadu, India.
129 http://www.organicgreenandnatural.com/2009/04/08/project-greenhands-%E2%80%93-compensating-the-earth/, last accessed on 10 March 2015.

Business organizations were contacted and GreenHands engaged them in making environmental care a part of their CSR initiatives (see Annexure 12.7 that lists out some of the business organizations that are associated with GreenHands). Jacques Rocher, President of the Yves Rocher Foundation mentioned in his blog, 'Out of this ecological initiative grew a human project. In fact, the people of Tamil Nadu are planting directly onto their parcels of land the trees that are most useful to them. They are planting fruit trees to meet an emergency food shortage and trees that reclaim the soil as a medium-term initiative. They are also planting construction wood to meet long-term goals.'

GreenHands utilized the already established goodwill of Isha to spread awareness about the green initiative. In order to develop a win-win partnership with other NGOs, the project offered the NGOs an array of activities that acted as a source of employment and income generation. This helped the NGOs in achieving their objectives. For GreenHands, the NGOs helped in taking the environmental initiative to large and diverse group of people. The NGOs also provided GreenHands with the needed manpower to implement the project.

PGH has also actively involved youth in its programs. Seeking to bring about a sense of awareness and reverence for nature in school and college-going kids, it has conducted various tree planting drives and mass awareness campaigns across schools and colleges. As a part of their efforts to involve children in ecological restoration efforts, PGH launched the Green School Movement in the year 2011. The mission of the Green School Movement is to create 'green consciousness' among school children through a change in their attitude, by involving them in sapling production and plantation. The project aims to create nurseries that will produce 18 million saplings by 2014, and will involve 450,000 school students from 9000 schools in 32 districts of Tamil Nadu. In 2011 as a pilot, a total of 600 schools in Erode and Coimbatore districts were chosen to be a part of this program, with a target of producing and distributing 2000 saplings each, every year. Almost 25,000 school children from nearly 503 schools contributed to the planting of 1.2 million saplings. In 2012, the project was initiated in Erode, Coimbatore, Krishnagiri districts of Tamil Nadu, and Union Territory of Pondicherry.

Some of the not-for-profit organizations that GreenHands partnered with included Eranda Foundation of UK [through Integrated Rural Development Center (IRDC)], Center for Low External Input Sustainable Agriculture (LEISA),[130] OAZONE,[131] National Agriculturist Awareness Movement (NAAM),[132] The Rotary Club,[133] The Lions Club,[134] The Indian Red Cross,[135] and Joint Action for Sustainable Livelihood (JASuL).[136] GreenHands also associated with Grow your Trees Foundation, GVN Trust, Velicham, Go Sakthi, Best Trust, etc. *Tamilaga Iyarkai Uzavar Iyakkam* (Tamilnadu Organic Farmers

---

130 *Note*: An organization whose mission was to promote organic farming.

131 *Note*: Engaged in rural development through water management projects.

132 *Note*: An India-based national organization working towards new farming methodologies.

133 *Note*: Rotary Clubs are located across the globe and its purpose is to bring together business and professional leaders to provide humanitarian service, encourage high ethical standards in all vocations, help build goodwill, and peace in the world.

Movement), founded by Dr Nammazvaar,[137] was another organization that GreenHands partnered with, to promote organic farming to farmers. Dr Nammazvaar visited many villages to promote awareness about GreenHands.

Resource Mobilization

Bhim, who had done the Isha Yoga programme, thought raising funds had been one of the difficult tasks. When GreenHands started preparing for the Guinness World Record endeavour, there was no money in the GreenHands account. There was no assured funding for the project. The initial support came from Isha Foundation. GreenHands spent approximately ₹40 for nurturing the sapling, planting it, and monitoring it for one year. Planting 114 million trees required substantial funding support.

'There is no assured funding. The theme of donor organizations varies every year. The risk is always there. We want to increase our focus on individual donors through web-based fund raising,' said K. Sekar, Project Director of Isha's Social Outreach programmes. GreenHands had a number of contribution options for donors. From 2007 onwards, there was a gradual improvement in the availability of funds. GreenHands also came out with a 'Gift of Trees' scheme were one can gift a donation of trees in the name of another person, with a monetary donation of ₹50 for each tree sapling that needs to be planted (see Annexure 12.8 for an example of 'Gift of Trees' certificate). GreenHands delivered a gift certificate to the donor or to the person on whose name the gift was made. In an interview given to Blue Planet Green Living, Sadhguru had mentioned the need for cash as a limiting factor in expansion of the project. A similar sentiment was echoed by Swami who said, 'Monetary support is necessary for the project. People are appreciative about the project. They now need to come forward and support the project.' GreenHands also came out with a 'World Environment Day' campaign where, for ₹100, one can plant a tree and GreenHands will do the planting, and post-planting care for two years till the tree sapling become self-sustainable. Through this campaign, the donor was also updated with the location coordinates where the tree sapling was planted and name of the farmer nurturing their trees.

PGH also explored partnership with for-profit organizations as an official tree planting partner. For its corporate partners, PGH provided them with detailed update about the farmers and farmlands where the agro-forestry saplings were planted. Post-planting status updates and digital photographs were shared with these partners. PGH asked for a minimum funding of ₹5,00,000 from these corporate partners, and in return, the

134 *Note:* Founded in United States, Lions Club motto is 'We Serve' and the organization focuses on activities related to sight conservation, hearing and speech conservation, diabetes awareness, youth outreach, international relations, environmental issues, and other programs that support the local communities where Lions live.

135 *Note:* A voluntary organization, which is part of the International Red Cross and Red Crescent organization. The Indian Red Cross engage in providing health and care to vulnerable people and communities.

136 *Note:* JASUL, based at Madurai, is a forum of several NGOs across Tamilnadu. The forum was created with the objective of preservation of natural water sources.

137 *Note:* A farmer and an agricultural scientist known for his experience in organic farming and agro-forestry.

corporate partner was able to list PGH as its official tree planting partner in the company website and other communication media. Two-thirds of the funding for PGH came from Yves Rocher Fondation, France. Individual donation and sapling sales contributed 19 per cent of the funding, while the remaining came from corporate funding.

Project Monitoring

GreenHands had an advisory board that included experts in forestry, organic farming, tree plantation, and related fields. They provided guidance to GreenHands at all levels of project implementation. Comprehensive records were maintained by GreenHands— starting from the collection of seeds, establishment of nurseries, and development of planting areas. Prior to the plantation, GreenHands conducted surveys to understand the environmental, social, and economic status of the region. GreenHands also conducted tests to check quality of soil and water. Based on these studies, recommendations were made on the type of action GreenHands should undertake. GreenHands registered the names of land owners who showed commitment to the cause. The landowners were also asked to make a formal commitment to plant and maintain trees (see Annexure 12.9 a sample of the commitment letter that a farmer has to sign). GreenHands also maintained a database of sapling distribution and planting. Follow-up and replanting requirements were done with the help of this database. GreenHands also maintained necessary support systems that helped in monitoring sapling development. These support systems included regular communication with regional offices (see Annexure 12.10 for details about plantation coordinating centres in TN). It was decided that a quarterly report would be released by GreenHands team for projects that were funded by corporate organizations. It was also decided that GreenHands website will be updated regularly (www.projectgreendhands.org) with outcomes and statistics, and the organization would come out with an annual report every year. Table 12.4 lists the result areas and the indicators used by GreenHands.

GreenHands expected many challenges in their project, and the risks were classified in different segments as shown in the following table (Table 12.5).

There were situations when maintenance of documentation was difficult. 'There are times when the usage of templates may not be effective. Volunteers come and go. There is also the necessity to ensure that information systems are aligned to local needs. Many grassroots level workers may not be having the system skills and basic English language skills. Due to the same, documentation was difficult during the initial stages of the project,' mentioned Maheshwari, who coordinated activities related to information systems. 'GreenHands have strong reporting system. We should now strengthen the evaluation based on the data we collect—project analysis, impact analysis, etc.," continued Maheshwari. She also observed that the human aspect also needed to be considered. Many volunteers had the inclination to be part of core activities and considered documentation related aspects as secondary. Swami echoed a similar sentiment. 'Collecting data from the field volunteers is a difficult thing. The activity

TABLE 12.4 GreenHands' result areas and their indicators

Result areas	Indicators
Nursery	Quantity of saplings, species of saplings, and survival rates
Planting	Number of trees planted, species, and location
Green cover	Geographical Information System (in implementation phase)
Maintenance	Surveys on sapling survival and growth
Volunteer participation	Registration numbers
Skill acquisition	Evaluation tests at the end of training period
Public mobilization	Number of events, number of participants in events

TABLE 12.5 Risks faced by GreenHands

Risk	Rising up to the challenge
Natural calamities	To undertake surveys after the calamity. This would be followed by replanting of saplings
Non-cooperation of villagers	Selection of villages that were having a harmonious relationship with other activities of Isha Foundation. Obtaining the official consent in advance from authorities and village heads
Financial risk	Application for third party funding
Nurturing of saplings	Usage of quality seeds, training to people, regular maintenance of saplings and nurseries

is done as a service and people do not want to keep a count on that. Even during the Guinness World Record initiative, we produced 11 lakh saplings, but we did not have documentation for that. We made a representation to the Guinness World Records only for 8.5 lakh because we only have records for 8.5 lakh sapling plantation.'

GreenHands believes that it had converted 65–70 per cent of the saplings it had planted to trees. 'Technically, it is not an easy job to assess the conversion figures. We did some random sampling. Based on the data we collected, we got technical inputs from a forest officer and from those inputs, we arrived at this figure. We would like the conversion rate to move up to 75 per cent,' mentioned Anand. To improve the conversion rate, GreenHands had been assessing the reasons on the variance in conversion rate at different regions. It found that conversion rate had been high in regions like Pudukkottai (as much as 80 per cent) while it is much lower in areas like Trichy (approximately 40 per cent). GreenHands had taken a decision that in regions like Trichy it will plant saplings in watershed areas only. Similar tailor-made solutions were evolved for all districts of TN.

People Dynamics

Sadhguru narrated[138] an incident that happened during his visit to Mysore for conducting a meditation program. There he met his English teacher who had taught him in school. 'And after it (the programme) was over, she came and hugged me and said, "Now I know why you didn't let me teach Robert Frost." I said, "Why would I not let you teach Robert Frost? I like Robert Frost." "No, no, do you remember you did not allow me to teach Robert Frost." I said, "Ma'am, why would I do that?" Then she reminded me and I remembered... She came and introduced Frost and she started, "Woods are lovely dark and deep..."[139] I said, "Stop it. Any man who calls a tree a wood, I don't want to listen to him." She said, "No, no, Robert Frost is a great poet." I said, "I don't care how great he is. If he calls a tree, a wood, I don't want to listen to him."'

The project started with the effort of a few people, and GreenHands did not have any formal departments. As the project started to scale up, they branched into two divisions. One is the operations—headed by zonal coordinators (who are in-charge of the nursery, planting, and monitoring work). The other is the Central Office team with the MIS, accounts, and fundraising team.

'The intensity and dedication with which people work here is unique. Whatever goals are set by Sadhguru, people will implement it here, whatever the constraint may be. If we look at the Guinness Record endeavour, it was a handful of people who drove the whole initiative,' mentioned Maheshwari. Anand recollected that he was sleeping only four hours during the months when Guinness World Record endeavour was going on. 'Here, we do not compare one person with the other. If they are giving their best, that is enough for me,' said Sekar. 'People are working here for something higher, which may not be visible outside. We are here for spiritual growth. I left a comfortable job and came to Isha. I wish to be with Sadhguru, and that's why I am here. He has provided me with a platform to be with him,' added Sekar. Sekar considered his role to be that of providing the volunteers with the basic needs like food and shelter and an activity platform where the volunteers can give their best.

GreenHands had found it challenging to get full-time volunteers who work exclusively on this project. 'We've been building the base in the past 2–3 years. Isha is having a number of social projects. We need to give importance and encourage all the projects,' opined Swami, in 2009 (see Annexure 12.11I for the organization structure of Project GreenHands).

---

138 *Note*: In a felicitation ceremony, when PGH won the *Indira Gandhi Pariyavaran Puraskar*, the highest award given by Government of India to individuals and organizations that have made significant and measurable contributions in the field of environment protection and improvement.

139 *Note*: From the famous poem titled 'Stopping By Woods On A Snowy Evening'

Transformatory Nature

'What has been most encouraging is the enthusiasm with which people have responded. Even a labourer earning daily wages to survive is willing to forgo one day's work to help plant saplings.'

Sadhguru

GreenHands has undergone major changes with its implantation approaches. In the earlier days of the project, GreenHands did not provide much focus on the type of trees that were provided to the villagers. Post 2005, the feedback was that villagers aspired for trees that were economically viable, like fruit trees and timber trees. 'There are times when I perceive that whatever we've done in earlier years were not that effective. Villagers were asking, "Why are you bringing Neem trees that we can raise ourselves?" And thus we started focusing on fruit bearing trees. We've been learning quite a lot. From 2007 onwards, we stopped sapling plantation on the roadside, and decided that somebody has to take responsibility for the saplings that are planted. We also demarcated the whole of Tamilnadu into eleven ecological zones, based on the soil condition and drought condition of the region. Then we listed down all drought resistant and economically viable trees that will grow in each of these zones. Later we selected those trees that grow in all these zones, except the Nilgiris Biosphere Reserve. Now, we distribute or plant only those trees,' stated Anand. This decision had been expected to increase the sustainability of the trees as these trees are drought resistant.

The volunteers has been feeling the transformation in their own lives. 'I feel I am fully utilized here. There had been immense personal growth here, as compared to my earlier work in a software firm. Earlier, I didn't know that I was ignorant, now I know that I am ignorant,' mentioned Maheshwari. Anand went through situations where he had to take up important responsibilities. 'This was during our preparation towards the Guinness Record endeavour. We've been meticulously planning for this (Guinness World Record) event for many months. We found despite all our prodding and communication to villagers, that only 3.5 lakh–4 lakh pits were dug by the end of September. Many of the villagers spent their time in political activities as the local body elections was coming up. Existence of pits gives a clue to how many saplings will be planted. A person who spent energy in digging the pit is certain to plant a sapling. With such a low number of pits dug, all of us were heartbroken. In one of the volunteer meeting I attended at St Joseph's college at Trichy, I saw young volunteers with tears on their eyes. Seeing all this, I told the group of volunteers that this initiative is not about breaking any kind of record. I told that we are here to give our 100 per cent, we've been giving our 100 per cent, and we will give our 100 per cent. I was only 21 then, and many of the volunteers there were much senior to me. I do not know from where such words came to me.'

While a number of volunteers associated with GreenHands came to the project due to their affiliation with Isha, there were many who took interest in the project though they did not have formal affiliation with Isha. Jayakumar K, Senior Lecturer, Bannari Amman Institute of Technology, came to know about this project through the internet.

'Though I have never participated directly in the project, it has created a craving in me to find an opportunity to make my presence in its activities,' said Jayakumar.

'There is a reason behind everything we do. Everything we do is logical. But the outcome is illogical. Our actions may inspire others in a number of ways, and we may not be aware of any of those. After our Guinness record endeavour, many people came forward with similar initiatives," remarked Ethirajulu. In the second half of 2007, government of TN came out with a 'Tree Cultivation in Private Lands in Tamilnadu' initiative. On 7 August 2008, people of Nokha Tehsil in Bikaner, Rajasthan, India, planted 105,000 saplings in three minutes and fifty seconds. On 11–12 July 2008 in the village of Chautaki in Bongaigaon, Assam, India, 300 people (villagers, NGOs, and government officials) came together to create a Guinness World record endeavour of planting 284,000 saplings in 24 hours. This record was later improved by Durango in Mexico where 348,000 saplings were planted in 24 hours by 300 people. On 14 June 2009, 300 soldiers of the 21 Jat regiment of Indian Army, with the support of district administration and the Forest department, planted 447,874 saplings in Sreegram reserve forest in Dhubri, Assam, thereby going beyond the record created by Mexico's National Forestry Commission (CONAFOR). 'Anything which has to happen on a large scale, has to be a movement, not a project. My mother has never seen Mahatma Gandhi. But, when he died, she cried. A movement touches everybody,' added Ethirajulu.

Expanding Endeavours

'It (GreenHands) is definitely carried out on a very large scale, which no other project has done at least I'm unaware of. However, the project needs revamping… Too many people are doing it, lacks innovativeness. (There is a) Need for better outreach mechanisms,' said Mangala Tewari (Mangala), Area Convenor and Associate Fellow, TERI (The Energy and Resources Institute), New Delhi. There were mixed responses to GreenHands' geographical expansion. On 22 March 2008 GreenHands was launched in Hyderabad with the sowing of 6000 seeds at Nanakramguda. 'Unfortunately the project never took off in New Delhi… if something materializes I will be the first one to take the lead in New Delhi,' mentioned Mangala. 'From where would we get the saplings? Which is best institution to target? And I'm still searching for my answers!,' added Mangala.

People at GreenHands were clear about the ill effects of the prevalent energy intensive agricultural model and environmental degradation. 'If we have to do something, we have to do it now. Sadhguru suggested that if we have to do something, it has to be done within 6–8 years time so that by the next 15 years we would have about 30 per cent green cover. We are sure that this project cannot be implemented if we wait beyond that time frame. If we become a desert land like Saudi Arabia, then our cost for nurturing saplings, planting them and monitoring them will spiral up, and we will not be in a position to implement this project,' said Ethirajulu. The organization had started the process of bringing together NGOs with similar objectives under a same platform and helped them in capacity building and creating linkages.

ANNEXURE 12.1

THE GUINNESS WORLD RECORD CERTIFICATE FOR
THE MASS TREE PLANTATION DRIVE IN 2006

ANNEXURE 12.2

CAMPAIGN MATERIALS USED IN THE 2006 TREE PLANTATION DRIVE

Number of posters	40,000
Number of handbills	8.5 lakh
Roadside hoardings	103
Mega hoardings	4
Newspaper advertisements	120
TV/radio advertisements	5
Media partner	Ananda Vikatan, a Tamil weekly
Signature campaign forms	1.1 lakh
Celebrity promotional video	2
Radio partner	Radio City

ANNEXURE 12.3

INVITATION TO A PHOTO EXHIBITION ABOUT PROJECT GREENHANDS

"Nothing resists the determination of ants."
-Victor Hugo

Project GreenHands
Greening Tamil Nadu

Isha Foundation and Alliance Française of Madras
invite you to the

Project Green Hands Photo Exhibition

Inauguration by Jacques Rocher,
Director of Sustainable Development
- Yves Rocher Group

on September 23rd, 11:00am
at Alliance Française of Madras

GUINNESS WORLD RECORDS

IN 2006, WITH THE SUPPORT OF 250,000 VOLUNTEERS, PROJECT GREENHANDS SET A GUINNESS WORLD RECORD BY PLANTING 852,587 TREES ON A SINGLE DAY.

For hundreds of thousands of volunteers in Tamil Nadu, global warming is an alarming signal to take action and reverse the disastrous environmental situation in the state.

The simplest, result-oriented measure is to plant trees. After all, only trees can provide us with oxygen and food, restore water, and protect us from scorching heat.

For the first time in Chennai, the work of Project GreenHands is presented to the public through a photo exhibition from 23rd September to 3rd October 2007 at Alliance Française, Madras.

Yves Rocher Group is the world leader in botanical beauty care and a major supporter of Project GreenHands.

Alliance Française de Madras

Location: *Alliance Française of Madras,*
40 College Street, Chennai 60006

Exhibition Dates: *23rd September through 3rd October*
Exhibition Timings: *Monday to Friday from 9am to 7pm*
and Saturday from 9:30am to 1pm

ISHA FOUNDATION

Isha Foundation in special consultative status with ECOSOC
of the United Nations is an international non-profit public service
organization dedicated to human wellbeing.

ANNEXURE 12.4

'SOUNDS OF ISHA' MUSIC CD ON PROJECT GREENHANDS

ANNEXURE 12.5

LIST OF TREE SAPLINGS CREATED IN THE GREENHANDS NURSERY

S. no.	Local name	Botanical name	Type of tree
1	Teak	Tectona grandis	Timber
2	Malai vembu	Melia azedarach	Timber
3	Mahogony	Swietenia Mahagoni	Timber and medicinal
4	Red sanders	Pterocarpus santalinoides	Timber
5	Kumil	Gmelina arborea	Timber
6	Vengai	Pterocarpus marsupium	Timber and medicinal
7	Palaa	Artocarpus heterophyllus	Fruit
8	Eti	Dalbergia latifolia	Timber
9	Karumarudu	Terminalia tomentosa	Timber
10	Poovarasu	Thespesia populnea	Timber
11	Perumaram	Ailanthus excelsa	Timber
12	Koyya	Psidium guajava	Fruit
13	Aranelli	Garuga pinnata	Fruit
14	Madhulai	Punica granatum	Fruit
15	Lemon	Citrus limonum	Fruit
16	Kariveppilai	Murraya koenigii	Spices
17	Mahilam	Mimusops elengi	Avenue
18	Sorgam	Simarouba glauca	Avenue
19	Rosia	Tabebuia rosea	Avenue
20	Jacaranda	Jacaranda mimosifolia	Avenue
21	Senbagam	Michelia champaca	Avenue
22	Iyalvagai	Peltophorum ferrugienum	Avenue
23	Racemosa	Colvillea racemosa	Avenue
24	Mandarai	Bauhinia purpurea	Avenue
25	Avellendae	Tabebuia avellanedae	Avenue
26	Argentea	Tabebuia argentea	Avenue
27	Badam	Prunus dulcis	Fruit
28	Poomardhu	Lagerstroemia speciosa	Avenue
29	Sara kondrai	Cassia fistula	Avenue
30	African Mahagony	Khaya senegalensis	Timber
31	Manja Kadambai	Haldina cordifolia	Timber
32	Sandal	Santalum album Linn	Timber

(Contd)

ANNEXURE 12.5 (*Contd*)

S. no.	Local name	Botanical name	Type of tree
33	Mungil	Bambusa vulgaris	Timber
34	Natuvagai	Albizia lebbeck	Timber
35	Vembu	Azadirachta indica	Avenue and timber
36	Pungan	Pongamia pinnata	Avenue
37	Neermaruthu	Terminalia arjuna	Avenue and timber
38	Naval	Syzygium cumini	Fruit
39	Thandrikai	Terminalia bellirica	Medicinal and timber
40	Kondrai	Cassia javanica	Avenue
41	Mayflower	Delonix regia	Avenue
42	Sivakundalam	Kigelia pinnata	Avenue
43	Vellai kadambu	Anthocephalus cadamba	Avenue
44	Thaneerkai maram	Spathodea campanulata	Avenue
45	Elai Porasa	Butea monosperma	Avenue
46	Mangium	Acacia mangium	Timber
47	Sisu	Dalbergia sissoo	Avenue and timber
48	Thanga arali	Tecoma stans	Avenue
49	Malli	Jasminum sambac	Avenue
50	Moringai	Moringa oleifera	Fruit
51	Maramalli	Millingtonia hortensis	Avenue
52	Nagalingam	Couroupita guianensis	Avenue
53	Karungali	Acacia catechu	Timber

ANNEXURE 12.6

PROCEDURE AND METHODOLOGY FOLLOWED FOR TREE PLANTING

Criteria for Choosing a Location for Tree Plantation

1. The planting location should be at least six feet away from the edge of the road/fence/compound wall. Multiple row plating is preferable. The space between each row is four'. The adjacent row planting location will be zigzag with respect to the previous or succeeding row.
2. The tree should not be placed below an electric line.
3. The location of the pit should not be where water logging takes place.
4. The tree should be planted either in protected area or in a place which is easily reachable for people to water and protect.
5. Watering and replanting should be scheduled and suitably monitored.
6. A minimum gap of seven feet and maximum gap of nine feet to be maintained between trees.
7. The seedling should not be planted in the shade of another grown tree.

Methodology of Tree Planting

1. Pit preparation

- For red soil and clay soil, the dimensions of the pit are 2' × 2' × 2'
- For sandy soil or loose soil the dimensions are 1.5' × 1.5' × 1.5'.
- The dug-out pit should be refilled with a mixture of compost and dug-out top soil.
- The compost should be evenly mixed with the soil.
- Green biomass (leaves) or non-composted material should not be put into the pit.

2. Planting

- The plastic cover should be removed carefully using blade or knife such that the clump of soil is not broken. This decides or ensures 70 per cent survival of the plant.
- If roots are grown out of the packet, it needs to be carefully cut before planting.
- The entire soil clump, holding the plant should be placed below ground level.
- After closing the pit, do not compress or harden the pit by stamping on it or by other means.
- Create a basin around the pit for better watering.
- Mulch the tree seedling after plantation with biomass (leaves or dried plant material)

ANNEXURE 12.7

LIST OF BUSINESS ORGANIZATIONS LINKED WITH GREENHANDS

International Partners

Yves Rocher Foundation, France; Price Waterhouse Coopers, UK; Give2Asia, Charity Aid Foundation,Data Source Mobility, US; Greenberg Quinlan Rosner Research Inc. UK; Monaco Modern Art, France; Association Arts & Environment, Germany.

National Partners

Suzlon Foundation, Indian Overseas Bank, L&T Construction, Chennai,

Mahindra Satyam, Hyderabad,

Mahindra & Mahindra, Hyderabad,

IBM, Oncor, Axis Mutual Fund, Zoho, Chennai,

Edelweiss, Mumbai,

Open Text, Hyderabad,

Aurobindo Limited, Hyderabad,

IRIS, ESSAR, Ordain Healthcare, Chennai,

Delphi, Banglore,

BPCL, Mumbai

AT&T, Banglore,

HAS India,

Edenred, Mumbai,

Albatross Fine Chemical (P) Ltd, Ananda Vikatan, Apollo Hospitals, Aravind Herbal Labs Pvt., Ashok Leyland, Cavinkare, Cognizant Technology, Covanta Energy, E.I.D Parry India Ltd, EB Department, Vallur Camp, Ecologic Ventures, Everest, Everest Construction, Everest Industries Ltd, GB Industry, GMR, Power Corporation, Henkel India Ltd, ICICI Lombard, Jayabharatham Furnitures, L&T Ltd, Life Insurance Corporation of India, Omkar Foundation, Orchid Chemicals & Pharma, PPN Power, Price Waterhouse Coopers, Raminium Builders, Bharat Petroleum, Sakthi sugars, Sakthi sugars, Salem Steel plant, SRF Gummidipoondi, State Bank of India, Suguna Poultry, , Take Solutions, TTK, Tube Investments, Visteon.

ANNEXURE 12.8

GIFT OF TREES CERTIFICATE GIVEN BY GREENHANDS

The Gift of Trees

In honour of ....

.... trees will be planted and nurtured by Project GreenHands of Isha Foundation in Tamil Nadu, Southern India.

This gift was made possible by...

"Trees and humans are in an intimate relationship. What they exhale, we inhale. What we exhale, they inhale. This is a constant relationship that nobody can afford to break or live without."

~ Sadhguru Jaggi Vasudev

Project GreenHands: **Raising the green cover of Tamil Nadu by 10%** in order to reverse desertification, reduce soil erosion, counteract poverty, rebuild communities, restore self sufficiency, recreate sustainability and survive climate change. Through education, mass people participation and agro-forestry implementation, 10 million trees have been planted in 5 years by 1 million people. 100 million more trees are needed to achieve the goal. Thank you for your vital contribution.

To donate, join in or learn more please visit **www.projectgreenhands.org**

PROJECT GreenHands

ANNEXURE 12.9

COMMITMENT LETTER SIGNED BY THE FARMER FOR THE AGROFORESTRY PROGRAMME

11. விவசாயம் மற்றும் மரம் வளர்ப்பில் பயிற்சி : ஆம் ☐ இல்லை ☐
அளித்தால் கலந்து கொள்வீர்களா? :

(i) ஆம் எனில்

    அ) நன்றாக மரம் வளர்ந்த தோட்டம் பார்ப்பது ☐

    ஆ) இயற்கை முறை விவசாயத் தோட்டம் பார்ப்பது ☐

    இ) விவசாயத்தில் ஊடுபயிராக மரம் வளர்ந்த தோட்டம் பார்ப்பது ☐

    ஈ) அடர்ந்த காடுகள் பார்ப்பது (மலை பிரதேசம்) ☐

    உ) உள்ளூரில் நடக்கும் விவசாய முகாமில் கலந்து கொள்வது ☐

    ஊ) விவசாய நிலத்தில் அடர்ந்த காடு உருவாக்கியவர்களின் தோட்டம் பார்ப்பது ☐

    எ) 100% மரம் வளர்ப்பதற்கான பயிற்சியில் கலந்து கொள்வது ☐

12. மரக்கன்று நடப்படும் இடத்தின் விவரம் : விவசாய நிலம்/ வீடுகளை சுற்றியுள்ள இடங்கள்/ பள்ளி/ கல்லூரி/ நிறுவனங்கள்/ அரசு அலுவலகங்கள்/ சாலையோரம்/ தொழிற்சாலை வளாகம்

13. இத்திட்டத்தில் நடப்படும் மரக்கன்றுகள் : கூண்டு/ வேலி/ சுற்றுச்சுவர்/ வீடு எவ்வாறு பாதுகாக்கப்படும்

14. தேவைப்படும் மரக்கன்றுகளின் எண்ணிக்கை : ....

உறுதி மொழி:

    மர ஆர்வலராகிய ....என்னும் நான், இந்த மரக்கன்றுகளை குழந்தைகளைப் போல் பாவித்து முழுமையாக பொறுப்பேற்று பாதுகாப்பேன் எனவும், எங்கள் தாய் மண்ணை பாதுகாக்கவும், வருங்கால சந்ததியினர்களுக்கு அர்ப்பணிப்பாகவும் என்பங்கினை செலுத்துவேன் எனவும் உறுதியளிக்கிறேன்.

                          கையொப்பம்

முன்பதிவு செய்தவரின் பெயர்:	மரக்கன்றுகள் வாங்கியவர் விவரம்:
பெயர் :	பெயர் : ....
இடம் :	இடம் : ....
நாள் :	நாள் : ....
நேரம் :	நேரம் : ....
முன்பதிவு செய்த நபர்:	மரக்கன்று வழங்கும் நபர்:
பெயர் :................	பெயர் :................
கையொப்பம்	கையொப்பம்

ANNEXURE 12.10

PLANTING CO-ORDINATION CENTRES IN TAMILNADU

Project GreenHands

84 Planting Co-ordination
Centers in Tamil Nadu

ANNEXURE 12.11

PROJECT GREENHANDS ORGANIZATION STRUCTURE

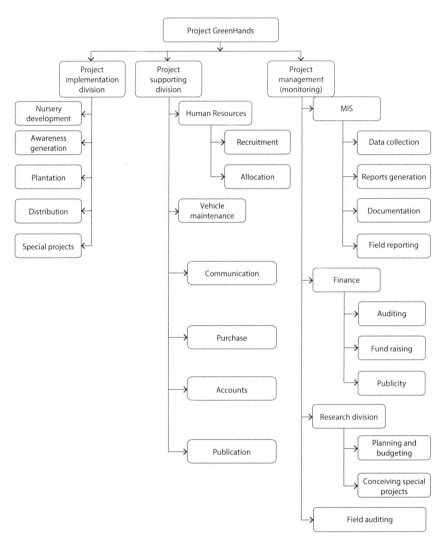

Discussion Questions

1. 'We wanted to make it a people's event.' One of the unique aspects of GreenHands was its people mobilization practices, an important element in any sustainability movement. What do you think contributed to GreenHands' ability to mobilize lakhs of people?

2. Prepare a SWOT analysis for Project GreenHands.

CASELET 1

AAROGYAPACHA AND JEEVANI

In December 1987, a group of researchers, led by Dr P Pushpangadan from The Tropical Botanical Gardens Research Institute (TBGRI), travelled to the forests of Western Ghat section in southern Kerala as part of All India Coordinated Research Project on Ethnobiology (AICRPE). Kani tribe, a tribe indigenous to the region, was a nomadic community of approximately 16,000 people. 'We went there to survey the Kani tribal settlements, but we got exhausted after a long walk. When they saw us tired, some of the Kani tribesmen, who were our guides, offered us fruits of a plant. We ate them and found that we could go on trekking for hours without fatigue,' says Dr Pushpangadan.[140]

Dr Pushpangadan was keen to know more about these fruits and their sources. Dr Pushpangadan asked them about the source of the fruits, and after receiving assurance that the information would not be misused, the Kanis showed him the fruits. These fruits belonged to a herb known as *Arogya pacha* (Trichopus zeylanicus), which in Malayalam language means, the healthy green.

Plathis, the healers among Kani tribe, are aware of the medicinal properties of the flora and fauna of the region, and this knowledge is passed on to the next generation orally. Using *arogya pacha*, the tribals were known to produce a concoction named as *malamarunnu* (the medicine from/of the mountain) which had been reported to cure liver diseases. The tribals never charged people who visited them for this treatment. While the fruits of *arogya pacha* showed anti-fatigue properties, leaves of the plant contained flavonoid glycosides, glycolipids, and other non-steroidal compounds with adaptogenic and immmuno-enhancing capabilities.

TBGRI developed a herbal drug from *arogya pacha* and the drug was patented as 'Jeevani'. In 1995, the commercial release rights was given to Arya Vaidya Pharmacy, Coimbatore for seven years, with a licence fee of ₹10 lakhs and a 2 per cent royalty fee from the profits on the sale of the drug. The licence fee and royalty was shared between TBGRI and the tribal community on an equal basis. A trust, Kerala Kani Welfare Trust, was formed and the amount of the tribal community was transferred to this trust. The interest accrued from this amount was used for the welfare activities of the tribe. Initially, TGBRI trained 25 tribal families to grow *arogya pacha* and were given seed money for cultivating the plant. This initiative has resulted in employment for the tribals, and each of the families earned ₹8000 in the first year of cultivation.

This project has led the Kani tribe to preserve and sustainably use their knowledge of biological resources, and this has also resulted in benefiting the community. The Kani tribe now lead a settled life in the forest of Agasthyamalai hills. UN has noted that this

---

140 http://www.rediff.com/news/2002/oct/11spec.htm/, last accessed on 9 October 2011.

is the first time that a local community has been rewarded with revenues for imparting knowledge about a rare medicinal plant resulting in a herbal drug.

Discussion Questions

1. Are you aware of other examples where indigenous people have benefited from monetization of an indigenous technical know-how?
2. What are the advantages and disadvantages in using an indigenous knowledge for commercial purposes? What are the advantages and disadvantages in providing monetary payment to indigenous people?

CASELET 2

EAST KOLKATA WETLANDS[141]

The East Kolkata Wetlands (EKW), located on the eastern fringes of Kolkata city is one of the largest assemblages of sewage fed fish ponds spread over an area of 12,500 ha. These wetlands form a part of the extensive inter-distributory wetland regimes formed by the Ganges Delta. EKW sustains the world's largest and perhaps oldest integrated resource recovery practice based on a combination of agriculture and aquaculture, and provides livelihood support to a large, economically underprivileged population of around 20,000 families which depend upon the various wetland products, primarily fish and vegetables for sustenance. Based on its immense ecological and socio-cultural importance, the Government of India declared EKW as a Wetland of International Importance under Ramsar Convention in 2003. The wetland system currently produces over 15,000 MT per annum from its 264 functioning aquaculture ponds, locally called bheries. Additionally, nearly 150 MT of vegetables are produced daily by subsistence farmers. Needless to say, EKW serves as the backbone of food security for Kolkata city.

EKW is a classic example of harnessing natural resources of the wetland system for fisheries and agriculture through ingenuity of local communities with their traditional knowledge. This forms the basis of its inclusion as one of 17 case studies around the world on wise use of wetlands by the Ramsar Convention. The wetland provides strong arguments for integration of traditional knowledge of local communities into conservation and management practices.

FROM A MALARIOUS JUNGLE TO WISE USE OF WETLANDS

EKW, presently widely hailed as an example of wise use of wetlands did not prominently figure as an ecological asset till about six decades ago. When Job Charnock laid its foundation in the Kolkata city on the levees of river Hooghly owing to its easy accessibility to the entire hinterland of Bengal, the wetland complex bordering the eastern fringes of the city was considered to be a locationally insignificant malarious jungle. These were called the salt lakes, serving as the backwater swamp and spill area of Bidyadhari River. The tidal effects of the Bay of Bengal made the water brackish and hence it was named Salt Lake. The wetlands in those days had utility only from the defence perspective owing to the challenges they presented in navigation.

Since the early 15th century, the eastward shift of the course of River Ganges brought metamorphic changes in the process of delta building in central and south Bengal.

---

141 *Note*: (c) East Kolkata Wetlands Management Authority and Wetlands International-South Asia. Sourced with permission from 'EAST KOLKATA WETLANDS'-the newsletter of East Kolkata Wetlands Management Authority and Wetlands International-South Asia. The newsletter can be accessed at http://www.wetlands.org/LinkClick.aspx?fileticket=zWFmETGLfzw%3d&tabid=56, last accessed on 30 September 2012.

A number of distributaries and re-distributaries were cut off from upland flow that signalled the end of those channels. Human interference in the region primarily in the form of channelization further quickened the process of silt deposition within the river beds, and finally the Bidyadhari became defunct by the end of the 18th century.

Kolkata grew to be, a large urban and trade centre virtually without any proper sewerage and solid waste management system, and thereby also subject to frequent drainage congestion, resulting in health impacts. The waste was initially dumped into river Hooghly, a practice which was later abandoned due to frequent outbreaks of malaria. A committee established to look into alternate solutions to the drainage problems recommended transferring all wastes to salt lakes, as the city had a natural eastwards elevation. The wetlands were nearly 8.5 feet below the highest point of the city. This recommendation prompted construction of a series of sewers and pumping stations towards the salt lakes. In 1864, a portion of the salt lakes was acquired for dumping solid waste. The first attempt at freshwater aquaculture was reported in 1918. Subsequent construction of waste water channels in the city increased access to wastewater, which in turn encouraged others to adopt wastewater aquaculture. Application of sewage was sequenced skilfully on the basis of detention time needed to improve the water quality appropriate for growing fish. The wetland system presently has 264 functioning bheries. The solid waste dumping area on the western periphery of the wetlands were converted to horticulture since 1876. The whole area has come to be recognized officially as Waste Recycling Region.

Having established a successful method of sewage-fed fisheries did not take the pressure of reclamation away from the wetland system. In fact, proposals for converting the wetland to accommodate the ever expanding Kolkata city were made as early as in the1830s. The post-independence surge of refugees to Kolkata city made the town planners look further into expansion of the urban area. This promoted reclaiming of nearly 1000 hectare of the northern portion of the wetland and hundreds of fish ponds for establishment of the Salt Lake city. In 1969, redistribution of land through land reforms led to further filling up of approximately 2500 hectares of water bodies for conversion into paddy fields.

However, there was also a gradual build-up of opinion on the environmental sustainability of the urban planning policies adopted by the government. A group of environmental experts questioned the reclamation of wetlands for urban settlements. In the 1980s, the Government of West Bengal initiated systematic research into the wetland and its waste recycling systems. Subsequently, a map of the waste recycling area was prepared in 1985. In 1992, a case study on EKW was presented in the expert committee meeting of the Ramsar Convention, and the site included as the only Indian case study on wise use of wetlands in a document published by the same name by the Ramsar Convention Secretariat, initiating the process of declaration of the site as a Wetland of International Importance. Therefore, when the idea of establishing a World Trade Centre on the wetland was mooted in 1991, a group of non-government organizations, notable of which was PUBLIC (People United for Better Living in Calcutta) filed a writ petition in the Calcutta High Court, asking directions of the state authorities to protect the wetlands and maintain their character, in particular preventing their reclamation as well as change in land use from agriculture to residential or commercial uses.

The court ruled in favour of maintaining the overall environmental values of the wetland system, and banned any conversion or changes in land use. Several suits and court decisions followed against developmental activities within the wetland area. The culmination was the notification of the The East Kolkata Wetlands (Conservation and Management) Act in 2006, which laid the foundation of the East Kolkata Wetland Management Authority and systematic implementation of principles of management of the Ramsar Site.

EAST KOLKATA WETLAND MANAGEMENT AUTHORITY (EKWMA)

The East Kolkata Wetlands (Conservation and Management) Act 2006 represented an important landmark for establishing an appropriate institutional regime for managing the Ramsar Site. The act took explicit cognizance of EKW as a Wetland of International Importance and its various ecosystem services, including regulation of water regime, and mechanism for waste water treatment, as a source for underground water recharging, and other socio cultural values. It also recognized the immense urbanization pressure on the wetland and the need to prevent its conversion for alternate usages.

The act defined the land use within the wetland as per revenue records, identifying each land parcel to be either substantially water dominated, under agriculture, or under settlement. Any further diminution of the wetland area, change in its (ecological) character, and land use was banned under the act.

It paved way for establishment of the East Kolkata Wetland Management Authority for conservation and management of the wetlands, and identified the following functions:
- Demarcation of the wetland boundaries
- Detecting changes in ecological character and land use, and enforcing land use control
- Preventing any unauthorized developmental projects, within the boundaries of the wetland system
- Preventing any mining, quarrying, blasting or any operation of similar nature to protect and conserve the wetland system
- Undertaking measures to abate pollution, and conserving the wetland biodiversity
- Promoting research and networking with other Ramsar sites
- Raising awareness on wetlands in general and EKW in particular
- Promoting conservation principles—like sewage fed fisheries and ecotourism

The act also lays a process wherein people living within the wetland area can apply for a permission to undertake any land use change. It also lays down exemplary punishment for not complying with the provisions of the act, which includes imprisonment of upto three years, fine upto ? ₹1,00,000, or both. An additional fine of ₹5000 a day is prescribed for every day such failure or contravention continues after the first conviction. Contravention to the act is identified as a cognizable and a non-bailable offence.

The authority has a broad-based structure and includes representation of all line departments and organizations. The Chief Secretary to the Government of West Bengal is the Chairman of the Authority, and the Secretary, Department of Environment (Government of West Bengal) its Member Secretary. The other members include the following:

- Secretaries of the state government departments of urban development, irrigation and waterways, fisheries, forests, municipal affairs, land and land reforms, panchayat, and rural development;
- Chairman and Member Secretary, West Bengal Pollution Control Board;
- Chief Executive Officer, Kolkata Metropolitan Development Authority;
- Commissioner, Kolkata Municipal Corporation;
- District Magistrates of the 24 Parganas (North and South);
- representative of Institute of Environmental Studies and Wetland Management;
- two nominated representatives of non-government organizations; and
- one representative of fishermen cooperative societies.

The office of the authority is headed by a Chief Technical Officer, who is in charge of the day-to-day affairs and functioning. The authority has a website www.ekwma,.com which provides details of the various interventions currently being undertaken by the agency.

Discussion Question

1. 'EKW is a classic example of harnessing natural resources of the wetland system for fisheries and agriculture through ingenuity of local communities with their traditional knowledge.' Explain.

CASELET 3

NARMADA BACHAO ANDOLAN AND THE SARDAR SAROVAR DAM PROJECT[142]

Narmada Bachao Andolan, which means 'Save River Narmada Movement' and the Sardar Sarovar Dam Project have been in national and international debate for almost three decades, thereby making the combined issue one of the longest protests against government authorities in India. The movement, led by Medha Patkar, voiced the concerns of the indigenous tribal villagers of the Narmada valley, questioned the cost-effectiveness of the project, and refuted the claimed advantages that a mega dam can bring through irrigation facilities and hydropower generation. Though the movement failed to stop the construction of the dam, it drew attention of the people to reflect on the claimed efficacy about building big dams.

ABOUT RIVER NARMADA AND SARDAR SAROVAR DAM

The river Narmada ran a 1312 km long-journey before joining the Arabian Sea at Bharuch, flowing through the three states of Madhya Pradesh (MP), Maharashtra, and Gujarat. About 90 per cent of the flow was in MP, and most of the remaining was in Gujarat, with a brief stretch through Maharashtra. A scheme was initiated in 1979 to construct a series of multi-purpose dams on the Narmada river. Among such 30 planned dams, Sardar Sarovar Dam (SSP) was the largest with a height of 163 metres and a length of 1210 metres.[143] The top reservoir level of the dam was 146.50 metre and the full reservoir level was 138.68 metre.[144] Through the construction of the dam, it was expected that benefits would reach the four states of Gujarat, Madhya Pradesh, Maharashtra, and Rajasthan. Narmada Control Authority (NCA), the representative body with official members from the states of Madhya Pradesh, Gujarat, Maharashtra, Rajasthan, and the Government of India, claim that the SSP proposes 'an annual irrigation of 17.92 lakh ha in Gujarat, 2.46 lakh ha in Rajasthan, and hydel power generation of 1450 MW'.[145] The proposed highlights of the dam project, as highlighted in the NCA website,[146] were as follows:

---

142 *Note*: This caselet is prepared as the basis for group discussion rather than to illustrate either effective or ineffective handling of a situation. The case is authored by Ajith Sankar R N. The author acknowledges and is thankful to the inputs provided by Zareen towards the preparation of this caselet. This caselet is released in the public domain. While the case writer holds the copyright to this case study, the reader may reproduce, distribute, publish, and transmit this case study in any form including photocopying, recording, or other electronic or mechanical methods provided that no text or figures are altered.

143 http://www.nca.gov.in/power_index.htm, last accessed on 14 August 2014.

144 http://www.nca.gov.in/news_index.htm, last accessed on 14 August 2014.

145 http://www.nca.gov.in/ssp_index.htm, last accessed on 7 July 2014.

146 www.nca.gov.in/ssp_index.htm, last accessed on 7 July 2014.

- The Narmada Main Canal, with a capacity of 1133 cumecs (40,000 cusecs) at the head regulator and 532 km length, would be the largest irrigation canal in the world.
- Irrigation to 17.92 lakh ha land of Gujarat covering 3360 villages of 62 talukas in 14 districts. Irrigation was also expected to benefit tribal areas of Maharashtra and drought-prone areas of Rajasthan.
- Generating 856–1007 million units per year of hydroelectricity.
- To supply 3571 MLD of drinkable water (2900 MLD for domestic consumption and 671 MLD for industrial consumption) to 8215 villages and 135 towns in Gujarat. To provide drinking water facilities to a population of about 13.71 lakh in 1107 villages and two towns in Jallore and Barmer districts of Rajasthan.
- Lower ratio of submergence to area irrigated—being 1.65 per cent of CCA against an average of 4–5 per cent of other major irrigation projects.

While the authorities used the above as reasons for justification for the construction of the dam, the history of the project was full of protests and struggles.

FORMATION OF NARMADA BACHAO ANDOLAN

In 1985, Medha Patkar, who was a researcher in her 30s, and her colleagues visited the project site and saw that there was a ban in the further construction of the dam. It was found by the team that this ban, by the Ministry of Environment and Forests (MoEF), was because of non-compliance of environmental standards. They also found that the indigenous people were unaware of the consequences associated with the construction of the dam. As the construction of the dam started, there was displacement of tribals, and they were also not given proper resettlement and rehabilitation. Medha Patkar was also able to generate support from people who were sceptical about the project and were also affected by the project. They formed the *Narmada Bachao Andolan* (NBA).

The movement started its activities by educating the villagers on the consequences of the project. NBA was also able to receive support from other local NGOs such as Arch-Vahini and Narmada Asargrastha Samiti (both based in Gujarat), Madhya Pradesh-based Narmada Ghati Nav Nirman Samiti and Maharashtra-based Narmada Dharangrastha Samiti, who were looking for fair rehabilitation plans or were opposed to dam construction. A number of social and environmental activists, including Baba Amte, supported the movement. Stating the reason for dissent among the dissenters, Patrick McCully, author of the book, *Silenced Rivers: The Ecology and Politics of Large Dams,*[147] said, 'Among their findings were that crucial environmental studies had not been conducted, that the number of people to be displaced was not known, that estimates of the amount of land to get irrigation water were wildly optimistic, and that while the supply of drinking water to some 40 million people in Gujarat was supposed to be one

---

147 Zed Books, London, 1996.

of the project's main benefits, the massive sums needed to build the pipes and pumps to deliver this water had been left out of the estimated project costs.'

WORLD BANK CONNECTION

In 1985, the World Bank made credits and loans totalling $450 million to the Government of India and the states of Gujarat, Maharashtra, and Madhya Pradesh, to help finance the dam and the canal. The bank also received another application for a disbursal of $350 million to complete the canal work, and a third application for an additional $90 million towards the Narmada Basin Development Project.

Following a series of protests by NBA activists and sympathisers in India and abroad, a detailed independent review of the project was done by the Morse Commission. This review was the first independent review undertaken by World Bank for any of its projects. Bradford Morse and Thomas R Berger, who were the reviewers, wrote a letter to the President of World Bank, stating, 'We think the Sardar Sarovar Projects as they stand are flawed, that resettlement and rehabilitation of all those displaced by the projects is not possible under prevailing circumstances, and that the environmental impacts of the projects have not been properly considered or adequately addressed. Moreover, we believe that the Bank shares responsibility with the borrower for the situation that has developed.'[148] The commission cited a number of reasons, detailed in their report for reaching this conclusion. The World Bank soon withdrew from this project.

NBA VS ELECTED GOVERNMENTS

From 1988, the members of NBA held talks with the government, explaining the flaws in the project and the environmental and social impact of the project. Protests, rallies, and hunger strikes followed. Many locals refused to be evacuated from the site, which met the possibility of drowning, especially during the rainy season. As protests gathered strength, government started using force to suppress the movement. Observer groups, constituting members from PUCL, DRAG, and Delhi Science Forum, on their field visits found human rights violations in submergence-zone villages.[149] A report by the Narmada International Human Rights Panel concluded gruesome and violent intrusions into human dignity, and held the Government of India, and the governments of Gujarat and Maharashtra responsible for such crimes.[150] In 1991, with the rising of the height of the dam to 32 meters, nearly 37,000 hectares of agricultural land were drowned, and villagers lost their homes. In 1995, the Supreme Court of India halted the construction of dam at a height of 80.3 metre, following a writ petition filed by NBA calling for a

---

148 http://www.ielrc.org/content/c9202.pdf, last accessed on 16 June 2014.
149 http://www.narmada.org/sardar-sarovar/hrvisit930708.html, last accessed on 14 August 2014.
150 http://www.narmada.org/sardar-sarovar/hrreport9310.html, last accessed on 14 August 2014.

comprehensive review of the project. NBA proposed alternate solutions to the dam. They showcased examples from parts of Rajasthan, Gujarat, and Madhya Pradesh, related to equitable distribution of water, revival of old water harvesting structures, and building of new ones. These solutions did not involve huge expenditure and were also environmental- friendly. An article in *The Economic Times*, in 1997, said, 'Meanwhile, resettlement of oustees because of the present height of the dam, 264 feet, is still not complete. Until last year, Gujarat had produced only 1700 acres of land for resettlement of oustees, scattered across numerous villages, contravening the conditions laid down for rehabilitation, which ask for resettlement in community units. This year, Gujarat increased this figure to 5700 acres, still scattered. At this point of time, it seems clear that producing land for rehabilitation is itself a tall order, and rehabilitation as agreed to is impossible.'[151] In 1999, however, the court gave the permission to raise the height to be increased to 88m.

As the dam construction progressed, NBA brought attention to the lack of canal development in command area and the lagging work in the construction of irrigation networks. It was also found that there was a huge short-fall in the power generation. An NBA press release, released in 2004, stated, 'The estimates of power generation at 110 meters, publicly declared, varied from 80MWs to 370MWs of power. The official documents such as one furnished to the Government of Maharashtra by Gujarat, however, could indicate that at 110mts dam height, only one of the five turbines at the Canal Head Power House could function and generate not more than 30 to 40MWs of power, that too only in good season, i.e., when adequate water is available in the river, in monsoon.'[152] In 2007, the NCA agreed to the illegality in raising the height of the dam to 121.92 metre and also agreed to the incompleteness and flaws in the rehabilitation of the people, who were affected by the project.[153] Following the heavy rains of 2013, the water level of the dam reached 131.10 metres; around 7000 people living in villages close to the Narmada river bank in the districts of Narmada, Bharuch, and Vadodara were evacuated and relocated.[154]

In its second interim report released in 2010, the committee constituted by the Ministry of Environment and Forests (MoEF) for assessing the status of compliance of environmental conditions and requirements to be fulfilled by project authorities of SSP and Indira Sagar Project (ISP), stated the following in its conclusion: 'The foregoing paragraphs reveal that project authorities of SSP and ISP have not taken due care of the environmental safeguard measures as stipulated during clearance of the these projects. In most of the cases, the Pari-Passu clause focusing simultaneous actions on environmental safe guard measures has not been respected. The compliances have been either partial

151 Lodaya, Kamal, 'SSP impasse: Is there a solution?', *The Economic Times*, 3 May 1997.
152 http://www.narmada.org/nba-press-releases/september-2004/Sept5.html, last accessed on 14 August 2014.
153 http://www.narmada.org/nba-press-releases/november-2007/Nov14.html, last accessed on 14 August 2014.
154 http://archive.indianexpress.com/news/7000-villagers-relocated-after-water-level-in-narmada-dam-crosses-130m/1159828/, last accessed on 16 June 2014.

or delayed and in a few cases not complied till today. Of the five parameters discussed in this report, the project authorities have grossly violated stipulations in respect of catchment area treatment, flora, fauna, and carrying and command area development, causing irreversible loss to the environment. The committee therefore recommends that no further reservoir filling either at SSP or at ISP be permitted till the catchment areas of both SSP and ISP are fully treated and all the outstanding requirements to protect and conserve flora and fauna, including preparation of master plan and creation of wildlife sanctuaries, are put in place. No further construction work on the canal network and no irrigation from even the existing network should be permitted till the various environmental parameters in the command area other than water management becomes Pari-Passu.'[155]

Reports like the above were used by NBA to generate public attention about the flaws in the project. In 2014, Government of India, through the NCA, was planning to grant clearance to permit installation of radial gates from the prevailing height of 121.92 metre to the final height of 138.68 metre. Questioning the benefits that may accrue from this decision, NBA stated, '…the canal work needs to be undertaken on a priority basis and the water ponded at 121.92 mts needs to be fully utilized and all pending measures on R&R (resettlement and rehabilitation), environmental compliance should be ensured, before raising the dam height further.'[156] NBA also asked the government to undertake a comprehensive multi-stakeholder review of this 70,000 crore project and the benefits that has come from this project.[157]

BATTLE LOST?

In a column in *The Telegraph*, Ramachandra Guha, a columnist, wrote, 'The NBA may have lost the battle it waged against the Sardar Sarovar Project. Yet its struggles made a considerable impact on popular consciousness. Had it not been for Patkar and her colleagues, the rights of those displaced by dams, factories, and highways would still be treated with a cavalier disregard in the press and by the urban middle class. Previously, those whose lands were taken over by public or private sector companies were paid a niggardly amount of money, which they were asked to take in the "national interest". Because of movements such as the NBA, there is now a nation-wide debate on providing just compensation to those who lose their homes and lands to development projects.'[158] A similar sentiment is echoed by McCully, saying, 'The NBA sees its role as much more than challenging a single dam or even dam building in general. Patkar and

155 http://www.indiaenvironmentportal.org.in/files/SECOND%20INTERIM%20REPORT%20OF%20THE%20 COMMITTEE%20FOR%20ASSESSMENT%20OF%20SURVEY.doc, last accessed on 7 July 2014.

156 http://www.indiaenvironmentportal.org.in/files/file/Urgent%20Letter%20to%20Narendra%20Modi-ji%20 on%20SSP.pdf, last accessed on 14 August 2014.

157 http://www.indiaenvironmentportal.org.in/files/file/Urgent%20Letter%20to%20Narendra%20Modi-ji%20 on%20SSP.pdf, last accessed on 14 August 2014.

158 http://www.telegraphindia.com/1130824/jsp/opinion/story_17254700.jsp, last accessed on 16 June 2014.

other NBA leaders have travelled throughout India supporting other struggles against destructive state and corporate development projects which strip the poor of their right to livelihood.'[159]

Discussion Questions

1. Explore different sources in internet related to Sardar Sarovar Dam Project and 'Narmada Bachao Andolan', and find out the environmental impacts of the Sardar Sarovar Dam Project.
2. What have been the short-term and long-term impacts of a movement like 'Narmada Bachao Andolan'?

---

159 McCully, Patrick, *Silenced Rivers: The Ecology and Politics of Large Dams*, Zed Books, London, 1996.

CASELET 4

EXAMPLES OF SUSTAINABLE TRANSPORTATION: GREEN TOMATO CARS, NEXTBIKE, TRANSMILENIO, DELHI METRO RAIL, AND NATURE AIR[160]

GREEN TOMATO CARS

Green Tomato Cars (GTC) was launched in London in the year 2006 by Tom Pakenham and Jonny Goldstone. It was the first company to provide eco-friendly car services in the UK. Starting with four cars of the Toyota Prius model, the number of cars with the company reached 40 in a year. In 2009, the number increased to 100 cars. By mid-2014, the company had 507 vehicles in its fleet. The company is expected to have a fleet size of 600 cars by the end of 2014.[161] GTC (http://www.greentomatocars.com) charged the same price as that of any other taxi, without charging anything extra for being green. 'Being green used to mean paying more for worse service... but we intend to emulate the best of the other cab firms if we are going to compete,' said Tom Pakenham.[162]

The company used Toyota Prius, which was a hybrid car having both petrol engine and electric motor. In 2011, GTC introduced large vehicles, which ran on bio-diesel. In 2012, it launched a fleet of cars that were fully electric. The company also offset its carbon emissions by 200 per cent (the company brought carbon credits for double the amount of carbon dioxide emitted from its operations) by planting of trees and implementation of energy-saving projects in India and Brazil. GTC had an effective fleet management system software that reduced the travel distance of a car, when it is unoccupied by a passenger. GTC also instituted ISO 14000, an environmental management system for its processes. For its sustainability initiatives, the company was recognized as the overall winner at the 'Sustainable City Awards', instituted by the City of London corporation.

While the company focused on green transportation, it also gave attention to its other services. The company implemented free Wifi services and audio systems within the vehicle, instituted a 24/7 hotline for booking, queries, complaints and suggestions, and booking through Twitter and iPhone applications. It also adopted the fare/share concept, where the passengers were able to share their taxi with other passengers on mutual understanding. 'Real-time Tracking', a software that helped the passenger confirm the location of the car and the time the vehicle would take to reach the passenger, was used by the company. After the booking, an automated text message was sent to the passenger regarding the details of the booking. The company also trained its drivers for safety and fuel efficient driving. GTC was rigorous in its driver selection process with only one from seven applicants being selected as drivers.

160 The author of this note is thankful to R. Dhivya, T.M. Vivekananda, Vimal Raja, Kumaresan, and Vishweshwaran for their inputs on writing this note.

161 http://www.fleetnews.co.uk/news/2014/6/2/corporate-car-service-launched-by-green-tomato-cars/52552/, last accessed on 6 June 2014.

162 http://www.treehugger.com/renewable-energy/green-tomato-cabs-in-london.html, last accessed on 8 June 2014.

British Sky Broadcasting Group plc (BskyB) was the first client for Green Tomato Cars. BskyB calculated its carbon footprint, and chose to reduce its carbon emission. Their agreement with Green Tomato Cars was part of the company's strategy to reduce its emissions. For this, the company used a strategy to encourage its employees and other staff members to travel in Green Tomato Cars. BskyB, in 2006, announced that it had achieved carbon-neutral status. Other major corporate clients of Green Tomato Cars included GlaxoSmithKline, News Limited, Buckingham Palace, BBC Television, Selfridges, etc. The company was also the official transfer service of Heathrow Airport.

As part of its social responsibility endeavours, GTC, since 2012, adopted 20 polar bears through the World Wildlife Fund (WWF), and conducted a campaign on climate change. The company also offered funded support to Macmillan, a charity institution that helps to design instruments for cancer treatment. In addition to focusing on greener initiatives, the company also set standards on broader aspects related to ethicality of business. The company shared its profits with its drivers and office staff, thereby becoming one of the few taxi companies in the world to institute a profit sharing plan for the drivers and office staff.

Green Tomato Cars widened their operations by franchising their cab service outside London, and expanded its operations in USA and Australia. In 2008, GTC was launched in Sydney through Green Limo service, and in 2014, it started its operation in the city of Washington.

Initially, the competitors for Green Tomato Cars were black taxies and other minicab operators. However, with its unique proposition, the business model and brand idea was replicated by numerous players. London now has a number of mini-cab service providers who operate with an eco-friendly tag. These include players like 'Climate Cars' and 'Go Green' cars. 'Climate Cars' claim to have the lowest CO_2 emission in the industry and offsetted all unavoidable emissions from its eco-friendly transport. 'Go Green Cars' have claimed that their operations results in the production of 60 per cent less CO_2, 98 per cent less NO_2, and 100 per cent less PM10, in comparison with the black taxi service of London.

NEXTBIKE

Nextbike GmbH (http://www.nextbike.de/en/), a rental bicycle (also referred to as 'bike') company was launched in the city of Leipzig, Germany, in 2004. This bike-sharing system allowed users to hire bicycles from various outlets in the city. By mid-2014, the company operated with more than 17,000 bicycles across the world. The three-speed geared bicycles were operated across more than 80 cities, in the countries of Austria, Azerbaijan, Bulgaria, Croatia, Cyprus, UAE (Dubai), Germany, Hungary, Latvia, New Zealand, Poland, Switzerland, Turkey, and the UK.

The bikes were held together at a centrally located bike stand, which had a fixing docking port and a rental terminal. The bicycles were automatically released for use when the payment was made through a credit card or a debit card. The user was able to make this payment through a console available in the stand. The company also developed an app that allowed the customer to book their cycle online. This app provided the customer with the information about the location from where the cycle could be picked up. The customer was also able to call a hotline, and obtain a code to release the bicycle's lock after making the payment. Nextbike also offered the option of a customer card. The company offered prepaid solutions too. The console had a card reader that identified the customer cards, e-tickets of public transport, and cards of car-sharing partners and other transportation service providers. The terminal was self-sufficient in terms of power supply, through solar cells and battery, and did not require connection to any power supply system (see Fig. 12.3).

In addition to offering CO_2-free transportation, Nextbike also offered an opportunity for transit advertising. Nextbike partnered with hotel companies like B&B Hotels, Radisson, Marriott, Novotel, Westin, etc., whereby the guests of these hotels used these bikes to explore the city of their stay. Companies providing green transportation options for their employees also partnered with Nextbike.

FIG. 12.3[163] NextBike Cycles parked in a solar powered cycle stand

163 NextBike, http://www.nextbike.de/en/, last accessed on 10 March 2015.. Used with permission.

TRANSMILENIO

The TransMilenio (http://www.transmilenio.gov.co/en), a Bus Rapid Transportation (BRT) system in Bogota, the capital city of Columbia, was able to provide a better mode of transport to the citizens of the city. In 2000, TransMilenio was opened for public, and in 2012, the system covered 112 kilometers across 12 lines. The system operated almost 2000 buses, and carried 2 million passengers on a daily basis.

With the population and the number of privately owned vehicles increasing at a rapid pace, traffic jams were also becoming frequent and longer in Bogota. During peak hours, traffic in Bogota was moving at 7 km/hour. To ease the citizens from this trouble, the TransMilenio was introduced. It was calculated that, in 1998, prior to the creation of TransMilenio, travelling a distance of 30 kilometers required two hours and 15 minutes. Following the introduction of Transmilenio, the same distance was covered in 55 minutes.

FIG.12.4[164]   TransMilenio buses near a bus station in Bogota, Columbia. One can see the exclusive lanes occupied by TransMilenio.

---

164 Photo by Carlos Felipe Pardo, used with permission. Image Source: https://www.flickr.com/photos/carlosfpardo/3794671537/, last accessed on 12 July 2014.

TransMilenio were given exclusive lanes on the roads (see Fig. 12.4). The system operated large-capacity buses and also had separate stations from where the passenger can board from, with some of the stations being elevated. Preboard ticketing, centralized fleet control, and operations for 18 hours daily were some of the positives attributed to TransMilenio. Due to the high frequency of these buses, and also because of the exclusive lanes, people realized that travelling through TransMilenio was faster than travelling through private vehicles. They also found it to be economical.

The buses of TransMilenio, designed by Volvo, were fitted with sensors to stop inter-bus collision. A plan to convert diesel powered vehicles to hybrid and full electric systems is in process. Some of the TransMilenio buses also had a solar powered generator that converted solar energy to electrical energy.

A C40 Cities Climate Leadership Group study indicated, 'The Bogotá TransMilenio system has attained a very high productivity level averaging 1600 passengers per day per bus, reducing travelling time by 32 per cent, eliminating 2109 public-service vehicles, reducing gas emissions by 40 per cent, and making zones around the trunk roads safer, thus decreasing accident rates by 90 per cent throughout the system.'[165] TransMilenio system helped in reducing the pollution level at Bogota (see Fig. 12.5). In 2012, the system made $25 million in carbon credits.

As per a report[166] prepared by Colombia's Ministry of Environment, Housing, and Territorial Planning, the system, between 2001 and 2006, helped in reducing sulphur

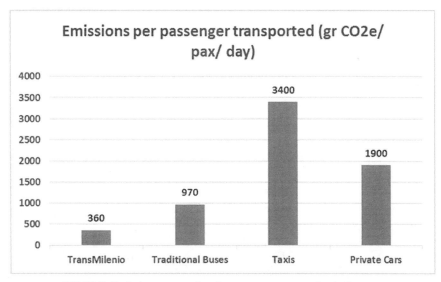

FIG.12.5 Emissions transmitted per passenger per day in Bogota

---

165 http://www.c40.org/case_studies/brt-system-reduced-traveling-time-32-reduced-gas-emissions-40-and-reduced-accidents-90, last accessed on 11 June 2014.

166 http://www.railway-mobility.org/docs/cop13/1COP13-D2-Paola_Betteli.pdf, last accessed on 11 June 2014.

dioxide, nitric oxide, and PM10 by 601 tonnes, 28,929 tonnes, and 3,823 tonnes respectively. It was estimated that the economic savings as a result of this reductions in emissions will amount to $229.7 million. TransMilenio also contributed to the savings of 534,692 barrels of fuel for the city, during this period.

DELHI METRO

Delhi Metro (http://www.delhimetrorail.com/), a rapid rail transit system operating in the National Capital Region (NCR) of India, started its operations in 2002. The metro now operates through 190 kilometres, through seven lines, connecting 137 stations and has a daily ridership of more than 23 lakh (2.3 million),. Planning for the metro work started in 1984. The first phase of this project began in 2002. Delhi Metro was the first metro in the world to receive ISO 14001[167] for the construction phase of the metro. By March 2013, the metro system was running 208 trains.

In 1997, Dr E. Sreedharan was appointed as the Managing Director of this ambitious project. Speaking about Sreedharan, Tim Colebatch, Economic Editor, The Age, comments, 'I dislike the "great men" approach to history, but in this case, it's indisputable. Infrastructure projects in India are usually characterized by political interference, corruption, delays, cost overruns, and inefficiency. The Delhi Metro broke the mould because they appointed a quietly brilliant, incorruptible, inspiring team leader as director, and gave him freedom to run it as he chose.'[168]

The metro reduced around 50–70 per cent of time that a citizen of Delhi uses to spend on travel, taking into consideration the time-spend on traffic jams. Travel through Delhi Metro resulted in the consumption of only one-fifth of the energy per passenger in comparison to the same passenger using road transport. Using the 'With Metro' and 'Without Metro' scenario modelling, it was estimated that Delhi Metro was able to remove more than 91,000 vehicles from the roads of Delhi on a daily basis,[169] thereby reducing traffic congestion, saving on fuel costs, reducing accidents, and saving on public health expenses.

The Bombardier Movia trains used by Delhi Metro (see Fig. 12.6) instituted energy saving technologies like regenerative breaking systems, from where energy created during breaking has been used to accelerate other trains in the same service lane, thereby saving 30 per cent of energy used in such operations. Delhi Metro became the first railway project in the world to claim carbon credits for the same. It was also the first transportation system in the world that was certified by United Nations to gain carbon credits for greenhouse gas emission reduction, estimated at 4.5 lakh tonnes[170] every year.

---

167 *Note*: A certification that acknowledges the setting of criteria for an environmental management system.
168 http://www.theage.com.au/comment/delhis-metro-success-a-lesson-for-australia-20130401-2h2w8.html, last accessed on 12 July 2014.
169 http://delhimetrorail.com/press_reldetails.aspx?id=746xECETA6Qlld, last accessed on 12 June 2014.
170 http://delhimetrorail.com/OtherDocuments/Annual-Repot11-12%28English%29.pdf, last accessed on 12 June 2014.

FIG. 12.6[171] A Bombardier train used in the Delhi Metro

Delhi Metro, for its energy efficiency initiatives, became the first metro project in the world to be registered with the Gold Standard certification for carbon mitigation projects.

Delhi Metro has also started the process of generating solar power from its metro stations. It was also announced that all stations to be constructed as part of the Phase III work of Delhi Metro will be designed as green buildings.[172] As part of its corporate social responsibility initiatives, Delhi Metro constructed a children's home, which is managed by the Salaam Balak Trust, and this home can accommodate 125 children. Delhi Metro, in association with Help Age India, also runs a 'Winter Age Home' between November and March. It also allows free-of-cost promotion of socially relevant messages by not-for-profit organizations at its stations through the medium of banners, canopies, and standees.

NATURE AIR

Nature Air (http://www.natureair.com/) is a carbon-neutral airline operating in San Jose, Costa Rica. The airline operated to 13 destinations within Costa Rica on a daily basis. It also operated to a location each in the neighbouring countries of Panama and Nicaragua, and also offered a number of charter services.

---

171 'DelhiMetroBlueLineBombardier' by WillaMissionary, licensed under Public domain via Wikimedia Commons, http://commons.wikimedia.org/wiki/File:DelhiMetroBlueLineBombardier.jpg#mediaviewer/File:DelhiMetroBlueLineBombardier.jpg, last accessed on 12 July 2014.

172 http://timesofindia.indiatimes.com/city/delhi/Metro-stations-to-be-rated-on-green-building-standards/articleshow/36985532.cms, last accessed on 12 July 2014.

The airline started operations in 1991 and was earlier known as Travel Air. In 2000, along with a change in the ownership, the name of the airline was changed to Nature Air. The airline operated a fleet of six planes, four of them belonging to the DeHaviland Twin Otter series 300 class and the other two belonging to Cessna 208B grand caravan class. The planes of Nature Air were painted in vibrant colours that represented tropical animals and destinations (see Fig. 12.7).

The airline became carbon neutral in 2004, thereby becoming the first airline in the world to achieve that merit. Nature Air's carbon emissions were calculated on the basis of the emissions caused by the burning of fuel by its planes, and also the emissions caused by its ground operations.[174] The airline could offset more than 6000 tonnes[175] of annual carbon emissions through the purchase of carbon credits that protected tropical forests in the Osa Peninsula, which is described by NatGeo as one of the most biologically diverse region, of the planet. The offsetting was done through National Forestry Financing Fund (FONAFIFO) under, Government of Costa Rica. To ensure

FIG.12.7[173] Vibrant paintings on a Nature Air airline

173 Image Source: http://www.natureair.com/nature_air_gallery/images/05.jpg, last accessed on 28 July 2014.
174 *Note*: For details of how the company calculated its emissions, visit http://www.natureair.com/carbonneutral/how-we-calculate.html
175 *Note:* 6320 tonnes in 2006

the effectivity of its carbon neutral program, the company conducted third-party audits to ensure that the biodiversity of the Osa region is conserved.

The company was also able to reduce its emissions by 7 per cent through efficiency improvements. Nature Air also participated in many environmental initiatives, and partnered with Rainforest Alliance to undergo verification for its sustainability practices. The ground vehicles of Nature Air used bio-diesel made from used cooking oils, collected from hotels and restaurants. This was done through Nature Air's sister concern, Aerotica. Employees of Nature Air also contributed to this effort by bringing used cooking oils from their homes. The company also started NatureKids foundation to teach English, computing, and environmental inputs to people from low-income families, enabling them access to create a better future.

The company had a 92 per cent on-time performance rate,[176] and also started e-ticketing services, making it the only airline in the Central American region to engage in such a practice. Nature Air significantly contributed to Nature Vacations, a carbon-neutral vacation program in Costa Rica, whereby tourists are given an opportunity to go through a travel itinerary that follows sustainability practices, such as, guided nature trails, stay at hotels that set industry standards in environment-friendliness, and road transportation through a bio-diesel van.

In 2008, Nature Air joined the Climate Neutral Network, an initiative of United Nations Environmental Programme to promote low-carbon societies and economies. Nature Air has won numerous awards for its sustainability practices. The company hopes to be carbon positive by 2021.

Discussion Questions

1. You are the mayor of a city. List out the parameters that you will take into consideration to ascertain the most effective sustainable transportation model for your city. Assume data for your city to be same as one of the cities in India.

2. In addition to the examples listed in this caselet, list out ten examples of various sustainable transportation models/practices from various countries, and write short-notes about them.

3. Compare and contrast the advantages and disadvantages of the sustainable transportation examples listed above.

---

176 *Note:* Nature Air claims that the industry standard is approximately 70+, while its nearest competitors average 55 per cent.

CASELET 5

THE NATURAL STEP[177]

Dominic and Suzanne Fielden are a husband-and-wife team in Canmore, Alberta, who care deeply about community, food, and celebration. They want their pizza company, The Rocky Mountain Flatbread Company (RMFC), to be a brand that stands for positive change in the world. When Suzanne learned that the Town of Canmore was working with The Natural Step, she came forward with her company as an 'early adopter' of sustainability.

BASELINE ANALYSIS

With support from other early adopters in Canmore, RMFC did a baseline analysis of the business. They noted where they were doing well, where they were contributing to violations of the sustainability principles, and areas they could improve upon.

Their strengths included the following:

- A partnership with the town and local schools to design and implement healthy cooking classes and responsible entrepreneur programs.
- Hiring people who share their vision and training them to be a part of a team that understands every aspect of the business. This resulted in greater staff retention in a community with a chronic seasonal turnover, confirming their conviction that a sustainable business means sustainable staffing.
- Using as many Canadian grown and organic ingredients as they could afford and were available, thereby supporting the local economy and contributing to a healthy natural environment.
- Using paints and varnishes containing fewer volatile organic compounds (VOC) for their renovations, thereby reducing their use of non-biodegradable or slow-to-biodegrade synthetic substances.
- Using recycled wood or wood from sustainable forests in their furniture and structural renovations. They were recycling paper, metal, glass, and plastics accepted at the municipal recycling centre, and they were fuelling their signature clay oven with salvage wood and deadfall.

The sustainability impacts analysis and key sustainability challenges included the following:

Sustainability principle 1—hydrocarbon and mined materials use

- RMFC's reliance on gas for food transport was the most obvious and the most difficult challenge. Both the business and its suppliers transport their goods in gas-fuelled vehicles. The business relies on fossil fuels as well, for heating the building and powering its electrical systems.

---

177 This caselet is authored by The Natural Step, Canada, and is available at http://www.naturalstep.ca/toolkits, last accessed on 2 March 2013. Used with permission.

Sustainability principle 2—PVC products, chlorine, dioxins, furans, and other organochlorine compounds
- Inexperienced at restaurant cleaning, the Fieldens signed on to the standard products package suggested by their supplier, which provided easy compliance with health and safety regulations. The baseline analysis, which revealed the negative impacts of the chemicals used in both water delivery and waste water disposal, led them to question their acceptance of these standard products.
- Although RMFC tries to use organic ingredients in their pizzas, the ingredients are not always available or affordable, so the company at times uses some products that have been exposed to various synthetic pesticides and fertilizers.

Sustainability principle 3—physical degradation of nature
- RMFC packages its products in boxes made of recycled cardboard, but require a substantial quantity of cardboard to deliver their product. Even though the cardboard is recycled, they continue to rely on harvested trees, and therefore impact forest ecosystems.
- The staff recycles all waste from the restaurant that can be recycled. Non-recyclables take up landfill space, and recyclables consume energy both in transport and during the recycling process.

Sustainability principle 4—human needs
- The global reliance on non-renewable fossil fuels is a major cause of political instability, social displacement, cultural upheaval, air, water, and land pollution, and other negative social phenomenon. The baseline analysis helped illuminate the extent to which RMFC—and Suzanne and Dominic as individuals—are dependent on fossil fuels and thus contribute to a global problem.
- In order to comply with health and safety standards, the company was using cleaning supplies that contained small quantities of chemicals that can be harmful to human and environmental health. The baseline analysis motivated them to revisit the question and seek a more sustainable solution.

COMPELLING VISION

As part of the process, the Rocky Mountain Flatbread Company revisited their company vision. It now reads:

'RMFC's vision is to be a restorative organization and be a part of restorative communities… This means to design our business in such a manner that our practices honour, support, and cooperate with nature's inherent ability to sustain life.'
- We will take personal responsibility for our social, ecological, and financial performance.
- Our vision also means being a part of and encouraging local government, non-governmental organizations (NGOs), businesses, and members of the public to work together to live and work in ways that support nature to sustain life.

RMFC STRATEGIC GOALS

In imagining what such a business would actually look like, the owners developed a list of strategic goals:

- We generate only benign emissions.
- We derive 100 per cent of our energy from renewable resources; we have a net carbon impact of zero—no net carbon will accumulate in the atmosphere as a result of our operations.
- Our organization has zero waste.
- Our fixtures and fittings come from recycled materials.
- We encourage people to make simple changes to their day-to-day lives that are more sustainable. We celebrate anything and anyone who represents community.
- We work closely with schools, NGOs, local government, and local businesses to explore how to live and work in sustainable ways.
- We work in partnership with schools to encourage responsible entrepreneurship.

The following is a snapshot of RMFC's sustainability impacts analysis:

Sustainability principal #1	Sustainability principle #2	Sustainability principle #3	Sustainability principle #4
Eliminate increasing concentrations of substances extracted from the earth's crust	Eliminate increasing concentrations of substances produced by society	Eliminate physical degradation of nature	Eliminate barriers that undermine people's ability to meet their needs
Sustainability challenge	**Sustainability challenge**	**Sustainability challenge**	**Sustainability challenge**
• Metals (vehicles and fixtures) • Trace metals (electronics, lightbulbs, computers) • Oil (diesel, gas, transport, food collection, heat, energy, packaging, chemicals, paints) • Other elements (fertilizers, pesticides, man-made chemicals, bleaching paper, cleaning products, paints) • CO_2 (propane, heat and cooking, diesel, and gas for transport)	• Emissions: NOX, volatile organic compounds (VOC) (energy, transport, paint) • Synthetic materials (flame retardants, plastic packaging, man-made pesticides from farming)	• Land ecosystems degradation (food, hydroenergy, paper, wood, cleaners, land fill space, extraction from lithosphere) • Aquatic ecosystems degradation (cleaning and drinking water, marine food, hydro-energy)	• Safe working environment (cleaning chemicals and smoke from fire)

(Contd)

Sustainability assets inventory	Sustainability assets inventory	Sustainability assets inventory	Sustainability assets inventory
• Locally grown ingredients (use as many locally grown ingredients as are available and affordable to reduce reliance on fossil fuels for transportation) • Recycling paper, plastics, and wood	• Organic materials (use as much locally grown ingredients as are available and affordable) • Low-VOC paints (use low-VOC finishes for renovations)	• Salvaged wood for oven	• Promoting responsible entrepreneurship (partnering with town, local schools, and businesses to learn about responsible entrepreneurship) • Partnering with Yellowstone to Yukon (conservation initiative) • Organic market • Support local clubs (selling our pizzas for fundraisers) • Work placements (students from Exshaw)

Discussion Question

1. Pick up a product that you consume. Detail the life-cycle of that product. You may use pictures, images, doodles, etc., to do this life-cycle mapping. What are the environmental impacts that are caused during the processes of extraction, production, distribution, consumption, and disposal of that product?

	Extraction	Production	Distribution	Consumption	Disposal
1st impact					
2nd impact					
3rd impact					
nth impact					

Now, read through the following concepts related to sustainability. What impact will these concepts have on the life-cycle of the product that you've chosen earlier?

Bio-mimicry, closed loop production, conscious consuming, consumer labelling, corporate social responsibility, cradle-to-cradle design, extended producer responsibility, fair trade, government accountability, green chemistry, local living economies, and zero waste

CASELET 6

SIACHEN PEACE PARK

Siachen (the place of roses) Glacier located in the Himalayan region is one of the world's longest glaciers, and this region's altitude ranges between 3620 metre (11,875 feet) to 5753 metre (18,875 feet). This region is the highest battlefield on Earth, with both India and Pakistan having military presence here. The nations have about 150 manned outposts along the glacier, and approximately 3000 troops from each side.[178] India controls the Siachen glacier, after a military operation in 1984, prior to which the territory remained unoccupied by both India and Pakistan.

The military presence in Siachen has resulted in human casualties amounting to an estimated 2700.[179] The Express Tribune, an English daily from Pakistan, quoted a Pakistani army officer, 'The real enemy is not the person sitting across the LoC (line of control), but the weather, which envelops a person from every side'.[180] Avalanches and high-altitude sickness has affected the soldiers of both India and Pakistan. In 2012, an avalanche resulted in the death of 138 Pakistani soldiers and civilians. Following this, Nawaz Sharif made a public reference of exploring withdrawal of its troops from Siachen Glacier. 'Let's not make it a matter of ego,' said Sharif.[181]

India and Pakistan incur huge expenses for maintaining military presence in this region. Retired Lt Gen. P.N. Hoon, a former Indian army official, says, 'We are spending 6–7 crores a day. Have we become such rich nations today?'.[182] Following the avalanche, Mr Pallam Raju, Minister of State for Defence said, 'They have their concerns, we have our concerns, but it does definitely take an economic toll. This money can be better spent on the development of both countries.'[183]

The presence of troops in the region has contributed to the creation of environmental pollution in the region. Aamir Ali, a mountaineer from India, commented, 'It is not easy to imagine the pollution caused by thousands of men living up there, with every item of necessity being flown in. Cans, drums, tetra packs of fruit juices, aluminium packaging; this can neither be burnt, nor destroyed, nor taken back. Imagine the human waste. This amounts to over 1000 kg a day; it is packed in metal drums and dropped into crevasses—up to 4000 drums a year. This, together with hundreds of tons of garbage, will then be our legacy to future generations when the glacier finally reaches the end of its journey. Heavy guns and equipment are flown in, but as a senior army officer remarked: Nothing

178 http://content.time.com/time/magazine/article/0,9171,1079528,00.html, last accessed on 10 March 2015.
179 http://www.bbc.com/news/world-asia-india-26967340, last accessed on 10 March 2015.
180 http://tribune.com.pk/story/365717/conferences-on-siachen-sooner-than-later-withdrawal-is-a-must/, last accessed on 10 March 2015.
181 http://tribune.com.pk/story/366272/worlds-highest-battleground-pakistan-should-lead-siachen-troop-pullout-says-nawaz/, last accessed on 10 March 2015.
182 http://www.dnaindia.com/india/report-india-welcomes-pakistans-call-to-demilitarise-siachen-glacier-1678153, last accessed on 10 March 2015.
183 http://www.dnaindia.com/india/report-india-welcomes-pakistans-call-to-demilitarise-siachen-glacier-1678153, last accessed on 10 March 2015.

will ever be flown back. The ibex are all gone. The wild roses—the area was famous for its wild roses; *Sia* means rose in the Balti language—have been cut for tent pegs or other uses, or for decoration.'[184]

There have been proposals to convert Siachen Glacier into a trans-boundary protected area (TBPA). There are a number of TBPAs across the world, which are also referred to as *Peace Parks*. Supporting the call to make Siachen a peace park, Ahmad Rafay Alam, an environment lawyer from Pakistan and a 'Yale World Fellow', states that, 'The platform is uncorrupted by Kashmir, the war on terror or other issues that form the composite dialogue. A declaration or accord recognizing both countries' commitment to protecting the environment and acknowledging the challenges of climate change could easily pave the way for a Siachen peace park management system, where elected representatives from either side act as co-chairs along with representatives from the armed forces and an international NGO (such as the IUCN or the WWF), and line ministries could set about demilitarising the Glacier and preparing a transition of control from the military to environment managers.'[185]

While there are issues to be addressed, primarily the mistrust arising from past experiences, there are voices looking forward to a sustainable solution for Siachen. 'As a young major posted in Jammu and Kashmir in the 1980s, I remember being upbeat about Rajiv Gandhi and Benazir Bhutto being the fresh new prime ministers of India and Pakistan, and actually telling my bosses that maybe we wouldn't have to spend another winter at Siachien,' says Harish Puri, in a *Letters to the Editor* column.[186] Harish Kapadia is a mountaineer and his son, an officer in the Gorkha Rifles of the Indian Army, died fighting terrorists in Kashmir. Kapadia says, 'On both sides of the LOC, it is said that to honour the blood of brave soldiers that has been spilled, not an inch of territory should be given up. One could say even with more force that the sacrifice of brave men could best be honoured by protecting this spectacular mountain area consecrated by their sacrifice… the concept of the trans-boundary peace park would fit well in giving a positive dimension to the process. It would work not only towards disengagement, but towards the creation of a park to protect the environment to allow the ibexes and snow leopards to roam, the wild roses to grow and the mountaineers to return to the Siachen Glacier…'[187]

Discussion Questions

1. Visit the website of various trans-boundary peace park initiatives existing across the globe, and list out the benefits that have accrued from their creation.
2. What would be the measures that could be evolved to create a trans-boundary peace park in a region known for protracted conflict?

184 http://www.harishkapadia.com/downloads/siachen-peace-park-proposal.pdf, Accessed on March 9, 2015, last accessed on 10 March 2015.
185 http://tribune.com.pk/story/366583/towards-a-siachen-peace-park/, last accessed on 10 March 2015.
186 http://tribune.com.pk/story/364693/damn-you-siachen-2/, last accessed on 10 March 2015.
187 http://www.harishkapadia.com/siachen-peace-park/, last accessed on 10 March 2015.

Index

A

Acid rain *111*
Adbusters *305*
Aichi biodiversity targets *345*
Air (Prevention and Control of Pollution) Act *416*
Akwé: Kon guidelines *402*
Algal bloom *120*
Anna Hazare *119*
Anthropocentrism *369, 370*
Aranyaka *38*
Ayurveda *78*

B

Basel convention *424*
Benefit-cost analysis or cost-benefit analysis *276*
Bhagavad Gita *38, 61, 62, 78*
Bible *78, 79*
Bioaccumulation *134*
Bioconcentration *134*
Biodiversity *329, 331–334, 344*
    Hotspots *336*
Biomagnification *134, 135*
Biosphere reserves *361, 362*
Bishnois *18*
Bottom of pyramid (BoP) *209*
Brundtland Commission *201*
Buddhism *54, 82, 83*
Buy nothing day *305*

C

Cap and trade mechanisms *442, 446*
Carbon disclosure project *244*
Carbon footprint *80, 263, 279*
Carbon intensity *166, 168, 169*
Carbon neutrality *223*
Carbon offsetting *223, 224*
Carbon rating *279*
Carbon trading *446*
Carrying capacity *30*
Central pollution control board *112*

Ceres *381*
Ceres principles *245*
Chipko movement *10*
Cleaner production *209*
Climate change *136, 145, 343*
Club of Rome *448*
Command and control *442*
Compost *312, 316*
Consumerism *304*
Convention on Biological Diversity *13, 424*
Convention on International Trade in Endangered Species of
    Wild Fauna and Flora (CITES) *426*
Convention on Migratory Species (CMS), *425*
Cradle to Cradle (C2C) *210*

D

Dalai Lama *130*
Dams *118*
Declaration *83*
    Buddhist *83*
    Christian *96*
    Hindu *86*
    Jain *87*
    Jewish *100*
Deep ecology *58–60*
Deforestation *170, 171*
Disaster management *146*
    Disaster management authority *147*

E

Earth charter *370*
Earth hour *155*
Earth overshoot day *262*
Earth summit *203*
Ecocentrism *369, 370*
Ecological economics *435*
Ecological footprint *261*
Ecological succession *29*
Ecology *1, 2*
Ecosia *177, 178*

Ecosystem *25*
   Aquatic *33*
   Desert *32*
   Forest *31*
   Grassland *31*
Ecosystem diversity *331*
Ecosystem services *268, 273, 274*
   Classification *269*
   Valuation *228*
Emissions *263*
   Direct *263*
   Indirect *263*
   Scope 1 *263, 264*
   Scope 2 *263, 264*
   Scope 3 *263, 264*
Energy *157*
   Alternate *158*
   Biomass *13*
   Non-renewable *158*
   Renewable *158, 160*
   Solar *158, 160, 161*
   Tidal *85*
   Wind *158, 163*
Energy efficiency *166*
Energy intensity *166, 168, 169*
Environment *2*
Environmental design management *258*
Environmental economics *433, 435*
Environmental impact assessment *279*
Environmental management *2*
Environmental management system *14, 255*
Environmental protection *9*
Environmental Protection Act *107, 416*
Environmental Protection Agency
 (EPA) *134, 186, 305*
Environmental risk management *257*
Ethical consumerism *378*
Extended producer responsibility *207, 313*
   Collective *313*
   Extended *313*
   Individual *313*
Externalization *436–438*
Extractive Industries Transparency
 Initiative *250*

F
Farming *65*
   Conventional *68*
   Factory *76*
   Natural *71, 73*
   Organic *68, 73*
   Permaculture *73*
   Sustainable *65*
Food chain *27*
Forests *418*
Framework Convention on Climate Change *13*

G
Gaia *59, 63, 64*
   Hypothesis *63, 64*
Genetic diversity *331*
Genuine progress indicator *451*
Global reporting initiative *241*
Global warming *136*
Green buildings *214*
Green investing *221*
Green marketing *229*
Greenpeace *108, 144*
Green product design *211*
Green Rating for Integrated Habitat
 Assessment (GRIHA) *216, 218*
Greenwashing *229*
Gross national happiness *452*

H
Habitat loss *338*
Hanuman *54*
Heliotropism *211*
Hinduism *38*
   Hindu *18, 38, 41, 86*
Honeycomb geometry *211*
Human–animal conflicts *132*

I
Incineration *309, 310*
Indian Green Building Council (IGBC) *216*
Industrial ecology *259*
Intergovernmental panel on climate change *136, 141*
International energy agency *157*
Invasive species *343*

ISO 14000 Standards *246*
IUCN Red List *344, 345*

J
Jainism *54*
   Jain *87–93*
Jambavan *54*
Jatayu *54*

K
Kailash Murthy *72, 73*
Khadin *189*
Kunds *188*

L
Law of the Rights of Mother Earth *426*
Law of Tolerance *30*
Leadership in Energy and Environmental
  Design' (LEED) *216*
Life cycle analysis *264, 265*
Living planet report *181, 261*

M
Marrakech *340*
Masanobu Fukuoka *71*
Mass Rapid Transport System (MRTS) *213*
Micheal Porter *203*
Montreal protocol *421*
Muslim *38*

N
Nakshatra *47*
National action plan on climate change *22*
National environment policy *21*
National water policy *23*
Natural buildings *214, 218*

O
Ocean acidification *120, 124*
OECD *157*
On climate change *3*
Oorani *187*
Organic architecture *214*
Ozone *109*
   Depletion *109*
   Ground-level *110*
   Imbalance *109*

P
Pani panchayats *119*
Payments for Ecosystem Services (PES) *458*
People's biodiversity register *362, 363*
Pigovian taxes *445*
Poaching *340*
Polluter pays principle *444*
Pollution *107, 122*
   Air *108*
   Light *126*
   Marine *120*
   Noise *124*
   Soil *120*
   Thermal *125*
   Water *112*
Pollution taxes *445*
Population *129*
Producer responsibility *313*
Project elephant *361*
Project tiger *359*

R
Rain water harvesting *185*
Ramsar convention on wetlands *423*
Recycling *310*
REDD+ *457*
Resettlement and rehabilitation *118*
Rights of nature *426*

S
Sabarimala *303, 304*
Sacred groves *51, 52*
Sadhguru Jaggi Vasudev 130
Sanatana Dharma *87*
Sanatan Dharma *38*
Sattwik *57*
Shareholder resolutions *380, 381*
Silent valley *19–21*
Slow food movement *398, 399*
Socially responsible investing *221*
Species diversity *331*
Sustainability *434*
Sustainability report *295*
Sustainability reporting *240*
Sustainable development *201, 203, 205*

Swami Chinmayananda *41*

T

Tankas *187*

The Economics of Ecosystems and Bio-diversity (TEEB) *6*

The International Union for Conservation of Nature and Natural Resources (IUCN) *8*

The Wild Life (Protection) Act, 1972 *417*

Tkarihwaié:ri Code of Ethical Conduct *403*

Triple bottom line *239*

True cost economics *440*

U

UN Global Compact *241*

United Nations Convention on the Law of the Sea (UNCLOS) *424*

United Nations Convention to Combat Desertification (UNCCD) *203*

United Nations Framework Convention on Climate Change (UNFCCC) *421*

UN Principles for Responsible Investment *241*

Upanishad *41, 61, 76*

V

Vaav/Bawdi/Barav *190*

Vahana *54*

Vasudhaiva Kutumbakam *412*

Vedas *39*

Vegetarian *81*

Vegetarianism *74*

Vishwamitra *39*

Vrikshayurveda *45, 46*

W

Waste *306*

    Construction and demolition *306*

    Disposal *309*

    Hazardous *307, 308*

    Industrial *306*

    Management *146, 308*

    Solid *306*

    Urban *314*

Waste-to-energy *165*

Water conflicts *115*

Water footprint *181*

    Blue *182*

    Green *182*

    Grey *182*

Water (Prevention and Control of Pollution) Act *416*

Y

Yagnas *57*